HENRY R. LUCE

Charles Scribner's Sons • New York

Maxwell Macmillan Canada • Toronto

Maxwell Macmillan International
New York • Oxford • Singapore • Sydney

HENRY R. LUCE

A POLITICAL PORTRAIT OF THE MAN WHO CREATED THE AMERICAN CENTURY

Robert E. Herzstein

Charles Scribner's Sons
Macmillan Publishing Company
866 Third Avenue
New York, NY 10022

Maxwell Macmillan Canada, Inc.
1200 Eglinton Avenue East
Suite 200
Don Mills, Ontario M3C 3N1

Macmillan Publishing Company is part
of the Maxwell Communication Group of Companies.

Library of Congress Cataloging-in-Publication Data
Herzstein, Robert Edwin.
Henry R. Luce: a political portrait of the man who created the
American century/ Robert E. Herzstein.
p.   cm.
Includes bibliographical references and index.
ISBN 0-684-19360-4
1. Luce, Henry Robinson, 1898–1967.   2. Journalists—United
States—Biography.   3. Publishers and publishing—United States—
Biography.   I. Title.
PN4874.L76H43   1994   93-42860   CIP
070.5'092—dc20
[B]

Macmillan Books are available
at special discounts for bulk purchases
for sales promotions, premiums,
fund-raising, or educational use.
For details, contact:

Special Sales Director
Macmillan Publishing Company
866 Third Avenue
New York, NY 10022

10   9   8   7   6   5   4   3   2   1

Printed in the United States of America

Book design by Liney Li

To the memory of Thomas L. Connelly

Friend, historian, colleague

CONTENTS

The Publisher
Who Wanted to Change
the World

Henry ("Harry") Robinson Luce was born in China on April 3, 1898. Three weeks later, on the other side of the globe, the United States Congress declared war on Spain. In the course of a conflict that had its origins in a crisis over Cuba, an expanding American nation gained a new empire, one which extended from the Caribbean to the South China Sea.

As a young man, Henry Luce took pride in his nation's new power and moral authority, and Theodore Roosevelt, an impassioned advocate of strength and purpose, was a hero in Harry's household. Luce became a global interventionist, and TR long remained his model. Expansion and empire were not to the liking of all Americans, however.

Writing soon after the Spanish War, Mark Twain spoke for many of his countrymen, too. Twain supported the policy of helping the Cubans become free men and women. He strenuously opposed President William McKinley's annexation of the Philippines, however, and the bloody repression of the Filipinos that followed it. After a horrible war in the jungles of the Philippines, the Americans prevailed. Mark Twain, a vice-president of the Anti-Imperialist League, wrote in bitterness that "*Thirty thousand killed a million*," meaning, 30,000 U.S. troops butchered an estimated one million Filipinos. The figures can be disputed, but Twain's point was clear: the United States had no right to be in the Philippines. As for China, which was much in the news, Twain offered this advice. He warned the U.S. government against meddling in the affairs of that troubled land, and concluded that "We have no more business in China than in any other nation that is not ours." Henry Luce could not have disagreed more. The Philippines were, Luce later argued, strategic America's expanding Pacific frontier. And the United States, he believed, had a *duty* to intervene in China.

Henry Luce's father, the Reverend H. W. Luce, labored as a missionary in Tengchow, China, where Harry was born. The Presbyterian minister and educator believed that Americans must convert and enlighten the Chinese, who could then modernize their country. Luce's son Harry would later advocate the extension of this mission to the whole world.

Less than ten months before Pearl Harbor, Henry R. Luce became the creator of what he called the "American Century." During that coming time of peace, Christian benevolence, and progress, Americans would, Luce believed, enrich humanity, and thereby realize their own, divinely ordained mission. "America cannot be responsible for the good behavior of the entire world," Luce admitted in 1941. "But," he added, "America is responsible, to herself as well as to history, for the world-environment in which she lives." In his sermonlike "American Century," Harry Luce described America as a world power, whose actions or inaction would determine the fate of democracy and capitalism. He called his country the "Good Samaritan," and demanded that the United States export food, technology, "Freedom," "Justice," and modern civilization to a world convulsed by tyranny and evil.

For forty years Henry R. Luce preached his ideals to millions upon millions of his countrymen. Luce helped to change the national mood because he was, in the words of the astute commentator Quincy Howe, "the most influential editor in the United States. . . . If there is any single individual in newspaper, magazine, or radio who has a greater influence on American public opinion," Howe added, "I do not know his name." In 1950 most Americans embraced, or at least accepted, policies that would have seemed outlandish to them ten years earlier. Henry Luce could take some pride in bipartisan support for a huge and permanent military establishment; for security alliances in Europe and Asia; for global intervention in the affairs of far-off peoples; for the dispatch of foreign aid to developing countries; and for the export of food to a myriad of hungry nations. When Henry Robinson Luce died in 1967, his remarkable prophecies of American prosperity and global power had been realized, many times over. Yet something was going very wrong.

Harry Luce lived to see his American Century endure a time of troubles. His beloved China was in the hands of Communists who hated America. As the head of Time Inc.'s magazine empire, Luce embraced the American commitment to an anticommunist Southeast Asia at a time in 1950 when most of his countrymen had never heard of Vietnam. In the 1960s, however, American involvement in Indochina became a national trauma. Thousands of Americans were engaged by 1967 in the kind of divisive and morally corrosive war against which Mark Twain had warned back in 1900. Meanwhile, great cities like Los Angeles, Detroit, and Washington were or would soon be in flames, as racial tensions boiled over onto their streets. Luce, who had so courageously advanced the cause of civil rights, was perplexed and horrified. His vaunted concept of the American Century, which had helped to define the nation's tasks, was in trouble.

Henry Luce's work and prophecies must be measured against his moral ideals, for Luce, a stern and intense human being, would have demanded no less. His record is flawed, but it is also filled with superb, even heroic chapters. Yet Luce's fascination lies in more than his brilliance and his power. He was at once driven, heroic, naive, and blind. John Billings sensed this when he wrote, "What a man—or rather what a mind, because as a man he is not really pleasant or attractive." Yet Billings realized that "Someday he will have to be written about in full, a job I would not relish."

This book records the history of Henry R. Luce's American Century, a powerful idea which this extraordinary publisher, entrepreneur, and salesman preached to two generations of Americans. A propagandist unequaled in the power to convey his ideas, and a man devoid of guile or hypocrisy, Henry Luce was, above all else, a believer in his God, his country, and his work. This credo gave him his strength and, ultimately, his power.

There is, however, a less happy side to this story. Luce, a man with unlimited faith in America's near omnipotence, had not prepared his readers for some of the complex, intractable, and seemingly insoluble problems of a troubled era.

As the century which he named ends, and the hundredth anniversary of Henry Robinson Luce's birth nears, it is time for an examination of the man's political ideas and their influence.

★ ★ ★

This book is heavily dependent on research conducted in a variety of archives and collections. The late Roy Larsen, longtime president of Time Inc., once observed, however, that much of his company's business reflected decisions reached through conversations, not memoranda or letters. In other words, documents and records offer the historian an incomplete picture of Henry Robinson Luce and his times. Only interviews with contemporaries can flesh out the archival records, by breathing life into figures long gone.

I have been fortunate in enjoying access to Henry R. Luce's family, co-workers, and friends.

When I went to the Manuscript Division of the Library of Congress, I discovered that researchers were barred from reading the papers of Henry R. Luce. I contacted Henry R. Luce's son, Mr. Henry Luce III, and explained the nature of my proposed book. He considered my request and generously granted me access in 1990. Used in conjunction with the voluminous papers of Clare Boothe Luce, the Henry Luce collection has proven to be invaluable.

I am equally grateful to Mrs. Elizabeth Moore, sister of the late Henry R. Luce. Mrs. Moore spent some time discussing her brother with me, and her recollections proved to be valuable as well as delightful.

The Theodore H. White papers were essential to my research on Luce and the great China crisis. The Manuscript Department of the Houghton Library at Harvard University is the repository for this collection. Ms. Caroline Preston assisted me as I worked my way through the White papers.

Professor John Kenneth Galbraith, who worked closely with Luce at *Fortune* in the mid-1940s, offered important insights into his former boss. I also appreciate the fact that Professor Galbraith gave me access to the relevant parts of his papers, stored in the John F. Kennedy Library, in South Boston, Massachusetts.

Mr. John Hersey, who was associated with the Luce publications during a crucial time in their history, is best known as a celebrated novelist. After corresponding with Mr. Hersey, I visited him on Martha's Vineyard in 1991. He offered vivid recollections of Henry Luce, along with incisive comments about his work and character. In addition, Mr. Hersey provided me with copies of important documents dating back to the Second World War. Sadly, Mr. Hersey passed away in 1993.

Professor Arthur Schlesinger, Jr., who wrote important articles for *Life* and *Fortune* in the 1940s, has provided me with interesting and useful recollections of Luce and Time Inc. during that important era.

Life researcher Barbara Kerr, who worked with Mr. Schlesinger, was most helpful during a long telephone interview.

I wanted to read the correspondence between William F. Buckley, Jr., and the Luces, which is stored in the Sterling Library at Yale University. I discovered that Mr. Buckley's permission was needed in order to research this massive correspondence. I thank him for granting it.

I met Mr. Henry A. Grunwald, former editor in chief of Time Inc.'s publications and later a distinguished ambassador to Austria, when he was preparing for his Senate confirmation hearings. Later, I interviewed Mr. Grunwald, and he responded in a helpful way to my inquiries about Henry R. Luce and Time Inc.

Mr. Herbert Brownell, former Attorney General and a power in Republican politics for half a century, shared his reminiscences of Luce with me. Mr. Brownell's unrivaled knowledge of GOP politics during the Roosevelt/Truman era placed many of my documents in clearer perspective.

The late Professor John King Fairbank of Harvard, the great historian of modern China, courteously replied to my inquiries. Unfortunately, he passed away in September 1991 before I could meet him.

Mr. Thomas Griffith, who has a knowledge of *Time* rivaled by few people, has given me a good sense of how Harry Luce and his magazines functioned.

Mr. Andrew Heiskell, who worked closely with Luce for almost three decades, participated in a massive and important oral history interview at Columbia University. He kindly gave me permission to read the transcripts of his interviews. I also wish to thank the Oral History Research Office at Columbia for its cooperation, in regard to this and several other useful transcripts.

Mr. Allen Grover, called by many "Luce's vice-president in charge of Luce," shared his rich treasure trove of Luce lore with me. Grover's memories of Harry Luce went back to the 1920s. Few men knew him so well, and none has been more patient in answering my questions. Sadly, Mr. Grover died in 1993.

Sidney James, a Time Inc. writer, editor, and executive, worked for and with Henry Luce for many years. He shared some of his recollections with me, and made available to me his rich array of private papers.

Robert Sherrod, who worked for *Time* and *Life* for many years, graciously contributed important data to my research and provided me with copies of correspondence stored in his private archive.

Mr. David Halberstam, a distinguished author, enriched our understanding of Luce and Time Inc. through his book *The Powers That Be*. He kindly authorized me to review his relevant research materials.

Halberstam's notes are stored at Boston University, as are the papers of the Time Inc. executive Ralph M. Ingersoll.

I wish to thank Mrs. Ralph Ingersoll, who graciously granted me access to her late husband's papers. Mr. Charles Niles, of the Department of Special Collections at the Mugar Library, courteously responded to my inquiries concerning the Halberstam and Ingersoll collections.

Several men affiliated with Time Inc. during the Luce era were generous with their time. The late Eliot Janeway, who had long been known as Luce's "ambassador to the New Deal," offered witty, blunt, and insightful comments about Luce and Time Inc.

Walter Guzzardi, Jr., worked closely with Henry Luce, and his recollections have been particularly valuable to me.

I am also happy to have interviewed Richard Clurman, long a major figure at Time Inc., and himself a chronicler of the company's recent history.

Irwin Ross, a writer who did important work for *Fortune*, was most helpful during our discussion of the Time Inc. culture. Julian Bach, an eminent literary agent who began working for *Life* in 1938, has provided valuable recollections of John Shaw Billings and Henry R. Luce. Hart Preston, who was one of *Life*'s talented photographers and a correspondent who covered much of Latin America, wrote me a long letter that turned out to be a highly informative account of his years with Time Inc.

The noted author Dorothy Sterling has enhanced my understanding of Time Inc. Her papers, which are stored in the Knight Library at the University of Oregon, are vital to the Luce researcher. I am grateful to Mr. J. Fraser Cocks III and the Special Collections Department for assisting me during my visit to the University of Oregon.

Mr. Douglas Auchincloss served for several years as an assistant to Henry Luce. He also worked in an executive capacity with C. D. Jackson in the Council for Democracy. This interventionist organization, which was active in 1940 and 1941, played an important part in Henry Luce's political evolution. Mr. Auchincloss' reminiscences provided me with insights into this important subject.

The late W. A. Swanberg, author of *Luce and His Empire*, was a gifted and honored biographer. He left his notes and papers to the Columbia University library, where I was able to use them. After several years of research, Swanberg concluded that Henry R. Luce was responsible for much of the anticommunist hysteria prevalent after the "loss" of China. Mr. Swanberg made his copious interview notes available to future researchers. In many, perhaps most, cases, Swanberg's subjects are deceased, so the interviews contain unique data. He must have known that other writers would come to entirely different conclusions about Henry R. Luce. I have benefited from my reading of the Swanberg notes, and I have indeed reached conclusions dissimilar to his.

Dr. Bernard R. Crystal and the staff of the Rare Book and Manuscript Library at Columbia assisted me as I researched the papers of W. A. Swanberg, Daniel Longwell, and the Institute of Pacific Relations.

I have been conducting research in the National Archives since 1969, and once again I find myself thanking its veteran archivists. John Taylor discovers relevant materials in the most unlikely places; he did so again in this instance. Richard L. Boylan, Eddie Reese, and Will Mahoney assisted me in finding sources relevant to Time Inc.'s relations with the armed forces and the War Department during World War II. Katherine G. Nicastro and David Pfeiffer, my guides to the records of the Department of State, were extremely helpful. Richard Von Doenhoff provided me with highly useful suggestions about the records of the Navy Department. Robert Wolfe, an old friend, has shown his usual courtesy, interest, and helpfulness.

Dr. Allen Stokes, Mr. Herb Hartsook, and the staff of the South Caroliniana Library at the University of South Carolina helped me as I spent many hours going through the John Shaw Billings papers.

Henry R. Luce's years at Yale College, and his activities as an alumnus, are important to anyone writing about Luce's ideology and beliefs. No repository is more important to the Luce researcher than the Manuscripts and Archives Division of Yale's Sterling Memorial Library. Ms. Judith Ann Schiff familiarized me with a rich array of Luce materials contained in various collections, including Yale-in-China. Mr. William R. Massa, Jr., was also most helpful during my several visits to this archive.

Princeton owns many manuscript collections important to the Luce researcher. Dr. Ben Primer and Ms. Jean Holliday, of the Seeley G. Mudd Manuscript Library, introduced me to important collections, including the papers of Bernard M. Baruch and other figures prominent in the Luce story.

I wish to thank Dr. James H. Hutson and the staff of the Manuscript Division of the Library of Congress. In researching the Henry R. Luce and Clare Boothe Luce papers, along with many other important collections, they showed me every professional courtesy.

Mr. Richard L. Popp, of the University of Chicago Library, made the correspondence between Robert M. Hutchins, William Benton, and

Henry R. Luce available to me. Mr. Philip Cronenwett and the Baker Library at Dartmouth College kindly assisted me as I researched the papers of Grenville Clark. Ms. Carolyn M. Picciano of the Connecticut State Library, Hartford, provided me with photocopies of correspondence relevant to the Luces' role in Connecticut politics.

Archivist David J. Haight and the staff of the Dwight D. Eisenhower Library in Abilene were highly knowledgeable and most supportive of my research.

Ms. Kathy Knox of the Robert W. Woodruff Library at Emory University photocopied relevant parts of the Philip J. Jaffe papers, and they have proven to be very useful to me.

Mr. James Tyler of the Olin Library at Cornell University mailed me photocopies of A. J. Liebling's important notes on Luce and Time Inc. Liebling was planning to write a series of articles on Luce for *Collier's* magazine. Unfortunately these pieces never appeared. Liebling's assistant in the late 1940s, Mr. James Munves, provided me with information about the context of the notes for the aborted *Collier's* articles.

Mr. Emil Moschella and the Freedom of Information Office of the FBI kindly mailed me copies of documents relevant to Henry Luce and Time Inc.

Ms. Carol A. Leadenham and the fine staff of the Hoover Institution on War, Revolution and Peace at Stanford turned an important research trip into a pleasant one. As always, information provided by Agnes F. Peterson resulted in more effective research and, I hope, a better book. Mr. Keith E. Eiler, a research fellow at Hoover, kindly supplied me with photocopies of very important correspondence between General Albert Wedemeyer and Henry R. Luce.

Archivist Dale C. Mayer and the staff of the Herbert Hoover Library, in West Branch, Iowa, generously assisted me during a 1989 visit to their archive. Curator Saundra Taylor of the Manuscripts Division of the Lilly Library at Indiana University corresponded with me in regard to the papers of Wendell L. Willkie. Subsequently, graduate student Karen Fouchereaux provided me with photocopies of Willkie's correspondence with the Luces.

Mr. Edward J. Boone, Jr., archivist at the MacArthur Memorial in Norfolk, Virginia, kindly mailed me photocopies of the MacArthur/Luce correspondence. Glenn S. Cook and the George C. Marshall Foundation were most helpful during my visit to the Marshall Library, in Lexington, Virginia. Ms. Karen L. Jania and the Bentley Historical Library at the University of Michigan made relevant parts of the Arthur Vandenberg papers available to me. The Special Collections Department of the Van Pelt Library at the University of Pennsylvania mailed me copies of Luce's correspondence with Lewis Mumford. I thank them all.

Ms. Wendy Thomas, of the Arthur and Elizabeth Schlesinger Library, at Radcliffe College, enabled me to research Luce-related materials contained in the Freda Kirchwey papers. Mr. Karl Kabelac and the Department of Rare Books at the Rush Rhees Library, University of Rochester, facilitated my use of the Thomas E. Dewey papers, an important source.

Mr. Thomas Rosenbaum, of the Rockefeller Archive Center, in Pocantico Hills, New York, proved to be a most intelligent and diligent archivist.

The excellent staff of the Franklin D. Roosevelt Library, in Hyde Park, assisted me in finding materials essential to the completion of this book. The Franklin and Eleanor Roosevelt Institute awarded me a generous research grant, and I thank both the FDR Library and FERI for their help.

Dr. Benedict K. Zobrist and the staff of the Harry S. Truman Library, in Independence, Missouri, were most courteous. Archivist Dennis Bilger not only helped me find documents, he located some of them himself and then pointed them out to me.

Curator Wendy E. Chmielewski, of the Swarthmore College Peace Collection, facilitated my use of records pertaining to Quaker activities in 1940 and 1941. Mary Ellen Chijioke, curator of the Friends Historical Library of Swarthmore, called records of a similar nature to my attention. Jack Sutters, of the American Friends Service Committee, in Philadelphia, made vital documents available to me during a visit to the AFSC archive.

Ms. Carolyn A. Davis and the George Arents Research Library at Syracuse University assisted me as I researched the papers of Robert Sherrod, Margaret Bourke-White, and other figures important to the Luce researcher.

Ms. Elaine Felsher and her colleagues at the Time Inc. Archive courteously responded to my questions. They shared some of their knowledge of the subject with me, and encouraged me as I continued to do research for this book.

Ms. Paula Williams and the United Negro College Fund, in New York City, made important records available to me. I appreciate the kind assistance rendered by this outstanding organization.

Ms. Laura Endicott and the staff of the Alderman Library, at the University of Virginia in Charlottesville, helped me when I made research inquiries about the papers of Louis Johnson and Edward R.

Stettinius. The staff at the Manuscripts Department of the Wisconsin State Historical Society, in Madison, helped me during two research trips.

Ms. Martha Lund Smalley, of the Divinity School Library at Yale, assisted me as I researched the missionary career of the Reverend Henry W. Luce. Seth Kasten, of the Burke Library at the Union Theological Seminary, provided me with copies of important correspondence.

Professor James L. Baughman of the University of Wisconsin, Madison, made useful suggestions and was generous in sharing his wide knowledge of Luce and Time Inc. with me. The author of the important book *Henry R. Luce and the Rise of the American News Media*, Professor Baughman will observe that my endnotes reflect my gratitude.

I want to pay a special tribute to my editor, Edward T. Chase. Ned Chase has been a friend for many years, but in this case he did more than express interest in my project. We discussed Luce at great length, and Ned Chase's insights helped me to organize my thoughts and plan this difficult project. But Ned contributed more than good questions and sharp criticisms. He introduced me to several of the people who worked with Luce—and sometimes against him—important Time Incers who had in common their knowledge of Henry R. Luce and a high regard for Ned Chase. I profited from their knowledge and share their opinion. I am also grateful to many other people at Scribners, including senior editor Bill Goldstein, associate editor Hamilton Cain, and assistant editor Charles Flowers.

My former dean, Dr. Carol M. Kay, and the University of South Carolina have been most supportive, as have been Dr. Peter Becker and my colleagues and students in the Department of History. My assistant, Ms. Liz Stewart, was most helpful as I worked to organize my files and prepare my manuscript for final editing. During the course of my research, I received a Carolina Research Professorship, which enabled me to travel to more archives and conduct more interviews than would otherwise have been the case.

This book reflects my view of Henry Luce's political ideas and their influence. I am responsible for all statements of fact and opinion contained in this work. They, and the interpretations advanced here are my own, except where otherwise indicated in the notes.

ROBERT EDWIN HERZSTEIN

HENRY R. LUCE

Summer 1940

A Visit to
Franklin D. Roosevelt's
White House

On Thursday afternoon, July 25, 1940, Henry Robinson and Clare Boothe Luce flew from New York City to Washington, D.C. The trip was uneventful, but the couple was soon complaining about the torrid Washington heat (99 degrees and humid). "It was the kind of day," Mrs. Luce noted, "you could fry one of the eggs that had been laid on the steps of the Capitol." After retrieving their luggage, the uncomfortable Luces hailed a taxi, not knowing that the White House had dispatched a car to meet them. This minor farce typified Henry Luce's awkward relations with President Roosevelt.

The Luces' cab pulled into the White House driveway at 5:45. Inside the building, an usher, accompanied by servants, escorted the guests to their bedroom, which was located on the northeast side of the mansion. During the 1939 visit of King George VI and Queen Elizabeth, the royal consort had slept in the four-poster that dominated the Luces' guest room. (Perhaps FDR was slyly commenting upon Clare's self-image.) To the relief of the Luces, their sparsely furnished, unattractive bedroom was air-conditioned. Clare, however, resented the fact that her dressing table was poorly lit.

Like Harry, Clare Luce disliked the President, whom both Luces viewed as a full-time opportunist and occasional demagogue. For years, Luce had scorned Roosevelt as a thoroughly political creature who, in Clare's graphic image, invariably held his moistened finger to the winds of public opinion. Despite their dislike for Roosevelt, however, Harry and Clare knew that this occasion would be a historic one. Churchill's England, bereft of her defeated French ally, now stood alone against the might of Hitler's Germany. Henry Luce, one of the most successful publishers in American history, had long been agonizing over "Time Inc.'s attitude and responsibilities in this critical hour of history." Now, Luce had arrived at the White House armed with a plan to help Britain, and strengthen America. In the days to come, both Luces recorded impressions of their evening with Roosevelt, and in describing that event, I draw upon their diaries.

Harry agreed with Clare that their guest room lacked charm, but a book of memoirs about the late President Woodrow Wilson, one of his heroes, quickly consoled him. Luce still bitterly resented what he saw as America's retreat to isolation following the Wilson presidency. In 1918, Harry Luce was training to become an officer in the U.S. Army. Young Luce hoped to ship out to France, where he could fight for his democratic and patriotic ideals. After Germany signed the armistice in November, however, he found himself back at Yale, where his fellow students soon voted him the college's "most brilliant" senior. Upon his graduation in 1920, Harry looked forward to helping America make the world safe for democracy, Christianity, and free enterprise. Instead, American leaders, and many of their fellow citizens, rejected Wilson's vision of American global leadership. "To hell with Europe!" was a commonly voiced sentiment. By 1939, Europe was again at war, and the totalitarian states were making bids for hegemony in Europe and Asia. At this dark juncture in July 1940, however, Henry Luce still believed that America was destined to change the world for the better.

Five weeks earlier, France's fabled armies had crumbled before the onslaught of the Wehrmacht. Prime Minister Winston Churchill believed that Hitler might order an invasion of England, perhaps in August or September. In the middle of May, and again in June 1940, Churchill had appealed in vain to FDR, asking that forty or fifty of 172 recently recommissioned American destroyers be handed over to Great Britain. The Royal Navy, the Prime Minister told FDR, needed the destroyers in order to defend supply lines essential to Britain's survival. On June 26, after France had collapsed, King George VI himself addressed an urgent appeal to Roosevelt, asking for the destroyers. Again, the President refused to act. In the waters around Britain, the Royal

Navy disposed in theory of about one hundred destroyers. By late July 1940, however, almost half of these had been damaged or sunk. Still, the White House remained silent.

Some of Roosevelt's military advisers feared that Britain might crack under the coming air attack by the Luftwaffe, or fall prey to starvation thanks to growing U-boat activity around the British Isles. If the island kingdom fell to Hitler, what would become of the U.S. destroyers? Another consideration troubled Roosevelt. The President assumed that the sale or gift of destroyers to Britain required congressional approval. Isolationists in the Congress, Roosevelt feared, would block the sale or transfer of American warships to Great Britain. On June 28, 1940, these members, ever suspicious of Roosevelt's intentions, managed to amend the law. The sale of military supplies to a foreign power was now illegal unless the relevant service chief certified them as inessential to the nation's defense.

Politics were never far from the President's mind, and the imminent campaign for the presidency complicated the destroyer issue. Roosevelt wanted to run as a peace candidate, whose measured gestures of aid for Britain in no way threatened to involve the United States in a new war. He thus needed to find a scheme that would convince Americans that the dispatch of destroyers to Britain was in their interests. And he wanted to make sure that the Republican presidential candidate, Wendell L. Willkie, supported any such transfer. On June 29, therefore, Roosevelt met with the famous Kansas editor William Allen White. A prominent Republican and the leader of the Committee to Defend America by Aiding the Allies, White was also friendly with Willkie.

Walter Johnson, a friend and biographer of White, suggests that the President "talked to White about trading destroyers to England for naval bases in the British possessions of the Western Hemisphere." This seems unlikely, for in the weeks ahead White, who was ever more anxious to secure the release of the warships to Britain, failed to make use of or even mention FDR's alleged suggestion. As late as July 25, White had not a clue about the "destroyer for bases deal," as it came to be known. This is not surprising, for the President met with the Kansan for a different reason. He wanted to secure White's support for a possible sale or lease of the destroyers. FDR wished to use William Allen White as an intermediary who could gain the backing of Wendell Willkie for the destroyer transfer.

Though the President was not ready to make the transfer, his meeting with White was not without issue. The Committee to Defend America worked to win public support for the dispatch of the destroyers, and White brought Willkie into the picture. On July 5 Clark Eichelberger wrote to White. A publisher, he suggested, should take over the public relations work of the Committee to Defend America. National Chairman Eichelberger, who ran the day-to-day operations of the "White Committee," added that "Our first thought is Henry Luce." William Allen White contacted Luce, offering him the position, but Harry turned him down. Though ardently interventionist, Luce feared that an official position with White could compromise his magazines. He preferred to act behind the scenes and let his magazines (and his wife) bask in the limelight.

Like the Luce press and other interventionist organs, the Committee to Defend America continued to bombard the public with a barrage of publicity favoring the sale or gift of destroyers to Britain. Its propaganda campaign, for example, soon made prominent use of the July 22 issues of *Time* and *Life*. Like Harry Luce, however, White remained perplexed by the President's inactivity. Writing to presidential speech writer Robert E. Sherwood on July 23, he noted that "If the President really wants to do it [i.e., transfer the destroyers]—it can be done." White added that "we must show him that the country will follow him in this matter." The Kansan was not particularly sanguine about the outcome, however. Somehow, he had not come up with the formula that would appeal to both the public and to FDR. On July 25, for example, the Committee to Defend America, which now had over 550 chapters, sent out 50,000 copies of its demand for the dispatch of destroyers to Britain. The urgent statement made no mention of a quid pro quo, or of any "deal." President Roosevelt was still searching for a device that would win the support of the public and the Congress. So the matter languished in late July 1940, even as the press concentrated ever more intently on the expected German onslaught against Great Britain.

Ostensibly, President Roosevelt had invited Harry Luce to the White House on July 25 for dinner, to be followed by the screening of a new movie. FDR and his guests would watch a full-length feature film produced by Time Inc.'s March of Time division. Called *The Ramparts We Watch*, the movie was generating much national interest. During this dark hour of the war, however, Harry Luce was more than the proud sponsor of a controversial film. In fact, the head of Time Inc. arrived at the White House as an unofficial spokesman, acting on behalf of powerful men known as the Century Group. Right now, aiding Britain was their common obsession.

The Century Group consisted mainly of "establishment" types, usually Eastern internationalists who believed in America's global mission and their own right and duty to influence United States foreign policy. They met at the meritocratic Century Association on West 43rd Street in New York City, hence the name Century Group. Formed on July 11 at a meeting convened across the street at the Columbia Club, the Century Group had thirty members, dominated by about a dozen activists. The men engaged in more than three hours of discussion. They agreed to send delegations to Secretary of State Cordell Hull and to Republican presidential candidate Wendell L. Willkie. In addition, those present decided to put more pressure on newspaper editors across the country. First, however, their group needed some money for the rental of an office. Ward Cheney, a silk manufacturer, donated $2,000 (of the necessary $3,500) to the group. The Century interventionists could now open a small office in suite 2940 in a building on 42nd Street, located around the corner from the Century Association. Directed by the Virginian Francis Pickens Miller, an energetic White Committee activist on leave from his post at the Council on Foreign Relations, the office became a busy center of interventionist activity. Its phone bank and secretarial staff acted as a conduit, linking the Century Group to the government, the British embassy, and the American media.

All members of the Century organization (at first dubbed the "Miller Group" by the press) shared a "common hatred of Hitler and of his system of society." Among these men one found the sixty-three-year-old Reverend Henry Sloane Coffin, the Presbyterian pastor of the Madison Avenue Church in New York City. The Century Group included Clark Eichelberger, ardent Wilsonian and friend of the ill-fated League of Nations; Roosevelt's friend and speechwriter, the famous playwright Robert Emmet Sherwood; and Ernest Hopkins, the longtime president of Dartmouth College. Henry Pitney Van Dusen, a forty-three-year-old professor at the Union Theological Seminary, was a prominent clerical advocate of the "social gospel," and a liberal Protestant activist whom Harry Luce greatly respected. The Century Group disseminated its propaganda through publishers and journalists like Barry Bingham and Herbert Agar, of the *Louisville Courier-Journal*, and Geoffrey Parsons, of the prestigious *New York Herald Tribune*. Inside information supplied to reporters like Charles Ross of the *St. Louis Post-Dispatch* soon made headlines. Though Henry Luce worried about becoming too public and controversial a figure (a role which might hurt his beloved Time Inc.), he felt honored to be included in such company.

The prominent and often wealthy individuals gathered together in the Century Group cherished religion, the Constitution, Anglo-Saxon liberties, and a free system of "production and trade." If they shared a common hero, it was Theodore Roosevelt, whose strength, patriotism, and righteousness particularly appealed to Harry Luce. The Century men wished to assist England in every possible way, even if U.S. actions incurred the risk of German retaliation. The Group feared German domination of the North Atlantic, and with it, a dark time when "the United States could be invaded from the Atlantic." The group's members operated with a sense of urgency, for the "British chances of success are at present doubtful. . . ." But they also felt driven by a can-do spirit, for if Britain received U.S. destroyers, she "could successfully withstand invasion."

Beyond the present emergency, men like Miller and Luce could see a new era dawning. The crisis of the British Empire was not all to the bad. If Americans could defeat the Nazis, then, Luce believed, their nation would be the undisputed architect of a new world order. First, however, Luce and men like Francis Miller would need to convince Americans that the present war was as much their concern as it was Great Britain's. Miller would soon suggest substituting the term "battle of the Atlantic" for the phrase "battle of Britain."

Henry Luce, all agreed, could effectively promote the interventionist cause through his powerful magazines. He was, however, a difficult ally. Francis Pickens Miller, a politically ambitious man, found Luce to be a tiresome moralist. Typically, Harry, who was a devout Presbyterian and an ardent lay theologian, insisted on turning exchanges about military strategy into "a discussion of what were a publisher's moral responsibilities at such a time." His harangues irritated Francis Miller, who had to keep order at these meetings. Harry, Miller complained, wanted his colleagues to act as a "group confessor." Worse still, Luce, Miller recalled, sometimes stammered to the point of inarticulateness. The insufferable Harry Luce was, however, the Century Group's emissary to 40 million American magazine readers and moviegoers. Luce also enjoyed access to the President, with whom he had last met on June 1, and Secretary of State Cordell Hull, with whom he conferred on July 13.

To the dismay of Luce and his colleagues at the Century, the Roosevelt administration did not appear ready to make a dramatic gesture to Churchill's hard-pressed Britain. After his futile conversation with Secretary Hull, Luce resolved to see the President in the near future. As always, the encounter would be personally unpleasant to both men, but present needs overshadowed their mutual aversion. Roosevelt knew that Harry Luce's publications had millions of readers. Besides, Republican Luce could if he wished act as a confidential go-between, linking the White House to both the Century Group and to GOP presidential candidate Wendell L. Willkie.

In 1939, and through the spring of 1940, Russell Davenport, managing editor of Luce's *Fortune* magazine, worked to convert lawyer and businessman Wendell Willkie into a national figure. Against all the odds, "Luce's man Willkie" had won the Republican presidential nomination a few weeks before the Luces arrived at the White House on July 25. Davenport was now Willkie's campaign manager, and both he and the candidate were constantly conferring with Harry Luce. If the Century Group hoped to induce the President to send warships to Britain, surely FDR would demand that Willkie endorse the controversial step. Here, too, the ever-driven Harry Luce might be expected to play a role.

In Luce's view, the United States was faced with a disaster in the making. He called upon his editors to "educate our readers to see that specific policies . . . can and do make sense." Among these policies were all-out aid for England, conscription, and the "elimination of Hitlerian interference. . . ." "We must," Luce added, "not only specify the Danger, but also urge where, when and how it must be met." By July 18, Luce had decided that countries and territories in and around the Caribbean basin "must be friendly to us." The same, he noted, was true of "Canada, Greenland, and various outlying points such as Bermuda." Clearly, Harry Luce intended to help England fight Hitler, while greatly extending America's defensive perimeters. Time Inc.'s chief now demanded that his editors "cultivate the Martial Spirit."

In this terrible summer of 1940, Henry Robinson Luce was a tall, slim, balding man of forty-two. He had in 1923 co-founded (with the late Briton Hadden) *Time*, the first newsmagazine. The brilliantly edited *Time* featured articles that read like short stories, replete with portraits of interesting personalities, sketched in snappy prose, and peppered with well-phrased wisecracks. *Time* skillfully conveyed its interpretation of events to its growing number of readers. Journalists and politicians routinely read *Time*; Roosevelt hated it but he nonetheless studied the magazine. In 1930 Luce created *Fortune*, which greatly influenced American business leaders and changed the way journalism covered private enterprise. By July 1940 *Fortune* was explaining defense needs to corporate executives and urging them to work with the government, not against it. The magazine exposed bottlenecks in the production of military hardware and sometimes helped to unclog them. It constantly warned that labor, management, and government must work together, in order to build the world's mightiest military machine.

In 1935, after a painful divorce, Henry Luce had married the former Clare Boothe Brokaw, a talented editor and an ambitious woman with a wide array of social contacts. A year later Luce began to publish *Life*, which within three years became the most popular magazine in the country. *Life*, with its wonderful pictures and interesting stories, helped restore America's morale during the last years of a terrible decade. By 1940 *Life*'s publicists claimed a readership of 17 to 20 million readers, in a country of 132 million. *Life*'s variety and appeal were akin to those of television from the 1950s on. Henry Luce's newsfilm effort, *The March of Time*, appeared on thousands of movie theater screens each month. The well-crafted visual images projected by *Life* and *The March of Time* skillfully conveyed Time Inc.'s opinions to almost one quarter of the nation. Time Inc.'s competitors lacked the power and influence of Luce's magazines and movies. Polls taken by Luce's friend Elmo Roper discerned changes in public opinion when all of Time Inc.'s media launched a sustained campaign on *one* issue.

In late July 1940, Harry Luce was far more than the great success story of the American magazine world. This son of missionaries was also a crusader, but unless Franklin D. Roosevelt acted, he might soon feel like Don Quixote. A clash of personalities made Luce's task more difficult.

By the time of the Luces' arrival in Washington on that hot summer day, Roosevelt had long since made up his mind about Harry Luce and his famous magazine, *Time*. He disliked Luce, whom he had met as recently as June 1, and resented much of what he read about himself and the Democratic New Deal in his magazines. Luce, a fervent Republican, had by 1936 become highly critical of Roosevelt. He personally scorned the President, and to the fury of the White House, Luce's magazines often conveyed this aversion to their readers. *Life*'s July 29 issue, for example, contained an article that compared Franklin D. Roosevelt to Adolf Hitler. In the contemptuous words of *Life*'s managing editor, John Shaw Billings, the recent 1940 Democratic convention was "a disgusting spectacle of machine politics." *Life* then savaged Roosevelt's renomination as a triumph for the "third termites," and compared the Chicago convention to the Nazi Reichstag, which routinely saluted every one of Hitler's appearances. The President, however, had no intention of confronting Luce on July 25 over this kind of slight. He badly needed Luce's support for his foreign policy, and *Life*, after all, was too popular to ignore. White House press aides Steve Early and Marvin McIntyre nevertheless kept a careful tally sheet of Harry's sins. One day, in calmer times, Roosevelt intended to settle this score.

On the evening of July 25, the President and the publisher would enjoy their cocktails, dine, watch a movie, then talk about serious foreign policy matters. Britain faced an imminent German attack. Closer to home, from Newfoundland to Trinidad, a weak Canada and a beleaguered Britain remained responsible for defending maritime lanes leading to the Atlantic and Gulf coasts of the United States. Henry Luce was coming to the White House armed with a plan, one that might help Britain, strengthen America, and provide Franklin D. Roosevelt with political cover. Despite his Republican partisanship, Harry was determined to put the interests of his country and of the Western world before his own political desires.

In September 1939, after the war in Europe had erupted, Britain agreed that American planes and ships might make use of port and air facilities in Trinidad, St. Lucia, and Bermuda. Little came of the proposal at that time, in part because few Americans felt threatened by the desultory war being fought in Europe. When the Germans attacked the Low Countries and France in May 1940, however, perceptions changed, and quickly. U-boat activity in the waters around England increased, and Americans anticipated a battle for supremacy in the Atlantic. Many Americans, including some so-called isolationists, suddenly saw the need to extend their country's Atlantic defense perimeter farther into the seas off the East and Gulf coasts. The astute British ambassador, Philip Kerr, Marquess of Lothian, wanted to make a generous gesture to the Americans. He hoped that a voluntary offer of Caribbean leases would later yield dividends. Churchill, however, rejected Lothian's proposal on May 29. Grumbling that the United States had done little to help the threatened Allies, he would grant nothing except "as part of a deal."

Late in June, as France prepared to sign an armistice with Hitler, Lothian advised the Foreign Office that many Americans were calling for access to British naval and air facilities in the Americas. The Foreign Office subsequently advised making an unconditional, unilateral offer of these bases to the United States, but once again the War Cabinet failed to act. Many officials were loath to give or bargain away pieces of the Empire, even at a time of national crisis. By early July 1940, however, Ambassador Lothian was implying that the United States might, under certain circumstances, seize the Caribbean bases and port facilities. Public opinion was veering in that direction. Lothian also knew that Frank Knox, the newly appointed Secretary of the Navy, was particularly anxious to secure these strategic assets. So, Lothian seemed to ask, why not bow to the inevitable and gain something in return for the bases?

Meanwhile, Roosevelt continued to puzzle over the destroyer dilemma. If he proposed that the Congress authorize a sale of the warships to Britain, isolationists might filibuster the measure to death. On July 19, 1940, presidential aide Benjamin Cohen suggested that the Congress be asked to permit the sale of the destroyers to Canada, provided that they were used in the defense of a broadly defined "American Hemisphere." After a few days of reflection, Roosevelt, though intrigued by the idea, refused to embrace Cohen's proposal. So, while Britain awaited the German assault, the old U.S. destroyers languished in American ports.

The Century Group planned to meet for dinner on July 25. Foremost on the minds of its members was the President's inactivity in regard to the overage destroyers. At some point before the forthcoming meeting of the full Century Group, Harry Luce, Henry P. Van Dusen, Francis Miller, and perhaps other activists held their own, preliminary conversation. This submeeting probably took place on Wednesday afternoon, July 24. Luce was the cause of this highly important encounter. He had to see Roosevelt on the evening of July 25, and would therefore miss a crucial Century Group dinner.

As a great promoter attuned to the country's mood, Luce knew what people would "buy" from their politicians. Most of his fellow Century interventionists, including Francis Miller and Henry P. Van Dusen, rejected the idea of demanding anything in return for the old destroyers. After all, by saving herself, England would be buying time for the United States. At this point, Harry Luce, as he so often did, interrupted. He opposed the gift of the destroyers to Britain. Knowing that Roosevelt would require political cover, Luce argued that the British must be asked to offer what he called a "quid pro quo," in return for the warships. Theologian Henry P. Van Dusen agreed, but not in a way calculated to calm Luce. Van Dusen proposed that the American side insist that Churchill neither surrender nor scuttle the British fleet. Instead, the remnants of a defeated Royal Navy would sail to Canadian or American ports. Luce scorned Van Dusen's proposal; it was not enough, he argued, to obtain such a promise from Churchill. After all, in the agony of invasion and defeat, a new and desperate British government could easily renege on Churchill's promise.

According to Francis Pickens Miller, Harry Luce thereupon proposed "these destroyers should be offered to Britain in return for immediate naval and air concessions in the Western Hemisphere." Luce made the argument that access to bases in this vast region would immeasurably increase American security. Then, Luce continued, the Navy could certify that some of its recommissioned destroyers were no longer essential to the defense of the United States. Roosevelt would be free to dispatch the old warships to Britain, while praising the deal as a boon to the defense of the Americas. Finally, Luce addressed the Willkie factor. While he thought that the Republican nominee would endorse the destroyer deal, Luce did not want to link FDR's approval to the GOP candidate's support. After all, the publisher argued, Willkie would find himself under extreme isolationist pressure, and if tried to accommodate the anti-interventionists, the proposed deal would fall through.

On July 25, while the Luces rested in their White House guest room, Francis Miller and seventeen of his allies in the Century Group duly arrived at the Century Association, in midtown Manhattan. A little after 7 P.M., Washington columnist and arch-insider Joseph Alsop addressed the group. Alsop, an ardent interventionist with close ties to the First Family, warned that Britain, lacking adequate sea power, might soon be open to German invasion. Using secret data culled from British intelligence operatives and diplomats, Alsop painted a bleak picture of Britain's naval strength. "Unless the British are given immediate additional destroyers," the journalist declared, "the odds are absolutely against defending the British isles." Alsop mentioned the possibility of sending the U.S. Navy destroyers to Canada, which could then turn some of its own ships over to Britain. After hearing Alsop, everyone present agreed that Miller should draw up a memorandum and present it to the President and other key officials. In the document, the Century interventionists would argue that one hundred destroyers could save Britain.

After Joseph Alsop and perhaps two other members of the Century Group had spoken, the assemblage tried to answer the following question: "What steps are to be taken to ensure action?" At this point, one member, probably Miller, reported on the "Wednesday afternoon conversation." Though Miller disliked the abrasive Harry Luce, the publisher's proposal had apparently impressed him and his colleagues. In Miller's notes on the July 25 meeting, the Century conferees agreed that the "The United States needs naval bases at Trinidad and other naval and/or air rights among the British possessions in the Western Hemisphere." Furthermore, "The United States, in the interest of its own national defense, should offer Britain destroyers in return for territorial concessions as specified by United States military and naval authorities." Thanks to Henry Luce's bold intervention, the Century

Group now had a plan, that "these destroyers should be offered to Britain in exchange for immediate naval and air concessions in British possessions in the Western hemisphere."

The Century men felt that public opinion "is not aroused on this issue," for people did not sense the imminent threat to "the Eastern approaches to [the Panama] Canal." Nor did Americans appreciate the need to provide "adequate defense for the Eastern seaboard. . . ." Perhaps so, but a Gallup poll of July 21 showed that 81 percent of those surveyed favored the purchase of strategic bases and port facilities in the Caribbean. Nevertheless, there would be much work for the Group's journalists in the days and weeks to come. Americans would have to be frightened and inspired at the same time. This was the kind of call that Harry Luce would readily answer. Few journalists took their trade so seriously; Luce was prepared to shoulder any burden imposed upon him by the divinely ordained American mission.

On its face, the destroyers-for-bases idea seemed to be the logical and perhaps inevitable solution to a perplexing problem. Late in July, the polls showed that Americans favored the export of all possible aid to beleaguered Britain. Only in hindsight, however, does the destroyer-for-bases proposal appear to have been inevitable. The public (and few private citizens) had not yet linked its two crucial elements.

On July 25, the day of the Luces' visit to the White House, Ambassador Lothian, who was in frequent consultation with the new Century Group, cabled a compelling telegram to the Foreign Office. He suggested that Churchill again alert Roosevelt to the imminent crisis confronting Great Britain. Lothian had spied a new opportunity, and within a day, Churchill began to draft an urgent cable to Roosevelt.

At 7:20 P.M., the Luces, who had refreshed themselves in their White House guest room, received a phone call from Roosevelt's secretary, "Missy" LeHand, who asked them to proceed to the place in the residence called the Oval Room. There, President Roosevelt, clad in a white linen suit, was sitting behind his desk, happily preparing his famous martinis. Clare believed that he was posing, as always, but Roosevelt impressed her as strong and pleasant—except for his hands, which appeared to tremble. Near the President stood (there was no place for them to sit) two Time Inc. executives and their wives, the Roy Larsens and the Louis de Rochemonts. With them were Missy LeHand and presidential aide Harry Hopkins. It had been a difficult, hot day, so Harry Luce, who was not much of a drinker, enjoyed two of Roosevelt's "excellent martinis." He bristled, however, when FDR, in an attempt at familiarity, again addressed him as "Henry." As Clare put it, "if people insist on using people's first names as a sign of familiarity they should make a point of using the right one." Eventually, Franklin Roosevelt turned his fabled charm on Clare, favoring her with some comments on the refugee situation in Europe. The President then tried a bit of flattery, telling Clare that "I worried terribly about you when you were over there [in Belgium]." Clare wondered how many other people had heard this line.

The President's guests walked downstairs to the dining room, where Clare sat to the right of the President. Roosevelt liked to tell a good story, and he expected everyone to listen. This time the tall tale concerned revolutionary chaos in Haiti during the First World War. According to the President's witty account, Assistant Secretary of the Navy Franklin Roosevelt had been responsible for sending the Marines to that country in 1915. Then, through an irony of history, it was President Roosevelt who in 1934 removed them. Clare Luce thought that the tale was "a very gory story full of murder and thunder," and one calculated to leave the impression that "Mr. Roosevelt had for all times settled the destiny of that particular corner of the Caribbean." Though she admired FDR's fabled conversational ability, she also resented his desire to "monopolize the conversation."

Clare Luce was notably self-centered herself, so she inevitably clashed with a President with so high a sense of self-esteem. "It rather galled and irritated me," wrote Clare, "that I am so insensible to his famous charm." FDR had already taken note of the slight. Clare disapproved of the President for another reason. When Mrs. Roosevelt was out of town (a frequent occurrence), Missy LeHand sometimes substituted for her as the President's hostess. Such was the case on this evening of July 25. According to some rumors, the relationship between the secretary and the Chief Executive was an intimate one. Clare greatly admired Eleanor Roosevelt, despite their political disagreements. She appears to have disliked Missy LeHand, however, and Clare made apparent her displeasure. Nor did she like Harry Hopkins, Roosevelt's closest associate.

Mrs. Luce insisted upon speaking, even as the President continued his performance. Boldly, she mentioned her admiration for two controversial ambassadors, Joseph P. Kennedy (London) and William C. Bullitt (Paris). Roosevelt responded in a discreet manner, describing them as "my temperamental ambassadors." Bullitt, of course, was an ardent and controversial interventionist, while Kennedy was reputed to be a defeatist and an isolationist. (Perhaps only FDR would have assembled such a diverse diplomatic duo at so critical a time in history.) If they were good diplomats, FDR continued, it was because they were political appointees. Career diplomats, Roosevelt claimed, knew too little about their own country. The President ascribed this insight to Harry Hopkins, who was seated at the dinner table. Neither Harry nor Clare Luce, however, was willing to give Hopkins credit for anything. To them, and to many other Republicans (and conservative Democrats), FDR's "Harry the Hop" represented the most repulsive kind of tax-and-spend-and-elect New Dealism. And Clare disagreed with Hopkins' view of diplomacy, though she did force herself to remain silent. Many years later, after serving as Dwight D. Eisenhower's ambassador to Italy, Mrs. Luce changed her opinion.

The entourage then turned to a brief discussion of domestic politics. Harry Luce disagreed with Missy LeHand, who feared that the country would vote for "appeasement" (meaning isolation and neutrality) in the fall elections. Not so, said Luce, whereupon it became clear that FDR believed he would win by denouncing "appeasement." Harry was puzzled by the President's comment, for Republican candidate Willkie was certainly no appeaser. Roosevelt, of course, intended to ignore Willkie and run against the Republican Party unless the race became too close to call.

The President and his guests, having enjoyed their coffee, returned to the second floor, where a large, miserably hot hallway contained a makeshift movie screen. The projectionist then ran Time Inc.'s new movie *The Ramparts We Watch*, which glorified the coming of the First World War to Main Street America in 1917. *Ramparts*, the product of Roy Larsen, Louis de Rochemont, and their dedicated technicians, cleverly blended staged reenactments with newsfilm footage. Luce and his colleagues at Time Inc. seemed to be calling for a rebirth of the anti-German patriotism that swept much of the country in those days. Or were they really justifying intervention in the European war in 1940?

The Ramparts We Watch was Time Inc.'s response to the millions of Americans who declared, "Once burned, twice shy," or, "No more interventions!" It portrayed the Germans as nasty aggressors, who in 1914 had turned thousands of Belgians into terrified refugees. Clare Luce, during a stint as a war correspondent for *Life*, had just covered the rout of the Allied armies in Belgium. Sobbing as the projector cast its images on the small screen, she wondered aloud whether Americans would come to the rescue, as they had in 1918. In an aside to Roosevelt, Mrs. Luce observed that we had gone to war in 1917 in order to preserve freedom of the seas, a right we surrendered in 1939. Roosevelt quickly agreed. Magnanimously, he blamed himself for America's inaction, but ascribed the real guilt to isolationists like William Randolph Hearst. Harry Luce despised the Hearst press, but he also believed that until recently, FDR himself had bent to the political winds.

The concluding scene of *The Ramparts We Watch* could not fail to stir Roosevelt and his assemblage. While the "Star-Spangled Banner" sounded in the distance, *Ramparts'* last frames showed Plymouth Rock, a symbol of freedom amidst the dangerous storms looming over the American homeland. The President's favorable reaction to *The Ramparts We Watch* was encouraging to Luce and his collaborators. Perhaps they had not worked in vain. The lights went on and the President and his guests left the stuffy corridor, where the air reeked of stale cigarette smoke.

Roosevelt then summoned Harry Luce to the Oval Room, whose doors shut behind them. Luce quickly came to the point. "My big question," he noted in his diary, was "has he or has he not made up his mind about sending destroyers to Great Britain?" In an interview granted many years later, Clare recalled that an impatient Harry Luce had suggested to President Roosevelt that the United States gain access to bases, airfields, and port facilities in the Caribbean region in return for the aging warships. FDR, however, seemed to say (Harry Luce was increasingly hard of hearing) that "it's out," meaning there would be *no* destroyer deal. Public opinion, he explained, would not stand for the proposed sale, since people were concerned first and foremost with the defense of *our* hemisphere. Clearly, FDR was worried about the polls. Though every sampling of public opinion revealed broad support for the general principle of aiding Britain, a large number of nervous Americans might oppose the dispatch of warships to a country on the verge of invasion. The heavily isolationist Congress was another thorn in Roosevelt's side. All of this discouraged Harry Luce.

The President then spied a ray of hope. He mused about giving the destroyers to the Canadians if they pledged to use them for hemispheric defense. Canada could then presumably turn some badly needed destroyers over to Britain. In addition, Roosevelt told Luce that he would soon invite congressional leaders to sail with him on his yacht and would try to bring them around. Presumably, his famous charm could once again work wonders. Then FDR slyly implied that he would go ahead with a destroyer deal only if *Time* and *Life* proposed it first. Clare Luce recalled her husband's version of the President's exact words. "Harry," Roosevelt pleaded, "I can't come out in favor of such a deal unless I can count on the support of the entire *Time-Life* organization for my foreign policy." Luce pledged his backing for measures intended to save England. Still, he could not get a firm commitment from Roosevelt. FDR, however, momentarily believed he had gained an important if highly volatile political ally.

Luce became confused and frustrated, and his *War Diary* reflects this sour mood. At such times Harry, agitated, would chain-smoke and stammer his way through a series of unwelcome interruptions. Franklin Roosevelt, by contrast, appeared serene, a mood that baffled Luce. "F.D.R. is very friendly and conveys an air of great confidence," Luce noted soon after the conversation, "though what in, I don't know. . . ." The President's good humor, interspersed with meditations on history, seemed to mock Luce's near frenzied intensity. FDR grandly confided to Luce that he felt reincarnated, as if he had been through all of this before. He implied to Harry that their generation would relive 1917, when the United States sent troops to Europe on behalf of the Allied cause. If so, Luce wondered, why did the President refuse to commit himself to the destroyer deal, even in principle?

Harry Luce finally left the President and rejoined Clare, who was engaged in an unpleasant conversation with Harry Hopkins, discussing the great issue of the day: how should Americans respond to the menace posed by Adolf Hitler? Hopkins declared that Roosevelt must be re-elected because he alone had not compromised with Hitler. Clare let pass this slur on her husband and Willkie. In her diary she predicted that Roosevelt would run again in 1944 if the world crisis lasted that long. This thought, which proved to be prophetic, horrified Harry and Clare. In fact, Harry Luce and Franklin D. Roosevelt found common ground only when confronting the prospect of Nazi hegemony in Europe. A Luce-Roosevelt alliance would, by its very nature, be both important and fragile.

On Friday morning (at 10:38 on July 26, according to the usher's precise records) the Luces left FDR's White House. Harry was glad to escape. Perhaps one small presidential gaffe summed up Harry Luce's attitude. "That God-damned President of yours," Harry more than once exploded in the presence of Democratic editors, "thinks he's being intimate when he calls me Henry. . . . I don't like that," he once growled to his Democratic friend William Benton. "My friends call me Harry."

On this same Friday, Harry Luce called on William Franklin Knox, the new Secretary of the Navy. The two men discussed American rearmament, and Frank Knox's optimism impressed Luce. On the same day, Luce visited the British embassy, where he chatted with the ambassador, Lord Lothian. The diplomat was in contact with other members of the Century Group, and he expected them to assist the British cause. Luce, however, could not impart good news, for he remained confused and angry about FDR's real intentions. Still, Lothian, like Roosevelt and Knox, was in a good mood, almost as if he expected a pleasant surprise. Luce, grasping at straws, talked about selling the overage destroyers to Canada, a possibility that intrigued the ambassador. After speaking with Luce, Lothian cabled London that "this is the moment to press the President about destroyers, etc." Within two days the ambassador was active on another front.

On July 28 Lord Lothian forwarded an alarmist memorandum to Whitney Shepardson—Rhodes Scholar, international investor, and prominent Republican—for distribution to the Century Group. Containing secret military information, the document painted a grim picture of Britain's situation. The facts, Lord Lothian told his allies, were so serious that "if [they] were known they would not be believed." Bemoaning the weakness of "politicians" (presumably Roosevelt and the members of Congress), Lothian warned that if Britain fell, "America itself is doomed." According to the Lothian memorandum, only sixty-eight Royal Navy destroyers remained "fit for active service," at a time when Britain faced an imminent German threat in her home waters. Lothian concluded that American destroyers "might make a decisive difference to the future of the war." The ambassador clearly hoped that the journalists affiliated with the Century Group would publicize Britain's dire need.

Henry Luce had promised both the Century Group and the President that his magazines would endorse any arrangement that would get the destroyers to Britain, while strengthening the defenses of the United States. He was as good as his word. *Time*'s July 29 issue was now in homes, offices, and libraries throughout the land. *Time* offered subscribers and the other media a "Strategic Geography of the Caribbean Sea." This highly unusual, striking, four-page essay, replete with detailed maps, made an eloquent case for obtaining the bases. An estimated 4 to 5 million readers learned that the Caribbean was the "only route for an attacker crossing the Atlantic to strike at the [Panama] Canal." The Dutch West Indies, *Time* warned, lay astride "the most valuable and most vulnerable area of the Caribbean . . . ," and formed "the first outpost of the U.S.'s maritime frontier." Axis bases in the region, *Time* continued, would pose a threat to both the Panama Canal and the southeastern United States. *Time* did more than make the case for gaining access to strategic bases and airfields. The magazine described the crucial importance of the Caribbean in some detail, by supplying readers with inside information gleaned from sources such as Army Intelligence, the Navy Department, and the British embassy. *Time* then argued that American-controlled bases would greatly extend the striking range of "the U.S. Fleet and land-based aircraft. . . ." *Time* favored gaining access to seas "1,000 to 2,000 miles beyond the Canal."

Time then showed that the perceived Axis threat to the Americas presented the United States with a wonderful opportunity. Thanks to the war—and presumably Britain's need for help—America could now move to dominate its eastern approaches by acquiring bases from Newfoundland to Trinidad. Harry Luce the supersalesman was at work, preparing the American people for a stunning transaction. He did not try to foreclose the President's options, for Roosevelt must have room to maneuver. The word "deal," therefore, did not appear in *Time.* Instead, Luce's Republican magazines implied that the use of bases essential to America's forward defenses was worth a substantial price. And the president who obtained access to them would certainly merit praise and perhaps reelection.

On July 29 Prime Minister Churchill concluded that the Germans might be preparing to land somewhere on Britain's south coast. On the high seas, Britain was about to endure a frightening fortnight. Before it was over, the Germans and Italians sank 135,000 tons of Allied and neutral shipping. On the same day, Lothian's pressure bore fruit. The War Cabinet finally decided to make a unilateral offer to the United States. Thanks to its decision, the Americans would receive the right to use British bases and facilities off the Atlantic Coast and in the Caribbean. First, however, Churchill again pleaded for the release of the destroyers. In a message to Roosevelt, which the Prime Minister drafted on Tuesday, July 30, he wrote that "It has now become most urgent for you to let us have the destroyers." If, the Prime Minister added, Britain could survive the "next three or four months," things might well take a turn for the better. But, he concluded, the Royal Navy must have the destroyers. "I am sure," Churchill cabled Roosevelt in a message which the President received on July 31, "that, with your comprehension of the sea affair, you will not let this crux of the battle go wrong for want of these destroyers."

Within days of the July 25 meeting of the Century Group, a memorandum prepared by Francis Pickens Miller was in the hands of a delegation composed of Century Group men. On Thursday, August 1, editor Herbert Agar, manufacturer Ward Cheney, and Clark Eichelberger, the power behind the Committee to Defend America, conferred with important figures in the Roosevelt administration. Agar and Eichelberger met with FDR, whom they presented with a copy of Miller's memorandum. This document contained Henry Luce's suggestion that the destroyers be traded for "naval and air concessions." The President, however, remained noncommittal, though he appears to have alerted Navy Secretary Frank Knox to the importance of the August 2 cabinet meeting. Knox, of course, already knew about the July 25 deliberations of the Century Group, thanks to his intermediary, journalist Joseph Alsop. The destroyer-for-bases idea intrigued Knox, an old newspaperman who knew a popular bargain when he saw one. Still, the President wanted to be "pushed" by public opinion, and, was worried about gaining Willkie's support for any destroyer deal.

Through Helen Hill Miller (Mrs. Francis P. Miller) and Whitney Shepardson, the Century Group was in close contact with Lord Lothian. The old, tiresome question remained: would Roosevelt act? Lothian, who within hours of the fact learned of the Century delegation's inconclusive meeting with the President, was beside himself with anxiety. On this evening of August 1 he acted like a condemned man who sees his only salvation fading away. On Thursday night, Lothian decided to telephone Knox, who was having dinner at home. Knox knew that Roosevelt intended to convene an important cabinet meeting on the next day. Lothian, however, was thinking only of his destroyers, and he was almost tearful as he repeatedly begged for immediate help. According to cabinet colleagues in whom Knox confided, the two men talked for a long time, as Lothian made his case to a sympathetic ally. Churchill, Lothian reported, had again lobbied the President to dispatch the destroyers now, but nothing had happened. Knox suddenly asked Lothian if England would "consider transferring to the United States . . . naval and air bases as we might need for our own fleet?" Lothian, who was groping for precisely this solution, realized that Knox had transformed the whole matter. The British War Cabinet, in fact, had already decided to make a unilateral gift of certain bases to the Americans. Lothian did not yet know this, but he himself had been urging such a course for many weeks. The War Cabinet's decision would make his job easier.

After speaking with Secretary Knox, Lord Lothian excitedly cabled London, telling the Foreign Office of the new possibilities. While mentioning the moribund Canada option, Lothian also noted that the destroyers might be obtained in return for the sale to the United States of bases in Newfoundland, in Bermuda, and in Trinidad and other islands in the Caribbean. Knox, Lothian reported, favored this second alternative, that is, he wanted to sell the destroyers, in return for gaining access to the bases. Such a deal would have an added virtue. If the bases were more important to the defense of the Americas than were the destroyers, the U.S. Navy could certify the warships as "inessential" to American security. A legal impediment to an agreement would thereby be overcome. Of course, the President would presumably have to go to the Congress, so a major problem still blocked the transaction.

On Friday, August 2, at 2 P.M., President Roosevelt convened a meeting of his cabinet. Cognizant of its importance, he took the unusual step of preparing his own account of the event. According to FDR, there occurred a "long discussion in regard to devising ways and means to sell directly or indirectly fifty or sixty World War old destroyers to Great Britain." Everyone wanted to do so, for all present were aware of the dangers confronting England. Frank Knox took the initiative, and it was clear that sentiment favored American access to "Britain's naval bases on our Atlantic Coast." Since the Americans were already leasing one naval base in Trinidad, that arrangement, the President agreed, could serve as a precedent for other such agreements.

On Saturday, August 3, FDR personally informed Ambassador Lothian of his cabinet's Friday deliberations. The embassy immediately cabled the Foreign Office. On this same August 3 Churchill replied, informing Lothian that "You should let Colonel Knox and others know that a request on these lines will be agreeable to us. . . ." Many details remained to be worked out, and FDR still worried about the political ramifications of any such agreement. Still, negotiations had begun, and by August 13 Churchill was willing to authorize the American use of British bases and port facilities from Newfoundland to British Guiana. Two days later, Churchill agreed to Roosevelt's proposal that the Americans take out ninety-nine-year leases on the bases and port facilities in question.

Problems remained, however, for the President wanted to show his public that he had crafted a good bargain for the United States. The agreement, FDR argued, should be in the form of a quid pro quo—destroyers for bases being the heart of it. "Quid pro quo," of course, was a phrase first used in this context by Henry R. Luce, probably on July 24, and again at the White House on July 25. Luce's expression kept cropping up without anyone associating him with it. Such anonymity would not have bothered him, as he was intent on achieving his goals, not flattering his ego.

The pieces that made up the destroyer agreement began to fall into place late in August. Difficulties lingered, however, and Lord Lothian again informed London that Roosevelt insisted on a quid pro quo kind of arrangement. Churchill demurred, but he later worked out a face-saving compromise with the President. The Prime Minister accepted Roosevelt's need to show the world he had struck a clever bargain, and in part the agreement would be what Luce had called the "quid pro quo." Wendell Willkie, though under pressure from isolationists like Representative Joseph Martin, indicated that he would not denounce the deal. Luce, who was so important to the Willkie enterprise, and *Fortune*'s Russell Davenport, the candidate's campaign manager, helped to win Willkie's acquiescence. And soon the Administration overcame the legal hurdles, thanks to a clever lawyer. Late in August, Attorney General Robert H. Jackson decided that the President, as commander in chief and constitutional steward of the nation's foreign policy, could conclude the destroyer exchange "as an Executive agreement, effective without awaiting ratification" by the Congress.

On September 3, 1940, the President informed Congress and the press that "The right to bases in Newfoundland and Bermuda are gifts—generously given and gladly received." However, Roosevelt also noted that "The other bases [in the Caribbean] have been acquired in exchange for 50 of our over-age destroyers." Speaking to reporters, a jovial President compared the destroyer deal to President Thomas Jefferson's Louisiana Purchase. America had strengthened her ability to project air and sea power into the far reaches of the Atlantic and the Caribbean. This greatly pleased *Life*, which boasted that the destroyer agreement was a "brilliant bargain for the U.S." The United States, according to the magazine, was now the world's leading naval power.

It was Henry Luce's bases-for-destroyers proposal that President Roosevelt had finally adopted. At his best, Harry Luce could envision the need for a product, then create it. In 1940 he was not the first person to demand that the United States obtain access to British bases, nor had he been the first to urge the dispatch of destroyers to Britain. But it was Harry Luce who turned the two proposals into a conceptual package. And it was Luce who understood that a master politician could "sell" the final product to the American people.

Franklin D. Roosevelt's decision had immense consequences. The destroyer-for-bases deal was the most dramatic American break with neutrality since the war began. The agreement was signed just as the Luftwaffe was preparing to challenge the Royal Air Force's supremacy in the skies over England. Winston Churchill felt that the "moral value" of the destroyer exchange "will be very great and widely felt." He proved to be right, for the American warships constituted a kind of pledge to the British people. Churchill later added that the agreement was "a decidedly unneutral act by the United States." The Americans, Churchill noted with satisfaction, "have justified the German Government in declaring war upon them." Lord Lothian, like the Prime Minister, saw the agreement as a "big thing," linking the United States ever more closely to Great Britain. The destroyer deal also sent a signal to maritime powers like neutral Spain and German-dominated France. Churchill believed that the failure of these powers to enter the war on the side of the Germans was in part due to the threat of American belligerency.

It took many months to refit the overage warships; by the winter of 1941, only a handful were battle worthy. Still, they performed well under Royal Navy command and made life more difficult for German U-boats. At a crucial moment in the naval war, Winston Churchill told Roosevelt that "We have . . . been able gradually to strengthen our escorting forces, thanks to the United States destroyers which were sent us. . . ." At home, the popularity of the destroyer deal made it easier for the Congress to support peacetime conscription. A little more than a week after the announcement of the destroyer exchange, selective service became the law. From Luce's vantage point, this, too, was a major achievement. Still, another result of the destroyer deal depressed him.

By pushing his innovative idea of a destroyer-for-bases exchange, Harry Luce had undermined the political prospects of Wendell Willkie. President Roosevelt, thanks in some measure to Time Inc.'s rave reviews in early September, was suddenly the decisive, farsighted, *bipartisan* leader of an imperiled nation. Wendell Willkie, by contrast, was in the lame position of endorsing the destroyer exchange before desperately denouncing the "dictatorial" tactics of the President. Willkie, who looked like a possible winner in August, started to dip in the opinion polls. Harry Luce's autumnal partisanship could not undo the damage that his patriotic advocacy had inflicted upon the Republican standard-bearer. Despite a revival in late October, Willkie was the third candidate to fall victim to a Roosevelt electoral landslide. Later, Henry Luce realized that the onset of the Battle of Britain, combined with FDR's wily response to it, had reelected the President.

As Luce had predicted, FDR in 1940 and 1941 continued to edge closer to war while promising peace and security. In fact, he wished to avoid entry into the war. Unrealistically, the President hoped that American military aid might enable the Allies to defeat Hitler. If Britain (and later, Russia) could not win on their own, then the United States would at some point—perhaps in 1943—jump in. To Luce, this kind of convoluted thinking was immoral and evasive. Roosevelt, he felt, should tell the nation that his policies carried in their wake the risk of war.

By using their new airfields in Newfoundland, Trinidad, or St. Lucia, American bombers could attack enemy fleets 1,000 miles to the east, thus blocking any attempted invasion of the Americas. Far to the south, U.S. warships, using port facilities in Trinidad, could now rove 2,500 miles into the Atlantic, thereby fighting more effectively against potential enemies—German U-boats and surface raiders. From April 1941 on, American warships, some of which cast anchor in Newfoundland and other British possessions, protected crucial maritime trade routes linking England to the Americas. Patrolling the huge area lying west of the meridian 26 West, the U.S. Navy was actively collaborating with the Royal Navy.

American naval commanders, whose warships often docked in British-owned ports, routinely alerted their Royal Navy counterparts of the presence of German surface raiders and submarines. Speaking of the President's ever bolder naval policies in 1941, Prime Minister Churchill observed to Roosevelt that "The action you have taken may well decide the Battle of the Atlantic in a favorable sense." In September 1941 an ever more confident FDR decided that "If German or Italian vessels of war enter the waters the protection of which is necessary for American defense, they do so at their own peril." This so-called shoot on sight order encouraged *Time*, which prematurely decided that the U.S. was now at war. Through his magazines and newsfilms, Henry Luce, unknown to most Americans, was preparing his vast audience for more unneutral acts.

Despite his bellicosity, the word "power" made Luce nervous, as if there were something sinful about its exercise. He once grudgingly admitted that he might have some "influence," but that was all. Yet what Henry Luce wanted to create was nothing less than a Christian, democratic, capitalist, and Americanized world. Sadly, this driven man who achieved so much in 1940 often felt himself hobbled by an intractable world. The wealthier and more powerful he became, the more frustrated Harry Luce felt. Nevertheless, a defiant Henry Robinson Luce displayed an unflagging commitment to Christianity, the American mission in this world, China, journalism, and the Republican Party.

1898

Tengchow, China

Henry R. Luce's father, the Reverend Henry ("Harry") Winters Luce, was descended from one Henry Luce, who in 1643 was among the first settlers to land on the island called Martha's Vineyard, Massachusetts. H. W. Luce was born in 1868, near Scranton, Pennsylvania. The Union had won the Civil War three years before his birth, and the United States had entered an era of industrial and commercial expansion. Nowhere was this more apparent than in the mining and industrial region around Scranton, where Harry Luce grew up in comfortable circumstances. His father, Van Rensselaer William Luce, was a moderately prosperous wholesale grocer. Van Rensselaer involved himself in numerous business and community affairs, and he and his wife, Adelia, were active in the Second Presbyterian Church.

Just under six feet tall, with reddish hair, blue eyes, and a pleasant smile, Harry Luce professed his Christian faith at the age of sixteen. Idealism and ambition were traits that marked his character. Sociable and highly intelligent, he displayed strong leadership qualities as well as occasional outbursts of temper. Young Luce freely acknowledged that his nature made it difficult for him to accept unwelcome decisions imposed by others.

Harry Luce enjoyed instructing young people, and soon emerged as a leader in the Young People's Society of Christian Endeavor, a national movement active during the 1880s. In Scranton, Luce also learned that service to a broader public required the cultivation of powerful groups and individuals. Yale College, a magnet to wealthy parents with college-age sons, was the ideal place to make such contacts. Harry Luce, like his 211 freshman classmates, pursued the traditional course of study: chapel attendance each morning, classes in Greek and Latin, mathematics, and Bible studies. Luce was also active in the Young Men's Christian Association, and during summers or vacations he worked in Scranton in various Christian missions. He did not neglect sports, for the YMCA believed in a healthy mind in a healthy body. Luce also earned a certificate in legal studies, which prepared him for entry into the world of Scranton's commercial elite.

In the spring of 1892, just before his graduation from Yale, Harry Luce became enmeshed in a painful conflict. In a devotional volume, he read words that inspired him to seek the Kingdom of God. Answering the call, Harry informed his parents of the momentous decision, and they supported their son. He entered the Union Theological Seminary and transferred after a year to the Princeton Theological Seminary, where he received his Bachelor of Divinity degree two years later. After graduation and a year's travel on behalf of the Student Volunteer Movement, he applied in 1896 to the Board of Foreign Missions of the Presbyterian Church, in Princeton. He asked to be recommended for service abroad. Luce's credentials were strong, and he persuasively listed his reasons for applying: (1) A love of Christ; (2) The need for missionaries, which exceeded the number of those willing and able to go; and (3) The fact that "Half a world has never heard of Christ." Luce wanted to work with the remarkable Dr. Calvin Mateer, the famous old missionary who continued to labor in China. Mateer had translated the Bible into Chinese, and at Tengchow, in Shantung province, he had established the first Christian college in China. His work appealed to Luce, for it combined deep faith with a strong belief in progress, science, and modern society.

Though impressed by Harry Luce's dedication and abilities, the board needed to make sure that he was the right man for this assignment. While he awaited the missionary board's decision, Luce met Elizabeth Middleton Root, a tall, attractive, talented young women who had come to Scranton while working for the Young Women's Christian Association. Elizabeth helped run a hostel catering to poor girls who labored in the factories of Scranton. Like the Luces, many other American Protestants believed that such work glorified the Lord, and thus bettered their own lives. In the view of advocates of this "Social Gospel," Christianity was more than a religion; it was a summons to social activism. The downtrodden masses of the Far East, like the workers in Scranton, offered a fertile field to courageous, socially minded Christians. Once he was formally accepted by the mission board, Harry became engaged to Elizabeth. Soon the Luces booked steamer passage to China.

In the autumn of 1897, the young couple arrived in Tengchow, where they took up their work as missionary educators. The Luces' vast new homeland was a troubled, explosive country, where an ancient, revered culture seemed unable and perhaps unwilling to confront the challenges posed by alien ideas and foreign aggressors. The Luces, however, believed that they could help ease China's passage into the modern world. Harry and Elizabeth could show the Chinese how to master the techniques of modern science. They would attempt to banish debilitating superstitions and prevent deadly epidemics.

Harry and Elizabeth Luce brought with them their American optimism and energy—the Reverend Luce called it "native Lucepower"—to Tengchow. Their mood reflected their nation's bustling, expansive, and "can-do" spirit. The Luces saw America as a providential land, selected to bring about the conversion of all peoples, perhaps in this generation. Their President, William McKinley, spoke for the Luces when he called for the Christianization of the Asian peoples. This evangelistic credo was founded on the faith that America, which was essentially good, must fulfill its destiny by doing unto others what God had done for the United States. The blessings of faith, liberty, and material progress must be offered to the suffering world.

The writer John Hersey, himself a "mishkid," or child of missionary parents, captured the evangelical spirit in his novel *The Call*. He has one evangelist explain that the English race had seized the East so that the heathens could listen to Americans preach the gospel. "God," says Hersey's Dr. Elting, "had a plan before we ever saw it." In his view, China, with enlightened American help, would overshadow and perhaps replace Britain's imperial order.

Harry and Elizabeth Luce worked hard to master Chinese. The Reverend Luce then taught his eager students the New Testament, the history of the Western world, and pedagogy. The busy couple examined candidates for admission to the church and baptized them. Harry and Elizabeth also taught Sunday school, and remained active in YMCA work. In the United States, the Reverend Luce's annual salary of $1,200 would have supported a rather modest life-style. In China, however, the Luces lived very well, for a laundry boy, gardener, chef (who learned to prepare food in the American style), and assorted servants waited on them. Nonetheless, however well off they were by Chinese standards, the Luces lived in segregated walled compounds, as privileged foreigners in a vulnerable world carved out by Westerners. Treaties forced on the Chinese by the artillery of powerful foreigners presumably guaranteed the safety of the missionaries, but at a price. Antiforeign and anti-Christian sentiments were rife. Banditry was endemic in the nearby countryside, while the central government was decadent and weak.

The filth and the degrading poverty, which were the lot of a long-suffering, patient, and highly cultured people, severely challenged those Americans and Chinese committed to change. Female infanticide was a common occurrence, and the birth of a girl provoked polite condolences from one's neighbors. Out of ten thousand Chinese women, one was literate. Progressive Westerners, including the Luces, preached social progress to people accustomed to seeing government as an oppressor, and change as a disaster.

For two years, Elizabeth and Harry Luce tended to their familial and professional duties, and life passed without untoward incident. On April 3, 1898, Elizabeth gave birth to the first of their four children—Henry Robinson Luce (the middle name was bestowed upon him in tribute to the Luces' Scranton pastor). Baptized by Calvin Mateer, the baby was healthy and alert. The Luces hired a Chinese *amah* or nursemaid/nanny, and little Harry later babbled a few words of Chinese before speaking English. The Luce family thrived, but outside their walled reservation, China was deteriorating.

Like the Luces, a large number of American missionaries hoped that the United States would emerge as China's protector. America, after all, was different from Russia or Japan; she was a democracy. The United States had, in the view of people like the Luces, acquired responsibilities and opportunities, not imperium, when its government annexed the Philippines, Guam, and other formerly Spanish territories. Leaders, among them President William McKinley himself, believed in the vast potential of the Chinese market, and one day, these optimists argued, the huge Chinese population, led by an educated, Christianized elite, might absorb American exports and capital, thus preventing future "panics"—economic downturns—in the United States. During the second year of Henry R. Luce's life (the Chinese servants called him "Small Boy Luce"), Secretary of State John Milton Hay addressed an appeal to Britain, Russia, and other concerned powers. He asked that they not discriminate against the commercial interests of foreign nations in their treaty ports and spheres of influence. The diplomatic notes did not commit the United States to action; rather, they expressed a self-interested, though pious hope. Meanwhile, the internal situation in China further eroded.

A violent Chinese revolt, led by the Righteous Harmony Band ("Boxers") against the foreigners and their concessions threatened both the missionaries and the precarious Chinese Empire. By the summer of 1900, the Boxers had slaughtered almost two hundred missionaries, along with fifty-three of their children. The Luces fled to the Shantung coast, where they boarded an American vessel. Once they were safe in Seoul, they learned that their dear friend Horace Pitkin had fallen victim to a mob while defending women seeking refuge in his mission at Paotingfu. The rioters beheaded him and burned his body. The Boxers ultimately massacred 30,000 converts to Christianity, but finally made a blunder that led to their own destruction. They laid siege to the foreign legations in Peking, an act that provoked a successful European and American intervention. The powers forced China to indemnify them for losses incurred due to Boxer depredations.

The Americans, anxious to maintain the Open Door, intervened again. Secretary Hay, believing that "the storm center of the world has gradually shifted to China," announced his support for the administrative and territorial integrity of the Chinese Empire. The Luces were proud of this display of American power and moral authority, which culminated in the rescue of the terrified foreigners in Peking. The two missionaries returned to their work, relieved and optimistic. The signs pointed to growing American involvement in China. But what did this mean? Not for the last time, American enthusiasm for China proved to be ambiguous in its application.

Although the small brick building that housed the Luces was a plain place with few modern conveniences, Elizabeth provided it with a cheerful decor. Meanwhile, the Luce family continued to grow. Little Harry (*amah*'s "Small Boy Luce") soon had three siblings, the girls Emmavail and Elizabeth, and Sheldon, the youngest child, who liked to play jokes on his more serious older brother. These Luce children started the day with a cold bath. They then studied their lessons, and sometimes played with the offspring of American and British missionaries. A nearby Chinese festival was certain to attract the kids, who loved to ride out of the compound on their gentle donkeys. The home was a busy place, where the parents studied the Bible together, often reading aloud to their children. Their library was well stocked, and Mrs. Luce often delighted the children with readings from Dickens and Shakespeare. Harry senior sometimes played a Beethoven sonata on the violin, while Elizabeth accompanied on the piano. On other occasions Mrs. Luce sang the *Lieder* of Franz Schubert. The annual arrival of a large order from Montgomery Ward & Co., was a major cause for celebration. In the summer the Luces repaired to a resort in Tsingtao, where they rented a cottage.

Little Harry, Small Boy Luce, thrived. Precocious and endlessly curious, the lad found enchantment in words and concepts. He rarely acted childishly. From the age of three, little Harry attended services conducted for the missionaries and their families. He also visited a Chinese church, and even before he could write, Harry junior requested that his mother write down some of his "sermons." In one photograph, the boy appears to be declaiming before an imagined throng of parishioners. The lad continued to enchant his parents with his antics, which included composing a handwritten "newspaper."

As a child, Harry knelt in prayer before going to bed, an act that became a lifelong habit. He learned to see himself as a sinner, but also as a boy determined to do good. Once, Harry sat in church with his parents and a stained window caught his eye. Upon a pane of glass was written a word reminiscent of his mother's maiden name, Root. Depicting Jesus with His disciples, the window displayed the words "I am the Vine and Ye are the Roots." Harry was surprised, and turned to his parents for an explanation. "I didn't know," he whispered, "that I was related to God."

The Reverend Luce was certain that he had never seen a child as bright as little Harry—with the possible exception of Elizabeth, known to all as Beth. Old Testament heroes awed the young boy, who saw himself as a Christian soldier. Indeed, one of Harry's favorite games, endlessly played, involved tin soldiers in fantasy armies, moving about while they laid siege to miniature fortresses. Little Harry, playing and preaching in his walled compound, soon regarded his American identity as a special goodness, as a form of grace. His sense of nationality isolated him from the people outside the compound and defined the life led by the Luces inside their plain home.

He might have spent a lifetime in Tengchow, preparing his lectures and nurturing his family, but the Reverend Harry Luce was an ambitious man. He was convinced that the Christian educational effort in China was hopelessly fragmented, as competing denominations vied for students, faculty, and money. Luce proposed uniting several colleges into one university. He believed that the present Tengchow College, located far to the north in Shantung, should move to a more central site, possibly to Wei hsien, near Tsinan fu, the capital of the province. Tsinan fu already housed a medical station, run by missionary doctors of British and American origins. Perhaps, Luce mused, the good doctors, whose ambitions for their school required expensive equipment and an ample endowment, might wish to unite with their collegiate brethren from Tengchow? A move to Wei hsien would make even more sense if the Presbyterians worked with the English Baptists, who ran their own school of theology in Shantung.

In 1904 the Reverend Luce's school relocated to Wei hsien, but this was the easy part, for without an endowment, the enterprise would fail. Competition for money was intense, and many feared for the future of Luce's ambitious plan. The Reverend Luce, however, hoped to create an endowment worth $200,000. His model was Calvin Mateer, who had constructed his college after receiving a donation from the widow of Cyrus Hall McCormick, founder of the International Harvester Company. In 1905 Harry Luce agreed to return to the United States, where he expected to raise large sums of money. His son later wrote that fund-raising on behalf of the Lord was the worst of all jobs, but the Reverend Luce never felt this way. If he did not exactly enjoy fund-raising, Harry Luce at least knew that he had a God-given obligation to solicit money. Luce could turn to old acquaintances in Scranton; at Yale College and at Union Theological Seminary he had made new contacts. The Luce family departed on their long voyage to the United States, where they arrived early in 1906.

The Luces, including young Harry and his sisters Emmavail and Beth, remained in California, while the Reverend Harry Luce journeyed by rail to Chicago. There, he intended to make use of a letter of introduction addressed to Mrs. Nettie Fowler McCormick. This enormously wealthy Presbyterian might, he hoped, finance the new campus at Wei hsien. The Reverend Luce checked into an inexpensive Chicago hotel and hurriedly readied himself for his important meeting with Mrs. McCormick. She invited him to a one o'clock luncheon. Harry, anxious about his mission, and still fatigued after the arduous journey from Shantung, appeared exhausted. Nettie graciously insisted that he take a nap. Mrs. McCormick later urged Harry to stay in her beautiful home, which he did. While he enjoyed having breakfast brought to him on an elegant silver service, Luce never neglected the business at hand.

Mrs. McCormick and her son Harold were impressed with the Reverend Luce. He might, they believed, have made a good businessman. This was high praise indeed, for it meant that Harry knew how to raise more funds from other sources, while putting the McCormick contributions to good use. Nettie eventually donated a small fortune—over $40,000—to the colleges at Wei hsien and Tsinan fu. In 1990s purchasing power, the McCormick gift would be equivalent in value to fifteen to twenty times that amount. Harry soon described Nettie as an inspiring woman of faith whose help had "doubled the efficiency of our life and work." In the process of making the rounds, the Reverend Luce later taught his son Harry valuable lessons about cultivating important people. He quoted scripture to young Harry, telling him not to say anything about others unless it was to praise them. Harry learned the value of hard work, and came to see money, not as a good in itself, but as a measure of one's success. As a boy he did not yet grasp the cost of his father's strenuous efforts. The Reverend Harry Luce pushed himself too hard, so much so that he soon developed a bad set of ulcers.

A lonely, aging woman, disappointed in some of her own family members, Nettie McCormick quickly became a kind of godmother to the Luce children. The Reverend Luce did everything in his power to encourage this relationship. On a subsequent visit to Chicago, he brought his brilliant child with him. Little Harry's demeanor, at once precocious and respectful, delighted the McCormick widow. She loved to hear Harry talk about his life in China, but one look convinced her that he needed better clothes. Nettie subsequently sent the Luces money so that the boy might wear new trousers and nicer, American jackets. Harry and Elizabeth encouraged Mrs. McCormick by sending her copies of little Harry's "sermonettes." "Abraham," wrote Small Boy Luce, "and many other people were good and holy. . . . He seeth the difference between the good and the wicked—so does man see the difference." Nettie became increasingly attached to this pious, precocious lad, and to his sister Beth as well. She finally insisted that the Luces live in a better house in Wei hsien, for which she paid. While not up to the latest American urban standards (no indoor plumbing), the residence was more comfortable than the cramped building in Tengchow.

The Reverend Luce assured Nettie that a recent visit by little Harry meant a lot to the boy. Luce senior waxed lyrical when describing Mrs. McCormick. He declared that "for grace of person, charm and manner, [and a] mental grasp of situations & conditions . . . I have never met her equal." The Luces were endlessly grateful to Mrs. McCormick, but on one point they demurred. Nettie wanted to keep little Harry as a companion for her grandchild Fowler, a proposal which the Luces quickly rejected.

A shrewd judge of character, Nettie McCormick has left us a prophetic portrait of little Henry R. Luce. She saw a boy whose brain worked like a "system of wheels," a child with incredible powers of perception and "great strength of will and character." Mrs. McCormick concluded that people would have a hard time keeping up with little Harry. One day, eight-year-old Harry warned his sister Emmavail not to walk on an icy path. She defied him and fell down. "Now," Harry responded, "that comes of not taking the advice of older and more experienced people, for I have lived at least two years longer in the world than you have!" Only in one respect did Nettie's appraisal of young Luce prove incomplete. She praised his independence, believing that it would prove to be "a fortress against the assaults of temptation." Temptation sometimes breached the fortress.

The Reverend Harry Luce's network continued to expand, for he tailored his approach to the interests and personality of his interlocutor. The ever thoughtful Mrs. McCormick arranged a meeting between Luce and Mr. John D. Rockefeller, Jr., who was much interested in medical missionary work in China. "Mr. Junior," as the Rockefellers called him, wrote to Nettie, praising Harry, for Luce had shown him that they shared common interests. Rockefeller later established the medical college at Tsinan fu, the first such institution where instruction took place in Chinese. Early on, young Harry learned that a powerful circle of contacts and friends could move the world. And in the spring of 1907, the Reverend Luce took the nine-year-old Harry to a missionary conference held in Tokyo. There, the conferees pledged themselves to evangelize the whole world in this generation. The challenge mandated a special role for American Christians. Harry junior long remembered his feeling that "Here surely, was the hand of Providence."

His parents decided to send Harry Luce to the British China Inland Mission School. Located in the port city of Chefoo, the boy arrived there via steamer and rail. Once again, Small Boy Luce was part of a minority. Run by rigid British disciplinarians, the school catered to the sons of English and American missionaries. The teachers sometimes beat Harry, for flogging was part of the school's code of discipline. Most of the students were British subjects, and the older youths among them lavished contempt on their American cousins. Forty years later, an angry Harry Luce could still recall the fistfights with "a little British bastard who had insulted my country." And new boys were expected to defer to older ones, a habit that did not come easily to young Luce. Pupils were not to associate with the Chinese who lived in the town, a prohibition which also cut against the Luce grain.

Harry could survive in this unpleasant world, since he understood its rules and could adapt to codes of discipline. His father ruled, however gently, at home; the headmaster reigned at school; and God, of course, governed all. Harry, however, understood the moral difference between the fair exercise of power and perverted customs like flogging and knuckle-rapping. He also found that he was capable of meeting the high scholastic standards of the grim place, though he required divine help in order to survive algebra examinations. His perfect grade, said Harry, "was all God." Determined to get into the fourth form, the boy did "not care if I die for it."

Upon seeing some British subjects mistreat the Chinese who crossed their path, Harry was repelled. And when he saw Germans beat rick-shaw boys, he felt better than ever about his American identity. Americans, Luce observed, never did such things. They *overpaid* their coolies, Harry proudly boasted. The Americans whom Harry knew were good people, and from them he learned to idealize his homeland. Harry never forgot the Fourth of July celebrations in Wei hsien, when Americans gathered together for patriotic displays, ice cream and cake, and the singing of "My Country, 'Tis of Thee." Born and raised abroad, Harry came to loathe the concept of the rootless cosmopolitan, of the man without a country. He desperately wanted a hometown. If he could not find it—and he never did—Luce could become the American voice of every man's imagined hometown. To this boy, the presence of the Americans in Shantung vindicated the providential act that had brought his ancestor to Martha's Vineyard more than two and a half centuries earlier. And if there was no role for the Luces in China, maybe the Almighty had made a mistake in creating America. This, of course, was unthinkable.

At the age of eight, Harry had given his parents a scare. Doctors ordered a tonsillectomy, for this procedure supposedly prevented heavy head colds, sore throats, and other diseases. The surgery proceeded without incident, but the anesthetic wore off too soon, possibly inducing trauma. Henceforth, Harry's speech was marred by a stammer. Many youths would thereafter have refused to engage in public speaking, fearing ridicule. Remarkably, Luce later insisted on debating with the best public speakers in his class, before highly critical referees. Through sheer "Lucepower," Harry stammered less in public than he did when conversing in his dormitory room.

Words had fascinated young Luce for more than a decade, as he preached, dictated, listened, and read. Now, Harry became editor in chief of a school newspaper, where he also displayed a natural business sense. He took this work very seriously indeed. As he put it, success or failure in his studies bring "me nearer or farther from man's chief goal—perfection." Young Harry was therefore suspicious of those comfortable with existing conditions. Though no revolutionary, he favored social and political change. By 1912 the boy could even refer to "conservatism" as the greatest evil in the world. This young critic, like his father, sided with the ecumenical movement against sectarianism; with the progressive trust-busters against entrenched corporate power; with the social reformers against oppression and neglect; and with Theodore Roosevelt's Bull Moose movement against President William H. Taft's political machine. Young Harry Luce grew up assuming that he was destined to become an activist, following a code that consisted of faith in God, self-reliance, and a will to succeed. One prayed for the *strength* that brought success. One earned earthly goods; one did not pray for them or merit them.

The Luces, meanwhile, welcomed the changes that were remaking Chinese society. Rumors reached Shantung, telling how new men, including an exile named Dr. Sun Yat-sen, intended to modernize China. Some missionaries feared for their privileges, but not the Luces. When he learned of the proclamation of the Chinese Republic in 1911, young Harry approved, so long as decent people came to power. The China of 1912, he hoped, was embarking on a rough road that ultimately would lead it into a modern, constitutional era.

After Chefoo, Harry had no trouble mastering the academic program at Hotchkiss. He participated in a full range of activities, choosing fields that challenged him. He continued to learn the declamatory techniques culled from sermons preached by Presbyterian pastors. (During Christmas break, Harry journeyed to New York City, where he boasted of having heard three sermons in a row!) He still stammered, but except when rehearsing speeches or debating skilled opponents, academic studies and classwork came easily to him. The Reverend Luce, however, was concerned about Harry's tendency to shoulder too many burdens. He warned his son against neglecting to "keep your body in good physical trim." Young Luce thus became a lifelong participant in various sporting activities, including tennis, hunting, and golf.

Harry's father, traveling about the United States raising money, kept in close contact with his gifted son. He praised the boy, advised him, and talked to him in great detail about his quest for funds. Encouraged by his ambitious father, young Harry stayed in touch with the Luce family patroness, the aging Nettie McCormick. She followed his career with great interest, and hoped that Harry would one day receive a call to serve the church.

At Hotchkiss, one teacher insisted that Luce study Greek, as a form of intellectual discipline. He excelled in the language, which he studied in the class of Dr. Lester Brown. Here, Harry was a classmate of a Brooklyn boy named Briton Hadden, who became his friend. Where Harry Luce was somewhat ponderous and somber, Brit Hadden possessed a sharp sense of humor. Students and faculty respected Harry; they liked Brit. And although Harry earned the highest grades in his class, and became captain of the debating team through sheer Luce-power, the vivacious Hadden quickly moved to the center of any group. Brit amused and entertained with his streetwise antics. Harry, by contrast, seemed to measure himself constantly against some unknown force. While Harry dutifully played football, Brit was crazy about baseball, though he had little talent for it. The boys grew to be friends as well as rivals.

As sophomores-to-be, Harry and Brit closely followed the events in Europe, where war had erupted in August 1914. The Luces were appalled at the carnage on the Western Front; the Reverend Luce bitterly told his son in late 1914 that truly Christian nations had never existed. Soon, many boys at Hotchkiss, as well as the Luce family, began to change their views. Alleged German atrocities in Belgium, and the Reich attacks on Allied and neutral shipping enraged most Americans. Young Harry told Mrs. McCormick that he now favored the export of armaments to the Allied powers. Remarkably, at the tender age of sixteen, Harry Luce was already predicting "America's leadership of the world at the close of the European war." He was prophetic, but to his profound disgust, American hegemony would have to await the end of a *second* European war.

Both Brit and Harry were attracted to journalism. Luce edited the *Hotchkiss Literary Monthly*, while Brit Hadden ran the *Hotchkiss Record*. Thanks to Brit's innovation, the *Record* contained an article on current happenings for "those of us who do not find time to read the detailed accounts in the daily papers." In this age of William Randolph Hearst's yellow journalism, most people read parochial or sensationalist newspapers, which lacked a national vision or market. Harry, however, possessed the preacher's desire to teach and persuade. The world was changing so fast and so violently that people needed to be informed and educated. Harry Luce concluded that he could "be of the greatest service in journalistic work and can by that way come nearest to the heart of the world." Anxious to begin his career, he sought out the eighty-year-old Dr. Lyman Abbott, editor of the famous religious journal *Outlook*. The old man's concept of a union between Christian thought and journalism appealed to Luce. In New York, the venerable Dr. Abbott urged that Luce articulate the ideals of his readers, without preaching down to them.

Harry Luce now assumed responsibility for the business dealings of the Hotchkiss *Lit*. He sold automobile advertising at the high price of two dollars per page, and Pierce Arrow and Dodge signed on. Luce would then mention this commitment to his next target, in order to impress yet another potential advertiser. During one vacation, the young man visited printers in order to obtain the lowest production costs for the magazine. He observed gigantic presses running off the October 1915 issue of *Scribner's Magazine*, and a fascinated Harry Luce came away musing about the power exercised by this union of words with modern technology.

Harry Luce was admitted to his father's alma mater, Yale College, after achieving the highest score in the country on the classical Greek entrance examination. Before moving to New Haven, Harry clerked in the business office of the Springfield, Massachusetts, *Republican*, his first job in journalism. Excited about associating with "all kinds and conditions of men," he sometimes escaped the office to see jail cells filled with disconsolate men, or tearful mothers bailing out wayward sons. Harry came away convinced that real journalism must embrace all kinds of experience, from politics to labor strikes.

His stint in Springfield helped to prepare Harry Luce for "heeling" (competing for a position on the board of) at the *Yale Daily News*. Brit

Hadden was again to be Luce's companion, for he, too, was heading for Yale and the *News*. Meanwhile Harry enjoyed the university president's matriculation sermon, but observed that "this fervid Xnity stuff" had alienated Brit Hadden. Both young men were soon working on the staff of the *News*, as associate members of its editorial board. Poor Harry's hometown was listed as "Tsinan, China."

By early 1917 the informal Yale debates about the war had sharpened. Most students believed that America's fate was linked to Britain's survival. The Americans had granted war loans, shipped food and munitions to the Allies, and suffered loss of life and property due to depredations inflicted by German U-boats. Unrestricted submarine warfare, when resumed by Berlin, might lead to war. Along with Luce, many bright young men, including Sinclair Lewis, Thorton Wilder (whom Luce had known at Chefoo), Walter Millis, Archibald Mac-Leish, and Stephen Vincent Benét, argued about neutrality and intervention. Harry, however, had long since chosen sides. Britain and France, he now believed, represented justice and civilization, engaged in a life-or-death struggle against Teutonic barbarism. Not everyone agreed, and a group of antiwar activists and radical reformers took out a large ad in the *Yale Daily News*. They argued that Wall Street, not the people, wanted war, that Germany was finished anyway. These dissenters protested in vain. By the late winter of 1917, Luce and most of the students were roused to a patriotic fever pitch. A dissenter's pacifist speech even provoked the student body into marching through New Haven singing "My Country, 'Tis of Thee," a Luce favorite since his China days. A month later, on April 6, 1917, the United States declared war.

The *News* campaigned for more patriotism and less drinking and carousing. Yale's student enrollment dropped from 3,300 to 2,000 young men, 1,300 of whom, including Harry Luce, volunteered for service in the Reserve Officer Training Corps. Luce summed up his credo by describing the war as "a world-wide struggle between right and wrong. . . ." He loved the heroic rhetoric of righteous struggle. "We cry for peace," asked Luce, "but is there any peace except the peace of the battle, I mean *in* the battle . . . [?]" Peace, the nineteen-year-old undergraduate concluded, came "through the blood of His cross." In Harry's view, one side was always right—or at least more right.

Luce quickly advanced from corporal to sergeant in the ROTC, and in August 1918 his Yale artillery element shipped out to Camp Jackson, near Columbia, South Carolina. There, Harry and Brit suffered through the searing heat of a Columbia summer. His officers decided that Harry

Luce would be a good propagandist. The future second lieutenant was soon lecturing the troops on American war aims, his speeches replete with righteous condemnations of the German crime in sinking the *Lusitania.* Luce also responded with enthusiasm to the ordinary demands of soldiering, though Brit Hadden was more flamboyant and assertive. Harry worked very hard, but he could not become a commissioned officer for another ten months or so, when he would reach the age of twenty-one.

The War Department soon lifted this restriction, however, so Brit and Harry received their commissions as second lieutenants in the field artillery. The young "shavetails" went into Columbia and smoked big cigars in celebration of their arrival as officers. Toward the end of this summer of 1918, their unit shipped out to join the Seventh Training Battery at Camp Zachary Taylor, near Louisville, where it underwent further training.

By this time, Lieutenant Henry R. Luce was a slim young man, about six feet tall, with blue-gray eyes and reddish brown hair combed back off his high forehead. Usually serious in demeanor, his brow furrowed in concentration, Harry drank less than his classmates, for his father opposed the habit. He did, however, smoke quit a bit, perhaps as an escape from pressures and anxieties.

Cheated of anticipated battle experience by the armistice of November 11, 1918, Luce and Hadden returned to Yale in time for the winter semester. Believing that war should be a leavening force, editor Luce, in a leader for the *Yale Literary Magazine*, called for greater dedication to intellectual pursuits. Men who had served in uniform could not, he claimed, easily return to the boyish insouciance of prewar times. This, of course, was wishful thinking, a tendency that sometimes blinded the ever serious Luce to less edifying realities. For most of his life, young Harry had been aware of dangers around him, threatening his America. Ever on the prowl for enemies, he had heard about what the Boxers did to Christians, and then he discovered the German menace. Now came the turn of the Bolsheviks. Luce gravely warned that ". . . if we do not intervene soon bolshevism will undermine the civilization of the world." More than most of his fellows, Luce saw himself as part of a great historical process, in which the war was a prelude to America's coming of age. Hadden often kidded Harry about carrying the world on his shoulders.

Harry Luce's style, then and later, was rarely felicitous, but his polemics did reveal an intellect wrestling with profound questions. Writing for the *Lit* during his senior year, Harry Luce published an essay on "The Integrity of the Mind," which criticized the majority of his classmates, who, he charged, embraced the Republican Party for selfish economic reasons. And Luce was at his literary best when celebrating patriotism, as in the prize-winning De Forest Oration, "When We Say America." Harry described the American experience as a multifaceted adventure, defined morally by the code bequeathed to the nation by the Puritans. The salient characteristic of the United States in 1920, Luce added, was *power*. He already favored American engagement in "every international difficulty." Luce envisioned a world twenty years hence, in which "American interests shall be respected, American citizens entitled to trade and to live in every corner of the globe, [and] American business ideals recognized wherever the trader goes. . . ." Harry also endorsed policies calculated to assist "the lame, the halt, and the blind among nations."

Luce's America would be the exponent of the kind of "muscular Christianity" espoused by Theodore Roosevelt. Power, inspired by philanthropy, would reshape the world. Young Luce thereby set out a program from which he never deviated. A powerful yet reverent America must dominate the world, while changing it for the better. A new meritocracy, consisting of moral, strong men, would then stand guard, defending the American-made world order.

Brit Hadden was the big man in the class of 1920, winning every campus election in which he ran. Harry Luce, however, was a better student, with a distinguished record as a prize-winning writer for the *Lit*. Luce's biography in his Yale classbook was long and impressive, but his classmates chose Hadden as "most likely to succeed." Though Harry was not always fun, his peers did declare him to be the "most brilliant" man in their class. Harry Luce resented the relativism of his professors, while Hadden fit right in with the skeptics and humorists. Luce, the Phi Beta Kappa bearing the weight of the world on his shoulders, often argued with Brit, but the two young men usually resolved their differences. Before graduation, a senior "tapped" both Luce and Hadden, signifying their election to the prestigious Skull & Bones Society, a secretive group of young men pledged to help each other throughout their lives.

After graduating, Brit Hadden moved to Clinton Street in Brooklyn and soon landed a job in the big city. Although a stint covering human-interest stories for the *New York World* exposed him to tough, jaded newspapermen, Hadden wanted to see more of life. Soon he and a couple of friends shipped out to South America. Brit's fun-loving ways had not changed: the young men booked first-class sleeping cabins on a steamship and paid for them by working as deckhands during the day. They were happy to do the work of the masses so long as they could also enjoy the privileges accorded to young men of their own social class.

A lark on a ship did not appeal to Harry Luce, who instead traveled to the Republican national convention in Chicago. He rode in the private railroad car of Rufus Patterson, father of Harry's Yale classmate Morehead Patterson. In Chicago Luce acquired a lifelong love for political shop talk, though he showed little enthusiasm for Warren G. Harding, the presidential nominee. Mediocrity repelled Harry, as did the kind of politics that produced the Harding nomination. Public life, he felt, should be molded by ideas and ideals. But how did one elevate the level of political discourse? Harry's experience in Chicago reinforced his belief in the potential benefits of savvy reportage.

He also sensed that changes in society could create an audience for a new kind of journalism. Economic growth and urbanization had greatly increased the size of the educated middle class, which desired better sources of information. Although America had become a global power, most newspapers remained provincial and poorly edited. There was no national press, and busy people were exposed to a hodgepodge of wire service dispatches and local news. Surely there was a real need for a journal *national* in scope, perceptive in its editing, and concise in format. In the past Luce and Hadden had discussed this kind of publication as a joint project, but Harry wanted some time for contemplation. He planned to tour Europe, then study at Oxford for two semesters. He would be able to do so thanks to his earnings as a business agent for the *News*, supplemented by a thousand-dollar graduation gift from Mrs. McCormick.

In 1920 Harry Luce and some fellow Yale men toured England, Wales, and Scotland, hiking and mountain climbing, before Luce headed for the Continent. He took the Orient Express from Paris to Constantinople, visiting cities in the Balkans and Central Europe. Wherever he went, Harry made contacts in the local American embassy and toured important historical monuments. He also tried to figure out how this ancient, Christian civilization comported with his vision of America's coming "moral and spiritual magnificence." Luce was like a man from the provinces, surveying his legacy so that he might transcend it.

Luce and his classmate Morehead Patterson settled down at Christ Church College, Oxford, where they enjoyed comfortable lodgings, complete with a servant. When not reading history, Harry went foxhunting, conversed about literature, and played chess and tennis. He

admired Oxford and the British intellectual elite, but came home convinced that American democracy would produce a more numerous and
useful meritocracy. Luce mused about this coming cohort of Americans, who would inaugurate their nation's age of global power and
service to humanity. Few Americans harbored such heroic visions in
1921. People rarely spoke any longer of making the world safe for
democracy, for the recent "war to end all wars" had evidently created
more problems than it had solved. Warren G. Harding had set the
new tone when he uttered a statement about the need for a return to
"normalcy." Harry was, however, entering an era molded by discordant sets of protagonists.

One heard much from men like H. L. Mencken and other sophisticated cynics who debunked old verities, while the country was awash
in talk of money and speculation. This was the age of the promoter,
of the "ad man," so Harry's experience in selling advertising could
contribute to his success. Cynicism was part of the national mood, but
so was nostalgia for a vanishing past. In some mythic time, small-town
virtues dominated society, and America, under God, went its own way.
Luce, despite his Yale degree and intellectual achievements, continued
to be one of these "small-town" boys, and the family life-style and
values that prevailed within the Tengchow compound were shared by
many other Americans. In his life as in his work, Harry Luce would
try to effect a union between traditional values, American evangelism,
and the modern age. As his son Henry Luce III later put it, Henry
Robinson Luce's guides were "faith and reason, Jerusalem and Ath-
ens. . . ."

1923

The Birth of *Time*

Harry Luce returned to the United States determined to invent a new form of journalism. First, however, the twenty-three-year-old Yale graduate needed to earn some money. In the summer of 1921 a gravely ill Nettie McCormick suggested that Harry contact her son Harold, who was president of the International Harvester Company. Harry took the train to Chicago, where the high unemployment rate reflected the bad times that had followed a brief postwar boom. Refusing a job that might cost another man his livelihood ("to hell with it"), Luce quickly found work as an assistant to Ben Hecht, the *Chicago Daily News'* popular columnist. The pay was meager ($20 a week plus car-fare), and the job did not challenge Luce's intellect. Diligent and curious, however, he scurried about Chicago, investigating human-interest stories that might merit a line or two in Hecht's column "One Thousand and One Afternoons." Unfortunately, Luce's curiosity ran in tandem with his literal-mindedness. Sometimes he sent in lengthy dispatches about trivial events or situations. By some accounts, Ben Hecht recommended that Luce be given his own beat, perhaps in the city room; he was too good to waste as a flunky. The columnist himself later contradicted this story, recalling that Luce buried him under an avalanche of useless, turgid material. Hecht added that ". . . this fellow is much *too* naive. . . . He's not going to go anywhere." It really did not matter, for Harry was just passing through. Late in 1921, after little more than a month with Ben Hecht, Luce received his pink slip.

Henry Luce and Brit Hadden decided to relocate to Baltimore, where they found jobs at the *News*. There, at the *Evening Sun*, the famous editor, critic, and writer Henry Louis Mencken was amusing sophisticated cynics with his lively jabs at hypocrisy and other human ailments. Clearly, snappy writing and irreverent cracks attracted modern middle-class urban readers. Luce took note of this fact. During their brief time at the *News*, Hadden and Luce learned more about the world of publishing, but what they saw only made them more critical of the daily press. Stories were unrelated to one another; the long, trivial article appeared next to a brief narrative. In a good newspaper, one could find most of the significant news, but this search required too much time. There was no national newspaper, and the syndication of popular columnists was still in its infancy.

A weekly magazine called the *Literary Digest* filled part of this void. The *Digest* pasted together last week's news stories, culled from a variety of sources. It did not rewrite these columns or articles, nor did it place them in any broader context. Read by busy people who did not have time to hunt for all the news or read the best columnists, the *Literary Digest* was very popular, and it enjoyed a circulation of about 900,000. Still, Luce and Hadden began to work on an alternative to the *Digest*. They often cut up the *New York Times*, pasted stories together, and sometimes rewrote them. Soon the young men had fabricated dummy issues of their proposed magazine.

In the winter of 1922, the two aspiring young journalists quit their jobs at the *News*. Hadden moved in with his family in Brooklyn; Luce lived with his parents in an apartment near Columbia University. The two men then found some office space in an old building on East 17th Street, in Manhattan. Hadden paid the rent, which was $55 per month. They now needed to raise lots of money, perhaps as much as $100,000, so Harry and Brit labored long hours, hammering out a prospectus for investors. This remarkable document reflected a sure sense of their magazine's potential readership. The prospectus spoke of a twenty-four-page magazine, with three columns on each page. The editors intended to place news stories in various departments, which included "National Affairs," "Foreign News," "the Professions," and "People."

The cataclysmic events of the age cried out for expert commentary, so the young editors proposed to summarize the views of leading columnists, such as Walter Lippmann of the *New York World*.

Harry promised to provide his readers with information about important religious thinkers and their disputes, such as the endless battle over the Darwinian theory of evolution. There were to be other innovations, too, though not all of them lasted. For example, fictitious interviews with persons prominent in the news enlivened the pages of the early *Time*. Other aspects of the magazine were more enduring. The young men realized that the magazine's name was "catchy." "Time" had a modern, no-nonsense flavor. *Time* was also, according to its prospectus, a dignified name, though Hadden, a master of the clever phrase, could not resist adding that "TIME will tell." Luce and Hadden intended to rewrite stories based upon newspaper accounts, but they would do so in a lively and provocative manner. Invariably, *Time*'s editors would concentrate on the personalities of their subjects, and their articles would all be of similar length, perhaps 400 words.

The two young journalists felt that they could attract a large readership, drawn from a pool of one million college graduates. Harry looked forward to the day when *Time* would be read by every alumnus and alumna in America. These people, Luce knew, wanted to make sense out of the revolutionary changes molding contemporary life. The automobile was remaking the country, typewriters were standard office fixtures, dresses were outrageously short, and dances were faster than ever. Women were voting, they sometimes smoked in public, and they were seen more often in the workplace. Radio was on the verge of becoming a national craze. The killing machines of war were more murderous than ever; totalitarian ideologies were emerging in Russia and Italy. Wall Street speculators were becoming national figures, often respected for their wisdom.

Time promised to explain this new world to its literate American inhabitants: once a week the magazine would spot trends and place the news in perspective. The new magazine promised to be "brief," and "interesting," because "TIME is valuable." A dummy issue, completed in December 1922, expressed sympathy for republican China, hostility to the powerful Ku Klux Klan, unusual compassion for the "Negro" cause, an open mind about the Fascist takeover in Italy, and little empathy for issues of Jewish concern.

Luce and Hadden did not intend to be reporters, nor did they wish to write editorials. Their rejection of the editorial format, however, should not be confused with objectivity. Harry and Brit freely acknowledged the biases they brought to *Time*. They believed in progress, science, enduring values, and tradition. Though Christian, Luce and Hadden repudiated both fundamentalist religion and Prohibition. Luce put it bluntly when he noted that he was not writing for "flat-world" types. He later summed up his journalistic credo when he avowed that "I am biased in favor of God, the Republican party, and free enterprise."

Luce and Hadden planned to present both sides of a debate, but they would then indicate which contender had submitted the stronger argument. To Luce there was a right position and a wrong one. So long as he was accurate in presenting the facts, he felt free to praise or condemn. The editors would bestow plaudits or blame in brief pieces, called "We Point with Pride" and "We View with Alarm." In a sense the whole "book" was to be a personal editorial, though Luce denied it. Of course, *Time* selected the facts, so problems could and did arise.

Brit Hadden wanted to amuse and inform; Harry Luce, perhaps reflecting another of his father's traits, wished to educate and *uplift* his readers. If Brit's great ability to tell a story could be harnessed to Harry Luce's curiosity, however, a new medium might evolve. Appearing on Friday morning, "with news up to and including the Wednesday immediately preceding," *Time* reflected the young men's unflagging self-confidence.

Luce and Hadden worked diligently through 1922 to attract a suitable list of investors. Brit's legendary charm made it hard for people to turn him down. He was particularly adept at approaching the wealthy relatives of Yale classmates. Luce, however, refused to turn to Mrs. McCormick, who was gravely ill, but did solicit her daughter, Anita McCormick Blaine, his "Aunt Anita." Responding enthusiastically to the venture, she agreed to buy fifty shares of stock, valued at $1,250. By October 1922 Harry and Brit had raised about $92,000, most of it in the form of preferred shares.

The young editors decided to retain 80 percent of the company's common stock, thus assuring their control of *Time*. Plans for incorporation progressed; the first copy of the magazine might be on sale within six months. Brit Hadden's cousin John S. Martin soon agreed to invest in the new publication. A bright but abrasive individual with great editorial abilities (when sober), Martin later decided to work with these two interesting men. Through Martin, Roy Edward Larsen (Harvard, 1921) heard about *Time*. Larsen, a shrewd man with editorial experience on the Harvard *Advocate*, realized that the new project required a dedicated circulation manager. Larsen's father, the head of a chain of theaters, advised him to go into banking, but Roy committed himself to *Time*. Luce, an undiplomatic man, often collected associates who displayed the finesse and social poise that he lacked, and Roy Larsen had these traits. More important still, Larsen, like Luce, possessed superb business acumen, but unlike Harry, he did not feel compelled to articulate "profound" ideas or edit copy. In 1922 Manfred Gottfried, a stable and hardworking Yale senior, became the future magazine's first "writer," constantly cutting, pasting, editing, and rewriting. Martin, Larsen, and Gottfried sensed the presence of promising careers in journalism, buried somewhere in the grubby offices on 17th Street.

These men were products of schools that shared the dominant, Protestant "Anglo–American" ethos of the time. When launched, *Time* was written by and for people much like themselves. Its small staff managed in cramped offices containing old bookcases and well-worn desks. "Editors" clipped newspapers and filed the articles in cubbyholes. Harry, working long hours and chain-smoking, would often run through Broadway traffic in order to grab the latest *New York Times* right off a delivery wagon. He frequently argued with Brit Hadden, but their work progressed. They prepared to launch the magazine in late February or early March 1923.

The magazine had decided to assemble an awesome list of charter subscribers. *Time* also asked each of its eighty investors to supply thirteen of their friends with subscription forms. The famous people who approved of the new venture included President Nicholas M. Butler of Columbia University; former Secretary of War Newton D. Baker; columnist Walter Lippmann; the recent Democratic Vice-Presidential candidate, Franklin D. Roosevelt; the popular Kansas journalist William Allen White; and Theodore Roosevelt, Jr.

A later age would describe the Luce/Larsen technique as "networking." This concept came naturally to Harry Luce, since he had spent years listening to his father's war stories of fund-raising. Some of Larsen's techniques were common in the magazine business, however. *Time* bought subscription lists from other publications and mailed 7,000 circulars to potential readers. Of those persons solicited, 6½ percent expressed interest in the new magazine. This was considered a good return. Potential subscribers discovered that the expensive magazine cost five dollars a year, but included a money-back guarantee. Luce and Larsen hoped to attract 25,000 subscribers, an unrealistic goal. The magazine did receive 6,000 orders, however, while newsstands agreed to accept a total of 5,000 additional copies to be sold retail at a cost of fifteen cents each. *Time* had even succeeded in attracting a few prestigious advertisers, who hoped to reach an upscale audience. The White Star cruise line bought a third of a page, as did Harper & Brothers, the

New York publisher. Propelled by optimism, *Time*'s small operation relocated to a better office on East 40th Street.

The first issue of *Time* was dated March 3, 1923. Its black-and-white cover (the famous red border did not appear until several years later) displayed a drawing of "Uncle Joe" Cannon, the legendary Speaker of the House of Representatives. The first page, containing a table of contents, clearly divided the magazine and the world into neat, easily mastered categories, ranging from "National Affairs" to "View with Alarm." *Time*'s brief news articles offered readers insights into the famous personalities of the day. "Milestones" provided gossipy tidbits of information about those who had married or died. Throughout the magazine, stories of significance appeared next to lighter items. An article about Italian Fascist negotiations with the Roman Catholic Church materialized next to a short piece describing King Victor Emmanuel III's coin collection. From the latter, readers picked up bits of inside information, learning, for example, that the King was a "numismatist." This combination of gossip, trivia, and arcane facts and words impressed many subscribers.

When important issues were at stake, one knew where *Time*'s editors stood. The magazine was against American isolationism, and anguished over persistent Franco-German hostility. The magazine approved of Italian Fascist leader Benito Mussolini, *Il Duce*, when the former revolutionary moved closer to Italian conservatives. By contrast, *Time*'s portrait of Soviet Bolshevism depicted a rotten government which sold grain abroad while its peasants starved at home. And *Time* was rarely balanced when grappling with the hot issue of Prohibition. Brit Hadden liked to party all night, as he sampled this or that speakeasy in Manhattan. Luce rarely took more than a drink or two, but he disliked the repressive, intrusive thrust of Prohibition. *Time* was therefore sympathetic to "wet" politicians like the Democrat Al Smith of New York. Prohibition, *Time* declared, was a "greased and perhaps blind pig." In decisions involving personal choice, Harry Luce believed in applying willpower rather than coercion, but personal interest played its part here, too. Luce and *Time* had a vested interest in the abolition of the "noble experiment." He planned to sell space to the liquor interests, when "Repeal" occurred.

Time was attracting the attention of quite a few journalists and opinion-makers. Advertisers remained cautious, but the staff again moved to bigger offices, located in a former brewery on East 39th Street. Roy Larsen, who was trying to vindicate his career choice, told his skeptical father that newsstand boys, even those hawking the papers in Grand Central Terminal, called *Time* a big success. Most readers seemed to enjoy the magazine, though its early issues sold a total of only 9,000 copies or so. Some patrons, however, took advantage of *Time*'s money-back offer.

One Charles Mohney, of Polk, Pennsylvania, discontinued his sub-scription when he spotted advertisements in *Time* for books advocating atheism or evolution. The New Testament, Mohney wrote, rebutted Charles Darwin's theory of evolution. Clearly, *Time* was not for Mr. Mohney. Nor was it for a lady in Bingham, Illinois, who asked that the magazine not be sent to her. "I dont want it," the lady wrote, "[because] I cante read." These setbacks did not bother Harry, for he rejected the patronage of such "flat-world" types. When Luce received a thoughtful critique from a more sophisticated reader, however, he paid more attention to it.

In August 1923 Henry Luce studied a letter written by a wealthy New Yorker who lived in the Hudson River valley. The note proved to be the prelude to a long, difficult, important, and ultimately hateful relationship. Franklin D. Roosevelt warned Harry Luce that *Time*, in its quest for brevity, "has made statements in regard to events which are not wholly fact." "FDR," as he often styled himself, observed that *Time* sometimes omitted important adjectives, thus conveying a false impression to its readers. He was the first reader (of whom we have a record) to bemoan one of *Time*'s most controversial and innovative techniques: the sly, colorful use or misuse of "qualifying words." Roosevelt, trying to recover from a severe bout with polio, did not accuse Luce of malice. Indeed, he acknowledged that spatial limitations had obliged *Time* to omit some important details. FDR concluded by offer-ing some friendly advice about how to increase *Time*'s circulation. He suggested that the magazine be sold by newsstands located in towns along the Hudson. Luce thanked Franklin Roosevelt, but he denied any attempt to distort the news. Luce was no psychologist, and he believed that if a story told most of the truth, presented accurate facts, and held its readers' attention, it was a good piece. Herein lay both *Time*'s appeal and its potential ability to gain readers and make enemies.

Harry Luce had been educated in a male world, had served in the all-male Army, and after graduating from Yale, he found himself in another male preserve, newspaper journalism. In Rome, on New Year's Eve in 1920, Harry's classmate Thornton Wilder introduced him to a student of Miss Risser's school. Lila Ross Hotz of Chicago, a pretty, sociable, poetic young woman was instantly attracted to the intense young editor. Harry began to court Miss Hotz, who fell deeply in love with him. Lila was devoted to travel, correspondence, warm friendships, and days filled with an endless array of parties and social events. Harry felt happy around her, and in 1923 the couple became engaged. Lila adopted Harry's enthusiasms as her own, and her emotional support made a sad event more bearable. Nettie McCormick, the Luces' patroness, died in the summer, after long and debilitating illnesses. Harry went to the funeral as the representative of the Luce family.

Lila worried endlessly about her fiancé's work habits. In her letters she wrote about Harry as she imagined him, bent over lists of subscribers, correcting copy, reading proofs. Luce, she knew, worked through much (sometimes all) of the night in his stuffy office, smoking up to five packs of cigarettes a day. Lila understood what *Time* meant to him. Corresponding from Paris, she once told Harry about her dogged, successful search for a copy of *Time*, or the "blessed paper," as she called it. Her playful phrases seemed to have been lost on Harry. In fact, she longed for a more poetic ("rugged yet refined!") Harry Luce.

Lila, who had a sizable inheritance, had trouble balancing a checking account. Her stepfather worried about her future, and he almost blocked her marriage to Harry Luce. Her guardian was dubious about these *Time* boys and their enterprise. He insisted that Harry pay himself a salary of $5,000 a year before he would permit him to marry Lila. Luce agreed, and the two young people were wed on December 22, 1923. There was no time for a honeymoon, though Harry promised a disappointed Lila that they would one day make a leisurely tour of Europe. As always, she was warm and deferential, cheerfully accepting Harry's obsession with his work. *Time*, after all, was struggling to succeed.

Manfred Gottfried believed that *Time* must read like a collection of short stories, each with a beginning and an end. The reader, he argued, must feel like an observer, going from "nowhere to somewhere." *Time*'s writers rose to meet Gottfried's challenge. Laird Goldsborough ("Goldy"), who soon wrote the entire Foreign News section by himself, provided an ample supply of readable stories. His untouched or even unchecked copy fit the mood of the era, and both *Time* and Goldsborough prospered. Filled with gossip about royalty and pithy portraits of famous people, Foreign News long remained Goldsborough's kingdom. New colleagues soon strengthened *Time*. Archibald MacLeish, a Yale alumnus, earned an extra ten dollars a week by writing about education. An aspiring poet with a family to support, MacLeish badly needed the money. Harry's sister Beth, who had graduated from Wellesley in 1924, contributed book reviews. Luce himself continued to write the religion section—religion, Harry insisted, must be treated seriously, for it was, he roared, "a Goddam good thing!"

Brit Hadden loved wisecracks, puns, and clever turns of phrase. Hadden created the famous *Time* style, while Luce tended mainly to business affairs. Brit reveled in editorial work, roaring with delight when reading a good line and growling with anger when offended by bad prose. Brit turned nouns into adjectives, so a man who was a teacher became "teacher Jones." An enthusiastic classicist, Hadden parodied Homer, describing people as "wild-eyed" or "long-whiskered." He invented new words, like "kudos" (for honorary degrees) and "tycoon" for men of wealth. *Time* created popular terms such as "cinemactor" and "socialite." Brit liked to print middle names, especially when their bearers despised them. Hadden made sure that his readers chuckled with him, often at the mental or physical shortcomings of his targets. Luce was uneasy with ridicule, but it sold magazines. Hadden's playful creativity was not limited to linguistic matters. He concocted "Peter Mathews," a fictional character whose name appeared on *Time*'s masthead. "Mathews" existed to take the blame for inaccurate statements corrected by irate readers.

Luce fantasized about the day when *Time* would have a few thousand dollars in the bank. The magazine lost almost $40,000 in 1923, but made a profit of about $700 in 1924. At the end of 1923, *Time*'s circulation stood at only 30,000, but about a year later the magazine sold 70,000 copies each week. The stock offering continued to do well, and investors showed their confidence by holding on to their shares. *Time* was winning over a small but growing reading clientele, in towns much like those skewered by Sinclair Lewis and Mencken. An upscale new publication, called *The New Yorker*, scorned the patronage of "the old lady in Dubuque." Harry, however, liked intelligent, well-read people, even if they did come from the provinces. He wanted that old lady to subscribe to *Time*, and soon she probably would.

Harry Luce never shared Hadden's enthusiasm for New York's sophistication. Luce, after all, respected many of the values dear to that old lady in Iowa. He was all in favor of marriage and the family, while Hadden always had a bevy of girlfriends, none of whom he took seriously. Brit Hadden lived at a madcap pace, and spent more than one night in jail for being drunk and disorderly. Harry disliked these bouts of boorish behavior, but he knew what Brit meant to *Time*, so they managed to work out a productive compromise. *Time* was like Hadden—smart-alecky and irreverent. Luce, however, made sure that the magazine did not drive away readers who bore traces of "Babbitry."

Time was attracting intelligent readers who had not attended Ivy

League schools, and circulation was growing in towns that lay outside the orbit of the New York media world. Harry Luce saw *Time* as a kind of weekly newspaper whose national mission reflected the growing integration of the American economy. The college-educated reader in Illinois or Colorado wanted more than he or she received from a local, provincial newspaper. Luce knew that his potential market was enormous. Falling farm prices affected more than the Midwest; Iowans watched the New York Stock Exchange with increasing interest. In politics, however, regionalism and local interests prevailed. When additional power flowed to Washington, *Time*, with its national orientation, would become essential reading to more and more people.

Since Luce preferred the Midwest to New York, he decided to move *Time* to Cleveland in the summer of 1925. Hadden strongly opposed this relocation to the "sticks." Brit could not match Harry's business acumen, however, and in his usual earnest and well-informed manner, Luce argued the case for Cleveland. By relocating, *Time* could rent more space for less money and cut other expenses as well. A local press offered excellent printing facilities, and by the end of the year, Luce had cultivated and won over many of Cleveland's business leaders. He had often mused about growing up in a normal American hometown, and, for the moment, he had found one. Hadden, however, derided the local citizenry as "Babbitts" and hated his new locale. An affordable printer soon came to Brit's rescue, and *Time* would return to his beloved New York City.

Since the end of 1924, circulation had increased by 50 percent, to 107,000 copies a week. *Time* averaged 111,000 copies by late 1926, and the company showed a small profit of about $8,000. At this point a skilled, innovative Chicago printer named T. E. Donnelley (of R. R. Donnelley & Sons), impressed by *Time*'s potential, approached Luce with an attractive offer. Donnelley claimed that he could print the magazine more cheaply in Chicago, without disturbing its publication schedule. This meant that *Time* could be published in New York and save money. Copy could be sent west on the 20th Century Limited express train. (Later, wires would be used to transmit both copy and pictures.) *Time* could now afford New York, which was, Luce had to admit, the media metropolis, and the magazine now moved back to the big city. More success followed, as *Time*'s snappier appearance and better graphics contributed to its burgeoning popularity. *Time*'s cover acquired its red border, and some advertisements appeared in four-color format. By 1928 circulation was pushing 200,000, while after-tax profits amounted to a solid $125,788.

Journalists and advertisers began to follow *Time* with interest. By the end of the decade, the magazine's clever style was influencing professors at schools of journalism. A good *Time* story, they believed, gave the reader a sense of immediacy, of watching a true tale unfold before one's eyes. In St. Louis, the *Post-Dispatch* reported that *Time* was "snippy, snappy, terse." Success sometimes provoked jealousy, too. *Time's* sole sources continued to be the daily press, well into the 1930s. Consequently, some newspaper editors resented the upstart scissors-and-paste magazine, and derided it as a parasite on their own work.

Time's readership was almost entirely upscale, a fact not lost on smart advertising firms. Only 18.8 percent of U.S. workers earned more than $5,000 per year; among *Time* subscribers, the figure reached 60 percent. Seventy-one percent of these readers owned their own homes, and most of them were upwardly mobile businessmen and professional people. Working with the steady, innovative circulation man Roy Larsen, Luce commissioned pioneering marketing surveys. Larsen also understood the potential importance of the new medium called radio, so early on *Time* sponsored a program entitled the "Pop Question Game." Asking questions answered by the latest issue of *Time*, the program awarded a prize to the person who mailed in a correct form. With business booming, Time Inc. reported a net profit of $400,000 in 1929.

A tragic event soon saddened Luce. Brit Hadden contracted a case of *streptococcus viridans*, or "blood poisoning." (A friend's cat may have scratched Brit, who was fond of animals.) Despite frequent transfusions of blood donated by Luce and other *Time* staffers, Hadden worsened and died on February 27, 1929. Emotionally drained, and physically depleted by repeated donations of blood, Harry experienced a brief and highly atypical period of depression. He even took a vacation, for despite his frequent differences with Hadden, he was devastated. Luce had known Hadden for half of his young life; he was now on his own, and so was *Time*.

To Harry Luce, Hadden had been a "rival since early Hotchkiss days," a man who challenged and stimulated his friends. "Race or rot," Harry liked to say, and Brit Hadden, whether pursuing pleasure or his plan for *Time*, was in a big hurry. Looking back on the creative relationship between these bright young men, one can scarcely imagine a more unlikely duo: Hadden, the perpetual adolescent, and Luce, the stern, mature man. Yet if Harry ever had a friend, it was Brit Hadden. Brit concealed his lack of ease with strangers by affecting a brash exterior. Harry found it difficult to make small talk, and in an elevator crowded with associates, he was likely to stare at his shoes. Indeed, Luce seemed to use Hadden as a complement to his own, more cerebral personality.

Harry Luce instinctively made use of people who displayed the traits he so sorely lacked. He admired Hadden as the popular "big man" in every school he attended. The mustachioed prankster and clever wordsmith proved to be the first in an emerging pattern. Luce, a stammerer who lacked glibness, vivacity, and social grace, would surround himself with men whose looks and talents compensated for his own ponderous quality. These same associates would project a favorable image and thereby help the company. When Brit died, Harry Luce lost his one friend, but he also mourned the death of a poet and writer who had invented the ever more famous (and notorious) *Time* style.

Having died young, like an athlete in his prime, Hadden left memories that would long enchant his friends. Time Inc. prospered, but Luce would never again permit himself to have a really close friend. None of his future confidants and associates dared engage in the kind of irreverent banter and (usually) friendly rivalry that had enlivened Brit Hadden's association with the ever-serious Harry Luce.

After his "vacation" following Brit's death, Luce returned to his many chores at *Time*. Despite a period of uncertainty, *Time* continued to rise in prominence. John S. Martin had edited National Affairs, along lines laid down by Hadden and Luce. After Hadden's death, Martin, who was Brit's cousin, became managing editor. An accomplished stylist as well as a hard-drinking eccentric, Martin ably carried on two of Brit Hadden's traditions.

Time was surviving, but one great worry bothered Harry Luce. Although he had lost his dynamic collaborator, he did not intend to lose *Time*. In his will, Briton Hadden had directed that his stock in Time Inc. not be sold by his family until forty-nine years after his death. He did this to ensure that Luce would maintain control of the company. Harry, however, wanted the Hadden shares immediately, and thought that he had a moral right to buy them. Brit's brother, Crowell Hadden III, anxious to raise some cash, offered to sell Hadden's stock to Luce for over a million dollars. Charles E. Stillman (Yale, 1926), the quiet financial prodigy who served as *Time*'s business manager, quickly put together a purchasers' syndicate. Luce borrowed a good deal of money, and he, Larsen, Stillman, and several other staffers bought most of the Hadden shares. Within two years the stock had almost tripled in value. Harry talked to Lila about buying a summer home for $100,000. By the age of thirty-two, Henry Luce was a rich man.

Good Fortune in
Bad Times

Main Street liked *Time*. Wall Street largely ignored the magazine, at a time when stock exchange averages were mesmerizing much of the country. People were talking about the imminent end of poverty, in an economy that would overcome the cycle of boom and bust. Luce liked the businessmen he had met in Cleveland, but he returned to New York with a condescending view of their culture and literacy. Capitalists, Luce concluded, needed their own literature. These men, who knew how to build factories, did not understand how their work related to the society around them. Businessmen, Harry believed, needed to examine their values, goals, and biases. Business magazines, unfortunately, usually looked like trade journals, or acted as shoddy guides to the thriving stock market. Luce wanted to create a literature for enterprise, but one that did not pander to the prejudices of its readers.

Luce's opinions were often unpredictable. In the 1920s this lifelong Republican freely criticized GOP administrations for their lack of direction. Harry Luce was probably one of the few Americans who voted for Democrat Al Smith in 1928, then switched to the hapless Herbert

Hoover in 1932. Speaking to Rochester businessmen in 1928, Harry Luce raised a troubling question. If the age of abundance had arrived, why were Americans cynical and apathetic about the political process? Luce found the answer in diverse social currents of the day. He pointed his finger at the eroding strength of organized religion; and at workers, who no longer automatically followed their divinely ordained "masters." Luce then attacked mediocre politicians, who failed to set goals and implement policies appropriate to a new age. Harry Luce, who tended to worship heroes, declared that the nation needed a "moral leader," a man who understood how to generate enthusiasm for "great national purposes."

Henry Luce's search for an aristocratic principle founded on morality and merit led him back to Edmund Burke, the eighteenth-century politician and philosopher. Burke, like Luce, welcomed change, so long as it respected tradition, honor, religion, and intellect. Luce particularly liked Burke's view of political morality. The Anglo-Irish statesman believed in politicians who respected themselves, public opinion, and history. Such men, Burke believed, had leisure time for reading, for reflection, and for conversation. As Luce later put it, "You must educate your conscience. It is not a child of nature." In Edmund Burke's view, the ideal leader braved all dangers in the "pursuit of honor and duty." Such a man, he believed, was the product of "a national aristocracy without which there is no nation." Luce concluded that the press must play a role in the search for this kind of leadership.

Harry Luce longed for the emergence of an entrepreneurial class that was aware of its responsibility. He thought that a corporation, like Time Inc. (he had abolished the comma), or the Federal Government, should be operated in the public interest. Luce knew that enterprise and innovation could not flourish in a repressive or collectivist environment. Business, Luce hoped, would provide the recruits for his new meritocracy. He saw both beauty and grandeur in industry, and Harry Luce envisioned a magazine that would educate both the entrepreneur and his fellow citizen on Main Street. The journal would have to be big, elaborate, beautiful, and expensive, in keeping with its subject and its mission. It must be printed on the finest paper, with cardboard covers, and contain brilliant writing. The publication would appear monthly, and cost an outrageous price—one dollar per issue.

Luce established an experimental department charged with planning the new magazine. He thought of calling it *Power*, but abandoned that title in favor of *Fortune*. The publication, Luce insisted, must be willing to offend the businessmen at whom it was aimed. *Fortune* would find out why things worked well or how they could work better. Still, some people warned Luce that corporation executives wanted to be the subjects of praise, not the objects of investigative reporting.

Henry Luce, like most of his contemporaries, had failed to sense the economic tremors beneath his feet. He paid little attention to warning signals such as the drastic fall in commodity prices. *Time* announced the debut of *Fortune* in its October 21, 1929, issue, which was on the stands at the time of the great Stock Exchange crash. Against the advice of some colleagues, Luce proposed that *Fortune* appear as scheduled, early in 1930. *Fortune* was a critical success, and readers marveled at articles printed on "wild wove antique," an expensive type of heavy paper. Owen Young, chairman of the board of the General Electric Company, reviewed *Fortune* and declared himself "overwhelmed." Advertisers raved about *Fortune*, too, so Time Inc. sold most of the year's ad space (at $500 per page) before the first issue had appeared. Few subscribers asked for refunds, so *Fortune* might not lose too much money. When the economy rebounded in the near future, the new magazine might even contribute to Time Inc.'s profits.

During these early years of the Depression, many people soon questioned the efficiency and durability of the free enterprise system. *Fortune* tried to show how the beleaguered capitalist could better serve society. The magazine even examined the roots of the labor troubles haunting the Ford Motor Company and expressed sympathy for trade unions. Luce advocated the creation of bigger banks with more branches so as to expand credit markets. He was convinced that psychological factors, combined with ignorance and bad government policies, prevented business from recovering. We have, or can have, enough to "live *on*," Harry declared, but we also need something to "live *for*."

Harry Luce realized that *Fortune* needed accomplished writers, not experienced business journalists. He claimed that he could turn a poet into a journalist more easily than he could convert a bookkeeper into a writer. Ralph McAllister ("Mac") Ingersoll, formerly of *The New Yorker*, was hard-driving, ambitious, and abrasive, but the new managing editor's contentious exchanges with editor in chief Luce resulted in a better *Fortune*. Ingersoll became a kind of in-house counselor to his boss. Mac suggested that Harry join certain prestigious men's clubs, and advised him on the new science of public relations. Meanwhile *Fortune* was constantly attracting bright new talent. Aspiring poets or writers, like young Archibald MacLeish, caught Luce's eye. He admired "Archie's" work for *Time*, and with a wife and three children, poet MacLeish needed to find a job that provided him with a "sabbatical" for part of each year. Fine, replied Luce, work for *Fortune* for three months of the year, or for twelve, depending on your financial needs. Once he had completed his assignment, MacLeish was free to devote his time to his art. At *Fortune*, MacLeish grew into a superb editor and writer; he also earned the 1932 Pulitzer Prize for poetry.

In 1930 Luce hired Russell Wheeler ("Mitch") Davenport, a fellow Bonesman (Yale, 1923). The son of a prominent metallurgist who served as a vice-president of the Bethlehem Steel Corporation, Davenport had twice earned the *croix de guerre* by driving a field ambulance during the war. His politics were libertarian, and his avocation was poetry. A dominant figure at *Fortune* and *Life* for more than a decade, Davenport was an intense, driven man. He suffered from hearing loss; when bored by a conversation, he simply removed his hearing aid. Once, when reminiscing about his pre-*Fortune* days, Davenport recalled being surrounded by "the intellectuals and the aesthetes, and by their books." While working at *Fortune*, he came to realize that those cliques of intellectuals and "Bohemians" did not understand America. At *Fortune*, Davenport observed, he felt like part of the "stream of America."

One day in 1929, during a visit to an advertising firm, Harry Luce had spotted some striking photographs of Cleveland's Otis Steel Co. The pictures gave Luce a feel for industrial civilization, "how it looks, how it meshes. . . ." After discovering the identity of the photographer, Luce dispatched a telegram to Margaret Bourke-White, inviting her to come to New York within a week, all expenses paid. Bourke-White knew little about *Time*, but suspected that Luce might want her to photograph politicians, who usually bored her. Still it was a free trip. In New York, Luce's interest in Bourke-White's photographs impressed her. She long remembered his jammed way of talking as well as his "almost frenzied intensity." Assured of Bourke-White's dedication—more like a calling or a mission, and that pleased Harry Luce—he asked her to work for him. This woman, Luce thought, captured the American energy and drive that spawned large factories and soaring skyscrapers. Luce's excitement was contagious, and Bourke-White accepted his offer.

Bourke-White soon set out to photograph industrial America, from shoe factories in Lynn, Massachusetts, to the steel mills of South Bend, Indiana. International Harvester, the Swift meat-packing industry, the George Washington Bridge, high coal rigs looming over Lake Superior, the latest (unfinished) Manhattan skyscraper—Bourke-White photographed them all. She took great personal risks, crawling out on ledges, risking pneumonia from the cold and heatstroke from the sun, all the while braving the skepticism and condescension of male industrialists.

By celebrating the strength, power, and even the beauty of American industry, Bourke-White, like *Fortune*, gained the attention of an influential audience. Archie MacLeish quickly recognized how Margaret Bourke-White's photography complemented *Fortune*'s literary efforts, and he helped to make her famous. And Luce the Republican did not let MacLeish's Democratic sentiments, or Bourke-White's incipient radicalism, undermine his fruitful collaboration with them.

Luce cared mainly about his gifted staff's performance. So long as the man turned in his copy, or edited it, Luce left him alone. Work-related ethics were another matter. Editors and writers were barred from trading in the shares of such corporations for thirty days after the relevant article had appeared. Nor were they to accept expensive gifts. All this was a novelty, but Luce was ahead of his time in another respect. He realized that the physical well-being of the staff contributed to the quality of the magazine. Luce wanted his top editors to enjoy long vacations—and this during a time of massive unemployment. He thought that even researchers should take one or two work days off each month. Despite these progressive management techniques, Harry Luce was in other ways a man of his time. He did not probe the obvious contradiction between his advocacy of good health and some of the products promoted by his publications. He himself smoked heavily, and his magazines advertised tobacco and (later) alcohol. And although Luce knew that many of his talented women researchers (usually referred to as Time Inc. as "the girls") might make good editors, he would not reconsider his males-only editorial policy.

Fortune's success owed a lot to the efforts of Associate Editor Eric Hodgins, who had graduated from the Massachusetts Institute of Technology. A talented journalist, Hodgins would become a legendary editor, who could be scathing in criticizing a first draft. Addressing one hapless writer, Hodgins commented that "This draft *subtracts* from the sum total of human knowledge." The debut of a major piece in *Fortune* was a challenge and an ordeal; editors sometimes labored through the night. Still, the system, broadly construed, worked well. Archibald MacLeish, like other editors, benefited from Luce's commitment to first-class research, and here a young man named Allen Grover made an important contribution.

Luce wanted to publish a series of articles on the Ivar Kreuger affair, a scandal that had attracted much attention. Kreuger, a Swedish financier, industrialist, and "match king," was also a fraud and a swindler. His suicide in 1932 caused a worldwide sensation. MacLeish agreed to write the articles, but Luce turned for additional help to Allen Grover (Yale,

1922). The tall, handsome, and graceful son of a bank president, Grover was trained as a statistician. He had worked for a Wall Street firm, but like many other brokerage houses, his failed in 1931. A friend introduced Grover to John S. Martin, who was a one-man recruiting team for Time Inc. In 1932 Luce gave Grover an important assignment. He was to travel through Europe, conducting research on the Ivar Kreuger scandal. Combining *Time*-like details about Kreuger's suicide with solid research, *Fortune* proceeded to create a new kind of investigative journalism.

Harry Luce soon imposed another task on Allen Grover. *Fortune*'s research department consisted of a few professionals, aided by former debutantes whose fathers described *Fortune* as a prestigious place to work. Besides, the presence of a daughter in *Fortune*'s office might (but rarely did) lead to a story about Daddy. The magazine's growing staff now required support and central direction. In April 1933 Luce asked Grover to take over the research department. Standards soon rose higher, as *Fortune* acquired the services of new recruits who had college degrees, and some knowledge of economics. The bolder among them would question an editor's use or misuse of their work. Allen Grover now enjoyed Luce's complete confidence. Grover could discreetly translate what pensive, stammering Harry *meant* to say.

In the beginning, *Fortune* had few enemies and many admirers, especially among business leaders. Times were getting worse, and the sumptuous appearance of a magazine gave these entrepreneurs and managers a good feeling. Some businessmen concluded that there must be something special about Luce and his "papers." *Fortune* claimed a circulation of 30,000 in 1930; nine years later, that figure had more than quadrupled. By 1934 *Fortune* was earning a small profit, for most of its audience continued to enjoy affluence and security. More than half of the magazine's readership consisted of persons listed in the *Social Register*, and a majority of *Fortune*'s subscribers were major business executives. The average subscriber earned more than $21,000 a year, a small fortune during the Depression.

Business leaders vied with one another to obtain favorable notice from the magazine. Disappointed suitors even spread the false rumor that Luce *sold* entry into the pages of *Fortune*, at the incredible fee of $50,000 per article. And despite its need for income, *Fortune* did not shy away from fights with advertisers. The powerful Matson Line objected to a *Fortune* article that alluded to the instability of certain of its ships. Mac Ingersoll and Harry Luce refused to retract the allegation, so the shippers canceled their contract.

"Good! Good!" responded Harry. "Ought to lose an account every month."

Harry Luce could afford to make such comments. Time Inc. earned $4.11 per share in 1931, *up* from $3.97 in 1930. At the end of 1930, *Time*'s circulation had passed 300,000, while the company owned more than $1.5 million in cash and marketable securities. In 1932 circulation stood at 420,000; three years later it had risen to more than half a million. While the country seemed mired in a permanent economic morass, Time Inc. was making money, more than $700,000 in the terrible year 1932. Over one third of *Time*'s subscribers still earned more than $10,000 per year—perhaps 1 percent of the nation's families did so.

Much to the joy of *Time*'s staff, the efficient John Billings, then National Affairs editor, became acting managing editor. Late in 1933, the strapping, handsome South Carolinian settled into his new position and ran *Time* for three years. For the next twenty years, Billings would play an important part in Luce's success as a publisher. In the 1920s he had begun to answer research queries for John Martin, receiving $25 a month. At National Affairs, his work consisted of constant editing and rewriting, but Billings survived, though not without travail. Martin was hard to please, and constantly rewrote and criticized Billings' copy. He also appreciated having Billings around, for the young man worked like a horse and did what he was told. Impressed, Martin soon appointed John Shaw Billings permanent National Affairs editor, promising him an eventual salary of $20,000.

At first Billings feared the intense, no-nonsense Harry Luce, but he soon came to admire his dynamic boss and wanted to know him better. After Hadden's death, he positioned himself to be Harry's confidant, but Luce no longer wished to have a best friend, at least not at Time Inc. John Shaw Billings slowly became indispensable to Luce, but as an editor, not as a friend. At home, in his Fifth Avenue penthouse, he wrote frequently about Luce. Billings' diary, which is a marvelous guide to the world of Time Inc., expresses much frustration over Harry's brusk manner and cold exterior. Still, Billings' resentment was tempered by admiration for Luce the editor and Luce the "thinking machine."

Harry Luce also kept a wary eye on the balance sheet. The company saved what money it could, while Charles Stillman and Roy Larsen searched for bargain-basement investment opportunities. The company's offices, located (since August 1931) on two floors in the fashionable Chrysler Building, were functional but not beautiful. Writers still labored behind old wooden desks, in crowded and cluttered quarters. Luce and his top editors worked in comfortable but sparsely decorated offices. Time Inc.'s employees, however, did enjoy some unique benefits. As early as 1929, Time Inc. introduced an employee stock ownership plan. Seventeen employees took part; the number rose to thirty-three four years later. Many of these people became wealthy because of the appreciation in the value of Time Inc.'s stock. In 1929, for example, Luce suggested that Billings buy some shares at $250 each. A few months later they were worth $500 per unit. While the stock market plummeted, Billings' Time Inc. shares continued to appreciate.

Time Inc. was evolving from a small operation, run by a bunch of Ivy League boys, to a medium-sized concern. The enterprise now expanded into broadcasting, for by 1933 radios had become commonplace items in almost 17 million American homes. The major radio networks lacked news divisions; occasionally, a commentator might read from the wire and briefly analyze a news story. *Time*, of course, owed much of its success to its dramatic, readable style. Why not apply some of its color to radio? Roy Larsen sketched out the idea for a radio program, and "The March of Time" first aired on the Columbia Broadcasting System in March 1931. The show used dramatic reenactments in reporting the news, and these "plays" engaged and amused listeners. Luce, who cared little for media other than print, muttered about the project's cost, but he paid for it. Once, when Time Inc. announced plans to drop the show, 22,000 letters poured in, opposing the move. Harry, who never bucked public opinion over trivial issues, relented.

Time Inc. was now a kind of collegial hierarchy, presided over by Harry Luce. The editor in chief wanted men about him who liked a good argument, and if a man did not believe what he wrote, Luce wanted no part of him. Ultimately, however, everyone knew who was boss. This situation sparked tensions that later affected some of his best editors. It was difficult for Harry to praise a staffer to his (much less her) face. He could be kind and gracious, but usually he displayed such traits in writing. Luce relied a great deal on a few valued associates, for the company was expanding very rapidly. At times colleagues even warned Luce against retreating into his managerial isolation. Their situation was in some ways rendered more difficult by the fact that Henry Luce did not give many direct orders to his managing editors. He expected, however, that *his* magazines would reflect his deeply held values and beliefs.

Henry R. Luce profited from his visionary ability to spot currents before they formed waves. His own code of behavior, however, typed him as a man of his time. Luce liked the company of intelligent, informed women—in a social setting. At work, Luce expected women to be secretaries or checkers. There were rare exceptions, such as Laura Z. Hobson, who wrote sparkling promotional material. When negotiating her salary, Luce warned her that no woman at Time Inc. could earn $7,000 a year, Hobson's current salary at a prominent department store. A beautiful, highly intelligent woman, Laura Hobson stood her ground, and Luce conceded the point. A few years later, however, when Harry established a "senior group" of profit-sharing editors, it was basically a male preserve. Luce's growing influence and wealth depended in some measure on female researchers, checkers, and typists who were, for the most part, strangers to him.

Henry Luce's journalism reflected a mix of personal experience, sentiment, prejudice, and solid narrative. Nowhere was this more apparent than in his coverage of China, a labor of love that ultimately touched the history of two great nations.

In 1932, accompanied by his brother-in-law, Leslie R. Severinghaus, Henry Luce sailed to the Far East as part of a journey around the world. Luce had not been in the land of his birth for twenty years. In China, he met and talked with all kinds of people, but he clearly preferred the company of wealthy and powerful Chinese. And converts to Christianity could easily gain access to Luce, despite his busy schedule. To Harry, China's predicament was a challenge, and America's generosity was an inspiration. In a north China village, for example, medical personnel, trained by the Rockefeller Foundation, faced the threat of a smallpox epidemic. Lacking modern vaccination equipment, these trainees disinfected sewing machine needles. The health workers then inoculated 21,605 Chinese and saved their lives. This kind of edifying tale gripped Luce, and he intended to convey it to his readers.

Capitalist Shanghai particularly fascinated Harry. An oasis of stability amid the turbulence convulsing much of China, Shanghai was home to many real estate and gold speculators. Luce found the Shanghai markets more exiting than the torpid American stock exchanges, though he overlooked the parasitical character of the Shanghai money-changers. On June 1 Harry Luce made the acquaintance of T. V. Soong, who had flown to Shanghai for his meeting with this American. Though he was suffering from a fever and had canceled all other appointments, Soong badly wanted to meet Harry Luce. Soong was careful to praise *Time* and *Fortune*, thereby inaugurating a long family tradition.

The thirty-eight-year-old T. V. Soong, a brother-in-law of strongman Chiang Kai-shek and son of a Christian Bible salesman, was a fabulously wealthy financier and political manipulator. Speaking softly, in perfect English, Soong expressed confidence in the new China. In Soong's vision, the government of Chiang Kai-shek, having disposed of warlords and Communists, would unite the huge nation. Then China could deal with any new Japanese depredations. As Luce excitedly mulled over reports of her great financial progress, he saw China as poised to move into Christian modernity. Surely, he believed, Americans would endeavor to help her.

To his delight, Harry Luce later journeyed to Beijing, where he visited a cabaret and danced with a beautiful young White Russian girl. He spent one night curled in a sleeping bag, next to a temple also on the Beijing Plain, near the Summer Palace. Luce met Pearl Buck, whose novel *The Good Earth* (1931) had become a bestseller. After his encounter with Buck, Luce endured long train rides through bandit-infested country. He sat in cramped, grubby compartments, but neither the dirt nor the lack of creature comforts bothered him. Though not known for nostalgia, Luce happily revisited the sites of his boyhood, such as the mission buildings in Wei hsien and the China Inland Mission School in Chefoo.

Like his father, Luce seemed to overlook or miss the tensions that kept Chinese society off balance. In Shantung the publisher realized that the local governor, Han Fu-chu, was loyal to the central government at Nanking. Local warlords disputed Han's authority, however, but Luce laughed the whole thing off, calling it "a typical Chinese muddle." Harry heard that "the President" (a general of the army), Chiang Kai-shek, was building himself a huge "White House," eight stories high. Luce listened to stories about the government's financial corruption and heard accusations leveled against Chiang's "medieval mind." In some Chinese universities, proto-Fascist groups of youth tormented students who adopted Western forms of dress and behavior. Luce, however, insisted that the ruling Guomindang movement would democratize China after she outgrew the pains that accompanied the advent of modernity. To Luce, reform must follow change, not precede it. Harry saw Soong (and perhaps himself) as a kind of midwife; when helping a woman give birth, one offered comfort and assistance, not criticism. The thirty-four-year-old millionaire could face unpleasant truths about China, but only if foreigners or other alien forces could be marked as the source of the country's ills. For the next fifteen years, *Time* began to regale its readers with the Chinese success story.

By the mid-1930s Henry Luce had decided that *Time* needed to be more responsible and more sensitive. Colorful and offensive physical descriptions became less pungent and occurred less frequently. Calling Mayor Fiorello H. La Guardia of New York City "fat, rancid, [and] garlic-smelling" might, editors decided, be counterproductive. As *Time* expanded, the cute adjectival descriptions ("tall, sleek, keen-minded, conscientious"—1930) became less elaborate. Two adjectives were now the norm, though they could still be brutal. The trend was clear, however. No less a historian than Bernard De Voto soon praised *Time* for both its accuracy and its stimulating style.

Luce wanted *Time* elevated to the status of a weekly national "newspaper," and he believed that a huge circulation opportunity existed west of Pittsburgh. Now he wanted to hire more stringers. These were local reporters who earned a few extra dollars by sending material to *Time*. Time Inc. had only one bureau in what New Yorkers called the hinterland, in Chicago. In 1935, however, the company opened a second one, in San Francisco. These bureaus sent story ideas to the Chrysler Building, answered questions, and sampled local opinion.

Time Inc.'s expansion became one of the great business stories of the era. While the economy stagnated, Wall Street put the company's book value at $47 million. In 1936 Luce's shares alone (more than 40 percent of the total equity) were worth over $20 million. Roy Larsen, the second-largest shareholder, earned $120,000 a year in dividends from his stock. These were staggering sums during the Depression. Harry Luce, moreover, did not neglect those who had stood by him during difficult times. John Billings received a small raise even in early 1932, when the company's growth momentarily stalled. By 1935 he was earning $25,000 a year. Billings was now able to buy his ancestral home and place of birth, Redcliffe, in South Carolina.

Before the end of the decade, thirty of the company's managers and editors (the "Senior Group") were earning, on average, a princely $19,000 per year. They might also receive bonuses, which added up to 20 percent of the company's profits after all charges. Less senior personnel could participate in generous incentive plans. By the mid-1930s, Henry Luce headed a widely respected publishing firm, but the tumultuous times ahead would test him and his company.

1935

Clare Boothe,
and a New *Life*

During the middle years of the 1930s, Harry Luce suffered through the greatest personal crisis of his life. Clare Boothe, whom Luce first met in 1934, precipitated Harry's marital turmoil. Slim, poised, blonde, and very smart, the thirty-one-year-old Clare Boothe was also a most accomplished editor. A glamorous divorcée, a shrewd observer of New York's social mores, and a very tough woman, she had endured many agonies. They began when her father, William "Billy" Boothe, an emotionally unstable musician, abandoned his family. He had turned his back on his adoring, nine-year-old daughter, a hurt that Clare neither forgot nor forgave. Her mother, Anna Clara Snyder Boothe, was a onetime aspiring actress and sometime chorus girl. Disappointed by her own failures in career and marriage, Anna now put her hopes in this beautiful young girl, Clare, and in her son, David. Her aspirations burdened the children, who sometimes retreated into their own imaginary worlds. David led a troubled life, while Clare survived by closely guarding her feelings. She remained ever vigilant against violation and betrayal. Sadly, she married a wealthy alcoholic, George Brokaw, who was both mentally and physically abusive. The union produced an unhappy daughter, Ann, who craved the affection and attention Clare was unable or unwilling to give her.

Mac Ingersoll, who worked with Luce at *Fortune*, steered clear of Clare Brokaw. He saw hers as a case of arrested emotional development, rendering her infantile and vindictive. In fact, Clare protected herself by making few personal commitments to her large array of prominent male friends. Though sexually active, Clare's comments reveal a woman who used sex rather than enjoyed it. (An architect once described Clare as a beautiful façade, but one which lacked central heating.) Clare knew rich and famous men; she socialized easily with them, gaining a reputation for both toughness and femininity. In concealing her inner psyche, Clare deftly used wit, ridicule, and fanciful narration as defenses against those who probed too deeply. Her sarcasm shielded her from unwanted intimacy, but it also created enemies, for, as she put it, "no good deed goes unpunished."

Clare Boothe's life was one long act, and one that dazzled her audience without reaching a satisfactory ending. She was professionally restless, embracing one career, only to toss it aside in two years, or three years, or four years. There was something self-destructive about Clare's abortive commitments. She became a playwright, achieved great popularity, then disappeared from Broadway; perhaps the most famous Congressperson in America, Clare Boothe ineptly sought higher office, only to leave the political stage entirely. An accomplished (if sometimes fanciful) storyteller, she never completed her memoirs. Clare was a shrewd observer rather than an original thinker. Her jibes and insults, endlessly repeated by persons who pretended to be shocked, attracted more attention than her ideas. Her most original creation was her own public persona.

Clare Boothe's vulnerability had steeled her, and she emerged as a shrewd judge of people—especially of their weaknesses. She talked her way into a central role in Condé Nast's publishing group, for office doors opened quickly when this beautiful, articulate young woman sought entry. She lunched with President Herbert Hoover, and later entertained New Dealers like Professor Raymond Moley. Clare enjoyed a close relationship with Bernard M. Baruch, the famed Wall Street speculator whom *Time*, to his disgust, called "speculator Baruch." Baruch was Clare's missing father; he may have been her lover. A generous man, he introduced her to the delights of his Hobcaw Barony, in South Carolina.

Clare Boothe had already met Harry Luce at least twice, without any dramatic results, when publisher Condé Nast introduced them at a party in the early 1930s. They discussed a mutual interest, the creation of a picture magazine. Luce was clearly interested in Clare, though as usual, he left the party early, and rather abruptly. Clare, however, saw beyond Harry's brusque manner. She spotted a man who was young, dynamic, brilliant, rich, and also vulnerable. He craved intellectual companionship, and was drawn to people possessing the social allure which he so obviously lacked. Clare again ran into Harry Luce when hostess Elsa Maxwell honored songwriter Cole Porter with a gala party at the Waldorf-Astoria. Spotting Harry walking by, bearing two glasses of champagne, Clare coyly blurted out, "Oh, Mr. Luce, is that champagne for me?" He stopped, and they chatted. Suddenly the power failed and all the lights went out. Harry impulsively asked Clare to accompany him down to the lobby, and once there, they stood about awkwardly. Harry finally managed to stammer a few important words. "Do you know," he asked, "that you are the great love of my life?" Harry hardly waited for an answer. Reverting to form, he pulled out his watch, explaining that he needed to leave. Before returning to retrieve his wife, however, Harry insisted on seeing Clare again. When he next met her, Harry, who was by his nature undemonstrative but intense, indicated that he *thought* he wanted to marry her. They agreed to wait a year before making a final decision.

By the late winter of 1935, a helpless and miserable Harry Luce could no longer function in this limbo. John Billings noticed that weeks went by without any word from him. At times he seemed depressed and listless; then he would suddenly sparkle with renewed energy. At one point Luce took Archie MacLeish aside and confided in him while they conversed at the Hotel Commodore. Luce, he observed, was "shaken, overwhelmed, infatuated," as if he were living through the fabled dark night of the soul. The Reverend Luce did not approve of divorce, so now, in addition to enduring diatribes against advertising liquor in *Time*, Harry could expect to hear a sermon on marriage vows. Harry's mother was even more hostile to his planned separation from Lila. And Harry's sister Beth, who was close to him, lectured her brother about his "selfish" nature. The publicity engendered by the liaison with Clare could only humiliate Lila Luce. And the fact that Lila was so devoted to him only made the situation more painful.

Harry Luce's curiosity quickly turned to fascination, however, just as Clare had planned. The virtuous Luce, moreover, did not want to have an affair with her, though this possibility doubtless existed for him, as it had for some of Clare's earlier suitors. Clare, in fact, appeared to harbor no qualms about destroying a marriage and splitting up a family. Allen Grover, whose tact and social poise were invaluable to Harry, later recalled that Luce had quickly, honestly, and brutally informed Lila of his decision to divorce her and marry Clare. This scene occurred in the late spring of 1935. Harry thereby caused great hurt to a woman who loved him.

Luce's honesty with Lila is interesting in the light of his fear of personal confrontations. At Time Inc., he rarely fired people; others carried out the unpleasant task for him. After Harry bared his feelings to Lila, she agreed to go on a vacation with their two boys, Henry ("Hank") and Peter Paul, while pondering the future. Lila realized that she was competing with a woman who was, as she later described Clare, "beautiful, brilliant, glamorous." Clare, Lila decided, was also "immoral" and "ruthless."

Shattered, Lila was convinced that Harry was making a big mistake. From time to time, over the next thirty years, he may have agreed with her, but not now. He decided to leave New York for a time to clear the air, to think. Foremost in his mind was the pursuit of Clare, who insisted that the couple endure a period of absence (and presumably, abstinence), so that Harry could decide if he really wanted to break up his marriage. Clare sailed to Europe, where she and a lady friend toured the Mediterranean, then spent some time enjoying the theater and the social scene in pre-Nazi Salzburg.

Clare Boothe was not after Luce's money, though he allegedly had an income, from Time Inc. stock, of almost $1 million a year. She earned a good salary, supplemented by alimony of $26,000 per year. She wanted to share Harry's power and help shape his growing media empire. Back in the summer of 1930, *Vanity Fair* put Henry R. Luce in its "Hall of Fame." The writer, associate editor Clare Boothe Brokaw, described Luce as a man whose "work fills his waking hours." Clare knew journalism, and she understood personalities far better than Harry could. The couple already realized that they shared a common interest in founding a picture magazine. Soon after they met, Clare told Harry how, only last year, she had mused about the possibility of buying a failed humor magazine named *Life*. In fact, Clare claimed, she had once made up a dummy for a magazine to be called "Life." Clare sailed to Europe thinking that she was to be the first managing editor of their new picture magazine.

Obsessed with his new love, Harry Luce was absent from the office much of the time. At Time Inc., however, his Experimental Department was mulling over an interesting idea.

Daniel Longwell was thirty-six when he came to Time Inc. His reputation as a promoter with good contacts in the publishing industry had preceded him. Born in Nebraska, and proud of his roots, Longwell liked to reminisce about his father's farm, southwest of Neosho, Missouri. An intense, nervous young man who was known to boast of his achievements, the impatient Longwell dropped out of college and entered the world of publishing. He learned about the retail side of the business by working as a clerk in a bookshop located in the busy Pennsylvania Station terminal, in New York. Longwell then embarked on a successful career in the world of books, rising to the post of promotion and publishing manager of Doubleday, Doran & Company. There, he generated the successful idea of publishing albums containing material culled from *The New Yorker*. Longwell thought himself a genius at promotion, and for a number of years, few disputed his evaluation.

Dan Longwell soon changed the course of publishing history. During this worst of times, he wanted to help Americans rediscover their heritage. Dan Longwell felt that Harry Luce, with his brilliance and drive, could make millions of newly impoverished Americans proud again. Longwell loved working with Luce, for he found him to be stimulating, open to arguments, and an innovative journalist. One trait particularly engaged Longwell. Luce never spoke about a mass audience. He intended to "edit up," in Longwell's phrase, not "down."

When Dan Longwell was planning a trip to England on Time Inc. business, Luce asked him for a personal favor. He requested that Longwell go to the Continent, where he could remind Clare Boothe of Harry's undying love. Longwell met Clare in Salzburg. He proceeded to inform Clare of Harry's concern and affection, and reported that Luce had left Lila. On his own, Longwell cautioned Clare against becoming involved in Time Inc.'s affairs, urging her to have babies instead. Clare shed some tears, informing Dan of her inability to bear more children. This was ominous information, if not to Luce, then to those who worked for him. Harry's colleagues expected nothing good to result from his infatuation with Miss Boothe.

While enmeshed in personal woes, Henry Luce was achieving new professional triumphs. After initial hesitation, he accepted Roy Larsen's advice and agreed to produce a film version of the "March of Time." The experiment was so successful that the new series won an Academy Award in 1936. *The March of Time*, declared the judges, had revolutionized the newsreel industry. Once again Luce had struck gold. Westbrook Van Voorhis' "sonorous and authoritative" voice soon became familiar to 15 million monthly moviegoers. Luce's foray into newsfilm documentaries augured well for a new venture in photographic journalism. People, Dan Longwell noted, could make very convincing actors. And since everyone loved the movies, why not devote a magazine to the portrayal of human beings?

Luce agreed that pictures could take readers to places otherwise closed to them. Each copy of an engaging new magazine, he realized, passed from hand to hand and might be read by ten people. There would be many purchasers and a constant influx of new subscribers. Luce also sensed that now, during this terrible Depression, people wanted to see pictures of modern consumer goods, even if they could not afford to buy them. Readers needed to imagine what the return of prosperity might bring them. And many of Luce's readers, recruits from the mailing lists of *Fortune* and *Time*, had plenty of money. The repeal of Prohibition resulted in a torrent of liquor advertisements. A thirsty country might respond well to huge, colorful ads for Four Roses or Johnnie Walker. Good advertising copy boosted sales; *Time* had proven this point. And if a publisher attracted enough advertisers, he could sell a big, richly illustrated, well-edited journal for a small price.

Dan Longwell showed Luce how new printing techniques could make appealing art available to millions of people—in color. Longwell and Luce both realized that a good picture magazine could attract high school graduates, who vastly outnumbered the college graduates favored by *Time*. Luce then decided to bid for the rights to the name "Life," and he ultimately paid $92,000 for this title.

Dan Longwell's appearance at Time Inc., and the project that resulted in *Life* magazine, marked a fork in the road. Editors and writers, few of them Ivy Leaguers, poured in from the Far West or the Middle West. Longwell's search for talented photographers even resulted in the employment of more Jews. Thanks to Daniel Longwell (and to Hitler's anti-Jewish legislation), the Experimental Department profited from German know-how. Longwell brought in Kurt Korff, former editor of the famous *Berliner Illustrierte Zeitung*, whom Luce agreed to hire at $5,000 a year as an adviser. Korff constantly reminded Luce that he must obtain the best photographs. A single outstanding picture could induce the casual reader to buy the magazine. Luce believed him; he always wanted people and copy of the highest quality. Korff, in turn, hired a photographer named Alfred ("Eisie") Eisenstaedt, who would soon make his mark. Carl Mydans, an employee of the Farm Security Administration, had already contributed to the documentary tradition. Mydans photographed people engaged in everyday activities; the resultant sequence of pictures told a story. Time Inc. acquired his services, too. Luce continued to ponder his options as he entered a new phase of his personal life.

After consulting her attorney, Lila Hotz Luce agreed to file for divorce in Reno. Her complaint was cruelty. The couple agreed to terms on property rights, and Lila received custody of the two children. A Reno court granted the divorce on October 5, 1935, and seven weeks later, in Greenwich, Connecticut, Clare Boothe married Henry R. Luce. After returning from a long honeymoon in Cuba, Clare clearly intended to change some of Harry's habits. Again, his co-workers worried, especially when the newly wed publisher left the office at a normal hour. Clare also vowed to improve Luce's appearance. Here, after all, was a prominent publisher who often wore baggy, unpressed slacks. Clare made sure that Harry became a well-dressed man, though Luce remained capable of coming to work wearing one black shoe and one brown one, topped off by a shirt sporting a badly frayed collar. Harry was ecstatic about his marriage; his staff was apprehensive. They feared that Clare harbored ambitions in regard to Time Inc. She did, of course, but if Harry was infatuated with Clare, he was in love with Time Inc. Ultimately, he alone would manage the company.

Clare soon wanted to buy a plantation near the Hobcaw Barony owned by her friend Bernard M. Baruch. Harry sent Dan Longwell to South Carolina, where he looked for a suitable property. Luce later purchased Mepkin for her, paying the sum of $150,000. Located forty miles north of historic Charleston, Mepkin had been the home of Henry Laurens, president of the Continental Congress. This South Carolina Low Country plantation consisted of more than 7,000 acres, replete with Negroes' cabins, Spanish moss, rice fields, and a meandering river. Mepkin became the Luces' very occasional refuge from the social and political pressures of New York. Though he spent relatively little time there, Harry Luce loved the place. Soon thereafter, the Luces purchased a fifty-nine-acre estate in fashionable Greenwich, Connecticut, within commuting distance of New York.

Luce's "Prospectus for a New Magazine" declared that the new magazine would watch the world and "see strange things—machines, armies, multitudes, shadows in the jungle and on the moon. . . ." The magazine would observe works of art, women and children. Like its audience, it expected to be "amazed" and "instructed." The magazine would clearly lack *Time's* supercilious detachment; it would not indulge in sardonic insults. Luce's prospectus combined Longwell's enthusiasm

with his own curiosity, and it was a winner. Longwell invented another
good promotional gimmick, suggesting that the magazine be bigger
than the popular *Saturday Evening Post.* Luce finally pointed out, with
some impatience, that the time for dummies and mockups and the
prospectus had passed. The new magazine, to be called *Life*, must
appear on the newsstands late in 1936.

Life's imminent debut confronted Luce with a new list of pressing
problems. Dan Longwell was not equipped to edit the new magazine,
for consistency and organization were not his strong points. Despite an
important career with Luce, Longwell peaked early. So in late 1936, on
the eve of *Life*'s much-awaited debut, John Billings assumed de facto
managing editorship of the project. Supremely confident as an editor,
Billings exuded strength, authority, and professionalism. He enjoyed
Luce's total confidence, and took orders well. The ever reliable Roy
Larsen was to be *Life*'s publisher, thus putting his considerable business
talents at the new magazine's disposal. Content at first, Billings soon
confided new frustrations to his diary. He complained that Longwell
was out with the flu, while the magazine had to go to press in seventeen
days. There was no real layout department; *Life* needed a good art
director. Despite all his fault-finding, however, John Billings was the
perfect team captain. He let others glitter, but reined them in when
their ideas contradicted Luce's vision of *Life*.

Life contained a Spectacle of the Week, and sections on cinema,
theater, art, sport, and the sciences. Joseph J. Thorndike, Jr., a quiet,
scholarly young man, was to edit the "President's Scrapbook," for
Roosevelt and his family were natural subjects for a picture-oriented
magazine. The magazine would attend parties, making it possible for
readers to see how fascinating people lived and played. Still, *Life*'s
survival would depend on its pictures, so Luce again turned to Margaret
Bourke-White, who had recently signed a contract with Time Inc. Its
terms provided that she would earn $12,000 a year, and Luce agreed
that this generous salary was a floor, not a ceiling. Harry Luce now
dispatched Bourke-White to the Northwest, where the Federal Government was building a network of huge dams, including one at Fort Peck,
Montana.

Moved by the plight of Dust Bowl farmers and afraid of the Fascist
wave engulfing Europe, Bourke-White had moved to the left. The New
Deal dam project suited her politics as well as her camera lens. Harry
Luce did not care; like Longwell and Korff, he wanted the best photographic art. The idea of sending Bourke-White on this mission was
vintage Luce, for the great construction project evoked the grandeur
and power of his America, Depression or not. Bourke-White captured

the spirit of Fort Peck's workers, as well as the immensity of their project. Here were barmaids and bouncers, cowboys and workers, children and ladies. Looking for a cover photograph, Luce instinctively reached for Bourke-White's shot of the dam. That one, he decided, *must* be on the cover of *Life*'s first issue (November 23, 1936).

Margaret Bourke-White later commented on *Life*'s treatment of photographers as "adults," and recalled their joy at working for Luce. Peter Stackpole, Tom McAvoy, Carl Mydans, "Eisie" Eisenstaedt, and many others responded to the spirit of *Life*. Luce expected total loyalty in return for the lifelong security he provided. For example, he assumed that Bourke-White would remain with Time Inc. forever. When she threatened to leave *Life*, Bourke-White temporarily became a "bitch" in Luce's eyes. His ire passed, but he remained a paternalistic employer. To Luce, Time Inc. was family, or, as he often put, "It's my life."

Luce had faith in the quality of *Life*, but would the magazine win over its readers? Donnelley's professional ability and the printer's new processes helped make *Life* an instant sensation. *Life*'s appeal cut across class and age lines. People overpaid by as much as one dollar in order to obtain a copy of the big new magazine. Parties were thrown, where the proud hostess displayed the precious trophy at an appropriate moment. Princeton freshmen voted *Life* their favorite magazine.

Luce had staked his career on a strange kind of magazine—profane, reverent, American, and unique, just like Harry Luce himself. During these early months of its existence, *Life*'s articles followed each other in a rather haphazard way. Luce realized that *Life* was "getting good," but needed to grow up, to improve. Its spontaneity, however, charmed readers; the magazine was full of surprises. *Life* took its subscribers to the theater, with Helen Hayes as a guide. It brought Americans to a village near the Amazon, showed them Greta Garbo in *Camille*, and introduced people to blowups of a black widow spider. *Life* also did much to popularize the work of contemporary American painters. It sponsored exhibitions of their art, and published a highly regarded book: *Modern American Painting*. Although the frenetic Dan Longwell deserved a good deal of credit for these achievements, he could be a problem. Too often, he bubbled over with unstructured zeal. As Billings, his managing editor, sourly noted, "He alone seems to realize the value of a good picture to sell a bad idea. . . ." Another talented editor soon arrived in-house.

Wilson Hicks, named picture editor in 1937, was required to examine 20,000 pictures a week, before Billings published about 250 of them in a single issue of *Life*. Once Billings decided on a story, he would tell Hicks what kinds of additional material he needed. If the pictures were

good, Hicks declared, *Life* "will write some words to go with them."
He viewed photographs as "words out of a camera with which stories
can be told." Hicks' department organized the photographs into categories, then showed likely winners to the managing editor. As Billings
put it, "I trust in God and Wilson Hicks for pictures."

John Billings' managerial talents co-existed with strong affinities and
lamentable prejudices, some of which had an impact on his magazine.
Billings loved railroads, the child actress Shirley Temple, and pretty
girls. These subjects often graced the pages of *Life*. He disliked stories
about Native Americans, South Americans, and refugees, so they rarely
appeared in the magazine. Luce, Billings, Hicks, and many other editors
and writers worked frantically, though the managing editor remained
outwardly calm amid the uproar. Sometimes *Life*'s editors would retire
to the spacious Cloud Club, atop the Chrysler Building, and debate
topics of interest to *Life*. Luce peppered his men with a barrage of
questions. What did people want? What did they think? The talented
young science and medicine editor, Andrew Heiskell, found that Luce
was not dogmatic, that he yielded to a good argument. Out of these
brainstorming sessions evolved some original ideas.

John Billings had to manage a difficult, diverse, and talented group
of people. David Cort, the foreign news editor, liked to tour nightclubs
until the sun rose. This penchant "made it difficult to get up at 9:00
A.M. . . . ." A cousin of Brit Hadden's, and hence a kind of untouchable,
Noel Busch was, according to a colleague, a man trying to act "like a
British dilettante." Yet this ignorant "Broadway sport," as Luce called
him, was a gifted writer and biographer. He would write many important "Close-up" pieces for *Life*, and later became the only editor to
whom Clare Luce would entrust her work. Many a Time Incer convinced himself that he would leave as soon as he had earned some
money. Then, the story went, the young editor would write the Great
American Novel or a good book of poetry. But the cost of living,
Luce's high wages, and personal factors usually kept frustrated literati
from straying far from Time Inc. Alcohol, love affairs, or resentment
sometimes took the place of literary achievement. Luce joked about
having deprived society of the work never written by many a second-
rate novelist or poet.

Life pioneered in multimedia presentations, many of which treated
artistic or religious themes. One issue reviewed Charles Laughton's
film performance in *Rembrandt*, while reproducing three of the master's
paintings, including "Storm on the Sea of Galilee." The Christmas issue
of *Life*, which inaugurated a tradition, published an article on the "Life
of Jesus Christ." The Reverend George A. Buttrick, pastor of Luce's

Madison Avenue Presbyterian Church, wrote the piece. Beautiful Renaissance paintings depicted various scenes in the story of Christ, from the Annunciation to the Crucifixion.

Life's high-minded articles about art and science, and provocative pieces on birth control or cancer or proper diet, taught valuable lessons. Yet these same pieces appeared amid aggressive advertisements for destructive, addictive products. Luce enriched his company by selling massive amounts of space to alcohol and tobacco manufacturers, and a review of *Life* reveals the extent of the magazine's dependence on female beauty. Clergymen often wrote angry letters about the contents of the magazine, but Luce resented their attacks on *Life*'s "cheesecake." He profited greatly, of course, from the prurient interest of his male readers.

Luce did not, however, seek confrontations with the postal authorities, for second-class mailing rates were the *Life*'s blood of his enterprise. The U.S. Post Office could ruin him. At one point, John Billings prepared to run a photograph of Thomas Hart Benton's painting "The Rape of Persephone." The picture contains a scene in which an old man, peeping through some bushes, stares at a nude girl. The Post Office objected to Benton's graphic depiction of the girl's pubic hair. A huge number of copies were ready for mailing, and Billings, after having negotiated with the Post Office, offered to print a new run, *sans* pubic hair. The government said no, and Time Inc. had to accept its decision. *Life*, however, was more willing to defy convention, when the issue at stake concerned reproductive freedom.

Some Catholics reacted badly to a *Life* article lauding the work of birth control advocate Margaret Sanger. At a time when almost all abortions were illegal throughout the nation, *Life* treated the subject in a frank manner. In a sympathetic article, *Life* reported that Sanger had once worked as a nurse. She recalled that one day a poor woman came to a doctor, asking for an abortion. Sanger overheard him refusing to perform the illegal operation. The woman sought outside help, and managed to procure a three-dollar abortion. She died as a result of the botched operation. More happily, *Life* celebrated a court decision handed down by a federal judge. Doctors, he ruled, could send contraceptives through the mail. Henry Luce's faith in science continued to embroil him in some nasty controversies. When it ran a piece on birth control, *Life* shocked some readers by including a photograph of a contraceptive device.

The most widely discussed magazine article of its day was *Life*'s "The Birth of a Baby." Joe Thorndike suggested that *Life* publish still photos taken from the film of that name. Much of New England banned the

April 11, 1938, issue of *Life*, which featured the offensive article. In Boston, a newsdealer, accused of selling obscene material, appeared in court. Though defended by an able attorney, Joseph Nye Welch, the dealer lost his case. In Pennsylvania, Governor George H. Earle ordered the magazine seized, and thirty-three cities banned this issue of *Life*. Roy Larsen himself forced a test case in New York City. He sold a copy of *Life*, and was summoned to appear in a Bronx courtroom. Charged with selling obscene material, Larsen was acquitted. Polls showed that 76 percent of respondents felt that the "Birth of a Baby" was not obscene. Eleanor Roosevelt praised *Life* for its enlightened decision, as did Dr. Thomas Parran, the Surgeon General of the United States. The issue was a sensation, and copies circulated privately at the price of one dollar apiece.

By 1938 *Life* was the most exciting big magazine in America. As Harry Luce had predicted, colorful, dramatically drawn advertisements added to its luster. People liked to savor pictures of the new Studebaker sedan, even if they couldn't afford to buy one. Fourteen people allegedly perused each copy, and the magazine claimed an audience of 17.3 million, though the figure fluctuated. All over the country, but especially in small towns located far from metropolitan areas, men and women eagerly awaited the latest issue of the big magazine. Overall, *Life* was upbeat at a time when people badly needed some good cheer. As Harry Luce blurted out when he particularly liked an issue of *Life*, "My God it is [swell]!," or "It's a humdinger!" America agreed, though the magazine, like the country, remained in the red.

Life's popularity almost destroyed Time, Inc. Not anticipating the demand for *Life*, Luce had underestimated its guaranteed circulation. Time Inc., having happily lured advertisers into signing long-term contracts, was thus committed to charging absurdly low rates. Anxious to sell a lot of copies, Luce sold the magazine for ten cents each. People, he believed, loved a bargain. Sales could, Harry hoped, stem the flow of red ink until the ad contracts expired. In fact, disaster loomed over the horizon. Time Inc. had netted over $2.7 million in 1936. That figure dipped to $168,430 in 1937, and dividends were cut. How ironic if creative exuberance, combined with an underestimation of popular demand, ruined Henry Luce.

The New Deal,
Labor, and Civil Rights

Back in 1932, Henry Luce had voted for President Herbert Hoover without feeling any antipathy toward the successful Democratic nominee, Governor Franklin Delano Roosevelt of New York. Theodore Roosevelt was one of Harry's heroes, and *Time* praised his distant cousin for his "breeding" and "good intentions." The magazine took note of FDR's large following and quoted him at length. And Luce approved of Roosevelt's support for the repeal of Prohibition. By March 1933 *Time* was speaking of FDR's inaugural address in tones of awe, and even favored the White House with an occasional fib. One article in *Time* described the polio-crippled President as standing up, before he went to bed, thus giving the impression that he could walk unassisted.

Soon after FDR's inauguration, Harry Luce and Archibald MacLeish called on him at the White House. This invitation to drink tea with the new President reflected Luce's increasing importance. The charming and witty Roosevelt, who knew that incorrigible Republicans owned most of the newspapers, had decided to woo the young, independent-minded magazine publisher.

Henry Luce liked to speak of a "man with the moral intelligence to understand what I'm talking about." An inveterate if sometimes premature hero-worshiper, he now convinced himself that FDR was this man. Luce emerged from tea at the White House exclaiming, "My God!" What a man!" Writing to John Billings, Luce referred to Roosevelt as "dynamic," as a man with "virtuosity." *Time* made Roosevelt its Man of the Year for 1933, and gave him favorable reviews. For the moment, Luce supported most New Deal legislation. He felt that these measures, which he termed "socialization," reflected an appropriate response to the failure of both business and government. The ultracapitalist *Time* looked kindly on the establishment of the Securities and Exchange Commission, and *Fortune* praised the administration's attacks upon unemployment. At times, readers complained personally to Luce, asking why his business magazine employed and encouraged "Reds" or New Dealers. Luce, in response to such questions, would invariably observe that "damned Republicans can't write."

More quickly than other publishers, Harry Luce realized that power was gravitating to Washington. The sleepy Southern town of 1927 was now the bustling home of bureaucrats, policymakers, and New Deal hangers-on. A new political elite came to power, and Luce took the lead in cultivating the White House and the expanding federal bureaucracy. He lunched with press secretary Stephen Early and then dispatched Allen Grover, a man of impressive demeanor, to Washington, asking that he contact Early. The press aide quickly responded, indicating that he would always be available to *Fortune*'s Grover. Louis de Rochemont, the producer of the *March of Time* films, also entered into a liaison with the White House. A favorable portrait of FDR in Luces' *March of Time* "delighted" the President. When the New Deal made $3 billion available for construction projects, Luce's *Architectural Forum* published an eighteen-page guide to the new law. Luce believed that private initiative, working with government, could engender the capital required for a boom in the construction industry. Luce, as the publisher of uniquely national media, was superbly positioned to profit from the growing nationalization of American life.

Despite Harry Luce's momentary euphoria about FDR, however, one finds the seeds of mutual disillusionment in the personalities of the two protagonists. Charm, a Roosevelt specialty, was never something that Luce admired, for he felt it was a superficial trait, rather like a nice suit. Men with charm were useful to Luce, but he would not have let any of them run his company. And from the beginning, Time Inc. antagonized this White House. Franklin D. Roosevelt, one recalls, had been the first (1923) reader to complain about *Time*'s selective truths. Roosevelt and his aides seemed to remember each slight, while quickly forgetting favorable notices. Even before FDR had taken office, *Time* had irritated the White House by referring to the governor's "shriveled legs." Later, the magazine mended its ways, and praised the President for his courage in recovering from polio. Other problems arose, however, and quickly.

Within weeks of FDR's inauguration, the White House complained that *Time* had printed off-the-record comments uttered by Roosevelt. Some time later, press aide Stephen Early protested against a "March of Time" radio broadcast. Early disliked the idea of an actor reading the role of FDR, and said so. "The March of Time" resumed this practice, but only after obtaining permission from the White House. And the program now told its listeners that the voice they heard was not that of the President. Both sides tried to maintain cordial relations, however, and the Roosevelt family helped to make *Life* a popular success. Eleanor Roosevelt was the most interesting First Lady since Dolley Madison, though Luce objected to her constant use of the term "I feel" (he preferred the phrase, "I think").

In the 1936 presidential campaign, Luce's magazines were relatively fair in their coverage. The President, an avid student of the new science of polling, keenly followed Elmo Roper's *Fortune* polls, of which Luce was justifiably proud. *Fortune* predicted that FDR would receive 61.7 percent of the vote; he obtained 60.5 percent. Advance copies of Roper's surveys made their way to the White House, where speechwriter Samuel Rosenman passed them on to the President. After Roosevelt had won in a landslide, *Time* concluded that he was "the ablest master of U.S. politics in a century."

FDR's relations with Time Inc. quickly soured again, however. *Life*'s publication of a photograph of him in a wheelchair caused a terrible row, for millions of Americans now saw that Roosevelt was a crippled man. Billings faced retaliation from the White House. An angry Postmaster General James A. Farley, an important Democratic operative, dressed down Harold "Hal" Horan, Time Inc.'s man in Washington, complaining that *Life*'s action was "one helluva way for your fellows to treat the Boss." No other magazine or newspaper, Farley claimed, had ever done such a thing, even in the middle of a campaign. The infuriated White House warned that a repetition would result in *Life* being barred from accompanying the President on future trips. More bad news soon reached New York. The President's mother, Sara Delano Roosevelt, objected to the appearance of near-nude figures in *Life*. The magazine, Farley agreed, displayed too much female flesh. Time Inc. retreated a bit on the issue of nudity, at least for the time being. And FDR did not again appear in *Life*'s pages as a helpless invalid.

Henry Luce's hostility toward FDR became more marked after 1936, and the White House itself grew more arrogant. Roosevelt, after all, had carried forty-six states in the recent election. FDR soon wanted to remake the Supreme Court, create a more liberal Democratic Party, and perhaps run for an unprecedented third term. Harry still smarted from Roosevelt's campaign attacks on big business, which he saw as sheer demagoguery, threatening free enterprise. At a dinner attended by Secretary of the Interior Harold Ickes, Luce criticized Roosevelt for undermining business.

Like the conservative Supreme Court, Henry Luce raised questions about Roosevelt's vaunted National Industrial Recovery Act. If industry adopted "codes" ("We do our part"), and promised to hire people and treat them in a certain way, would the state intervene to "enforce" them? Luce feared that higher taxes, imposed by one-party big government, would sap the entrepreneur of both his will and his money. And he soon wondered if Harry Hopkins' Works Progress Administration would really put people to work building roads and schools. Or, as Harry feared, would millions of people convert meaningless relief work into a life-style? In the latter scenario, a permanent class of "reliefers" emerged, draining society of its capital and individuals of their morale. Elmo Roper later recalled Harry's fear that "FDR would make this a nation of handouts." *Fortune* now seized on the British term "welfare state," converting it into a nasty synonym for the New Deal.

President Roosevelt, Luce argued, cynically divided class against class and thereby made political hay out of economic misery. Luce also attacked those, like the President, who "spoke as if American industry was not part of America." And Luce feared Roosevelt's fiscal irresponsibility. A prudent man with Time Inc.'s money, Harry had come to detest Roosevelt's budget deficits. This amused FDR, who later commented that Luce nearly went "bust" due to losses incurred by *Life* (True, Luce once replied to the President, but he eventually balanced *his* budget!). Yet Luce continued to criticize big business, for without its blunders, FDR would not have won his great mandate.

Increasingly, Luce looked to the free press as the last firewall between democratic capitalism and the forces that could destroy it. He did not mouth the usual self-serving phrases about his First Amendment "rights." There was, Luce declared, no freedom of the press without "some corresponding duty." He wanted to sell and promote, but he also wanted to teach and inspire. Luce feared and disdained a press dominated by selfish business interests, but he also saw a danger in giving the people what they wanted. Advertisers, Luce knew, hoped to sell their products, period, just as irresponsible publishers wanted to peddle their newspapers. Junk sold well, Luce believed, and he particularly loathed the press owned by publisher and "yellow journalist" William Randolph Hearst. Luce argued that newspapers devoted too much of their energy ("70%") to entertainment. Freedom of the press, said Harry, could thereby degenerate into a device "to seduce [the people] to their own enslavement." Where the press faltered, evil men gained power. Looking at the course of "modern dictatorships," Luce warned that a failed press was the prelude to barbarism and tyranny.

Henry Luce's comments on barbarism reflected his careful study of José Ortega y Gasset's powerful book *The Revolt of the Masses*. This influential little volume argued that "mass man" had triumphed in Europe. His species, Ortega wrote, could be found in all social classes. Mass man was the product of modern technology, including the media. He could not, however, maintain the technology that made him possible, for he was a barbarian, a destroyer, one who reviled humanity and creativity. Ortega hoped that people who possessed "excellence and superiority" would band together to defend civilization, where it still existed. Ortega's field of reference was the Europe of communism and fascism, but Luce adapted his warning to the American scene.

Ironically, Luce himself had been unduly tolerant of a certain foreign Fascist, so much so that his enemies sometimes accused him of being one. When Henry Luce took up residence in a new penthouse office, irreverent wits at Time Inc. joked about "il Luce," a pun on Mussolini's title, *il Duce* ("the leader"). In 1934 a full issue of *Fortune* had lauded Mussolini as a decisive leader who had remade Italy. Later, however, Luce, like many other Americans, turned against *il Duce*, rejecting his corporative state as incompatible with "democracy and liberty."

At home, Luce and his magazines opposed the excesses of demagogic anti-communists. Congressman Martin Dies' investigative committee met with contempt from *Life*. The magazine was outspoken in denouncing Dies' "smear," which accused liberals and labor of disloyalty and communism (Dies, in his hunt for publicity, had even attacked John Billings' little idol, Shirley Temple). *Life* expressed sympathy for a schoolteacher who lost her job because of such libels. Luce thus refused to align himself with the numerous anti-Communist hysterics who looked for Reds in the New Deal or in the White House.

A well-managed and potentially prosperous company, Time, Inc. now employed 641 people in New York City and maintained branch offices in five cities. These drew on the work of 399 stringers. By 1937

Luce's company was preparing to move into its new Time & Life Building, on the prestigious Rockefeller Plaza. Henry Luce's own class interest now stoked his growing contempt for Roosevelt. He complained about the taxes that Time Inc. paid, and two of Luce's magazines (*Time* and *Fortune*) appealed to those who were still fairly well off despite the Depression. If such citizens had suffered economic reverses, they tended to blame Roosevelt for their setbacks. They condemned the New Deal for the faltering stock market and feared the devaluation or erosion of the dollar. Luce's upper-middle-class readers did not like the idea of government competing with private industry, as in the case of electric power utilities. *Fortune* sourly noted that in 1899 the Federal Government had absorbed 6.2 percent of the national product; by 1936 that figure has risen to about 14 percent. Luce viewed much of this growth as inevitable, given the abuses of the past. He feared its consequences, however.

Henry R. Luce had attracted backers and readers who resented FDR's usurpation of power. Reared during a more tranquil time, these upper-class Americans—overwhelmingly Protestant and Republican—had grown accustomed to running things pretty much as they pleased. The war had interrupted their lives, but these people enjoyed a good decade during the 1920s. Then came the Depression and the New Deal, which challenged the authority of big businessmen, bankers, and the old-line Republican publishers. In effect, Roosevelt had since 1935 declared war on *their* acquisition of wealth. To perpetuate his own power, FDR forged alliances with his social inferiors, with the downtrodden, the middle classes, and newly emerging ethnic groups, often Jews or urban Catholics. Suddenly the leading voice in the land made the proprietors of the nation feel like moral lepers.

Thanks to his father and mother, Harry Luce had received a chance to enter a higher social class. He lived comfortably in Connecticut and owned a plantation in South Carolina. Though not an Astor or a Rockefeller socially or financially, Luce had acquired an interest in the preservation of their wealth. In addition, Harry had become the chief spokesman (through *Fortune*) of a reformed entrepreneurial and managerial elite, which was now ready to assert *its* right to rule the country.

Despite *Fortune*'s discovery of this managerial elite, grand old names impressed Harry Luce. He was soon listed in the *Social Register* and purchased a box at the Metropolitan Opera. John Hersey long remembered a night at the opera with Harry Luce. Hersey was surprised when an awed Luce pointed excitedly to people sitting in the boxes known as the Diamond Horseshoe. "There's an Astor!" he whispered. "There's a Vanderbilt!" Luce had come into friendly contact with the old elite, just in time to hear Franklin D. Roosevelt vilify it as the baleful relic of a failed era.

Fortune was the voice of an intelligent, modern capitalism. As such, the magazine often offended ultraconservatives, like the men who ran U.S. Steel. *Fortune*'s famous articles on that company were largely the work of Yale man Dwight Macdonald, who disdained the world of business. He wanted to make some money, then retire to write literary criticism. A political leftist, though not yet a renegade Marxist, Macdonald had become skeptical about the future of capitalism. His first two articles demonstrated that U.S. Steel had done little for its shareholders and used outmoded technology. U.S. Steel was antilabor and engaged in monopolistic pricing practices. Macdonald's third article, which was really a radical critique of the company, never appeared, for Luce dismissed Macdonald's last piece as an editorial. He continued to employ editors and writers whose politics were left-wing, but Luce would not allow *Fortune* to become an upscale version of the *Daily Worker*. Macdonald's two pieces enraged the company's directors, but *Fortune* changed the way U.S. Steel did business. The articles paved the way for the company's collective bargaining agreement with John L. Lewis' Congress of Industrial Organizations. *Fortune* thus helped to undermine the old "public be damned" attitude.

Henry R. Luce's publications advocated reconciliation, not confrontation, between unions and management. His editors opened the pages of *Fortune* to the controversial Lewis, who defended the National Labor Relations Act against its detractors. *Fortune* also exposed the miserable working conditions of "underemployed, underfed" migrant workers. And during the last years of the decade, *Time* openly sympathized with many a "sit-down" strike. The conservative John Billings glumly complained that *Time* publisher (since 1937) Mac Ingersoll had "revolutionized and sovietized things."

When *Life* covered the bitter confrontations between Ford and its auto workers at the River Rouge plant, the strikers came out looking a lot better than the thugs Ford used against them. *Life* showed that the police were to blame for violence unleashed by a CIO march in South Chicago. It touched the conscience of the nation with a brilliant sequence of photographs made by Louis van Dyke showing company "bulls" (police) arresting hobos in the Albany railyards of the New York Central Railroad.

Although the magazine played down class differences—as if to say, "What a wonderful world in which to be an American!"—Harry Luce realized that the patriarchal age of employer-worker relations was over, at least in other companies. He accepted unions as economic instruments dedicated to the welfare of their members. Luce believed that collective bargaining, as defined by article 7A of the National Industrial Recovery Act, made sense. This right, he added, was a fundamental one in a liberal, capitalist order, so Luce did not rejoice when the Supreme Court tossed out the entire NIRA. When the Congress promptly replaced it with the Wagner Act, Luce endorsed that, too. Meanwhile, he had a chance to practice what *Fortune* preached.

Meeting in 1936, editors, writers, and researchers at Time Inc. organized a chapter of the Newspaper Guild, which was affiliated with the American Federation of Labor. Some of its pioneers included major figures in Luce's company, such as Wilder Hobson, Russell Davenport, Archibald MacLeish, Joseph Kastner, and Thomas S. Matthews. MacLeish, a strong proponent of the union shop and collective bargaining, helped formulate the Guild's negotiating position. Luce seemed unalarmed by the Guild, though he had some qualms about its specific demands. He did not in any way penalize those of his associates who remained active in the union.

Time Inc. was Harry Luce's missionary compound. The young proprietor paid the highest editorial wages in New York. Benefits, stock options, medical insurance—Luce pioneered in these areas. The company was also far ahead of its time in respect to maternity leave. A pregnant woman could take six months off without fearing for her job. If she did not return to work, the former employee received severance pay. Despite Archie MacLeish's appeals, however, Luce would not agree to recognize a "union shop," controlled by a highly politicized Guild. Nor did he accept the Guild's demand for compulsory arbitration. Mac Ingersoll, however, diligently negotiated with the Guild on behalf of Time Inc., and the two parties finally signed a contract in December 1938. The agreement contained clauses detailing job descriptions, wages, and severance pay. The contract also provided for a standard forty-hour workweek. Time Inc. extended these benefits and terms to the promotion department and a few other units as well. Secretaries, however, and those low-wage earners who most needed help, were not protected by the new contract.

Many Communists were active in the Guild, and they soon plagued Luce and his associates. Early in 1939, "Communist Party Members at Time Inc." published several issues of a broadside cleverly entitled *High*

Time. Well written, nicely printed, and carefully edited, *High Time* followed the Communist line, but the paper also featured inside information about major personalities at Time Inc. People Luce had trusted and paid well were subverting his company from the inside. Outraged, Luce claimed that Time Inc.'s name had suffered grievous damage. He vilified *High Time* as "gossip," a strange charge, given some of the material that ran in *Time.* What most bothered Luce was *High Time*'s betrayal of group journalism, which, he said in all seriousness, depended on "free speech in confidence." This unfortunate, contradictory phrase met with scorn, and *High Time* continued to appear.

Luce and Roy Larsen considered taking drastic action. One plan would have required that each editor ask his underlings if he or she was a Communist. This proposal failed to win acceptance, thanks to opposition voiced by Allen Grover and Manfred Gottfried. The Communists, after all, would deny their guilt, while innocent people would be demoralized. Instead, the company hired a detective, who discovered the identity of *High Time*'s printer. The investigator determined that the CP wanted to provoke discussion by printing *High Time.* Then the party would spot likely targets for recruitment. Once word spread that the detective was at work, the broadsheet vanished as quickly and mysteriously as it had appeared.

During Roosevelt's tumultuous second term, Harry Luce came to view the New Deal as collectivist and demagogic. *Fortune* surveys, which revealed broad public opposition to the redistribution or confiscation of wealth, encouraged Luce. By the winter of 1938, 73.1 percent of respondents advocated a balanced budget. 58.1 percent favored removing the government from competition with private enterprise, and a plurality of respondents opposed a government takeover of the power utilities. Only 43.7 percent of those polled endorsed a third term for Roosevelt, compared to 52.6 percent in early 1937. A year later *Fortune* concluded that Roosevelt had not "succeeded in selling the New Deal's economic . . . ideas to the American people." While admitting that Roosevelt was still personally popular, *Life* happily noted that the New Deal was not. Luce understood, however, that social class played a key role: the upper classes opposed Roosevelt, while a solid majority of other income groups backed him.

As the 1938 midterm elections approached, *Time* published stories accusing FDR of everything from nepotism to political incompetence. The New Deal and the welfare state, Luce believed, could perpetuate

themselves only by sabotaging economic recovery. *Life* published devastating photographs of a Democratic Party dinner, to which *Life* photographer Tom McAvoy had managed to gain access. Hidden from
view, McAvoy photographed the partygoers through a telephoto lens.
Life's readers soon met the tribunes of the downtrodden, frolicking in
the midst of the "Roosevelt recession." Smoking cigarettes and imbib-
ing large quantities of alcohol, *Life*'s Democrats were "happy drinkers"
toasting the President while the economy spiraled downward.

After the Republicans made major gains in the House and the Senate,
in November 1938, *Life* published a provocative photomontage. Called
"Speaking of Dictators," the spread showed Hitler, Mussolini, and
Stalin engaged in various activities, ranging from public speaking to
swimming. Next to the dictators appeared FDR, so the story's message
was unmistakable. *Life* subscribers could only be amazed, enraged,
or delighted. On a more serious level, Luce now applied the phrase
"Roosevelt depression" to the economic downturn of 1938. He looked
forward to a Republican resurgence. And Luce was coming to hate
Franklin D. Roosevelt.

A Time Incer once recalled a revealing incident. One day Harry
Luce picked up a copy of *Time*, and a brief sentence about a lynching
caught his eye. Banging his fist on a table, Luce angrily declared that
"A man's life is worth more than a line!" The race issue increased Luce's
unease about FDR, whose Southern allies blocked all attempt to repeal
poll taxes or pass a federal antilynching bill.

Henry Luce's liberalism rested upon the assumption that "democracy
is meaningless if the pursuit of happiness is invalid." Preventing other
people from pursuing happiness was, Harry Luce believed, a sin. He
had great personal sympathy for the black cause, for he, too, had grown
up surrounded by an oppressed people of a different race. And Harry
Luce sympathized with Negroes for another good reason: American
blacks were almost all Protestants, and had helped to build his blessed
America.

Even before *Time* appeared, a dummy issue contained a scathing
series of quotations taken from a Ku Klux Klan publication. The Klan,
with 4 million members, was no joke, but Luce and Hadden selected
items calculated to expose its barbarity while subjecting it to cruel
ridicule. "Nigger writes insulting letter to young white girl" provided
the magazine with a good quotation. A related anecdote told the story
of a Klan official who came to a Newark hospital for children. He

donated $50 to the institution—but had to remove his robes lest he frighten the beneficiaries of his largesse.

From its inception, *Time* favored black self-help movements. The most famous of these was led by the Jamaican Marcus Garvey, who tried to organize a migration of African-Americans out of the United States, to Africa and the West Indies. Garvey advocated the "complete freedom of the Negro economically and culturally," so that he might become a "full man." Without endorsing Garvey's work or his methods, *Time* linked Garvey's rise and fall (jail for mail fraud and subsequent deportation) to the plight of oppressed blacks in this country. *Time* continued to regale its readers with lurid stories about lynchings, while tallying the number of racially motivated murders. And to the dismay of many Southerners, Walter White, head of the National Association for the Advancement of Colored People, was featured on the cover of *Time*. The lead story noted that eight men and boys had been lynched in 1937, bringing the total number of lynching victims since 1882 to about 5,000. Yet a federal antilynching bill could not prevail over a Senate filibuster.

Time Inc.'s magazines did not merely dwell on tragedies and failures. They tried to present a positive image of American blacks. *Life*, for example, showed that "Negroes" were ready to move up the social ladder, since a substantial number of black doctors, lawyers, tycoons, and scientists flourished in America. The great singer and actor Paul Robeson, the son of an ex-slave, was fond of the Soviet Union, a nation Luce despised. Writing of Robeson's visit to the Moscow Conservatory, however, *Life* magazine sardonically observed that Robeson was engaged in "his lifelong search for white people who will think he is as good as they think they are."

Life's photographers also captured sad scenes of Southern poverty. One saw a black farmer riding a watermelon wagon to market, as if he were trapped in a time warp. In 1936 the magazine soon to be known as *Life* dispatched Alfred Eisenstaedt, a German Jew, to the South. As his writer companion, Dan Longwell chose Robert Sherrod, a young reporter who worked out of Luce's small Chicago office. Longwell was blunt: "Keep after cotton and colored people." Yet he also insisted that Eisenstaedt capture the blacks' "humanity." And *Life* quickly discovered that "redneck" politicians were as grotesque as characters in a gothic novel. Senator Theodore G. Bilbo, of Mississippi (whom *Time* dubbed "prince of the peckerwoods"), and Governor Gene Talmadge, of Georgia, were among Time Inc.'s favorite gargoyles.

While many Americans smugly shook their heads over Europe's

murderous ethnic squabbles, *Life* boldly addressed America's own "minority problem." The magazine described 14 million "Negroes" as the "most glaring refutation of the American fetish that all men are created free and equal." One of *Life*'s more famous photographs depicted black victims of the great 1937 Ohio Valley flood as they waited in line for food relief. Looming over them stood a billboard advertisement, commissioned by the National Association of Manufacturers. "World's Highest Standard of Living," read the sign, which concluded that "there's no way like the American Way." From the billboard a happy and prosperous white family (in a new car, of course) smiled down as they drove forward into the American dream.

In his search for a solution to the racial problem, Henry Luce began to probe the gulf separating the South from the rest of the nation. He concluded that agricultural diversification, combined with better public education, could help to "restore the South to her rightful place in the nation." He also believed that a heavy dose of industrial capitalism could work wonders. Economic progress and a national perspective would, Luce hoped, erode resistance to the advance of the blacks.

Henry Luce's magazines were nonetheless a product of their time, and were not immune to stereotypes. The Savoy Ballroom in Harlem, a famous dance spot, was a perfect subject for a "Life Goes to a Party" feature. One saw working class blacks doing "barbaric" dances, and kissing passionately; *Life* described them as engaged in a wild frenzy. Time Inc. hired few blacks and no black editors. The company also accepted advertising that portrayed African-Americans as menial workers, such as servile bellhops. An otherwise fine picture story about the Memphis Negro Fair used the offensive word "Pickaninnies" when reporting on the fair's "healthiest baby contest."

As a Republican, Harry Luce reacted with consternation to the desertion of his party by black Americans. Their vast migration to Northern cities, which had greatly accelerated during the Great War, was beginning to change American politics. While Roosevelt rarely spoke about "Negro issues" as such, his policies often appealed to blacks. A quarter of a million blacks were enrolled in the New Deal's Civilian Conservation Corps, while thousands of black farmers received federal loans. A few blacks occupied important posts in federal agencies; many more depended on New Deal programs for their survival. Eleanor Roosevelt's dedication to civil rights reinforced black allegiance to the President, and by the late 1930s, most blacks were voting Democratic.

By 1938 Harry Luce looked forward to the blessed day when a liberal Republican, perhaps a progressive businessman committed to civil rights, would oust the New Dealers from power. Then, he argued, a socially aware business community, cleansed of its sins, would collaborate with a new, enlightened President. Luce had no doubt that the economy would be the big issue in 1940. This was a pleasant prospect, he felt, since how could their obvious economic failures reelect the Democrats?

Time,

Anti-Semitism,

and Fascism

Henry Luce had not foreseen the magnitude of the European crisis. As late as 1937, he failed to pose the central question of his time: what was Adolf Hitler all about, and how did his plans for Europe affect America? Soon, however, Luce began to ask important questions about Hitlerism. Slowly, then at an accelerated pace, he also probed the changing Jewish role in the United States.

Few of the young Ivy League WASPs around Harry Luce would have considered themselves intolerant, much less anti-Semitic. They were, however, subject to the prejudices of their time and their class. Like Franklin Roosevelt, who considered this a "Protestant" country, Luce and his colleagues wanted to ensure continued rule by "the presumptive heirs of the national estate" (*Time*). Though young Jewish men studied at Yale, Harry's contacts with them were few and far between. In the early 1920s he and his friends from Yale would have associated Jews with urban ghettos like New York's Lower East Side. They assumed that the Jews were interested in money, observed strange dietary laws, were clannish, and often spoke exotic languages.

Although not explicitly anti-Semitic, Luce was insensitive to Jewish concerns. Time Inc. employed few Jews. And a dummy issue of *Time*, which appeared three months before the magazine's debut, foreshadowed future slurs. One read that the murderous pogroms in Jassy, Romania, resulted from unreasonable demands voiced by Jewish medical students. These young men, believing that their dead must receive a "decent burial," had refused to provide corpses for dissection. In its very first issue *Time* slandered Jews by alleging that the male Polish Jew gives thanks in his prayers that he is not "a dog, a woman, or a Christian." *Time* waited fifteen years before admitting that it had erred on this point. An early issue of *Time* made another dangerous accusation when it charged that the Soviet leaders were mostly "of Jewish blood." Before it was a year old, *Time* had managed to equate Jewry with communism, anti-Christian movements, and asocial behavior. A few years later, many of *Time*'s vindictive comments about Jews owed their inspiration to one unusual editor.

Working late on a Friday night, *Time* staffers might hear the regular thump-thump of a walking stick as the handicapped, overweight Laird Shields Goldsborough slowly proceeded to his office. Reclining on an old couch in his choice corner room, "Goldy" wrote page after page of copy, dropping the sheets on the floor as he finished them. Long the Foreign News editor of *Time*, he evoked the name of every aristocrat and statesman whom he had interviewed. Luce grumbled about Goldy's expense account, but he admired the man's ability to gain access to highly placed European leaders: personalities sold magazines. Respecting only the upper classes, Laird Goldsborough made the mistake of portraying Hitler and other grubby demagogues as nothing more than bizarre, ill-mannered upstarts.

Adolf Hitler's first great national breakthrough, in the election of September 14, 1930, was the subject of a major piece in *Time*. Readers learned that the Jews, terrified of him, were behaving like uncovered conspirators: "With her plump, black-eyed brood, Jewess after rich Jewess scuttled out of the Germany. . . ." In sketching the probable fate of the Jews under Nazi rule, *Time* foresaw a kind of second-class, segregated citizenship. The magazine did not particularly object to this outcome. By the end of March 1933, however, Hitler had begun to fashion his Nazi dictatorship. Early in April, Jew-baiter Julius Streicher organized the infamous Nazi boycott of Jewish retail businesses ("Germans! Defend Yourselves! Don't Buy from Jews!"). *Time* depicted this brutal action as a short-lived stunt that only hurt Germany. Old President Paul von Hindenburg, *Time* added, had reprimanded Hitler for the boycott, which quickly ended. *Time* failed to see that this so-called boycott against Jewish atrocity propaganda foreshadowed genocide.

Sometimes, however, the blind foretell the future. *Time*, describing Hitler's June 30, 1934, Blood Purge, smelled the "stench of sizzling human flesh [that] filled the furnaces of German crematoriums. . . ." Goldsborough continually described financier Bernard M. Baruch as "Jew Baruch," and Premier Léon Blum of France as "Jew Blum." Leon Trotsky was usually tailed by the phrase ("*née* Bronstein). While discussing a demand for more Jewish ballplayers, *Time* slyly recalled that Jews, who had seen "many diamonds on their brethren," would now like to see more of their brethren on the baseball diamond.

In a more dangerous vein, *Time* regaled its readers with anecdotes about Jewish criminality. The magazine carefully listed the ill-gotten gains allegedly earned by Jewish owners of saloons, bordellos, and the numbers rackets. *Time* did not ask about the social origins of this antisocial behavior. This was a dangerous tactic in the 1930s. Now, while many Americans suffered, some Jews, enjoying the fruits of their recent social, economic, and educational progress, were more visible than ever before. They advised Roosevelt (Bernard M. Baruch, Felix Frankfurter, Samuel Rosenman, Henry Morgenthau, and Benjamin Cohen), and dominated the Hollywood fantasy factories and the New York garment trades. Hard times in the United States, moreover, fostered a search for scapegoats. In 1937, 29 percent of those queried by Gallup believed that anti-Semitism was on the rise. When Elmo Roper, Luce's pollster, asked respondents to name the ethnic group to whom "you object," the Jews won, with 32 percent. A staggering 53 percent of those Americans answering Roper's questions displayed signs of strong anti-Jewish feelings. These sentiments ranged from the advocacy of deportation (10 percent), to "toleration," granted to Jews if they avoided places "where they are not wanted" (11 percent). When asked if Jews had too much power in this country, 41 percent said "yes." Only 39 percent of polled respondents believed that Jews should be treated like everyone else.

Americans feared for their jobs; if they were unemployed, they reacted badly to appeals for increased immigration. Sympathy for victims of Hitler, concluded *Fortune*, did not imply a "hearty welcome." Despite Nazi pogroms, 71 percent of the American public opposed the admission of a "larger number of Jewish exiles." The explosive word was "refugee," which many respondents equated with "Jews" (some people called these victims of persecution "refujews"). *Time* wished the refugees good luck and suggested that they emigrate to Palestine.

In the 1930s John Shaw Billings observed that the men who ran Time Inc. spoke the same language, were roughly the same age, and shared the same basic ideas and principles. This unanimity had been a source of strength, but now, in a new age, conformity placed limits on the company's intellectual and social development. These same men also harbored the prejudices common among their peers. Billings, for example, called himself "anti-Semitic at heart," and he was right. Digs at Jews pepper the pages of his voluminous diaries, where one reads about a "repulsive Jewess," a fat Jew opening a "greasy paper bag," and Jews frying odoriferous onions. Billings, one must note, kept these views to himself, and worked in a fully professional manner with his few Jewish associates, for by the mid-1930s Alfred Eisenstaedt, Laura Z. Hobson, and other Jews were emerging as important figures in the organization.

Sadly, Henry Luce's literal-mindedness did not always serve him well. He *knew* that he did not hate Jews. If Goldy identified a Jew as such, or printed his "real" last name, well, all that was factual, was it not? In Luce's own circle, composed mostly of upper-class Protestant males of about thirty-five years of age, he did not need to justify this opinion. Now, as *Time*'s circulation rose, thanks in some measure to an influx of well-educated Jewish readers, complaints began to pour in. Luce blithely assured readers that *Time* opposed religious or ethnic prejudice, but Jews still wondered why, in *Time*'s view, the *New York Times* was "Jewish-sympathizing," and why Haile Selassie, Emperor of Ethiopia, was a "Semitic tradesman." To Henry Luce, the phrase "Jew Blum" represented a statement of fact, not an accusation. But *Time* rarely said "Anglican George V" or "Protestant Roosevelt." Those adjectives, Luce lamely argued, did not reveal as much. As much—about what?

Archibald MacLeish harbored some of the prejudices typical of his time, but at least he was confronting them. MacLeish badly wanted to publish articles on the Jewish question, in *Fortune*. Fearing that the pre-Hitler German experience might repeat itself in America, MacLeish told a surprised Henry Luce that Jews believed *Time* was anti-Semitic. His proposed articles, he added, might dispel that image. Archie MacLeish's arguments impressed Luce, but other colleagues reacted badly to them. Some believed that the series could only invite trouble, and recommended that MacLeish drop it.

MacLeish remained obstinate, and *Fortune*'s long-awaited "Survey on Anti-Semitism" was due to appear in January 1936, while "Jews in America" was scheduled for February. Concerned Jews worried about the outcome, but *Fortune* sent questionnaires to prominent Jewish leaders, and MacLeish shared his thoughts and his drafts with many of them. When published, the *Fortune* pieces elicited so much comment that Random House agreed to publish them in book form.

Though well researched and intelligent, *Fortune*'s articles were also

timid and wrongheaded. The Jews, said *Fortune*, might *appear* to be
prominent in some professions and industries. Breathing a sigh of relief,
the magazine then concluded that they played "little or no part in the
great commercial houses." (This denial would have surprised Herbert
Lehman, Otto Kahn, Paul Warburg, and Bernard Baruch.) *Fortune* also
believed that certain Jews were predisposed to display an affinity for
Marxism. Other Jews, it advised, would be wise to be less "aggressive."
And *Fortune* played down the extent of anti-Semitic agitation, since
"only" 15,000 Americans spent most of their time agitating against
Jews. *Fortune*'s articles on Jews did some good, but only because most
other popular publications were afraid of broaching the subject. Luce
and Time Inc. were learning things they needed to know, but the gap
between education and the formulation of editorial policy remained
wide.

Harry Luce did have his moments of pessimism about America's
future, but he never gave way to despair. Despite the cynicism and the
unemployment, popular faith in the Constitution and the two-party
system remained strong. The United States had not suffered massive
human losses during the last war; its territory lay unscathed. Americans
had grown richer through intervention in Europe, and no neighboring
state challenged the nation's borders or patronized a discontented ethnic
minority within them.

Luce's blueprint for the future—sketched out in numerous memos,
speeches, the occasional letter or unsigned editorial—mandated a new
world economic order, led by American capitalism. When the public
debate concerned questions of foreign policy and defense, however, he
was reluctant to lead. Like President Roosevelt, Harry Luce was not
ready to commit American prestige to the solution of the problems
tormenting Europe and Asia. Neither man was prepared to defy the
popular consensus on foreign policy. Most Americans regretted America's entry into the last war, and many of them ascribed that blunder to
British fabrications about German atrocities in Belgium. To some,
wicked arms merchants were the culprits. At one point, the Luce media
lent credibility to this charge.

The diplomat Norman H. Davis, a confidant of FDR, had given
Harry Luce an idea for a story on the "merchants of death." *Fortune*
subsequently highlighted the international armaments trade, in an exposé that President Nicholas M. Butler of Columbia called the "greatest
sensation since the World War." In part due to *Fortune*'s powerful

essay, Congress passed the Neutrality Acts of 1935–1937, and Roosevelt signed them. Designed to keep the United States out of war, the new laws would prevent Americans from aiding belligerent powers. No pacifist, Luce feared the results of his own lurid exposé ("killing is their business"). Uneasy about the *Fortune* essay, Harry Luce mumbled something about how he might soon advocate building "the biggest navy in the world." But despite this disclaimer, even Luce catered to, and was profiting from the antimilitarist and anti-interventionist national mood. In 1937, for instance, *Life* published a moving story about Americans who were honoring their war dead in a French cemetery. "Nothing," *Life* wrote, "in all the clipped and ordered memorial calm is allowed to remind visitors of the way men once hung there on barbed wire with gaping wounds, writhed in the mud with legs or arms blown away. . . ."

Fortune's exposé of the arms merchants was not a fluke. Revulsion against the last war bred illusions about the next one. In 1934 former Secretary of State Frank Kellogg had declared that "There is no more chance of war with Japan, than a war with Timbuktu." In the summer of 1935 *The March of Time* lauded U.S. Army maneuvers as those of a "modern army." The same film calmly told its vast audiences that this "modern" army was sixteenth in size among armies of the world. Coupled with this statistic was better news. Audiences heard that the odds against another American intervention in a "major conflict" were 100 to 1; the odds stood at 500 to 1 against invasion of the U.S. by a foreign power.

A year later, Dan Longwell, a military buff, wrote a memorandum that clashed with this smug, safe consensus. He postulated a Japanese-U.S. naval war, centered on Guam and other Pacific islands. The Japanese, Longwell added, might even attack Hawaii, though not "in this generation." Longwell's idea about an attack on Pearl Harbor inspired a *Life* article that elicited little reader response—Longwell was known as a kind of scatterbrained enthusiast who pursued the strangest fantasies. Meanwhile, *Time*'s Laird Goldsborough continued to tell silly stories about European royalty while ignoring the implications for Americans of fascism and militarism. Goldsborough's picture of Europe—non-threatening, violent, amusing, and above all, distant—satisfied most readers of *Time*. The era of disillusion, of Depression, of the Neutrality Acts, this was Goldy's *Time*.

Although Laird Goldsborough laughed at any suggestion that the United States had a stake in preventing Fascist aggression, angry debates soon erupted at Time Inc. over the direction of *Time*. After the Italians had wantonly attacked Ethiopia in October 1935, newsreels brought scenes of the carnage to local theaters, and the violence disgusted many *Time* readers. In July, in a cover story on Mussolini, *Time* adopted a more restrained tone, though it still promised that Italy would treat Ethiopia in a "Christian" manner.

The Spanish Civil War, which began during the turbulent summer of 1936, proved to be a divisive subject at Time Inc. A democratic "Popular Front" government, supported by liberals, socialists, and Communists, confronted a right-wing rebellion led by General Francisco Franco. *Time* immediately decided that the General's fascist-minded supporters were, according to Goldsborough, ". . . men of property, men of god and men of the sword."

Mac Ingersoll, an ambitious man, was soon general manager of Time Inc. This job did not give him license to meddle in editorial matters, but Mac felt that he must correct *Time*'s coverage of Spain. He formed an alliance with the eloquent Archibald MacLeish, *Fortune*'s ardent exponent of antifascist activism. To Ingersoll and MacLeish, Goldsborough's writing trivialized a great moral issue. These two dissidents decided to put Luce's concept of objectivity to good use. Objectivity, Luce often said, was a false god. A magazine should weigh the moral merits of arguments put forth by both sides in a dispute then decide which disputant had made the stronger case. Fine, said Goldsborough's critics, let us apply that dictum to the European crisis. Clearly, Ingersoll implied, the Ethiopians and the Spanish Republic would come out on top.

Mac Ingersoll was unrelenting in his appeal to Luce's conscience. *Time*, he argued, must fight for democracy. Ingersoll even sent copies of his memoranda to Goldsborough's nominal boss, John Shaw Billings. If he expected support from that quarter, he was mistaken. Billings, secure in the knowledge that Luce supported Goldy, angrily denounced Ingersoll's "offensive language" and praised Goldsborough's "unbiased" reportage. Ingersoll retreated, at which point Billings graciously told him to forget the incident. Goldy had won a battle, but the campaign dragged on. Goldsborough counter-attacked, complaining about *Fortune*'s use of the word "Fascist." MacLeish responded that he would happily define it if *Time* explained what it meant when it called people "red," "reddish," "pink," and "pinko." Goldy then repeated his charge that MacLeish was following the Soviet line.

Harry Luce had not yet committed himself to a policy, so his senior editors expressed differing views when they reported on Spain. *Life*, for example, pleased its pro-Franco readers when pictures showed how leftists ("Loyalists") lynched priests and fired on monarchist crowds.

Life's most striking Spanish pieces, however, usually gratified Americans who detested Franco. The picture magazine went out of its way to praise a pro-Loyalist film, MacLeish's *The Spanish Earth*. Ernest Hemingway wrote the captions that accompanied the still shots adopted from the movie. Robert Capa, a brilliant young photographer, provided *Life* with grim but powerful pictures of a Spanish soldier, shot through the head on the Cordoba front. *Time*, however, wearily resigned itself to a Franco victory.

In 1937 both Luce and FDR made one daring speech on foreign policy, addresses that pointed to new and frightening possibilities. When President Roosevelt spoke in Chicago in October, he failed to identify the aggressors whom he denounced. FDR did, however, speculate about the need to "quarantine" predator nations. Since the address did not fall into the category of foreign news, Goldsborough did not get to ridicule it. But *Time*, which was pleased with Roosevelt's speech, overreacted when claiming that FDR had just ended fifteen years of isolation. Such hyperbole quickly yielded to a more modest appraisal, and *Time* finally decided that Roosevelt had tossed some pieties to the public. Luce, hoping to hear a clarion call, concluded that FDR had soothed the public with beautiful words, signifying very little.

Harry Luce was becoming a more effective public speaker, though he would never approach FDR's eloquence. He wrote out his talks in longhand, then rehearsed by reading them to Clare. Two months after Roosevelt spoke in Chicago, Luce addressed a group of Yale alumni, assembled in Montclair, New Jersey. At times he seemed to be speaking extemporaneously, since Luce had a phenomenal memory. He rarely stumbled over a word. Luce stunned his audience, which had expected to attend a nostalgic social gathering. On that autumn day in 1937, Henry Luce warned of a coming world war. Worse still, he prophesied that the United States would enter the conflict.

Luce spoke movingly of Memorial Hall, at Yale, which honored 212 Yale men who had died in the World War. If this grim warning failed to move his audience, Luce's next comment struck home, hard. He predicted that the casualties incurred in the next war would include the names of people "right here in this room." Luce did not predict the war's outcome, but he sounded pessimistic, for how could a nation that seemed to spurn the ideals of its fathers fight and win a big war? Luce seemed to be saying that we had better damned well figure out what was worth dying for. Otherwise, he warned, in thirty years (1967), the U.S.A. was unlikely to be a "decent place to live in."

By 1938 Harry Luce feared that young people, reared on pacifist and anti-interventionist doctrines, would refuse to fight for the American idea. Wanting to speak directly to American youth, he addressed the Founders' Day Convocation at Rollins College, in Florida, on February 21, 1938. Luce began by defining man as a moral animal. To Luce, Marxists, Freudians, and cynics were purveyors of fool's gold. He was also suspicious of talk about "economic man" and "social reform." If man's material welfare was uniquely important, demagogues who pandered to it could shout their way into power. Luce thus saw economic challenges as moral and political problems. And if we think in moral terms, he believed, we will not be tempted to solve problems through force. To Henry Luce, democracy was a doctrine based on freedom, and was thus "an act of faith." Turning to American disillusionment with the 1917 war, Luce excoriated the fashionable crusade "against all the icons of morality." America, he argued, had done the *right* thing in 1917, and had acted *wrongly* after 1919. Today, Luce continued, the world was again enmeshed in a "gigantic drama," and its outcome would depend on American youth.

Early in 1938, Luce styled himself editorial director of Time Inc., presaging a time when the three major magazines, and Luce's other media outlets, would speak with a single voice. Laird Goldsborough's stylistic flair, his sense of drama, and his love of gossip no longer captured the mood of the day. And given the rising threat of Nazism, Goldsborough's contempt for Jews was an embarrassment. In response to past derelictions, *Time*'s new publisher, Mac Ingersoll, professionalized the staff. Morale among researchers improved, for *Time*'s foreign stories were becoming more serious, reflecting fewer ethnic biases. And *Time*'s anti-Semitic innuendos decreased in number.

Luce's other productions were still ahead of *Time* in their anti-Nazi fervor. *Life*'s Christmas 1937 issue, for example, featured "Christmas in Naziland," where German children played with toy tanks beneath trees bedecked with figures of hanging Jews. At Louis de Rochemont's *March of Time*, a documentary called *Inside Nazi Germany* was causing a stir. As the most daring anti-Nazi film to be seen on American screens, *Inside Nazi Germany* enraged Nazis and triggered an avalanche of comment in the press. The film was, however, a kind of stage show, using actors with fake accents. And except for brief references to Nazi subversion, neither the broadcast nor the film argued that Hitler's brutality might threaten American interests.

At Time Inc., the certainty of a Nationalist victory in Spain frightened pro-Loyalist staffers. Ingersoll and his co-workers therefore redoubled their efforts to oust Goldsborough from Foreign News. They had found a perfect anti-Fascist replacement, too. Robert Neville, newly recruited by Time Inc., had traveled to wartime Spain and returned home a strong advocate of the loyalist cause. When Neville wrote copy, *Time* sounded like a publicity front for the Spanish Republic. Meanwhile, Goldy, who was ill or otherwise absent much of the time, began to decline, helped along by hostile pranksters. He could not find his cane or his notes. His phone would be left off the hook. By 1938 *Time* was a bit more critical of Hitler, and it no longer glorified *il Duce*. Over at *Life*, John Billings even grumbled about *Time* going Bolshevik. Luce, however, refused to shunt Goldy aside. But history was moving too fast for Goldsborough.

Supported by a sizable Nazi minority, Hitler seized Austria in March 1938. *Life* expressed concern about the fate of 365,000 Jews trapped in the enlarged German Reich. Its readers saw the word *Jude* scrawled on windows in Berlin, and Jewish prisoners scrubbing walls in Vienna. At *Time*, Mac Ingersoll confronted Frank Norris, whom he had accused of defending Hitler. "Now," Ingersoll asked, "will you believe the guy is a bastard?" Goldsborough was harder to convince. Even after the *Anschluss, Time* looked askance at the idea of a Western/Soviet alliance against Hitler, and still supported the appeasement policy promoted by Prime Minister Neville Chamberlain.

Though Luce had not yet formulated a coherent foreign policy, events in Asia were pushing him further toward global intervention. *Time*'s view of General Chiang Kai-shek and his Japanese neighbor had changed since 1932. *Time* had earlier described Chiang as a remote, egotistical, and possibly corrupt politician. Referring to "dictator Chiang," *Time* expressed concern about the General's early alliance with the Communists. Luce had paid little attention to Japan during his 1932 visit to Shanghai or Beijing, though Japan had already seized Manchuria. Examining life in "Manchukuo" (formerly Manchuria), *The March of Time* praised the economic progress made under the Japanese administration. As late as 1935, *Time* implied that Chiang's Guomindang Party, *in alliance with Japan*, might create a progressive new order in the Far East. *Time* saw the Japanese Army as a bulwark against Russia and communism, and in the autumn of that year *The March of Time* even produced a documentary ambiguously entitled "Japan-China."

Chiang Kai-shek had been fighting the Communists for almost a decade, and this struggle redounded to his benefit at Time Inc. Since 1927, *Life* noted with satisfaction, Chiang's forces usually restricted public beheadings and mass executions to Communists. The General had driven the Reds from their southern strongholds to remote sanctuaries far to the north. True, corruption and oppression endured, but China's leadership refused to succumb to it. *Time*, while admitting that some of Chiang's "Blue Shirt" bully boys were "spies, *agents provocateurs* and throat-slitters," gave his government high marks. By the summer of 1936, *Time*'s Chiang was "sagacious," as he (albeit, reluctantly) united China for her coming struggle with Japan. The Communists, of course, along with many jailed liberals and intellectuals, would have disagreed with this apotheosis of Chiang and his Soong in-laws.

Life regaled readers with stories about the legendary T. V. ("Charlie") Soong. Americans learned that Charlie had emigrated to America, where he obtained a good education and converted to Christianity. Soong then returned to his homeland, where he established a publishing house that printed Bibles. Charlie became very rich, married a Christian woman, and raised five children. He made sure that his children knew all about the United States, and learned the finest manners of the Chinese upper classes. Soong's saga embodied Harry Luce's idea of Chinese progress. Christianity, modernization, tradition, and wealth marched hand in hand.

In Luce's version of the Soong story, American know-how was bringing China into the modern world. In *Life*'s view, Chiang's alliance with T. V. Soong had created a government dedicated to "democracy and peace." T.V.'s sister, Mme. Chiang (Mei-ling Soong), the beautiful and poised First Lady, soon became one of *Life*'s heroines. A devout Methodist, her "New Life Movement" tried to infuse Chinese virtues with Christian faith. The Luce publications clearly preferred Mei-ling to her American counterpart, Eleanor Roosevelt.

When Japan attacked China in the summer of 1937, *Life* wondered if Chiang Kai-shek would resist the powerful invader. When he decided to fight, Chiang emerged, in Harry Luce's eyes, as the greatest man in the Far East. As Chiang's ill-equipped armies fell back before the enemy onslaught, *Time* hailed him as stoic and courageous. The Luce publications, however, were apprehensive about China's future. Could she withstand this massive assault, and would America help her? For the first time, *Time* sourly contrasted Chiang's faith in America with the do-nothing policy of the U.S.A.

For years *Time*, like Chiang, had depicted the Reds as bandits. The magazine worked to counteract romanticized, pro-Communist stories about Mao Tse-tung's revolutionary movement. When Japan threatened to invade China, however, the Luce publications changed their line. In early 1937 *Life* published a remarkable series of photographs shot by an adventurous journalist named Edgar Snow. A thirty-one-year-old Missouri-born correspondent, Snow had trekked to China's remote north, near Yenan, and discovered a disciplined military force ready to fight Japan under the leadership of Communists. These Chinese were doing calisthenics, training for war, playing tennis, and marching in youth groups. Their drills seemed to be progressive and patriotic; their activities impressed Americans who wished China well. *Time* now wanted to present its readers with more information about these Communists.

When Edgar Snow published his sensational *Red Star Over China* in 1937, *Time* called the book a journalistic coup. Snow had interviewed Red generals like Chu Teh and Lin-Piao, and learned to respect the amiable but tough Chou En-lai. He became friendly with the Communists' undisputed leader, Mao Tse-tung, who recounted the story of his life. Snow eagerly wrote everything down. The journalist heard the heroic story of the Communists' Long March. Driven from their communes in Kiangsi by Chiang's "anti-bandit campaigns," the Communists made their long trek to safety in Yenan, in the north. Of 90,000 fighters and dependents who started on the march, only 20,000 finished the journey, 368 days later. The Communists, Snow added, had played a big role in Chiang's recent and belated adherence to the anti-Japanese cause.

The Luce publications also made America aware of the grim cost of Japanese aggression. Readers saw a moving photograph of a weeping Chinese mother holding her dead child, killed during the brutal bombing of Canton. But few photographs packed the emotional punch of a picture printed by *Life* in the spring of 1938. The Japanese had just bombed Shanghai. Near the South Station, amid the panic and the ruins, a small child sat alone, crying. Reproduced countless times, the picture appeared on movie screens, in newspapers, and of course, in *Life*. The magazine estimated that 136 million Americans saw the image of that same child.

The tragic story of China's ragged refugees only reinforced *Life*'s faith in their cause. With great ingenuity, Chinese engineers and workers living in threatened cities disassembled industrial plants. They then carried machine tools and other precious equipment to safety in inland towns. There, they rebuilt their factories, and workers prepared to produce more armaments. What could not be saved was destroyed. Millions of refugees, clutching their meager belongings, were now heading up the Yangtze toward Chungking. In a remote city surrounded by arid gorges, many Chinese finally found temporary shelter. With awe, *Life* described how students and professors, pupils and teachers reopened their schools in China's temporary capital.

By the autumn of 1938, *Time* had concluded that the Chinese nation was "unbeatable." And if the Chinese were virtuous victims, *Life's* Japanese were automatons in uniform. The magazine compared the Japanese soldier to a cockroach, "superbly adapted to getting along on almost nothing." He could bath himself in scorching water and endure every discomfort. *Life* spoke of tough, machinelike soldiers who carried weapons dating from 1918. Time Inc. helped to convince Americans that the Japanese were sadistic, disciplined fanatics, but were militarily inferior to the great Western powers.

Not for the last time, Henry Luce's magazines ignored facts that might undermine readers' faith in China. *Life* glorified China's scorched-earth tactics but refused to tell readers about the damage they inflicted on peasants. At first *Life* denied that Chiang's authorities were blowing up river dikes and flooding the plains. These inundations, of course, engulfed both onrushing Japanese troops and the huts and fields of peasants. Finally, *Life* admitted that the Chinese Army had blown up the dikes along the Yellow River. While remaining silent about the horrors inflicted on Chinese peasants by these tactics, *Life* gloated over the damage meted out to the Japanese enemy. Why then, Luce wondered, did the West trade with Japan and sell her strategic materials like scrap metal and high-octane fuels? As *Fortune* pointed out, in 1938 Americans were exporting $169,567,000 worth of goods to Japan, while they imported products valued at $148,186,000. The Depression dragged on, and one did not easily dismiss a favorable balance of trade. (Commerce with China was worth one third of America's trade with Japan.)

Earlier than most publications, *Fortune* portrayed Japan as a potential industrial competitor for shrinking world markets. And in September 1938 Luce's military expert, Major George Fielding Eliot, published an intriguing article on "The Impossible War with Japan." Eliot tried to prove that a successful Japanese attack "upon Hawaii is a strategical impossibility. . . ." Eliot's view reflected wishful thinking, in which many of his countrymen also indulged. The very fact that he wrote the article, however, showed that people were worried. *The March of Time*, however, promised that the United States was creating "a new Gibraltar in the Pacific," at Pearl Harbor. The movie seemed to say that (1) War would not come, and (2) If it did, America was impregnable in the Pacific. Add to this the overestimation of China's fighting power, and the contempt lavished on the Japanese Army, and one had a made-in-America recipe for catastrophe.

More than ever, Henry Luce became convinced that only a failure of will prevented the West, especially America, from redeeming the East. He clung to this view for the rest of his life.

The Campaign
Against Appeasement

Though fretting about China, Henry Luce could not ignore the convulsions unsettling Central Europe, nor could he overlook *Time*'s problems. Threats of war and colorful demagogues seemed perfect subjects for the magazine's editors and readers, yet *Time*'s circulation was declining. Mac Ingersoll ascribed this paradox to Goldsborough's Foreign News. Calling Goldy a "tired, tired Jesuit," Ingersoll again pressed for his removal. At this point Time Inc. was in a state of editorial turmoil, for Ingersoll's ambitions had outreached his grasp. Suspicious of both Ingersoll and Goldsborough, Harry now decided that he wanted to see the crisis, first hand, and he sailed to Europe in the spring.

Late in May 1938, a new emergency erupted, as the Nazis began to demand freedom and autonomy for their "persecuted" brethren in the Sudetenland region of Czechoslovakia. Luce did not understand German, nor did he know much about German history, but he was a quick study. In the Reich, Harry observed that people seemed content with the regime. Families had enough to eat, and most Germans did not walk around trembling with fear of their imminent arrest by the sinister

Gestapo. Luce concluded that totalitarianism had its seductive aspects. What Harry saw only confirmed his view that some must live better if all were to "have enough." Luce, however, did not completely understand the Nazi phenomenon. He could not resist making a silly analogy between Hitler's *Autobahnen* and Roosevelt's Tennessee Valley Authority. And Luce thought that the Nazi "Blood and Soil" theory reflected a people's deep-rooted sense of living on a hallowed piece of land. This was absurd, for *Blut und Boden* was merely a vulgar Nazi slogan, imposed upon an indifferent society by politicians and crackpots. Nor did Luce realize that the "Sudeten" Germans in the Czech borderlands were merely tools of Nazi policy. Luce's conclusion was on the mark, however: popular support for the Nazi regime, combined with German discipline, made Hitler a threat to the world.

In Germany, Henry Luce finally grasped the full ferocity of Nazi anti-Semitism. He heard that Jews were being arrested in great numbers, and saw that virulent anti-Jewish propaganda infected much of German life. Luce also noted that the Austrians made even better Nazis than the Germans. Later he would vividly recall one incident that took place in Vienna. He was to lunch at the American consulate. Upon approaching the building, Luce had to push his way through a crowd of desperate Jews, pleading for entry visas. This grim sight moved him, and he concluded that these "undesirables" might strengthen the "spirit of progress and patriotism" in the U.S.A.

Luce learned important lessons in Central Europe, but he had still not laid down a clear policy. *Time* feared an arms race, economic disaster, and war; *Fortune* endorsed rearmament. Nevertheless, Luce's trip to Prague had an important result: Czech President Eduard Beneš convinced Harry that Soviet Russia might yet become a valuable ally of the democracies. Luce decided to rethink *Time*'s coverage of the Soviet Union in the light of the threat posed by Germany.

As he traveled to various capitals, Henry Luce received the kind of treatment usually accorded to important foreign dignitaries. In Paris leaders of the French press threw a big cocktail party for Harry and Clare. Luce, however, mostly wanted to seek out good sources. While in France, Luce arranged for some of his *March of Time* film people to meet with Ambassador William C. Bullitt. He did the same thing in Britain, where he chatted with Ambassador Joseph P. Kennedy. Luce liked Kennedy, and the two men conversed often on their return voyage to America. Kennedy became a valued friend of Harry Luce, and a crucial news source.

Soon after arriving back in New York in June, Harry Luce composed a long memorandum about his experiences in Europe. While fearful of war, he found grounds for hope. Luce admired the plucky Czechs and respected their democracy. He also convinced himself that the Czechs would fight, alongside powerful allies. Luce now advocated the creation of an antiaggressor front, but one consisting solely of *European* nations. If the coalition blocked Hitler, Americans could presumably cheer it on from the safety of distant sidelines. Luce, however, was not yet ready to call for the repeal of the neutrality laws. The prospects for a real antiaggressor front thus looked dim. The May crisis had passed, but Hitler's minions soon resumed their subversion of the Czech state. *Fortune*, following Luce, praised Czech democracy, and lauded its modern army, yet the magazine feared that the Czechs might one day slide into the German orbit, while "France and Britain sit helplessly by." Germany would then achieve "European supremacy."

Luce's flagship magazine continued to reflect rather than lead public opinion. This reticence aggravated Mac Ingersoll. How, he asked, could Harry endorse *Time*'s continued indifference to the implications of the greatest evil of the day? Luce finally agreed that *Time* had become mediocre. He also had to note that *Time*'s operating profit dropped by $2 million in 1938. Ingersoll suggested that Luce and Time Inc. had dissipated their energies. The company had, he argued, undertaken too many new projects during the past eight years: *Fortune, The March of Time, Life*. This charge annoyed Luce, who was proud of his "great successes," conceived in a "period of great human crisis." He began to mull over one possible solution: rid himself of both Goldsborough and Ingersoll. Mac Ingersoll soon solved the easy half of the problem. Anxious to found his own newspaper, he agreed to leave early in 1939.

In September 1938 Hitler again threatened the Czechs, and the Western powers capitulated to him at Munich. For the moment, "peace" was preserved. *Time*, which at first reported that France was standing by its Czech ally, initially seemed unconcerned about Premier Édouard Daladier's surrender to Germany. Almost immediately, however, Luce had second thoughts about Munich. By the middle of October, *Time* (like Roosevelt) compared Munich to paying protection to a criminal. The payoff might not prevent what *Time*, in an early use of the term, called the "Second World War." Luce was still searching for an editorial policy appropriate to America's potential place in a shattered world.

In Paris, Herschel Grynzspan, a troubled young Polish Jew, fatally wounded a German diplomat. On the night of November 9, 1938, the Nazis retaliated by launching a nationwide campaign of terror against the Jews. They arrested more than 20,000 of their victims and burned synagogues throughout the Reich. *Reichskristallnacht* or "Reich Crystal

Night," so called because of the broken glass from synagogues and stores that littered German streets, stunned the world.

Defying the efforts of German censors, *Life* obtained a few photographs of the pogrom's aftermath. *Time* eloquently denounced this modern barbarism, and published detailed information about atrocities inflicted on Jewish prisoners in Nazi concentration camps, like Sachsenhausen. "The March of Time" radio program reenacted the German pogrom. Millions of people heard this broadcast, which helped to convey the full horrors of Jew-hatred to Americans. Profoundly disgusted, FDR recalled the American ambassador to Germany, and *Time* heartily endorsed the President's move.

"The March of Time" made clear that Jews were begging for visas, though it refused to endorse their issuance by the State Department. Instead, the documentary pointed the Jews toward new homes in Africa and South America. This same issue of "The March of Time" did, however, break new ground. It implied that Hitler would *exterminate* the Jews with fire and sword unless the democracies removed them from his grasp. Time Inc., however, still displayed little moral courage while walking through the political minefield known as the refugee issue. Harry Luce felt sorry for the Jews and despised Nazi bullies, but he failed to develop a coherent policy on the refugees. For the next six and a half years, Luce, like Roosevelt, would concentrate on destroying Hitler, not upon saving the Jews.

Crystal Night made it impossible to defend any accommodation with Hitler. Henry Luce now convened his newly formed "Policy Committee," as if Time Inc. were about to formulate new American foreign policy. Among the committee's members were Ingersoll, Larsen, Hodgins, Gottfried, Ralph D. Paine, and Longwell. While Allen Grover took notes, the committee deliberated. Despite a thorough discussion of Munich, the group could not formulate a strategy. Luce, who had already named himself editorial director, decided to shed some more of his business responsibilities and again edit several issues of *Time*.

Late in November, after two long years of futile pressure applied by MacLeish and Ingersoll, Luce decided to rid Foreign News of Laird Goldsborough. The beleaguered editor felt helpless and became seriously ill; Billings, never one to suppress an unkind thought, believed him to be mad. A few days later, Luce finally shunted Goldsborough aside. On December 8 Harry informed all writers and editors that Goldsborough was now beginning his "long over-due sabbatical year."

Luce praised him highly for his thirteen years of brilliant service, but for Goldsborough, an extended vacation proved a prelude to oblivion.

Sadly, this troubled man refused to see that his *Time* had passed. Although Goldy tried to make a comeback less than a year later, he was even more erratic. He wandered about in a kind of daze, a pathetic figure scorned by most of his former colleagues. Harry Luce tried to help him by contacting a staffer at *Time* who had befriended Goldsborough. Luce asked this book reviewer to sneak Goldy into the "back of the book." Whittaker Chambers readily agreed to help, for he shared Goldsborough's dread of communism, but managing editor Manfred Gottfried would have none of it. Many years later, Laird Goldsborough, holding his gold-tipped cane, jumped out of a window in the Time-Life Building. Luce dutifully attended the funeral, where Goldy's relatives and friends ignored him.

Time's Christmas 1938 issue depicted a Nativity scene, above St. Matthew's question, "Where is He that is born King of the Jews?" This was moving, but neither Luce nor his staff had thought through the implications of their recent conversion. They did not yet advocate aligning the United States with a broad anti-German front. Although bolder, Luce kept one eye on public opinion, and the public was confused. Half of those Americans polled by Gallup or Roper believed that Hitler wanted to rule Europe, and more than 60 percent of the respondents concluded that war would engulf both Europe and the United States. A majority of the people felt that the U.S. should "at any cost" stand with the democracies in opposition to fascist aggression. But when asked about sending troops overseas, a *larger majority said no*.

Everyone at *Time* agreed that Adolf Hitler must be named Man of the Year for 1938, but the editors planned to use a rather flattering, official portrait of the *Führer* on its cover. Mac Ingersoll, in Luce's absence, rejected this plan as obscene. Instead, he used a frightening drawing sketched by Austrian refugee Rudolph Charles von Ripper. This picture depicted Hitler as an "unholy organist," playing his "hymn of hate." Above the organ pipes, one saw a wheel, to which were chained the corpses of recent victims. This cover, the most powerful in *Time*'s history, enraged Luce. He did not disagree with its message; rather, Ingersoll's insubordination angered him. Luce quickly calmed down, but he and Ingersoll drifted further apart.

In describing Man of the Year Hitler, *Time* derided Prime Minister Neville Chamberlain, whose peace with honor had "achieved neither." Winston Churchill, whom Goldsborough had once portrayed as a warmongering babbler, was now installed as *Life*'s "most resolute and capable member of the Conservative Party." And Time Inc. would soon discover hitherto unseen virtues in Franklin D. Roosevelt.

Franklin Roosevelt often responded magnificently to daunting challenges. The crisis in Europe would again test him, and at just the right time. His plan for reforming the Supreme Court had been ignominiously defeated in 1937; he had subsequently failed to purge conservative Democrats. The New Deal lacked its old fire, and presidents never ran for third terms. On paper at least, FDR was a lame duck, badly in need of a new cause. Massive rearmament could put many of the almost 10 million unemployed back to work. The reinvigorated economy in turn might reelect Roosevelt or another New Dealer in 1940. Henry R. Luce shuddered at this prospect (*Fortune*'s polls indicated that FDR could win), but he put his country ahead of his partisanship. He just hoped that Roosevelt would do the same thing.

Guns, ships, and battalions proved to be tailor-made subjects for *Life* and *Time*. Dramatic captions and striking photographs conveyed a sense of power, excitement, and national purpose. *Time* lauded plans to build two 45,000-ton battleships, the biggest in U.S. history. *Fortune* explained rearmament to its interested readers. Industry could certainly profit from government contracts, which would in turn create jobs. *Life* grew even bolder. Even before Luce totally soured on Munich, the picture magazine shocked readers with its headline "America Gets Ready to Fight Germany, Italy and Japan."

A *Life* editorial bitterly attacked those Americans who had turned their backs on Woodrow Wilson's "call for a crusade to make the world safe for democracy." Dan Longwell became a kind of admiral-in-residence, as his magazine sounded trumpets that had been silent for almost twenty years. Pacifists and isolationists abhorred his displays, but *Life* posed a difficult question: Was America prepared to use its weapons on behalf of "morality and justice"?

In March 1939 Hitler violated the Munich pact by occupying Bohemia and Moravia. *Time*, relying heavily on information provided by Ambassador Bullitt and his colleagues in Europe, had already warned that Hitler might attack Poland. *Time* believed that Daladier and Chamberlain were finally awakening from their disastrous slumber. And the magazine was now much friendlier to Franklin Roosevelt. In April *Time* endorsed Roosevelt's plan to extend the principle of cash and carry. This scheme would enable belligerents (presumably Britain and France) to buy weapons from the United States if they paid cash for these goods and hauled them away on their own merchant ships. Predicting "even greater deeds by Franklin Roosevelt," *Time* lambasted those isolationists who derided FDR's foreign policy.

Several senior editors at Time Inc. were suspicious of Luce's belated interventionism. They feared that in the coming months Harry might again turn on Roosevelt, who could be running for reelection. When these editors confronted Luce with an invitation to dinner, however, he was prepared for their criticism, and he turned the tables on them. Harry decided to play the host and invite his colleagues to dine with him at his Waldorf Towers apartment. Among Luce's guests were Thomas Matthews and Frank Norris of *Time*, and Charles ("Wert") Wertenbaker of *Fortune*. With Goldsborough out of the way, these men were moving to institute a kind of collective leadership. Luce's colleagues now wanted to hear from their boss.

Thomas Matthews, the son of an Episcopal bishop, had studied at Princeton and Oxford. He displayed marked literary talent and as "back of the book editor" Matthews had long been working to make *Time* a respectable contributor to national discourse. He despised the magazine's clever adjectives, nasty cracks, and eccentric sentence structures. His efforts bore fruit in the late 1930s, though *Time*'s fixation on double adjectives continued to bedevil him. Matthews saw the boss as an uneasy, friendless man who did "nothing but work." And Harry, he knew, could be rude and dogmatic. In moments of despair, Matthews would go up to see "Uncle" John Billings, who listened patiently to his tales of woe. Yet Matthews also admired Harry Luce as a self-proclaimed sinner who wished to make the world a better place. And he respected a man whose stammer spurred him on to greater effort.

At their dinner, Tom Matthews and his colleagues discovered that Harry Luce had anticipated their tough questions. All these men agreed that *Time* enjoyed vast power. Would Luce use it for political purposes? Yes, he replied, if "I thought the Republic was in danger." In the past, *Time* had amused, scolded, and sometimes informed its readers. Luce now intended to *mold* public opinion. Scattered bits of bias would yield to a coherent message. Tom Matthews soon took over *Time*'s all-important National Affairs department. Luce had convinced him that *Time* would play the activist in addressing the current crisis.

Harry Luce was asserting direct editorial control over his magazines. Editors could still argue, but at a certain point they must yield to the consensus—which Luce would define. Perhaps nothing symbolized Luce's faith in American globalism better than a *Life* cover that showed the Statue of Liberty standing against a dark-blue background. "America's Future" was its theme. Harry Luce's dream of America's global mission had endured, and he would define it for a skeptical, frightened nation.

After meeting the Luces, George Bernard Shaw had called Harry "Mr. Boothe," for he was the husband of the more famous Clare Boothe Luce. After producing the sensation known as *Life*, Luce had become a public figure, however, but his personal entry onto the national stage was awkward. By the autumn of 1936, Harold Ross' *New Yorker* was well established as a sophisticated, bemused observer of contemporary urban mores. Ross' attention was now drawn to the upstart creator of the famous, all-too-clever *Time*. *Time*'s stylistic foibles presented a good satirist with wonderful raw material, and a talented writer named Wolcott Gibbs set to work. Ross shared his galley proofs with Time Inc., whereupon Luce grew very agitated. Harry, whose *Fortune* had pushed aside the curtain of anonymity shielding corporate executives, now demanded privacy for himself. *Time* marketed personalities, but its editor in chief wanted to be let alone. Unfortunately, a tough Harold Ross would not alter his decision. *Life*'s colorful Alexander King, a witty Viennese immigrant and raconteur, occasionally referred to Luce's "dangerous integrity." According to King, this quality inspired Luce's "frenzied intensity." In reacting to the Gibbs piece, an angry Harry Luce again displayed his paucity of psychological insight, not to speak of his lack of any sense of humor.

The *New Yorker* printed its profile of Henry Robinson Luce in late November 1936, portraying him as a wunderkind of journalism. Gibbs took Luce seriously, describing him as a "baby tycoon" (*Time* had invented the phrase "tycoon"). Gibbs noted that 8 or 9 million people listened to "The March of Time" on the radio. He also observed that the newsfilm version appeared thirteen times a year, in more than 6,000 theaters, coast-to-coast. Twelve million people watched *The March of Time* newsfilms each month, and later that figure rose to 20 million. Gibbs speculated that Luce might wish to become President. He did not know it, but the idea sometimes intrigued the publisher.

The *New Yorker*'s parody of *Time* quickly became legendary. "Backward ran sentences until reeled the mind," wrote Wolcott Gibbs. Playfully, *The New Yorker* concluded with a *Time*-like observation: "Where it all will end, knows God!" This anguishing episode hurt Luce's feelings, but it did him no damage. To the contrary, to be satirized by that rising star, *The New Yorker*, brought one to the attention of thousands of affluent people. After the *New Yorker* fiasco, however, Harry Luce usually avoided potential interviewers.

The *Los Angeles Times* now viewed *Time* as the "most powerful single element in journalism," and marveled at Henry Luce's "Horatio Alger"

story. The radical writer and ex–Time Incer Dwight Macdonald decided that Luce controlled a "gadget" that put ideas "into 30,000,000
heads." He accused Time Inc. of being entrenched in the "industrial-
financial plutocracy," though Macdonald had reason to know better.
At their worst, Luce's magazines disguised their ignorance by affecting a
pose of omniscience. At their best, his publications displayed impressive
integrity, fortified by superb research. Luce now decided that *Time*
should be the "most powerful publication in America."

Despite it sales slump in the late 1930s, *Time* was already a national
institution. In 1936 the company sold over 641,000 copies of the magazine each week. *Life* had broken out of the class and income range
prescribed by Luce's other efforts, and Time Inc. soon (1941) claimed
that almost 20 million people a week were reading *Life*—or looking at
it. *Life*'s ideal subjects were upper-class colleges, nice clothes, people
with wholesome morals, movies, fancy automobiles, chic parties, and
polite tennis matches. By January 1939, *Life* was finally making money,
and it turned a profit of $225,000 in the first quarter. During the year,
the company as a whole earned a $3 million profit. Luce's Senior Group
now consisted of thirty-one people, who received a percentage of these
earnings. Luce spread his wealth around, granting editors and managers
stock options and cash bonuses, thereby creating a new class of potential
millionaires. He even joked about dinners accompanied by the music
of jingling cash registers, but John Billings had a better line. Everything
was going well, he noted, except for Hitler, who made trouble every
time the Billingses planned a long, peaceful weekend in South Carolina.

Behind the scenes, *Life* was acquiring a unique knowledge of American opinion-makers. In *Life*'s publicity department, Otis Swift quietly
assembled files on 80,000 "public-opinion-forming citizens." The company learned, for example, that Princeton freshmen had voted *Life* their
favorite magazine. One day these young men would dominate the
boardrooms, faculty clubs, officers' quarters, and bureaucracies of the
nation. By then, Luce hoped, they would all be reading *Time* and
Fortune as well as *Life*. Indeed, *Time* already seemed to be everywhere,
as its red-bordered cover appeared in living rooms, on newsstands,
even in classrooms. From 1936, Time Inc. provided thousands of
schools with teaching aids of all kinds. It mailed free quizzes to school
administrators for use in social studies classes. Throughout the country,
pupils answered questions by offering Time Inc.'s version of world
events.

One heard that everyone who was anyone read *Time*, or cited it, or
borrowed clever bits of prose from it. Writing in 1939 or early 1940,
press critic Quincy Howe praised Luce as a "magazine genius," who

might well become the most powerful man in his branch of journalism. Howe observed that the great editor reacts like his reading public—but in advance of them. Luce, Howe concluded, was a brilliant editor. Success spawned imitators, and in 1933 a new publication called *News-Week* emerged—a smaller, blander, and less controversial *Time*. Much later, *Newsweek* evolved into a prime competitor, but for the moment, Luce dominated the newsmagazine field.

There were, of course, dissenters who objected even to the lovable *Life*. J. L. Brown, attacking "Picture Magazines and Morons" in the *American Mercury*, dismissed *Life* as a scandalmongering picture show aimed at illiterates. Brown admitted, however, that commercially, *Life* represented a "minor miracle." Jacques Barzun, a Columbia University professor, scorned *Time*. "More dull error," he observed, "could not be compressed into so few words." (Barzun much later worked as a consultant to a book project—created by *Life*.) *Time*'s critics grew in direct proportion to its rising circulation. Some Catholics disliked the magazine's occasional criticism of General Franco. Jews still resented *Time*'s infrequent slights, while anti-Semites objected to Time Inc.'s new sympathy for the Jews of Europe.

As Time Inc. gained international notoriety, it engendered complaints that reached the Department of State. The Cuban government seized and banned copies of the magazine after *Time* labeled President Fulgencio Batista a dictator. Japan banned an issue in 1936, over an alleged insult to the Emperor Hirohito. Luce rarely apologized for such transgressions. He had even refused to reprimand Foreign News when an issue of *Time* provoked the wrath of British censors.

_1939_

Toward
Collaboration with
Roosevelt

On the afternoon of April 20, 1939, Henry Luce walked into the ball-room of the Biltmore Hotel in Manhattan, where an audience of more than 600 executives waited to hear from him. Mostly women, these members of the Fashion Group were leaders in the world of dress and design. Luce made some small talk about the importance of the fashion world to _Life_. He then addressed graver problems, such as the social progress achieved by the people of China. He quickly moved on to the subject of war. He repeated the national pieties, hoping that the United States would not again become a belligerent power. Luce strongly endorsed President Roosevelt's recent appeal to the dictators, which called on them to refrain from committing new acts of aggression. Luce hoped to see the advent of "some kind of General World Peace Conference."

Elmo Roper's polls, which were a prominent part of _Fortune_, showed that people feared war and thought that Germany would unleash it. Most Americans believed that their country would be drawn in, but they hoped it would stay out. They approved of Roosevelt's performance in foreign affairs, and a large majority thought that if the two Axis powers, Italy and Germany, defeated Britain and France, they would then wage war against the U.S.A. Eighty-seven percent of the nation favored training college men as aviators, but 83 percent opposed sending these men overseas, even to help the democracies. These contradictions bothered Luce. To Luce, there must be a cause—meaning an idea—worth fighting for, not just a coastline that required protection. Harry hoped that the United States would act on the basis of its "moral sentiments." Did he favor war? Not quite yet, though he believed that Americans would not tolerate the defeat of France and Britain. On May 1, 1939, *Time* inaugurated a lavish "Background for War" section. Spurred by fear of Germany, the magazine was adjusting its foreign policy priorities.

In London, Major Vernon Bartlett, M.P., quipped that "We shall not be able to enjoy ourselves until Franco's widow tells Stalin on his deathbed that Hitler has been assassinated at Mussolini's funeral." This clever comment might have amused *Time* just a few months earlier. Luce, however, had come to believe that Hitler, not Stalin, was threatening the West in 1939. By the late spring, *Time* finally absolved Soviet Russia of any revolutionary intentions. Stalin, it added, had a respectable fighting force and could become a valuable partner of the West. Then, after musing about a Western alliance with Soviet Russia, *Time* decided that Stalin might ally himself with Germany. Though unlikely, this dark prospect frightened *Time*. Such a coalition would enable Germany to fight a long war, which was supposed to be Britain's strong suit.

On the home front, *Time* harshly attacked benighted anti-interventionists. For the first time, Colonel Charles Augustus Lindbergh, Jr., drew the magazine's full measure of contempt. In a cover story entitled "The Press v. Lindbergh," Luce's men set to work. "Lindy," *Time* wrote, had been a hero for too long. The magazine did not frighten Lindbergh, who was a stubborn, courageous, and determined man. In fact, Luce and Lindbergh were defining different visions of America's role in the world. For more than two years, they and their spouses, Clare Boothe and Anne Morrow, would argue about whether America should accommodate herself to the rising totalitarian current. Or should the United States counterattack and try to forge a better world? Roosevelt's enemies, the Lindberghs, were now Harry Luce's adversaries, too.

By 1939 Time Inc.'s magazines, radio shows, and movies were reaching over 40 million people a month, almost a quarter of the American population. Judging by their income and related data, most of these people appear to have been Republicans or independents. Gaining Harry Luce's support would be a *coup* for the White House. The Luces and the Roosevelts had met three or four times in the past, but their chemistry was poor. On one occasion, Roosevelt made a joke about *Life*'s financial tribulations. "Well, Mr. President," answered Harry, "I've got *my* next year's budget balanced." Roosevelt laughed, as he often did, but this light moment did not lead to a friendship.

Clare Luce, on the other hand, greatly admired the First Lady, and Eleanor Roosevelt took an interest in Mrs. Luce's work as a Broadway playwright. Mrs. Roosevelt understood Clare's vulnerabilities and spoke bluntly to her about them. She advised Clare to overcome her mood swings, bitterness, and past hurts. In her nice way, Eleanor seemed to disapprove of Clare's past, and she disparaged the sometimes nasty dialogue that enlivened Mrs. Luce's Broadway hits. Wallowing in mean dialogue was, to Eleanor, an escape, not a cure.

Although Clare was not able to overcome her past so easily, some of her subsequent work may have profited from Mrs. Roosevelt's advice. In 1939 Broadway produced Clare Luce's play *Margin for Error*, a political morality tale in which a Jewish cop solved the murder of a repulsive Nazi diplomat. An eloquent plea for tolerance, *Margin for Error* was a success. Harry was very proud of Clare, though he never understood the venomous wit that inspired much of her work. Still, Clare Luce had come to share Harry's revulsion against Nazism.

June Hamilty Rhodes, managing director of the Bureau of Fashion Trends, had deeply appreciated Henry Luce's Biltmore speech. Miss Rhodes also enjoyed access to the White House, and penned an urgent note to her dear friend "Missy" LeHand, Roosevelt's private secretary. Henry Luce, said Rhodes, was on the President's side and "is capable of great leadership." And, given public opinion, "we need him so badly." Rhodes attributed profound influence to Luce's magazines, and told LeHand that their support would greatly strengthen Roosevelt. Four days later Roosevelt curtly answered Rhodes. He had seen the Luces quite recently, and expressed no enthusiasm about another visit.

Four days after this cool response, Adolf Hitler dismissed Roosevelt's recent appeal for peace as the work of an arrogant interloper. Some days later, the German authorities banned *Time*. Apparently Luce and Roosevelt were attracting the same contempt. Indeed, FDR faced vehement domestic opposition as he confronted the dictators. Some called him a warmonger; extremists labeled him a tool of the Jews. Like Roosevelt, Luce had come to see that anti-Semitism and the rise of fascism were related. Clearly, Roosevelt would need allies in his struggle against this poison. Perhaps a meeting with Harry Luce would be in order after all. While FDR prepared to confer with Luce, the publisher was delving more deeply into the question of anti-Semitism.

Time's coverage of Jewish issues remained spotty and erratic, but the magazine did publish a long, moving account of a ghostly "Endless Voyage." The steamer *St. Louis*, carrying 937 helpless German Jews, tried to dock in the United States, or in a Caribbean country, but failed to secure permission. The vessel sailed back to the Reich. *Time* bemoaned the fate of these Jews but refused to advocate a change in American immigration policy. *Life*, meanwhile, published an article by the noted writer John Gunther, in which the Zionist leader Chaim Weizmann was depicted as a sympathetic figure. Palestine, not America, Time Inc. implied, should be the Jews' destination.

Harry Luce, however, now understood that anti-Semitism threatened not just the Jews, but democracy itself. If people believing in a Jewish conspiracy could destroy a democracy, then who was safe? Since *Fortune* had broached the question of anti-Semitism in 1936, Luce now turned to managing editor Russell Davenport for some answers. Davenport did not believe that Jew-hatred was a clear and present danger to this democracy, but he did not underestimate its potential power. If the American economy did not revive, Davenport concluded, then the "psychosis" of anti-Semitism could grow stronger. Davenport, who was proud of *Fortune*'s articles on the Jews, favored confronting the issue head-on. He also wanted to describe the contributions of Jews to the American economy. This approach would presumably counter the comments of those who argued that Germany had grown stronger after expelling its Jews. In conclusion, Davenport urged that the Luce magazines expose hate groups.

At *Fortune*, Del Paine reported back to Harry Luce on May 12, 1939. Ironically, Paine's memorandum raised the same question that had confronted MacLeish back in 1935. Was it best to expose American anti-Semitism or smarter to ignore it? *Time*, according to Paine, gave free publicity to the anti-Semitic priest Father Charles Coughlin, when writing about his tirades, so perhaps it was better to ignore him. Other advisers argued that since *Time* influenced so many people, it must work to discredit anti-Semitism, wherever it lurked. Del Paine, however, was more cautious than Davenport. He advised Luce that *Life*, with its huge, presumably less educated readership, avoid the issue of anti-Semitism altogether. *Fortune*, which reached a smaller, more sophisticated audience, could better control reactions to its exposure of anti-Semitism. Paine recommended that *Time* publish stories about efforts to combat intolerance.

Despite *Time*'s more respectful attitude, Jews continued to find signs of malice or insensitivity in Luce's magazines. Mrs. David Sarnoff, for instance, the wife of the president of the Radio Corporation of America, complained to Russell Davenport. She was greatly agitated, for *Life* had published an advertisement purchased by the Valley Ranch, in Wyoming. Mrs. Sarnoff claimed that she had attempted to send her sons there for the summer, but Valley Ranch would not accept Hebrew patronage. Davenport contacted Luce, suggesting that *Life* be on guard against accepting advertising from anti-Semites. This incident caused John Billings one more headache, but his magazine acted more cautiously in the future.

Fortune, meanwhile, continued to worry about American anti-Semitism. Was it a prelude to fascism or merely a socially disruptive prejudice, doomed to disappear? Helen Walker and Judith Pequignot, researchers at *Fortune*, suggested that the magazine conduct a survey measuring the strength of American anti-Semitism. Then, *Fortune*, understanding the enemy, could combat this hateful prejudice. The researchers also proposed that Jews in New York be questioned by Roper. Their responses would presumably refute anti-Semitic allegations, among them charges that most or all Jews were radicals, cheats, rich, racially distinct, and "too damn smart."

A nervous Russell Davenport commissioned the survey, which was scheduled to appear in the October 1939 issue of *Fortune*. In the course of its polling, *Fortune* discovered that at least half of Roper's Gentile respondents harbored anti-Jewish sentiments. Davenport strongly urged that Time Inc. suppress this information, then use it later, in a sanitized form. *Fortune* decided not to publish its data. Distracted by the outbreak of war in Europe, the magazine concluded that anti-Semitism could wait.

Overall, however, Luce's magazines were doing a better job of covering issues of concern to Jewish readers. Indeed, Time Inc., which Jews had once accused of rampant anti-Semitism, now became a target of men who blasted FDR as "Rosenfeld," a "Jew," and a "warmonger." Borderline psychopaths and Jew-haters like William Dudley Pelley, head of the "Silver Shirts," distributed leaflets denouncing *Life*'s attacks on American Nazis and Fascists. The crude sheet labeled *Life*'s Andrew Heiskell and David Cort, and other Time Incers, as "Jewish." So Henry

R. Luce, of all people, now found himself allied with Franklin D. Roosevelt—and "the Jews."

FDR canceled a May 10, 1939, luncheon date with Secretary of the Interior Harold Ickes. Instead, he invited Henry R. Luce to visit the White House. Luce took the train to Washington, where his lunch with Roosevelt went badly. The publisher, with his usual bluntness, suggested that the President speak frankly to the American people. If the United States had an interest in Germany's defeat, then the President should say so. FDR, however, intended to sell rearmament as a *defensive* measure, and hoped to dissuade Hitler from committing further acts of aggression. The President asked for support, but revealed no long-term goals. Luce wanted firm answers, commitments, perhaps a call to arms. He went home disappointed, but the publisher redoubled Time Inc.'s efforts on behalf of rearmament, and intensified its opposition to appeasement.

FDR needed the cooperation of industrialists and financiers, as he worked to rearm the nation. Much of the big-business community, however, hated the New Deal, and wanted to do business with the Axis powers. Luce and *Fortune* could help make FDR's case, precisely because they had recently opposed many of his domestic policies. *Fortune* now argued that businessmen must go to Washington in order to take rearmament out of the hands of New Dealers. *Fortune* also told its constituents that patriotism and profits beckoned businessmen to FDR's Washington.

A few days after Luce lunched with Roosevelt, Dan Longwell took some friends down to the docks along the Hudson, where the gleaming ships of the majestic American war fleet were anchored. Longwell knew that ships and guns could do more for *Life* than anything except pretty girls and cute animals, and he often succeeded in bringing his naval extravaganzas to its readers. *Life*'s preparedness campaign quickly gained the attention of military leaders, Congressmen, Senators, and government officials.

As Harry Luce prepared to begin his interventionist campaign, he retained the services of Raymond Leslie Buell, a well-known academic critic of isolation. Buell, who had headed the important Foreign Policy Association, wrote long memoranda about the world situation to Luce. A dry, professorial presence, Buell established the famous *Fortune* Round Table. Working with Luce and other *Fortune* editors, he would pick a controversial topic related to America's stake in the global crisis.

Fortune then invited prominent businessmen to a retreat, where experts in business, economics, and politics debated the issue at hand. At the very least, they clarified their differences. Articles and special supplements in *Fortune* then shared the conferees' conclusions with the broader public. The Round Tables influenced public opinion and attracted the attention of influential players, from Wall Street to the Council on Foreign Relations, from the Senate to the White House. Luce liked the Round Table idea, for it combined a search for truth with the power to shape policy.

Harry Luce felt compelled to confront issues that many Americans wished to avoid. He berated the "stuffed dummy of impartiality," and he would never let this mannequin prevent Time Inc. from telling the truth. If the West failed to revive its faith in itself, Luce added, civilization was doomed. From his reading of Ortega y Gasset, Luce learned that mass man, enraged and armed, could "destroy the civilization which bred him out of the darkness." Luce was not singling out the working man or the unemployed when he referred to "mass man." To the contrary, he found this phenomenon most troubling when it appeared in the middle and upper classes. Educated people, he felt, should reject the instant gratification, irrationality, and anti-intellectualism typified by "mass man." Where, Luce asked, was their allegiance to higher ideals, their unselfish devotion to great causes? Now, he believed, Americans were paying a high price for the cynical laughter that had debased the land during two lost decades. Henry Luce hoped to redeem his generation, which had betrayed the promise of 1918. He looked ahead to the day when America could realize what Luce named the "Great Society."

In the spring of 1939, at about the time he lunched with Roosevelt, Luce turned to the most eminent journalist of the day. Few Americans possessed the breadth of vision and the intellectual depth of Walter Lippmann. Writing a widely syndicated column for the *New York Herald Tribune*, Lippmann conveyed his thoughts in prose that was at once magisterial and readable. If anyone could explain America's stake in the European confrontation, it was Lippmann. Born in New York City in 1889, Lippmann graduated from Harvard in 1909. In 1914 he co-founded an influential and progressive journal called *The New Republic*. Lippmann then drew closer to the presidency of Woodrow Wilson. When war broke out, Lippmann condemned German militarism and aggression and supported the democratic Allies, Britain and France.

After America entered the conflict, Lippmann joined the staff of Newton D. Baker, Secretary of War. He coined the phrase about making "a world that is safe for democracy," and emerged from the war with great hopes for the postwar order. Yet the Senate rejected Wilson's peace treaty, and with it the League of Nations. Lippmann blamed the President, as well as a confused public, for this fiasco. As a result, a disillusioned Walter Lippmann sourly commented that "I'm not going to spend my life writing bugle calls." In the years following the war, Lippmann became a famous columnist, and to *Time*, which placed him on its March 30, 1931, cover, he was the great spokesman for American liberalism. In 1937 *Time* again so honored Lippmann, but this time the magazine praised him for moving to the right.

Like many other Americans, Lippmann supported most of the neutrality legislation. Even as a quasi-isolationist, however, he emphasized the importance of Anglo-American solidarity. And as Germany grew more powerful, Lippmann became alarmed. The American public, he argued, had accepted a false history of the 1917 adventure. He was returning to his earlier, outspoken interventionism, and this reversion attracted the attention of Harry Luce.

Believing that the present generation had misread the history of the recent past, Luce offered Walter Lippmann a new pulpit. As a syndicated columnist, he could claim to reach 10 million Americans and Canadians, who read his column in 160 newspapers. Lippmann's audience was largely a Republican elite, often consisting of families led by businessmen, bankers, civil servants, lawyers, intellectuals, professors, and the like. Luce, by contrast, could bring Lippmann to a readership of 20 million Americans from all walks of life. *Life* commissioned an article from him, entitled "The American Destiny." With Billings' usual expert editing, Lippmann's article ran on June 5, 1939.

Lippmann began by pointing to two paradoxes troubling many Americans. Today, this rich and free continent seemed unable to overcome poverty at home. And the nation watched helplessly while civilization collapsed across the seas. Now, Lippmann decided, people believed in very little, saved too little, worked too little, and were too averse to risk. This nation, he argued, simply could not accept German domination of Western Europe and of the North Atlantic sea-lanes. Again and again, Lippmann observed that the Reich's triumph threatened American military, economic, and political interests. The United States, he concluded, occupied center stage in the Western world, and its destiny was to play the leading role. A clarion call, Lippmann's article summoned Americans to a destiny they could no longer evade.

Harry Luce could not have chosen a better messenger. A brilliant, inspiring piece of journalism, "The American Destiny" provoked widespread discussion. Requests to reprint the article poured in from other publications. *Time*, Luce's flagship, quickly echoed Lippmann's arguments. Even if Americans wished to remain neutral—and they did—their nation must necessarily affect the world balance of power.

During this tense summer of 1939, Harry Luce decided that he must again visit Europe. He and Clare intended to see people in London, Paris, Warsaw, and Bucharest. In Britain, Luce sensed that the appeasers had weakened, while Winston Churchill was champing at the bit. He wanted to wage war, and Time Inc. encouraged him. In late June, Harry journeyed to Paris, where *Time*'s attacks on France's weak foreign policy were creating fresh problems for its editor in chief. Early in May, *Time* had reported that the French government, concerned about pro-Fascist propaganda in the press, intended to crack down on journalists who accepted foreign money. *Time* then described the French press as the "sewer of world journalism." The magazine accused French journalists of accepting Nazi money in return for covering the news in ways favorable to Berlin. The Paris Press Association heatedly objected to *Time*'s article, which in its view had caused "incalculable harm" to the French press. The Association sued Luce for 5 million francs, and a hearing was scheduled for October.

Hitler and Mussolini had banned Time Inc. from their realms, and Henry Luce was anxious to maintain some toehold on the Continent. *Life*, moreover, was dispatching its own representative to Paris, and the "sewer" imbroglio would not make Sherry Mangan's job any easier. Luce's first reaction was to stand by the *Time* article; now he had second thoughts about this whole affair. He was working for Franco-American solidarity against Hitler, so this was no time for a debilitating quarrel among friends. A somewhat contrite Harry Luce responded to the Association, noting that he had not read the article before it appeared. He almost apologized for *Time*'s broad-brushed attack on French journalism, and promised to be more careful in the future. Counsel for the Association demanded that *Time* publish a stronger retraction. Several days later, however, the French police arrested two French journalists who were supposedly on the German payroll.

The police, according to rumors, had unearthed evidence of alleged treachery while investigating *l'affaire Luce*. Important journalists, including Georges Bidault of *L'Aube*, now rushed to Time Inc.'s defense, and the Association vs. Luce became moot. *Time* then published its clarification, which was really a veiled apology. Still, the affair troubled Luce: a democracy on the brink of war depended on a corrupted press, which sued foreigners who told the truth. Luce revised his opinion of French strength, though he continued to express confidence in France's army.

Wherever he went, Harry Luce tried to stiffen the European backbone. He waxed enthusiastic about America's "super-colossal rearmament." His misleading hyperbole reflected a wish, not reality, for America's army was tiny and ill-equipped. Other misunderstandings marred Luce's visit to potential opponents of the Nazis. When he said something, Harry meant it, and he assumed that his interlocutors were equally sincere. If a Romanian politician said he would fight Hitler, that was that. Luce concluded that the future "allies" had created a front which might deter Hitler from attacking them. He was wrong. Nevertheless, unlike most observers, Harry faced the unimaginable: the Greater German Reich might make a revolutionary deal with the USSR.

Armageddon

Henry Luce arrived back in New York at noon on August 14, 1939, and immediately organized a meeting with his senior editors. In a fighting mood, he insisted that the Poles would resist Nazi demands. Three days later, Luce presided over a luncheon, held in the RCA Building. He boasted about the virtues of Polish nationalism. Clearly, Luce expected too much of Hitler's next victim.

The stunning "Hitler–Stalin" nonaggression pact of August 23, 1939, provided for the partition of much of Eastern Europe into German and Soviet areas of interest. Luce lamely ascribed the treaty to Nazi weakness, when it really represented a brilliant, opportunistic triumph for Hitler. Any power confronting Germany now had to do so without the help of 200 million Soviet citizens. At home, Communists soon joined the ranks of those opposed to aiding Poland, Britain, and France. Not entirely unhappy about this development, Luce could now maneuver to aid democracies, rather than worry about including the Soviet Union in a struggle on behalf of civilized man.

Needing an outlet for his frustration, Luce angrily complained about *Life*'s August 29 cover, which displayed not Hitler or Stalin but the actress Rosalind Russell. *Time* had already printed a million copies of its forthcoming cover, which featured comedian Jack Benny, but Luce soon scrapped him in favor of Winston Churchill, Britain's new First Lord of the Admiralty. *Time* also rushed a special supplement on "The Background for War" into print. The section offered readers some shrewd insights into the looming crisis, predicting, for example, that Italy would stay out of the war, at least for the time being.

On September 1, 1939, German artillery fired across the Polish border, and German planes bombed enemy towns and rail junctions. On September 3 Britain and France declared war on Germany. The Poles, as Luce had predicted, fought valiantly, but the German armies knifed through Poland. President Roosevelt favored the democratic cause, but, as required by law, he proclaimed American neutrality.

Thanks to the crisis, Luce devoted even more time to the editorial side. He resigned as president and chief executive officer of Time Inc., where Roy Larsen assumed the presidency. Luce retained the titles editor in chief and chairman of the board, but he could now concentrate on policy, meaning the war. *Life* published a special war issue on September 25, and by this time it had obtained photos of the Polish campaign. Luce, however, was unhappy with this issue. He felt that *Life* was too easy on Hitler and was overly critical of Britain. As a result, John Billings complained that "Longwell, Luce and Larsen put helping the Allies ahead of keeping the U.S. out of war—" This was probably true, but Billings did not seem to realize that Luce did not object to propaganda, which, after all, had originally meant propagation of the true faith.

In fact, Harry Luce wanted to change the mind of the American people. Most Americans sympathized with the Allies, but fewer than one sixth of those polled would favor going to war even if the Allies were in "real danger of losing." Luce supported repeal of the arms embargo, but at home, life went on pretty much as before. Luce anxiously awaited word from Roosevelt; he craved bold leadership. Instead, the President reassured the nation of his desire to keep war away from these shores. By October, polls indicated that 62 percent of respondents favored repeal. Finally, Roosevelt advocated lifting the arms embargo while endorsing a popular, albeit modest, rearmament program.

Luce expected a long world war, and if the United States languished on the sidelines, its result would be uncertain. Luce hoped that war would unify the American people, and he searched for the requisite words of inspiration. Rarely an admirer of columnist Heywood Broun,

Luce now drew strength from his statement that "This [war] is not a backroom brawl. This is Armageddon."

Like Henry Luce, the new Army Chief of Staff, General George C. Marshall, was struggling against a legacy bequeathed him by twenty years of neglect, disillusionment, and isolation. The magnificent American army of 1918 was a memory, and Marshall's task was a daunting one. On July 1, 1939, the United States Army contained about 174,000 men, scattered throughout the country. The Army had the "framework" for three or so divisions, but only on paper. In training, troops fired rationed rounds of ammunition from the barrels of thirty-four-year-old rifles. They had ancient field artillery and few armored vehicles. On the eve of the war, the U.S. Army still numbered only 210,000 soldiers. On September 8, 1939, Roosevelt authorized a meager increase to 227,000. At the same time, he expanded the National Guard to a potential strength of 235,000. Heavily politicized and lightly armed Guard divisions faced a tough challenge. So did the Army Air Corps, which was outdated and small. As proposed by Roosevelt, the Air Corps would eventually grow to a strength of 5,500 planes. The armed forces also moved to strengthen coastal installations from Newfoundland to Panama. Yet all of this was pitifully inadequate.

George Marshall understood that in a democracy, people needed to see what kind of defense their tax dollars were buying. He knew that *Time* and *Life* reached readers whose support was vital, so the General went out of his way to answer questions posed by Time Inc.'s correspondents. Though not a vain man, General Marshall appreciated Time Inc.'s tributes to his leadership qualities. And Marshall had ensured his stature, in Luce's eyes, by refusing to politicize his job. When *Life*, America's cheerleader, endorsed rearmament, Marshall found that Congress was more receptive to his requests. It was thanks to *Life*, George Marshall claimed, that the Army had gained six months in its campaign to modernize its matériel. Time Inc., which had spent years attempting to sap popular confidence in the New Deal, soon emerged as a powerful supporter of Franklin Roosevelt's chief military planner.

Edward K. Thompson, an Army reservist since 1928, had joined *Life* in 1937. He avidly researched stories that told Americans how the Marines trained their recruits. Thompson used his military connections to great advantage as he constantly investigated new weapons systems. Roy Alexander, who had served in the Marines and was a pilot in the National Guard, had recently accepted a position at *Time*. He, too, gained access to well-placed military and civilian officials, to the benefit of the magazine's editors and readers. Army intelligence (G-2), for example, cooperated with *Time*, which sometimes received secret information.

If the war took a dramatic turn, *Time* would be ready to deal with the latest developments. It now expanded to a record 116 pages, many of them covering war-related issues. And through *Fortune*, Henry Luce made a unilateral truce with the New Deal. Business conditions were certainly improving, though millions of men and women still lacked steady work. A famous Round Table meeting decided that the United States must create more jobs, while safeguarding the "social gains of the past few years." The Round Table also called for the use of both deficit spending and private initiative in the fight against unemployment. Meanwhile, Luce urged cooperation between government, labor, and capital.

For the moment, Harry Luce believed that the democracies were militarily secure. France was still in the field, and *Time* indicated that the "completed" Maginot Line was impregnable. Britain was increasing the strength of her Royal Air Force, too. Then, as the months passed, the Allies seemed to be waging a passive, "phony war." And how could one blockade and starve out a Reich that enjoyed access to the agricultural and mineral riches of Poland and the Ukraine? In January 1940 *Fortune*'s Round Table again convened. A nervous group agreed that a totalitarian victory would threaten America's "political and economic institutions."

While not advocating full repeal of the neutrality laws, the Round Table sought to increase aid to the Allies; it also called for more rearmament, and, quaintly enough, favored paying for it through higher taxation. All present agreed that international trade and free institutions flourished or fell in tandem. In a totalitarian world, even the vast American continent would suffer from restraints placed on its foreign commerce. *Fortune*'s conferees feared a German victory, but they were also prepared to challenge Japan's bid for hegemony in East Asia. The Round Table therefore opposed the sale of strategic materials to Japan, and considered advocating an embargo on all exports to that aggressor.

Fortune posited a grim scenario. If Russia and Japan joined Germany, and the Allies fell, the victorious Reich might seize strategic points that formed a line stretching from Newfoundland to the Bahamas. Fighting alone, the U.S. Navy could not defend all of the Americas, with their far-flung trade routes. *Fortune* then speculated about Axis air attacks on the Americas, a concern that impressed some readers as science fiction. After all, no bombs had leveled German or French cities, much less Canadian ones. Barring a sudden German victory, few Americans feared an invasion. Time Inc.'s articles, however, were trying to prepare readers for an emergency that could arise in the event of a catastrophe in Europe. For most citizens, however, life went on as before, except that a modest war boom revived certain sectors of the economy. Still, people were not enthusiastic about creating jobs through war. Not many men rushed to join the Army, and even fewer taxpayers wished to quadruple its size.

Harry Luce had come to believe that democratic states could not co-exist with totalitarian regimes. Forced in upon itself, an isolated America would become autarchic, militarist, and quasi-totalitarian. In order to forestall such a turn, Luce demanded a two-front effort. Abroad, one must aid the Allies. At home, one must arm, while re-newing the nation's commitment to human liberty and the life of the spirit. In *Time*'s words, if Britain fell, the U.S. alone would remain to "guard the rights of man."

Harry Luce hurriedly wrote to Archibald MacLeish, then Librarian of Congress and a friend and admirer of the President. He wanted MacLeish to intercede with Roosevelt, asking that FDR address a dinner hosted by the Foreign Missions Conference of North America. This occasion, said Luce in all seriousness, was a good time for people to be reminded of the Ten Commandments and of Jesus Christ. FDR asked that MacLeish convey his regrets to Harry Luce. He was "terribly sorry," but he rarely traveled for the purpose of making a speech. The President, however, did agree to speak on the radio in March, to a convocation of the Christian Foreign Service. Leaders of the Conference conveyed their thanks to Luce.

In a powerful editorial in *Fortune*, Henry Luce now called for a re-newal of Christian faith. He demanded that the churches provide "spiri-tual leadership" to a nation out of touch with its mission. Luce spoke scornfully of churches that had asked Americans to die in a war against the Kaiser, but now mouthed pacifist and isolationist pieties. Disillu-sionment with a past war, Luce argued, could not justify neutrality in 1940. A few weeks later, Luce himself called the White House, asking for an appointment with Roosevelt. The President gave him fifteen minutes on very short notice, but Luce did not come away with any great insights. Harry Luce still could not fathom Roosevelt's intentions.

Both men, however, needed each other, so they repaired the frayed ties binding Time Inc. to the White House. Intermediaries played a role here, for Luce admired some of the men around FDR. Archie MacLeish, and through him, Associate Justice Felix Frankfurter, the President's friend and valued adviser, were among Luce's contacts. Harry dined with them, and tried to believe their kind words about the President.

Time Inc. had given Frankfurter highly favorable press notices, and Luce had a wonderful time conversing with this brilliant, canny Supreme Court justice. This was Luce's ideal kind of dinner, since it was filled with intense intellectual discussion. Harry also relished the "inside" political chatter. (A few years earlier, Frankfurter would doubtless have been *Time*'s "Jew Frankfurter," crony of the President.)

During the winter of 1940 little fighting occurred on the Western Front. To most Americans, World War II was a distant conflict, one that might even dissipate for lack of action. Almost alone, the Luce publications demanded that industry adopt wartime production schedules. Aviation, steel, and Allied purchases of war matériel were subjects that dominated *Fortune*'s pages, issue after issue. As *Fortune* showed, there was money to be made through war contracts. Luce preferred a war economy, run by businessmen, to the stagnant economic management associated with the declining New Deal. And he hoped to profit from Britain's economic decline. Thanks to the war, old trading patterns would dissolve, and American entrepreneurs could rush to fill orders formerly served by British exporters. When nay-sayers warned against "overproducing" aircraft, *Fortune* offered the opposite advice to U.S. aviation manufacturers. If America built large numbers of aircraft for the Allies and for itself, "U.S. aircraft makers will be in a position to dominate the world market. . . ."

By February 1940 *Fortune* was talking about the establishment of a *pax americana*, an Atlantic civilization dominated by the United States. *Fortune* was coy about the process leading to this new American order, though it did speak admiringly of the *pax romana*. And the Romans, after all, had conquered much of their empire. Indeed, *Fortune*'s scenarios seemed to cry out for U.S. entry into the war, but the magazine refused to go that far. Luce would decide when to make this call.

In March Franklin Roosevelt (whom *Time* had just anointed as Man of the Decade) delivered a broadcast address to the Christian convocation, wherein he appealed for a just peace, based on brotherhood and freedom. Though he briefly mentioned God, Roosevelt did not speak of Christianity and the just war nor of the Christian basis of a postwar peace. The President said nothing about America's role in molding the peace. Though again disappointed, Luce conveyed his appreciation to Roosevelt.

Clare Boothe, who was traveling about Europe as a *Life* correspondent and author, now provided Harry with depressing information. Clare toured the Maginot Line, and interviewed many military, political, and diplomatic leaders. Her blunt questions antagonized some of these men, for they were not used to such an outspoken woman. The Allies, Mrs. Luce concluded, had no plans for waging war. As Clare traveled about, the Germans were preparing to strike. On April 8 the "phony war" came to a dramatic end, as Nazi air, naval, and land forces attacked Denmark and Norway. Within a few weeks the Germans were poised to expel British forces from Norway. *Time* urged Congress to appropriate almost a billion dollars for America's small army.

When she had departed for Europe, Clare Boothe had not shared Harry's ardent interventionism. She feared that the United States was not ready for war. Now she concluded that Harry was right; America would have to arm, and would again go to war. Clare suggested that Harry come to Europe, where, she said, the "curtain is about to go up on the greatest show the world has ever seen." Her feel for melodrama served her well. At this point Harry received a second summons to Europe, from Ambassador William C. Bullitt. In Bullitt's view, France's hour of trial was dawning.

Luce was unhappy about the cables dispatched to New York by *Time*'s European staff. He felt they lacked punch and provided little guidance. Correspondent Sherry Mangan and Paris bureau chief Del Paine pointed out that French censorship subverted their efforts. Luce wondered what was going on, and decided to see for himself. Miss Thrasher booked his airline tickets, and Harry packed his bags, but bad weather forced him to sail on the Italian luxury liner *Rex*. The publisher, whose schedule included visits to Italy, France, England, Holland, and Belgium, was due to sail home from Genoa on May 18.

On the way over, Luce concentrated his thoughts and wrote them down in a letter to Roy Larsen. He correctly guessed that the Germans might strike anywhere on the Western Front, but would not attack the Maginot Line. Mussolini, Luce added, would soon join Hitler. If the Allies could withstand the imminent attack, Luce wrote, they could win a long war. But Harry also feared that Hitler might soon control the air, then destroy inbound shipping around the British Isles. At that point his forces could invade England. Luce was already thinking about how to assist the Royal Navy. He also cried out for more dynamic Allied leaders and asked that more planes be dispatched to Britain and France.

In his letter to Roy Larsen, Harry Luce concluded that Time Inc. had yet to "realize its tremendous potential power." Perhaps the same was true of Britain. On April 29, 1940, *Life* placed Britain's "warlord," Winston Churchill, on its cover. The hapless Neville Chamberlain, however, remained Prime Minister, while rumors about Allied successes in Norway failed to materialize. Harry Luce became more alarmed as he discussed the crisis with foreign and American officials. On May 2 he cabled an urgent message to New York. Referring to terrible shortcomings in Allied aviation, Harry recommended that the United States sell the democracies two or even three thousand more airplanes.

While Luce feared catastrophe, most Americans seemed oblivious to the danger of an Allied collapse. This was, however, an election year, and Luce hoped that politics might strengthen American willpower. Luce started to ponder the current crop of Republican presidential candidates and what he saw discouraged him. Gallup indicated that 95 percent of Republicans favored an isolationist candidate in 1940. And when the pollster pitted Thomas E. Dewey against FDR, Roosevelt narrowly won. A New York district attorney and "racket buster," Dewey had no foreign policy experience. He tended to avoid controversy in this area, and would presumably cultivate mainstream Republican leaders, most of whom were in favor of neutrality and nonintervention.

On the evening of May 9, Harry and Clare Luce traveled from Holland to Brussels, where Ambassador John Cudahy welcomed them. The Luces were houseguests of the ambassador, who knew that Harry was supposed to interview King Leopold III the next day. After dinner the Luces retired for the evening. While they slept, Ambassador Cudahy learned of the German attack, and telephoned the White House. Before 6 A.M., a maid knocked on the Luces' door. When she entered, the woman excitedly informed them that "*les allemands reviennent!*" The Germans were returning. Clare, who relished drama, observed that "the show has begun." Bombs landed nearby, but neither of the Luces lost their composure. Harry rarely experienced physical fear, and Clare was equally cool under fire. She soon seized her chance to make a grand entry into the forbidden world of *Life*.

Henry Luce headed for the nearest cable office and dispatched historic messages to New York. He could not refrain from commenting that Belgium's foreign policy was based on neutrality, and that Leopold III had tried to isolate his country from the war, with disastrous results. Before the Germans attacked, Belgian officers were not allowed to consult with their British and French counterparts. Too many Americans, Luce argued, had also put their faith in isolation and neutrality, and Hitler was happy with this "impotence of American opinion." He wished that all the "pious pacifists" could be in Belgium, to watch the Germans shatter another peaceful nation. In New York, John Billings read Luce's cables, and even this cool customer became agitated while mulling over their ominous message. He cursed the Germans, who had twice brought war to his world. A bit dazed by it all, Billings now believed that the Allies might lose the war. From luncheon companion Walter Lippmann, who was trying to interpret a world gone mad, Billings heard that twenty years of stupidity had returned to haunt his nation.

Luce approved of President Roosevelt's sharp comments about the latest German aggression. Although he had even hinted that he might support FDR unless the Republicans nominated someone closer to *Time*'s view of things, he now expressed an interest in a candidate who stood at only 5 percent in the polls. Though not a famous national figure, Wendell Lewis Willkie had impressed Luce. For the moment, however, Harry had to report on fast-breaking wartime developments. The Luces hired a car and drove to Paris, where the defeatism of the upper classes appalled them. He did not say so publicly, but Harry feared meeting the same kind of people in New York. When he left France, Luce joked about returning with an American army.

Clare continued to write, and her dispatches were often brilliant. *Life* readers who trusted in neutrality, or isolation, could read Clare's gripping story "Der Tag," which described that unforgettable day, May 10, 1940. Clare vividly depicted a crisis that uprooted and terrified citizens. She understood the politics of defeatism, but she also narrated a very human story, filled with touching scenes. Clare loved to tell the tale of an old Belgian refugee whose cart was pulled by three Flemish sheep dogs. To her, this story proved the ability of the human being to survive when all seemed lost.

On May 20, 1940, Harry Luce flew back to New York on a Pan Am clipper. He had hardly unpacked his bags before summoning senior editors to an evening meeting at the River Club, where he spoke non-stop for three hours. Everyone, Luce noted, had underestimated the striking power of the Nazis. In his desire to awaken the public, Harry soon sought out new allies, such as Kansas journalist William Allen White, a founder of the newly formed Committee to Defend America by Aiding the Allies.

White was an American legend, Republican, independent, and a man possessed of uncommon good sense. His Committee was aware of Luce's views, and knew that Harry had been in Brussels during the onset of the Blitz. White and his colleagues immediately concluded that Time Inc. could greatly assist them. His group offered to acquire radio time if Henry R. Luce would broadcast two addresses within the next week or so. This was a new experience for Luce, and he doubtless worried that he might stammer. Still, the gravity of the situation overcame any qualms he may have felt.

Henry Luce also wanted to write a powerful editorial for *Life*, which would demand that all available help be sent to the faltering Allies. This was, Billings glumly noted, a "dangerous proposal," for one could not predict the reaction of the American people. The crisis in France and Belgium might, after all, reinforce isolationist sentiment rather than undermine it. And some Republicans would certainly try to ride the neutrality issue into the White House. At *Time*, an equally reticent Manfred Gottfried wanted to avoid frightening the nation. Luce over-ruled him, for he saw himself standing before Armageddon. As a reli-gious man, Luce would not have believed that accident alone had accounted for his presence in Brussels.

Luce and the
Willkie Candidacy

On May 22, 1940, Harry Luce sat before a microphone in the studio of radio station WJZ. On a coast-to-coast hookup called the Blue Network, he argued that only *superior* force would stop the aggressors. If Harry was right, then American intervention alone could defeat Hitler. In his heart Luce believed this to be true, but he refused to draw so drastic a conclusion. Instead, he supported the President's efforts to strengthen America's defenses. Even if the Allies prevailed, Luce concluded, they would emerge from this war weaker than before. Only the United States, he said, could then restore "some justice and decency" to a devastated world. Luce demanded that her citizens prepare to fight for the ideals that defined America. In his view, these guiding principles must be freedom, justice, progress, democracy, and brotherhood.

Life grimly warned its readers that Hitler's ambitions might transcend Europe's shores. The magazine painted a scenario in which the poorly armed Western Hemisphere confronted a powerful German Europe. *Life* quickly endorsed Roosevelt's call for a $1.2 billion supplemental defense appropriation. And the President won strong support from Time Inc. when he appealed for the production of 50,000 warplanes a year. Luce complained, however, that democracies rarely fostered the "will to fight." He intended to mobilize Time Inc. as a kind of herald, calling the nation to arms. Billings, Gottfried, and their senior colleagues, who were often reluctant soldiers, soon marched to the beat of Luce's war drums.

Henry Luce repeated a phrase familiar to him since childhood days. We stand at Armageddon, he again declared. Only a few months earlier, these words sounded a bit melodramatic, but no longer. Luce was not referring to some ancient battle; rather, he had in mind the imminent clash between faith and Satan, good and evil. Harry took as his guides the books of Ezekiel, Zechariah, Mark, and Revelation. The false prophets and the beast—perhaps advocates of neutrality, and Adolf Hitler—were arrayed against the Kingdom of Israel. By "Israel," Luce understood the Judeo-Christian fabric of Western civilization, into which man had woven the secular achievements of his culture. Like his Calvinist forebears, Harry Luce saw himself as a modern-day Israelite. And in tomorrow's struggle, God would intervene to save the Israelites from their evil foes. Luce believed that the United States had become the guardian of everything that promised man a decent future. And he had concluded that Nazi tyranny, more than any other evil force, blocked humanity's march toward the Kingdom of Heaven.

Buoyed by the good response to his radio address, Luce convinced himself that Americans were ready to make sacrifices. Harry feared, however, that New Dealers might create an inefficient and highly politicized war machine. To counter such a move, Luce called for the establishment of a competent, nonpartisan, and independent War Industries Board, which would bring the best businessmen to Washington. Yet all this would take time, and Luce was so frustrated that he suddenly became an advocate of premature war. He wanted to publish an editorial in *Life* that would effectively declare war. He would also urge that Americans be allowed to enlist in the Allied armies. The more cautious Roy Larsen felt that Luce's draft was confused, and John Billings argued that a *Life* editorial should be a major event, a "sixteen inch gun" that must never fire wildly.

In Paris, Time Inc.'s operations were in disarray. This was unfortunate, for the company had dispatched five crack photographers to France, including Tom McAvoy and Carl Mydans. The rapidity of the German advance, combined with French military censorship, had sabotaged effective coverage of the front. For the moment, however, the Germans were not heading toward the capital, so Time Inc.'s Paris bureau continued to function. Hoping to improve its coverage, *Life* sent Andrew Heiskell to Paris. Twenty-five years old, and unusually tall, the savvy Heiskell had grown up in Europe and spoke several languages, including French. *Life* hoped that he would be able to lighten the hand of harsh French censors. The young man obtained passage on a flying boat, made his way to neutral Lisbon, then bravely proceeded to Paris. He had little time to carry out his assignment, however, for the German panzers, rushing past and around stunned enemy troops, headed for the Channel. During the last days of May, most of the British Expeditionary Force evacuated the Continent at Dunkirk. The Germans were now routing the encircled Allied armies and might soon strike at Paris.

A few days later, Prime Minister Winston Churchill's stirring words electrified Luce and much of the West. Rejecting any compromise with Hitler, Churchill pledged to fight on until the new world came to the "rescue and the liberation of the old." In an overwrought mood, Henry Luce tried to make another appointment with Roosevelt, telling the White House that the President would want to hear what he had to say. Luce received a positive response, but the exact hour of the meeting was left open. As June 1 neared, Luce asked about the time of his appointment with the President. He needed to know, he explained, because CBS was planning to air his speech on Saturday evening. On Saturday morning press secretary Steve Early informed the press room that "At 11:30 the President" would meet briefly with "Mr. Harry Luce of LIFE, TIME and FORTUNE, who has just returned from Europe." Luce rushed over to the White House, where he saw Roosevelt. As usual, the atmosphere was unpleasant. FDR did most of the talking, and Luce felt that the President was patronizing him, as if he were a Yale "sub-freshman." Luce would not be sidetracked, however. He made his plea for dispatching aircraft to the Allies, and tried to convey a sense of urgency to a concerned but politically cautious President. Roosevelt refused to commit himself to Luce's schemes. Though he, too, admired Winston Churchill, FDR was uncertain about the prospects for British survival. Of course, he tried to flatter and manipulate Luce, for his administration more than ever needed the support of Time Inc. As was his pattern, FDR wanted Luce to help transform public opinion so that Roosevelt would be "forced" to pursue goals to which he was inwardly committed.

Perplexed by Roosevelt's inactivity, Harry Luce again appealed to the American people. He took to the airwaves later that day. Luce spoke in his usual staccato, no-nonsense tone. His speech again elicited favorable reviews. If the Allies lost, Luce warned, Hitler would be our enemy. If Britain survived this challenge, however, Germany would most likely lose the war. Luce called for a pledge that this nation would never accept Hitler's conquests. He advocated the appropriation of billions of dollars in aid to the Allies and appealed for national unity in this hour of crisis. While praising Roosevelt, Luce had kind words for Herbert Hoover, as he lobbied for a kind of coalition government. Within a few weeks the President nominated two Republicans to important positions in his cabinet: Henry L. Stimson (War) and Frank Knox (Navy).

Life now devoted a special issue to "America and the World." Walter Lippmann, whose article dominated the magazine, brushed aside the daily headlines. In his essay Lippmann told Americans what they confronted and how they must respond. Lippmann knew that the Atlantic was a bridge, not a moat. Clichés about avoiding entanglements had paralyzed the nation. The free nations of Europe crumbled, and America now faced powerful enemies. "To our unready and unwilling hands," wrote Lippmann in his grand prose, "there has been confided the task of maintaining a seat of order and of freedom. . . ."

At *Time*, the National Affairs and Foreign News editors rallied around the President, declaring that Roosevelt "spoke for the nation" when he advocated an Allied victory. The trouble was that the June 10 issue of *Time* could not resist alluding to Roosevelt's inability to walk. Though praising him for overcoming a great infirmity, *Time* had again violated a code of silence observed by most of the media. On this same June 10, Benito Mussolini declared war on Britain and France, whereupon a dyspeptic John Billings called him a "jackel," a "vulture," and a "maggot." *Life*, repeating an argument often propounded by Harry Luce, argued that, like it or not, Americans would once again have to field great armies and navies.

In Paris, Sherry Mangan and a small staff prepared to follow the French government as it fled south, toward Tours. The staffers packed their luggage, then crammed it into seven automobiles. Dodging German fighter-bombers, the group eventually reached Tours, just in time for a German air attack. In New York, Billings returned to his penthouse apartment, where he wrote in his diary as if dazed. "We thought France was invincible," Billings noted, then sighed, "Too bad—too bad!"

After finding refuge in southern France, Andy Heiskell and photographer Carl Mydans decided to turn around and cover the sad story of German troops marching into Paris. Harassed by French militia, who thought they might be German spies, Heiskell and Mydans reached a point twelve miles south of Paris. The Germans, however, had already entered the city; so the young journalists abruptly reversed course. They headed south and finally reached the border, eventually arriving in Lisbon. This adventure was symbolic of the enterprise created by Harry Luce. As infuriating as he might be, Luce brought out that last, untapped ounce of energy in his people.

As the French armies crumbled, Luce found reason for hope in the United States. The disaster in Flanders was good for the political fortunes of Wendell Willkie. According to pollster George Gallup, the dark-horse candidate was now the favorite of 29 percent of Republicans polled. This figure represented an enormous leap forward, though Tom Dewey easily led the pack. *Fortune* had discovered Wendell Willkie several years earlier, when this young businessman fought a memorable battle on behalf of the private utilities industry. A big, outgoing man, Willkie's hoosier twang reflected his upbringing in the small town of Elwood, Indiana. The Willkie family revered the great progressive politicians of the day: Theodore Roosevelt, Robert La Follette, and Woodrow Wilson. Willkie, a German-American, staunchly supported the American war effort, and the day after Congress declared war in 1917, the young man enlisted in the Army. After he returned from the war, lawyer Willkie became active in Democratic politics. He was even a delegate to the party's tumultuous 1924 national convention, where the issue of the Ku Klux Klan split the Democrats. Willkie shared Harry Luce's passion for civil rights, and he stalwartly fought the powerful Klan. He also felt that the Republicans had turned their faces away while vast concentrations of economic power undermined the American economy. Willkie thus endorsed FDR in 1932, and donated a small amount of money to his cause.

A co-counsel for Commonwealth & Southern (C&S), the large utilities holding company, Wendell Willkie became its president in January 1933. The new chief executive officer usually supported the early New Deal, though he quickly soured on Roosevelt. Wendell Willkie got into the fight of his life when C&S's subsidiary, the Tennessee Electric Power Co. (TEPCO), fell victim to the New Deal's publicly owned Tennessee Valley Authority. Backed by enormous federal resources, the TVA, Willkie charged, practiced unfair competition. In the ensuing struggle, Willkie lost a battle but won a war. TEPCO went out of business, but TVA officials, in a much publicized photo opportunity, handed Willkie a compensatory check for $78.6 million. This photogenic, principled, articulate businessman was now a celebrity within corporate circles.

During the Depression, the "big" businessman had become a national whipping boy, for some very good reasons. Willkie bid fair to refurbish his image, so Harry Luce and Russell Davenport elevated him to the status of a hero. Here was a businessman, preached *Life*, who wanted to invest $3 billion in a stricken economy. Instead of helping him, or getting out of Willkie's way, the government had frightened off potential investors. Sound on business matters, in favor of civil rights, and no reactionary when it came to social legislation, Wendell Willkie was Luce's answer to the New Deal. Hitler's victories, combined with the efforts of Luce and his operatives, now decreased the odds against Willkie's long-shot candidacy. *Fortune*'s Russell Davenport could provide Willkie with some good rhetoric, while Harry Luce lectured him on the appropriate American response to the crisis in Europe and Asia. Luce, according to some of his close associates, fancied himself a secretary of state.

Fortune, in its survey of the Republican Party, now reserved a high place for Willkie. The party had made impressive gains in the last congressional elections, but the GOP, of course, had not faced Roosevelt back in 1938. Luce and *Fortune* were looking for a man who could make the case against FDR or any successor Democrat. This 1940 candidate would have to avoid splitting the party, while winning the votes of disenchanted Democrats. He must have a strong personality, and a face and voice suited to the picture media and radio. Henry Luce concluded that Willkie could forge a modern, progressive, internationalist Republican Party. Luce encouraged his editors as they publicized Willkie's achievements. Soon, millions of people read a spate of articles about Wendell Willkie. *Time* placed him on its cover, and its article about him was one long profession of love. The forty-seven-year-old Willkie had some problems, too, though neither Luce nor Davenport cared to ponder them. He smoked too much and occasionally took one drink too many. He was overweight, drove himself too hard, and was struggling through a troubled marriage. In time, public adulation became Willkie's narcotic.

Before Hitler's latest Blitz, Henry Luce had offhandedly resigned himself to a Taft or Dewey candidacy. Luce tried to be nice to Senator Robert A. Taft of Ohio, a Yale man, but Bob Taft, hardworking and highly intelligent, still emerged as "dull, prosy, [and] colorless." Though the Senator sometimes courted Luce, Taft made little progress in the pages of *Time* and *Life*. Henry Luce was the first publisher who stuck the "can't win" label on Taft, and the Senator never shook it off, in 1940, 1948, or 1952. Young Tom Dewey, by contrast, had received his share of praise from the Luce publications. In 1936 *Time* even de-

scribed Dewey, who was of average height, as "tall" and "handsome."
The magazine's enthusiasm, however, did not keep pace with Dewey's
ambition.

Back in the autumn of 1938, when Luce badly wanted to crush the
New Dealers, Dewey was running for Governor of New York. A
week before the election, *Life* portrayed him as the "white hope of the
Republican Party," but its article intimated dutiful support rather than
enthusiasm. Tom Dewey lost the hotly contested election, though he
came close to unseating the popular incumbent, Herbert Lehman.
Dewey did not blame *Life* for his defeat, but he was convinced that
Luce and his editors disliked him. By 1940 Thomas E. Dewey was
running for President and leading in the polls. *Time*, though lauding
him for his success in fighting New York crime, again restrained its
ardor. The newsmagazine even repeated a nasty comment that helped
to bury the New Yorker's quadrennial presidential bids: *Time* noted
that people said that you had to know Tom Dewey before you could
dislike him. Cold, methodical, ambitious, a great young racket-buster
in New York City—and totally innocent of foreign policy experience—
this was the Dewey whom Luce presented to millions of Americans.

In April 1940 *Fortune*'s publication of Willkie's famous article "We the
People" had converted its author into a viable, if long-shot candidate.
Davenport wrote most of "We the People," which displayed Willkie's
appealing platform to *Fortune*'s readers. Luce's ideas dominated the
essay, which called for the unshackling of individual initiative. Wendell
Willkie described himself as a civil libertarian, a businessman, and a
crusader against the abuses of the New Deal. He endorsed a policy of
supporting the Allies and cogently outlined the American stake in a free
global economy. Willkie soon made inroads, though Dewey remained
far ahead of him both in the polls and in pledged delegates.

During the spring of 1940, Wendell Willkie assumed the mantle of
those Republicans who accepted much of the New Deal while rejecting
Roosevelt's alleged excesses. Hubert Kay, assigned to write a *Life* story
on Willkie, was unabashedly enthusiastic about his man. Wendell Willkie, said *Life*, was scholarly, witty, and knew how to enjoy himself.
Twenty years later, people came to speak of television candidates. In
the language of 1940, one might say that only two photogenic candidates were *Life* candidates: Wendell L. Willkie and Franklin D. Roosevelt.

Ten days before Hitler struck in the West, Russell Davenport resigned
as managing editor of *Fortune*. As campaign manager, Davenport
worked day and night, in a virtual frenzy, trying to bring about Willkie's nomination. The candidate responded well to Davenport's combi-

nation of enthusiasm and intellect. The new campaign director (Willkie named him the "Zealot") fed the candidate's ego and his ambition. Davenport, however, would ultimately prove to be a disaster as a campaign manager, for he lacked discipline and administrative ability, as did Willkie. For the moment, however, the campaign moved forward.

Henry Luce's doubts about the prodigy Dewey were growing. In this spring of 1940, the racket-buster's heroic assaults on mob figures suddenly seemed like colorful, almost irrelevant anecdotes. Later, wags would describe the humorless Dewey as a casualty of the Second World War, and the joke contained much truth. To most Americans, Hitler, not mobster "Lucky" Luciano, was now Public Enemy No. 1. Prosecutor Thomas E. Dewey, however, was unschooled in foreign affairs and military policy. Just weeks earlier, Dewey's cautious comments about the war crisis sounded like common sense, but now they came across as opportunism compounded by inexperience. The nation's mood was fearful and contradictory, but it was shifting even as Dewey stubbornly stuck to his bland, isolationist generalities. Taft was even worse, at least from Luce's viewpoint. In fact, the Senator forthrightly stated that he preferred a Nazi victory to America's entry into the war. This stand pleased ardent isolationists, but polls showed that rank-and-file Republicans, as well as Democrats, greatly feared Germany.

Throughout the country, affluent young (and not so young) Republicans organized Willkie Clubs, dedicated to their man's nomination and election. The Willkie Clubs arose thanks largely to Oren Root, a twenty-seven-year-old cousin of Henry Luce. Root took copies of Willkie's "We the People" and mailed them to Republican clubs throughout the nation. Though Luce did not know Oren Root, the young man's efforts impressed him. Luce and his magazines now helped to turn the Willkie campaign into a national groundswell. Cynical supporters of Taft and Dewey, bitter about Willkie's growing strength, responded by vilifying Wall Street internationalists for foisting this ex–Democrat on the GOP. Alice Roosevelt Longworth, a Washington hostess known for her sharp tongue and isolationist politics, responded tartly to the Willkie boom. When told that the Willkie Clubs represented the grass roots, she replied, yes, the "grass roots of ten thousand country clubs." Luce bristled at this suggestion, for Willkie, like Taft and Dewey, had grown to manhood in the heartland of the country. The fact remained, though, that Willkie supporters most often lived in suburban places like Westchester and Fairfield counties.

While he mulled over his next move, Henry Luce journeyed to New Haven for his Yale reunion. Everyone there seemed to buttonhole him, for his old classmates thought that Harry must know more than anyone about developments overseas. Luce engaged in lively debates and exchanges, and came home convinced that his generation was a pretty good one. Of course, Harry still found much to criticize in the public's attitudes toward momentous questions of the day. In one poll, for instance, almost two thirds of Gallup's respondents favored some form of conscription. Young men of draft age, however, were evenly divided. Luce ascribed this uncertainty to twenty years of pacifism and disillusionment. Even among the youth, however, the *trend* favored rearmament and conscription. The same momentum now propelled Willkie's candidacy forward. Unfortunately for Luce, the dynamics of world crisis also augured well for Franklin Roosevelt's third run.

Time Inc.'s editorial staff was, like America itself, divided over the issues of war, neutrality, and intervention. Luce, Mitch Davenport, Raymond Buell, Roy Larsen, David Cort, and other interventionists shared a viewpoint alien to many of their senior colleagues. Men of similar age and background found themselves engaged in vitriolic arguments, and old friendships frayed. Politics spoiled many a coffee break and shortened more than a few cocktail hours. Billings and Larsen (though the president of Time Inc. was an interventionist himself) tried to maintain peace in Time Inc.'s offices at Rockefeller Center. Billings never confronted Luce; rather, he smoothed his feathers. Luce never retaliated against those who questioned his advocacy of intervention, for he expected colleagues to speak their minds in editorial meetings. When Noel Busch clashed with Dan Longwell at a luncheon held at the Louis XIV restaurant, Luce enjoyed the spectacle. Reminded that Roosevelt's advisers also fought among themselves, Luce once commented, "Well, you know, that's not all bad."

By June 1940, *Time* and *Life* virtually demanded that Willkie be nominated. Dissatisfied with a *Life* piece on the case for the GOP, Luce curtly informed Billings that he would write it himself. John Billings, ever sensitive to an imagined slight, resented Luce's heavy-handed demands for action. Luce, he growled (privately, of course) should act like a journalist, not a champion of controversial causes. The polls, however, contained good news for both Willkie and Luce. A growing minority of polled respondents did *not* believe that entry into the last war had been a mistake. Americans now feared that Germany might win the war, and almost half of them soon believed that Hitler's defeat was *more important* than the preservation of American neutrality. On the eve of the Republican convention, those who held this opinion were in the majority for the first time. As the convention neared, however, Luce and Davenport still faced an uphill battle against Taft and Dewey. Their Republican supporters did not want to elect an interventionist. And to Luce's horror, the Republicans adopted an isolationist, mealy-mouthed platform. This document contrasted completely with Willkie's candidacy, both in style and substance.

Defying precedent and odds, Wendell Willkie's hardworking campaign supporters packed the galleries at their convention, which met in Philadelphia at the end of June. The anti-Willkie forces were divided among themselves, and demoralized; a discredited foreign policy had gone up in smoke as the German Army forced an armistice on defeated France. Screaming "We want Willkie!," the candidate's enthusiasts cheered the balloting, which eventually resulted in Willkie's nomination. Harry Luce had the time of his life, acting like the political insider he never was, and taking pride in a candidacy hatched by his magazines.

Ecstatic over the Willkie nomination, *Time* discarded any sense of caution. Its National Affairs section read like press releases for a candidate. To *Time*, Willkie was principled, honest, blunt, and a possible winner—even in the South. Willkie, impressed by his own success, began to rely ever more on Luce. Miss Thrasher, Luce's very efficient secretary, always let Willkie come in without an appointment. The candidate then listened carefully to Harry's monologues and accepted most of his advice. Harry and Clare were also raising money for Willkie, and both Luces contributed ideas and phrases to his more important speeches. In addition, Luce soon gave Ray Buell a leave of absence so that Willkie could draw on Buell's vast knowledge of international affairs. Luce himself informed Willkie about China's myriad problems.

In 1939 Luce had launched a new, more strident campaign on China's behalf. His publications repeatedly denounced Japan while demanding more aid for China. *The March of Time* insisted that America fortify Guam, despite Japanese warnings against such a move. *Life* hailed FDR's grant of modest commercial credits to China and supported his decision to embargo the export of certain strategic materials to Japan. Gallup had already reported that 51 percent of polled Americans favored such a course. By the spring of 1940, *Life* depicted an accelerating arms race between the Japanese and American navies. At the same time, the Luce publications continued to underestimate both Japan's strength and her sense of desperation. Gloating that Japan was dependent on the U.S.A. for 56 percent of her "essential war materials," *Life* assumed that an embargo would alter Japanese behavior for the better.

Life constantly professed its faith in China's staying power. Despite such bravado, however, Luce was worried. *Time* was even willing to accept a partial Japanese withdrawal from China, one that would still leave Tokyo in control of Manchuria and five adjacent provinces. Hitler's victories in Europe only increased Luce's apprehension about Asia. He now feared a Japanese attack on mineral-rich European empires in Southeast Asia, and questioned the readiness of the U.S. Pacific Fleet.

Encounters
with the Kennedys

Sometime in June 1940, the Roosevelt White House made a major miscalculation, one that ultimately hurt Luce. Press Secretary Steve Early heard that Henry Luce had called a staff meeting at Time Inc. At that gathering, the top brass of the company had supposedly decided to endorse Roosevelt for a third term. Early and his boss overlooked the publisher's commitment to Wendell Willkie, widely known as "Luce's man," and the White House continued courting Henry Luce. In June, when Roosevelt briefly considered appointing a high-level liaison to the press, Harry Luce's name surfaced. The head of Time Inc. was, however, suspicious of the idea, and nothing came of it. Unfortunately, the false Early/Roosevelt rumor about Luce's political endorsement would soon convince the President that the publisher had double-crossed him.

The White House's fascination with Time Inc.'s growing influence was well founded. Indeed, the Gallup and Roper polls were beginning to reveal a striking pattern. When Luce's publications and movies articulated a *single, coherent message*, the polls reflected changes in public attitudes, usually about four to six weeks after they had launched their propaganda blitz. Time Inc., of course, was but one factor changing

American attitudes toward aid to Britain. Still, if one compares the readership of the Luce press to the circulation of even the largest newspapers, Time Inc. came out way ahead. As for *Time*'s direct competition, *Newsweek* was growing, but it had not yet captured a large share of the newsmagazine market. The *Saturday Evening Post* was traditional and conservative; *Collier's* and *Look* rarely advocated strong foreign policy positions, certainly nothing that compared to the endless interventionist drumbeat pounded out by Luce's magazines. *Life*'s rivals were not edited by missionary types like Davenport and Luce, and their magazines lacked *Life*'s prestige.

Where newspapers were weak or one-sided, *Time* grew strong. Even the *New York Times*, the great newspaper of record, had few outlets beyond the Greater New York area. Nonresidents received the *Times* in the mail several days later, and it was not sold outside New York except at the few newsstands displaying three-day-old out-of-town newspapers. So, the farther one traveled from New York, the more one saw and heard of Time Inc.'s magazines. The Luce press became an influential counter-medium in Chicago and Washington, where the *Tribune* and the *Times-Herald* supported anti-interventionist policies.

Henry Luce controlled a conglomerate. Its influence resembled that of television networks and cable companies in the 1990s, except that the Luce media often followed the same line. And Luce's ideas even reached people who did not read his magazines. Local newspapers, which were often inadequate in peacetime, were incapable of covering the global crisis. Newspaper reporters had long imitated *Time*-style, even as they affected to despise magazine journalism. Now they often repeated *Time*'s version of recent events, and quotations from *Life* and *Fortune* editorials cropped up all the time in America's newspapers. In fact, the *New York Times*' weekly review of the news was itself a tribute to *Time*.

In 1940 Harry Luce was forging new alliances, partnerships that brought him into contact with people who possessed great wealth and power. Luce's allies recruited him as a man who could bring their ideas to the attention of the public. Most of their interventionist cliques consisted of relatively young men, and Luce himself was only forty-two. His colleagues were usually of Anglo-Saxon (or similar) heritage. These men had grown up after the turn of the century, in a prosperous America. Like Luce, his fellow interventionists resented the Japanese or Nazi upstarts as savages who threatened to overturn their secure and reasonably moral world.

Henry Luce's co-workers (to isolationists: co-conspirators) had usually graduated from Ivy League or other elite colleges. Most, but not
all of these men had inherited substantial sums of "old" money. Luce
had not, but he respected those who bore grand names and possessed
substantial wealth. These men were often his social superiors, and their
respect was important to Harry. Henry P. Van Dusen of the Union
Theological Seminary, whom Luce greatly admired, often conferred
with Harry, as did Francis Pickens Miller, a director of the Council on
Foreign Relations. Like Walter Lippmann, these men quickly discovered that Luce could be of unique assistance to their interventionist
network.

Prime Minister Winston Churchill had repeatedly requested the dispatch of overage American destroyers to Britain, but the President,
fearing both American public opinion and a British collapse, refused to
commit himself. *Fortune's* polls only reinforced Roosevelt's caution.
Roper reported that two thirds of his respondents favored giving aid to
the Allies; yet almost as many people opposed entry into the war, under
any circumstances. According to Gallup, a bare majority of Americans
wished to give *more* aid to England, but a plurality of Americans also
believed that Germany would win the war. Fretful over the state of
public opinion, *Time* relentlessly assailed the anti-interventionists. In
fact, never had Harry Luce been so frustrated with a President as now.

Rather than sending the warships to Churchill, FDR emphasized
the Nazi threat to Latin America or Nazi subversion in the Western
Hemisphere. This was very good politics, and the data proved it. In
the summer, *Fortune's* polls showed that 93.6 percent of Roper's respondents were willing to spend until the nation acquired an adequate defense. A majority of Americans also favored the purchase of British and
French colonies in this hemisphere. Roosevelt therefore concluded that
further aid to Britain would have to be sold as a measure vital to
America's hemispheric defense. *Life* promptly fired another round of
salvos. Except for Britain, the magazine observed, the United States
was friendless in the world. If Hitler dominated Europe, the American
way of life was doomed to decay. *Life* told a grim joke: Hitler orders
10,000 new tanks from General Motors. The company asks him for the
delivery address. Never mind, says the *Führer*, we will "pick them up
on our way through Detroit."

On the evening of July 11, 1940, Henry Luce participated in an
important discussion, which was held in a private room at New York's
Columbia Club. Prominent men from several walks of life had assem-

bled to discuss the wartime crisis. Harry and his colleagues quickly agreed that the security of the United States depended on the viability of the British fleet and the British Commonwealth. In order to guarantee England's survival, Luce boldly proposed that the United States grant war loans to Great Britain and dispatch American warships to the waters around England. Both of these measures would have violated various laws, however, so Luce was stymied. Fearing the worst, the current issue of *Time* painted a frightening scenario: in the event of British capitulation, the U.S.A. would have to abandon the Pacific, while its Atlantic fleet faced the combined might of the Axis and former Allied navies.

The public was far more supportive of Luce's proposed humanitarian gestures. *Time* proudly reported that the Justice Department had cut through red tape, thereby "allowing British children to come in as fast as they could be sent." The magazine did not compare this benevolence to the fate of an abortive Senate bill that would have brought 20,000 mainly Jewish children to the U.S.A. That bill, which Roosevelt refused to endorse, had died in committee in 1939, and no one moved to revive it now. Some isolationists, most Nazis, and many anti–Semites claimed ever more loudly that intervention was "Jewish warmongering."

The Columbia Club group was prepared to ship food to Britain in American ships. Luce and his colleagues even mentioned the dread words "under their own convoys if need be." The term "convoy" conjured up images of the 1917 intervention, and was controversial. The Columbia Club group did develop one highly marketable proposal, however. Some of its members were in touch with lawyer Allen W. Dulles, a key figure at the Council of Foreign Relations. Dulles, who argued in favor of U.S. access to British bases and airfields in the Atlantic and the Caribbean, impressed his colleagues, especially Luce. The group also decided that the British government, in return for American assistance, should promise that it "would not surrender the surviving part of [its] fleet to Germany." This plan, however, would come to nought, unless Roosevelt acted on it.

The Columbia Club group therefore suggested that several of its members, including Harry Luce, negotiate with the Roosevelt administration. Given reports of an imminent German assault on the Home Islands, there was little time to lose. On Saturday, July 13, 1940, Luce, accompanied by the Reverend Henry Sloane Coffin, went to see Secretary of State Cordell Hull. The two men did not achieve very much, for Roosevelt alone would decide about the destroyers, and FDR remained silent. Luce also tried to see General George Marshall, but the Chief of Staff, who was usually accessible to Luce's agents, was suddenly unavailable to their boss.

He had good reason to avoid Time Inc. Marshall was doing his best to keep the Army out of the President's reelection calculations. The Democratic convention had not yet "drafted" FDR for a third term, but Marshall knew how the Luce magazines felt about that prospect. Since Luce was reputedly one of the most powerful publishers in the country, and a Republican, Marshall could not afford to be caught in a political crossfire. Luce, undismayed by Marshall's sudden reticence, now planned to take his proposal directly to Roosevelt. He would have to await the conclusion of the Democratic convention, which would presumably renominate Roosevelt on July 15.

The determined Harry Luce felt frustrated. True, the Congress had appropriated billions for defense, much more than FDR had requested. And Willkie, not Taft, was the GOP nominee. People were coming to accept the idea of conscription, and of a large, two-ocean navy. No draft bill had passed the Congress, however, and Luce still denounced the American "phobia" about war. Armed struggle was, he announced, part of life, like pain or pleasure. One must accept the *risks* of war, but sadly, his nation refused to do so. Luce disliked Administration talk of aid measures "short of war," since these soothing words only lulled people into dreaming about risk-free options.

On July 17, 1940, Harry Luce completed a memorandum, which he circulated to all members of his Senior Group. In words that were harsh and unyielding, Luce insisted that America's neighbors to the south behave in a "manner agreeable to us." The same was true, Luce added, of Canada, Greenland, and other areas. Luce favored extending American protection to new regions, in a kind of American-led North Atlantic Alliance system. But where was the leadership? Luce decided that *Life* and *Time* must sound the tocsin of national peril; they must evoke the martial spirit.

By July, Henry Luce had become active in the so-called Century Group. After meeting at the Columbia Club, the group relocated to a building located across the street, hence its name. This small, self-selected coterie of interventionists met fortnightly from July 25 at the prestigious Century Association, a meritocratic men's club located at 11 West 43rd Street, in Manhattan. These men agreed that if Britain fell, America must dominate the seas, and they had no doubt that the United States could achieve this goal. Henry Luce was one of the Group's main conduits to the Roosevelt administration. His power came from his access to the public.

At this juncture, *Life* again turned to the most respected pundit in the country. With Billings' skillful editorial assistance, Walter Lippmann examined the "Economic Consequences of a German Victory." *Life* published the article on July 22, 1940, and in it, Lippmann warned against sirens luring Americans toward dangerous shoals. It was foolish to believe that freedom, as Americans understood it, could survive a totalitarian victory. Lippmann predicted that a Nazi triumph over Britain would enable Berlin, Tokyo, and Moscow to control the flow of world trade. The United States, he said, would become either a dependency of foreign tyrants or a nation existing in a permanent state of siege. Lippmann concluded that American freedom could not survive an Axis victory over Great Britain.

Francis Pickens Miller, a mainstay of the Century Group, was increasingly nervous about Britain's ability to maintain control of the North Atlantic. Miller again asked that Luce alert the nation to Britain's immediate need for fifty destroyers. Luce replied that everything was now up to the President. He did promise, however, that Time Inc. would go all-out in covering the imminent Battle of Britain. Luce now inaugurated an intensified multimedia campaign, one that emphasized America's stake in Britain's survival. His magazines showed that America's defense required U.S. access to strategic bases in the Caribbean region. Combining good text with strong graphics, *Life* offered heavy coverage of strategic defense issues. In July 1940 Major George F. Eliot dominated two issues of *Life*. Aided by striking maps, Eliot argued that a passive defense of the American mainland would lead to disaster. He urged that the United States build or lease military strongpoints in Newfoundland, Greenland, Trinidad, Brazil, and Bermuda.

During these turbulent months in 1940, Harry Luce's relationship with Ambassador Joseph Kennedy played a potentially important if hidden role in the presidential campaign. Harry Luce and Joseph Patrick Kennedy had come to know each other in prewar days. Although the two men invariably disagreed when their discussions turned to foreign policy—Kennedy cared little about China, and dismissed Luce's doubts about Chamberlain and appeasement—other factors drew them together. The ambassador had wealth and power, and Luce was attracted to men who possessed them. Luce admired Kennedy as a hardheaded, blunt-spoken businessman in an Administration larded with anticapitalist New Dealers.

The photogenic Kennedy clan (nine children) had become standard copy in the pages of *Time* and *Life*, even before Luce really knew the *paterfamilias*. *Time* had expressed delight when Roosevelt appointed Kennedy to the chairmanship of the Securities and Exchange Commission. Joseph Kennedy appeared twice on *Time*'s cover, and *Fortune* ran a feature story about his achievements. And *Life* soon became a kind of Kennedy family album. Late in 1937, millions of its readers met a smiling Joe Kennedy, the proud patriarch, surrounded by his wife, Rose, and their large brood of appealing children. Some months later, *Life* managed to contrast the levelheaded Kennedy (a "great Democrat") with the New Dealers who had created the "Roosevelt Depression." *Life* described Kennedy as one of "few efficient businessmen still loyal [to Roosevelt]," and lauded Kennedy's work as chairman of the Maritime Commission. Joe Kennedy was, gushed *Life*, a "dynamic, freckle-faced Boston Irishman" and an able, pragmatic man who served his nation well. And Joseph Kennedy harbored great ambitions for his sons, especially for Joe Jr., a student at Harvard. *Life* could help them launch political careers, and, as Luce later recalled, "Joe Kennedy was not in favor of any of his sons starting at the bottom."

By 1940 Henry Luce was trying to cut a deal with Joseph P. Kennedy. Luce knew from Clare, who had heard it from the Ambassador, that Kennedy was threatening to come home and "endorse the Republican candidate for president." In fact, the Ambassador believed that the recently published *German White Book*, which was based on captured Polish diplomatic documents, proved that FDR had pushed the Allies into war. Luce planned a sensational scenario, which would unfold when the Ambassador returned to the United States. The Luces would meet him at the airport in Queens, take him to the Waldorf for a brief rest, then bring him to a radio studio. Speaking on a nationwide hook-up, Ambassador Kennedy would stun the nation by endorsing Willkie. Rose Kennedy, however, admired the President and thought him to be the most charming man in the world. She believed that Joe would appear to be an ingrate if he turned on the President who had showered high honors upon him. And Kennedy had a loose tongue, so Roosevelt grew suspicious and refused to let the Ambassador visit the United States. The Ambassador seethed, but he stayed in England as that country prepared for a German siege.

During the early summer, polls now showed that Willkie was closing in on Roosevelt. Joseph Kennedy enjoyed high standing among Irish Catholics, a key voting bloc in hotly contested states like Massachusetts, Connecticut, and New York. "Old Joe," however, already knew something that Harry Luce would later learn. Franklin D. Roosevelt was a powerful, jealous, and sometimes vengeful political personality. The Ambassador's far-flung, multifarious business enterprises mandated good relations with Roosevelt and his federal regulators. On the other hand, Kennedy had heard about Luce's virtual creation of the Willkie candidacy, and that was something to be pondered. Joseph Kennedy knew what the Luce publications had done for him, and was aware of their importance to the futures of Joe Jr. and young Jack.

During the winter of 1940, John Fitzgerald Kennedy, a senior at Harvard, was trying to answer a question that bedeviled much of the Western world. Could a democracy, which loved peace, prepare for war? John F. "Jack" Kennedy proposed to write a senior thesis, as required of students wishing to graduate with honors in political science. Instead of blaming the discredited Neville Chamberlain and his appeasement policy, Jack Kennedy wrote a long senior thesis that tried to explain why Munich happened.

This intelligent and well-read young man, thin and frail but gifted with a marvelous smile, now emerged as the author of a controversial and remarkably subtle thesis. Assisted by five stenographers, Jack Kennedy rushed to complete his paper by the deadline, March 15, 1940. He produced a work twice as long as the average thesis, and young Kennedy's faculty readers divided over the virtues of "Appeasement at Munich." The committee described the thesis as "badly written," though it also found it "interesting and intelligent." Ultimately, the faculty readers awarded the thesis the designation *cum laude plus*.

The young man's great strength lay clearly in analysis, not narrative. Jack Kennedy's work rejected ideology, as well as emotion, and the thesis was neither profascist nor antifascist. John Kennedy skillfully examined trends in British politics and public opinion. Pacifism was widely in vogue, and until late in the 1930s the Labour Party opposed most rearmament measures. The Tories, too, favored budget cuts, except for funds earmarked for the Royal Navy. And despite revulsion against the persecution of the Jews and other Nazi atrocities, the British public was not ready to rearm. People advocated collective security without wanting to pay for it. Politicians, Jack Kennedy wrote, therefore gave the nation what it wanted, which was peace, very modest rearmament, and frequent reassurances.

The result of British weakness was the Munich conference, which perpetuated the illusion of peace. Of course, Ambassador Kennedy admired his good friend Neville Chamberlain, and Jack was not anxious to embarrass his father. Appeasement, John F. Kennedy concluded, bought time for rearmament. As he put it, Munich had been "the price [the British government] had to pay for the year of grace." As appeasement, however, fell victim to new aggressions, England be-stirred herself.

One could argue that the author had blamed democracy itself for Britain's lack of preparedness. Certainly, John F. Kennedy concluded that only imminent danger could rouse a democracy out of its lethargy. More importantly, Jack Kennedy drew some lessons for Americans to ponder. Democracies, he concluded, must be willing to demand sacrifices, even as they strove to maintain their high standard of living. Toward the end of his thesis, Jack Kennedy speculated about the future. If Hitler conquered the Allies, he wrote, Americans, though protected in some measure by the ocean, would have to duplicate the sacrifices being made by Britons. Americans, however, might not have as much time to prepare for war. Kennedy's premonition of impending disaster was on the mark.

Joseph Kennedy had been closely watching son Jack's progress. Am-bitious for his boy, the Ambassador decided that Jack should publish his thesis. A quality book, he wrote, "really makes the grade with high-class people [and] stands you in good stead for years to come." Following his father's advice, Jack Kennedy sought the counsel of the powerful *New York Times* columnist Arthur Krock, who agreed to read the thesis. Krock liked the work and recommended publication. He suggested that Kennedy call the book *Why England Slept*, a sort of play on Churchill's volume of speeches, *While England Slept*. The Ambassa-dor proudly showed the typescript to friends in London. He even hired an editor to go over Jack's copy. Arthur Krock subsequently told young Kennedy to rewrite the book, which he agreed to do.

It was not easy to find a publisher, however. Harper & Row rejected *Why England Slept* because its editorial board believed that the stupen-dous events in France had overtaken the book. Wilfred Funk, Inc., however, decided otherwise. Impressed by young Kennedy's manu-script and by his powerful sponsors, Funk planned to rush the book into print. *Why England Slept* might be available in the bookstores by midsummer.

In July 1940 Ambassador Kennedy called Henry Luce from London, asking him to write a foreword to Jack's book. Arthur Krock resented this slight, but Joe Kennedy felt that Luce could do more for Jack. Harry Luce duly read the galley proofs and agreed to write the fore-word. When Jack Kennedy later made the rounds, promoting *Why England Slept*, he found that Henry Luce's name opened doors. Review-ers often mentioned Luce's foreword to the book or quoted parts of it. And as he toured the nation, the personable young man with the Har-vard/Boston accent veered closer to Luce's positions.

The
Ramparts We Watch

At Time Inc., a monumental film was in production. Louis de Rochemont's March of Time unit would soon release *The Ramparts We Watch*, which represented Harry Luce's most vehement attack on cynicism and isolation. De Rochemont began thinking about this kind of movie in December 1938 as the Munich-cobbled "peace" began to turn sour. Those prepared to endorse the project included some of FDR's favorite collaborators. Librarian of Congress Archibald MacLeish blamed the pathetic state of American preparedness on two decades of disillusionment. Too many young people, he argued, had found nothing worth fighting for. Robert Sherwood, a distinguished playwright and occasional speechwriter for FDR, concurred.

While France fell, de Rochemont's people hurriedly edited *The Ramparts We Watch*. Luce's latest appeal for the Allied cause would be released as German honor guards goose-stepped through the streets of Paris. By this time, the usually calm Roy Larsen talked of little besides *The Ramparts We Watch*. Roosevelt, who had often requested copies of the *March of Time* documentaries, realized that powerful film propaganda could change public attitudes, and he never underestimated the impact of Harry Luce's productions.

The Ramparts We Watch was sure to provoke controversy, which film moguls disliked (Jack Warner had supposedly said that if he wanted to send a message, he'd use Western Union). Many of these Hollywood studio owners and producers were Jewish, however, and Hitler's victories confronted them with a challenge that could no longer be evaded. In addition, film producers feared federal intervention, not in Europe, but in their own business affairs. Roosevelt might well win a third term, so movie magnates and theater-chain owners were more receptive to feature films that sent a message favorable to the President's policies. Meanwhile, the publicity campaign for naval aid to Britain, in which Luce was so active, had succeeded.

A *Fortune* poll, which Elmo Roper shared with the White House, indicated that 70.2 percent of the nation favored the dispatch of the destroyers to Britain. Roosevelt carefully studied the polling data. He remained silent on the subject of those warships, however, despite Churchill's ever more urgent entreaties. Columnist Joseph Alsop, like Harry Luce, worried that the U.S. warships would arrive in Britain too late or not at all. Alsop therefore decided to visit his friend Interior Secretary Harold Ickes, who was an ardent interventionist. Harry Luce, Alsop told the Secretary, wanted to talk to the President, immediately. Ickes called Hyde Park that same evening, only to discover that Luce had already made an appointment. Among other things, Harry Luce was thinking about a movie that might interest the White House.

The President was indeed anxious to see the movie, which was scheduled to open in Washington on July 23, 1940. FDR therefore decided to invite the people responsible for *The Ramparts We Watch* to the White House, where everyone would enjoy a private screening. The guests included de Rochemont, Roy Larsen, and Luce, along with their spouses. Afterward, FDR would speak privately with Harry Luce. On July 25 the Luces flew to Washington as representatives of a powerful group of interventionists.* Still, Harry came away disappointed. FDR seemed to solicit support both for the destroyer deal and for his own campaign, but he refused to commit himself to anything in return. The next day Luce called on Lord Lothian, the British Ambassador, as well as Frank Knox, the Secretary of the Navy, and discussed the destroyer

---

*See Chapter One for a more detailed description of Luce's encounter with Roosevelt on July 25.

question with both men. In his conversation with Lothian, he complained that Roosevelt's attitude was not encouraging. Harry mentioned the possibility of having Canada, a belligerent power, request the destroyers. Although he disliked this kind of subterfuge, Roosevelt's hesitancy left him grasping at straws.

Luce did not intend to remain on the sidelines, however. He now emerged as the coordinator of a press and radio campaign on behalf of the destroyer project. The publisher mobilized leading commentators and columnists, such as Joseph Alsop, Mark Sullivan, Raymond G. Swing, and Elmer Davis. At the same time, Time Inc.'s magazines, movies, newsreels, documentaries, supplements, and school materials argued the case for national selective service. *Life*, for example, wrote approvingly of the proposed draft of 400,000 young men, and the magazine lauded those Americans who crossed the border in order to join Canadian regiments fighting Hitler. Elmo Roper, polling for *Fortune*, now showed that the public accepted conscription by growing margins.

At this point Harry Luce received troubling counsel from a valued associate. The usually optimistic Dan Longwell expressed his belief that England would probably lose the war. At about the same time, President Roy Larsen gave Luce some pessimistic advice about the war's probable impact on Time Inc. Larsen believed that the signs of a war boom were misleading. Time Inc., he wrote, might have to tighten its belt as profits decreased and good people left the company to work for the government. Their departure would deprive the company of needed personnel, and dim Time Inc.'s financial prospects. Adding to all this gloom was Luce's concern about governmental mismanagement of the economy. Implicitly, both Longwell and Larsen were advising caution and retrenchment. The idea of retreat, however, was incompatible with Henry Luce's character and anathema to his global messianism. As a result, his magazines and motion pictures reflected neither Longwell's pessimism nor Larsen's caution.

In August *The Ramparts We Watch* opened in theaters throughout the nation. The film glorified the 1917–1918 war effort, in a stoutly nonpartisan manner. The film showed an old photograph of Wendell Willkie, who had joined the Army and served in 1918 as a second lieutenant. Then *The Ramparts We Watch* used footage of Assistant Secretary of the Navy Franklin D. Roosevelt visiting the Western Front late in 1918. In its last scene, *Ramparts* suddenly switched from 1918 to the present. A fifth column, intoned the narrator, was undermining America, but strong men like candidates Willkie and Roosevelt—now shown in scenes from 1940 newsreels—were uniting the nation in support of freedom.

Insofar as the film made audiences aware of the need to defend democracy against cynicism and isolation, *Ramparts* did its job. The movie pleased the interventionist *New York Post*, which likened *Ramparts* to an old tune that "sounds better, more convincing, than during the skeptical years." Not everyone agreed. Historian Charles A. Beard criticized the film's historical inaccuracies. *Ramparts*, for example, failed to depict the widespread hostility to intervention, and it ignored "lynch propaganda" directed against German-Americans in 1917. Isolationists, encouraged by the presence of a prestigious ally like Beard, launched a broad counterattack against *The Ramparts We Watch*. Otis Ferguson, film critic for the influential *New Republic*, described the movie as a "stinking little tent show," and "smooth as oil." The film, charged Ferguson, employed "high and noble emotions" to sell a discredited cause, intervention. The *New York World-Telegram* attacked *The Ramparts We Watch* for its "emotional hysteria" and labeled it "flagrant pleas for our entry into World War II." The newspaper was right on both counts.

The Ramparts We Watch received publicity boosts from two unlikely sources. The pro-Nazi *Amerikadeutscher Volksbund* (the "Bund") threatened to disrupt showings of the movie, thus making decent people more sympathetic to it. Diplomat/propagandist Ulrich von Gienanth snarled that "Germany is not a small country and she will not permit such things to be done to her." His embassy denounced the March of Time for using "pirated" footage from the Nazi propaganda film *Baptism of Fire*. Von Gienanth threatened a lawsuit, but soon dropped the whole matter, presumably because he understood that his statements were grist for the interventionist propaganda mill.

The Pennsylvania Board of Censors, however, banned part of the film's last reel, which contained bombing scenes taken from *Baptism of Fire*. Fearing the movie's "terrifying effect on the masses," the board lectured producer de Rochemont on his duty to the nation. "The thing you are doing," replied de Rochemont, "is promoting appeasement— surrendering to fear—the most dangerous thing facing America today." Unmoved, the board decided that the last scenes of the film clashed with "the American way of life." In all, however, *The Ramparts We Watch* was a mixed blessing for Luce's cause. The sentimental movie stoked the embers of idealism, played up conscription, and attacked Germany, which was all to the good, but *The Ramparts We Watch* never appealed to a mass audience.

★ ★ ★

John F. Kennedy's *Why England Slept* had appeared in bookstores in late July and August 1940, and by October it was selling well. The young author graciously presented Harry Luce with an autographed copy. In his foreword to the book, Luce had overlooked certain uncongenial aspects of *Why England Slept*. Kennedy's work, for example, did not take a stand on aiding Britain. In his foreword, and through other promotions, Luce converted Jack Kennedy's ambiguous book into a stirring appeal for rearmament and intervention.

Dan Longwell exaggerated when he boasted that "TIME and LIFE are the two most important book mediums in the country." Yet Kennedy owed much to Henry Luce. Luce later reviewed *Why England Slept* and heavily promoted it. His foreword ("no mean appraiser of young genius") caught the eye of the *New York Times Book Review*. The result was a long "rave" review, the kind that launches best-sellers. *Time*, referring to Jack as the son of "philoprogenitive" Joseph Kennedy, praised the book as "timely" and "objective." *Why England Slept* sold 40,000 copies in the United States, thanks in substantial measure to a large number ordered by Joseph P. Kennedy.

In early September the prospects for the Burke-Wadsworth conscription bill suddenly improved, especially after Roosevelt, then Willkie, endorsed it. *Time* now circulated a special brochure, which again promoted selective service. The supplement defined service as a national obligation, irrespective of one's social class. And as if to illustrate the terrible alternative to full mobilization, *Life* published excerpts from Clare Luce's brilliant new book, *Europe in the Spring*. This sad, incisive portrait of European lassitude, decadence, and defeat sounded a warning that Americans ignored at their own peril.

When Harry Luce was crusading for one of his cherished causes, however, he was subject to delusions. In the middle of the summer he convinced himself that Wendell Willkie could defeat Franklin Roosevelt. True, *Fortune*'s August survey showed Willkie trailing Roosevelt by a mere 2.5 percent, a figure that fell within the margin of polling error. The campaign had not yet begun, however, and in this time of crisis, Roosevelt, of all presidents, would doubtless be resourceful. Moreover, Luce's zeal blinded him to his candidate's defects and caused him to ignore Roosevelt's virtues. Luce forgave Willkie when he began to pander to Republican antiwar sentiment. And he would not admit that FDR's "dilatory tactics" had met their equal in Willkie's confused and opportunistic lurchings. He defended his man, though after Willkie lost, Luce retroactively condemned his appeal to the peace constituency. The candidate was indeed trying to mollify the isolationists, with very limited success. In contrast to Willkie, Roosevelt could speak for most of his party when addressing the issue of aid for Britain. The conservative South, though often cool to elements of the New Deal, overwhelmingly supported Roosevelt's foreign policy and defense initiatives. If Willkie, on the other hand, could not unite his own party in a time of international crisis, how could he unify the nation?

In the middle of August, the Luftwaffe assaulted the Royal Air Force and its bases. Putting doubts aside, *Life* was the first major magazine to place its faith in the RAF's prowess. The interventionist press, led by the Luce media, soon felt vindicated by events. Without prior congressional approval, Roosevelt announced on September 3, 1940, that the United States would send those fifty old destroyers to Britain. This deal, of course, represented the outcome of a proposal advanced by Henry Luce and his Century Group.

The dispatch of the ships shored up British morale, and in the process, the United States acquired access to a vital number of bases, port facilities, and airfields. *Time* described this boon as equivalent to obtaining 2,500 new warplanes. *Life* credited Roosevelt with a "bold stroke," one for which it had been agitating since July 15. *Life* even congratulated FDR for doing an "excellent job" of educating the nation about the danger confronting the United States.

Privately, Harry Luce gave all the credit for the destroyer deal to Wendell Willkie—and none to Roosevelt. In September *Time* praised Willkie for refusing to pander to isolationists, an accolade that proved premature. Nevertheless, Willkie soon criticized Roosevelt for circumventing the Congress in a high-handed, perhaps dictatorial manner. Harry Luce now pouted that "I want nothing more done for Britain on the personal and exclusive authority of Franklin D. Roosevelt."

Most Americans, however, believed that the President had acted in a manner appropriate to the crisis at hand. Many observers had claimed that no president would institute peacetime conscription during a political campaign. FDR's signing of the Burke-Wadsworth bill two weeks later again confounded his critics. Although firmly behind Willkie, Luce still needed to collaborate with Roosevelt on behalf of aid to Britain and the full wartime mobilization of the economy. FDR, after all, would be president for the next four months.

Fighting Roosevelt

Recent successes in his struggles for the Willkie nomination, the destroyer deal, and conscription contributed to Harry Luce's increasing optimism. He ardently believed that Willkie, guided by *Fortune*'s Mitch Davenport, would somehow transform the GOP into an interventionist party. Certainly, Willkie sometimes uttered words that justified Harry Luce's pride of authorship. Speaking in Madison Square Garden toward the end of a grueling campaign, Willkie strongly advocated racial equality. There, and on other occasions, he even uttered words usually avoided by national politicians—like "Christian and Jew," "Negro and white." Harry, who was committed to civil rights, was moved. To Luce, Willkie's campaign was a crusade, not a news story. Time Inc.'s Charles Stillman and John Martin contributed to Willkie's speeches, which Mitch Davenport rewrote and the candidate delivered.

Unfortunately, the early euphoria generated by Willkie's crusade quickly dissipated. Russell Davenport was meant to be an editor, political philosopher, and poet, not a campaign director. Willkie was irrepressible and unpredictable; in fact, he was unmanageable. The candidate seemed buoyed by the size and enthusiasm of the roaring crowds; he sometimes sounded as if he were trying to shout his way into the White House. The Willkie campaign train was unusually chaotic, cramped, and grubby. In this late summer and early autumn of 1940, Time Incers aboard Willkie's train cabled blunt stories to Tom Matthews, *Time*'s National Affairs editor. Matthews, though a Willkie man, was an independent-minded editor, and harbored traditional notions of fairness and objectivity. Some jarring notes began to sound, and they annoyed Harry Luce. Reporters disgusted with *Time*'s puff pieces on Willkie were in revolt.

In September *Time* published a big story. The widely cited piece depicted the Willkie/Luce "Crusade for Free Men in a Free Land" as a fallible political campaign, perhaps a fiasco. *Time* described the fetid atmosphere aboard the campaign train, where reporters drank and played cards. Meanwhile, Willkie was shouting himself hoarse, as his standing in the polls deteriorated. *Time* mused that events would tell whether Willkie was presidential material, instead of a "fatter, louder Alf Landon." Cynical reporters, reminded of Willkie's impressive crowds, laughed at Bob Sherrod's rejoinder, as printed in *Time*: Yes, people came from miles around to see Willkie, but they would also come to stare if a dead whale, lying on a flatcar, rolled into town. Felix Belair, *Time*'s new Washington bureau chief, informed Luce of the favorable reaction to *Time*'s objective coverage. This praise did nothing to mollify Luce, who disliked what he had read. Harry Luce longed for victory, not impartiality.

Luce contacted Manfred Gottfried and Tom Matthews, urgently trying to redirect *Time*'s coverage of his candidate. He even went over the heads of his editors to writers who worked for National Affairs. This ploy irritated the usually placid Gottfried, who told Luce to lay off or edit the department himself. Luce then called Tom Matthews on a Wednesday, berating him for *Time*'s terrible slights. An angry Matthews explained that Wednesday was his day of rest, between long days and nights of preparing *Time* for the printers. If Luce ever again disturbed him on Wednesday, Matthews would quit. Harry later apologized, and felt like "crawling into a hole." He remained bitter, however, for Luce felt betrayed by his flagship magazine. Still, he did not like to give orders. Luce hoped that his editors would see the light.

The editor in chief strongly "suggested" that his editors pay attention to issues other than Willkie's sore throat and campaign foibles. Harry proposed that *Time* devote more coverage to the third-term issue and to Roosevelt's inadequacies in foreign policy. The war, Luce argued, demonstrated that FDR had saddled the country with a paltry defense structure. Luce became even more generous with his advice. He wanted

Time to blast Roosevelt for his ties to the urban political machines. Luce also suggested that *Time*'s campaign coverage include the names of prominent people who had endorsed Willkie. Some of these ideas bore fruit in the magazine, but *Time*'s enthusiasm seemed muted. *Life*, however, was more accommodating, thanks to John Billings. The managing editor rewrote Willkie speeches so that *Life* could build articles and short pieces around them. *Life* (which still lacked a formal editorial page) clearly supported Willkie, but it, too, occasionally suffered from the kind of objectivity that so infuriated Luce. *Life*, for example, reported that Willkie was losing his voice, and was enmeshed in a sadly amateurish campaign. To make things worse, Henry Luce received an appreciative telegram from Henry A. Wallace, Roosevelt's vice-presidential candidate, thanking Luce for the fairness of his publications.

Luce did everything he could to save Wendell Willkie. He tried his hand at major campaign speeches; he raised money; and he agitated among his friends, colleagues, and acquaintances. It was all in vain. Willkie, having sampled the wine of victory, now tried to drain the whole cup. He desperately accused Roosevelt of dictatorial ambitions, appeasement, and warmongering. The charges all aired within a few weeks, and the candidate ignored their contradictory implications. Luce was no model of consistency, either. Undeterred by the facts, he argued that Willkie had done more for defense and national unity than any man in the United States. He berated Roosevelt for his "delay and dilatory tactics," but also argued that FDR's perceived "overeagerness for war" undermined his ability to lead the nation. Henry Luce concluded that Roosevelt was lying, that he "as much as admitted that to me in private conversation." In other words, FDR knew that America would somehow become involved in a shooting war. It is doubtful, however, if the President "lied" to Harry Luce. Instead, he probably foresaw the possibility of war, but preferred to avoid it, so long as other powers could destroy Hitler and contain Japan.

The White House played politics with enormous skill, and FDR managed to stay in the interventionist mainstream. He talked about aid to Britain short of war and told the nation that this assistance would help to keep the war away from American shores. Germany might yet win the war, but, as *Time* showed week after week, Hitler's victory was no longer certain. Americans listened to the rich voice of Edward R. Murrow, who broadcast from defiant London. "England can take it" became a widespread conviction, and *Time* speculated that Churchill might be the greatest Prime Minister in British history. To Walter Lippmann, and to many other interventionists, Willkie had picked the worst time to accuse Roosevelt of warmongering. And if FDR helped Britain, and she survived the Nazi onslaught, who needed Willkie? Lippmann shocked Harry Luce further by endorsing Roosevelt. Willkie, Lippmann concluded, was pandering to isolationist sentiment.

In a preelection article published by *Fortune*, Russell Davenport eloquently laid out the case for Willkie. To Luce's annoyance, editor John Chamberlain proceeded to make a powerful counterargument on behalf of Roosevelt. Like many isolationists, Chamberlain supported a stronger defense for the nation, and he had concluded that Roosevelt would be more effective in "pushing rearmament." For the first time in weeks, however, *Time* pleased Luce as it listed his "good reasons" for supporting Willkie. Willkie, *Time* observed, was not allied with machine bosses like Ed Flynn and Frank Hague. Nonetheless, *Time* showed that Roosevelt was again gaining in the polls and would probably receive as many as 500 electoral votes.

Some of the most famous and admired women in America—Eleanor Roosevelt, Clare Luce, Dorothy Thompson, and Anne Lindbergh—were soon caught up in the political debate about war, peace, and foreign policy. Thompson, a highly influential syndicated columnist, now hammered another nail into Wendell Willkie's coffin. Like Lippmann, she had come to prefer Roosevelt out of fear of Republican isolationism. Second only to Luce in its enthusiasm for Willkie, her employer, the *New York Herald Tribune* refused to renew Thompson's contract when it expired some months later. Her apostasy also enraged Clare Luce, who decided to debate her. The two women had worked together on behalf of Willkie's nomination, and Clare, as always, took the slight personally. Her good friend Bernard Baruch paid for the much publicized radio broadcast. As debaters, the two women were evenly matched. Clare, however, remained angry. Speaking for the United Republican Finance Committee, she attacked Thompson in her nastiest speech of the campaign. Clare concocted a kind of play, explaining Thompson's political choice by imputing it to hysteria, anxiety, and fear.

Clare changed her mood as often as she embarked on new adventures. After the debate she sent a gracious cable to Thompson, and the two women resumed their friendship. Clare resented the fact that the sexist press had turned their political exchange into a kind of feline confrontation, but who could blame the newspapers? Clare's own language had long provided observers with generous amounts of vituperation. Indeed, her behavior during the campaign only contributed to Franklin Roosevelt's growing contempt for Harry Luce. By contrast, the President later went out of his way to recognize Dorothy Thompson's great service in "arousing all Americans to the necessity of eternal vigilance. . . ."

Ever the cynic, John Billings concluded that Harry's wife was much like Dorothy Thompson—"except that Clare has smaller breasts to beat in public."

Though Clare Luce failed to save Willkie, she did acquire a taste for a new kind of performance. At the pinnacle of her career as a playwright, Clare was turning to a new pursuit, politics. The publication of *Europe in the Spring* made Clare a famous author as well as a public polemicist. In this incarnation, she had embarked on her third or fourth career, depending on how (and what) one counted. Clare seemed to derive pleasure from attacking equally famous women whose views had antagonized Harry. Luce would not launch these sorties, for it would be ungentlemanly to ridicule a woman. So it was Clare Boothe who now readied herself for a political offensive against Anne Morrow Lindbergh, author of *The Wave of the Future*. This little best-seller advocated a modus vivendi with the totalitarian and Fascist regimes that threatened the democracies. Clare Luce counterattacked, and then returned to her flamboyant work on behalf of the Republican ticket.

Clare Luce's advocacy of Willkie failed to convert Elizabeth R. Luce, Harry's mother. Mrs. Luce admired Roosevelt and voted for him in 1940. In fact, Mrs. Luce, who resented Clare's marriage to Harry, went out of her way to defend Dorothy Thompson. She wrote to the columnist, applauding Thompson's endorsement of Roosevelt. The journalist replied to Mrs. Luce, expressing her outrage over being attacked "by a woman whom one has liked and admired and consistently defended against her catty women 'friends'—I am talking about Harry's wife, Clare—. . ." The columnist, tired and angry, expressed the wish that Mrs. Luce might convince her "powerful son" that a vote for Willkie was a vote for fascism. Thompson concluded with a melodramatic touch, describing how she prayed on her knees every night, that "it" [fascism/Willkie] would fail in America.

The Luces had done their best for Willkie. They had provided his campaign with the maximum allowed under the Hatch Act, $14,700— in 1990s dollars well over $100,000. The campaign ground toward its end, but the Luces believed that a dramatic gesture could still turn the tide.

For months the Luce duo had awaited the return of Ambassador Kennedy, who might articulate the case for a change. Joseph Kennedy was angry at Roosevelt and his advisers, who had leaked derogatory material about him to the media. *Time*, by contrast, was ready to forgive Kennedy for expressing doubts about Britain's ability to survive. Harry Luce, encouraged by Kennedy's indiscreet and highly negative comments about FDR, anxiously awaited the Ambassador's arrival in New York. Toward the end of the campaign, the Ambassador finally arrived home, expecting to be caught up in all the last-minute, anxious politicking. When he arrived, however, Kennedy was greeted by Administration officials bearing letters from the White House. The Ambassador, Roosevelt had decreed, was to proceed to Washington and issue no statement before conferring with the President. While Joe and Rose Kennedy flew to Washington, the Luces impatiently awaited word from their purloined ambassador. The isolationalist America Firsters, FDR, and Willkie (through Luce) were all engaged in a struggle for the political soul of Joseph Patrick Kennedy. In the White House, President Roosevelt worked on the Kennedys, and he knew which buttons to press. The Ambassador was a man with widespread business interests, and he did not want to antagonize the Administration.

In a highly effective radio broadcast, Joseph Kennedy soon endorsed Roosevelt for reelection, citing the President's experience, *dedication to peace,* and effectiveness as reasons for his decision. The Luces were shocked. Not until 1956 would Clare know something else, which Joe Kennedy confided to her: Roosevelt had agreed to support Joseph Kennedy, Jr., for governor of Massachusetts. The President, boosted by Kennedy's support, now promised Bostonians and all Americans that he would not send their boys to fight in foreign wars. To Luce, this was an outright lie, but the die was cast. Roosevelt was the safe choice, as Kennedy had shown. On the eve of the election, Justice Frankfurter, whom Luce so admired, penned a note to FDR. He defined Roosevelt's historic mission as working to "make our beloved country continue to be effective and aggressive on the side of civilization."

As for Willkie, "The train rolled on," in *Time*'s playful phrase. The GOP candidate received a decent popular vote, but in the electoral college, FDR won by a landslide. Harry Luce failed to take pride in *Fortune*'s polling, though Roper came within 0.6 percent of predicting the popular vote. Luce was crushed, and he now convinced himself that Willkie should have risked a greater defeat by admitting that Americans *would*—and perhaps *should* (after appropriate national debate)—go to war. In an eloquent statement, gracious except for its omission of the winner's name, Luce praised the work of his staffers. He called for national unity and a frank discussion of the grave issues confronting the nation. *Life* again proposed that business, labor, and government work

together on behalf of national defense. *Life* agreed that the election had
ratified the New Deal, but also concluded that it was time for Roosevelt
to stop attacking big business.

If Luce believed that his magazines had been too friendly to the
Democrats, an unimpeachable source was about to be set him straight.
Many of Time Inc.'s alleged campaign sins had aggravated the White
House. Press Secretary Steve Early, for example, charged that Luce and
Davenport had suppressed a *Fortune* poll that gave FDR 56 percent of the
straw vote. "Believing in the general objectivity of your publications,"
Early coyly added, "I would greatly appreciate word from you regard-
ing these reports." The charge failed to impress Luce. Most likely it
was intended as a warning to Time Inc., at the beginning of the stretch
drive. A short time later, *Time*'s "election special" infuriated Franklin
Roosevelt, and a couple of weeks after the election, FDR decided to
reprimand Luce.

Time's "election extra" story described election night at Roosevelt's
Hyde Park home. Based on copy filed by Felix Belair, it exuded smugness. In a draft letter to Henry Luce, President Roosevelt released his
pent-up rage, made worse by seven years of reading *Time*'s account of
his presidency. He had not, wrote Roosevelt, been sitting apart from
the other guests, he had never removed his jacket, his collar was never
unbuttoned, he had not been alone in the room with Miss LeHand, and
he had not lined up a row of freshly sharpened pencils. After indicting
Time for sensationalism and inaccuracy, the President accused it of
deliberate misrepresentation. People, he said, liked to read *Time* because
of its style. They were becoming aware of the fact, however, that
the magazine often published erroneous data. Toward the end of this
extraordinary letter, Roosevelt's tone turned threatening: *Time*, the
President solemnly concluded, was harming American democracy.

Cooler heads prevailed in the White House, and the President decided
not to send Harry Luce his vitriolic letter. Instead, the President provided Lowell Mellett, of the Office of Government Reports, with a
copy of his note. Mellett, a skilled public relations expert, then discussed
the Luce problem with the White House press office. FDR soon ordered
Steve Early to do one of two things: either revise the letter and prepare
it for the President's signature or write a letter to Luce in Early's own
words. Lowell Mellett duly rewrote FDR's nasty letter. He preserved
Roosevelt's sense of indignation and added a warning of his own.
Journalists, said Mellett, "shall not knowingly and willingly abuse the

freedom of the press." FDR thought that since sweet-talking the Luces in July had gotten him nowhere, a little bullying would help.

Henry Luce received the Mellett/Roosevelt letter on December 11, 1940. Overlooking the implied threats, Luce thanked Mellett for the "spirit of your letter." A semi-apology may be detected in Luce's comment that the extra edition of *Time* went to press on a "completely abnormal rush schedule." He also promised to check into Mellett's allegations. Like Roosevelt, Luce pondered this dispute for some time. Harry could not ignore this challenge. On Christmas eve he responded in greater detail to Mellett's letter. Luce brushed aside Roosevelt's specific charges as irrelevant, since the letter really attacked the "theory and practice of TIME." Defiantly, Luce accused Mellett of disliking *Time*. Then, after dismissing his aversion as unimportant, Luce accurately observed that readers "consider it [*Time*] to be the major advance in journalism in our time."

FDR's current obsession was no aberration. Rather, Mellett's ugly exchange with Henry Luce proved a harbinger of an intensified feud. Roosevelt, a great man, had descended to a petty level that rendered him incapable of appreciating Time Inc.'s services to the nation. And Harry Luce, the most important and innovative publisher of his day, was unable to see things from FDR's viewpoint.

Lowell Mellett provided FDR with a copy of Harry Luce's letter, which Roosevelt contemptuously dismissed as a "slippery reply." Referring to *Time* as an "incendiary bomb," the President noted that the magazine made "false reporting extremely attractive." And Henry Luce, the President concluded, lacked courage, for he refused to admit that he had sinned. Roosevelt sporadically brooded over this incident for about six weeks. Luce and *Time* were beginning to haunt him.

During these last weeks of 1940, Winston Churchill urgently regaled Roosevelt with facts about Britain's dire need for help. As he prepared to move boldly, Roosevelt knew that he would again require the backing of interventionist publishers like Harry Luce. When it came to national security questions, Luce remained perfectly willing to work with the President. Otherwise he followed his own instincts.

As the winter of 1941 drew near, humanitarian groups feared that the British blockade could lead to the starvation of many Belgians, Norwegians, Frenchmen, and other occupied peoples. Henry Luce knew little about the state of European agriculture, but hunger remained a lifelong concern. Luce particularly admired the efforts of Herbert

Hoover, who had fed millions of Belgians during World War I. In 1940 the former President proposed that American food be shipped to German-occupied territories. To the British government, fighting for its life, relaxation of the blockade meant undermining its own war effort. Britain wanted none of Hoover's plan, and *Time* refused to endorse Hoover's recommendation. Its editors wondered if the food would reach the suffering Belgian masses.

The food issue grew more heated when the Friends Peace Committee, the American Friends Service Committee (AFSC), and other pacifist groups endorsed the Hoover plan. An angry British government argued that any relief supplies shipped to Belgium would strengthen the German war economy. Besides, Churchill's government added, if the Belgians were hungry, they owed their plight to Nazi looting. Luce, however, could not overlook the prospect of mass starvation. Clare Luce defended the Hoover plan, in the face of objections voiced by Anglophile skeptics. *Life* now listed the pros and the cons of the Hoover plan and leaned toward helping the young, the very old, and other endangered persons. The magazine was vague about the details, however, and recommended the dispatch of a commission of inquiry.

Luce soon found himself in the minority, when he informed the Century Group of his desire to feed the Belgians. He now decided to sever his formal ties to this historic group of interventionists. Even without the tensions provoked by the thorny food issue, Luce probably would have departed. He had decided that, as a publisher, he should not be a permanent member of a "policy-promoting group outside of my own organization." Luce's real motive stemmed from his concern about Time Inc.'s reputation. In September the *St. Louis Post-Dispatch* had published a sensational article by Charles Ross. The piece showed that a small group of influential men, including one Henry R. Luce, had helped to engender the destroyer deal. This kind of publicity, Luce feared, could undermine the reputation of his publications.

After Christmas, President Roosevelt sketched out an imaginative plan that would allow cash-starved Britain to pay for badly needed American goods. Under what became known as "lease-lend" or "lend-lease," the United States government would commission and finance the production of armaments destined for the war machines of states whose survival was in the interests of this country. The President, of course, would make this determination. The U.S. government would then purchase the goods produced by American industry and agriculture, with monies appropriated by Congress. The friendly government would "lease" these products for the duration of the war or would acquire them by taking out a kind of mortgage or "loan." The loan

Henry Robinson Luce as a senior at Yale College, 1920.
Sterling Memorial Library, Yale University

Briton Hadden, Luce's collaborator
and friendly rival, 1920.
Sterling Memorial Library, Yale University

In 1925, Hadden and Luce proudly show the
latest issue of *Time* to Cleveland's city manager, William R. Hopkins.
Western Historical Manuscript Collection, Columbia, Missouri

Clare Boothe and her daughter Ann, at about the time Clare became involved with Henry R. Luce. She sent this photograph to her good friend, financier Bernard M. Baruch.
Princeton University Library

Luce invariably worked, even while trying to relax. Henry and Clare Luce on their honeymoon, at the Casa Mason, Jimenitas, near Havana, Cuba, late 1935 or early 1936.
Courtesy of Mugar Library, Boston University

Henry R. Luce, editor-in-chief of *Time* and *Life*, circa 1938.
Princeton University Library

Billings, Luce, and Longwell at work in the late 1930s.
South Caroliniana Library

Laird Goldsborough dominated Foreign News until Luce ousted him in late 1938.
Here "Goldy" and his wife, Florence, sail to Europe on the *Normandie*
in April, 1937.
South Caroliniana Library

Ralph M. Ingersoll, general manager of Time, Inc.,
who left the company in 1939 after a tumultuous decade there.
Courtesy of Mugar Library, Boston University

Archibald MacLeish of
Fortune magazine, who
engaged Henry Luce in intense
discussions on subjects
ranging from anti-Semitism
to the Spanish Civil War.
Library of Congress

*L*ife's winning team, 1940. From left to right: Daniel Longwell,
Wilson Hicks (standing), John Billings, and Roy Larsen.
South Caroliniana Library

*F*ormer President Herbert Hoover's
plan to feed the peoples of occupied
Europe enmeshed Henry Luce in yet
another controversy.
Courtesy of Richmond Times-Dispatch

*F*rancis Pickens Miller, a prominent
leader of the "Century Group,"
disliked Henry Luce, but worked with
him on behalf of aid to Britain
in the summer of 1940.
The University of Virginia Library

Preparing to scan the sky for enemy bombers.
Central Park, New York City, 1941, as photographed from
his balcony by *Life*'s John Shaw Billings.
South Caroliniana Library

President Franklin D. Roosevelt
signing the declaration of war
against the Japanese Empire,
December 8, 1941.
Courtesy of FDR Library

would be repaid after the war by returning the armaments or goods of equivalent value. Roosevelt pledged to transform American industry into the "arsenal of democracy."

Henry Luce intended to support the Lend-Lease proposal, but he did not like some of what he heard. *Life* wondered how American industry, with all its bottlenecks, would fill orders submitted by the British Purchasing Commission *and* the United States government. And Roosevelt aggravated Luce in two other ways. He again pledged to retain the "social gains" achieved by the New Deal. To Luce, this was dishonest, for Roosevelt was promising guns and butter. In addition the President assured the nation that Lend-Lease would keep America out of the war. As always, FDR's logic rankled Luce: edge closer to war, the President seemed to say, in order to avoid it. *Time*, by contrast, boldly proclaimed that the United States was already in a new kind of "undeclared, short-of-fighting war. . . ."

Berlin wanted to defeat Lend-Lease and postpone American entry into the war. Elements in the German government, possibly including Hitler himself, now appeared interested in some kind of negotiated peace. Since Hitler planned to attack Russia in May 1941, a compromise in the West would spare Germany a two-front war. Berlin thus had good cause to look with favor on peace talks in America. Edgar Ansel Mowrer, of the *Chicago Daily News*, soon warned the White House of an imminent German-inspired "peace offensive. The President was alarmed, for such a rumor could have a devastating effect on British morale.

By late December 1940, an unlikely figure emerged as an important player in the movement for a compromise peace. To the historian, Malcolm R. Lovell is a perplexing figure. A shadowy, self-proclaimed Quaker humanitarian, Lovell was unprepossessing. He lacked wealth or real power, but his trail leads to important places, such as the German embassy, the American Friends Service Committee, and the White House. People were frequently suspicious of his motives, but famous men dined with him. A contradictory figure, Lovell enjoyed a close relationship with British diplomats while cultivating his ties to Hans Thomsen, chargé d'affaires at the German embassy. An advocate of peace, Lovell was also a supporter of Jewish causes and called for the unlimited admission of Jewish refugees into the United States. Lovell shared Harry Luce's antiracist sentiments, too, and at one point he had considered devoting his life to "our underprivileged colored people."

The FBI's raw data, which were sometimes unreliable and even scurrilous, told the story of an alleged financial schemer, crook, money launderer, and confidence man. The FBI portrayed Lovell as a man who had failed in business, profited from a suspicious fire, and moved from scheme to scam. The data did not indicate that anyone had ever indicted Lovell, much less convicted him. Still, read in the quiet of a White House office, the FBI raw file was devastating. To the Federal Bureau of Investigation, Malcolm Lovell was an appeaser with suspicious friends.

Shortly before Christmas 1940, Lovell contacted Harry Luce. Lovell did not press the issue of food relief. Instead, he emphasized his friendship with Hans Thomsen and talked about a negotiated peace. He clearly wished to bring Luce into contact with Thomsen, who may have put the tenacious Quaker up to his latest mission. After all, if Luce, who enjoyed access to much of the American public, suddenly endorsed a negotiated peace, Roosevelt would be embarrassed. New proposals for aid to Britain would suffer a body blow if *Life* and *Time* preached peace, instead of Lend-Lease and rearmament.

Luce's motives in agreeing to a dangerous encounter were complex and varied. England had survived the Battle of Britain, but how long could she withstand an assault by German bombers and U-boats? Luce feared that Britain, despite her heroism, might give up the fight, so he began to flirt with the idea of a negotiated *truce*. Malcolm Lovell, sensing that he was making progress, asked Luce a question: if Hitler agreed to cease hostilities and withdraw from Western Europe, would American public opinion be receptive to a negotiated peace? Luce evaded the question. First, he wanted to see what Germany proposed. Judging by his private comments to his trusted associate John Billings, Luce hoped that Hitler would give up some of his gains, whereupon an armed "peace" would prevail. At some point, of course, the Germans would resume their march through Europe. This third act in the German drama would not resemble 1939, however, for Luce assumed that a fully mobilized United States would then become a belligerent power. The strengthened Allies would win a smashing victory, whereupon the United States would take the lead in reshaping the world.

On December 23, 1940, Henry Luce told an annoyed John Billings to await his phone call. Like a good boy, Billings returned to his Fifth Avenue duplex apartment and glumly sat there, waiting for a summons that never came. The next day Billings learned that the abortive call concerned a meeting arranged by one Malcolm Lovell. Luce seemed ready to listen to the German "proposal," though Billings viewed it as a fantasy. There the matter rested, though Allen Grover and editor John Hersey may have met with Lovell, preparatory to Luce's next risk-filled move. Henry Luce had professional reasons for meeting Hans Thomsen, dangerous though such an encounter might be. *Time*, banned in Germany by the Propaganda Ministry in May 1939, would profit by gaining entry into Hitler's Europe. And *Life* wanted to send former ambassador John Cudahy to Berlin and occupied Europe. Cudahy's mission for *Life* would, of course, require a German visa.

Malcolm Lovell soon told Hans Thomsen of Henry Luce's interest in a European peace settlement and added that the publisher wanted to investigate conditions in Germany. Lovell's meaning was clear: a very powerful interventionist publisher needed help from the German authorities. Even if Thomsen discounted some of Lovell's eternal optimism, this project was worth a gamble. On January 2, 1941, the German diplomat caught a train for New York, where he headed for Malcolm Lovell's apartment. Early that same evening, John Billings had William, his liveried chauffeur, drive him to the Waldorf, where he took the elevator up to the Luces' apartment.

Luce spoke excitedly about the forthcoming meeting with Dr. Thomsen. After a cocktail with Allen Grover, Luce and his colleagues were driven to East 38th Street, where a butler admitted them to Malcolm Lovell's sparsely furnished apartment. Their host introduced the three men to Hans Thomsen, a suave, middle-aged diplomat who, Billings observed, spoke "perfect English." Lovell, whom Billings described as a "commonplace-looking" little man, stayed in the background. There was tension in the air, for Luce and his colleagues were openly hostile to Thomsen. Despite the chilly atmosphere, however, all guests remained civil. After dinner the group repaired to the living room, where the butler offered them cigarettes. Mrs. Lovell, wearing a blue gown, made a brief appearance, served coffee, then departed for the evening.

Hans Thomsen was maddeningly vague as Luce barked questions and demanded answers. The German diplomat calmly puffed on his pipe. Luce wanted to know about Hitler's *real* aims. Did he want to conquer the world? The Nazi diplomat tried to parry Luce's thrusts by bringing up some grievances of his own. He claimed that *Fortune* was anti-German; he ridiculed Time Inc.'s speculation about a possible German invasion of South America or the United States. Luce would not yield on any point. The hours passed, while Billings glumly wondered if the evening would ever end. After midnight, Lovell reminded his guests that Thomsen needed to catch the train to Washington. Luce left feeling that he had probably wasted his time—a thought calculated to worsen his mood.

The FBI soon caught wind of the Luce/Thomsen encounter. Driven by patriotism or self-interest (perhaps both), Malcolm Lovell provided

American intelligence with information gleaned from his many conversations with Hans Thomsen. Still, one searches in vain for the logic behind Luce's decision to meet Thomsen. Had word of the meeting leaked out, Luce's reputation would have suffered, for even as he was preparing to meet Thomsen, *Time* strongly endorsed FDR's rejection of all the Nazi-inspired "talk of peace." Sometimes, Harry Luce admitted, "we [at Time Inc.] may do harm where we mean to do good." Two weeks after Luce's meeting with Lovell, the White House heard from the FBI. Roosevelt was highly indignant. Worse still, he soon learned that John Cudahy would visit Germany—on behalf of the Luce publications.

On January 21, 1941, the day after his third-term inauguration, FDR dictated a highly confidential memorandum, suggesting that Eleanor Roosevelt discuss Lovell's activities with her friend the Quaker Clarence Pickett. Roosevelt accused Lovell of working for "appeasement," and proposed that Pickett send Lovell to China to do some relief work. A few days after Roosevelt sent his note about Lovell to Eleanor, Cudahy visited Billings and mentioned that he intended to interview Adolf Hitler. FDR did not yet know about this specific plan. For the moment, moreover, he had no intention of exposing the Luce/Thomsen meeting. He needed the backing of *Life* and *Time*, which were strident supporters of Lend-Lease. In fact, when Time Inc. launched its promotion of the proposed law known as H.R. 1776, subsequent polls reflected some movement in public opinion. Roosevelt therefore controlled his temper, and Luce went on with his work, oblivious to the danger lurking around him.

Early in the new year, Harry Luce drafted a major editorial for *Life*. The essay soon landed on the desk of John Shaw Billings. To the managing editor of *Life*, Luce's messianic moods inevitably bore ill tidings. "He's too busy," Billings would complain, "saving the nation to pay any attention to his magazines." This time, however, *Life*'s managing editor understood the importance of this article to Harry, to *Life*, and to the nation. Billings carefully edited the manuscript, clarifying this or that point, raising questions, moving paragraphs around, deleting copy. He then returned the product to Luce. There followed more drafts, conferences, and delays.

Henry Luce believed that the United States was already *in* the war, though it was unprepared to *wage* war. He therefore intended to create an ideological program that would proclaim American war aims while preparing the way for postwar American hegemony. Luce wished to engage in a preemptive editorial strike. He would demonstrate that political liberty and free enterprise—not the New Deal—could guide the nation to a prosperous and decent future. Luce's editorial was called "The Risks of War."

From these shores, Luce argued, democracy and capitalism must go forth, until, with America help, humanity advanced toward the City of God. To Harry Luce, an America divested of its global purpose was an absurdity. Now he favored going to war "at a time of our choosing against an enemy of our choosing with an outcome of our choosing." He wanted to force a national debate on the question of declaring war. This was precisely the kind of confrontation that President Roosevelt had successfully avoided.

1941

Henry Luce's
American Century

John Shaw Billings liked to call Henry Robinson Luce a "thinking machine." Though Billings often doubted it, Luce was also a human being. By 1941 Luce was rapidly balding. His narrow, deeply set eyes (*Time* would have described him as "gimlet-eyed"), placed beneath an impressive forehead, conveyed the look of a man constantly mulling over weighty problems. Still slim and muscular, Luce often paced the floor of his office, barking orders, picking up and slamming down phones. He smoked constantly, sometimes snuffing out a cigarette almost as soon as he had lit it, and his fingers and teeth bore witness to this addiction. Luce's baggy clothes reflected his lack of interest in fashion, despite Clare's elegant contributions to his wardrobe. He continued to enjoy a cocktail or two before dinner, rarely more. His evenings revolved around people who interested him, and at dinners or banquets, Harry learned what he could from those seated beside him. He did not mean to offend, but his manners were uncommonly brusque. Luce would often fumble for a cigarette, then fail to offer one to his companion. He was uninterested in the furniture and paintings surrounding him in the apartments or homes he visited. Harry's indif-

ference to normal social interaction irritated *Life*'s aristocratic John Billings, for Luce expected his editors to be at his beck and call. One ring
of a senior editor's telephone meant that Harry was on the line. Every
editor's door was open to Luce; the reverse was not true.

At tense times, Harry Luce would have his driver swing east—if
Clare had the car, he would hail a cab—then north, to a comfortable
apartment located at 1000 Park Avenue. There he would visit his sister
Beth. When Elizabeth had been born, precocious little Harry believed
that the baby was a present for him. People sometimes commented that
Beth Moore had Harry's brains, along with the charm and consideration
for others which he so sorely lacked. Once ensconced in Beth's apartment, Luce would pour out his concerns, troubles, and hopes. Harry,
frustrated when Beth's telephone was busy, had the telephone company
install a private line that connected his office to her apartment.

Reporting to his Senior Group, Henry Luce observed that his company had earned $3 million in 1940, after taxes. Time Inc. had generated
gross revenues of $37 million—few in that group recalled how Luce
and Brit Hadden had scrounged around to come up with their first
$92,000. Despite these enormous figures, Luce was in a foul mood.
Speaking with emotion, he indicated that he wanted to shake things
up, to bring about change. America, he believed, was a "special dispen-
sation—under Providence." An annoyed John Billings knew that something special was in the hopper. Harry wanted to get out of New York
and into the heartland. He needed to gauge how a cross section of the
prosperous American middle class (the only class he really understood)
reacted to his arguments. First Luce accepted an invitation to speak in
Pasadena before a meeting of the Association of American Colleges.
Harry worked through his drafts, then decided he had hit the right
note.

He began by challenging his audience. Ten years ago, he observed,
we thought the worst had befallen us when the economy failed. Greater,
unforeseen evils awaited us, however. In a world filled with ever-
increasing horrors, Luce, the American optimist, looked ahead to a time
that could surpass "the greatness or goodness of any of the past ages of
men." He might not live to see this millennium, however, for the
twentieth century could condemn civilization to "a gigantic and rotten
death." To Luce, the world would soon enter either "an American
century" or a time of decline and, finally, doom. He concluded that
"there is no possibility of the survival of American civilization except
as it survives as a world power." Since humans are flawed creatures,

they needed to use force against the evil men who block the triumph of morality, freedom, democracy, and free enterprise. His character forced Luce to imagine the future in either/or terms. The world would be either mostly good or terribly evil. Luce could not imagine that it might be both.

To Henry Luce, the American frontier now encompassed the world, one which hungered for food and hope and American know-how. He advocated the dispatch of American technicians, engineers, doctors, and road builders to foreign lands. Luce thereby anticipated the Peace Corps, as created twenty years later by his young friend John F. Kennedy. In Pasadena, Luce called for feeding *all* "of the hungry people of the world." He coupled this bold plan with a demand for unleashing the untapped productive capacity of the American farmer. A few days later, Luce spoke in Tulsa, at a dinner hosted by the Mid-Continent Oil and Gas Association. There, Luce lauded American industry and praised John D. Rockefeller as "the greatest organizing genius in all business history." He decried the antibusiness talk that had disfigured the New Deal. Although he tepidly praised Roosevelt's appeal for Lend-Lease, Luce assailed the uncertainty surrounding the nation's foreign policy. His prose sounded uncommonly lyrical, however, when Luce concluded that "we can no longer escape the burden of our own destiny." He added that "Ours is the power, ours is the opportunity—and ours will be the responsibility whether we like it or not."

Henry Luce had talked to teachers and oilmen about war and peace. He now turned to automobile dealers. Traveling to Pittsburgh, the publisher addressed their national trade association, where he contrasted American anxiety with British determination. The English people, he observed, knew what they had to do. Americans, on the other hand, were uncertain and sullen. People wanted to be deceived, Luce continued, but he intended to tell the truth. "I say," he dramatically declared, "that we are already *in* the war." Luce ridiculed a policy that called for preparedness *and* neutrality while taking the country closer to war. He attacked an Administration that talked about Hitler's threat to the Americas, yet permitted the German embassy (and Hans Thomsen!— irony remained absent from Luce's calculations) to operate quite openly. If Americans slid into the war thanks to Roosevelt's devious maneuvers, the results could be disastrous. In Luce's view, the President would then augment his own powers while allowing the people to wallow in confusion. Mistrusting FDR, Luce feared that a triumphant collectivism or socialism could emerge in the wake of a flaccid war effort.

After speaking in Pittsburgh, Luce received an important letter from

Sidney L. James, the young Missourian who headed Time Inc.'s small Chicago bureau. James, a shrewd newspaperman who understood the American heartland, was part of the second generation of Time Incers. He had joined the company in 1936, as Ivy League domination of the company yielded to an influx of young journalists from the Midwest and the Far West. The great issue was the war, and James addressed it. People in the Midwest, he wrote, could not imagine the wail of screaming air-raid sirens. Oklahomans, James added, were confused about the need to aid Britain, for they did not understand how their own security depended upon her survival.

Harry Luce quickly responded to James' demand for clarification. As he explained things, Britain, fighting alone, could not win the war. Germany, aided by Japan and Russia, might ultimately dominate much of the world. Sid James believed that Harry Luce was on the right track, and urged him to take to the airwaves, but Luce had a different pulpit in mind: *Life* magazine. His call for an American Century coincided with favorable developments in the war. Italy faced grave difficulties in Africa and the Balkans, where Britons and Greeks had taken the offensive. Though the situation in the North Atlantic was ominous, there were no signs of a British collapse. The public opinion struggle at home was going well, too. Lend-Lease was heading for a surprisingly easy victory, and *Life*, of course, helped it along.

By early February 1941, Harry Luce was scribbling like mad, rewriting his visionary editorial. The publisher's name was now familiar to 27 percent of the polled public, while almost everyone seemed to know of, or read, one or more of his magazines. Dan Longwell cheered him on, urging Luce to write a kind of "modern Federalist papers for this world [of] A.D. 1941." The managing editor of *Life* recoiled at this prospect, for Billings feared that Luce was "so busy being a Great Personage that he has forgotten the source of his greatness—the magazines we put out for him." Though Luce complained about some of his editor's deletions, Billings improved the boss's copy. He suggested, for example, that instead of calling the piece "We Americans," Luce entitle it "The American Century." A grateful Harry Luce later inscribed an offprint of his article, "To my editor."

"The American Century" appeared in the February 17, 1941, issue of *Life*, dominating the magazine. In magisterial yet translucent prose, Luce equated a happy future with American hegemony. He continued to fulminate against the sins of 1919, when Americans turned their backs on world power and global responsibility. Unlike most of his fellow citizens, Luce had never bought the schoolboy claptrap about the United States being an ever peace-loving nation, antimilitarist and isolationist. Luce knew that this country, conceived in war, had remained united thanks to a great but bloody civil war. Luce wanted to bury isolationism, just as the Civil War had resolved the argument over slavery. He spoke of using the Bill of Rights and other constitutional wonders as "our free gift to all peoples." Luce insisted that this new internationalism be "of the people, by the people and for the people."

Henry Luce argued that American culture had already illuminated the path to his new century. Throughout the world, people listened to American jazz and watched Hollywood's films. (He might have added that Nazis, Fascists, and Communists feared both Duke Ellington and Frank Capra.) Luce noted that American slang transcended borders, as did the demand for American machinery. Describing the United States as the "powerhouse from which the ideals spread throughout the world . . . ," Luce foresaw an American Century in which the U.S.A. reigned supreme. This coming age would fulfill history as tensions evaporated and wars became obsolete.

A family friend, James A. Linen, Jr., referring to Luce's "new world order," told Luce's mother that her son's "missionary appeal" reminded him of Dr. Luce's need to go forth and save the Chinese, almost a half century before.

"The American Century" reached millions of people through *Life*, but the essay quickly traveled beyond the world of "Big Red." Time Inc. offered copies free of charge, and distributed thousands of them. Luce's company also promoted "The American Century" by buying space in newspapers like the *New York Times*. The April *Reader's Digest*, which had its own huge clientele, reprinted "The American Century," as did the *Washington Post*. The essay also solidified some of Luce's important alliances. Walter Lippmann, writing to Harry's father, noted that his own recent article in *Life* followed in the path of "The American Century." "Nothing," Lippmann added, "could please me more than that." Robert Sherwood called the Luce article "magnificent," and used it to bash the isolationists one more time.

Over at the Department of State, Stanley K. Hornbeck carefully excerpted Luce's article. He also cited "The American Century" in a memorandum forwarded to the powerful Under Secretary of State, Sumner Welles. Hornbeck, who had once dismissed *Life* in the most condescending manner, had obviously changed his mind. This turnabout reflected *Life*'s new seriousness of purpose, but Hornbeck's interest had other ramifications. As a key player in formulating Far Eastern policy, Stanley Hornbeck dealt with a region of pressing concern to

Harry Luce. "The American Century," Hornbeck believed, could have an impact on U.S. policy toward China and Japan.

"The American Century" provoked a heated controversy about America's role in the world. The essay elicited almost 5,000 letters, many of them thoughtful, even anguished. Some readers saw Luce's work as "a light in the distance," after years of stumbling about in the "semi-darkness." Businessman, federal regulators, editors, college presidents, engineers, and journalists raved about Luce's article. Douglas Fairbanks, Jr., called it "superb," while other critics praised "The American Century" for damning the "mean-spirited" concept of aid short of war. The Reverend Luce's old colleagues on the Presbyterian Board of Foreign Missions praised Harry's essay. From Hollywood, mogul Samuel Goldwyn, famous for his malapropisms, declared that "The American Century" had hit "the nail on the head."

The people who praised "The American Century" were important men and women in their institutions and communities. Luce had given the more ardent interventionist minority (perhaps 20 percent of public opinion) a platform and a program. At Iowa State College, Professor John A. Vieg wanted to distribute hundreds of copies to "leading students on this campus." In Memphis, hardware wholesaler Edmond Orgill contacted Episcopal bishop James M. Maxon, and the bishop agreed to summarize "The American Century" for a meeting of the Rotary Club. In many high schools and colleges, the essay became required reading. In some municipal offices, copies were distributed to city employees. Luce's essay inspired numerous metaphors. One believer referred to the article as a rope thrown to a drowning man. Another called it "lean meat among all the fat."

Men who had served in the Great War, a crusade "to make the world safe for democracy," thanked Luce for reviving memories of their youthful idealism. In moving letters, some of these veterans remembered their sorrow when Woodrow Wilson's League of Nations went down to defeat. And they often expressed sadness over the needless war that had followed in the wake of America's retreat to "normalcy." Luce's essay rekindled the faith of J. W. Dafoe, who had served on the Canadian delegation to the Versailles peace conference. This old man wrote that the U.S.A. was destined to lead the democracies, and "[that] day seems to be at hand." George Gordon Coulton, a distinguished historian of the English Reformation, was eighty-two years old. Writing from the University of Toronto, he accepted Luce's terms for an

Anglo-American alliance. ". . . I would far rather that we [Britons] were second in such a partnership," wrote the venerable scholar, "than that the cause of liberty should suffer."

A whole gamut of critics, ranging from Republicans to pacifists and progressives, vehemently dissented. The isolationist Senator Robert A. Taft, Republican of Ohio, argued that Americans could not impose their system on the world. Luce's globalism, Taft correctly predicted, would require a huge peacetime military establishment. Harry Luce's friend Bruce Barton, a leading advertising executive, did not believe that America, even in alliance with Britain, could shoulder Luce's global burdens. Respected Socialist Norman Thomas attacked Luce for his imperialism, which would have Americans police the lesser peoples of the world. Vice-President Henry A. Wallace, who was equally progressive but more moderate in his choice of words, also objected to the phrase "American Century," preferring "The Century of the Common Man." Wallace later admitted, however, that he found much to admire in Luce's concept.

To the editors of *The Nation*, "Luce Thinking" was just a new type of imperialism, one that endangered democracy. In *The Nation*, Freda Kirchwey compared Harry's idea to Nazi concepts like the "New Order" and *Lebensraum*. Oswald Garrison Villard, a veteran antiwar activist, believed that interventionism was now a kind of politically correct form of thought control. To this old pacifist, Roosevelt was trying to become the "President of the World." Villard saw Luce and Roosevelt as men with evil, global designs. "The American Century," he wrote, mixed aggression with imperialism, resulting in a kind of American *Mein Kampf.*

Comparing "The American Century" to *Mein Kampf* was not only farfetched, it was funny. Nazi and Fascist "journalists," after all, were vilifying Luce's essay as a dangerous piece of enemy propaganda! Italy now banned all sales of *Time*. Giovanni Ansaldo, editor of *Il Telegrafo*, angrily portrayed Luce as an unsentimental spokesman for the American governing class. According to this Fascist, American leaders, Luce included, wished to rule the world. Ansaldo foresaw an evil "American Century" in which their new Yankee rulers treated Europeans like Hawaiians or Filipinos. The Fascist propagandist triumphantly concluded that Luce must be a Jew. This hilarious charge amused Dorothy Thompson, as did similar Nazi accusations leveled against herself and other Americans. She wrote to Harry, slyly suggesting that "you, Franklin and Eleanor Roosevelt, Sinclair Lewis, Henry Mencken and I become charter members of the Lost Ten Tribes Society." Thompson wickedly concluded that our "folks have been keeping something from us!"

In Germany, Nazi print and broadcast "journalists" attacked Luce at great length, and for long periods of time. Mixing fact and fantasy, Dr. Richard Sallet, a leading writer for the official *Völkische Beobachter*, published a major essay on Luce. "The American Century" had "created a considerable sensation," wrote Sallet. To Sallet, Luce was an imperialist spokesman for a barbaric country. Thanks to Luce, Roosevelt had established a "Division for Foreign Propaganda." Sallet added that the American Century reflected "moral depravity behind hypocritical arrogance, [and a] plutocratic pretense of stupidity and cunning. . . ." Ironically, those opposed to the American Century spied a fact that eluded Harry Luce. Their Fascist enemies correctly lumped Luce and Roosevelt together, as twin proponents of an American global mission.

Fortune, meanwhile, was preparing to devote an entire issue to answering the question, "What will total war for the U.S.A. mean to you?" *Time* predicted with some accuracy that the United States would achieve full mobilization in 1944, then win the war in 1945. Luce's magazines were filled with advertisements making use of military themes. On page after page, one saw articles about military equipment, strategy, and tactics. *Life* promoted products used by models clad in cute navylike "uniforms." One unhappy reader of *Life* observed that Luce had uncapped a volcano.

Indeed, many letters to *Life*'s editor were critical of Luce. Some readers puzzled over the contradiction between Henry Luce's American future and the tawdry liquor advertisements or "lewd" photographs that degraded *Life*. One troubled reader contrasted Luce's high purpose with the "decrepit tendencies" inherit in the magazine's consumerism. An amusing letter noted that "You boys who peddle sex and preach are like the saloon keeper who moralizes—your influence summarizes your ambitions." Other readers disliked Luce's high-minded pretensions. "Get down off that pulpit, boy," wrote one Colin K. Lee of Bowling Green, Missouri. "You're no Billy Sunday." Another, less literate critic wrote that "Just owning a magazine don't make a man that smart." This gentleman, after admitting that he "may not be educated," reminded Harry Luce that "we *aint* in the war." An irate writer from Indiana informed Luce that "I am among those who will continue to regard you and your kind as god damn fools." Some other angry readers denounced Luce's "white man's burden." After embracing Luce's global mission, said these naysayers, America would wake up with a terrific hangover.

A more troubling response came from Gail Goodin of Chestnut Hill, Pennsylvania. Miss Goodin expressed her heartfelt rejection of war. As she put it, she valued her brother more than all the "gold in the world," and angrily refused to donate him to Luce's war. Harry's friend, Joe Kennedy, felt exactly the same way about his two draft-age sons. "I say," Miss Goodin concluded, "to hell with the British!" This same lady asked a disturbing question: How could a country which had so many poor and hungry people dare to reform the whole world? And pro-labor readers asked how Luce could save all of mankind when he printed his magazines on "scab presses" at the Donnelley plant? The editors of *Life* responded rather lamely when they addressed fears that war would undermine social progress at home. They argued that domestic reform would take place even as the United States mastered the global crisis.

Public opinion surveys indicated that the percentage of Americans favoring war hovered stubbornly around 15 to 20 percent. Among Luce's more prominent readers, however, one senses a new, more belligerent mood. *Time* reported that almost half the polled persons listed in *Who's Who* favored going to war. And the self-described "war-monger" Harry Luce now found a new ally in Dorothy Thompson. She respected Luce, and *Time* had helped to make her a national celebrity. When "The American Century" appeared, Thompson greeted the piece as a kind of revelation, as a "historic document" that would help to create a new, Anglo-Saxon world order.

Dan Longwell, writing to Harry Luce, referred to Thompson's column as wonderful publicity for the most important piece ever published by *Life*. In fact, Dorothy Thompson unashamedly embraced a kind of American imperialism, in which the United States would be "in a top place in whatever 'new order' prevails after this war."

In the nineteenth century, the French observer Alexis de Tocqueville observed that the future might see the rise of two rival global powers, Russia and the United States of America. Luce's 1941 vision had room for just one.

All through the American Century conflict, Luce continued to agonize over the problem of malnutrition in occupied Europe. After all, he was talking about feeding the postwar world, while the press wrote of imminent famine in Europe. To Dorothy Thompson, however, it was inconceivable that the architect of "The American Century" could advocate a policy that would undermine the Allied war effort. In February 1941 Mrs. Roosevelt invited Thompson to visit the first family. After her discussions at the White House, Thompson approached Luce about a new plan and suggested that the Americans offer food to France, along with stringent political conditions. If France or Germany rejected the new plan, they would lose the propaganda battle. Luce accepted much of Thompson's proposal. *Life* soon suggested that a modified Hoover plan be tried in unoccupied France and in Belgium. In the case of France, the French government would make (as yet unformulated) political concessions to Britain and the United States.

Henry Luce tried to forge a synthesis, but this proved to be impossible. The Vichy government was not about to defy Berlin, while British Ambassador Lord Halifax coldly noted that "liberating [the French] is far more important than feeding them." "Nothing could be done," FDR agreed, until "Hitler was beaten." The food issue soon receded from the public debate.

To Save China

Even as German troops marched into Paris, Harry Luce had argued that the "Pacific [problem] is far more important even than speedy aid to the Allies." Though moved by the plight of Belgians and Frenchmen, Luce liked to remind his audiences of the greater human suffering endured by millions of Chinese. Relief agencies estimated that 50 million miserable war refugees cluttered China's roads and towns.

Aware of Anglo-American weakness in the Far East, Luce was willing to negotiate a broad settlement with Japan, but only on terms acceptable to China. As England grew stronger and America rearmed in 1941, Luce advocated a harsher policy toward Japan. He felt compelled to act, because his fellow "warmongers" were usually Anglophiles who knew little about Asia. In fact, many of these men and women viewed Asia as an appendage of the British Empire, which still clung to India. To Luce, however, a resurgent China, aided by America, was destined to displace British influence in the East.

Harry Luce, unlike many of his countrymen, rarely used racist language. He did sometimes refer to the Japanese as a "savage race" or as "little men," but he usually preferred to attack their culture. Luce chuckled indulgently about Chinese who believed in good-luck charms, but he condemned Japan's Shinto religion ("the way of the gods") as a savage cult. Luce decided that Japan owed its alleged modernization to techniques copied from Western hygiene, shipbuilding, industry, commercial radio, advertising, and of course, weaponry. The Japanese, in Luce's view, had thereby Westernized their material culture without changing age-old mores.

Luce's China, though backward in technology, was steadily progressing toward a revolutionary goal. To Harry, the Three Principles of Sun Yat-sen—national unity, government by the people, and livelihood for the people—held the promise of China's redemption. From their ancient civilization, Luce argued, the Chinese had inherited patience, fortitude, and family solidarity. They were now applying this benign legacy to the tasks confronting China as she sought to fulfill the democratic promise of a better life for all.

When it came to helping China, Harry Luce was willing to embrace unlikely partners. After Japan threatened to annihilate China in 1937, *Life* saw the USSR as a counterpoise to Japan's growing power, for the Chinese resistance was heavily dependent on Soviet aid. For the next five years, however, Luce agonized over a touchy question. Would Joseph Stalin support Chinese unity against Japan, or would he advance the sectarian schemes of Chinese Communists? At this desperate moment, Luce and *Life* were willing to give the USSR the benefit of their many doubts. Harry would never be happy about being allied with Russia, but "isolated America" could not be choosy. In an interesting aside, *Life* predicted that Hitler might attack Russia, thus giving the United States more time for rearmament.

For the moment, Harry Luce could do little to satisfy the military requirements of the Chinese armies, but he could help the suffering Chinese people. He had long agonized over the scattered, sometimes competitive fund-raising that passed for "China relief." Attempts to create a united relief organization in the late 1930s had failed. Since the outbreak of the war, Luce had worked anew to create a coherent plan for assisting China. In his proposal, member agencies would continue to cultivate their own sources of revenue. At the same time they would collaborate as colleagues, within a broader, umbrella organization. Agencies, Luce added, would need to reorient their publicity so as to solicit funds in a common drive. He offered another inducement: If the prominent agencies agreed to his plan, Luce himself might give them $20,000, or even $25,000, provided that other sources matched his gift. And if the major charities supported a "united organization," Luce would promise to assemble a "representative group of outstanding

American leaders to serve as Directors of the organization. . . ." In addition, Harry would make sure that the new entity enjoyed access to a "substantial initial operating fund. . . ."

Luce contacted people affiliated with Pearl Buck's China Emergency Relief Committee, Inc., on which he had served. Buck's honorary chairman, Mrs. Eleanor Roosevelt, personified humanitarian idealism, and she supported new measures intended to assist China. Buck also approved of Luce's proposed merger. Luce acquired the services of Paul G. Hoffman, head of the Studebaker Motor Company and long a favorite of *Fortune*. Hollywood producer David O. Selznick, aware of *Life*'s ability to make or break a movie, also agreed to serve with Luce. William C. Bullitt, a diplomat with political ambitions, joined Luce's new board. Drawing on family contacts, Luce happily added James G. Blaine, Thomas Lamont, and John D. Rockefeller III, the Quaker Rufus Jones, and Wendell Willkie to his campaign committee. By the end of 1940, most of the major China relief agencies were on board.

The American Bureau for Medical Aid to China (ABMAC), founded in 1937, brought medicines and surgical instruments to Chinese field hospitals and military personnel. ABMAC's affiliate, the Emergency Medical Service, directed by Dr. Robert K. S. Lim, trained badly needed physicians and medical officers. The American Friends Service Committee (AFSC) joined Harry's relief drive, too. The Friends' ambulances patrolled China's war zones, where their drivers braved Japanese bombs as they rushed to rescue wounded soldiers and injured civilians. The Church Committee for China Relief, which represented American Protestant churches, maintained some 200 mission stations in both occupied and free China. These sanctuaries provided civilians with food, shelter, and clothing.

The Industrial Cooperatives (INDUSCO) dispensed capital to uprooted Chinese workers and small employers. Through 3,000 cooperatives, employing over 70,000 people, INDUSCO promoted the revival of small industry in a land ravaged by war. Luce likened INDUSCO to a "guerilla industry," since the cooperatives manufactured shoes and blankets for needy Chinese troops. Here, too, Luce called on acquaintances and friends. Ida Pruitt, who had been a classmate of Harry's at the British school in Chefoo, was a leading figure in INDUSCO's support apparatus. Luce also helped to form the American Committee in Aid of Chinese Industrial Cooperatives, which attracted the support of prominent citizens like Henry Stimson, former Secretary of State and a strong opponent of Japanese aggression. Luce himself acted as temporary chairman of the Provisional Committee to Cooperate with the Chinese Industrial Cooperatives. He soon found new allies.

The China Aid Council provided aid to guerrillas who were fighting behind Japanese lines or in remote areas adjacent to enemy-held territory. The Council also worked with the American Committee for Chinese War Orphans, which helped to keep 4 million children alive. Mme. Chiang, who called these kids "warphans," financed camps for them and exploited them for publicity and fund-raising. Who indeed could resist the darling little "warphans," tiny hands outstretched, as they begged for a bowl of rice?

Meanwhile, Harry Luce continued to raise large sums of money for his Christian colleges in China, through their American boards. The Rockefeller Foundation came through with a gift of $85,000, and in March 1939 Luce himself bestowed a gift of more than $18,000 on ABCCC. After the European war broke out, Harry donated more than $32,000 to this beloved cause. The Christian colleges now controlled endowments of over $7 million, most of which they invested through New York City banks. These schools received additional support from about 20,000 of their graduates. The Christian colleges employed 783 teachers, most of whom were native Chinese. Defying the ravages of war, 7,734 students were attending the schools in 1941. The Associated Boards also established textile cooperatives and trained hospital workers.

Henry Luce's vision of an all-embracing China relief coalition was nearing reality. Luce addressed his task with energy and enthusiasm, and he "drafted" certain colleagues to help him. Otis P. Swift, *Life*'s capable publicity director, was on loan to the new charity, and other Time Incers soon joined him. By early January 1941, the major relief agencies had approved a "plan of agreement" devised by Luce. After assembling his fledgling National Committee, Luce made arrangements for the distribution of funds. A campaign committee would investigate present agency needs and disburse monies accordingly. Since additional funds would be raised in the future, more cash could eventually be allocated to worthy causes. Luce called his new organization "United China Appeal."

Because of his enormous faith in his own China projects, Luce tended to ignore voices warning of new troubles, including that of his Chungking correspondent, Theodore Harold White. A bright, intense young man, Teddy White was only twenty-five years old in 1941. His life reads like a chapter in the Jewish-American success story. White emerged from a modest Boston background, having grown up in lower middle-class Dorchester. As a boy, he attended the prestigious Boston

Latin School and also pursued his Hebrew studies in night school. By
adolescence, White wanted to find the gateway to a bigger world.
Harvard College was only a few miles from Dorchester, but to Teddy,
and others like him, it opened up new worlds of experience. Teddy
White received a scholarship and entered Harvard in 1934. He could
not afford to live on campus, so he commuted from Dorchester.

At the end of his sophomore year, chance brought Teddy White into
contact with a young instructor named John King Fairbank. Dr. Fairbank,
a student of Chinese history and culture, had gone to Exeter, Harvard,
and Oxford. Tall, dignified in bearing, and impressive in demeanor, Fairbank was a WASP from the Midwest and Ivy League down to his fingertips. To White, Fairbank came from a different world, one refined by
social grace and marked by personal self-assurance. Teddy White was
of medium height, thin and intense, even nervous, with slightly buck
teeth and poor eyesight.

Teddy White and John Fairbank, however, had much in common.
Both men were ambitious, and loved politics and history. And they
learned from each other. As a tutor, Fairbank introduced an excited
Teddy White to great thinkers of the past and present, ranging from
Thomas Aquinas to Alfred North Whitehead. When Fairbank taught a
new course on contemporary China, White was his prime pupil. Soon
Teddy became the only undergraduate majoring in Chinese history,
but he was really majoring in Fairbank. They shared left-of-center, anti-
Fascist politics, and both men hoped that China would survive Japan's
assault. Teddy wrote his senior thesis on Japan's "Twenty-one De-
mands," which had threatened China's independence during the First
World War.

As to his future, Professor Fairbank did not believe that Teddy would
ultimately be happy as a diplomat or a scholar. This may have been his
way of deflecting White from attempting a career barred to most people
of his background. Ever so tactfully, Fairbank suggested an alternative
path, perhaps less prestigious, but certainly more adventurous than
diplomacy or professing. Why not become a journalist? Fairbank knew
that people like Agnes Smedley and Edgar Snow had brought the China
story to the attention of readers throughout the West. They, too, were,
in the jargon of the day, "progressive." As graduation neared, Professor
Fairbank gave Teddy White his presents: six letters of introduction plus
an old typewriter. Teddy did not even wait for the commencement
exercises. In 1938, even before he had graduated, he boarded a bus and
headed for the University of Michigan at Ann Arbor. There, White
intended to learn spoken Chinese. Thanks to Fairbank, White also
gained access to Edward C. Carter, William Lockwood, and William

L. Holland, influential directors of the Institute of Pacific Relations (IPR). Fairbank then put White in touch with progressive China-watchers, such as the people who published the journals *Amerasia* and *Far Eastern Survey*. Later, Fairbank brought White to the attention of a scholar named Owen Lattimore, editor of *Pacific Affairs*. White soon received a grant-in-aid from the IPR and a traveling fellowship from Harvard. These funds would enable him to study local government in both occupied and free China.

Theodore sailed for China, where in the spring of 1939 he landed a job with Hollington Tong, who ran a Publicity Board for the Chinese government. Tong's propaganda agency worked to win sympathy for the Chungking regime among people who could provide China with arms, investments, and loans. While White enjoyed working with "Holly" Tong, he resented his suppression of unpleasant facts. The Chinese people, White realized, lacked basic freedoms. Nor had Teddy ever seen such horrible working conditions. He never forgot the little seven-year-old girls who worked themselves to death in textile factories, to be discarded in the evening like so much garbage. Teddy White did not blame the war-ravaged Chinese government for these conditions, but he was privately (and sometimes loudly) critical of the ubiquitous glorification of the Chinese leaders. Stranded somewhere between Hollington Tong and the real world of China, White grew restless.

In April 1939 Harry Luce received a letter that proved to have historic significance. Edward Carter, of the Institute of Pacific Relations, was sailing for Japan and China. He wanted to meet scholars working with the Institute and learn more about their research. Carter knew that Luce supported the IPR and he hoped that Harry might be able to provide him with a knowledgeable assistant. John Hersey, a young Yale graduate whom Luce admired, had been working for *Time* since October 1937. Hersey impressed Carter, who believed that the young writer would make an excellent secretary. He asked Luce to release Hersey for a few months. Under Carter's terms, Hersey could not file stories while he was assisting him, but he would be present at meetings with important scholars and leaders. This experience, along with his travels through the turbulent Far East, would provide Hersey with invaluable background information. Later, of course, he could file stories if he chose to remain in China on his own. Harry Luce readily agreed to these terms.

John Hersey sailed to the Orient, and in Chungking, he met Teddy White. The two men were a study in surface contrasts. Hersey was tall, athletic, handsome, and polished. White was still the short, rather slight Jewish boy from Dorchester, blinking out at the world from behind wire-rimmed eyeglasses. The two young men were contemporaries, however, and they shared a common aversion to fascism, fortified by their deep love for beleaguered China. Impressed by White's energy and enthusiasm, Hersey suggested that he work as a stringer for Time Inc. White, impatient with Tong's operation, accepted *Time*'s terms. For the moment, Teddy remained with Tong, as he prepared to dispatch *Time*'s copy. Hersey, meanwhile, was expected to return to New York, where editorial work awaited him. A man who wanted to be in the front lines himself, he felt envious of White's situation. "Help China beat the goddam Japs," was John Hersey's parting advice to White.

Teddy White was happy to work for the prestigious Time Inc., believing that this assignment would free him from restraints imposed by Tong's propaganda mill. This faith proved misplaced, but White plunged into his job with enthusiasm. His contact in New York was David Hulburd, Time Inc.'s director of incoming cable traffic. Hulburd asked White to write confidential reports each week. He made it clear to Teddy that he wanted firsthand observations and gripping anecdotes, not finished articles. So White wrote about INDUSCO, guerrilla warfare, Manchukuo, and everything else he could investigate or experience. He received from five to twenty dollars for each dispatch.

David Hulburd was a shrewd man, widely regarded at Time Inc. as a political weathervane. China, of course, was Harry Luce's special love. Rumors around the company suggested that John Hersey, who had hired White, stood high in Luce's favor. None of this was lost on Hulburd, who also realized that White's dispatches were highly original. Teddy White's copy gave its readers a sense of what it was like to live and fight in China. This, Hulburd knew, was the kind of reportage that could boost the reputation of *Time*. The astute Hulburd decided to sweeten White's terms of employment. This was important, for White worried about the financial needs of his family. Teddy would now receive a regular stipend of $25 per month, plus another $25 if he would agree to write four mailers a month.

Tensions with Tong escalated after White went to work for *Time*, for his boss wanted to censor all of Teddy's Time Inc. material. This would not do, for, in White's words, such tutelage would require that he "paint the Chinese as white as angels or portray the future of this war in too-roseate" colors. White thus decided to resign from his job with Tong. He assumed that Time Inc. wanted the unvarnished truth, so he proceeded to write insightful reports. Chinese censorship, however, plagued the young correspondent. There were military censors, postal censors, and political censors. The Guomindang (ruling party) bigwigs were particularly sensitive to reports about internal political

bickering among the Chinese leaders. They also frowned upon speculation about China's relations with the Soviet Union. White sometimes
provided Hulburd with sensitive military information about the Chinese Army, which could not be published. New tensions arose as Teddy
warned New York against printing prohibited material. If traced to
him in Chungking, White feared, he could lose his access to important
sources. Hersey tried to calm Teddy down by noting that some of his
hushhush material had already appeared in the *New York Times* or
elsewhere. Hersey reminded White that no one could accuse him of
supplying everything on China printed in the magazine.

White remained unconvinced. He felt compelled to tell New York
the truth, but feared the consequences of its publication in *Time*. In the
light of later developments, this situation was not devoid of irony. In
the years ahead, White revised his attitude and he accused Luce of *not*
publishing the truths he had unearthed in China.

Whether he was drinking with other reporters, interviewing a subject, inspecting a war front, or sunning himself in the nude atop the
press hostel building, Teddy White was always planning his next move,
for no matter how grim the situation, he loved his work. White noted
that events in China would transpire whether he was there or not. Since
they were so fascinating, Teddy felt he was "darned lucky that I've got
a whack at the observing rather than someone else." Possessing a fine
eye for human detail, White spotted deeper problems where others saw
anecdotes. At one point, White reported, the three Soong sisters had
decided to show themselves to the people. The crowds were curious
and appreciative, White noted, but the police were clearly hostile to
them. Indeed, they even roughed up well-meaning Chinese who attempted to approach the Soongs. This incident provided White with
an ominous insight into the gulf between elites and governed, one that
Chiang Kai-shek never bridged. (Most likely, Harry Luce would have
seen only the enthusiasm, not the use of excessive force.) White, however, wanted to equate antifascism with democracy, and such events
confused, then angered him. The liberal elements in the ruling Guomindang, wrote Teddy White, were losing out to the feared secret police
known as the Tai Li men. In a devastating despatch, which failed to
pass the Chungking censors, White described the head of these police
as the "Chinese Himmler." How could Chiang change China for the
better if he depended on such men?

Teddy could see that the Europeans in Asia were in full retreat.
After the fall of France, he wrote, the British had appeased Japan by
temporarily shutting down the Burma Road, while the French in Indochina blocked the shipment of vital exports to China. Teddy visited

Hanoi, where he judged the French colonials to be "stupid or cruel."
White reported that some Chinese leaders spoke of turning away from
the West; perhaps they would form an alliance with Russia or make
peace with Japan. News from the front was bad. The Japanese had taken
Ichang, on the Yangtze, east of Chungking. Given their ability to move
into Indochina, the enemy might mount a two-pronged offensive, from
the east, and through Yunnan, from the southwest. White reported that
the Chinese, however, continued to resist. And even if Britain and
France appeased Japan, Russia and America remained China's potential
allies.

   Despite these encouraging words, Teddy White was growing cynical
about the Chiang regime. He described H. H. Kung, a powerful financier married to a Soong sister, as a "fat, double-chinned, pot-bellied
bastard." He also saw Kung as powerful, vain, indecisive, and weak.
Signs of the failed war effort were ubiquitous, White noted, while
China was unable to fend off crippling blows. Enemy saboteurs were
active even in Chungking, where they blew up an arsenal. This town,
which contained many emergency dwellings made of bamboo and mud,
was vulnerable to fire, bombs, and plague. Chiang's personalized style
of government, White added, was undermining the war effort. T. V.
Soong could not work with Kung, his brother-in-law, so their troubled
relationship subverted the financial side of the war effort. The Chinese
had no real air force left, reported White. When supplies for the army
ran out, how would China continue to fight? Teddy White greatly
admired the Chinese resistance, but he now began to question its staying
power. His pessimism intensified in the autumn of 1940, but his mood
often changed from day to day.

   Teddy White did provide *Time* with favorable anecdotes about
Chiang Kai-shek, as the magazine worked to brighten the image of the
Chinese leader. White described Chiang as a ruthless and stubborn man,
determined to regain control of all China. Calm and self-controlled,
White's Chiang consulted with his powerful National Military Council
on a daily basis, where his "Olympian" tranquillity reassured "all who
come into contact with him." And the young journalist could not
praise Madame Chiang highly enough; he was long infatuated with her.
Madame's legs turned his head; Teddy described her figure as "probably
the best in Chungking." Teddy White's Mei-ling (Madame Chiang)
was brave, self-assured, and anxious to bring American efficiency to
ancient China. She believed in the "democratic process," White decided, and expressed her credo in perfect American English. To Teddy
White, Mei-ling Soong was a philanthropist, a social worker, and the
patroness of the New Life movement. He implied that she was a force

for Americanization, as she manipulated her more "Oriental" and tradition-minded husband. When Teddy White praised the Chiangs, *Time* printed his copy almost verbatim. No one contributed more than Teddy White to the growing Chiang cult in the United States.

In the winter of 1941, White dispensed some more badly needed good news, and it, too, reflected well on Chiang. The Generalissimo had rejected peace feelers from Wang Ching-wei's puppet government. Wang, based in occupied Nanking, was a creation of the Japanese Army. By rebuffing him, Chungking gave notice that it would stay in the war. More good news followed. After visiting the great British base at Singapore, White had pronounced it "impregnable." Time, he reported in the late autumn of 1940, was running out for Japan, for China was growing stronger each day. White did note, however, that the Japanese were building up their bases in Tonkin, Indochina. This could be an ominous development, for the enemy might be preparing new offensives against southern China.

Although Harry Luce liked White's emphasis on the increasing strength of China, Teddy White was also telling a second story, one that grated on Luce's ears. White reminded New York that the Guomindang's organization owed a good deal to Soviet, totalitarian models, while Chiang himself exhibited marked xenophobic tendencies. His generals ruled almost every province, while the National Military Council involved itself in every aspect of Chinese life. While White admired the "Whampoa men," who were graduates of the famous academy founded by Chiang, he questioned their commitment to social change. In fact these army commanders seemed to see themselves as allies of the wealthy classes and protectors of the social status quo. Chiang's generals espoused nationalism and industrialization, but opposed land reform. Other prominent Chinese, like the famous Ch'en brothers, were outright reactionaries, who wanted to prevent modernization from destroying China's "great rural family." White questioned the influence of Luce's cherished INDUSCO cooperatives, themselves experiments in democracy and equality. And he constantly warned New York against underestimating China's need for land reform.

In 1939 an enthusiastic Teddy White had reported that the United Front alliance between the Communists and the Guomindang held firm. Toward the end of that year, moreover, White had visited areas of the Shansi front, where Communist officers impressed him with their determination and ability. They were clearly gaining the allegiance of many Chinese, he noted. Some of Professor Fairbank's progressive friends, however, feared that Guomindang (KMT) reactionaries would jeopardize Chungking's alliance with the Chinese Communists. White replied that Stalin, who could tolerate Hitler, would have no qualms about working with Chiang. Like other observers, White assumed that Stalin wanted to help unite China so that Chiang could fight Japanese aggression. He also believed that the Chinese Communists were heavily dependent on Moscow. It followed that Russian pressure on Mao's Communists, combined with Soviet aid to Chiang, would strengthen the United Front. Meanwhile, Soviet aid continued to roll into China via overland routes in the northwest.

By late 1940 White reported that the Communists were exploiting the land reform issue to good effect. As a consequence, many Guomindang feared the Reds more than the Japanese. White's own perspective was that of a liberal antifascist, skeptical of Communists but willing to work with them against an evil enemy. Teddy White hoped that Chiang would outfox the Marxists by initiating a program of land reform, though he found few signs that this was happening. Instead, White saw a government that refused to plumb the "depths of the misery of the Chinese people. . . ."

Almost none of this vital material found its way into Time, but Teddy White himself was partly to blame for this omission. He provided New York with reams of anecdotal material lauding the Chinese resistance and glorifying the Chiangs. White constantly worried about losing access to Guomindang officialdom and cautioned Time against printing censored material. White did warn his editors, however, that the Soongs were widely despised as "foreign [and] Americanized." Indeed, he predicted that they would one day fall, though Teddy seemed to believe in the Generalissimo's personal durability. China, White cautiously concluded, would hold together, "so long as external pressure demands it."

Editors familiar with Harry Luce's views were puzzled by White's contradictory copy. Teddy White was indeed a chronicler of Chinese valor, but he was also a Cassandra, bringing news of Chiang's mounting number of failures. Editors therefore took the safe path, and Time omitted most of Teddy's lengthy criticisms of the KMT. Foreign news editor Frank Norris obligingly portrayed Chiang as Luce wanted to see him. Aided by a wife depicted as an Asian Joan of Arc, Chiang emerged in the pages of Time as a hero struggling to modernize and democratize China. The Guomindang, while imperfect, served Western interests by holding off a barbaric foe. The West, in turn, must arm and assist China.

Concerned with what China could be, or should become, Harry Luce often ignored what China really was. To Luce, the situation described by White only reinforced the argument for a stronger American policy. China, in his view, was America's special responsibility. She must never be lost to Russia, Japan, or any other potential master.

The Distant
Specter of Chinese
Communism

Henry Luce could have learned a good deal about Chinese communism by reading a remarkable manuscript, now lodged in the library of the Yale Divinity School. Written in 1940, the *Brief Outline of the History of Chinese Communism* was objective in its approach, and as such, it stood almost alone. The *Brief Outline* was the work of Harry's seventy-one-year-old father, the Reverend Henry Winters Luce.

As Dr. Luce liked to say, he had spent the first part of his life explaining the West to Chinese; now he tried to increase the West's knowledge of the East. So, at an advanced age, the Reverend Luce joined the planning committee of the Interpreters' Institutes. In this capacity he taught seminars that educated faculty at theological seminaries. The *Brief Outline* reflected Dr. Luce's desire to interpret an aspect of contemporary China that remained unknown to many Americans. He had written a unique document, something without precedent in the colleges of the United States. A handful of professors in the 1930s taught courses on Marxism; few, if any, devoted an entire part of a semester to Chinese communism.

Early in his outline, the Reverend Luce stressed a point that rarely appeared in *Time*'s lengthy articles about China: he noted that the Guomindang movement reflected years of Soviet tutelage. The author went so far as to claim that the founder of the Guomindang, the revered Sun Yat-sen, "was endeavoring to [adopt] Communistic ideas to Chinese conditions." The Communist Party, founded in 1921, had entered into a United Front with the KMT in order to fight their mutual enemy, the northern warlords. Chiang Kai-shek, trained in Moscow, succeeded Sun, who died in March 1925. Supported by the Communists, Chiang then marched north in a successful campaign against the warlords.

Dr. Luce offered his appraisal of the Red rulers, which sometimes relied on a writer out of favor at Rockefeller Center. By 1940 the radical journalist Edgar Snow was anathema to *Time*'s editor in chief, but not to the Reverend Luce. Relying heavily on Snow, the senior Luce provided a portrait of Mao Tse-tung, the forty-seven-year-old leader of the Communists. He noted that the young Mao had read widely in the Western classics, showing a special interest in Lincoln, Gladstone, Rousseau, and other great figures. Luce added that Mao used George Washington as a revolutionary model. The Founding Father, like the Chinese rebels, had fought for years before winning a war and building his nation.

The Reverend Luce argued that the Chiang regime was a one-party dictatorship. Poverty and misery, he added, provided Communist propagandists with their opportunities. Luce, moreover, decided that the Chinese Communists were nothing like their Soviet counterparts. The Chinese Marxists, he wrote, opposed the nationalization of the land. Instead, they wished to distribute it to small farmers and peasants. In Luce's account, Mao sought to gain political power through "mass action." A reader of Dr. Luce's *Outline* would conclude that Chiang was more authoritarian than Mao. In words that might later have landed him before a congressional committee, the senior Luce wrote that the Communists cultivated a "democratic spirit."

The Reverend Luce sensed that the Communists were convincing many Chinese that China belonged to its people. As proof he cited the rules governing the behavior of Mao's soldiers. The militiaman, according to the "code of the Red soldier," must be honest, courteous, and clean. By describing the rules imposed on its soldiers by the Red Army, Luce was providing readers with an attractive alternative to the lice-infested, ignorant, and half-starved peasant conscripts who filled Chiang's "300" divisions. He was teaching material flatly hostile to

Time's version of Chinese affairs. He appears not to have discussed this discrepancy with his son.

During the winter of 1940–1941, Theodore White reported that friction between Chungking and the Communists encouraged the Japanese, who were launching a major offensive on the Shansi front. Teddy White blamed Chiang for this crisis, for he believed that Communist leaders, including both the Soviets and Chou En-lai, had been conciliatory. After meeting Chou, the Communist representative in Chungking, in 1939, Teddy White came to admire Chou's relaxed style, his sharp mind, and his ever-present wit. Through Chou, White made the acquaintance of Tung Pi-wu, one of the legendary founders of the Chinese Communist Party. These Communists, White believed, wanted a united China. Chiang, however, unimpressed and fearful, was anxious to confront the Red "bandits," who had moved south. In White's view, Chiang, confident of more American aid, had decided to annihilate some of his Communist enemies.

As Teddy White told the story, the New Fourth Army, containing about 100,000 men, had occupied positions on both banks of the Yangtze. Chiang wanted to evacuate this force, whose activities represented an illegal expansion of Communist power. In January 1941 the Generalissimo's eager local commanders issued an ultimatum to the New Fourth Army. The Communists quickly agreed to leave their positions and move to north Anhwei. Ten thousand of their fighters were preparing to cross the river when government forces gratuitously attacked and decimated them. The Nationalists killed the Communist chief of staff and court-martialed the commander of the New Fourth Army. Teddy White reported that this fratricidal episode dismayed many Chinese. At about the same time, White recorded an ominous rumor. He had heard that Chiang was ready to strike a deal with Japan. Under its putative terms, the Japanese would occupy all of China north of the Yellow River, while Chiang would hold the south. The two former enemies would then proceed to destroy the Communists in their midst. "The two groups," White glumly concluded, "stand at the end of tolerance." To Luce's annoyance, Teddy White was predicting civil war.

Henry Luce wanted China to win the war without having to face a powerful Communist challenge in its aftermath. *Time* thus ignored White's cabled report on the melee along the Yangtze. Instead, *Time* blamed the New Fourth Army for its own fatalities. This story further eroded White's faith in his New York editors. Chiang, they wrote, had "prevented internal disorder by disarming and disbanding the Communist" army. *Time* omitted the bloody details, then sidestepped the bitter results of the Yangtze troubles. White concluded that the Guomindang and the Communists each wanted to reorganize China along lines that excluded cooperation with the other.

Teddy White, like his boss, did not really know the Reds, except for those Communists he had met in Chungking. He had already concluded, however, that communism was an indigenous movement, responding to local rural needs. In fact, Teddy's comments confirmed the insights imparted by the Reverend Luce in his outline history. The Communists, after all, had lowered rents without nationalizing the land. Although White was critical of their heavy-handed methods, he decided that the Communists were "good people." By contrast, the KMT seemed remote, corrupt, paranoid, and authoritarian. Harry Luce was willing to read this kind of thing; publishing it was out of the question. In Harry's view, generous Americans and grateful Chinese, having won their common war, would build a new civilization in East Asia. The Communists could only endanger Luce's goal.

Harry Luce's support for the tattered United Front in China weakened each day. In March *Time* published an ambiguous review of Edgar Snow's book *The Battle for Asia*. Snow was a prime mover behind the Chinese industrial cooperative movement, which Luce patronized. Snow, however, believed that the Chinese guerrillas were better fighters than Chiang's soldiers. *Time* therefore concluded that Edgar Snow had written "one long left-wing editorial." But had he really done so? Teddy White soon corroborated some of Snow's military judgments.

By 1941 Teddy White was regularly cabling shocking stories to New York. If published, they were sure to disillusion Americans. Visiting the central China front in the spring, White inspected one of Chungking's divisions, in the 6th War Area. Obviously, the government wanted White to see crack troops, and he did. Still, troubling signs caught Teddy's eye. Most of Chiang's generals were in their thirties, graduates of his Whampoa Military Academy, and totally loyal to the Generalissimo. The inflow of supplies to them depended on their friends and contacts. These highly politicized officers, White observed, were pro-American, but many Chinese generals, according to White, lived in a dream world. Their divisions lacked artillery and air cover, but Chiang's field commanders believed in coming miracles to be performed by American aid. Like their friend and spokesman Harry Luce, these men believed that America could do anything. Americans and Chinese were sowing seeds that could only nurture mutual disillusionment.

Meanwhile, 200 miserably outfitted regular army divisions plus 100 reserve and militia units faced 800,000 seasoned Japanese troops. The Chinese soldier, according to Teddy White, was a peasant, and he could endure almost anything. He was, however, filthy and lice-infested. The Japanese, White observed, bombed him from airplanes, shelled him with artillery, and gassed him. Somehow the front lines held. In fact, they had moved very little in three years. Sadly, Chungking seemed to forget about its front-line units except when the Japanese launched a dangerous offensive. The Army, White concluded, "ignores Chung-king," which in turn is "ignorant of the army." Chiang and his aides lived in a world molded by political manipulations and conspiracies. The Japanese soldier, moreover, was not about to crack. He looted the land and alienated civilians, but he was a fine fighting man. From Indochina, good Japanese divisions were poised to attack Chungking's Yunnan flank, and such an assault could block the import of vital goods via the reopened Burma Road lifeline. *Time* insisted, however, that China would prevail if she received vast amounts of artillery and war-planes. White was not so sure.

Luce carefully read White's dispatches, often scrawling "home" across the top of the first page. There, he and Clare could study them at their leisure. Luce then selected what he liked from these dispatches and ignored the rest. In Chungking, Teddy White was reading dated issues of *Time* with ever greater apprehension. This was important, for few American newspapers wrote very much about China. Millions of people were getting much of their news about Chiang from *Time* and *Life*. Teddy White faced a new dilemma, for he had completed a manu-script for Random House, but as he bluntly told Fairbank, it was no good. In order to tell the truth, White would have to explode myths to which *Time* pledged weekly allegiance. To suppress the truth, on the other hand, would make the manuscript worthless. White could have told his story in 1941; instead, his sensational revelations about China appeared five years later, in the changed world of 1946. The delay had historical consequences, replete with tragic overtones.

In Harry Luce's view, a correspondent was indeed supposed to report facts, but an editor needed to print the truth. If the facts clashed with the higher truth, they would have to yield to it. With Japan edging closer to war against the West, the order of battle was becoming clear, at least to Luce: Americans and Chinese would fight Japan. White's negativism, therefore, grated on Harry's nerves even when independent sources confirmed some of Teddy's more controversial insights. In February 1941, for example, Lauchlin Currie, an administrative assis-tant to President Roosevelt, made a three-week-long fact-finding tour of China. A professor who had taught courses in banking at Harvard,

Currie returned to Washington highly critical of the Chungking regime. Like Teddy White and the Reverend Luce, Currie understood the need for drastic land reform measures. In his report to Roosevelt, he described the Guomindang as both anti-Communist and repressive, but despite his criticisms of the Chiang regime, Currie, like Teddy White, recommended that China receive military aid commensurate with her needs. By this time Currie also recognized Henry Luce's leadership role in maintaining "America's interest and support in China's struggle." Luce appreciated Currie's support of China and ignored his criticisms of her government.

On the American home front, Harry Luce could take heart from the Roper polls published in *Fortune*. According to these surveys, Americans were becoming more hostile to Japan, in part due to her recently concluded (April 1941) Neutrality Pact with the Soviets. *Time* believed that the pact would enable Japan to launch an attack against the mineral and rice-rich lands of Southeast Asia. Again, Luce spoke of Armageddon, while *Time* foresaw a war between Britain and China, on one side, and Russia and the Axis, on the other. More than half of polled Americans now supported policies intended to keep Japan out of Southeast Asia. The Gallup Poll reported that 39 percent of polled respondents would even risk war in order to prevent Japan from seizing the Dutch East Indies and Singapore.

Helping beleaguered China, however, was no easy task. Lauchlin Currie found that statistics on Chinese production were confusing and sometimes irrelevant, so it was hard to measure Chinese needs. In late April 1941 Chiang warned Washington of sinking Chinese morale, so in May China became eligible for Lend-Lease assistance. Currie, now the director of Lend-Lease assistance for China, wrote to Chiang, telling him that $45 million in aid would be forthcoming. Currie hinted at additional disbursements, some of which would come from prior allotments to Britain. Currie's hope that Chungking would now undertake radical reform measures quickly dissipated.

Harry Luce, encouraged by China's inclusion in the Lend-Lease program, intensified his efforts. United China Relief (UCR), Luce's umbrella organization, was efficiently organized into several major committees. For the position of chairman of the National Committee on Chinese Participation (the Appeal's liaison in China), Luce needed someone who exuded prestige and power. He succeeded in recruiting T. V. Soong for the post. The chairman of the National Committee on Disbursements was the IPR's Edward C. Carter. Thomas E. Dewey, who was anxious to cultivate Luce and improve his coverage in *Time*, agreed to serve as the Greater New York chairman of United China

Relief. B. A. Garside, a longtime friend of the Reverend Luce, worked as executive director of the appeal. A dedicated worker with many contacts in the missionary community, Garside labored tirelessly on behalf of fund-raising for China. He ran United China Relief along lines laid down by Harry Luce.

With 409 agencies trying to raise money for victims of the war, unity offered a decided advantage to these benefactors of China. With the help of his colleagues, Luce hoped to raise a fortune, $5 million, a sum that far exceeded present contributions. The goal proved to be beyond Luce's reach, but the lofty figure served its purpose. Within weeks more than 100 communities played host to China relief campaign committees. The national headquarters, located in New York, was Harry's chief concern. Luce personally put up $50,000 for its needs, thus providing UCR with rent money, furniture, phones, and clerical personnel. Located at 1790 Broadway, UCR divided incoming monies among its constituent agencies, according to their needs. When contributions passed $2,190,000, Carter's committee would review their requirements, then disburse the monies accordingly. The first order of business was publicity. Prodded by Luce and his associates, prominent writers, advertising firms, and broadcasting companies offered to help. UCR mailed out 25,000 appeals in May, and an effective series of radio presentations publicized its drive. The mailing resulted in a phenomenal 6,500 replies, producing an income of $50,000.

The widespread and pitiful image of poor China, slowly bleeding to death, was anathema to Harry Luce, and he worked to change it. UCR's propaganda showed the Chinese as resisters, who had halted the "Japs" in their tracks.

Harry Luce had not been in his Chinese homeland for almost a decade. The journey would be arduous, even dangerous, but Luce needed to reaffirm his faith. He wanted to encourage the students in the Christian colleges and greet the heroes and heroines described by *Time* and *Life*. And he hoped to meet this energetic young Jewish man, Teddy White, who could provide fresh information about the Chinese resistance and Chinese needs. Then, strengthened and energized, Luce could bring the China story to millions of Americans, first hand.

Within weeks of the debut of "The American Century," Harry Luce's secretary, Miss Corinne Thrasher, contacted Pan American World Airlines and booked two round-trip tickets to the Far East. The Luces intended to make an extended tour of the Pacific basin, where they would visit America's far-flung outposts, among which they numbered embattled China. As April approached, Harry and Clare Luce obtained their passports, traveler's checks, and letters of credit. Health certificates indicated that the Luces were inoculated against smallpox, cholera, and typhoid. Under Pan Am's rules, each passenger could bring along only two suitcases, a small one and a larger grip. The trip was sure to be adventurous, but it would also be grueling and uncomfortable, for the Luces planned to cram every possible experience into their brief itinerary.

On April 24, 1941, Harry Luce headed for the West Coast. Clare had left New York three days before, with her cameras and notepads. Arriving in San Francisco, Luce joined his wife at the elegant Mark Hopkins Hotel. On Monday afternoon the Luces boarded a Pan Am clipper and made their way toward places whose names would soon become familiar to Americans: Midway, Guam, and Manila. Bernard M. "Bernie" Baruch, Clare's wealthy and affectionate friend, playfully cabled a telegram welcoming her to each stop on her way to the Far East. On May 5 Harry and Clare arrived in China, where they refreshed themselves in the Hong Kong Hotel. On Wednesday, May 7, before sunrise, the couple boarded a plane for Chungking, located in the mountainous, remote interior of China.

After flying over Japanese-occupied territory, the Luces arrived in China's temporary capital. There, in the small airport, Chiang's officials, complete with limousine and driver, greeted their guests like heads of state. Porters carried the Luces and their baggage up the steps of cliffs, which led to the city. In Chungking proper, an automobile provided by H. H. Kung awaited Harry and Clare, who were beginning their two-week foray into China. Kung, the head of the government, invited the Americans to take tea and other refreshments with him. Later, the Luces enjoyed a sumptuous dinner, at which Harry conversed with General Ho Ying-chin, the war minister. Harry was happy as a lark, talking about China, with Chinese, in order to help China. He later fell asleep under mosquito nets provided by the Kung household.

Harry Luce eventually called on American Ambassador Nelson T. Johnson, a longtime contact. The Ambassador had spent more than thirty years studying China or serving there. Japan, the Ambassador claimed, intended to eliminate all Western interests in China. Johnson, fifty-four, an ambitious career diplomat, was aware of *Time*'s growing influence; he had cultivated Luce for years. *Time*, meanwhile, had discreetly used Johnson as a major source, even placing him on its cover late in 1939.

The Nazis had bombed Luce while he was the guest of the American Ambassador to Belgium. Now, during Johnson's reception, the Japanese Air Force attacked Chungking. A bomb landed twenty feet from Clare's feet as she stood on an ornate terrace overlooking the city. To Luce's delight, the Chinese were wonderful at improvisation and repairs. They quickly restored the overcrowded town to working condition. Luce was proud, for their diligence showed that the Chinese, like the Londoners, could take the terror that rained down upon them. Why, Luce wondered, had Americans donated $23 million to Britian in the last twelve months, while presenting China with a meager $1 million?

Life tried to right the balance, and rushed to cover the suffering inflicted on the Chinese by Japan. *Life* published disturbing photographs of a recent Japanese air raid, showing some of the 4,000 people who had suffocated in their shelters. Equating Japanese bombings with Nazi terror seemed appropriate to Harry, whose contempt for Japan increased with each air raid. This, he concluded, was a good time to toughen American policy in the Far East.

United China Relief

During his Chungking visit, Teddy White served Harry Luce as a kind of guide, in an early version of a *Time* tradition. When Luce traveled, his retainers were expected to meet him, tell him about the locals, and attend to his needs. White, who was very anxious to please, had an easy task because Luce enjoyed everything around him. Soon after touring part of Chungking, Luce again heard the wail of air-raid sirens. Impressed by the calm demeanor of the civilian population, Luce relished even this grim experience.

Henry Luce was endlessly curious about everything, and White could usually answer his questions. (Teddy later referred to these dialogues as conversations with a vacuum cleaner.) Often, the two men hired a rickshaw and traveled around the town. Delighted by everything he saw, Luce recalled his boyhood Chinese. He wanted to talk to everyone, and asked White to correct his mistakes. And Teddy fascinated Harry Luce. He had seen China at war, and exuded enormous energy and curiosity. To White, Luce was a big man in all senses, a powerful boss who offered him access to worlds beyond Dorchester, Harvard, or Chungking. White's combination of brains and drive appealed to

Harry Luce, and gave him insights into a rising generation of Jewish-Americans. These people would prove to be important to the growing success of Time Inc. Luce viewed Teddy White as the future Far Eastern editor of *Time*.

On the surface, the Calvinist Yankee and the intense young Jew made an incongruous pair, despite their common affinities for China and journalism. White, however, harbored real affection for Harry Luce, and through all their later crises, the attachment never totally dissipated. Luce liked Teddy, and even permitted White to cut him off in midsentence, though he once warned, "Don't interrupt me too much, Teddy." White would soon become the first correspondent to have a by-line in *Time*. Though disappointed with much of *Time*'s China coverage, White admired its improved (thanks to Tom Matthews) sections on the arts, literature, the press, music, and theater. He realized that the "back of the book" was bringing new information to busy middle-class readers, like the people who lived in triple-decker homes in Dorchester.

One of Henry R. Luce's great moments occurred when he finally met the leader himself, a "slim wraithlike figure in khaki," Generalissimo Chiang Kai-shek. Reserved and monosyllabic when it suited him, Chiang impressed Luce with his decisive "yes" and "no" answers. Luce saw nothing of Chiang's tantrums, which often troubled observers. Like many other Americans, he was much taken with Madame Chiang, whom he provided with a fresh supply of hard-to-obtain American cigarettes. He also offered the Chiangs flattering photographs of themselves, which delighted the Generalissimo. Madame Chiang reciprocated, presenting the Luces with beautiful incense burners and other expensive gifts. Like White, Luce had spent a lifetime looking for heroes. Theodore Roosevelt had never let him down, but Luce's early attraction to FDR left him feeling betrayed. Now he found new heroes, and gushed that the Chiangs "will be remembered for centuries and centuries."

The Luces, oblivious to discomfort and grave danger, insisted on visiting a heavily contested sector of the front. Chiang's military machine, working with Hollington Tong's propaganda apparatus, obliged them. Harry and Clare soon found themselves sitting cramped up in a Beechcraft plane, heading for remote Sian. There, they rode in an automobile for some distance, then a train. When the tracks ended, the Luces mounted Mongolian ponies and rode to the banks of the Yellow River. Across the water, mounted on cliffs, stood the massed guns of the Japanese Imperial Army. Luce inspected units of the Chinese forces. Perhaps only Harry would have discovered men who claimed to be reading the works of Sun Yat-sen. From his hosts Luce learned that these soldiers enjoyed a good diet, observed the principles of sound hygiene, and grew vegetables in their spare time.

Harry Luce vaguely wondered whether these troops were "typical," but he ultimately decided that the crack 167th Division was no better than many others. Deeply impressed, he raved about its "superb morale" and made sure that *Life* featured its story. Harry was in a state of suspended euphoria, which White, for reasons of courtesy and self-interest, did not try to dissipate. Divisive issues remained undiscussed. Harry ignored, or perhaps did not see, the simmering xenophobia that permeated the Guomindang. Nor did he want to discuss press censorship with Teddy White. At home, *Time* devoted a major article to the wartime speeches of Chiang Kai-shek. In its review *Time* blasted Edgar Snow, Agnes Smedley, and the French writer André Malraux because those authors depicted Chiang as a Fascist whose officers wantonly slaughtered Communists.

Harry and Clare Luce enjoyed all the carefully orchestrated propaganda displays, which featured singing children and defiant anti-Japanese stage plays. Luce was not a victim of Holly Tong's public relations machine; he was seeing what he wanted to see. In her diary, Clare confessed to "confusion in my own mind about China," but here she ultimately followed her husband's guidance. Luce cabled suggestions back to Allen Grover, asking that *Life* prepare stories about China's war effort. Chiang, declared the *March of Time*, was one of "the best statesmen and chiefs China has ever known," while China was "enjoying a rebirth as a free republic." Luce was celebrating China, not visiting it.

Harry Luce, of course, heard rumors about corruption, but he countered them by referring interlocutors to examples of American malfeasance. He was not totally rigid. As a result of conversations with Eliot Janeway, Currie, and White, Luce appealed to Chiang, urging him to liberalize the Guomindang and reform the government. Harry, however, had no intention of tying strings to his support for China. Friendly advice was in order, but putting pressure on the government would be inappropriate. Chiang, who felt nothing but loathing for liberal democracy and dissent, was a shrewd man; he knew he could ignore Luce's advice while retaining his support.

In fact, the Generalissimo was husbanding his resources while he awaited the advent of an avenging angel: America. Once the Americans freed him from the Japanese threat, Chiang intended to crush the Reds. In fact, conflicting visions of China left little room for compromise. If

Japan struck on all of China's fronts, the Guomindang and the Communists would probably cooperate. Barring such a development, they pursued their own selfish goals. Writing in April, Ambassador Johnson had predicted that Harry would not like the China of the future. Postwar China, Johnson believed, would become antiforeign and isolated. Luce vehemently disagreed.

On May 20, 1941, the Luces flew back to Hong Kong before starting their long journey home. Prior to leaving China, Harry turned to Teddy White. "You're coming back with us," he declared. White, immensely pleased, looked forward to learning more about Luce while visiting New York City. To Luce, White's companionship offered a way of prolonging his China trip. White, they decided, would write an article for *Fortune*, where he could tell the real story of the Chiangs. The Luces intended to take White home to their elegant wooded estate near Greenwich, where he would meet famous journalists like Walter Duranty and John Gunther. And Luce could also bestow rewards on White, such as good pay and stock options. These bonuses would mean a lot to Teddy's family, whose memories of the Depression were vivid. To a boy from Dorchester, who had saved pennies in order to reach Harvard Square, such vistas were overwhelming.

As always, Harry Luce craved comradeship; he wanted to be a buddy, a regular guy. This goal continued to elude him, however, for since Brit Hadden's death, Harry drew back from intimacy. Gratuitously, he warned Teddy White not to come too close, for Luce's door would be closed to him, except by appointment. And if Teddy White wanted to work his way up, he would need to become an editor, back in New York. By-line or not, work in the field was a trap, with several false doors. *Time* was an editor's magazine, where well-paid "correspondents" wrote copy that often disappeared into file cabinets. If White returned to Chungking, his growing irritation over *Time*'s China coverage would doubtless erupt into a major crisis. But if Teddy edited in New York, he would jump out of his skin, itching to reach the front lines in the global struggle. For the moment, White enjoyed himself. Flying to Guam, the Philippines, Wake, Midway, Honolulu, then San Francisco, he conversed endlessly with Harry Luce.

On the way home, the Luces met General Douglas MacArthur, Marshal of the Philippine Army, who delighted both Luces. MacArthur exuded a sense of drama and history; one quality appealed to Clare, the other to Harry. A great actor and a handsome man, MacArthur was perfectly suited to *Life*. Within a few months, *Time*, too, was talking about General MacArthur in reverential terms.

Harry Luce arrived home during the last week of May, all fired up with enthusiasm for his task. John Billings, however, heard a discordant note amid all the happy reunions. One day at lunch, White and Luce got into an argument. Apparently Teddy believed that civil strife would engulf China after the end of the current war. Luce vigorously demurred. Soon, however, both men turned to other, less volatile subjects, such as General MacArthur.

Back in the United States, Harry Luce became the nation's preeminent spokesman for Chinese war relief. He sometimes addressed large audiences through full radio network hookups. His stammer held no terrors for him now, as he traveled the country. Luce loved to quote the expatriate writer Gertrude Stein (an unlikely ally), who had declared that "the only way for America to save herself is for America to save China!" Saving China meant redeeming the promise of American honor. Alluding to China's 450 million souls, Luce exalted their endurance. He then praised the 5,000 American missionaries who still, despite all hardships, ministered to China's material and spiritual hunger. Luce affectionately described the Chinese as people who naturally loved Mei-kwa, America.

If sour critics alluded to Guomindang corruption, Luce became irritated. He sometimes excused Chinese graft and privilege, ascribing them to the demoralizing effects of three years of war and blockade. And besides, did not America (read: Democrat-controlled big cities) have its fair share of corrupt politicians? To those Americans who lauded the Communist guerrillas or criticized Chiang's war effort, Luce counseled silence. Chiang, Luce argued, was closer to the front than were his American critics, and he could better judge its needs. Half of Chiang's divisions, Luce claimed, contained first-rate soldiers, who were ready to fight on. In fact, a lack of manpower, long supply lines, fear of the Soviets, and the size of China contributed more to Japan's failure to resolve her "China Incident." And Luce angrily rejected the arguments propounded by people who complacently suggested that China could easily "absorb" an outnumbered conqueror. Did these critics, Luce asked, expect England to absorb Hitler? He also referred to the Chinese Communist armies as "overpraised."

Harry Luce's idealized Chinese peasant was a kind of Asian student of Dale Carnegie and John Calvin, anxious to improve himself through hard work. Luce even described conscripted workers along the Burma Road as patriots who labored "partly for pay but most of all for their country." Though warned by Teddy White, Henry Luce tended to dismiss or play down the disastrous effects of inflation on Chinese morale. This was ironic, for in 1941, Kurt Bloch, an expert on the subject, joined the editorial board of *Fortune*. Bloch pointed out that the Chinese government was doing little about the rising inflationary spiral, which would one day lead to disaster. When Harry thought about China, he was less interested in markets or supply and demand than in heroism, armies, offensives, and victories. There was nothing wrong with the Chinese economy, he believed, that American money, experts, and goodwill could not fix.

Within weeks of Luce's return to New York, *Time*'s June 16, 1941, cover featured General Chen Cheng, the defender of Chungking. After celebrating the durability of the Chinese soldier, *Time*, straining credulity, linked the future of the Middle East and Southeast Asia to the fate of China's 6th War Front. From Chungking, however, came an encouraging, pleading letter from Dr. Wang Shih-chieh, who worked for the Ministry of Publicity. Dr. Wang flattered and gently cajoled, as he praised *Fortune* and one of Mrs. Luce's "inspiring" speeches on China. Chungking wanted more of the same, much more, and Luce intended to oblige.

John Hersey was a soft-spoken but persistent dissenter. He had risen sharply in Luce's esteem since first coming to *Time* as a rookie several years before. Then the young Yale graduate had taken the "*Time* test," an ordeal required of all prospective writers. An editor tossed a bunch of news clippings at Hersey, who had to write a *Time*-like piece based on them. A departmental editor would judge the product. After passing the test, Hersey was on probation for three more months. What really impressed his bosses, however, was a Hersey memorandum that detailed all of *Time*'s defects. Of course Harry had known Hersey while he was still studying at Yale, so there was little doubt about his splendid future with the company.

By 1941 the twenty-seven-year-old associate editor was reminding Harry Luce of unpleasant truths about his China. Hersey had visited the country, including its Japanese-occupied coastal ports. The Chinese people, Hersey concluded, were resisting Japan, but in 1941 they remained largely feudal and superstitious. Luce, greatly annoyed, countered by describing China as a country fighting for democracy, not merely for survival (he disliked those who merely fought to survive). Luce would listen to the tall young man, argue with him, then praise China's "extraordinary" degree of freedom. This statement would have surprised dissidents incarcerated in Chiang's prisons.

John Hersey was trying to correct Harry Luce's vision, but faith usually triumphed over reportage. One argument between Luce and young Hersey, over an article for *Fortune*, resulted in an uneasy, amusing compromise: China was part democratic and part feudal! Luce believed that Hersey should be happy with this settlement. Indeed, Luce had big plans for this young man. People at Time Inc. whispered that Hersey might one day be managing editor of *Time*. When arguments passed, they were, in Harry's phrase, "spilled milk." Luce, however, did not expect well-paid editors to defy him over a long period of time.

In China, Luce had confused propaganda displays with spontaneous demonstrations of faith. Inspired by Madame Chiang, Luce quoted her words to American audiences. She had cried, ". . . why don't you wake up!" then exclaimed, "don't you know the world's on fire!" Luce's magazines were becoming permanent fund-raising organs for United China Relief. In a move that disturbed some of his colleagues, Luce decided to request donations from Time Inc.'s employees. Time Incers received invitations to a private showing of the color film *Ku Kan*, a celebration of China that would presumably stimulate their generosity. Teddy White and John Hersey, among others, were pressed into service. Shortly thereafter, they distributed a touching memorandum, providing information about China's needs. Then UCR collectors went from office to office, asking for money. People donated, "for Harry." Billings soon placed Madame Chiang on the cover of *Life*, where Margaret Bourke-White's photographs did justice to her subject's dignity and beauty. United China Relief could only benefit from such displays. In fact, it was impossible to separate UCR's appeals from the "factual" material in *Life* or *Time*.

Harry Luce drew on personal contacts that sometimes reached back three or more decades. The McCormick family's International Harvester Company gave UCR $20,000, and Luce supplemented this amount by appealing directly to old friends. In June 1941, for example, he traveled to Chicago. Mrs. Anita Blaine received an invitation to Harry's forthcoming UCR speech, scheduled for delivery at the Drake Hotel. Mrs. Blaine promptly pledged a generous $1,000 contribution, which made her a member of the China Relief Legion. Co-sponsored by Madame Chiang and author Pearl Buck, this honorary corps consisted of substantial contributors to the medical relief of China. Later in the year Luce sought funds for newspaper promotions announcing an important radio address by "the greatest woman of the Orient in modern times."

Madame Chiang, in turn, lavishly praised the Luces for "helping the American people understand the significance of China's struggle." The Luces' recent visit, Madame Chiang added, had "renewed our faith in the ultimate victory of the Democracies." Privately, Madame shared a concern with Clare, for she had heard rumors about the negotiations between Washington and Tokyo. Madame Chiang clearly hoped that Harry would work to prevent further appeasement of Japan. "America," she concluded, "will soon have to face the issue of war or dishonor in the Pacific."

Luce was for the moment less critical of Franklin Roosevelt, who on May 27, 1941, had proclaimed an Unlimited National Emergency. U.S. relations with Japan were also entering a more dangerous phase. Convinced that hostilities would erupt in 1941, Luce did not flinch, for no one, he argued, had ever figured out how to win a war without fighting it. It was possible, he thought, that Japan would respond to American pressure by adopting a more conciliatory attitude. What, however, if Tokyo refused to relent? Then, Luce responded, America would have to go to war. In Luce's view, the West plus China could win their war in the Pacific in a year or less. China's armies, he argued, were wearing down the Japanese war machine, readying it for the kill. Harry Luce now convinced himself that an American air corps, consisting of perhaps 1,500 planes, could put Japan on the defensive.

Luce did not content himself with preaching to the public about the export of arms to China. In June he decided to approach the Secretary of War on China's behalf. Henry L. Stimson listened carefully, as Luce spoke excitedly about Chinese military discipline and related matters. In talks with other influential men and women, Luce harped on Christianity's growing influence in China and ignored the xenophobia that was rife in the Guomindang. Arranged marriages, he noted, were becoming less common. With Western help, modern-minded Chinese doctors were fighting previously ineradicable diseases.

Luce's propaganda onslaught was hard to evade. Reaching the public through press, radio, and speeches, millions of Americans heard his message. *Life*, with its powerful photographs, was especially effective. Who could resist the little "warphans," trying to survive on nothing in embattled Chungking? In Chicago, children wrote letters responding to Madame Chiang's appeal on behalf of these Chinese kids. *Time* noted that one dollar could support a Chinese civilian for three weeks. In Indiana, Paul Hoffman, Luce's industrialist friend, agreed to head a UCR drive. He raised $16,000, in part by organizing a "Chinese" meal in South Bend. There, sitting under a portrait of Chiang, people tried to eat chow mein by using chopsticks. China *must* be helped, *Life* rashly concluded, for it, too, was a democracy.

UCR held big rallies, including one in Madison Square Garden,

where 15,000 Americans cheered long and hard for China. A deluge of
checks, some as high as $10,000, fattened the coffers of UCR. Luce was
particularly happy about his Los Angeles operations. There, Hollywood
mogul David Selznick chaired the movie industry's UCR drive. Beholden to *Life* for the success of many a film, Selznick had good reason
to humor Luce. So did producer Louis B. Mayer, who contributed
$1,000 to UCR. In Los Angeles' Chinatown, 100,000 people attended
a fund-raiser for China relief. UCR thus netted $100,000, thanks in
large measure to the presence of Claudette Colbert, Jack Benny, Betty
Grable, and other stars.

At the River Club, in New York, a group of men and women, clad
in "Chinese" outfits, attended a UCR benefit. Mrs. Edith Willkie, John
D. Rockefeller III, Thomas Lamont, Thomas J. Watson of IBM, and
Mrs. Dwight Morrow graced the occasion. *Life* attended the party, and
featured the occasion in a multipage spread. The Yenching connection,
which had brought Dr. Luce into contact with the Rockefeller operations in China, also proved lucrative. After Luce contributed $50,000
to UCR, the Rockefeller Foundation, John D. Rockefeller, Jr., and John
D. Rockefeller III donated $10,000 to the organization. Old supporters
of Harry Luce, such as Mrs. William L. Harkness and Thomas W.
Lamont, made large gifts to China Relief. In all, Luce and his colleagues
had raised more than $2,350,000 since April. Late in the year, Harry
happily corrected this figure, which was then approaching $3 million.
This figure was over and above the amounts individually solicited by
the member agencies. United China Relief's total income did not reach
the unrealistic goal of $5 million, but it came within a million of that
amount. Appropriately, UCR's board of directors soon honored Harry
Luce, for "without his leadership and devotion the movement could
not have gone forward." *Cue* magazine, the widely read entertainment
weekly, saluted Luce for "his farseeing efforts to turn the eyes of the
American people across the Pacific as well as the Atlantic." This view
of Luce, often repeated in the coming decades, did not always precede
a salute.

Cue applauded Luce, but in New York City an ominous mishap
occurred. On a breezy spring day, Wendell Willkie and Governor Herbert Lehman were reviewing a UCR-organized parade. The highlight
of the festivities was to be a dragon, modeled on those fashioned in
Chiang's homeland. The animal, made of paper and lightweight wood
and held together by ropes, symbolized the heroic Chinese resistance,

led by Chiang Kai-shek. The fake monster, however, was an unwieldy creation, a full block in length. The cardboard beast could not withstand a sudden gush of powerful winds, which smashed its legs and torso to pieces. Only the beast's head was intact, as this casualty of America's China fantasy lay dead on the pavement.

Crusading
for Democracy and
Mobilization

Back on August 12, 1940, a group of patriotic activists had organized the Council for Democracy (CFD). Participating in the deliberations were Freda Kirchwey of *The Nation*, a leftist; Ohio Republican Charles P. Taft, a moderate; and Colonel William Donovan, a flamboyant war hero. Harry Luce's designated choreographer was Charles Douglas ("C. D.") Jackson. At CFD, Jackson acted as Luce's surrogate, much as B. A. Garside did in the Broadway offices of United China Relief. The new Council depended heavily on Luce for its early funding. When the CFD succeeded in raising its first $85,000, for example, $35,000 came from Harry Luce. He continued to give the occasional "loan" of $5,000, and Luce was not overly concerned about repayment.

Widely traveled since the days of his childhood in Switzerland, C. D. Jackson possessed the credentials so important to Harry Luce. A Princeton man, Jackson spoke fluent French, which he taught there. His father's death forced C.D. to take over the family's marble and stone import business. The Depression, however, soon compelled him to sell the family concern, and Jackson, after talking to a friend at *Fortune*, approached Harry Luce for a job. He became Luce's assistant in 1931. C. D. Jackson was an able, energetic jack-of-all-trades. He was well spoken and sophisticated, yet exuded a hearty air of good fellowship. Jackson also liked to gossip, and he was later known to tell tales about the alleged travails of Harry and Clare. C.D.'s presence often lightened a room darkened by Luce's ponderous impatience. By 1937 Jackson was *Life*'s general manager; he soon bore the title vice-president of Time Inc. Jackson was an imaginative public relations man, too. By 1941 this self-styled "sucker for a crusade" had become an outspoken interventionist. As the Council for Democracy's first president, Jackson served his cause well.

C. D. Jackson had intended to work for the CFD only until it could function without him. For about eight months he headed the organization, which set up midtown offices at 285 Madison Avenue. There, he directed a multimedia national promotional campaign. To help C.D., Luce assigned Douglas Auchincloss, his own able young assistant, to the Council. The young executive vice-president did most of the CFD's administrative work, and there was a great deal of it. Jackson hoped that the CFD would unite people *against their enemies*, primarily Nazis, Fascists, and isolationists. The Council worked closely with community activists, and it appealed to nostalgia, pride, and fear. The early results sometimes disappointed Jackson, who sneered about "cheesy" events featuring "a lot of God Bless America and anti-communist talk." The Council quickly refined its techniques, however. Its ambitious new program required the use of all the major communications media, including radio, press, film, advertising, and publishing.

The CFD's radio program, "Speaking of Liberty," was heard every Thursday night for nineteen weeks, on forty-one radio stations scattered across the nation. Letters poured in praising the series, so later in the year NBC broadcast a second set of programs. The Council even fielded foreign-language radio programs, including one for Italian speakers in the U.S.A. And in an unprecedented move, the CFD broadcast a German-language program to the Reich. The important new group, called Loyal Americans of German Descent, owed its inception to the Council for Democracy. The Council also inspired The March of Time's release, "Americans All," a moving tribute to the national melting pot. The Council for Democracy attracted 28,000 people to a rally in Bridgeport, Connecticut. Preparedness had been good for this depressed industrial town, and Socialist Mayor Jasper McLevy was pleased to show his appreciation. Two weeks later, in Madison Square Garden, the CFD staged a large National Emergency Rally. Before 20,000 enthusiastic people, speakers voiced unstinting support for President Roosevelt's foreign policy.

Roosevelt had considered establishing an agency "to combat subversive propaganda." Luce's name had surfaced as a possible director, but the project came to naught. There was no need for such an agency, the White House decided, for private groups could make appropriate propaganda without being nailed as Administration puppets. In fact, the Administration engaged in secret collusion with the Council for Democracy. Archibald MacLeish, a Roosevelt favorite and Librarian of Congress, defended this collaboration as one of "the functions of government and private agencies under present conditions." White House aide Lowell Mellett coyly added that private groups had the right "to influence the people." Luce's Council for Democracy pleased the White House by making pro-Allied, antitotalitarian propaganda. FDR, however, now suspected Harry himself of aiding and abetting the Nazi cause.

Former Ambassador John Cudahy was about to travel about Europe on assignment from *Life*. The White House watched him closely, for FDR viewed Cudahy as an appeaser out to make trouble for him and for Britain. Luce's correspondent was, in Roosevelt's view, a dangerous man. FDR and Churchill were in no mood for new, confusing "peace offers" from Germans—or Americans. Late in February 1941, the President had learned that Cudahy was in Bermuda. According to Assistant Secretary of State Adolf A. Berle, Jr., Cudahy was heading for Europe as a correspondent for *Life*. Secretary Berle added that Cudahy purported to be on a "private mission for President Roosevelt." Actually, Berle noted, Cudahy was going to Berlin in order to probe Germany's peace terms. The day after receiving Berle's memorandum, Roosevelt dictated a note to Under Secretary of State Sumner Welles. He wanted to discuss the Cudahy situation with his old friend.

The publisher's latest gambit perplexed the President. How could the author of "The American Century," who called for war, support "appeasement" by a bleeding heart like John Cudahy? In fact, Harry Luce merely wanted access to a sensational news story, and as always he was willing to pay very well. Allen Grover and John Billings offered Cudahy the generous sum of $10,000 for at least four articles. Three weeks later, the President told Steve Early that he wanted to see Luce within the next few days. Appointments secretary "Pa" Watson dutifully cabled the publisher, asking him to stop by the White House on Friday, February 28, at 12:30 P.M. Whatever his private view, Luce expressed delight at the prospect and planned to depart for Washington. The President suddenly caught cold, however, and abruptly canceled the appointment. Luce was puzzled, but Bob Sherrod, who now worked in Time Inc.'s Washington bureau, soon provided him with information gleaned from White House insider Thomas "Tommy the Cork" Corcoran. According to Corcoran, Roosevelt had hoped to discuss "the Chinese situation" with Harry. This seems unlikely, but it was the kind of story calculated to disarm Luce. Roosevelt's sudden cold probably stemmed from presidential anger over the Cudahy mission.

In early March 1941, the press learned of Cudahy's travels. A rumor soon made the rounds, alleging that the former diplomat was going to interview Hitler. Questioned about his onetime friend, the President airily responded, "Oh, no, he's a newspaperman." This coy, sarcastic dismissal was vintage FDR, but under his surface calm there lurked growing rage. In fact, Noel Busch of *Life* had suggested that Cudahy interview Hitler. The dictator, who wished to keep the United States out of the war, might be happy to talk to the American people. *Life* would be a marvelous forum.

President Roosevelt soon demanded detailed information about John Cudahy's travels. The former ambassador became the object of a formidable international intelligence operation, conducted in the United States and abroad. Two weeks after Ambassador Alexander W. Weddell lunched with Cudahy in Spain, FDR dispatched an angry memorandum to Sumner Welles. The President claimed that while Cudahy was in Madrid, he had bad-mouthed the Administration. Luce's correspondent, Roosevelt feared, would write a series of "amazingly unintelligent articles." These pieces would, FDR predicted, "get enormous acclaim . . . in Germany." Hinting at blackmail, Roosevelt told Welles why Luce needed to "know this probability beforehand. . . ." If Cudahy did meet with Hitler, or publish articles supportive of Nazi propaganda, the White House could then "prove that Luce knew about it beforehand. . . ."

Luce did know about "it" beforehand. In April Cudahy was due in Berlin. Henry Luce had issued general guidelines to him in case he met the *Führer*. Suggesting that the Ambassador take careful notes and keep a diary, Luce again wished to learn the precise nature of Hitler's war aims. Anticipating the obvious charge, Luce did not believe that Cudahy would be taken in by the Germans. He may have been wrong. In fact, a high German Foreign Office official bragged that Cudahy "might be very useful in bringing the German viewpoint before the United States."

In early April 1941, as German tanks rolled through Yugoslavia and Bulgaria, then into Greece, Cudahy prepared a draft article for *Life*. He had met with German officials, who offered him their views about postwar trade between the Reich and the Americas. Cudahy praised these men for their cooperation. Without his knowledge, someone in the American embassy obtained a copy of his draft and cabled it to Sumner Welles. The embassy was convinced that Cudahy had fallen for propaganda glorifying the New Order. To the irritable White House, Luce and Cudahy were flirting with treachery, at the worst possible time. The Germans were pressing the British in North Africa. The United Kingdom's shipping losses in the North Atlantic threatened her long-term survival, while German bombs rained down on English cities. Some observers even believed that Hitler would try to invade Britain. Many interventionists, some of them in Luce's circle, demanded that the President institute convoys in the North Atlantic.

In the midst of these crises, John Cudahy pressed ahead, preparing for a possible interview with Hitler himself. The White House, which prided itself on understanding and using the media, could not get a handle on Luce's way of operating. The facts were simpler, and less duplicitous than FDR imagined. Harry Luce wanted a scoop, but he also wanted to expose the Nazi "New Order" as a fig leaf for German despotism. Such an exposé could hurt the cause of those pacifist and isolationists who still clamored for a compromise peace.

The U.S. embassy in Berlin soon learned that John Cudahy was about to meet with Foreign Minister Joachim von Ribbentrop. As seen by the White House, this encounter proved to be a disaster. At his May 4 meeting, Cudahy seemed to be offering advice on how to manipulate Roosevelt. Berlin must, he said, warn FDR of the dangers inherent in his pro-British policy. Cudahy added that Americans, fearful of war, would then deter Roosevelt from instituting a convoy system. The White House obtained some of this material in draft form even before it appeared in *Life* or in syndication. And in a conversation with Propaganda Minister Joseph Goebbels, John Cudahy learned that Britain would be defeated that summer. Germany, however, could not, and did not wish to invade the Americas. In fact, Goebbels added, Berlin hoped that the poor relations between the two nations, which had not resulted from German actions, would improve. Goebbels' pitch backfired badly. In the American press, newspapers carried headlines like "U.S. Invasion Study Admitted by Nazis."

A telegram from Cudahy, which the former Ambassador had cabled from Berlin on May 6, landed in the hands of Roosevelt's press aides. The message consisted of a draft article for *Life*. Cudahy's tone was preemptory, as he demanded that the Hoover food plan be implemented in Belgium. Just as this nettlesome issue had faded from the public view, Cudahy was reviving it. Herbert Hoover, a prime enemy of the White House, observed that the article "may possibly save the lives of more children than any one man has ever saved before by a magazine article." To the White House, Luce was waffling again on the food plan, while giving the Nazis a propaganda outlet in the United States. Worse was to come.

On May 23, 1941, John Cudahy finally obtained his interview with Hitler. He was the first American reporter to speak with the dictator since the fall of France. Cudahy traveled up to the Berghof, near Berchtesgaden, and spent several hours with the German leader. Hitler, however, despite Cudahy's prompting, refused to discuss his war aims, much less the future of Axis-dominated Europe. He did, however, warn Roosevelt that "American escorts for convoys meant war." At *Life*, Billings tried to soften the blow by contacting Steve Early at the White House. When Billings asked Early if he wanted to read an advance copy of the interview, the press secretary turned him down. Irritated, Billings responded in kind (but to his diary only), calling Early a man whom "I despise." FDR blamed Luce for this whole fiasco. Some of Harry Luce's colleagues tended to agree. Tom Matthews labeled the Cudahy interview a "blow for appeasement." Ray Buell agreed that *Life* was being used by the Nazis in their propaganda campaign.

Life's editors were concerned about public reaction to the Cudahy interview, and their editorial work showed it. Billings' introductory comments, though accompanied by a box containing a few of Roosevelt's anti-Nazi statements, failed to mollify the White House. While Roosevelt praised the *New York Times* for dissecting the Cudahy material, he did not laud *Life* for doing the same thing. Less than a week after the *Life* article appeared, Roosevelt asked that Luce be contacted. He left the time and date open. FDR did not give a reason for his request, which the Cudahy article may have provoked. The public furor over the interview quickly dissipated, but the White House would not soon forget the affair.

In fact, Cudahy had made no attempt to conceal anything from the American embassy or from State Department officials. Though Sumner Welles would not see him, Cudahy duly passed on private information to Cordell Hull. He could not mollify the Administration, however. The White House's surrogates attacked *Life* for offering Hitler the ultimate propaganda forum. Speaking to the press, Roosevelt implied that Cudahy was working for the Germans on behalf of American appeasers. The White House drew back from cutting all ties to Luce and Time Inc., however. The occasional alliance endured, and it soon paid dividends to the President. Luce's productions became more venomous than ever in their treatment of Roosevelt's isolationist enemies.

The March of Time produced a film called *Peace by Adolf Hitler*. This scathing "documentary" attacked Senator Burton K. Wheeler (Democrat of Montana) and other isolationists (but not Cudahy) as mouthpieces for Hitler. The "documentary" mimicked Nazis, who denounced Roosevelt as a bloodthirsty warmonger. *Life*'s Hubert Kay depicted Wheeler as a kind of shifty demagogue, who may have been dabbling in anti-Semitism. And the White House, which was anxious to destroy Charles Lindbergh's credibility, found an ally in *Life*. Edmond Taylor's forthcoming *Life* article would, said John Billings, show that what Charles A. Lindbergh, Jr., "says is down the Nazi alley." In a cover story, *Time* soon snidely and unfairly lumped America First head Robert Wood together with "Jew-haters, Roosevelt-haters," and other demagogues. Colonel McCormick's *Chicago Tribune*, wrote *Time*, had risen to "new heights of isolationist frenzy." McCormick, for one, never forgave Luce, and a new feud was born. Perhaps only Luce could have managed to infuriate both Colonel McCormick and the *Chicago Tribune*'s archenemy, Franklin Delano Roosevelt.

For months Luce's publications hammered away at Lindbergh. In the middle of September 1941, this frustrated America Firster openly attacked American Jews as warmongers. *Time*, like most of the media, promptly placed America First in the company of "impeccable Americans, Bundists, Fascists [and] Coughlinites." Harry Luce gloated that Lindbergh was "for the moment at least, a dead bunny." Writing to his friend Laura Hobson, Luce added that ". . . I am hoping that there is still enough left of the true American instinct to agree deeply on tolerance whenever the occasion again arises." In Roosevelt's fight against Lindbergh and America First, Luce proved to be the most stalwart and effective of allies.

In May 1941 FDR received important news from Chungking. Germany, Chiang Kai-shek predicted, would attack the Soviet Union within a month and half. That meant June 27 or June 28 at the latest. *Time*, to its credit, had long been alerting readers to Soviet-German tensions. In fact, in copy filed before June 22, the day of Hitler's invasion of Russia, the magazine's sources reported heavy troop movements near the Soviet-German border in Poland. At *Life*, picture editor Wilson Hicks predicted that Germany would soon attack Russia, and with fabulous timing, he dispatched Margaret Bourke-White to Moscow.

Accompanied by her husband, novelist Erskine Caldwell, the eminent photographer arrived in Russia a month before the German assault. While narrowly escaping death from an enemy bomb, Bourke-White snapped exclusive, sensational photographs of a German air attack. Wilson Hicks had boasted that his global picture operations were now stronger than "those of all the newspapers of the United States combined. . . ." Bourke-White showed that he was speaking the truth. Looking like gigantic fireworks, the explosions over Moscow soon offered Americans their first real glimpse of the Russian home front during an attack.

Harry Luce's America seemed to be sitting on the sidelines while the world burned. To Luce, FDR's cautious policy embodied a concept of "extreme limited liability." He repeatedly commented that "to win a war without fighting is a good trick if you know how to do it." Then he would invariably add: "I don't." To the disgust of Henry Luce, however, more Americans now thought that the Allies might win— without the need for direct U.S. involvement in the war.

After Hitler's invasion of the Soviet Union, 47 percent of polled Americans thought that Germany would defeat Russia. In late July, Gallup found that 34 percent of those questioned favored a compromise peace with Germany. In this scenario, the Reich surrendered western and northern Europe, while retaining her conquered Russian territory. Right through the middle of August, *Time* gave dreary accounts of Soviet losses in both lives and territory. With each passing week, however, the press became more sanguine about Russia's prospects for survival.

Harry Hopkins, who had flown to Moscow in order to assess Russia's fighting ability, was Roosevelt's personal emissary to Stalin. Hopkins, despite his unpleasant encounter with Clare Luce in the White House a year earlier during the screening of *The Ramparts We Watch*, was aware of *Life*'s hold on the American public. He interceded with Stalin, and Bourke-White took some striking pictures of him. Stalin, Bourke-White concluded, was strong, but a person "with a great deal of charm and a magnetic personality."

The Moscow that *Life* showed curious Americans was a city preparing for a siege. Children played in nurseries, kids loved their war games, but everyone was soon ready for the German assault. To Americans, these remarkable photographs offered a glimpse of a distant, newly hopeful world. The myth of German invincibility, undermined by Britain, might be shattered in Russia. John Hersey, who wrote about the Russian front for *Time*'s Foreign News, began to express enthusiasm for the Red Army. In Russia, Hersey saw a nation fighting for its future, and a people that would not be conquered. Hersey and *Time* portrayed Stalin as a formidable war leader and a man in touch with his people. Occasionally *Time*'s Foreign News even criticized Britain for failing to give more assistance to beleaguered Russia. *Time* supported the immediate dispatch of American aid to the USSR. Suddenly *Life* was optimistic about the apparent end of official Soviet atheism. In a major story on "Religion in Russia," *Life* claimed that various faiths were flourishing in the Soviet Union.

A global alliance was taking shape, and one could follow its shadowy emergence in Luce's magazines. China was still in the field; Britain was growing stronger each day; the Red Army refused to collapse; and the United States was finally gearing up its great industrial machine. A sense of inevitability about entry into the war permeated much of the nation. So did the feeling that an Allied victory was possible without America, but certain if the United States entered the war. Luce, however, feared fatalism, and continued to support the work of the Council for Democracy, which had become more aggressive.

Though Luce attended at least one meeting of the CFD's executive committee, he left daily operations in the hands of others. Still, several members of the CFD's high command grew nervous about its reputation as a "Time Inc. propaganda subsidiary." This, of course, is exactly what it was. C. D. Jackson was restless anyway, so, having carried out his assignment, he relinquished the presidency to Ernest Angell. Chaired by Harvard professor Carl J. Friedrich, the CFD's board now included labor leaders David Dubinsky and A. Phillip Randolph, and editor William Allen White. Other allies of Harry Luce soon joined, among them the interventionists Hamilton Fish Armstrong, Herbert Agar, and Dorothy Thompson.

Despite his discreet absence from most CFD functions, Harry Luce could not escape new controversies. Sensing the slide toward war, isolationists lashed out at convenient—and effective—targets. *Uncensored*, a widely circulated newsletter, enjoyed the active support of anti-interventionists like Oswald Garrison Villard and *Fortune*'s own John Chamberlain. In August 1941 the paper accused the CFD of warmongering. Referring to C. D. Jackson as "smooth young trouble-shooter for Henry Luce" (an accurate description), *Uncensored* complained about the CFD's secrecy. As a holding company, rather than a membership organization, the Council was not required to publicize the names of its contributors. And according to *Uncensored*, the Council, allegedly because of its support for Roosevelt, enjoyed tax-exempt, "educational" status. Other activist groups, however, found themselves subjected not only to taxation, "but also to investigation by the FBI." This was true, for while the White House helped the Council for Democracy, the FBI spied on America First.

Senate isolationists, led by Gerald P. Nye, senior Senator from North Dakota, shared *Uncensored*'s frustration. Nye decided to investigate the Hollywood motion picture industry, where, he was convinced, foreign-born producers were turning out warmongering propaganda. The Senator quickly added that he had "splendid Jewish friends," though he did not identify them. Nye labeled *The March of Time* "the purest kind of manufactured propaganda of a most brutal nature." Describing *The March of Time* as "part actuality, part fiction," Nye even resented the newsreel's attacks on Hitler's recent peace offensive.

Senator Nye opened his antipropaganda circus in September 1941. His accusations soon ran afoul of Luce's friend Wendell Willkie, Hollywood's defense counsel. *Life* happily noted that the witch-hunters had not seen most of the movies they were attacking. Sarcastically, Nye's critics wondered if the Senator would be happy if Hollywood produced a given number of anti-Nazi films, then balanced them by creating an identical number of *pro-Nazi* movies. Displaying a disturbing mixture of ignorance, anti-Semitism, and Anglophobia, the Nye hearings adjourned amid a hail of ridicule. In fact, surveys indicated that most polled respondents preferred war-related newsreels and short features to newsfilms offering more traditional themes.

A few days after Harry Luce published "The American Century," Daniel Longwell surveyed the grim world facing the United States. "I think," he concluded, "that if the U.S. Government didn't have *Life* Magazine, it would have to invent it." Longwell described *Life* as an intermediary between a confused public and the rapidly expanding armed forces. "[We] must," he added, "attempt to be the big educator of the kind of world [in which] we are evidently going to live." This would be *Life*'s war. As Harry Luce liked to point out, Time Inc. had been "at war" since 1939, and he was waiting for the President and the nation to catch up with it.

Washington was changing very quickly, for the once provincial capital was being invaded by industrialists, bureaucrats, military men, contractors, secretaries, and seekers of opportunity. Channels of communication between Time Inc. and the rapidly multiplying agencies of government needed to be streamlined. Harry Luce again turned for help to Allen Grover, appointing him chairman of the War Plans Committee at Time Inc. Grover now found himself charged with addressing problems arising between the company and "various Washington Departments including the Army and Navy." Luce was relying on Grover's ability to act with discretion. Touchy issues involving state secrets and censorship were sure to arise.

Harry Luce's company was becoming ever more important to the American defense effort. Like Harry Luce, General George C. Marshall was particularly pleased with *Life*'s July 7, 1941, issue, which depicted the "Arming of America." That magazine introduced a dynamic major general named George S. Patton, Jr., to the American people. The commanding general of the Second Armored Division, standing on his tank, represented the daring, younger generation of American army commanders. And a lead article on new weapons depicted a light landing craft that could carry armored vehicles. In an uncanny premonition of Omaha Beach and Saipan, *Life* then published pictures of a modern landing operation.

Life knew that Americans were worried about their young draftees. In a picture story, the magazine featured a few of the 25,000 soldiers and young trainees encamped at Camp Jackson, near Columbia, South Carolina. *Life* sympathized with the lonely soldier, on leave in a city he did not know. Respectable local girls, of course, did not mix with these selectees. The young soldiers did not find much to do except for the occasional visit to a bowling alley, hamburger stand, or movie house on Main Street. Hinting at a morale and health problem that grew as more young men flocked to the training centers, *Life* admitted that some of these boys visited "roadhouse girls," and described venereal disease as a threat to the national defense. *Life*, however, usually balanced this sort of story with a more upbeat look at "national defense." One piece showed Russell Sage College in Troy, New York, where pretty coeds were busily at work. Clad in appealing garments, the young ladies repaired radios, tuned automobiles, and learned radio technology. One girl, wearing shorts, tinkered beneath a truck. *Life* coyly advised that "Shorts may be more comfortable for this work, but overalls afford more protection." Thus did the national magazine leaven the national burden with a bit of cheesecake.

War proved to be good for business. The near-prosperity boosted *Life*'s sales while further undercutting its call for sacrifice. The good life seemed within reach to many more people, since well-paying defense jobs were now plentiful. *Life*'s warnings about battles in the North Atlantic competed with full-page advertisements hawking Calvert whiskey and Thanksgiving turkeys. In one striking but typical ad, a factory worker and a machine gunner draw their patriotic strength from Fleischmann's Enriched Yeast. While *Fortune* was worrying about producing synthetic rubber, *Life* published a two-page advertising spread glorifying rubber-made products manufactured by Firestone. This rubber importer, which could soon lose access to its Southeast Asian sources, was urging American consumers to buy more, not less of its product.

By 1941 *Fortune* had become an intermediary in the dialogue between the burgeoning defense establishment and the Roosevelt administration. *Fortune*'s original, sometimes scathing portraits of American managers enhanced its reputation among government officials suspicious of big business. Progressive, innovative businessmen also admired the magazine, but less sympathetic readers charged that *Fortune* "could have been written in the Kremlin." The magazine's reputation for detachment and criticism served it well, however. Superbly researched, clearly written, and independent-minded, *Fortune* relentlessly attacked production bottlenecks in war plants and administrative confusion in Washington. The magazine also convinced many executives of the government's need for their talent.

Some of these "dollar-a-year" men, such as Edward R. Stettinius, chairman of the board of U.S. Steel, were soon working closely with Eric Hodgins, publisher of *Fortune* magazine. *Fortune*'s Forum of Executive Opinion provided the Roosevelt administration with important insights into the thinking of leading businessmen. The results were interesting, and in some cases surprising. Most of these executives confessed that they had no idea what they were supposed to do on "mobilization day." And many reported disquieting shortages of skilled labor, which was vital to the expansion of the machine tool industry. By late 1940 the government was busily working to sort out urgent priorities among defense procurement needs. Interviewed many years later, Eric Hodgins gave a good deal of credit for this new efficiency to "*Fortune*—and when I say *Fortune*, I mean Harry Luce. . . ."

Time Inc. was a beneficiary of the new wave of defense spending. Ed Stettinius, who was rapidly rising in the new defense bureaucracy, proved to be an invaluable resource for Time Inc. Stettinius, who was two years younger than Harry Luce, was a handsome man with prematurely silver hair and the manners of an accomplished actor. He knew how to get along with the New Dealers, and accepted organized labor as a fact of life. Early on, he became the object of a prolonged courtship carried on by *Time*'s Charles Wertenbaker, a wealthy Virginian. The two men quickly became "Ed" and "Charlie." Wertenbaker, working in concert with Eric Hodgins, gave Stettinius his full support. As the ambitious Stettinius wrote to Noel Busch at *Life*, "I shall always stand ready to meet you half way in any reasonable undertaking." Ed Stettinius sometimes brought *Fortune*'s draft articles to the attention of

General Marshall and other important officers. When Wertenbaker once needed to see George Marshall, he dropped the name of his good friend Ed Stettinius and Marshall immediately granted the interview.

In 1941 Secretary of War Henry Stimson drew a bit closer to Harry Luce. In a note thanking Luce for a "kind article," Stimson provided him with a brief personal account of a recent trip to the state of Washington, where the Secretary had reviewed troops on maneuver. Praising their "courage, physique, and morale," the Secretary seemed to be trading better coverage for inside tidbits. Indeed, even *Time*, hitherto so critical of the confused and jammed defense effort, was turning optimistic by September 1941. Still, Luce's magazines could rarely resist a chance to snipe at Roosevelt, while demanding a better performance from American industry. These jibes did not go unnoticed. The President had only recently compared some of *Life*'s production figures to statistics available at the War Department and in the Office of Production Management. *Life*, FDR complained, had failed to ask for these figures before publishing its own, erroneous ones.

Life and *Time* and *Fortune* constantly advocated better relations between labor and capital. Henry Ford was notoriously antilabor, and his hostility impeded a stronger defense effort. In an article examining the conversion of Ford's huge River Rouge complex to "wartime use," *Life* argued that proper organization, supported by good labor-management relations, could unleash America's might. The March of Time, by way of example, produced a film on *Labor and Defense*, which praised 9 million organized workers for their commitment to national defense. Luce quickly approved of an article about Sidney Hillman and the CIO, which was highly favorable. When industrialists argued that paying overtime wages at the rate of time and a half caused inflation, *Time* cited figures supportive of labor's position. General Motors, the magazine noted, had in 1940 earned profits equal to 50 percent of wages paid. On issues related to race, Luce also continued to be "progressive" in his views.

Few publishers and fewer White House aides paid attention to the race issue in defense except when confronted by a crisis or a near riot. Harry Luce was an exception to this general rule of neglect. To Luce, blacks were an important part of America's defense potential, and he refused to censor his own views about racial justice. The Luce publications continued to laud black achievements and give publicity to the black plight. As Eliot Janeway eloquently put it in *Life*, ". . . our treatment of the Negroes is the great blot across the old belief of ours that all men are created equal." *Time* alone published more about Negroes in the military than all other national magazines put together.

An article about the famous 369th Infantry Regiment, of the New York National Guard, drew much favorable comment. This coastal artillery unit, *Time* sadly observed, was unique, since "there is no other place for Negroes in the Army." *Time* also told the story of the first regiment of Negro engineers, working at Fort Bragg, while *Life* followed a "Negro" private from basic training, to furlough at home in Warsaw, North Carolina. *Time* wrote about the first black flying force in the U.S. Army. The newsmagazine also brought the problems of the black soldier to the attention of millions of Americans, by recounting grievances reported in the Negro press. Luce's magazines were still not free of ethnic stereotypes, however. *Life's* young black selectee goes home to North Carolina and enjoys a watermelon, while sitting on a wagon pulled by a mule. And "Unlike most Negroes, Raymond does not like dancing." *Time* and *Life* occasionally spoke of "jive" and "pickaninnies," though more out of ignorance than malevolence. At no point, however, did these magazine really understand that the war could unleash racial turbulence beyond anything foreseen by Harry Luce. Still, by equating racial justice with patriotism, *Life* helped to promote change for the better in both the Army and in society.

In the summer of 1941, the Administration, preoccupied with other issues, failed to grasp the extent of congressional support for mustering out 669,500 one-year trainees when their term of service ended in October. At this crucial point, *Life* strongly endorsed the judgment of General Marshall, who wanted to keep his men in uniform beyond the one-year time frame. Luce's powerful arguments for retention of the draftees helped to win over some influential citizens, who contacted their Congressmen. In the House, only twenty-one Republicans voted for the continuation of service beyond the stipulated year. By the narrowest of margins—a single vote—Marshall's army was saved. Had the Luce press adopted the position advocated by the Republican leadership in the House, the General's new force would have faced extinction. Instead, the armed forces continued to grow, and by October 1, 1941, about 1.8 million men filled the ranks of thirty-four divisions and other units.

General Marshall was happy to assist his supporters in the media. When *Time* and *Life* wanted new and exclusive color photographs of the General, he waited in his quarters, after hours, until technicians arrived with their equipment. After the German invasion of Russia, *Life* gained access to secret maps of that campaign. The atlas came from the Army's G-2, or intelligence branch. When *Fortune* planned to devote an entire issue to air power, Roy Alexander and Charles Murphy requested an interview with the overworked General. After receiving their request, Marshall gave a typically terse order to his secretary: "Arrange this," he commanded. After carefully studying *Life*'s July 4 special issue on preparedness, Marshall praised the magazine for "awakening the American people to the fact [that] their Army is not willing to be caught unprepared." The General added that "It is indeed gratifying to have the cooperation and assistance of your great magazine in building up the defenses of our nation. . . ." And *Life* returned Marshall's compliment. Despite the War Department's belated objection to such an accolade, the magazine labeled Marshall a "military genius."

Life's Dan Longwell had predicted in February 1941 that war might soon erupt in the Pacific, a belief that only strengthened his legendary devotion to the Navy. On the thirty-first floor of Rockefeller Center, he constantly buttonholed his colleagues with new ideas for Navy-oriented stories. The Navy was a marvelous subject for *Life*, in which Wilson Hicks' photographers displayed gleaming warships with big guns ready to fire. Set against the backdrop of harbors and high seas, *Life*'s subscribers met smartly clad officers, who commanded well-trained sailors.

Life's special issue on the Navy caught the eye of Admiral Harold R. Stark, Chief of Naval Operations, who called it to the attention of his colleagues. By August 1940 Dan Longwell was commuting to Washington almost every week, discussing defense issues with the Army and the Navy. From the Commandant of the Marine Corps, Longwell learned about the amphibious landing exercises carried out by troops in training. This was important information, which offered readers a glimpse of coming battles in the Pacific. *Life* was ahead of its competitors, once again.

By the autumn of 1941, the Luce press was writing about a potential trading bloc of free nations and regions, consisting of the U.S.A., the British Empire, and Latin America. Given American potential, it was clear to *Fortune* that the U.S.A. would lead this alignment. Instead of accepting autarchic trade blocs in a largely totalitarian world, *Fortune* advocated the inauguration of global free trade in a Hitler-free environment. These expansionist policy positions, expressed in clear, confident prose, attracted a growing body of supporters both inside and outside Time Inc.

One important recruit was the Assistant Secretary of the Navy, James V. Forrestal, the former president of Wall Street's Dillion, Read & Co.

After reading *Life*'s special issue on the Navy, Forrestal contacted Dan Longwell, telling him how much that effort had helped the Navy. The Secretary quickly decided that Harry Luce's "The American Century" offered the most feasible blueprint for the construction of a new world order. "We cannot," Forrestal declared, "avoid our world responsibilities. . . ." Pointing to America's "potential world leadership," Forrestal repeated Luce's harsh condemnation of isolation. Speaking to the Union League in Philadelphia, Forrestal bemoaned America's past failure to maintain her great fleet. Jim Forrestal, following Luce, looked to a modern two-ocean navy as the guarantor of American global hegemony. In words that echoed Luce's phrases, Forrestal foresaw a postwar order dominated by the United States. Through its ties to men like Marshall and Stettinius and Forrestal, Time Inc. anticipated the advent of a new, defense-oriented complex, comprised of industry, government, and the media.

With Rockefeller in
Latin America

Harry Luce and the senior editors of *Fortune* had long been aware of unfortunate factors troubling Latin American–U.S. relations. In part, these gloomy developments reflected the onset of bad economic times. U.S. trade with Latin America had declined by about 75 percent between 1929 and 1933. In 1929 the U.S. absorbed 34 percent of Latin America's exports; by 1934 that figure had dipped to 29.4 percent. In 1936 Brazil was importing more cars from the Reich than from Great Britain. In that year Brazil also purchased 86,000 tons of coal from the Reich; a year later the figure reached an alarming (to the State Department) 200,000 tons. By 1937 the Germans were providing 26 percent of Chile's foreign goods, and 17.7 percent of Mexico's imports.

Franklin Roosevelt wanted to secure a paramount position for American exporters within his ever more broadly defined "Western Hemisphere." As early as December 1935, Roosevelt had thought about assisting Latin American countries with "supplies of one kind or another." Diplomatic engagement and sensitivity to other viewpoints replaced gunboat diplomacy and the dispatch of Marines. When Mexico nationalized American oil properties, Roosevelt responded with tact rather than bluster, thus winning points for his Good Neighbor Policy.

If Henry Luce did not pursue a subject through the usual flurry of memos and conversations, his editors were free to do their best, or their worst. *Life*, for example, wrote about Brazil in words that were "condescending and contemptuous." In an article filled with ethnic clichés, *Life* described Brazilians as a charming, lazy, racially mixed bunch who inhabited a failed society. *Fortune* was soon doing much better by Latin America, and the magazine enjoyed enormous prestige there. In 1938 *Fortune* published a stunning series of articles on South America, the most striking of which appeared in October.

Called "Mexico in Revolution" and illustrated by the great Mexican muralist Diego Rivera, *Fortune*'s essay was both probing and fair. The article explained the Mexican government's nationalization measures to smug or angry Americans. Poverty was endemic in Mexico, where per capita income averaged $36. *Fortune* concluded that "revolutionary nationalism" was here to stay; the peasants wanted land, and the workers demanded decent treatment. *Fortune*'s attitude was useful to the White House, where President Roosevelt worked to reach a compromise agreement with Mexico regarding its expropriations of foreign properties. And soon fascism seemed a greater threat than did nationalization.

For years FDR had been receiving private warnings about Nazi activities in South America. By 1940 he was reading memorandums that described South American officers as Axis sympathizers, ready to join a Nazi invader. *Time* soon feared that "90 million Americans" to the south might one day be working for Hitler. To win the hearts and minds of Latins, the President now turned to a man whose energy, wealth, and family connections could serve a newly aggressive American foreign policy.

Following the fall of France, the young millionaire Nelson A. Rockefeller wanted to do something important for the American cause in a region of interest to himself and his family. In August 1940 FDR decided to name Rockefeller Coordinator of the Commercial and Cultural Relations Between the American Republics. Less than a year later Rockefeller found himself heading its successor, the Office of the Coordinator of Inter-American Affairs (OCIAA). Disposing of public and private resources, Nelson Rockefeller worked to convince Latin elites and middle classes that alignment with "Yanqui" policy was in their own interest. After decades of American incursions and exploitation, this would not be an easy sell. Fueled by large amounts of goodwill and cash, the

Office of the Coordinator dispatched employees and allies to the lands south of the Rio Grande. In Rockefeller's view, American exports, from movies to magazines to airplanes, were weapons in his arsenal. Though not opposed to modest social reform, he stressed economic development and Pan-American accommodation.

Like Henry Luce, Nelson A. Rockefeller was aware of the long-term economic benefits that could accrue to his country. The war had disrupted normal trade patterns; where the European powers lost out, the United States might gain. Rockefeller believed that a global mission beckoned American entrepreneurs. He expected that Americans, not Germans or Italians or Japanese, would fill the gap left by defeated France and beleaguered Britain. A new network was emerging, and Roosevelt, Rockefeller, and Luce were building it.

A grandson of John D. Rockefeller, a Dartmouth graduate, and heir to one of the great American fortunes, young Nelson Aldrich Rockefeller became an avid patron of Latin American architecture, painting, and sculpture. In 1935 his avocation took him to Caracas, where he studied at the Venezuelan Museum of Modern Art. Rockefeller returned to New York, committed to the establishment of the Museum of Modern Art (MOMA), on West 53rd Street, between Fifth and Sixth avenues. This patronage brought the young man into contact with Harry Luce.

Though no expert on modern art, Henry Luce devoted considerable space in his magazines to Rockefeller's worthy venture. To him, the MOMA, erected in the midst of a harrowing Depression and frightening world crises, exemplified America's dedication to civilization. Yet Nelson Rockefeller's appeal to Luce transcended art. Harry fondly recalled how Nelson's father, John D. Rockefeller, Jr. ("Mr. Junior" to his staff), had, thanks to Mrs. Nettie McCormick, helped the Reverend Luce during his arduous fund-raising days. For his part, young Rockefeller appreciated the importance of Luce's media, which heartily supported the creation of MOMA. Among other kindnesses, Luce provided the museum's staff with temporary offices in the nearby Time-Life Building. When some of MOMA's directors importuned Luce, he placed the young Rockefeller on the cover of *Time*. The story, whose appearance coincided with the formal opening of the Museum, depicted Nelson Rockefeller as a kind of Renaissance man, at once an oil magnate and an art connoisseur.

Rockefeller contacted the Museum's board of trustees and suggested that its members, all wealthy and prestigious people, meet with Harry Luce. Rockefeller later proposed that Harry become a director, and the publisher dined with MOMA's board in November. Two months later Rockefeller personally notified the delighted publisher of his election. Within weeks the two friends again dined together when the Museum opened its Italian masters exhibition. Nelson Rockefeller's friendship with Harry even survived an unwelcome piece in *Fortune*. Russell Davenport provided Rockefeller with the draft of an article about the old Standard Oil Company of New Jersey. The piece showed how its founder, John D. Rockefeller, had brutally crushed competitors, including a group of Cleveland oil refiners. Nelson objected, but *Fortune* went ahead with the piece. Despite his resentment, Rockefeller and his family continued to work with Luce. Young Nelson, after all, harbored political ambitions. A determined self-promoter possessed of adequate talent and enormous drive, Nelson Rockefeller nurtured his friendship with Luce and his sister, Beth Luce Moore. When he became Latin American coordinator, Rockefeller found that Time Inc. was extremely useful.

Producer Louis de Rochemont learned that Rockefeller wanted to subsidize the export of *March of Time* films to Latin countries. Accordingly, The March of Time promised to produce two documentaries celebrating hemispheric solidarity. Nelson Rockefeller took note of this commitment and relayed it, with much other information, to the White House. *Fortune* also began to work closely with the Rockefeller office, and was soon waging what it called "political warfare." Working behind the scenes with American companies and the State Department, *Fortune* pushed the export of American know-how and industrial genius to South America. American corporations were moving into a vacuum created by a capital outflow from Argentina and other Latin countries back to Britain.

Somewhat cynically, *Fortune* told U.S. companies how they could sell a bit of their stock to favored "natives," thereby averting potential expropriations. American companies could displace Axis interests, make money, and foster hemispheric defense, all at once. In addition, American business, working with the Rockefeller operation, was pouring millions of dollars' worth of advertising into Latin America. This publicity sparked a demand for North American products among Latin elites.

Harry Luce wanted to preside over a company whose global influence reflected the growing importance of the United States. He therefore created a Latin American Committee, chaired by financial adviser Charles Stillman. In Stillman's view, the new American excitement about things Latin was not transient. In his opinion Time Inc. should tell Latin Americans about the United States, while explaining Latin America to North Americans. In the short run, Stillman noted, the company would derive little financial benefit from this twofold effort. In the long run, however, Time Inc. would reap a bountiful harvest in readers and goodwill. Stillman put the company's effort in the category of pro bono work. His colleagues were not sure about the feasibility of Time Inc.'s sudden involvement in Latin America, but Harry Luce was committed to expansion.

Ever the imaginative promoter, Luce had long been mulling over the prospects for an air edition of *Time*. The image of *Time* winging its way to influential Americans and other English-speakers in far-flung countries pleased Harry. Forces external to Time Inc. now made the air edition a reality. New planes and special subsidies sharply decreased costs, so that subscribers could now receive an air edition of *Time* for $10 per year. By the spring of 1941, 20,000 copies of the Air Express Edition of *Time* were heading southward in Juan Trippe's Pan American clippers, and Time Inc. could boast about publishing the world's first "plane-delivered magazine."

After some internal discussion and much external polling, Time Inc. decided against adjusting the contents of the air edition so as to mollify errant Latin leaders. The magazine's jibes at its least favorite Latin politicians occasionally unnerved Nelson Rockefeller, but by and large, *Time* proved a powerful advocate of American foreign policy goals. Luce strengthened *Time*'s personnel roster in Rio and Buenos Aires. And along with the English-language air edition, *Time* now published a syndicated service in Spanish. Each week the magazine translated an 8,000-word summary of its current issue for use in South America. Eventually, twenty newspapers, with a total circulation of one million copies, carried this version of *Time*.

Juan Trippe, of Pan American World Airlines, viewed the air edition as a great public relations coup. Writing to FDR, Trippe happily observed that his planes carried *Time* to Mexico, Colombia, and Peru. They also ferried reels of *The March of Time*, whose Spanish edition (*La Marcha del Tiempo*) soon played in 500 Latin American movie theaters. To Luce, Trippe was a great American entrepreneur, so *Life* detailed his many achievements. By 1941 Pan Am's planes flew over five continents and carried 400,000 passengers a year. *Life* noted that Pan Am helped to expel competing Axis airlines from major air routes in South America.

Pan American was to be the air arm of the American Century, and like Luce, Juan Trippe felt no compunction about working with his government. According to the records of the Military Intelligence Division, Pan American employees supplied the War Department with intelligence data. By 1941 Trippe's airline regularly flew representatives of American commerce, culture, and military intelligence into South America. U.S. businessmen arrived to take defense orders, and American entertainers and other celebrities flew southward on patriotic missions. Military officers went to South America, where they trained armies. All of this activity served Nelson Rockefeller's purposes, but he added a few touches of his own. By using economic pressure, Rockefeller could deny the benefits of burgeoning U.S. import orders to defiant South American companies. *Life* supported Rockefeller's blacklist, which helped to purge Latin American payrolls of alleged Axis sympathizers and spies. Luce also joined Rockefeller's Advisory Committee on Policy, designed to make South America safe for U.S. interests.

Ambassador to Chile Claude Bowers, a presidential friend of long standing, continually warned FDR of Nazi subversion in Chile. Roosevelt shared some of these stories with the press, since they bolstered public support for his foreign and defense policies. Following the President's lead, Luce's magazines grimly warned readers about the Axis threat in this hemisphere. Labeling the German community in Chile "a kind of foreign fungus," *Life* sounded the alarm over the alleged 500,000 "German Storm Troopers" in South America. The magazine published "Nazis in Chile," featuring photographs depicting an alarming array of Nazis, arms upraised in the Hitler salute. Photographed by the talented Hart Preston, who knew a lot about South America, the pictures exposed the brazen antics of the Nazi "Trojan Horse."

Time Inc. and the White House appeared to be working together, but as usual harmony yielded to turbulence. Ambassador Bowers approved of *Life*'s article on Chile, but one gaffe annoyed him. President Pedro Aguirre Cerda had exchanged pro forma notes with Hitler on the occasion of a national holiday. *Life*, Bowers told an irate President Roosevelt, had implied that Aguirre was a pro-Nazi. Worse still, Bowers added, *Life* had taken a formal message out of its proper context. Speaking of Time Inc., Bowers concluded that "these people always must do something to hurt."

The President, distracted by more pressing matters, did not complain to Luce. Worse was to come, however. In the autumn of 1941, *Time*, reverting to its Haddenesque style of yesteryear, described Aguirre as an ailing incompetent. He was, *Time* implied, about to leave office, perhaps to spend "more and more time with the red wine he cultivates."

In fact, Aguirre was at death's door, and he crossed the threshold a few days later. Harry Hopkins, no fan of the Luces, promptly forwarded a memorandum to Roosevelt, suggesting that he find a way to denounce the *Time* article. FDR quickly mobilized his allies, and no less a personage than Sumner Welles protested to Felix Belair of Time Inc. Roosevelt himself decided to vilify *Time* at his next press conference.

According to the President, the newsmagazine had published a "disgusting lie," akin to "Nazi propaganda against the United States." In aggrieved, self-righteous tones, the President implicitly accused *Time* of lying, slander, murder, and treason. For the first time in eight years or more, the United States, Roosevelt complained, had to apologize to a foreign power. Overcome by anger, FDR did not realize that he was boosting *Time*'s credibility. Henry Luce had to respond, and when he did, the Aguirre case became a *cause célèbre* in the U.S. press. Luce defended *Time*'s article, which reflected stories culled from a number of reliable sources. In words that could only enrage the White House, Luce ascribed Roosevelt's outburst to "the pressure of international politics." He rebuffed the President's attack on the free press, and most editorial writers supported *Time*.

While Roosevelt and Luce bickered, their common operations in Latin America were succeeding. Most of the region's governments had moved closer to the United States and Britain. Local Nazis found themselves harassed, arrested, or expelled. American influence had never been stronger. In the event of war, the resources and manpower of South America appeared to be less vulnerable to German blandishments or foreign subversion.

Late in November 1941, after promising to file a complete report on the Aguirre incident at a later date, Harry Luce turned to more pressing business. War threatened in the Far East.

The Day of Wrath

Twenty-eight years earlier, in 1913, Assistant Secretary of the Navy
Franklin Delano Roosevelt had received a letter from his distant cousin,
former President Theodore Roosevelt. TR had warned the young Secretary against weakening the Pacific fleet. Either keep the fleet strong,
advised Cousin Teddy, or remove all battleships from the region. In
the event of a crisis, he added, trouble with Japan "will come suddenly."
It would be unpardonable to be caught unprepared.

Henry Luce's journey to China in May 1941 had first taken him to
Hawaii, where he visited the American naval base at Pearl Harbor. At
the time, talk was rife about an impending crisis in Southeast Asia.
Luce's inspection tour convinced him that the Navy needed more ships,
but its gunners' "anti-aircraft marksmanship" impressed him. Though
stirred by the fighting spirit of American sailors, Harry Luce was uneasy
about what he had heard from their commanding officer, Admiral
Husband E. Kimmel. The Admiral said something to Harry about "not
biting off more than we can chew." In June, however, *Time*'s Robert
Sherrod filed a reassuring report, gleaned from information supplied

by a "high naval source." The Navy was shifting most of its strength to the Atlantic, since "Hawaii is impregnable."

To Harry Luce, Admiral Kimmel's cautionary words smacked of defeatism, but he read no deeper meaning into them until he met with Under Secretary of State Sumner Welles. As Luce recounted the story, Welles, using his finger, drew a line across a map of Southeast Asia. If Japan crossed that trip wire, "there would be war." Grenville Clark, a prominent lawyer, heard an even more disquieting rumor. The father of the 1940 conscription movement had just talked with his good friend Harry B. Cabot. Clark, to his shock, learned from Cabot that "we would get into war via [a] clash with Japan."

Luce believed that Franklin Roosevelt, unlike his great cousin, had relegated Asia to a dimly lit arena reserved for minor sideshows, and Harry resented it. *Time* bemoaned the fact that "the people of the U.S. remained unaware of the battle of the Pacific now underway." While sniping at FDR, Luce and his publications fell prey to their own enduring illusions. *Time*, for example, approvingly quoted Ambassador Bill Bullitt, who argued that only China's resistance prevented Japan from waging a combined "sea war against the British or ourselves. . . ." And, *Time* added, Japan could not conquer heroic China. Missing from *Time*'s coverage was any sense of the despair haunting Japanese military leaders. Some Tokyo newspapers even spoke of a war in which all the Axis powers would combine to attack the great democracies. Despite this ominous sign, *Time*, lacking its usual omniscience, could not predict who would prevail in Tokyo, the statesmen or the warriors.

Luce's magazines seemed confused in other ways, too. In *Life*'s sensational article on Singapore and a possible war with Japan, the American fleet steams out of Pearl Harbor and heads for the lifelines linking Japan to Southeast Asia. American flying fortresses, departing from bases in Guam or China, then reduce Tokyo to "a smoking rubble." *Life*, however, sensed the vulnerability of vaunted Singapore, which it described as the key to the region. Indeed, *Life* concluded that "Half the world falls to Japan with Singapore."

During the summer, *Time*, like most publications expressing a view on the subject, favored an American embargo on all oil exports to Japan. In July the Japanese prepared to seize bases and airfields around Saigon as well as the naval facilities on Camranh Bay. From these positions Japan could launch attacks on Singapore, the East Indies, the Philippines, or Thailand. President Roosevelt embargoed the export to Japan of high-octane fuels and crude oil, and on July 26 he froze Japanese assets in the United States. The President also recalled to duty General Douglas MacArthur, a move that delighted the Luces and his many other admirers. MacArthur was to command the Philippine armed forces, now placed under the authority of the U.S. Army. Confrontation was rapidly replacing "appeasement," and *Time* approved.

Most editorials supported Roosevelt's toughening position, seeing it as "a healthy warning to the Japanese." Newspapers predicted that, should war come, the American Navy would immediately blockade Japan while Army Air Corps bombers fire-bombed her papier-mâché cities. Fletcher Pratt, a reputable authority on military subjects, described the Japanese as having "defects of the tubes of the inner ear. . . ." This flaw, said Pratt, gave them "a defective sense of balance," and for this reason they could not be good aviators.

On September 12 nine of General MacArthur's new model B-17 "flying fortress" heavy bombers arrived in Manila. One day, MacArthur expected, those planes would threaten Japan herself. Everywhere, as she looked around, Japan now saw friends, allies, or dependencies of the United States. From Vladivostok to Pearl Harbor and Singapore and Chungking, Japanese military planners perceived encirclement, embargoes, strangulation, and doom.

While the Far Eastern situation grew critical, new fighting erupted in the Atlantic. A big picture spread in *Life* showed the wounded destroyer *Kearny* (torpedoed by a German submarine on October 17), then described the mothers of its dead as the first "Gold Star Mothers of World War II." On October 31 a German submarine sank an escort warship, the U.S. destroyer *Reuben James*, killing 155 crewmen and officers. Henry Luce once again declared war, as he attempted to jolt the public into action. The United States, *Life* decided, "was now at war with its inevitable enemy, Nazi Germany," and *Time* chastised "men [who] still talk of avoiding war." "The U.S.," *Time* insisted, "is at war with Germany." The nation was finally spending more money each day on defense than was Great Britain. Yet where was its sense of crisis? "The President," complained *Time*, "was still being cagey. . . ." Only 26 percent of those Americans questioned by Gallup favored declaring war on Germany. Too many Americans, Luce felt, failed to understand the magnitude of the challenge confronting them. He himself, however, was partly to blame for their confusion.

Time might be waging word-war, but Henry Luce, the prophet of war and redemption, remained the greatest purveyor of consumerism in America. *Time* demanded war, then placed actress Rita Hayworth on its November 10 cover. Though Americans believed that the United

States would enter the war, few of them sensed any imminent danger, certainly none that touched their daily lives. Dan Longwell, however, received a shock, when columnist Walter Lippmann suddenly posed a frightening question: "Do you realize," asked Lippmann, "we are only a month or so away from a war with Japan?" Longwell, who was habitually optimistic, now gave Luce a gloomy forecast. Writing on November 3, Longwell believed that the United States faced a "long and devastating war in all the oceans. . . ."

Stunning confirmation of this prophecy arrived in Washington in November. Malcolm Lovell, last seen introducing Harry Luce to German *chargé* Hans Thomsen, was an intelligence asset of Colonel William J. ("Wild Bill") Donovan, the newly (July 11) appointed Coordinator of Information. On Thursday, November 13, 1941, Colonel Donovan hurriedly dispatched a messenger to Roosevelt, bearing the letter from Lovell. Relying on his conversations with Hans Thomsen, Lovell reported that if Japan went to war, Germany would immediately follow suit. Thomsen also predicted that Japan, fearing strangulation, would strike in the very near future. If Donovan was right, then Japan had already set the timer and cocked the trigger.

Believing in the Great Man Theory of History, Harry and Clare Luce turned to a new savior, General Douglas MacArthur. Their genuflection was important to the ambitious General, so MacArthur cultivated the Luces. In MacArthur, Luce spied qualities that he missed in the White House. Like Harry Luce, MacArthur had long railed against the "propaganda of the peace cranks." To Luce, MacArthur was a man who knew the Far East and understood the great sweep of its history. *Life* now declared that Corregidor fortress in the Philippines was the "Gibraltar of the Pacific."

A talented, ambitious woman who hated being spurned by "Harry's little people," Clare Luce interviewed General MacArthur at length. She submitted her article to *Life*, where John Shaw Billings privately dismissed it as seventy-three pages of junk. Harry, however, pronounced it "good stuff," and fearing an outburst from Clare, he pressed for immediate publication. A group of editors, among them John Hersey, Tom Matthews, and Manfred Gottfried, then decided to discuss Clare's manuscript with Harry. This was a bad day for Luce. Matthews thought little of the piece on MacArthur, and Gottfried supported his colleague. Predictably, Harry moaned and groaned, begging his editors, "Don't do this to me! Don't do this to me!" Luce feared Clare's hurt and wrath, and paced back and forth, urging that his editors tell *Time's*

readers about Clare's scoop. Roy Alexander, meanwhile, hurried toward the meeting room and quickly opened the door. To John Hersey's
dismay, the doorknob smashed into the editor in chief's back, knocking
him over. Luce, undeterred by the omen, still wanted to publish his
wife's article. Billings stalled, suggesting that Clare's hagiography be
published when the Pacific crisis erupted into war. Harry agreed, for
he greatly respected Billings. Ultimately, however, Harry's decision to
publish was a wise one. Though Clare had again defied sexist convention, this time by involving herself so deeply in military matters, her
essay on MacArthur was a real coup. And *Life*'s timing would prove
to be perfect.

While Clare's editors revised her piece on MacArthur, important
news from Bob Sherrod arrived in the *Time* office of David Hulburd,
the News Bureau chief. On Saturday morning, November 15, as Sherrod was preparing to leave for the Carolinas, where he would cover
some Army maneuvers, he received a surprise summons to the War
Department. There, seven Washington correspondents listened carefully to General George C. Marshall, whose comments were, Sherrod
noted, of a highly confidential nature. Before finally departing for the
Carolinas, Sherrod typed a letter to Harry Luce, summarizing Marshall's comments. According to Sherrod, George Marshall, a well-
organized man, spoke rapidly but clearly as he stood before a large map
of the Pacific.

Using circles and arrows, Marshall imparted startling news to his
small audience. In the General's scenario, the Japanese would attack
somewhere in Asia, probably between December 1 and December 10. If
Marshall was right, the Japanese aggression would occur before General
MacArthur had completed his own preparations. MacArthur was trying
to train ten Filipino divisions, some of which would allegedly be ready
for battle in a month. The Chief of Staff, therefore, hoped for a reprieve,
so the White House needed to keep stalling Japan. Then Marshall made
a stunning comment. The Americans, he declared, were preparing for
"an offensive war against Japan."

According to George Marshall, the Japanese did not realize what was
going on in the Philippines. Thirty-five flying fortresses were already
based in the islands, and eighty more were scheduled to arrive in the
near future. Marshall did not mention it, but by March 1942 the Army
planned to base 470 modern warplanes in the Philippines. New 75mm
and 105mm artillery pieces were also on their way to those islands, along
with 100 tanks and new dive bombers. Marshall left the impression that
the United States was already in fine shape for a defensive battle but
needed to buy time for its offensive operations.

In George Marshall's wildly optimistic scenario, Japan was surrounded, from Alaska to Siberia, from Australia to India. Marshall spoke of B-17s and B-24s, which would take off from bases in the Philippines and China. The Soviets, Marshall assumed, would also go to war against Japan, so Vladivostok would play host to American warplanes. If the Japanese attacked after the Americans were ready, the U.S. would fight a virtual war of extermination, during which Japan's paper cities would go up in flames. As Bob Sherrod took detailed notes, the General warned that military data about the U.S. buildup in the Philippines must not appear in the American press. The U.S. government, Marshall explained, intended to leak the material to moderates in the Japanese leadership. After learning more about American power, these prudent realists might brake Japan's quickening march toward war. In Sherrod's words, "We want to put up a big front to the Japanese, without forcing them into face-saving war measures." Time Inc. followed Marshall's instructions, and the next issue of *Life* commented on the coming war with Japan—in a bland paragraph on page 36. In fact, General Marshall's statements to the correspondents were overly optimistic, and his countrymen still viewed Japan as a nuisance more than a dire threat.

Negotiations had, for all practical purposes, stalled. Speaking to his "War Council" on November 25, FDR predicted that Japan would attack without warning, but where, he did not know. Stimson soon informed the President of new information, gleaned from the "Magic" intercepts of Japanese diplomatic messages. Japan might attack Guam or the Philippines; she would certainly invade Southeast Asia. The State Department cobbled together a program intended to put the onus for the break in relations on Japan. The "Ten-Point" program, presented to the Japanese diplomats on the afternoon of November 26, was propaganda.

Henry Luce's earlier misgivings about Admiral Husband E. Kimmel's preparations at Pearl Harbor were justified, but he appears to have put them out of his mind. Intelligence unavailable to Luce had warned in late March 1941 that the likely launching point for an attack on Pearl Harbor was located 233 miles from Oahu. In April, just before Luce's visit to Pearl Harbor, air commanders in Hawaii had also concluded that "the most likely and dangerous form of attack on Oahu would be an air attack." Kimmel himself had seen Pearl Harbor as a possible target of Japanese aircraft, submarines, or sabotage. Yet on a typical morning in 1941, American spotter planes rarely went out farther than

200 miles. Pearl Harbor's carrier-based aircraft lacked sufficient range, according to American experts. Besides, sending planes out on a 360-degree search pattern would undermine plans for supporting the fleet when it steamed out toward the western Pacific. The Navy's coordination with the Army was defective, and there was no plan for permanent manning of antiaircraft batteries around Pearl Harbor.

On November 27 the Navy Department wired war warnings to commands in the Pacific, declaring that "an aggressive move by Japan is expected within the next few days." General Marshall sent an urgent message to the Western Defense Command, alerting it to the imminence of Japanese action. Japan, according to Marshall's warning, must cast the first stone, but American forces should not construe restraint as dictating "a course of action that might jeopardize your defense."

Insofar as he feared attack, Admiral Kimmel expected incursions into the harbor by submarines, while the Army worried about sabotage directed against its planes at Hickham Field. This fear of treachery proved to be a miscalculation and a prelude to disaster. Placed in the center of the fields, wing to wing in order to avoid attacks along the perimeter of the base, the U.S. Army Air Corps planes were sitting ducks in the event of an air attack. And despite the dangerous international situation, Kimmel's ships routinely sailed out of the harbor on Tuesday, usually returning to port on Friday. Japanese spies knew this.

Japan's Pearl Harbor Task Forces fleet had steamed out of Hitokappu Bay on November 25, at 1600 hours, Eastern Standard Time. The Japanese carriers proceeded toward Oahu under cover of a radio blackout. Intelligence officers in the U.S. Navy did have access to about 10 percent of Japan's naval signal traffic, but much of this information consisted of weather reports. Nobody in Washington—or in Hawaii—knew where Japan was hiding her "missing" carriers.

Around December 1, George Gallup found that 52 percent of polled Americans expected war in the near future. "The Japanese people," warned *Time* in its December 8 issue, "were told by their leaders that the U.S. sought to destroy them." *Time* foresaw an imminent Japanese attack, perhaps against the Burma Road or Thailand, but thought that Tokyo might back down. If not, "every man was at battle stations," intoned *Time*, for "This was the last act of the drama." Actually, the curtain was just rising, and Japan was pulling its strings.

At *Life*, Dan Longwell, Joe Thorndike, John Billings, and Noel Busch had finally finished recasting Clare Luce's article on General MacArthur. Dan Longwell then made the decision to put MacArthur on the cover of the December 8 issue, which would be available at newsstands by December 5. Yet many of *Life*'s editorial comments belied MacArthur's confidence, for its editors fretted about a distant war "for which the American nation was not yet fully prepared." In these days of looming crisis, *Time* junked its planned cover. Instead of Walt Disney's cute elephant, Dumbo, Admiral Kimmel would grace the famous cover. Later, Eric Hodgins wickedly suggested that it would have been better to have stuck with Dumbo.

In early December the Japanese carrier fleet steaming toward Pearl Harbor continued to maintain radio silence. It received but one message from home, a noncoded phrase indicating that the attack should be carried out as planned. American commands in the Pacific learned on December 3 that Japanese diplomats were preparing to destroy their codes and secret documents. On the same day, however, Winston Churchill, perhaps referring to Singapore or the East Indies, called a Japanese attack "a remote contingency." The U.S. Army's Military Intelligence Division predicted on December 5 that Japan's most likely goal was the "occupation of Thailand." The American naval authorities did not believe that the Japanese Navy could attack Pearl Harbor with any prospect of success. With so much to tempt her in Southeast Asia, why would Japan undertake a foolhardy operation thousands of miles from home?

Sitting in his study at 1200 Fifth Avenue, John Billings made an ominous entry in his diary. "The Jap negotiations," he wrote, "have gone sour—there's no telling what will happen next." Billings, however, quickly reverted to wishful thinking, for he expected that things would drift along as before. In fact, Foreign Minister Joachim von Ribbentrop had promised Ambassador Hiroshi Oshima that, in the event of a war between Japan and the United States, Germany "would join the war immediately."

On December 6, 1941, President Roosevelt and his aides drafted a last-minute appeal to the Emperor Hirohito. FDR called for the immediate "withdrawal of the Japanese forces from Indo-China." At the very least, this hopeless plea could be used as good wartime propaganda. The appeal was cabled to Ambassador Grew at 9 P.M. After some delay, Grew demanded to see the Emperor, but he quickly learned that the negotiations were terminated.

The Japanese finally responded to the American "Ten Point" plan, in a long, multifaceted note relayed to their Washington embassy on the evening of December 6. The Japanese answer was blunt and unyielding. Thanks to the American attitude, Tokyo wrote, "it is impossible to reach an agreement through further negotiations." The Americans intercepted and read the message, which a naval aide brought to the President. FDR, who was in conference with Harry Hopkins, passed the document on to his redoubtable adviser, adding the comment "this means war."

The Japanese assault on Pearl Harbor, carried out in two waves on December 7, incapacitated most of the Pacific fleet, and cost 2,403 brave men their lives. Had Japan's carrier fleet remained in the area, it could have inflicted even greater damage, and thrown the Americans onto the defensive for more than six months. Admiral Yamamoto, however, had other ideas. He wished to conserve his precious carriers and their tankers, which the Japanese admirals planned to employ in their far-flung Asiatic operations. The Japanese fleet therefore failed to sink either of its adversary's absent aircraft carriers. The American battleships suffered most, but they proved more expendable than carriers, destroyers, and cruisers, which for the most part survived. Indeed, most of the damaged ships could be salvaged, and Pearl Harbor's dry docks were soon back at work. The Japanese attackers also failed to demolish Pearl Harbor's fuel tanks, or its power plant, nor did they cripple Oahu as a base for future operations. Soon after the raid on Pearl Harbor, the man who helped to craft the assault, Admiral Yamamoto, observed that "This war will give us much trouble in the future. The fact that we have had a small success at Pearl Harbor is nothing. . . . People should think things over and realize how serious the situation is."

In Greenwich, Connecticut, on this Sunday afternoon, the Luces were entertaining an array of distinguished guests. When Clare received the news of Pearl Harbor, she playfully teased those "appeasers" and "isolationists" who were present at her table. In his penthouse in New York, John Billings arose from his customary Sunday afternoon nap. As he dressed for dinner, Billings switched on his radio. Hearing of the Japanese attack, he changed his plans and rushed to his own battle post, *Life*'s editorial offices at Rockefeller Center. Billings thought immediately about putting out a special issue of *Life*. *Time* soon decided that the "Japs" had been "brilliant, thorough, audacious." They had also committed "murder masked by a toothy smile."

At the office, Billings conferred with Harry Luce, who was quite cheerful. Teddy White, who remained home on leave from China, later recalled the reason for Harry's elation. All the good guys stood on one side, ready to corner the bad guys, and Luce liked the simple moral choice that now confronted the country. While many Americans thought only of survival or retaliation, Henry R. Luce, who was absolutely confident of eventual victory, already looked forward to a post-war American Century.

The Home Front,
the War,
and the Holocaust

Late on Sunday, December 7, 1941, editors and assistants rushed in and out of offices at Time Inc., as everyone groped for more information about the terrible event at Pearl Harbor. At one point Harry Luce left his busy colleagues and phoned his parents, who now learned about the attack on Hawaii. He and the Reverend Luce talked about the implications of the Japanese attack for both America and China. The ailing Dr. Luce had said his last goodbye to Harry, for later that evening he died in his sleep at the age of seventy-two. Upon hearing the sad news, several of Harry's friends had the same thought: How fortunate you were, cabled Bernard Baruch, in having been "able to give him the news . . . which made it look as if his life's work was coming to fruition." "He lived long enough," Harry agreed, "to know that we were on the same side as the Chinese." By working to redeem China, Luce felt that he honored the memory of his late father.

Even in the wake of Pearl Harbor, Harry Luce found himself compelled to struggle against misguided "Europe-firsters," who tended to ignore the Far Eastern theaters of war. The polls bedeviled Luce, however, for Gallup reported that 64 percent of the people believed that

Germany, not Japan (15 percent) represented the greater threat to the
U.S. Indeed, after the first shock passed, many Americans reverted
to comfortable reveries about the "Japs." *Life*'s Josh Billings proudly
characterized his nation as calm and "united like steel." *Life* denounced
Japanese duplicity, but confidently described Japan as having committed
national suicide. In a rehearsal of its role as first cheerleader for the
armed forces, *Life* predicted that the Americans would hold the line in
Asia, then strike back quickly and land a devasting blow. Apparently
this was to be a kind of Hollywood war, a Western set in the Far
East, with ships, Marines, and bugles coming to the rescue. Frank
McNaughton, who wrote copy for *Time*, later recalled that Americans
regarded the "little Jap . . . as something of a joke, a nuisance, a belligerent little snot that the U.S. could smack down in a month, well, maybe
six months. . . ." American overconfidence, fortified by Luce's liberal
racial attitude, caused *Time* to defy hysteria about "Japs" on the West
Coast. The magazine dismissed charges of disloyalty leveled against the
79,642 Nisei, or Japanese-Americans.

Luce drafted a powerful editorial, "The Day of Wrath," which came
close to blaming the President for Pearl Harbor. He agreed to revise
the editorial, but senior editors still found the piece too anti-Roosevelt.
The revised essay appeared in *Life*, where Luce steeled his public for
the hard battles to come. Harry also decided to offer his support to the
nation's leader. In a carefully crafted, handwritten note to FDR, Luce
referred back to the controversy over the death of President Aguirre of
Chile. Swallowing his pride he bravely noted that he had suffered "as
tough a wallop as I ever had to take." Without apologizing for his past
transgressions, Harry added that "I can take worse ones." Go win the
war, I will help—this was the gist of Luce's first message.

In a longer letter to Roosevelt, written the very next day, Luce hinted
at conflicts to come. Proud of Time Inc.'s role in preparing the people
for war, Luce assured the President of his company's commitment to
winning the war, but he warned FDR that Time Inc. intended to speak
frankly when criticism was in order. Luce would of course keep his
comments "within the limits of patriotism." FDR's response should
have troubled Luce. The President, after graciously thanking Harry for
his "patriotism" and "sportsmanship," proudly alluded to the new
spirit of national unity. Pointedly, Roosevelt did not respond to Luce's
promise to maintain a critical stance.

During these first weeks of the war, *Life* continued to calm popular
fears. The magazine decided that if the Nazis bombed Manhattan, they
would lose 90 percent of their attack force, and American casualties
would be low. *Life* also decided that the fall of Singapore might not,

after all, signify the loss of "half the world." Retreating British forces could then make common cause with the Dutch troops in the Netherlands East Indies. Harry Luce quickly dismissed these reassuring bits of fantasy. He warned that Americans *could* lose the war in the Far East. *Life* advised reinforcing the beleaguered American positions in the Far East. Then, after smashing Japan, the Allies could attack the isolated Nazi colossus.

Terrible events combined to rob Luce and his country of their quick victory. The fall of Singapore and an imminent disaster in the Philippines provoked a startling piece in *Life*. After citing the President, who warned of Axis attacks against American coastal installations and inland cities, *Life* speculated gloomily about a U.S. collapse. In an apocalyptic scenario, combined Axis fleets attack the United States. Aided by 100,000 fifth columnists, the Nazis and "Japs" land on the two coasts and then converge before the invader "pours up the Mississippi Valley." John Billings, like many Americans, worried about losing the war. He wondered why the U.S. forces were incapable of launching offensives. Fighting this war, Billings added, was like being in a losing game in which one was not permitted to quit. In March *Life* reported on a Japanese submarine that had lobbed a few inoffensive shells at an oil field located in Ellwood, California, twelve miles north of Santa Barbara. Americans heard that their industrial production was making great strides, but in fact, shortages of rubber undermined the war economy.

Assistant Secretary of War John McCloy, who directed the ongoing evacuation of the Japanese-Americans from their West Coast homes, believed that this operation was "largely a public relations matter." He hoped that the media would tell the story of the Army's role in this evacuation. Presumably, a publication like *Life* could help to allay Americans fears of Japanese subversion. So Time Inc., which had only recently dismissed rumors of "fifth column" activity by Nisei, now approved of their deportation to "reception centers" run by the Army. By April 1942 *Life* was enthusiastic about the internment of "West Coast Japs." Soon, these people, most of whom were loyal American citizens, would find themselves living in grim "relocation centers" set up by the newly established War Relocation Authority. Americans, hearing about defeat after defeat in the Pacific, would see in *Life* that their Army had won a victory over the "enemy" in California.

Henry Luce was angry about defeats and production bottlenecks; he wanted to shock America. Even though 54 percent of the population could boast of at least one relative in the armed forces, Luce's America was, to her shame, fighting a phony "Hollywood war." In his office, he railed against the incompetents running the war effort. Don't people know there is a war on? he asked. When the President requested that everyone do his part, however, Luce heard only the vague appeal of a politician. The trade unions, *Life* claimed, were putting too much pressure on the War Labor Board, which granted hefty wage increases to the steelworkers. Luce's magazines exposed poor labor relations in and around Detroit, where confusion, bad morale, and management thuggery sparked wildcat strikes and other unseemly clashes. Price controls, Luce believed, were failing despite the efforts of the Office of Price Administration (OPA).

Life wanted to levy heavier taxes so as to soak up excess purchasing power. Harry Luce wanted to pay for the war, not borrow against the credit of future generations. *Time*, meanwhile, mercilessly pilloried the government for presiding over an inefficient selective service system. Disappointed with Roosevelt and Washington, *Life* hoped that people, working in their own communities, would establish effective scrap-metal-salvage programs. They could thereby minimize some of the damage done by War Production Board snafus. *Time* criticized drivers for opposing the rationing of gasoline and upbraided the Administration for waiting too long before developing a synthetic rubber program. "Nobody I know," Billings commented, "but Longwell thinks the war is being well run." In his frustration, Luce gave commands, canceled all vacations, and ordered that no editor be more than six hours away from a telephone.

Henry Luce preached sacrifice but not austerity. He seemed to believe that a determined America could both win the war and enjoy the bounty offered by its fruited plain. To Luce, this approach to life was not contradictory. If the United States could one day put 10 million men in the field, it could also enjoy a magazine that claimed 4 million subscribers. *Life*, with its consumer fantasies and bright pictures, *was* America. Speaking to a group of advertising salesmen, Luce described *Life*'s editors as the "real historians of the day." He had made a good point, for America's magazine recorded both the heroic and mundane aspects of a global struggle. The preservation of the fantasies and dreams produced by his picture magazine was one of Harry Luce's war aims. Indeed, he was fighting for the American Way of *Life*.

While outgunned American forces fought to hold Corregidor, *Life* fussed over dancer and actress Ginger Rogers, a Dan Longwell favorite, and hawked colorful displays of alcohol, cigarettes, and hair dryers. Later in the war, Time Inc. discovered that American servicemen did not want to read sanitized, special editions of *Life*. They loved the advertisements, for soldiers and sailors and airmen saw *Life*'s ads as a promise of a better tomorrow. With his uncanny sense of the market, Harry Luce knew that the abundance promised by *Life* during the Depression might soon be within the grasp of millions of readers.

Luce would and did cap executive salaries, but he had no intention of shrinking the massive bulk of *Life*, unless paper restrictions forced him to do so. To Harry Luce, more and bigger usually meant better if they bore an American trademark: more faith, more territory, more subscribers, a bigger gross national product, more soldiers, more victories, more money. *Life* was soon taking up 134 pages; late in 1942 the magazine grew to 156 pages. Crammed with advertisements, the magazine bragged about its circulation of over 4 million copies per week.

In 1940 Luce had expanded *Time*'s operations in Washington, the city that he saw as the future political and military capital of the American Century. Time Inc. rented an office on the second floor of an old brownstone building on K Street. Employing about a half dozen people, *Time*'s D.C. bureau chief was former *New York Times* reporter Felix Belair. *Time* lured him away from the *Times* with a staggering $5,000 raise, which increased Belair's pay to a hefty $12,000. To Luce, Belair's good access to the President, combined with his healthy skepticism about FDR, made him an attractive catch. Belair, aided by capable correspondents like Robert Sherrod, provided New York with a stream of original stories.

Felix Belair tried to run a professional office, but he clearly missed the city room atmosphere of a premier newspaper. The office camaraderie, where old-timers, fueled by whiskey and smelling of stale smoke, traded war stories, did not comport with Time Inc.'s residually Ivy League, serious-yet-flippant style. At one point Belair made the mistake of asking Harry Luce why he worked so hard. Luce's response—"Felix, sometimes I actually think you're a hedonist"—was really an accusation. Belair, expecting frequent visits from Luce and other Time Inc. bigshots, felt compelled to publish a prissy set of proper office rules. It must have galled Belair to outlaw time-tested habits, such as stamping out cigarettes on the floor, drinking in the office, or getting intoxicated in public places. Defensively, he observed that office "whiskey leads to abuses that have led in most organizations to prohibitions. . . ." This rule amused Bob Sherrod, who recalled that Belair sometimes started working on his own bottle before 10 A.M.

By the summer of 1941, Felix Belair felt neglected, for managing editor Manfred Gottfried wielded a heavy pencil. Luce informed him that editors in New York combined his material with information culled from the *New York Times*, the wire services, and *Time's* researchers. As Harry Luce put it, there were three sides to every story—your side, my side, and the truth. Like a soldier at his post, Belair scratched his head, then labored on, standing watch while Harry Luce extended his *Time*-tested formula to the whole world.

Felix Belair thought he was putting out a well-informed weekly newspaper, but Harry Luce was intent on producing a journalistic sermon. He wanted to explain the world to a confused public. Belair, unlike Luce, used traditional definitions of the term "objectivity." With Clare talking openly of pursuing a career in politics, the Luces sought the advice of several Time Incers. Don't do it, advised Belair, *Time* would be unable to cover you in an objective fashion. For the moment, Clare agreed, or said she did, but Harry primly responded that readers would believe what they read in *Time*, period. When Belair left *Time*, it was with a sense of mutual relief, but during this war, he did his job well.

By midsummer 1942, Harry Luce was cheered by signs of the impending onset of a real rather than a "Hollywood" war. In the Solomon Islands, Marines launched an offensive of their own. Luce, commemorating their bloody sacrifice, described the Marines' assault as a "valiant effort . . . to lift America out of fifth or sixth place in the war-world to the supreme position to which she belongs." He believed that victory would be possible only if the home front achieved total mobilization. In factories and mines, on farms and in offices, everyone must produce at a fever pitch. Now, his agitation, which influenced both readers and the Administration, was showing results. Throughout the government, officials interested in more efficient war mobilization worked with Time Inc.'s people. *Time* even discovered grounds for optimism in the hapless, hated Office of Price Administration. There, Frank McNaughton had tapped a valuable new source, Deputy Administrator John Kenneth Galbraith.

The towering, Canadian-born economics professor, then thirty-four, possessed a sardonic wit and a keen intellect, both of which he enjoyed putting on display. So long as McNaughton did not attribute his information to the economist, Galbraith was willing to work with him. The professor told McNaughton about the problems facing OPA, as every special interest group, from farmers to congressional blocs, worked to undermine relevant price control regulations. Galbraith cogently argued that OPA could not function if it bargained with all these clamoring groups. Instead, he worked to establish an across-the-board approach to pricing problems. OPA was heavily dependent on the War Production Board, which determined production and consumption priorities. Now that the WPB was working more efficiently, Galbraith saw better days ahead for the OPA. Though it would never be popular, the OPA might emerge from the suffocating thicket grown by competing special interests. By the autumn of 1942, John Kenneth Galbraith had gained the admiration of several Time Incers. Outspoken and independent, this talented liberal academician could make major contributions to Luce's plans for the reconstruction of the global economy. *Fortune* later decided that Galbraith would be an asset to its board of editors.

Finally, after a decade or more of stagnation, the nation's vast productive machine roared into action. By late 1942, *Life* boasted of factories that could assemble a cargo ship in four and a half days. From *Time's* Roy Alexander, an expert on air power with high-ranking sources in the Army Air Forces, Luce heard about the damage inflicted on the enemy by America's growing fleet of Flying Fortresses. The "Hollywood" war, ignominious and self-defeating, was passing from the scene, unlamented by Harry Luce.

During this long war, Time Inc. needed to navigate its way through a sea of new clearance requirements. The Roosevelt administration, ever sensitive to the vagaries of public opinion, had placed a powerful Bureau of Public Relations (BPR) in the War Department. The Bureau was answerable only to the Secretary of War, and through him, to the White House. The man who directed the BPR, Brigadier General Alexander D. Surles, was an efficient but cautious officer who won the respect of the press. While a stunned nation mulled over the news from Pearl Harbor, Surles put the BPR's contingency plans into effect. He would always try to give a break to a friendly reporter, but he was not a man with whom one trifled. The BPR chief recorded every official telephone conversation to which he was a party.

The BPR accredited war correspondents. Surles therefore suggested that Time Inc. provide him with separate personnel lists for each of its magazines, along with the names of proposed war photographers. At Time Inc., John Billings drafted *Life's* wish list. This operation was immensely important, for *Life* would rise or fall with the quality and quantity of its pictures from the fronts. Unlike most of their competitors, *Life's* picture editors had long since figured out how to arrange a sequence of pictures so as to narrate a dramatic story. Under the Army's pool reporting system, the written word or captions did not have to be shared with rival companies. Sympathetic or ambitious Army officers and censors, understanding the importance of *Life*, made certain that the release date for photographs did not sabotage the magazine's publication schedule. This was *Life*'s war, and Luce's people seized their chance. Steve Early soon noted with alarm that *Life*'s cameramen were better than the Navy photographers—one fourth of whom the magazine's personnel had trained. Early, a loyal spear-carrier for the President, had to face the fact that when FDR traveled, he could not take thirty photographers with him. So one had to choose, and *Life* usually won the draw.

Thanks to their sources, Luce's editors were better informed than most of their rivals, but good reporting, striking photographs, and inside stories told only part of Time Inc.'s wartime story. Dan Longwell, for example, used American artists when writing *Life*'s saga of this epic war. Longwell, realizing that color film took a long time to develop, quickly assembled a group of fifteen artist-correspondents, who accompanied units to distant battlefields. After the Army had engaged more than a dozen of its own artists, Congress stepped in. Fearing in 1943 that these painter-soldiers would do little more than sketch and glorify their commanding generals, the politicians ordered the Army to cease its artistic endeavors.

Longwell spotted an opportunity for *Life*. He went to see Assistant Secretary of War John McCloy and arranged to take over the Army's art project. Proudly, Longwell had now doubled the size of *Life*'s staff of artists. Luce's picture magazine subsequently displayed some of the best work of its combat artists. Tom Lea, for example, depicted the last step of a mortally wounded Marine, dripping blood as his mangled left arm hung limply above the gory beach. *Life*'s prestige, its reputation for telling the truth, had soared to new heights. The War Department took note.

When Harry Luce came to town, General Surles helped Felix Belair line up an impressive array of leading military officers, who would be happy to meet with the head of Time Inc. If Belair or a Time Inc. executive, like Eric Hodgins, wanted to lunch with Surles, he could usually set up the appointment on very short notice. If Surles had an important press release, he would alert Belair to it, and make certain he received it before *Time* closed out copy for its forthcoming issue. At other times, Surles even let Belair review a release before it became generally available. Since *Time* would not appear for several days, the information would not reach the public with undue haste. *Time*, with leisure to mull over the implications of the document, could then produce a better story.

Life's Ed Thompson once joked that the Army had its own definition of a military secret, namely, "something known only to the high command, the enemy and *Life* magazine." In *Time*'s cramped, smoky Washington office, George Tames, a young photographer, marveled at the amount of confidential material lying about. Before a major Allied amphibious operation occurred, Tames saw plans for various stages of the invasion. Up in New York, Billings, ever concerned about espionage, warned staffers against leaving confidential material in the wrong places.

The energetic Ed Thompson often rushed back and forth between Washington and Rockefeller Center, hurriedly trying to clear pictures with the censors. A grumpy John Billings, who liked to be home by 6 P.M., sometimes had to sit in his office until 9 or 10, awaiting Thompson's return. Ed Thompson sometimes displayed a short temper, and vainly proposed defying the censors altogether. Usually, Billings was able to calm him down, and Time Inc. cooperated with the War and Navy departments. But the ever self-pitying Billings often complained about the nervous strain imposed by the need "to hear yes or no from Washington on everything."

Luce's company was forced to work with a second public relations bureaucracy. The civilian Office of Censorship (OC), established by Roosevelt twelve days after Pearl Harbor, regulated communications passing between the U.S.A. and foreign countries. In the case of Time Inc., for example, the OC's mandate covered all cables dispatched from London to New York, reels of *The March of Time* flown to London or Santiago, and the air editions of *Time* sent to South America. The Office's first wartime (acting) director was the FBI's J. Edgar Hoover. Hoover might have inflicted much misery upon Time Inc., for the FBI Director disliked *Life*'s coverage of his sanctified Bureau, and was no admirer of the pro–civil rights *Time*.

Some weeks later, the Office of Censorship received a broader assignment along with a new chief. The OC was now to coordinate the voluntary self-censorship of the American media. All information detrimental to the "effective prosecution of the war" must be withheld. The Director enjoyed full authority, for he was accountable to no other office or agency. His Office of Censorship worked, where appropriate, with the armed forces and with Surles' BPR. And happily for the free press, J. Edgar Hoover soon yielded to Byron Price, the acting general manager of the Associated Press wire service. Price was an improvement over Hoover, and was even willing to correct the President. After arguing with FDR, Price once noted that Roosevelt actually believed that the OC could *order* the press to desist from publishing contested information.

A fifty-one-year-old native of Indiana, Byron Price had joined the AP way back in 1912. An effective and fair-minded administrator, Price did not view the newspapers as adversaries. He also believed in self-policing by the media, for he saw himself as a traffic cop, not a detective. The Office of Censorship's *Code of Wartime Practices* laid down certain general regulations that the press was expected to observe. Publications were not to print various kinds of photographs or maps, lest they assist the enemy. Barring an announcement by the White House, the press was not to report on the travels or whereabouts of President Roosevelt.

Soon after Byron Price promulgated his code, Harry Luce contacted Eric Hodgins, who would be in charge of Time Inc.'s compliance with wartime press regulations. Problems were sure to arise, and they did. Price observed that the "eccentric" Henry R. Luce had rejected the system of voluntary censorship, and claimed that Luce's men were probing to see how they could evade this or that rule. Price's distaste for *Time* was common among newspaper reporters. Luce, however wealthy and influential, was still the outsider, a successful novice whose magazines challenged the precepts of working journalism. To Price, Luce was a "parasite" and a "pariah," who fed off the hard work of honest newspaper reporters.

A striking example of *Time*'s potentially imprudent behavior occurred when the magazine learned that the Danish physicist Dr. Niels Bohr was in the United States. The media did not know this, and the government, which was heavily committed to the nuclear Manhattan Project, wanted to maintain absolute secrecy. Hodgins duly told Time Incers to stay away from the story. On several other occasions, the OC reprimanded Time Inc. for alluding to the whereabouts of the President. Actually, the company's record was remarkably good. Between Pearl Harbor and the end of July 1944, the OC accused Luce's magazines of only seventeen violations of the Code, such as the "premature disclosure of results of naval action." Still, relations between Time Inc. and Byron Price remained tense. As wags at *Time* might have put it, the Price of vigilance was eternal suspicion.

While Eric Hodgins struggled with the Office of Censorship, Dan Longwell cultivated sources close to his beloved Navy. In once instance, Harry Luce paved the way for him. As Harry told Assistant Secretary James V. Forrestal, "much of the future of the world dates (in my mind) from the day you [Forrestal] went to Washington." Forrestal reciprocated, and wherever possible, he did favors for the Luce publications. Often, to the chagrin of its rivals, *Life* seemed to get first crack at newly released pictures of naval combat. Such an event occurred in the summer of 1942, when the magazine obtained photographs of a sinking Japanese destroyer, as viewed through the periscope of a U.S. submarine. In 1942 the Navy assigned a censor to *Life* in order to facilitate the flow of declassified text and pictures to its millions of readers. *Life* led the field with a sensational story detailing Japanese mistreatment of U.S. prisoners of war.

Life, which brought the war home to American readers, was also helping to wage it. John Billings growled when the government demanded that he be fingerprinted because Time Inc. did "so much secret work for the Army and Navy." The Office of Naval Intelligence, for example, had turned for help to Andrew Heiskell, the young, multitalented general manager of *Life*. American servicemen, according to ONI, were frequently firing at their own ships and planes. If they could clearly identify the enemy, such incidents could presumably be avoided. Once a week Heiskell commuted to Washington, where he helped to set up a magazine called *The U.S. Army-Navy Journal of Recognition*. This publication, which looked a bit like *Life*, made use of the talents of photographers Margaret Bourke-White and Carl Mydans. *Recognition*, a restricted item, trained thousands of recruits on the appearance of enemy aircraft and warships.

The top-secret Office of Strategic Services also drew upon Time Inc.'s personnel and resources. The OSS had heard about *Life*'s detailed biographical files and wanted access to them. Time Inc., through its War Tasks Division, complied. Intelligence operatives descended on the company's offices and pored through its records. And when William ("Wild Bill") Donovan, head of the OSS, needed additional intelligence about Japan, he turned to Ralph ("Del") Paine, managing editor of *Fortune*. Donovan requested a list of Time Inc. personnel who had worked on the special Japanese issue of *Fortune*. These people could then be debriefed. OSS believed that it was gaining access to useful information about the Japanese war economy, military machine, and mentality.

In New York, OSS official Allen Dulles asked for a roster of Time Inc.'s overseas correspondents. The company complied, and Dulles prepared to interview these men when they returned to the United States. He also indicated that the OSS might wish to use the correspondents in intelligence work. Time Inc. did not object, but requested that such assignments be arranged through the company's executive offices. In return for these patriotic favors, *Time* and its sister publications were granted entrée to leading intelligence officers, including Colonel Donovan. C. D. Jackson, for example, went on a secret mission to

Turkey, where he helped to deprive the Axis of vital strategic ores. Raymond Buell learned a good deal about the OSS's underground work against the Axis and shared it with Harry Luce.

Luce delighted in secret knowledge. The writer Eliot Janeway later recalled that the best way to manipulate Harry Luce was to look around, lean forward, then whisper these words to him: "Harry, keep this to yourself, but . . ." Luce would listen intently, then store the esoteric bit of information in his mind. Now, Harry Luce knew some very big secrets, and he sometimes could not resist hinting at his inside knowledge. Even as American forces prepared to attack North Africa in November 1942, Luce suggested that the invasion was coming. Speaking to Billings, he mumbled something about General Dwight David Eisenhower, apparently a name to reckon with.

The Navy and War departments, grateful—with some exceptions— for the work done by Luce's magazines, gave them valuable, often confidential information. Assistant Secretary of War Robert Lovett, for example, came to New York, where Roy Larsen arranged a private dinner for him. Lovett provided his guests with some hitherto classified information about the strength of the Luftwaffe's fighter units. When *Fortune* planned a piece on the organization of the Japanese Imperial Army, Eric Hodgins called with a request for General Surles. No, the General replied, a Time Inc. staffer could not see what the U.S. Army Manual, prepared by Intelligence (G-2), said about his subject. Instead, Surles promised Hodgins that a colonel in G-2 would orally brief *Fortune*'s representative, imparting information gleaned from the manual. When *Fortune* needed information about Russia, its editors hoped to procure material from G-2 and the OSS. Accumulating IOUs with Time Inc., Surles responded that "They're pretty close mouthed over there but I'll certainly do what I can." He usually kept his promise.

Throughout the war, General George Marshall continued to evince a lively interest in Time Inc.'s coverage. Within weeks of Pearl Harbor, Luce was on his way to the War Department, where he spoke with the Chief of Staff. Though reserving his right to criticize the conduct of the war, Luce pledged to build up the public's "honest fundamental understanding" of the military and its problems. *Life* further burnished Marshall's image, calling him a "man of the people" and America's "greatest chief of staff." By the middle war years, Marshall was routinely doing favors for Luce and his magazines. When *Life* requested that Yosuf Karsh be permitted to photograph the General, the session took place a scant two days later.

Even more revealing was Marshall's own involvement in the genesis of major stories. The General's staff decided that the Army would profit from broader public knowledge of its work. Marshall then suggested that *Time* and *Life* cover the training of an infantry replacement unit, and follow its progress from boot camp to the front lines. General Surles became involved in the project; on Time Inc.'s side, correspondent James Shepley and *Life* photographer Tom McAvoy were the point men. Marshall found it easy to work with Shepley, who later played a crucial role in his dealings with both Harry Luce and China. And by constantly praising his political and public relations gifts, *Life* seemed to be grooming George Marshall for postwar tasks in Luce's American Century.

New wartime problems constantly confronted Luce, his publishers, and their managerial colleagues. Wages did not keep up with inflation, and one had to deal with government bureaucracies that had not existed a few years, or even months, before. Many good men left to enlist in the armed forces, sometimes quite suddenly. By the spring of 1942, 20 percent of the men previously employed at Time Inc. were serving their country. In many departments, fewer people grappled with a heavier workload. As Andrew Heiskell realized, scarcity and ubiquitous federal controls limited one's ability to reward good work.

In comments made during *Time*'s twentieth-anniversary dinner on March 11, 1943, Henry Luce described his company in almost military terms, ascribing its success to discipline, loyalty, responsibility, and courage. Luce observed that "we require discipline and we require freedom." But how could one reconcile the two? In fact, Time Inc. had evolved into a hierarchy whose patriarch was often out of town, preoccupied, or remote from most of his staff. One correspondent later complained that "I saw Roosevelt, Marshall [Admiral Ernest J.], King, but Luce was too busy." Luce's remedy for this problem consisted of greater centralization. He remained uneasy about giving orders, but from now on, he decided, senior editors, managing editors, and even assistant managing editors must bring their disagreements to the attention of the editor in chief. Luce still wanted to argue, but more than ever he expected his editors to forge some semblance of unity when covering the momentous issues of the day.

The war was a hard one, and in 1943 it was far from over. *Life* shocked many readers when its story about the battle for Buna depicted the stench and the maggots and the dead "Japs." Photographer George Strock's bloated, stinking bodies brought home a war of extermination. Later, *Life* listed every American killed in action, a stunning and moving tribute that sounded a warning of worse to come. *Life* also helped to fan the racist wave of anti-Japanese hatred when its Picture of the Week showed a girl thanking her Navy beau for his gift of an autographed "Jap skull." Reader reaction was quite negative, but the magazine nonetheless approved of General W. E. Lynd, who observed that the "Japs" don't retreat, "You just kill them." In a calmer but no less racist vein, *Life* decided that the Japanese displayed unique physical and mental characteristics. The magazine was careful to differentiate between Japanese smirks and Chinese smiles. Did Luce agree? Apparently not, but he did nothing to curb *Life*'s excesses.

Relentlessly, *Life*'s photographers traveled the globe, searching for the heroic, the sad, and the gory in the human face of war. Some of these camerapeople logged 150,000 miles during the war, and one correspondent, William Chickering, was killed in a kamikaze attack off the coast of Luzon. Margaret Bourke-White became the first woman to fly on a bombing mission, when American planes raided a German airfield in Tunisia. The great photographer Robert Capa jumped with the 82nd Airborne Division when it opened up a new front in Sicily.

To Henry Robinson Luce, the arrival of Americans anywhere on the globe was grounds for rejoicing. *Time* cheered the doughboys who had landed in Algiers. Most Americans wanted to win the war, bring the boys home, then return to their normal lives. Not Henry Luce. Instead of farm boys from Nebraska, or factory workers from Detroit, *Time* saw these young men as symbols of "a new era in the unfolding of mankind." And Time Inc.'s growth, like America's victory on Guadalcanal, in North Africa, or at the workshop bench in Gary or Detroit, vindicated Harry Luce's faith. *Life* now offered five times more foreign coverage than any other mass circulation weekly. On the other hand, the Luce publications, like most of the media, avoided issues that might dampen morale, and therein lay a tragedy.

Henry Luce's magazines did not adequately cover the extermination of the Jewish people in Nazi-occupied Europe. Indeed, once the United States went to war, *Life* usually avoided Jewish issues.

Like many malcontents suffering from low self-esteem, managing editor John Billings projected his misery onto external victims, with Jews in the lead. Speaking of his staff at *Life* during the war, Billings observed (with some exaggeration) that "We're all anti-Semitic, only some of us have better self-control than others." If Jews entertained him, however, or stirred his conscience from a safe distance, Billings could tolerate them. He liked the music of Irving Berlin and sympathized with Jewish victims of the Nazis so long as they appeared in a book or on the screen of a Hollywood movie. If despised "Jewy-looking Jews" sat near him in a nice restaurant, however, Billings reacted badly. When his brother, the noted artist Henry Billings, took a Jewish lover, John Shaw described her as an unattractive "Jew woman." Had John Billings felt differently about the Jews, he might have offered *Life*'s readers more material on the plight of the Jewish people in Europe. And had Luce been less distracted by other, more "American" issues, he might have changed *Life*'s direction.

Life sometimes exposed wartime extremist groups, arguing that hate-mongering would divide America and undermine morale. *Life* admitted that subversive thoughts occurred to many Americans, but barely mentioned their anti-Jewish component. The article "Voices of Defeat" was a rare exception. In this lengthy exposé, *Life* showed how extremists cursed President "Rosenfeld" and his "Jewish war." The magazine, however, missed the main point, for anti-Semitism was not the sole property of far-right fringe groups like the shattered Christian Front. Luce, however, refused to confront the fact of widespread dislike for the Jews; he wanted to unite the nation, not polarize it. All issues, except those which unambiguously contributed to the war effort, must be pushed aside.

During the Holocaust, not a single issue in *The March of Time* news-film series treated the fate of European Jewry. On infrequent occasions, however, *Time* did recount stories of horrors inflicted on Jewish victims. After Hitler had conquered Poland, *Time* reported on Jewish deportations from the ghettos of Posen and Lodz to a "reservation" near Lublin. There, the magazine noted, the Jews were "virtual slaves." *Time* rarely followed up with sequels, however, as it did when covering stories that gripped its imagination. Between July and September 1942, *Time* did not run a single story about atrocities inflicted upon the Jews. Stories about crimes committed against Serbs or Russians or Poles, however, appeared with some frequency throughout that year. *Time*'s two wartime cover stories on Nazi police chief Heinrich Himmler hardly touched upon the Reichsführer SS's most hideous persecution.

Harry Luce, who was always anxious to expose Roosevelt as a devious opportunist, failed to harass him over at least two issues—Jewish refugees and the plight of Jews in occupied Europe. Here, Luce missed a great opportunity. Rabbi Stephen S. Wise, chairman of the World Jewish Congress, announced in November 1942 that a Nazi "extermination campaign" had resulted in the murder of 2 million Jews. Early in 1943, polling data showed that 47 percent of respondents believed

that the Nazis had indeed killed 2 million Jews. Stories about the Holocaust had already circulated in respectable newspapers, though they
rarely garnered appropriate publicity.

In the winter of 1943, *Time* did a major story on "total murder,"
which was based on reports distributed by the American Jewish Congress. In a desperate request to the United Nations powers, the AJC
asked that 5 million Jews be rescued from occupied Europe. *Time*
argued that this was a challenge which ". . . the United Nations could
not in conscience ignore." The magazine suggested that some imperiled
Jews could be transported to neutral countries, where they would be
exchanged for Axis prisoners of war. *Time* failed to pursue the issue,
however, and when Wise finally met Billings, little came of the encounter. Concerned about *Life*'s coverage of Zionism and the Palestine issue,
Rabbi Wise hoped to affect the magazine's policy. Billings' records do
not even hint at a discussion of the Jewish nightmare in Europe. And
the Wise/Billings meeting represented but one missed opportunity.

Kurt Bloch, himself a refugee, was an esteemed member of *Fortune*'s
staff. In the spring of 1943, Bloch received a letter from a friend or
relative in England, who provided him with information about a Jewish
woman in Berlin. According to his informant, the lady had committed
suicide, for "she would not wait to be deported to Poland." Nor was
this unfortunate woman a unique case. "[We] are afraid," wrote Bloch's
source, "that . . . there is little hope for any of our friends and relatives
under Hitler to live to see the end of the Nazis." Bloch's contact warned
that, given the present level of Allied inactivity, not a single victim
would be snatched from Hitler's voracious death machine. Had Wise
or Bloch forcefully confronted Billings or Luce, a major story might
have appeared.

After the Red Army captured the Maidanek death camp, near Lublin
in Poland, *Life* ran a series of devastating pictures. Framed in black
borders, they showed crematoria, mass graves, clothes of victims, and
heaped rubble composed of burned, pulverized bones and skeletons.
The date was August 21, 1944, more than two and a half years after the
Nazi bureaucracy had committed itself to the "Final Solution of the
Jewish Question." *Time*, using copy filed by Moscow correspondent
Richard Lauterbach, told readers that the Nazis had murdered 18,000
victims on a single day, using Zyklon B gas. By this time, the Nazis
had directly or indirectly killed more than 5 million Jews.

A story that appears sporadically, then disappears for long periods of
time, provokes doubt and erases memory. By 1944, in an incredible
reversal, Gallup reported that only 15 percent of the public believed

that the Nazis had killed more than 2 million people in their concentration camps. By largely neglecting the Holocaust, *Time* and other media had actually *increased* public skepticism about its reality. Measured against Luce's professed values, Time Inc.'s coverage of the Holocaust was woefully inadequate.

1943

The Reorganization
of the World

Writing to Yale alumni in 1940, Harry Luce had envisioned a future that might offer "years of hope rather than years of cruelty and folly." In a series of speeches delivered between 1942 and 1944, he sketched out the postwar order for which he longed. "If a nation ever had a mission," he declared in 1942, "that nation is America." Today, wrote Luce, there can be no internationalism "which is not inspired by American leadership." The United States, Luce ordained, must "fashion a bridge to carry [mankind] across the chasm of horror which yawns between one epoch and another." At the root of Luce's ideology lay a Christian faith in human equality, fortified by a commitment to the idea of progress. He proudly pledged himself to creating "a finer and more liberal epoch than man has ever known."

Harry Luce's American Century was thus reverent, generous, and humanitarian; it also brooked no rivals, took the world for its stage, and assumed its own moral superiority. As Luce put it, "I want America to be different—always—to have a purpose—until all men are free." Once the Allies had destroyed the Axis, what forces would stand between Henry Luce's America and its redemptive global mission? The

British Empire was entering its final crisis; Soviet Russia was backward and bloodied; France had been defeated; and Italy was about to surrender. Japan could not defeat China, and the Americans were counterattacking along the Japanese periphery. Fascism was in disgrace, nazism repulsive, and communism unworkable.

Harry Luce's postwar world would be one in which disparate peoples developed a community of ideals. Americans, Luce foresaw, would travel abroad as never before, linking together peoples who had seen little of one another. His listeners sometimes scoffed, but Harry Luce foresaw a gross national product of hundreds of billions of dollars. Abundance would increase leisure time, which men and women could use to forge a society of "goodness and beauty." Artists would beautify the country, while the "craftsmanship of industrial design" made it efficient and comfortable. Speaking of his "great society," Luce saw no impediments blocking its progress. As Luce saw things, "if we [Americans] have anything on our minds we must do something about it. . . ." *Time* and especially *Life* would play their part in disseminating the blessings of the American order.

Luce's vision of postwar America contradicted the popular mood. Most Americans, the polls said, expected an economic downturn after the wartime boom. They feared the downsizing of the war economy, which would eliminate jobs in war industries. Americans anticipated a time when there would be more government controls, fewer jobs, and lower wages. Luce swam against this stream. *Life* noted that General Motors had turned out about $50 million worth of military goods in the first quarter of 1941. Less than two years later, that figure had risen to $750 million. By 1943 almost 300,000 men and women were engaged in GM's war work. To Luce, these figures bore witness to a new, probably *permanent* burst of productivity on the part of both labor and management.

Life attracted a lot of consumer attention when it unveiled a department dedicated to the marvels of "Postwar Living." The magazine prophesied a world in which newly prosperous middle and working class citizens shopped for conveniences and luxuries. Everyone, *Life* observed, needed new homes, autos, radios, and appliances, so factories would be humming and wages would rise. Television would be a reality, and the sky would be filled with civilian airliners. Men, *Life* said, would have jobs; their wives would enjoy new stoves and Frigidaires. Government was not about to return to the modest role it had once played in national life, and this bothered Luce. Still, Henry Luce, prodded by Charles Stillman, finally accepted some of the tenets of Keynesian economics. Jack Jessup convinced him that government must provide hard-pressed individuals with some modicum of social security. Luce reluctantly agreed, but he preferred to dwell on the glories of individual initiative.

Life celebrated American oilmen who, working with the government's Petroleum Reserves Corporation, built a $150 million pipeline across Saudi Arabia. Only 6 percent of the Allies' oil currently came from this region. In the future, *Life* believed, that figure would rise, and since Britain still controlled most Middle Eastern oil, *Life* hoped that Saudi Arabia would become a dependable, American-controlled source of energy. The Luce publications also lauded the work of Harry Luce's friend Paul Gray Hoffman, the head of the Studebaker Company. Paul Hoffman shared Luce's faith that American capitalism, if given the chance, would not disappoint the nation. Indeed, Hoffman concluded that postwar industry would be capable of exceeding prewar production figures by 40 percent. Jack Jessup, who conveyed many of Luce's ideas to *Life*'s reading public, now called for less regulation, more individual initiative, a reformed tax code, and fewer farm subsidies.

Henry Luce sometimes acted as if Time Inc. were his own republic, with himself as foreign minister. Back in the summer of 1941, Luce had asked a group of associates to examine "which or what combination of [postwar] . . . alternatives will the U.S. take for itself?" Formally inaugurated on December 18, eleven days after Pearl Harbor, the new "Q Department" answered to Luce's foreign policy adviser, Raymond Leslie Buell. Buell's postwar materials could generate articles for Luce's magazines, thus giving Time Inc. primacy in this new field. Eight months later, CBS copied Luce's example and established its own postwar group.

In August 1942 Jack Jessup became editor in chief of the Postwar Department. In 1943 Luce changed it into a Policy Formulation Committee. Drawing on the researchers and secretarial staff of the former Postwar Department, the new group answered directly to Luce. Consisting of himself, Grover, Buell, Jessup, and others, the Policy Committee also advised Time Inc.'s managing editors. Through these consultations, Luce hoped to coordinate the sometimes disparate editorial tendencies of his three major publications.

In 1944 the Committee yielded to the Foreign Policy Advisory Department, headed by Ray Buell. "Your job, Ray," he once reminded the sometimes abstruse Buell, "is to maintain orderly procedure." Still, Luce enjoyed the intellectual discussions engendered by Buell's scholarly memoranda. He also relished the confidential nature of these postwar operations. Since the Q Department had access to sensitive materials, including military secrets, readers were required to return documents to Buell's operation within one week after their release. There could be spies at Time Inc., warned Charles Stillman, and there were certainly too many loose tongues babbling away in the corridors and offices at Rockefeller Center.

At first few readers seemed engaged in postwar issues. As Clare Luce put it, Americans wanted to win the war; they were not interested in phrases like "winning the peace and reorganizing the world." Luce's postwar operations eventually yielded dividends, however. By the spring of 1943, Time Inc. claimed that more than half a million Americans had read one or more of *Fortune*'s essays on the postwar world. These materials, supplemented by articles and essays in *Time* and *Life*, became part of curricula in more than 400 schools and colleges. Time Inc. also made sure that advance copies of its postwar publications reached important individuals in business and government. Vice-President Wallace forwarded materials from *Fortune* to President Roosevelt. And Wendell Willkie was ". . . convinced that Life Magazine is the foremost medium by which to provoke and promote a sizable volume of thought [*sic*] along these lines."

As the Allies took the offensive-against the Axis, Henry Luce continued to ponder the postwar world. At a 1943 brainstorming session of his Postwar Committee, Luce raised many relevant issues. Germany, he decided, must be punished, then "Europeanized." For a number of years, Germany would have to work for Europe, which she had plundered and tormented. Turning to the rest of the continent, Luce argued that Europeans, who looked to the U.S. for spiritual guidance, feared a recurrence of American isolationism. He therefore hoped that a congressional resolution would commit the United States to postwar cooperation with its allies.

Ever the law-and-order disciplinarian, Luce argued that European governments-in-exile, some of which were reactionary, would have to return to power. These regimes could provide their homelands with "order and security." In fact, undemocratic regimes could thereby thwart the yearning for freedom felt by millions of their former subjects. Not for the last time, Harry Luce refused to admit that liberty might come into conflict with an American-backed world order.

In 1943 Luce unveiled a more detailed plan for the postwar era, grandly entitled "The Reorganization of the World." To Allen Grover, Luce's startling document represented "Harry's idea of what might be done if human beings just had the wit to do it." The U.S., Luce wrote, must be stronger than any "other two nations combined." She would develop her "heritage of political freedom" while becoming "creative, fraternal [and] reverent." American taxpayers would have to help build postwar Europe by offering her billions of dollars. Then a revived continent would create a United States of Europe, sponsored by Britain, the U.S.A., and the Soviet Union. In Luce's plan, a federated Europe would adopt a charter of civil liberties akin to the Bill of Rights.

Harry Luce then grappled briefly with other global theaters. He hoped that the Russians would "develop a prosperous and noble [postwar] society." The other United Nations, Luce promised, would not try to isolate the USSR. Rather, they would assist her, and "seek her cooperation" in world affairs. When he turned to "Greater China," Luce expected that America, in league with her Chinese friends, would lead Asia into a "renaissance of a great Chinese civilization." Anticoloni-alist America would ensure the orderly emergence of a United States of India, free of European domination. Liberated from her colonial burden, Britain, Luce argued, would be stronger. Working with the U.S.A., the British Commonwealth could then "establish a capitalistic orderly trading system for the world, in which all peoples may partici-pate. . . ."

Latin Americans, Luce believed, would one day determine "what organic relations they will wish to establish in and with the world." He foresaw an era of trusteeship for much of Africa, which would be "treated as a great corporate treasure-house and playground, trusteed for the benefit of all mankind." Luce assumed that ex-colonial peoples would respond with gratitude to those who wanted to aid them. The Anglo-Americans, under U.S. leadership, would then create a "world-girdling system of trade and freedom." Racial conflicts and national wars would diminish. Capitalism, free trade, and civil rights would prevail over nationalism, poverty, and hatred. Mankind would develop an international "common law," that is, one respected by all peoples. Presiding over this time without equal would be Luce's God, rediscov-ered by grateful men and women who could not "live by bread alone." The war, *Life* concluded, was about to enter its decisive, *American* phase, and the "zero hour" was approaching.

As he scanned the horizon, Henry Luce devoted some kind words to Great Britain. He cheered the RAF's fighter pilots and praised the defiant speeches of Winston Churchill, but inwardly questioned the viability of the British Empire. As an American nationalist, Luce ex-pected the United States to replace Britain as the leader of the English-speaking world. He thus treated the declining Empire in a manner reminiscent of a respectful yet anxious heir-to-be: he worried about his legacy while exuding concern for his ill relative. Harry paid particularly close attention to the "white Dominions" of Australia and Canada, where he hoped to deepen American influence and expand the operations of Time Inc. *Time* did not bother to disguise Luce's ambition when it wrote that ". . . Australia's present plight, and future welfare, are problems which once concerned Britain and Australia, but are now primarily the concern of the U.S. and Australia."

To Luce, much of Britain's future depended on her management of the Indian problem. In 1939 *Life* had annoyed certain British officials by publishing a highly favorable essay on the Indian Congress Party leader Jawaharlal Nehru, a Cambridge-educated Brahman. Though Nehru was a Socialist, *Life* admired the man who demanded that the British grant "full democracy to 350,000,000 Indians who want freedom." Like the British liberal Thomas Babington Macauley (1800-1859), Luce felt that in giving "freedom to India, [Englishmen] should feel themselves standing on a most magnificent pinnacle of history." *Time*, in reporting that the British had arrested Nehru for the ninth time, advocated diplomatic intervention by the United Nations, and especially by the Americans.

By and large, though, British officialdom was content with its relations with Time Inc. Luce, after all, had been an interventionist and "warmonger" since the early days of the war. As one official had put it, ". . . we are far from unmindful of the help which *Life* has already given to our cause." Brendan Bracken, Churchill's close confidant and minister of information, carefully cultivated Time Inc.'s London staffers. Aware of isolationist Anglophobia in the United States, Bracken once told a sympathetic Walter Graebner that "You can do a lot for us in America by nailing any lies about Britain." Early in 1942 the British government decided to invite Harry Luce to London.

Luce arrived in London late in February, at a particularly bad time. The fortress island of Singapore, with its 130,000 defenders, had fallen to Japan only days before. Everywhere, Harry asked questions, studied production figures, looked around, and made notes. Luce concluded that the British government had failed to tell its people about the weakened condition of the Empire.

The day after he returned home, in late March, Luce drafted a long, incisive memorandum, which he later distributed to senior editors and influential friends. In this document, Luce wrote that a "victorious America . . . must inevitably seek to establish a world wide influence." Harry Luce also honored the British commitment to "international law" and the "ideas of justice," which he hoped to extend to the whole

world. Luce concluded that Britain's "supremacy is over but she may
largely determine what and who comes after." Singapore's fall had
shocked Britons, who were not prepared for the day when England
"might live and the Empire go down." The self-governing Dominions,
Luce observed with satisfaction, now looked to themselves, *or to the
Americans*, for their protection.

Despite his fault-finding, Luce had not come away from England
unmoved. He had found a people whose "churches were empty," but
whose hearts were filled with Christian yearning. A poetic Luce recalled
the summer of 1940, when "you [Britain] recaptured for one finest hour
an unsurpassed greatness." Like a proud but grateful heir, Luce hoped
that postimperial England would not allow herself to slip into a degrading, Socialist retirement. Instead, he expected that the British people,
having rediscovered Christianity, would lift themselves "above the
barbarism to which they will not surrender."

During these terrible months of Allied defeat, Harry Luce was not
about to undermine his imperiled British ally. By the autumn of 1942,
however, Allied troops were winning victories, and were poised to
launch offensives in both the Southwest Pacific and North Africa. Luce
was now willing to provoke a debate about the future of the British
Empire. "An Open Letter from the Editors of *Life* to the People of
England" caused an enormous uproar, mostly in Britain. Russell
Davenport's October 12 editorial sounded threatening: *Life* spoke,
Davenport assured Britain, for 134 million Americans. It warned its
stunned British friends that "we are sure we are *not* fighting . . . to hold
the British Empire together." According to *Life*, Americans believed
that Britain would sacrifice common goals in favor of selfish measures
calculated to preserve the Empire. If England did so, Davenport threatened, "you will lose the war [,] . . . because you will lose us." *Life* then
opened the painful Indian wound and suggested that Britain would have
to resolve this problem by adherence to the ideal of self-government.
"In order to have our own freedom," wrote the eloquent Davenport,
"we are learning that others must have freedom." Davenport, who had
worked closely with Luce before publishing his Open Letter, concluded
that Britain's opposition to free trade, combined with her haughty
attitude toward Asia, could harm American interests.

Britons, who had been fighting for their lives in 1939, 1940, and
1941, while Americans were absorbed in baseball's pennant races, were
not amused. On the left, Kingsley Martin, since 1931 the editor of
the influential *New Statesman*, mocked Luce as the "American Cecil
Rhodes." The Conservative Randolph Churchill, ranting to Tom Mat-

thews, accused Harry Luce, an "irresponsible press autocrat," of "unscrupulous sensationalism." Harry, he thought, wanted to be President, and thanks to this ambition, Luce was trying to gain the support of isolationist Anglophobes. *Time*-hating isolationists like Senator Nye of North Dakota gleefully denounced the interventionist Luce for endangering America's alliance with Great Britain.

Though Luce approved of Davenport's editorial, he disliked the ensuing uproar. Luce wanted to expand his worldwide operations, and the hostility of Britons concerned him. Mitch Davenport wanted to refute the arguments advanced by critics of the Open Letter; Harry wished to let the matter die quietly. Yet the uproar did not subside, so Luce issued a contrite statement, which regretted the misunderstanding and boasted of *Life*'s long struggle against Hitlerism. He hoped that *all* Allied powers would renounce imperialism and outline their plans for the postwar world. Yet the furor boiled over again. In "A Communication," published by *Life*, Vernon Bartlett, Member of Parliament, cruelly compared the Open Letter to Dr. Goebbels' best Nazi propaganda. He defended his country, arguing that Britain had gone to war on behalf of human freedom, not imperialism. Luce, after reaffirming his admiration for Winston Churchill, had to listen in pained silence as thirty or so members of the British press corps attacked him. "May God forgive you, I can't," declared one overwrought British correspondent.

Clare Luce, meanwhile, was supporting a strident campaign endorsed by the India League and the American Civil Liberties Union. Demanding the release of Nehru from his latest British jail, Mrs. Luce spoke in the "most barbed anti-imperialist style." Clare, who could sketch deft images with a cruel pen, compared Indians to animals in a well-maintained (British) zoo. The analogy with German concentration camps was too obvious to be ignored. Henry Luce spoke in softer tones, but he, too, attacked the "insufferable snobbishness of the sahibs," and eloquently declared that "The injunction to be your brothers' keepers is no warrant for any form of slavery." Even if the Indians fought a bloody civil war after independence, Britain had no right to rule them. "If [Churchill] was fighting for empire," *Time* scolded, "he might risk losing the war." Such statements greatly annoyed British observers, but they reflected widely held American views. According to a 1943 poll, almost a third of the GIs surveyed believed that Britain was working to control the world, not build democracy. Thirty-nine percent of U.S. military personnel questioned in the Middle East theater did not like their British allies.

Luce hoped that the United States could induce Britain to liberate

India, by offering a tradeoff to Churchill. Harry drafted a plan that would have the Americans forge an international order based on free trade. If England cooperated, she could expect to prosper, but only if she first divested herself of the golden albatross called India. Britain would clearly be a junior partner in a world reorganized by American genius, but she would be honored for her great traditions of justice and law. If, however, Britain protected the status quo, she would lapse into collectivism, and fail to play her assigned role in the American Century.

Henry Luce's plan for a peaceful, American-ordered postwar world rested upon the following six premises:

1. The United States would emerge from the war with enormous power and prestige. Of all Luce's presuppositions, this one appeared to be the surest bet. Luce's other assumptions fell into what FDR would have called the "iffy" category, to wit—

2. Britain would avoid the pitfalls of socialism while peacefully divesting herself of the incubus of empire.

3. An internationally oriented Republican Party would soon come to power in the United States.

4. The Chinese government would survive and grow stronger.

5. The postwar world would avoid the polarization induced by prolonged and widespread ideological conflict.

6. The West would still enjoy good relations with the Soviet Union.

While a Yale undergraduate, Henry Luce had described V. I. Lenin's revolutionary Bolshevism as an affront to civilization. During the immediate prewar and war years, however, Luce no longer sounded the tocsin for an anti-Bolshevik crusade. Other concerns—such as Adolf Hitler and the Great Depression—were more pressing. Despite its aversion to communism, Time Inc. began to portray Soviet Russia as a kind of status quo power. Stalin, according to *The March of Time*, wished to maintain peace in Europe while postponing "any world revolution . . . [,] indefinitely." *The March of Time* also argued that Russian industrial efficiency was improving as the Russian people struggled toward the goal of self-sufficiency. By June 1941, when the Nazis attacked the USSR, Harry viewed Russia with mild hostility tempered by hope.

Henry R. Luce's editors soon portrayed dictator Stalin as the personification of the surprising Russian resistance. By depicting the Soviets as a hard-fighting, fully mobilized ally, Luce's magazines called attention to the indifferent state of the American war effort through much of 1942. Self-consciously, *Time* ridiculed those Westerners who had once portrayed Stalin as "a sort of unwashed Genghis Khan with blood

dripping from its fingertips"—a good description of Harry Luce's prose
in years past. In the summer, when German armies drove toward the
Volga and Stalingrad, *Time* feared a Soviet collapse or a Russian deal
with the Nazis. This, intoned *Time*, was Russia's "gravest hour."

By September 1942, while Stalingrad held out—a "second Verdun,"
according to John Shaw Billings—Luce was complaining about Russia's
lack of friendship for the Americans. Wendell Willkie, whose recent
interview with Stalin soon appeared in *Life*, gave Luce further pause
for thought. The dictator, at his charming best, had coyly conveyed a
warning to the Americans. Grateful for America's help, Stalin admon-
ished his ally against adopting a patronizing tone toward the USSR.
And as the Soviet leader and his foreign admirers demanded a second
front in Europe, *Life* restrained its enthusiasm for the venture.

By 1943 talk about our heroic Soviet ally was heard throughout the
land, from the White House to the field headquarters of American
generals. Luce, however, continued to harbor premature and highly
unfashionable suspicions of Russia—when he personally edited *Time*,
the newsmagazine voiced scant enthusiasm for Stalin. *Time*'s Foreign
News, however, usually reflected the pro-Soviet views of editor Charles
Wertenbaker. At the end of 1942, *Time* concluded that the Germans
were losing the war, thanks to Soviet successes. Stalin was named Man
of the Year, and *Time* marveled at how Americans resembled Russians,
and how much these two nations could learn from each other. In *Time*'s
view, the Soviets needed to show more respect for the rights of the
individual, while Americans could use a dose of Russian discipline. This
argument left Luce unimpressed, but like a good soldier in the cause of
Allied solidarity, he was cautious in his public statements.

While the remnants of the German Sixth Army were surrendering at
Stalingrad, Harry Luce conversed with Under Secretary of State Sumner Welles. A confidant of Roosevelt, Welles hoped to organize the
world in cooperation with Soviet Russia and other Allied powers. Luce,
however, suggested an alternative approach. If the USSR proved to be
uncooperative, why not plan for a postwar order without her? Welles,
unimpressed, evaded the implications of Luce's scheme, and Luce returned from Washington irritated with Roosevelt's refusal to force Russia's hand.

Luce's increasing concern about Russia coincided with the temporary
departure of Charles Wertenbaker. Wert left to cover the Tunisian
campaign, and he did not return to Foreign News for several months.
Since John Osborne, his successor, was less enthusiastic about the Soviets, *Time* now hinted at postwar trouble if the USSR wanted to annex
territory beyond the Baltic states and parts of Finland.

After Stalingrad, editorial signs of Luce's inner qualms started to surface. *Time*'s February 22, 1943, cover asked, "What kind of victory does Russia want?" The Soviet Union, according to the newsmagazine, was a secretive, possibly expansionist state. *Time*'s editors and correspondents, however, did not speak with a single voice, for Luce himself was undecided about what line to follow. While he pondered the Russian puzzle, *Life* published a celebrated issue on the Soviet Union. Among those involved in the production was Walter Graebner, just back from Russia.

Walter Graebner's book *Round Trip to Russia* argued that Russia did not intend to conquer Europe nor revolutionize the world. A minor celebrity of the moment, Graebner spoke on the radio, gave interviews, participated in war bond drives, and addressed distinguished audiences. He was also involved in the "Russian Issue," to be published by *Life* on March 29, 1943. The Soviet Society for Cultural Relations had provided Graebner with about 10,000 photographs; *Life*'s editors selected around 1,000 of them. Now copies would have to be made, but Moscow lacked the requisite photographic paper. The paper existed, but only in besieged Leningrad. Despite the siege, the Soviets flew the precious material to Moscow. When prints were made of several hundred pictures, U.S. Ambassador Admiral William H. Standley dispatched them to New York in a diplomatic pouch.

Life's March 29 cover featured Margaret Bourke-White's striking portrait of Stalin. Inside, the magazine proclaimed its admiration for the Russian people, while reproducing beautiful photographs devoted to Russia's history, culture, sports, and even religion. In a question-and-answer session with former Ambassador to Moscow Joseph E. Davies, *Life* even opened its pages to an apologist for the Stalin regime. Davies, author of the best-selling book *Mission to Moscow*, told Americans that Stalin's Russia wanted peace and offered goodwill to the West. In the former Ambassador's view, the Soviets did not covet land lying beyond the territories taken from them in 1941.

Life's special issue contained more than this pro-Soviet fluff. In the spirit of realism, *Life* argued that Russians feared encirclement by the West, while Americans nurtured well-founded suspicions of the Soviets. Ten million Russians had already died in this war, so the West must treat the Soviets with sympathy and respect. *Life*, however, also recommended that Russia address concerns expressed by Americans. Luce and Davenport, for example, resented Soviet secrecy, which prevented Americans from seeing how the Red Army used its Lend-Lease assistance. And for the first time, the magazine used a phrase that later circulated as common currency in American political debate. Afraid that the Soviets would establish "satellite states" around their periphery, *Life* argued that the U.S. could not prevent this from happening. The magazine warned, however, that such expansionism would poison postwar relations between Russia and the West.

Four fifths of the reader response to *Life*'s special issue was positive, for most Americans clearly wanted to work with the Soviets after the war. The liberal *New Republic*, which was no admirer of Henry Luce, praised *Life*'s acceptance of the Russian Revolution as a first for a big capitalist publication. Fellow travelers and admirers of the Soviet war effort lauded the magazine for dispelling years of "vile distortions and venomous lies that the American press had been perpetrating on the people for 25 years." The Soviets themselves loved the issue, and used it in their propaganda.

Roper's polls, which Luce carefully studied, continued to reflect Americans' respect for Russia. Only 9 percent of Gallup's sample named Britain as the nation doing the most to win the war: the figures for the U.S. and Russia were 55 percent and 32 percent, respectively. Luce the trend-spotter did not buck public opinion unless he was ready to break with it. *Time* was sometimes critical of the Soviets, but rarely hostile to them. The magazine rejected the idea of reconstituting an anti-Soviet *cordon sanitaire* in Eastern Europe, and acknowledged Stalin's need for secure boundaries—without defining them. By 1943 *Time* wanted to believe the best of the Communist partisans in Yugoslavia, since they were clearly inflicting heavy losses on the German occupation forces. Late in April 1943, when Nazi Propaganda Minister Joseph Goebbels announced that the Germans had uncovered mass graves of Polish officers, murdered in the Katyn Forest by Soviet police in 1940, the Russians denounced the story as a Nazi lie. *Time*'s editors, anxious to preserve Allied unity, decided to pay tribute to Allied unity despite private concerns about Russian perfidy. Besides, *Time* defensively noted, the Germans had killed many more Poles than had the Russians.

By the summer of 1943, the Allies had won the Battle of the Atlantic, and the Germans were in full retreat in southern Russia and the Ukraine. Hitler was clearly losing the war, but this fact only intensified Harry Luce's concern about America's policy—or lack of it—regarding the Soviets. As usual in such cases, he scrawled a memorandum clarifying his views. Wise colleagues then interpreted these opinions as guidelines.

Harry Luce's memorandum to managing editors was openly critical of the be-kind-to-Stalin policy. He noted that Time Inc. had always favored freedom of speech. In the interests of wartime solidarity, Luce added, his magazines had made an exception of Russia. After the war, however, Time Inc. might have to stop apologizing for her. As Luce put it, he favored opposing governments that scored lower than "50%" on his "tests of political freedom." Although *Time* still pursued a cautious course, the newsmagazine wondered whether the prominence of the Moscow-sponsored National Committee of Free Germany (consisting of German POWs and steered by German Communists) foreshadowed a German-Soviet alliance. If it did, then the Russians would one day dominate all of Europe.

By October 1943 Harry Luce had decided that Stalin understood one thing: power. When Secretary of State Cordell Hull visited Moscow, *Time* warned that the West was ill-equipped to deal with the "toughest ruler in the modern world." *Time* printed a map exposing Stalin's alleged designs on the Baltic Republics, eastern Poland, and Romanian Bessarabia, and called for blunt discussions with Stalin. Western leaders, *Time* argued, should emphasize their growing ground, air, and naval strength throughout the world. Worried about Russian expansionism, *Life*'s editorial page praised the Moscow foreign ministers' declaration that the great powers agree not to "employ their military forces within other states, except . . . after joint consultation." Still, *Life* was aware of the fact that 81 percent of polled Americans hoped to collaborate with the Soviets in building a peaceful postwar world.

Before Roosevelt's summit meeting with Stalin and Churchill in Tehran, *Time* described the President as a realist who knew how to compromise. After Tehran, *Time* continued to sway back and forth as it appraised Soviet intentions. Perhaps, *Time* ominously speculated, the Soviets, after achieving their unstated goals in Eastern *and Central* Europe, would join the postwar international order. In the early winter of 1944, Luce was still a concerned citizen searching for a policy. Then, in a flurry of conferences and memoranda, he demanded a full reevaluation of Soviet goals and American foreign policy options.

Perhaps no other publishing company in the United States could have responded to Luce's request, but Time Inc., with its various foreign policy committees was a kind of ink-stained, Rockefeller Center version of the Department of State. Driven by Luce's curiosity, intellect, and obsessive desire to ask and answer the right questions, editors and publishers now found themselves engaged in high-level strategic and political debates. Foreign policy adviser Raymond Leslie Buell, an expert on Eastern Europe, greatly influenced Luce's thinking. Responding to

Harry's questions, Ray Buell supplied his colleagues at Time Inc. with a bulky portfolio on Russia.

Buell's Russia was an immensely strong, totalitarian regime, which could act decisively. American democracy, by contrast, moved more slowly. Following classical geopolitical theory, Buell's Russia sought to control the "heartland" of Eurasia. Poland, Ray Buell told Harry Luce, would prove to be a test of Soviet intentions, but the fate of post-Hitler Germany was even more important. Buell predicted that the wartime alliance would probably fragment over the future of Germany, "not to mention the whole question of the economic reconstruction of Europe."

The West, Ray Buell warned, must deprive the Soviets of the German powerhouse. Buell, anticipating later policy, demanded that the West ally itself with "democratic forces in Germany," thereby staunching the westward expansion of the USSR. If the West failed to prevent the Soviet domination of Germany, Buell added, Britain might accommodate herself to Russian hegemony. This development, in his alarmist view, would lead to a war in which the United States stood alone. In a more optimistic vein, Buell suggested that the West create an "Atlantic Union," under British and American leadership. Of course, he added, the Soviets could join his Atlantic Union—if they liberalized their regime and acceded to a Western military presence in the Baltic area. Stalin would hardly agree to such terms. Overall, Ray Buell painted a bleak picture, one which appealed to Luce's growing mistrust of the Soviet Union.

On January 26, 1944, John K. Jessup, acting for Harry Luce, convened a council of Time Inc.'s senior editors. Meeting in the Carpenter Suite at the Waldorf, the conferees discussed Buell's memoranda at length. As a professional, Buell had ably presented the discussants with alternative scenarios. In the happy one, Russia was cooperative, while the gloomy prognosis assumed that she was a menace. It was clear that Buell himself feared the rise of an expansionist, messianic state poised to dominate Europe. Better to prepare for this eventuality and be wrong than to ignore it and be destroyed.

Henry R. Luce's American age of benevolence was supposed to follow a time of troubles and turmoil. Now, if Buell was right, the American Century might encompass a struggle against a new and dangerous enemy.

Luce tended to come down on Buell's side, in part because of the supposed threat to China represented by a truculent Soviet Union. In his wartime correspondence with Douglas MacArthur, Luce boasted of having "insisted that the Pacific War is of no less importance than the European." And Luce shared MacArthur's belief that "the focus of the next ten thousand years of human history will not be Europe but Asia and the Pacific." As in 1938 and 1939, Luce's reaction to China's plight affected his policies toward Europe.

China:
Truth-Telling and
Mythmaking

Henry Luce's alliance with Soviet Russia was based on a shared commitment to the defeat of a common enemy, the Greater German Reich. In the Far East, by contrast, Luce had an ally he loved, but one of questionable military value to the United States. Luce tirelessly attempted to convince both Washington and the public that China needed and deserved more assistance. Through his magazines, he challenged the widespread view of the Chinese as an apathetic, antlike mass of victims.

Life's deification of a heroic Chiang Kai-shek helped to define the Chinese leader for millions of American readers. Teddy White contributed to this cult in the late winter of 1942, when *Life* portrayed Chiang, "the leader of fighting China," as a man who was helping to decide "the destiny of all Asia." Surely, the magazine declared, this leader deserved more military assistance. But helping China was a more complex challenge than *Life* acknowledged. An incident involving White himself hinted at miseries to come.

A few weeks after Pearl Harbor, Teddy White wrote to T. V. Soong, offering to dispatch cables to his editors in New York. *Time*, he hoped, could then generate some interest in helping China. White, assuming that he had clearance from Soong, typed the draft of his cable and presented it to the Chinese censors for approval. The putative dispatch sat on a bureaucrat's desk while *Time*'s deadlines came and passed, unheeded. Finally White wrote to Soong, complaining about the situation. Meanwhile, White's cable had received the approval of both H. H. Kung and the U.S. Army. Apparently, however, three censors in Free China were one too few. A disgusted Teddy White learned that Foreign Minister Soong's own office would have to approve of the cable.

After Pearl Harbor, the Allies had agreed that Chiang would be supreme commander of all forces fighting in the China theater. General Joseph W. Stilwell (promoted to Lieutenant General in late February) was to serve as the Generalissimo's chief of staff. Stilwell, soon named Commanding General of U.S. Army Forces in the China–Burma–India theater, would control all Chinese forces assigned to him by Chiang. He was also charged with the distribution of U.S. aid to China. A blunt-spoken, often sarcastic man, Stilwell had commanded the III Corps in California. Late in February 1942, "Vinegar Joe" Stilwell, a lean and tough old soldier, arrived in Calcutta, then flew on to Chungking. Events in the south, where the British feared a disaster in Burma, quickly drew him back to the Indian theater. Rangoon fell to the Japanese invaders on March 7, and the enemy pushed farther into Burma.

Commanded by Britain's General H. R. L. G. Alexander, a collection of Chinese, Indians, and Britons endured the horrors of retreat through devastated villages, jungles, and mountains. Stilwell's hastily assembled Chinese divisions proved inadequate to their task. They, too, fell back amid confusion and defeat, fleeing toward India while the air stank of the bodies shattered by Japanese bombs. In late April the Allies lost the use of the Burma Road, which had been a major lifeline to isolated China. The Japanese divisions then drove toward Lashio and Mandalay and into Yunnan before supply problems brought them to a halt. Roosevelt feared that the Japanese seizure of the Burma Road might lead to the collapse of China. Then a large number of Japanese troops could attack India or even Australia while throwing the Western powers out of East Asia. In Chungking, U.S. Ambassador Clarence E. Gauss, a blunt man, argued that China was a "minor asset," which could soon become a "major liability." In Washington, General Marshall worried about Chiang's lack of support for Allied military efforts in both Burma and Yunnan.

Clare Boothe, a war correspondent for *Life*, flew out to India with Stilwell. Showing extraordinary bravery and coolness under fire, she covered the dismal Burma retreat for the magazine. The General considered Clare good company, and before disaster befell the Allied forces in Burma, Clare would sometimes provide a drink for Stilwell and his aides. Later, as she typed away in the dank heat, Clare created a new legend for the readers of Harry's picture magazine. In *Life*'s pantheon of heroes, Fighting Joe Stilwell, commander of Chinese and Americans, now took his place alongside Douglas MacArthur—and Chiang Kai-shek.

In fact, Chiang Kai-shek was an insecure ruler whose view of the outside world contained equal measures of illusion, ignorance, and suspicion. At the moment, Chiang entertained fantasies about the imminent arrival of U.S. Army divisions in China. After the GIs failed to appear, the Generalissimo charged that Washington was diverting promised bombers to India without consulting either Stilwell or himself. Stilwell now faced the most difficult challenge of his career, for he intended to forge a first-rate Chinese army. Thinner, and suffering from jungle itch acquired during the Burma retreat, Stilwell drilled his trainees and suffered at their side. Obsessed with reopening the Burma Road, the General demanded more and more Chinese troops. Tragically, the blunt, occasionally crude Stilwell was no diplomat. He disliked Chungking, which he saw as a rancid place, reeking with intrigue and duplicity. He found Chiang to be "ignorant, arbitrary [and] stubborn," and frequently referred to him as "Peanut."

Detached from the people, Chiang relied heavily on cronies, a few generals who shared his background, and the Guomindang party organization. He sullenly tried to treat the impatient and usually absent Stilwell as a foreign subordinate, on a par with, but far more dangerous than his Chinese generals. Chiang feared that crack troops, trained and armed by American officers in Burma, India, and Yunnan, would not be loyal to their head of state. Unlike Stilwell, the "Gimo" did not want to waste his best units fighting Japan, for the Americans would presumably eclipse the Rising Sun. Chiang wished to conserve these precious divisions so that he might one day use them against Communists and other internal foes.

Chiang felt that the Americans were failing him. A year into the Pacific war, the War Department had stationed only 17,000 troops in the China–Burma–India theater. Chiang began to blame Stilwell for Washington's paltry shipments of transport and military assistance. Madame Chiang, a cunning manipulator, wanted the White House to know that China might collapse. The ever resourceful Madame Chiang turned for support to her friend Clare Luce, who had visited the Chiangs while reporting on the Burma campaign. When she returned to the States, Clare briefed Assistant Secretary of State A. A. Berle, Jr. She

endorsed Chinese complaints about the paltry level of American assistance. Mrs. Luce, as if programmed by the Chiangs, suggested that the
Chinese might cease fighting altogether. Informed about the conversation, State's Far Eastern Affairs expert Stanley Hornbeck angrily criticized Clare's mix of "truth, half-truth, hearsay account and horseback
judgment." Clare Boothe Luce was an effective spokeswoman for the
Chiangs, and this is what irritated the State Department.

More American supplies began to arrive in the China theater, but
Chiang continued to complain about their unfair distribution. Badly
needed military equipment, industrial supplies, and oil were stored in
India and Burma. This vital matériel could reach China only by flying
it over the daunting "Hump," the high mountains separating the Allied
depots in India from airfields around Kunming and other towns in
Yunnan. The Americans, however, possessed only limited transport
capacity. Undeterred, the Chinese authorities insisted that a higher
percentage of Lend-Lease stockpiles stored in Burma or India be handed
over to China. Stilwell, who controlled the distribution of these goods,
could not agree. He planned to train thirty modern Chinese divisions,
and this goal required the supply of Lend-Lease matériel to Stilwell's
forces in Yunnan and Burma. Eventually Stilwell planned to liberate
northern Burma. With supplies flowing into China on a reopened
Burma Road, he could equip a vast new Chinese army, perhaps ninety
divisions or more. These crack units would take the offensive against
the Japanese occupier while Allied forces landed on the coast of China.
An unhappy Chiang looked for an alternative to Stilwell and his strategy.

Before the war, Colonel Claire Chennault's "Flying Tigers" (officially called the American Volunteer Group, or AVG) staffed fighting
China's only air arm. Chennault, a swarthy Texan whose calm demeanor masked an iron will, had equipped his men with the famous
and highly effective P-40 fighter aircraft. Overestimating the results
which his new bombers could achieve, Chennault now promised to
defeat the enemy within a year. His plan, however, required a massive
diversion of precious supplies flown in over the Hump. At first, Joe
Stilwell was happy about Chennault's presence, but soon it became
clear to both men that they were on a collision course. Stilwell, under
great pressure from all sides, could not provide anyone with adequate
supplies ("Trying to manure a ten-acre field with sparrow shit" was
Stilwell's earthy metaphor for his task). To Chennault, every ton of
supplies diverted to Stilwell postponed the day of reckoning with Japan.

Character differences played their part in disrupting Chennault's relationship with Stilwell. Joe Stilwell was an old-fashioned puritan who

exploded when he discovered that Chennault had supplied aviators based in Kunming with "clean" Indian prostitutes (flown in over the Hump). It was soon clear to Chennault that he could expedite his victory-through-air-power plan only if Marshall recalled Stilwell. Roosevelt was not prepared to make this change, so the animosities festered. And while these Americans and their clients quarreled about China, the Chungking government intensified its appeal to its friends in the United States.

Chiang's propagandists turned first to Harry Luce. In the words of China's foreign minister, "it is indeed the supreme good fortune of China that, at this crisis in her national life, she has found in you [Luce] and your family such staunch and devoted friends." When the news from China was bad, Luce amplified his rhetoric. Referring to 2.5 million Chinese war dead and 10 million wounded or killed civilians, *Life* lauded those Americans who had supplied beleaguered China with nearly $7 million in relief funds. China, Luce orated, was fighting "to greet a new sun shining upon a universal humanity from a universal heaven." Referring to his 1941 visit to a war zone on the Yellow River, Luce described that point as the pivot of the northern front. There, he insisted, China had halted Japan, so freedom had won a battle for "the entire world."

Rarely had an American so overstated China's contribution to the worldwide war against aggression.

Disconcerting notes sometimes disturbed Harry Luce's reveries. As early as 1942, he had come by secret information that directly contradicted much of what his magazines published about China.

Professor David Rowe, like Luce the son of missionary parents, was a professor of Chinese and Japanese history at Princeton. After working in America's Chungking embassy, Rowe went on a special mission to China, where he gathered information for Colonel Donovan's OSS. Rowe confided in his friend Ray Buell, who in June 1942 wrote an important follow-through memorandum to Luce and other interested Time Incers. Rowe warned of growing imperialist tendencies among Chinese officials. And Rowe sharply contradicted Ambassador to Washington Hu Shih, for China, according to the professor, was not moving toward democracy and reform.

Even more ominously, Rowe spoke of a regime that had dedicated itself to maintaining "the dominant privileges of a landed gentry and a military class. . . ." Professor Rowe, Buell reported, was highly critical of *Time*, *Life*, and *Fortune*, for the Luce publications too often overlooked Chungking's power struggles, corruption, and inefficiency. Rowe concluded that by disguising China's desperate plight, Luce's magazines were performing a real disservice to the American people.

Henry Luce could not accept these purported facts. *His* China was at stake, and Luce had no intention of undermining her valiant struggle. The inflation issue provided a case in point. *Time* finally admitted that prices in China had risen 3400 percent since 1937, but the magazine tended to blame the Allies (they gave too little help) for China's plight. Then *Time* praised H. H. Kung for China's modest successes in her lagging fight against inflation. Within a month Ray Buell got the point, for he served at Luce's pleasure. In July 1942 Buell distanced himself from Rowe's cruel but accurate comments about China. In the mildest terms, Buell admitted that many Chinese did not always agree with Chiang "on the problems of peacetime administration and government." He praised those young Chinese who wished to build a modern, reformed China. Though calling for land reform, Buell hailed the non-reformer Chiang as a great soldier and statesman.

While working in Chungking, Teddy White felt frustrated, as *Time*'s coverage of Chinese issues veered sharply away from his own. Worse still, White noticed that U.S. Army officers in the China theater constantly cited Luce's magazines when backing up their own statements. Writing to a colleague back in the United States, White expressed concern about the growing gap between legend and reality. He concluded that "the less legends we create in this war, the better Time Inc. is going to look after it's all over."

In Washington, China was of growing concern to the White House. Lauchlin Currie, who wanted to become Ambassador to China, told FDR that Chiang was planning to implement an anti-Soviet policy before annihilating the Chinese Communists. Any such policy would of course cause more problems for the White House. Having revisited China, Currie also decided that General Stilwell was incapable of achieving a "fruitful or healthy relationship with Chiang." He therefore recommended that the War Department relieve the General. Chief of Staff Marshall, however, who was a great admirer of Joe Stilwell, continued to support his man in China, so Stilwell remained in the field.

Ray Buell might provide Luce with reassurance, but Teddy White took a different tack. Despite the crises confronting Chiang, White wrote that "There were to be no changes in personnel, party or government." By November 1942, White was bitter about the Guomindang, which he labeled a one-party dictatorship like Russia's, replete with purges, cells, and spies. White had a more personal reason for loathing the KMT, for its censors mangled his copy. White also detested the dominant "CC clique," which consisted of two far-right-wing brothers, Minister of Education Ch'en Liu, and Chiang aide Ch'en Kuo-fu. And by the winter of 1943 Teddy White was less sanguine about China's reserves of strength. He alerted New York, and after reading White's dispatches, Harry Luce actually fretted about a possible Chinese collapse.

Publicly, however, Luce kept up his brave front. His speeches reached thousands of Americans, and his addresses were invariably upbeat. When Henry Luce spoke of Chiang, he portrayed him as a kind of John Calvin, leading his people into a new Reformation. Luce described Chinese suffering as a kind of purification rite, imposed upon an innocent people by the sword of a "savage and perverted race." When Harry delivered a sermon on China in a church, preceded and followed by processionals, anthems, and organ postludes, he would describe China as the ultimate challenge to American Christendom. If we faltered there, he argued, "we fail totally." The Burma Road might fall, but Harry Luce held out.

Once, Luce was delivering a speech in the Beverly Wilshire Hotel before an audience of Hollywood eminences. With some emotion, Harry recalled a time in Chungking when Japanese bombs fell nearby. Suddenly, as Luce was speaking, the lights in the ballroom went out, thanks to a power blackout. The busboys hurried to find some candles, then, in the dimly lit hall, against the flicker of small flames, Harry Luce returned to his text. There he stood, barely visible at the end of his cigarette, preparing to complete his speech. No ill omen could deter him from finishing his appointed task.

Luce's work for China was part of a family effort. Since Pearl Harbor, Harry Luce, Beth Moore, and Clare Luce had beat the drums for China relief. Beth Moore served as chairwoman of the Greater New York Women's Committee of UCR, and she often attended meetings of UCR's executive committee. Clare Luce proved useful in several respects. Thanks to her longtime friend, financier Bernard M. Baruch, UCR received a gift of $100,000 in government bonds, though Baruch made clear that Clare was to control the disbursement of these funds. Clare even solicited a statement from her friend General Stilwell. Approved by the War Department, Clare's blurb bore Stilwell's name: "I have seen the Chinese fighting and I have heard them talk about America and in their bitter relentless struggle I know how much they are looking to us Americans. . . ."

United China Relief's propaganda network fanned out through the country, with speakers addressing citizens at several thousand meetings each year. A "Cheer China" show at the Radio City Music Hall in New York featured Fred Waring and his glee club, actress Helen Hayes, musician Harry James, and actor Adolphe Menjou. Luce was in constant touch with Hollywood producers and motion picture executives, 200 of whom agreed to help him raise money for China. Producer David O. Selznick led Hollywood's UCR drive, and "David," Luce happily wrote, "wants to build a show which will send 40,000,000 Americans to bed weeping for China and emptying their pocketbooks." The irrepressible Sam Goldwyn promised Luce $1,000, while Daryl Zanuck, Luce noted, "is crazy to do a China picture." Working through community groups, labor unions, and corporations, the UCR eventually raised $7 million. Local affiliates received pledges totaling more than $2.2 million in additional gifts.

Thousands of Americans saw one of the four motion pictures produced by UCR. These half-hour presentations owed their technical expertise to the staff of *The March of Time*. Personnel borrowed from Time Inc. also published many UCR posters, school materials, brochures, and newsletters. UCR's slick and highly readable eight-page *News of China* targeted thousands of people. Numerous American schools made use of UCR's pamphlets about China, along with its sample examinations, pedagogic guides, and maps. United China Relief appealed to the emotions, too. Gut-wrenching, illustrated booklets featured Chinese soldiers, defending little homeless orphans. Uncle Sam shook hands with a Chinese soldier, as a picture told Americans that China was "struggling victoriously toward Democracy as we did 150 years ago." Luce's view of America's obligation to a resurgent China reached thousands of children, aged five to eighteen, boys and girls who came of age during the late 1940s and early 1950s. More young Americans were starting to see China as America's ally, and her special responsibility. China, Luce was teaching, was indeed ours to lose.

Harry Luce was ever on the prowl for new public relations successes, and late in 1942 he struck gold. Thanks to Luce's prodding, Madame Chiang agreed to tour the United States. *Life*'s photographers would trail in her wake, and Luce believed that Madame's electrifying presence would greatly facilitate his work as a UCR fund-raiser. In February 1943 Luce began to plan a gala reception for her in New York. He invited John D. Rockefeller, Jr., and other distinguished citizens to join him as members of the Citizens Committee to Welcome Madame Chiang Kai-shek. Luce himself served as associate chairman.

Before speaking in New York City, Madame addressed Congressmen and Senators in Washington. *Life* hailed her speech as Jeffersonian, as Time Inc. launched a month-long celebration of Asia's greatest lady. The visit, however, produced headaches in the White House, for Madame had come seeking (cajoling or demanding, some said) more aid. Madame Chiang argued that Japan was more dangerous than Hitler, and concluded that the United States "will need China in the future just as much as China needs the United States now." This was absurd on the face of it, but the hyperbole comported with Harry Luce's faith, so *Life*, spurred on by its insistent editor in chief, shared Madame's insight with its readers.

Time placed Madame Chiang on its March 1, 1943, cover, after deciding that "She and China know what endurance means." The magazine lauded Madame (Wellesley, class of 1917) as a woman who embodied the Chinese resistance, and praised the American contribution to her country's progress. *Time* did not realize, however, that this aloof woman ("The only thing Oriental about me is my face") might also personify the gap separating China's peasant masses from Chungking's governmental elite.

Time's uncritical tribute to the grand lady was available at newsstands when Madame Chiang made her long-heralded appearance in Madison Square Garden. On March 2, hours before she was to speak in the Garden, Luce and his sister Beth (Clare Luce was busy in Washington) hosted a formal dinner at the Waldorf for Madame Chiang. Harry had invited nine Northeastern governors and their wives, in addition to Wendell Willkie; John D. Rockefeller, Jr.; General H. H. ("Hap") Arnold, commander of the U.S. Army Air Force; and other luminaries. Luce's aide, Wesley Bailey, wrote the text of each governor's toast to Madame, who was staying in her own suite in the same hotel. The assemblage duly convened in the elegant Jansen Suite at 6:30, and awaited Madame Chiang. That moody lady, however, decided that she would not appear. Perhaps she felt that visiting mere governors offended her dignity. Instead of proceeding to the Jansen Suite, Madame finally sent word that she would receive the guests, without their wives, in *her* suite.

Host Harry Luce took this slight in stride. Though mumbling to John Billings about Madame's excessive sense of royalty, Harry never lost sight of the reason for her visit. She was here to win support for China, and that more than made up for this difficulty. Later, Harry and his guests entered limousines and drove to the Garden. Once seated in his box, Luce was joined by Dr. and Mrs. Walter Judd, of Minnesota. Judd, formerly a medical missionary to China, had just won a seat in

Congress. No one, not even Harry Luce, could exceed him in loyalty
to the China of Chiang Kai-shek. Harry made sure that other allies
from his ever-growing China network appeared on the platform with
Madame Chiang. Despite Madame Chiang's dinnertime gaffe, Harry
was ecstatic about the evening. She gave a scintillating performance, as
20,000 Americans cheered her on.

Madame later made her way to Chicago and Los Angeles, accompanied by Wesley Bailey. In the Hollywood Bowl, the beautiful and
dignified First Lady addressed 30,000 supporters. Millions of Americans
who could not be in Hollywood saw the event through the eyes of *Life*,
which featured a big spread on Madame's appearance there. Thomas
Watson, head of IBM, paid for the printing of *First Lady of China*, a
glossy souvenir of Madame Chiang's forty-six-day tour of the U.S.
Replete with beautiful photographs, the slim volume provided China-
relief fund-raisers with a useful promotion. This publication, like all
other UCR propaganda, laid the blame for China's misery solely at the
door of the "savage and perverted" Japanese invader.

Within days of Madame Chiang's glorious appearance in New York,
the Luces were in possession of a devastating memorandum. Dated
March 9, 1943, a surviving copy of the document, which was strictly
confidential, lacks the name of its author and addressee. The writer,
who appears to have been a high civilian or military figure with access
to Stilwell, claimed that China was letting its allies fight the war. The
writer also exposed the foibles of Chiang's high command, including
its venality and shifting feudal loyalties. Most disturbing of all was the
author's contention that the only accomplished Chinese units were the
Communist forces, along with the troops whom Stilwell was training
at Ramgarh, in India. The writer noted that the brisk smuggling trade
between Free and occupied China enriched corrupt Guomindang officials. The Chinese, the author added, would clean up their act only if
they felt that their allies would deprive them of badly needed equipment. He noted that the false heroics ascribed to the Chinese by the
U.S. media only played into the hands of corrupt KMT leaders. The
author of the memorandum described General Stilwell as a symbol of
opposition to "incompetence and corruption."

Time's readers did not see any of this material, and the latest Luce/
Jessup editorials in *Life* again rejected the idea of making aid to China
conditional on reforms in Chungking.

While Madame Chiang accepted the applause of Congressmen and
other Americans, a disaster struck millions of Chinese. The famine in

Honan province was one of the great tragedies of the war, but the Chungking government tried to prevent the world from learning about it. Teddy White, in one of his finest hours, refused to accept this grotesque censorship. Unoccupied Honan, located near the front south and west of the Yellow River, had once contained about 32 million people. No rains had come in 1942, so now, in the winter of 1943, a famine occurred. As White described things, millions of people fled the province, but 1 to 2 million more Chinese were too weak or too poor to get out, and succumbed to the horrors of famine. White insisted on seeing the victims of the latest Chinese catastrophe.

Accompanied by American correspondent Harrison Forman, Teddy White smelled stinking bodies polluting the land, saw dogs munching on corpses, and watched people eating leaves and bark. He never forgot these horrors. Most devastating of all, White discovered that the authorities had foreseen this disaster, but had done little to prepare people for it. By a fluke, an incompetent or selfless official in the Loyang telegraph office dispatched White's cables directly to New York instead of forwarding them to Chungking for censorship. Later, there would be hell to pay, but this blunder meant that Time Inc. received a full report on the Honan famine. In the preceding year, White cabled, droughts had devastated the wheat crops. The government, however, had shipped only a paltry amount of grain into the endangered province, for Chiang had ignored reports of extreme distress in Honan. Now, in the midst of famine, inaction and corruption continued to exact a huge human toll. Army officers were selling supplies at exorbitant prices to relief organizations, and officials refused to remit taxes to starving peasants.

Even more discouraging to Theodore White was his employer's misuse of unique cable copy. Time published only a truncated version of White's dispatches, where one read about some of the suffering in Honan. White later convinced himself that even this inadequate article helped to save "a few thousand lives." Yet Time ignored most of White's data about corrupt Guomindang and army officials, which clearly showed much of the misery could have been avoided. When White returned to Chungking, Chinese censors, never generous with him, eviscerated his copy. In his original dispatch, White had written of "administrative bedlam," corrupt government officials, greedy money-changers, and indifferent bureaucrats. When the censors finished with his work, Chiang's government emerged nearly blameless. The blockade, combined with Japanese depredations, had allegedly caused the Honan famine.

Young Teddy White would not give up. Enraged, he appealed to the American embassy, which stuffed his uncensored dispatches into diplomatic pouches and forwarded them to the State Department. There, copies made their way to the White House. After comparing *Time*'s coverage to White's cables, Lauchlin Currie recommended that the President read the dispatches. Currie did more: he circulated copies to Harry Hopkins, Mrs. Roosevelt, Lend-Lease administrator Stettinius, and other important officials. Currie urged that persons privy to the White dispatches must keep quiet about Teddy's role in disseminating them. Otherwise, Currie warned, T. V. Soong, who had sources in both the embassy and on Stilwell's staff, would retaliate against White. The Soongs, he knew, were accustomed to buying favors and punishing transgressors.

Theodore White wanted to make sure that the Honan tragedy led to reforms in China. Madame Sun Yat-sen was willing to listen to him, as was the liberal leader, Dr. Sun Fo. Through Madame Sun, White gained access to her brother-in-law, Generalissimo Chiang Kai-shek, who listened to him for twenty minutes and jotted down some notes. Belatedly, the government took some action, but White had turned suspicious officials into rabid enemies. Chungking bureaucrats called him a liar and worse. They once again cracked down on the liberal press, blaming it for helping White make pro-Communist propaganda. More than ever, the reactionary Ch'en brothers seemed to control the government. Teddy White now discovered that frightened or hostile sources slammed their doors in his face.

Madame Chiang asked that Harry Luce fire White, which the publisher refused to do. White managed to hang on, but Chinese weakness, magnified by the government's heavy-handed incapacity, cast a pall over his subsequent reporting. Teddy White emerged from the Honan debacle convinced that China was nearing collapse. His disgust with *Time* mounted, as did his doubts about his own future at Time Inc. The story that mattered most to Teddy White had failed to change the policies of *Time*'s editor in chief.

Teddy White's Harvard mentor and patron, Professor John King Fairbank, was working in Chungking for the Office of War Information. He, too, had reached some depressing conclusions. The Chinese government, said Fairbank, was ever more isolated from its people and their massive problems. In Fairbank's view, the Chungking government felt besieged by enemies without and within. The Ch'en brothers, he argued, were creating a police state, complete with semifascist trappings. White's onetime professor resented the sight of the Guomindang's political hacks forcing ideological instruction on liberal professors. Fairbank shared his views with sympathetic observers, including a diplomat named John Paton Davies, Jr.

Davies, like Harry Luce, was born in China to missionary parents. White, who later befriended him, recalled Davies as young, handsome, and "a rising star of the Foreign Service." Fluent in Chinese, Davies was endlessly curious about the new China born in revolution and war. A political adviser to Stilwell, Davies foresaw the specter of civil war. If Chiang attacked the Communists, Davies wrote, Yenan would turn to the Soviet Union for support. His fellow officer, Jack Service, had already decided that a corrupt, upper-class clique governed the Guomindang. Davies and Service also concluded that Chiang, not the Communists, was destroying China's United Front. The United States, they argued, should withhold support from the Generalissimo until he and the KMT changed their quasi-fascist policies.

President Roosevelt, however, was not prepared to take such drastic action. Indeed, he criticized Stilwell for adopting too harsh a tone in addressing the "undisputed leader of 400,000,000 people." Like many Chinese and most Americans, FDR assumed that Chiang was the only man who could keep China together. Few reporters on the scene believed this any longer. An authoritarian, almost fascist Chinese government, journalist Eric Sevareid claimed, was "sitting out the war." Chungking, he added, was fooling no one but "the sentimental American public." Stilwell described Chiang's army as "rotten with corruption," and he, too, warned against illusions harbored by the American public. Stilwell was regularly venting some of his rage in the presence of correspondents, including Teddy White.

Since Luce yielded to no one in his loyalty to China, the bad news from Chungking troubled him, and he finally decided that a response was in order. If the wrong "experts" (presumably liberals and Communists) explained China's troubles to the American people, cynicism might displace enthusiasm. Luce, aware of his own reputation as a friend of Chungking, acknowledged the need to let the people hear from a respected outside source. After agonizing long and hard over an essay written by Pearl Buck, Luce decided to publish it in *Life* in May 1943.

Pearl Buck, the child of missionaries and a 1938 Nobel Prize laureate, knew that most Americans were unaware of dangerous trends in her beloved China. When they learned about them, Buck feared, they would turn away from China, thereby "throwing away a nation of people who could and would save democracy with us. . . ." As edited by *Life*, she expressed her views with sympathy and ever so much discretion. In her widely read *Life* article, "A Warning About China," Buck portrayed a beleaguered country whose liberals could no longer speak freely about the need for democracy. Who was to blame? Buck attributed some of China's plight to her allies, which refused to provide adequate assistance. She defended the Chinese, who deserved "neither adoration nor condemnation." Rather, they merited "understanding and help." In case *Life*'s readers did not get the point, the magazine editorialized that China's plight arose from America's "failure to understand . . . the necessity of helping China. . . ."

From Chungking, U.S. *chargé d'affaires* George Atcheson notified the State Department that the situation was "seriously deteriorating in all respects." China, he believed, might be headed for ruin. Her leaders, Atcheson added, did not lead; rather, they impeded action. He predicted that the regime in power might collapse within a year, and "Foreign loans will no longer help." A respected voice in the Congress also challenged the optimistic view of China. In September 1943 a Republican, Senator Henry Cabot Lodge, Jr., of Massachusetts, observed that Americans visiting China were becoming disillusioned with our ally. They expected to see millions of Chinese resisting Japan. Instead, Lodge observed, Americans were surprised when their preconceptions fell victim to a troubling reality.

In the summer of 1943 Henry Luce wrote an important memorandum to his managing editors. Ever given to hyperbole when speaking of Asia, Luce decided that the "long-range happiness of the U.S." depended upon good relations with Asia. As always, Luce decided that there were "plenty of reasons for the faith." Every ambiguous hint of democratization again impressed *Time* as a step on the way to "a mighty upsurge of prosperity and democracy." Japan, according to the ever optimistic newsmagazine, was showing signs of weakness; China had survived the Honan famine; China was developing its own air force; Chiang had grown in stature.

Responding to such effusions, Teddy White hardly knew where to begin his indictment. He pointed out that China produced only 10,000 tons of steel each year. As in ages past, cabled White, most peasants lived and died in their villages. "The peasant is China," wrote Teddy White. A few lucky farmers had access to modern medicine, but not many. Meanwhile, small and landless peasants were worse off than ever, thanks to the inroads made by an imperfect capitalism. White recommended that China institute a sweeping program of land reform. Grasping at straws, he sought solace in the reformist speeches of Dr. Sun Fo. Sun, the president of the Legislative *Yuan* (governing body) and a leading liberal, shared White's commitment to democratization. It soon became evident, however, that Sun Fo wielded little power.

Theodore White's dismal portrait resembled the picture of China sketched by Kurt Bloch, *Fortune*'s expert on the Chinese economy. In a long memorandum to Harry Luce, Bloch warned that China lacked skilled and honest administrators. He stressed China's need for Western assistance, but was not optimistic about its effect. No matter who did what for China, Bloch continued, the growing hatred between Communists and Guomindang would undermine postwar reconstruction. Bloch warned Luce against sticking to his "pollyanna" approach while ignoring the need for more democracy in China. But Bloch's most disturbing observation concerned international power politics. Officially, Roosevelt would soon recognize China as an equal of the other leading Allied powers. In fact, Bloch argued, China might not be the country that replaced defeated Japan in East Asian power politics.

Around Thanksgiving, Luce cabled T. V. Soong, warning him that "recent reports from experts regarding conditions in China are very unfavorable." Harry hoped that the government would make "vigorous efforts to improve [the] situation."

With America on the offensive in the Southwest Pacific theater, Luce began to think about the contours of the postwar East Asian order. He now designed an American security belt that stretched from Alaska and the Aleutians to Iwo Jima, Okinawa, and the Philippines. Instead of exterminating the Japanese people, fighting on until unconditional surrender, or occupying Japan, Luce proposed that the Allies supervise her disarmament. Grasping the importance of the sacred Emperor to the Japanese nation, Luce would let Japan determine its own constitutional order. He wanted to invite a reformed and disarmed Japan into a postwar world created by the Americans. Presumably, Stalin would be locked out of this new East Asian order. Luce's vision became a prophecy.

In early November 1943, good news arrived from Moscow, where the Big Three foreign ministers had convened. The Soviets, who were at peace in the Pacific, did not wish to antagonize Japan, so Chiang's representative could not formally attend the Moscow conference. Still, the foreign ministers recognized China as a great power, and Chungking was particularly fond of the sixth part of the Allied declaration. There, the Allies pledged not to use their armed forces beyond their borders, "except for the purposes envisaged in this declaration and after joint consultation." Chiang believed that this agreement could shield him from the Red Army, which, if the Americans had their way, would one day launch an attack on Japanese forces from bases located near Manchuria and Inner Mongolia. Chiang, however, made a concession, too. Bowing to Allied pressure, the Generalissimo agreed that "we should clearly recognize that the Chinese Communist problem is a purely political problem and should be solved by political means."

In this autumn of 1943, Roosevelt wanted to gain new insights into the China problem. In Patrick J. Hurley, FDR found an Oklahoma lawyer/politician who was ready to take a fresh look at the entire China Theater of Operations. Hurley soon concluded that China would not really contribute to a major Allied offensive against Japan, since Chiang was saving his forces for a postwar struggle against his internal enemies. If Hurley's report was accurate, then Chiang was insecure, insincere, and perhaps incompetent.

Americans knew nothing of the Hurley report. Instead, newsreels treated movie audiences to a kind of updated version of Madame Chiang's gala visit to the U.S.A. Not far from the great pyramids, Chiang had finally met FDR and Churchill as a supposed equal. While the cameras rolled in Egypt, the Generalissimo and FDR smiled and appeared to chat, though Chiang knew no English. *Time* celebrated Cairo as a Chinese triumph, but in fact, the Cairo meetings had a darker side. Roosevelt referred to the possibility of using Communist troops in the war against Japan, an idea that frightened Chiang. FDR also suggested that Chiang form a unity government with the Communists, a proposal that was anathema to Chungking. And Chiang, for all his smiles at Cairo, worried about concessions that Roosevelt might make to Stalin. The President's military advisers wished to bring the Soviet Union into the war against Japan at the earliest opportunity. Chiang wondered whether he would be the one to pay the entry price.

In fact, Roosevelt had quickly grown weary of the Generalissimo. Speaking of Chiang, FDR told Stilwell that the Americans might have to "look for some other man or group of men to carry on." In January 1944, moreover, Roosevelt turned down Chiang's request for further financial aid. Inflation and speculation, said FDR, were running rampant, even though the Chinese government had promised to curb these deadly ills. The President was also disgusted with Chungking's failure to cooperate with the latest Allied offensive in Burma. FDR referred to Chiang as a man of "limited" military knowledge, commanding troops who fought "badly." This change of heart would have shocked millions of Americans, who had come to equate Chinese resistance with heroic Generalissimo Chiang and beautiful Madame Chiang.

Since early 1943, textile importer Alfred Kohlberg had been concerned about bottlenecks and inefficiencies choking the China relief effort. An embittered antileftist, Kohlberg was an ardent supporter of conservatives in the Guomindang, including Chiang. Now the chairman of the Executive Committee of the American Bureau for Medical Aid to China (ABMAC), Kohlberg had heard that more than 30 million Chinese suffered from malaria, cholera, and dysentery. Blood banks lacked funds, while other Chinese medical relief operations failed to operate efficiently.

An inveterate collector of news clippings, diverse data, and biographical information, Kohlberg loved to investigate people and organizations. On April 20, 1943, ABMAC authorized an inquiry, so Kohlberg traveled to China, where he examined the work of Chinese agencies assisted by the bureau. To his dismay, Kohlberg found that large amounts of medical supplies were rotting in storage depots and warehouses. The energetic American visitor also concluded that some vitally needed drugs were being stolen for subsequent sale on the black market. Kohlberg appealed to the American embassy for help, but before achieving any results, he became involved in a dispute that marked the beginning of a nasty chapter in American history.

According to the agreement signed by UCR and ABMAC, United China Relief turned a certain amount of money over to the bureau. ABMAC then disbursed these funds to Chinese medical personnel, while both ABMAC and UCR took responsibility for monitoring the efforts of their Chinese beneficiaries. The combative Kohlberg, however, charged that UCR's Chungking officials lacked the requisite military experience and medical knowledge. He further complained that Dwight Edwards, China Field Director for UCR, had carried out investigations that undermined the work of ABMAC and sowed confusion among Chinese officials. Kohlberg believed that ABMAC should be supporting agencies that worked to meet "urgent needs at the front." He therefore lavished high praise on the Emergency Medical Service Training Schools, or EMSTS, a service operated by the Ministry of Military Affairs.

After touring the Changsha front, scene of repeated Japanese assaults, Kohlberg decided that EMSTS graduates were rendering yeoman service. He also concluded that the soldiers, "excepting new recruits," were in good condition. They lived, he claimed, in spotless barracks and ate nourishing food. Writing to Madame Chiang, Kohlberg lauded the sanitary and medical conditions in Hunan's 9th War Area. Unfortunately for Kohlberg, Dr. W. S. Flowers, of the British Red Cross, totally discredited his appraisal of China's military prowess. Flowers noted that his Chinese hosts had taken Kohlberg on a highly selective tour of "one small area on this front." According to Flowers, there was "wide-spread semistarvation and malnutrition amongst both civilians and military." Two Red Cross doctors with enormous experience on China's war fronts also rebutted Kohlberg's glowing testimonials to Chiang's army. Doctors Kamieniecki and Schoen spoke of a typical division, where in less than a year, thousands of men died or fell ill. Even the dead were not spared: corrupt generals indulged in a "coffin racket," in which they raked off a percentage of the profits earned in a very brisk trade. Lurking behind these outrages was an assumption ascribed to their perpetrators: "Never mind, the thing we have plenty of in China are men."

Alfred Kohlberg returned to the United States, determined to destroy Dwight Edwards. He soon found powerful allies in scholar-diplomat Hu Shih and writer Lin Yutang. These men also blamed UCR's Chungking office for many of ABMAC's problems. Using information provided by Lin, Kohlberg accused Edwards of putting undue pressure on the Chinese government, which badly needed his UCR disbursements. Kohlberg appealed his case to the board of directors of UCR. He proposed that Edwards be invited to New York for a debate, but the UCR's executive committee rejected this suggestion. Instead, the UCR established a three-man special committee, which would hear Kohlberg's arguments, then report back to the full executive committee.

The special committee, consisting of James G. Blaine, Paul G. Hoffman, and Henry R. Luce, listened to Kohlberg on February 29, 1944, for three hours. The plaintiff argued that Dwight Edwards had treated Chinese medical personnel with disrespect. Further, Kohlberg charged that Edwards' inaccurate reports had resulted in UCR's decision to stop funding EMSTS's valuable work. Though Henry Luce left before the session concluded, he, like his colleagues, was predisposed to support Edwards, a Princeton alumnus long active in the YMCA movement in China. Most Chinese, Luce knew, held Dwight Edwards in very high regard. Kohlberg, by contrast, appeared to be an energetic troublemaker with a personal ax to grind. Besides, though Kohlberg might be sincerely devoted to China, he was not part of the Christian philanthropic network.

While Kohlberg was importing Chinese textiles, Dwight Edwards was working in China for the people, for all of thirty-eight years. What most impressed the special committee, however, was Kohlberg's inability to document his charges. Luce's committee therefore found that Edwards' actions had not adversely affected UCR's support of ABMAC's programs. Luce and his colleagues did, however, make a very minor concession to Kohlberg. They recommended on March 28 that improvements be made in ABMAC's disbursement procedures. Concluding with a ringing endorsement of Dwight Edwards, the Luce inquiry angered Alfred Kohlberg. He appealed its decision to the UCR board of directors, which endorsed Luce's conclusions.

From these obscure beginnings, a poisonous debate over American actions in China began to infect American politics. Luce had no idea of what would sprout from the Kohlberg affair. Though they started out on opposite sides of the debate, and departed on unfriendly terms, Luce had not seen the last of Alfred Kohlberg. Ironically, their views often coincided in the years ahead. A self-important man with an immense ego and energy to spare, Kohlberg later surfaced as a sometime ally of Henry Luce, in the so-called China Lobby.

By 1944 Chiang Kai-shek was embracing an authoritarian if not xenophobic ideology. *Time* learned that Chiang's new book, *China's Destiny*, which had not appeared in foreign translation, was a bitter diatribe against Western imperialism, the Open Door, the missionary movement, and foreign influence in general. China, Chiang wrote, was not oppressed; therefore Chinese did not need to struggle for liberty. While lauding modern progress in science and technology, Chiang wanted to move forward without bearing the burden of Western-style democracy. Chiang now urged a return to ancient virtues, and expressed open hostility to Western-style capitalism. In Sun Fo's view, *China's Destiny* attacked the ideologies of democracy and communism, which prevailed in states allied with or friendly to China. Ambassador Clarence Gauss sadly reported that Chiang's government and party were now in the hands of "reactionaries." As Chiang's troubles multiplied, American interest in the Yenan Communists intensified.

In February 1944 the White House asked that Chiang permit American military observers to visit the Communist-controlled regions of the north. Chiang parried this thrust by attacking the Reds for plotting new aggressions. In March the Generalissimo accused the Communists of expanding their operations in the Yellow River valley. Without producing evidence, Chiang argued that this action proved that the Russians and their Chinese allies were working in league with the hated enemy, Japan. Roosevelt, however, refused to go for the bait, and Secretary of State Cordell Hull dismissed the claim as "fraudulent and lying propaganda."

Relations with China were now badly frayed. Teddy White felt that solutions could be found "if a lot of our fascist-countrymen don't fuck things up." White believed that the Communists had created an effective army of 500,000 men. He even claimed that this army was "holding down more of Japan's land force than General MacArthur and Admiral

Halsey combined." White saw the Communists as a *possible* force for positive change, while the Chungking government stubbornly fought for one thing—the preservation of its own power over an exploited people. Naturally, Chinese censors butchered White's dispatches. The Guomindang claimed that White vastly exaggerated Communist strength and failed to grasp the illegal, opportunistic nature of the Marxist movement in China. *Time* cooperated with Chiang and contradicted its own Theodore White. Using material provided by a defector named Wang Shih-wei, the newsmagazine claimed that the people governed by Communist leader Mao Tse-tung were unhappy, overtaxed, and underfed. *Time* supported Chiang's blockade of the Red "border regions," and laid the blame for armed clashes at the door of the Communists.

Jack Service and other informed Foreign Service officers disagreed. Americans who shared their views often described the "so-called Communists" as agrarian reformers, who looked to America for support and inspiration. If John Paton Davies was right, the Communists would be attractive allies in the event of American landings on the north China coast. FDR again informed Chiang that he looked forward to the arrival of American military observers in the Communist-controlled regions. These men could then supply the President with an accurate picture of the situation. Chiang deflected the American proposal, though some Chinese felt that direct contacts with the Reds might disabuse Americans of their "romantic" view of the Communists. Chiang, however, feared that the Americans might force him to make major concessions to the Communists.

At Time Inc., Kurt Bloch concluded that isolation and the Japanese blockade had badly affected the Chinese government. Xenophobic and reactionary, Chiang's regime now encompassed corruption without "equal in Chinese history." Other reliable sources confirmed Bloch's pessimistic prognosis.

In a moment of anguish shared with "Daddy" Kung, Henry Luce confessed his great fear. "Nothing would cause me greater unhappiness," he wrote, "than if my primary obligations to my fellow citizens should conflict with my love for China and the friendships there which I value so highly."

Working to
Modernize the Republican
Party

China was dear to Henry Luce, but so was the Republican Party. A highly partisan supporter, anxious to help his "second church" return to power, Luce continued to fight in the political wars. He remained convinced that Republicans committed to free enterprise and internationalism could one day take control of the White House and the Congress.

In his quest for change, Luce knew that able young candidates would have to displace the reactionary mossbacks who had so tarnished the image of the Grand Old Party. Thomas E. Dewey, the former racketbusting prosecutor, was young, independent, and honest, but he was also standoffish and cold. In 1942 Dewey badly wanted Harry Luce's support, but did not intend to court him. Luce respected Dewey, though he did not particularly like him. He did, however, see the candidate for Governor of New York State as a potential winner. By contrast, ties of friendship and ideology bound Luce to Wendell L. Willkie, whose impressive presidential bid in 1940 owed so much to Time Inc. Willkie, however, provoked the animosity of Republican regulars and isolationists, still a rather numerous group. To make things more difficult for Harry Luce, Willkie and Dewey detested each other.

In 1942 Wendell Willkie remained Luce's friend, and *Life* cheered as "the right wing of the Republican Party crumbled before the onslaught of Wendell Willkie. . . ." When Willkie toured some battlefronts, *Life* sounded like his echo. Willkie's eloquent appeals for freedom and his attacks on colonialism elicited this comment from Luce's picture magazine: "The Republican Party stands in dire need of a foreign policy, and Wendell Willkie is on the way to it." Willkie's ghostwritten manifesto, *One World*, sold 200,000 copies within a week of its appearance in 1943. Admirers of the candidate now formed the Republican Postwar Policy Association in order to promote Willkie's zealous if ill-defined brand of internationalism.

Republican regulars, who had never trusted Wendell Willkie, dug in their heels. To some of Tom Dewey's potential supporters, Willkie was no more than a global New Dealer, traipsing around his one world on behalf of Franklin D. Roosevelt. Harry now did his best to widen Willkie's circle of acquaintances by bringing him into contact with church leaders, China Relief crusaders, and other interested observers. Still, Luce worried about his friend's inability to woo party leaders. In fact, Wendell Willkie could be vain, temperamental, and difficult; these qualities would not endear him to the crass politicians whose support was essential to his nomination. Luce began to wonder whether Willkie could build a nuts-and-bolts organization, one broad enough to house both regulars and progressives. Harry Luce liked Wendell Willkie, but he loved the Republican Party more.

New York Governor Herbert Lehman had narrowly defeated the thirty-six-year-old Dewey for Governor back in 1938. By the winter of 1942, Dewey's star was again in the ascendant. Only weeks after Pearl Harbor, advertising executive Bruce Barton, a friend of Harry Luce, started a Dewey-for-Governor movement. Willkie wanted to block Dewey's nomination, for he viewed the ambitious young (forty) man as a rival for the 1944 Republican presidential nomination. Luce remained above this fray, but two of his closest associates, C. D. Jackson and Russell Davenport, were busily organizing an abortive draft Willkie movement. Their boomlet elicited a sarcastic comment from John Billings. "Politics is like malaria," he wrote, "it keeps coming back in chills & fever—& [Russell] Davenport has it bad."

Henry Luce hoped that Dewey would win the governorship, and Willkie the presidency. He also longed for the day when the GOP would regain control of Congress. This goal mandated the selection of attractive new faces, and after much hesitation, Clare Boothe decided to run for the U.S. House of Representatives in Connecticut's Fourth District. Once again, Clare abandoned one highly visible career to enter a new, even more public arena. She quickly tired of her various professional roles, but when she played them, she pulled out all the stops. Supported by her proud husband, Clare vigorously contested the Fairfield County seat once occupied (1939–1941) by her stepfather, Dr. Albert E. Austin.

John Billings observed that Clare Luce was "more like an actress than a politician." She was, he added, "theatrical in essence. . . ." This was true, but her desire for personal publicity, which Harry avoided like the plague, was consonant with her star quality. A tough and imaginative campaigner, Clare transformed some of Harry's convoluted ideas into slogans or partisan rhetoric. Instead of denouncing the failure to produce synthetic products, she declared (in a phrase later borrowed by Douglas MacArthur) that there was a substitute for rubber, but "there is no substitute for Victory." Mrs. Luce courted the small but potentially pivotal black vote, and went out of her way to praise organized labor. Helped by Bernard Baruch and other friends, Clare could draw on resources available to few other candidates. The Luces put up $7,900 for the campaign, and though the Democrats sharply attacked "the Luce millions" and the "Time-Life-Fortune Axis," Time Inc. was most useful to Clare.

Prodded by Harry Luce and his associates, Time Inc. researchers helped with facts and figures. Wes Bailey, Luce's assistant and trouble-shooter, assisted Clare and worked to keep Harry out of the publicity surrounding the campaign. When Clare needed help with her keynote speech to the Connecticut Republican convention, she turned to Russell Davenport. Willi Schlamm and John Chamberlain also provided Clare with ideas for speeches, while *Life* photographers assembled attractive portfolios showing Clare as a globe-trotting journalist. During the campaign, *Time* cleverly supported Clare by citing other sources. "Blonde, beautiful, brilliant," gushed the *New York Daily News*. *Time* decided that Clare (also) showed a "cool certainty of poise that tongue-ties men; she likes chocolate milkshakes. . . ."

A foreign dignitary holding a vested interest in Clare Luce's success sent her best wishes, along with an exquisite eggshell porcelain bowl. Madame Chiang, who knew all about politics, thought that Clare could make a real contribution to public life. Presumably, Madame was think-ing of China's interests. Though Billings and Longwell were happy to be rid of correspondent Clare Boothe, they now had to worry about covering her highly newsworthy and photogenic political antics. Luce did not pressure Billings, however, and he, along with Longwell and

Hicks, decided that a *Life* close-up on Clare should not appear until after the election.

Certainly, Clare, who had not yet reached forty, knew how to mesmerize males; she had been doing so for more than a generation. Wendell Willkie, who was infatuated with her, accompanied Clare on a campaign swing from Stamford to Bridgeport. Riding through Willkie country (fine homes, suburbia, and station wagons), Clare garnered more publicity and perhaps a few extra votes. Many blue-collar workers lived in the Fourth District, particularly near the war industries located in and around Bridgeport. When addressing these men and women, she concealed her intense dislike of Roosevelt. Immediately upon her election, Clare Boothe Luce became a nationwide political celebrity. The flashbulbs popped and the newsreel cameras rolled when she arrived at the Capitol, and she kept them busy for the next four years. Harry was delighted with Clare's well-publicized victory. The passion of early romance had dissipated, but in its place was emerging a partnership, replete with a competitive edge.

Harry Luce was in a particularly good mood after these November 1942 elections. Many people felt that the war was not being well run, and the Republicans made major gains on all levels. To Harry, Clare's victory was the icing on the cake. Dewey was elected Governor by a plurality of 600,000 votes. Wendell Willkie, who had never won an election, now faced a dangerous rival for the 1944 nomination. According to Frank McNaughton, whose political sources Luce respected, Willkie remained unpopular with congressional Republicans.

Time now offered Willkie some helpful advice. He would, the magazine suggested, have to cultivate the party professionals. This would not be an easy task. To Willkie, politics meant action, personal contacts, and the projection of a kind of animal energy. He professed grand principles, but he also devoured the adulation, applause, and enthusiasm offered up like incense by countless crowds of well-dressed Willkie-ites. Willkie referred to politics as "the Sport of Kings," but Luce did not believe that politics existed for the pleasure of its practitioners. After 1942 Luce no longer discouraged his editors from taking critical looks at Willkie. John Chamberlain had endorsed Roosevelt in 1940. Now he was writing a piece for *Fortune* without the candidate's help, for Willkie feared that "John Chamberlain will distort my position. . . ."

Dewey badly wanted good notices from *Time* and *Life*, for in the past these magazines had hurt him. Dewey's people mistrusted Luce, however, for they felt that if Willkie faded, *Time* would turn to a different alternative, perhaps to California's charismatic Governor, Earl Warren. Though *Time* reported that Dewey had passed Willkie in a straw poll, the magazine snidely referred to the noncandidate as a "glamor boy." Late in July 1943, *Time* still insisted that Willkie was winning over Republican professionals in the Midwest. The magazine proudly referred to Willkie's *One World* as the "fastest-selling book in U.S. publishing history." Anyone, *Time* argued, could beat Roosevelt on domestic issues. In a long, personal note to his friend, Harry Luce argued that Willkie could make headway by attacking the "economic waste and even chaos" for which Roosevelt was responsible. Only Willkie, moreover, could defeat the New Deal in the foreign policy arena.

In Luce's opinion, the Democratic coalition was growing brittle. The GOP, however, could not merely be *against* the New Deal. Rather, the party had to embrace alternative programs. Luce insisted that the 1944 Republican platform be liberal (a word he liked), embracing free trade, individual initiative, civil rights, and an American-guided postwar international order: "History is a machine which does not easily go into reverse." Luce accepted the gains made by organized labor, and he praised the Republicans, meaning people like Clare Luce, who "no longer treated labor unions as strange and foreign creations." Luce intended to preserve much of the New Deal while reorienting politics toward state and local entities. The federal government would help to plan the postwar order, but Washington must be prepared to lift wartime controls when the war ended.

Meanwhile, Willkie's penchant for impractical, overblown rhetoric about the future was starting to grate on Harry's nerves. Though giving Willkie full credit for the GOP's emergence from its "long foreign policy sleep," *Life* now placed its favorite son in the company of other Republican politicians. In the summer of 1943, Harry's friend Bruce Barton told Dewey that Willkie could not be nominated, but "you can and will be." A poll surveying the presidential choices of 1940 Republican delegates showed that almost two thirds of these men and women favored the New York Governor. Republican sources reported that Willkie had lost ground in Michigan and Virginia, and Harry could not ignore all the Republican grumbling about his man. Luce himself finally admitted that "too many Republicans think that [Willkie is] a big lot of just what they don't want."

During the summer of 1943, Harry Luce continued to search for a recipe that would ensure victory in 1944. To that end, he solicited the views of his friend pollster Elmo Roper, who suggested that people were most concerned about two issues: full employment after the war and "world peace through world cooperation." In August 1943 Luce addressed senior staff on the issue of Willkie's candidacy. Editors were nervous, for they feared a repeat of the 1940 debacle when Luce's partisanship had eroded public faith in *Time* without electing Willkie. Harry thus surprised his colleagues by adopting a wait-and-see attitude toward Willkie. Furthermore, he agreed to offer *Time*'s readers frank accounts of Willkie's campaign. This augured ill for Wendell Willkie. Meanwhile Thomas Dewey was strengthening his rather meager foreign policy credentials.

Henry Luce, whose relationship with Governor Dewey was a purely formal one, was coming to have a high regard for John Foster Dulles, the New Yorker's foreign policy adviser. Dulles, an international lawyer schooled in the teachings of his Presbyterian church, felt compelled to apply Christian principles to the great problems of the day. "If history teaches anything," Dulles preached, "it is that no nation is great and no nation is strong unless its people are imbued with a faith." Luce could not have agreed more. Speaking of Dulles after his death, Henry Luce observed that "I'd rather have people who have convictions than to play around as if these convictions don't amount to anything." A prominent Presbyterian layman, Dulles had long been active in the Federal Council of Churches, and at Dulles' urging, the council established a commission to Study the Bases of a Just and Durable Peace. In 1941 Dulles accepted the chairmanship of the new commission.

Dulles advocated the recognition of global interdependence. All nations, he wrote, deserved access to markets and raw materials. The wealthier, more enlightened countries would thus have to agree to place certain limitations on their own sovereign powers. Dulles, however, was politically astute, and he was not planning to bargain away American sovereignty. Rather, he set out long-term goals while jealously safeguarding the nation's current interests.

On March 18, 1943, Dulles and his supporters, assembled at a luncheon meeting in the RCA Building at Rockefeller Center, gave the world their "Six Pillars of Peace." They recognized that change "is the one thing that is inevitable" and advocated eventual self-rule by all peoples. The commission favored the establishment of an arms control regime and supported the creation of an effective international organization. Governor Dewey, whose 1940 foreign policy utterances had been vaguely isolationist, endorsed the Six Pillars.

John Foster Dulles and his many supporters in the churches now took their case to the nation. Beginning with a convocation in the Cathedral of St. John the Divine in New York, they fanned out across America, ultimately visiting 102 cities. Dulles and some of his colleagues soon met with Roosevelt, who praised their plan as a "splendid one." *Life* publicized the Dulles program at great length, and Dulles, who harbored political ambitions, began to cultivate Luce and his editors. Willkie, who had tried and failed to recruit Dulles as an adviser, was left out of this new entente.

Roosevelt was concentrating on winning the war. Ever mindful of the sad fate of Woodrow Wilson, FDR refused to say anything substantive about a postwar international organization. Others moved into the breach. In the Senate, Joseph Ball, a Minnesota Republican, sponsored a resolution that endorsed a United Nations organization. The world body would deter aggressors or punish them when the need arose. *Time*, which now featured a subsection on the "Postwar," depicted the Ball resolution as a reaction against "Two decades of a false peace." The newsmagazine also supported a related House resolution sponsored by William J. Fulbright, a young Arkansas Democrat. To Russell Davenport, an unreconstructed Willkie man, the Ball and Fulbright resolutions showed that Americans were preparing to embrace global democracy and brotherhood. A onetime isolationist, Republican Arthur Vandenberg of Michigan, also supported an international organization so long as membership did not undermine American sovereignty. And to *Time*'s delight, even "throaty, balding" Representative Karl Mundt, an ardent isolationist, embraced the idea of global interdependence in the postwar world. The public debate about the postwar world had begun.

Harrison Spangler, the plodding regular who chaired the GOP's National Committee, had formed the Republican Postwar Advisory Council. Chairman Spangler expected that his council would offset Willkie's more internationalist Republican Postwar Policy Association. The Republicans, Spangler believed, had to formulate a policy that, in *Time*'s words, "would offend no one." *Time*, however, was optimistic about the forthcoming conference on Mackinac Island, Michigan, where forty-three members of Spangler's council planned to discuss matters of political interest. The magazine, reverting to its old style, quickly dismissed chairman Spangler as a "fat little waddling type." Later, Frank McNaughton caricatured Spangler as a "portly, aging" man from "corn-hog Iowa." Spangler, McNaughton decided, was as "simple and sincere as an Iowa farmer could be." Enraged, Spangler replied to *Time* that he was five-foot-nine and weighed only 163 pounds. And he felt that his Republican council deserved to be taken seriously. *Time*'s treatment of Spangler, which had party bigwigs laughing their heads off, showed why people in the know sometimes despised a magazine they felt compelled to read.

Wendell Willkie's campaign, meanwhile, was stumbling, for the Midwestern Republican organizations were lining up against their 1940 standard-bearer. In 1943, on the eve of Mackinac, party regulars in Missouri showed their contempt for their former presidential candidate. The 1940 delegates to the Republican national convention published an open letter to Willkie in which they confronted him with questions of the "Have you stopped beating your wife?" variety. Led by Grover Dalton, state party chairman, the delegates asked if Willkie wanted to make the U.S. a member of a "world supranational state." The good Republicans also wanted to know if Willkie was an absolute free trader; if he favored unrestricted immigration to the United States; if he would further define what he meant when endorsing a "liberal platform." Willkie soon met with these hostile politicos, but his short temper hurt him badly. "I don't know whether you're going to support me or not and I don't give a damn," yelled Willkie. "You're a bunch of political liabilities . . . ," he added.

Governor Dewey, on the other hand, climbed steadily in the polls. Imbued with growing confidence, he opened up a new front. Though supposedly lacking flair and imagination, Dewey now decided to make an important statement on foreign policy. On the eve of the Mackinac meeting, he surprised his fellow Republicans by advocating a postwar alliance with Great Britain. Henry Luce was flattered, since the first Republican to propose such a pact was none other than Connecticut's Clare Boothe Luce. The press reaction was mixed. Dewey, growled the *Chicago Tribune*, "has finished the pilgrimage to Downing Street by way of Wall Street." As the *New York Times* saw it, however, "Mr. Dewey was regarded as having moved into the class of advanced Republican thinkers on international affairs—vying with Wendell L. Willkie. . . ."

The Eastern conferees scheduled to attend Mackinac boarded a steamer at Buffalo, then sailed toward Detroit. There, Senator Arthur Vandenberg joined them, and the party proceeded north to Mackinac Island. Chairman Spangler, "from the bottom of his compromising heart" (*Time*) hoped to issue a vaguely internationalist statement about postwar foreign policy. Vandenberg duly prepared a bland draft resolution for Spangler, but the eighteen governors wanted stronger language. Though Spangler was, according to one critic, "old, slow, seared [and] befuddled," his council made a Republican commitment to "Responsible participation by the United States in a postwar cooperative organization among sovereign nations. . . ." *Time*, looking ahead to the 1944 battle, decided that the Mackinac manifesto was the "greatest tactical advance made by the Republican Party in years." Henry Luce happily awaited the day when the GOP guided the "nation's destiny," as seen in the "grand perspective of history."

On November 1, 1943, the Big Four Allied powers declared that they intended to establish a "general international organization, based on the principle of the sovereign equality of all peace-loving states . . . for the maintenance of international peace and security." Secretary of State Cordell Hull and President Roosevelt hoped that the U.S., Great Britain, the USSR, and China would act jointly to prevent or punish aggression. These "four policemen" would refrain from establishing spheres of influence, so balance of power policies would no longer be necessary. From the State Department came talk of an eight-member council on which the four great powers would hold permanent seats. Some observers claimed that the Big Four would also be able to veto unwelcome proposals, but no one was sure. The process moved forward slowly, in part because Roosevelt was planning to run for a fourth term.

Henry Luce now entered into a lively correspondence with John Foster Dulles. Dulles approved of the November 1 declaration, but he hoped that the four policemen would be temporary guardians. In the longer run, Dulles expected that Britain, China, the U.S., and the USSR would surrender some of their sovereign powers "to international institutions drawing their vitality from the whole family of nations." Together, these enlightened states could then create a real "international law." The Federal Council of Churches, Dulles assured Luce, supported "world government as an ultimate ideal. . . ." Henry Luce now worked to reconcile his faith in the American mission with the Dulles brand of internationalism. He did not want to embrace the nationalist politics of "mere expediency." At the same time, Americans, and no one else, were now *"citizens of a vastly powerful state continuously exerting its power."*

Wildly ambitious for his nation and moved by his own vision of the coming era, Harry Luce sometimes lost sight of the warning dinned into him since early youth: men, even Americans, were fallible and sinful. They could overreach, and must often fail.

Roosevelt's Revenge

Franklin D. Roosevelt was the first in a long line of Lucephobic Democrats. The President viewed Time Inc. as a dangerously powerful Republican monopoly that wielded national influence. This vendetta featured two protagonists, however, and Luce's hatred for Franklin Roosevelt matched FDR's contempt for Time Inc. "This is almost a private feud between HRL and FDR . . . ," wrote John Shaw Billings.

The White House did not take kindly to a magazine (*Life*) that noted that the four sons of "Eleanor Roosevelt" (but not of Franklin Roosevelt?) were in uniform. That jibe was bad enough, but worse came later. In one issue, *Life*'s table of contents featured a piece called "The Fighting Roosevelt Family." But when the reader turned the page, he or she saw that the story concerned the family of *Theodore* Roosevelt! FDR had once consoled a fellow victim of *Time*'s wisecracks by remarking that "I have gone through the same sort of thing well over a hundred times in the past few years."

Harry Luce did not understand that *Time*'s jibes often caused pain and embarrassment, for he was a man devoted to policy studies and ideas. His magazines, however, flourished thanks to their ability to personalize every story. *Time*'s success thus puzzled the often naive and insensitive Harry Luce, and the indignation its stories provoked among their victims completely befuddled him. If attacked, Luce always asked if the facts in a story were accurate, not if the article was snide or one-sided.

Early in January 1942, *Life* irritated the Administration by running a story about bases used by the American air forces in Brazil. From these airfields the AAF and the British RAF flew bombers over to Africa. The U.S. had asked that the Brazilians not publicize the uses to which these bases were put. Now *Life* had done so, to the embarrassment of the Brazilian authorities. Angry Brazilians even claimed that *Life*'s photos were faked, but they were authentic. Axis agents in Brazil allegedly bought up copies of *Life* and distributed them to local army officers offended by this latest bout of Yankee arrogance. Even though managing editor John Billings had secured the approval of the U.S. military censors, *Life*'s article irritated American diplomats. The American embassy in Rio described *Life*'s story as "harmful and indiscreet." Sumner Welles brought the matter to Roosevelt's attention, whereupon the President complained to Press Secretary Steve Early. "I am a little tired," wrote Roosevelt, "of calling matters like this to the attention of Henry Luce and his associates."

In a memorandum to his press secretary, FDR reaffirmed his contempt for *Life*'s sin, and three days later Harry Luce came to the White House, where he regaled Steve Early with his side of the story. The offensive article, Harry noted, had gone to press before Pearl Harbor. Pointedly, Luce included the Army, the Navy, and the U.S. embassy in his list of cooperative bureaucracies. He did admit that *Life* had erred in a caption, wherein a Brazilian base became a "U.S. Field."

Luce then made an impassioned defense of his work. He reminded Early that Time Inc. had been preparing the country "for this struggle" for "200 weeks." And Luce insisted that he wished to serve his country "on all fronts." Early had to admit that Time Inc. was not to blame for the airfield fiasco, that U.S. and Brazilian officials had been careless in releasing the offensive photographs. The press secretary told Roosevelt about his meeting with Luce, thinking that the matter had been resolved. The President, however, apparently had plenty of time to spend on Harry Luce. How would Americans feel, asked Roosevelt, if a caption appearing in a foreign magazine described "A British Air Field in the U.S."?

Within days of the airfield incident, Roosevelt attacked *Time*'s coverage of the recent conference on hemispheric solidarity, convened in Rio de Janeiro. The magazine had referred to Rio as a "big round-up," a phrase that offended Latin sensibilities. According to FDR, *Time* and *Life* had thereby exhibited an "unpatriotic" attitude that was "harmful to the United States to a very great degree." Early shared this message with Felix Belair by way of a warning. Billings understated matters when he observed that Roosevelt "doesn't like *Life*—or *Time*—or Henry Luce. . . ." Ominously, the President wondered out loud about how to counter Luce's malevolence. Harry wanted to fight back, but colleagues such as C. D. Jackson and Dan Longwell considered the feud potentially disastrous to Time Inc. They counseled Luce to "eat crow with the President." A few days later Harry Luce headed for Washington.

Convinced that the White House had overreacted to Time Inc.'s stories, Luce went to see Early but accomplished nothing. He then visited the War Department, where he saw General Marshall, an admirer of *Life, Time*, and *Fortune*. Even Marshall, who usually spoke in a calm, gracious manner, coldly enumerated *Time*'s sins, then warned that Luce's publications had better "behave themselves." A depressed Harry Luce returned to New York, convinced that FDR had forced Marshall to upbraid him. Billings then pointed out that being nice to the Administration "really meant liking F.D.R. who *is* the government." Luce agreed that his publications would have to be kinder to "Washington," but could not bring himself to be solicitous of Roosevelt.

In March 1942, while Allied resistance collapsed throughout East Asia, FDR continued to add to his detailed inventory of Harry Luce's sins and errors. In its issue dated February 16, *Time* had offended his majesty, Faruk I, King of Egypt, eliciting an angry response from the Egyptian minister in Washington. The diplomat protested to Under Secretary of State Sumner Welles, who contacted the White House. Roosevelt then suggested that Early bring this matter to Luce's attention. According to Welles, the "chief editor of *Time*" then apologized to the Egyptian minister. Nothing, however, could assuage FDR's anger. Again and again he returned to the attack, telling his friend Sumner Welles that "it is time to build up a complete case [against Luce]." No sooner had the Egyptian matter died down than the President aired a new grievance.

At a cabinet meeting held on March 13, 1942, he noted that an Army plane had flown correspondent Clare Luce across the Atlantic to Egypt. An indignant Roosevelt asked whether the Army should provide a civilian with scarce transport space. The bureaucracy sprang into action, and the War Department investigated the weighty matter. It turned out that Ambassador Laurence Steinhardt, who was preparing to leave for

Turkey, had received a suggestion from the President. The German armies in Russia might launch a spring offensive, which could well drive Turkey into the Axis camp. Roosevelt therefore hoped to counter German pressure on Turkey, and he suggested that the U.S. media laud the virtues of neutral Turkey and its valiant people. Steinhardt, who believed that Time Inc. was ideally suited to this task, invited the Luces to join him on his trip to Ankara. Harry Luce, who was otherwise engaged, declined, but Clare agreed to go as Mr. Steinhardt's assistant. Ambassador Steinhardt's explanation did not mollify Mr. Roosevelt. Subsequently, the War Department decided that the Secretary of War or someone designated by him must approve before a civilian could take up space on a military aircraft. Clare's journey would come back to haunt Harry in the years ahead.

During the war, what one citizen called Mrs. Luce's "vitriol-tipped tongue" frequently and effectively lashed Franklin Roosevelt and his supporters. Clare Luce's 1943 maiden speech in the House of Representatives was one of the celebrated addresses of its day. On the surface, Clare was talking to her colleagues about air transport routes and landing facilities, hardly a topic calculated to ignite a public debate. In this instance, as in many others, however, she took some of Harry's ideas and packaged them in wittier, and sometimes nastier, wrappings. A later age would have referred to her jibes as perfect "sound bytes."

Harry and Clare insisted that the rapid wartime expansion of American aviation must not be throttled after the war. Vice-President Henry A. Wallace, on the other hand, had recently called for "freedom of the air—he wished to internationalize air routes and abolish exclusive landing rights and privileges. Clare made the liberal Vice-President seem like a dreamy, wooly-minded fool. In fact, her speech marked the beginning of the end of Wallace's career. Rejecting Wallace's globalism, Representative Luce proposed that American airlines control American airspace, airports, and landing rights. In a demagogic aside, Mrs. Luce conjured up the image of a British competitor using Lend–Lease planes as part of a plot to undermine American airlines. Clare was not merely spouting ideology, however. She was helping her political ally, Connecticut politician Sam Pryor, who had important ties to Pan American World Airlines. In her most famous *bon mot*, Clare called Henry Wallace's plan "globaloney."

Eleanor Roosevelt tried to defend the Vice-President by asserting that all nations must have "free access to the world's travel lanes." In an exposé published in *Collier's Magazine*, Frank Gervasi attacked "The

Globaloney Girl." Clare replied with a little parody, which she wisely
kept to herself:

> There was an old whore from Bengazi
> Who slept with both Fascist and Nazi
> But she drew the line at Gervasi

Clare had won the debate, however. She appealed to American nationalism, and delighted isolationists by twisting the tail of the British lion.
The Hearst press, which had long hated Luce and his magazines, congratulated Clare for her good sense. London's diplomats in Washington
were dismayed, especially when Clare's speech elicited more than 2,000
letters of support. Though Clare coyly protested that she favored a
postwar alliance with Britain, she was clearly pandering to Republican
Anglophobia.

Harry was proud of his wife's speech. As he naively wrote to a
dubious but ever gracious Henry A. Wallace, ". . . I believe [Clare]
performed a service." Piously, *Time* thanked Mrs. Luce for opening an
important public debate, though the magazine gently reprimanded her,
too. So did *Fortune*, whereupon Harry groaned to his fellow editors,
"How could you do this to me?" Nothing so infuriated Clare as her
treatment at the hands of "Harry's little people."

In March 1943, when the President invited new members of Congress
to a social gathering at the White House, Clare Luce drafted a long
letter, dated March 7. Her office provided this broadside to the press
even before the White House had read it. In the acerbic document, the
Connecticut Congresswoman alluded to a "calamitous cramping of war
industry." Mrs. Luce reminded FDR that "power has a tendency to
corrupt." After paying homage to labor, one of her key constituents,
Clare expressed a wish that the Republicans be returned to power. Steve
Early indignantly noted that Clare Luce had turned a social invitation
into a political platform.

In fact, much of the criticism leveled against Clare was sexist and
partisan. Former Senator Harry B. Hawes told the White House that
the Congresswoman's name should be spelled "clearly loose," for "the
background is loose and wild." Essayist E. B. White, writing in *The
New Yorker*, published a clever satire in which he accepted Clare's
invitation to visit Fairfield County. In White's takeoff, the writer releases his response to the press before his hostess sees it. Librettist
Howard Dietz provided the White House with a witty poem called "Au
Clare de la Luce." The President liked Dietz's doggerel, one stanza of
which read as follows:

And when it's mealtime, never stoop
To see the letters in the soup.
The ghosts may form like homing birds
"My God," you'll cry, "I ate my words!"

Undeterred, Clare Luce intensified her attack on the Administration's foreign policy. In a long diatribe, she linked Roosevelt to isolationism, Munich, and appeasement, and criticized him for displaying contempt for Free France's Charles de Gaulle. In 1943, however, FDR struck back and deeply wounded Harry Luce.

Ever since the autumn of 1942, Harry Luce had been hoping to revisit China. He had not been "home" since the spring of 1941, and he wanted to bolster China's war effort. In 1943 he applied to the proper authorities for permission to visit the "Pacific theater or theatres." Soon after being told to pick up the requisite papers at an Army facility in New York, Luce received bad news. Due to the shortage of transport space, publishers, editors, and executives could not visit combat areas. Luce did not give up easily, and decided that he would travel to the Far East as an accredited correspondent. By the end of January 1943 he was ready to leave. Luce made sure his passport was in order and took care to have the required inoculations. Delay followed delay, however, and a frustrated Harry Luce contacted General Surles, head of the War Department's public relations office.

At the War Department, Surles seemed to think that Harry would soon be winging his way across the Pacific. Luce, encouraged by the visit, went to see the Chief of Staff, with whom he had a very friendly talk. General Marshall requested that Luce, while in theater, look into certain matters for him, then report back for debriefing. Luce left the Chief of Staff's office convinced that he would be able to visit the Far East at some point after March 10. So far as Luce knew, he could fly as soon as the Army provided him with a seat on a transport plane. He waited impatiently, then decided to call on John McCloy at the War Department. The White House, said McCloy, wanted to issue an order banning publishers from visiting theaters of war. McCloy asked that Luce keep this matter to himself.

March 10 came and passed, and Luce grew more apprehensive. Could Felix Belair and Jim Shepley, his men in Washington, expedite matters? On March 15 Belair learned that something had gone wrong. He called General Surles, who told him that a publisher could not travel to a war theater. Surles blamed the "Ferry command and the boat people" for the edict, which he ascribed to the pressing demand for a minuscule amount of spare transport space. A frustrated Felix Belair complained that somebody had "pulled a rug out from under us." Surles, who was playing the role assigned to him, sympathized, observing that "a damn policy hit me square in the face and that's all there was to it." Belair, however, was angry, and not easily put off. "Well God Almighty," he observed, "a policy doesn't operate against a [Chief of Staff]—he seemed to be all for it [Luce's trip]." Knowing how badly Luce wanted to visit the Pacific, Belair feared for his job. As he told Surles, "it certainly makes me look awfully bad here."

General Surles comforted Belair, explaining that no one could blame him for a War Department ruling. Belair decided to appeal to Marshall unless Surles objected. Surles did not, and he even encouraged Belair by denying that a "civilian objection" had barred Luce from the Pacific. Belair could do nothing about the matter, but to his delight, Luce took the news very well. This reaction was misleading, for Harry interpreted the ban as a temporary setback, not a defeat. Immediately, Luce began to hatch inept schemes, and again brought Shepley and Belair into the picture. Maybe he could fly to Honolulu; perhaps he could appeal to the Navy.

James Shepley could not learn much about the new ban on travel by publishers. Surles only told him that Luce had run "into a policy that's going to knock him out of a trip." Shepley decided to interpret the phrase "working press" very broadly, so much so that Harry Luce fit that description. The agile Surles, however, mumbled something about the "second part" of the decree, which banned media from adding new correspondents to their rosters in theater. Time Inc. certainly kept reporters in the Pacific and China, including such stars as John Hersey. When Shepley forlornly asked about appealing to Marshall, Surles discouraged him. A higher authority, he explained, had made this "WD [War Department] decision."

While an impatient Harry Luce cooled his heels in New York, his unseen tormenter inflicted a slight on another Time Incer. Young John Hersey, who had come to *Time* as a $35-per-week rookie, had steadily risen in Luce's esteem. Luce saw this associate editor as a future managing editor of *Time*. After Pearl Harbor, Hersey, like many of his colleagues, wanted to cover the war, and he was soon serving in the Pacific theater. The Americans were finally launching a counteroffensive against Japan, and in August 1942 the Marines hit the beaches on Guadalcanal. The fighting was bloody beyond belief, and John Hersey recorded his impressions of the worst of it.

On October 7, 1942, war correspondent Hersey accompanied the 7th Marine Regiment of the 1st Division as that unit engaged the enemy in tough fighting east of the Matanikau River. Wanting to get closer to the fighting, he climbed down a steep hill into a forbidding ravine. There, a battalion of Marines was coming under heavy Japanese mortar and machine-gun fire. John Hersey spotted several wounded men, and without hesitation he rushed to remove them from the line of fire. He brought them to a first-aid station some distance from the fighting, thereby saving their lives. The next day Hersey performed a similar feat of heroism at a different sector of the front. According to the commanding officer of the 7th Marines, John Hersey's conduct was "outstandingly conspicuous by reason of his being an observer and therefore not required to undergo the dangers which he subjected himself to." The commanding general of the 1st Marine Division recommended that the Secretary of the Navy award Hersey the Silver Star. Responsible officers at each superior level concurred, and by December 17, 1942, Admiral William F. Halsey, commander of the South Pacific Force, had endorsed the recommendation.

In January 1943 Alfred A. Knopf published John Hersey's book about the Marines, called *Into the Valley*. The slim volume received much critical and popular acclaim. In February the Navy's Board of Awards concurred in the matter of the Silver Star, and on March 8 Secretary of the Navy Frank Knox signed a memorandum that informed the White House of his favorable recommendation. The President's naval aide received Knox's note, and on March 22 he, too, suggested that Roosevelt approve the award. One small technicality stood between Hersey and his medal. President Roosevelt wanted to review decorations of this kind if civilians were the recipients. Still, the outcome of the war weighed in the balance, and one would assume that FDR was preoccupied with important strategic issues. On March 23, however, a noncommittal President dictated a memorandum to press aide William D. Hassett. Roosevelt did not question Hersey's valor, nor the judgment of commanders who recommended him for the Silver Star. Instead, the President asked for an inquiry into "type and kind of story written by John Hersey. . . ."

Bill Hassett, who knew how to maneuver around political Washington, turned to the Office of War Information, where his friend Henry F. Pringle set some wheels in motion. Pringle asked for help from Chester Kerr, chief of the OWI's book division. Kerr, who had roomed with Hersey at Yale, provided Pringle with a biography of the correspondent, from his birth in 1914 through his days with *Time*. Hersey, Kerr wrote, "will inherit Henry Luce's mantle, and in general I believe that will be a fine thing for the country and for *Time*." Pringle, who also knew something about Hersey's work, endorsed Kerr's report, which landed with a thud on Bill Hassett's desk on March 24.

The next day Roosevelt, who was devoting a lot of time to this relatively minor matter, dictated a memorandum to Frank Knox. On its surface, the memo affected an affable tone. John Hersey, said the President, appeared to have "done good work for *Time* magazine for six years." FDR, however, questioned the wisdom of bestowing this high medal on a civilian correspondent serving at the front. He wondered whether "bringing in wounded in the midst of a fight" merited such a distinction. Disregarding Halsey, Knox, and his own aide, Roosevelt decided that anyone "who had red blood in his veins . . . would do the same thing." John Hersey would never see his Silver Star, and in its place, he received a letter of commendation from Secretary Knox and congratulations from Henry Luce. It was not until 1991, two years prior to his death, that John Hersey learned about his elusive decoration.

President Roosevelt vetoed John Hersey's Silver Star on March 25, 1943, while Harry Luce was still hoping to depart for the Far East. The next day General Surles received a phone call from General Henry ("Hap") Arnold, whose air forces would have to ferry Luce to the Pacific theater. "What," asked Arnold, "was the prohibition put on Henry Luce going out to a combat zone?" Surles would only say that Luce could not go, period. He promised to supply more information, but not over the phone. Hard-driving James Shepley still tried to work around the ban, and when speaking to military personnel, he implied that the Navy had agreed to send Luce to the Pacific. When informed of Shepley's maneuver, Surles curtly replied, "Well, I know different." On March 27 Harry Luce appealed directly to General Marshall. Reminding him of their conversation, Harry self-consciously admitted that he was not a "regular correspondent." Still, he felt responsible for millions of weekly readers and viewers, and could better serve them by visiting the Pacific theater.

Meanwhile, Felix Belair again called General Surles, and angrily observed that "I've had my head against a stone wall for about 3 weeks." Surles again tried to console him, and asked that Belair keep quiet while they both worked to mollify Luce. He suggested to Belair that the three men have lunch together. Luce, he added, should understand that situations sometimes change from week to week. Belair brushed aside these nice words, for he thought that he knew "who has queered this thing." Felix Belair had already figured out that neither the War Department nor the Navy Department had killed Luce's proposed trip. He decided to keep his insight from Luce, however, for Belair feared that Harry would somehow retaliate in *Time* against the villain. If Harry did so, Belair believed, he himself would lose access to key news sources. On March 29 Luce visited Secretary Stimson, just to chat, for he sensed that Stimson had nothing to do with the "no publishers" rule. He did not mention his proposed trip to the Pacific.

On March 31 George Marshall told Harry Luce part of the truth. According to the Chief of Staff, a "critical shortage of transportation" prevented Luce from visiting the Pacific. Marshall spoke kind words about Time Inc.'s "strong support" for the Army, and he seemed to be unhappy about having to give Harry Luce the bad news. Luce replied, with a cold, formal note containing two sentences. Who, he wondered, had intervened to derail his plans? The editor in chief had his suspicions, but he could not back them up with evidence. So Harry Luce continued to belabor his associates, asking them to intervene on his behalf.

Allen Grover, a liberal with good contacts in the Roosevelt administration, tried to put pressure on John McCloy at the War Department. According to Grover, his boss was not asking that he be allowed to cover a theater of war. Rather, Luce wished "to visit the capital [Chungking] of the country with which he has long had a very close connection." McCloy, who was aware of the ban on publishers, turned for advice to Steve Early at the White House. Early told McCloy that presidential assistant General Edwin ("Pa") Watson advised the War Department in cases like this one. "Not a single exception to this policy has been made . . . ," Early added. In fact, the ban proved to be a flexible one, except in the case of Harry Luce. In September 1943 a frustrated Luce finally appealed his ban to Secretary of War Stimson, a Yale man with strong Republican credentials. John McCloy, forewarned by Grover's intervention, alerted Stimson to the purpose of Luce's forthcoming visit. Luce duly arrived at the War Department, where he strenuously objected to this obvious instance of discrimination. He insisted to Stimson that he was not a "publisher," but a working editor in chief. He also raised the banner of press freedom. An uncomfortable Henry Stimson tried to calm Luce down, and perhaps inadvertently fed Harry's suspicions. Stimson admitted that the White House was afraid of stories that could derail its war strategy. Once again Harry left Washington empty-handed.

Henry Luce's clever, determined, and invisible enemy was moving the goal each time Luce advanced a few yards. Clearly, Roosevelt wanted to hide behind a fog of anonymity, for two reasons. He did not want the wartime public to learn of his feud with a leading publisher, and he did not need more grief from Luce's magazines. In October 1943 Luce decided to confront the elusive source of his misery. Writing to Roosevelt, he observed that "only you can lift the ban which prohibits me from visiting any active theatre of war except England." Luce requested an appointment so that he could make his case. He received a courteous note from Roosevelt, addressed (intentionally?) to "Dear Henry," a name Luce detested. After a delay caused by a presidential flu, Luce learned that he was to see FDR on November 8 at 2:15.

At the worst time for Luce, another flap over *Time* and *Life* unsettled the touchy souls in the White House. George Kennan, the First Secretary in the American legation in Lisbon, had complained to the Department of State; evidently, Luce's correspondents were snooping into sensitive, ongoing diplomatic negotiations in Portugal. Secretary Hull informed the White House of Time Inc.'s latest transgression just as Luce was preparing for his trip to Washington. Though the incident quickly blew over, it did nothing to redeem Luce in the eyes of the White House. Kennan's complaint was included in the file on Luce prepared for the presidential dossier.

On the morning on November 8, 1943, Steve Early informed the White House press corps of the President's daily schedule, which included an afternoon meeting with Henry Luce. Early noted that Luce had "asked for the appointment, and wrote the President a letter asking to come in." These words made Luce sound like the supplicant he was. The meeting yielded nothing, for Luce bumbled into a heated argument with an unamused President. FDR did tell "Henry" that he would speak with General Marshall, but this was just an evasive ploy: the Chief of Staff had nothing to do with the ban. On his way out of the President's office, Luce ran into Marshall, but nothing came of their awkward encounter. Harry Luce would have been even more enraged had he known about a folder in Roosevelt's Official File. There, an unknown hand had scrawled "re censorship" on a page containing a summary of correspondence with Luce.

Felix Belair, who labored under renewed pressure from Luce, appealed to General Surles for help. Could he not wire General Stilwell, asking him to authorize a visit by Luce? Surles, an adept player, said no, he could only contact Stilwell if Luce had already received the authorization to visit that theater of war. According to a presidential order, the State Department now had to secure the approval of the Joint

Chiefs of Staff "before authorizing travel by civilians into or through the designated areas of active operation. . . ." Luce had fallen victim to an almost comic runaround. When he approached the War or Navy departments, they referred his travel request to the State Department. State, however, needed to obtain the agreement of the Joint Chiefs before acting on Luce's application. The Chiefs, of course, would not approve such a request without the permission of the White House, which had instituted the ban in the first place.

Harry Luce's travel request died, suffocated in a maze of bureaucratic regulations over which he had no control. More than ever, he felt like a man boxing with shadows. Referring derisively to "Papa Roosevelt," Luce told Charlie Wertenbaker that the President fit the "Führer pattern."

While Harry wrestled with New Deal officialdom, Clare found that the White House had not forgotten her, either. Early in 1944 Congresswoman Luce, a member of the House Committee on Military Affairs, ran into a stone wall when she tried to visit the Mediterranean theater of operations. Defiantly, Clare informed General Surles that "I'm going to New York tonight to pack my things." She could have saved herself the trouble.

Henry Luce could not create his better world if Franklin Roosevelt won reelection. His quadrennial obsession with presidential politics now seized hold of him once again. In late October 1943, *Life* still hailed Willkie as an internationalist capable of skewering the New Dealers. *Time*, however, started to examine alternatives to Willkie. A cover story on the handsome but limited Governor John Bricker (an "honest Harding," William Allen White once called him) dismayed Willkie's fans. If idealism was out of style, however, then Willkie's reputation for "one world" internationalism might hurt, not help him in 1944. The shrewd Mrs. Luce, who was always quick to spot a small but deadly harpoon sticking out of an otherwise healthy whale, wrote a sharply worded memorandum to her husband, noting that too many Time Incers, Harry included, failed to understand "practical politics." As for candidates, Clare recommended that they behave like good politicians, "or they share the fate of Willkie—which is to say, the party rejects them." Representative Luce wrote this in December 1943 about a man who she had called a "global Abraham Lincoln" just a year before. Early in 1944 *Time* suggested, not for the last time, that a Thomas E. Dewey–Earl Warren ticket might be a winner.

January 1944 was a dreadful month for the Luces. Ann Clare Brokaw, nineteen years old, was now a senior at Stanford. Harry Luce treated Clare's only child like a daughter, and the shy, somewhat awkward girl responded well to his fatherly friendship. Ann was driving back to Stanford from San Francisco, where she had visited her mother. Suddenly, another vehicle smashed into the open convertible in which Ann was riding. Her car careened off the road, hitting a tree. The force of impact threw Ann out of the automobile, killing her. Harry immediately flew to the West Coast to be with Clare, and they later returned to Mepkin, in South Carolina, where the Luces buried Ann. The tragedy brought Harry and Clare closer together. The couple's shared passion for politics—his permanent, hers more transient—soon offered an escape from their mutual sorrow. And Clare began to think about converting to Catholicism.

In February Harry Luce laid out his political program for 1944, for he assumed that *Time* could influence the outcome of the election. He also admitted, or boasted, that the newsmagazine was not "immaculately immune from prejudice. . . ." As if to prove the point, Harry argued that Roosevelt was a charlatan who was now playing the role of the social reformer turned internationalist. In his memorandum, Luce reiterated his support for Willkie, but he lacked enthusiasm. Indeed, Harry angrily rejected the idea that the fate of Republican liberalism rose or fell with the Willkie candidacy. After all, he cracked, the party could reject Willkie for unrelated reasons, like "halitosis." And when Willkie spoke out on domestic issues, he sometimes left Luce cold. Willkie talked about bringing together labor and management, which sounded fine. Luce, however, feared that Wendell did not appreciate the gulf between himself and the more fervent New Dealers.

Within weeks of Luce's memorandum, *Life* devoted a full page to a photograph of Governor Dewey. Unfortunately, he looked like a small mannequin sitting on thick telephone books. An amused reader responded that "If you remove the telephone books from under Tom Dewey you will have a good picture of him trying to fill President Roosevelt's chair." Harry was giving Dewey another look, but he had not warmed to the New York Governor. In the polls, however, Dewey was pulling further ahead of Willkie, who now had the support of only 19.6 percent of surveyed respondents. Much of the New Yorker's appeal stemmed from his prosecutorial skills, which he used to good effect against alleged New Deal excesses. Luce seemed to crave some of this partisan ideological spice, while Willkie preferred to dream out loud about his "One World."

While Wendell Willkie floundered, the Luces looked closely at other presidential possibilities. For years, Clare had admired General Douglas

MacArthur, her "hero warrior strutting the beleaguered ramparts." She knew that MacArthur was a poseur and an actor, but, as she happily told the General, "every day is MacArthur day with me." Clare's photograph of him on the Pearl Harbor–era cover of *Life* remained a famous testament to the General's appeal to a frightened nation. For a few weeks Clare seems to have seen herself as a director, choreographing a production in which MacArthur played a presidential role. Henry Luce saw MacArthur as an Asia-firster, whose moral code embodied sound Republican principles. Unbashedly religious, Harry admired MacArthur's public professions of faith in the Savior. Eastern liberals might not like the General, but their aversion did not bother Luce. Besides, an invitation from the General might enable Harry to visit the Pacific theater of war.

General MacArthur made glamorous copy for *Life*, which helped to transform him into the hero of the Pacific. Clare Luce defended MacArthur against those who called him a Fascist. Being histrionic herself, she did not see the General's fits of grandiose rhetoric as anything more than "high-flown" language." When Clare interviewed MacArthur for *Life*, she would let him review her copy in exchange for extra bits of important information. John Billings, always anxious to believe the worst, believed that "she might be secretly in love with [MacArthur]." *Time*, however, occasionally sniped at this "colorful, often theatrical soldier . . . ," who spoke in "rounded periods, full of historical allusions." At times MacArthur believed that the Luce publications were part of some conspiracy against him. After the war, he growled, these magazines were through. John Billings concluded that MacArthur "is a vain prima donna and there is no pleasing him."

Clare's idea of a MacArthur candidacy was immensely impractical. A wartime commander, on the verge of his biggest battles, does not win friends by resigning in order to fight a political campaign against his own commander in chief. Dewey, therefore, continued to build his lead. In fact, Harry Luce had flirted with the wrong general. Prophetically, *Time* later chose General Dwight David Eisenhower as Man of the Year for 1944.

Clashes
with Teddy White
Over China

In Chungking, Teddy White eagerly awaited Harry's arrival. Anxious to tell Luce and the readers of *Life* about the growing crisis in China, White decided that Luce's visit "will probably directly affect the entire policy of Time, Life and Fortune with regard to the Far East." When his boss could not visit him in the spring of 1944, White decided to fly back to the United States, where he intended to confront Luce.

Though White and Luce were very different individuals—one an ardent antifascist and Jewish secularist, the other a Christian with a mystical faith in America—mutual respect and a shared devotion to China had turned them into friends. White found Harry stimulating, intense, a man capable of deep thought and great moral anguish. Dealing with Luce in this matter of China was, Teddy White later recalled, a "god-dam inspiring experience." Touched by the meaning of China in his own life, Henry Luce immersed himself in the "sheer joy and sorrow of the subject." Teddy hoped that their friendship would endure, though his proposed essay for *Life* became the occasion for the "inevitable clash" between White's beliefs and Luce's policy. Their debates about China foreshadowed a momentous controversy that would disrupt American politics for a generation.

Once he was back at Rockefeller Center, White unleashed a torrent of long-suppressed resentment. An angry White indicted Chiang's government for repression, incompetence, xenophobia (including the anti-American variety), and corruption. The entire Soong clan, White argued, was crooked. Luce devoted many hours to reading White's draft article, and for a brief time White convinced himself that Time Inc. was changing its China policy. Harry Luce, however, soon decided that White had failed to grasp the real sources of China's current plight. In Luce's view, the relentless Japanese blockade, along with a lack of American aid, was largely responsible.

In Henry Luce's judgment, a nation that had done little for China when she stood alone had no right to pressure her in this time of pain and turmoil. As Luce saw things, Chiang was trying to carry out reforms that were compatible with the great Chinese cultural tradition.

Teddy White responded that Chiang ruled through corrupt cliques of secret police, Tammany-style politicians, greedy landlords, and officious censors. True, the government, like the country, suffered from the Japanese blockade, but even so, a better regime would have alleviated the pain inflicted by a cruel war. In White's interpretation, Chiang had fallen back upon a kind of reactionary, stale ideology that was part Confucian and part Fascist. If Chiang persisted in his course, White darkly prophesied, liberals would be pushed to join the Communists. China, White added, desperately needed new land laws and more respect for basic human rights.

While Henry Luce dissected and often discarded White's arguments, Teddy's draft article for *Life* ran the censorship gauntlet. He was in a great rush to publish his piece on China, but everyone seemed to be messing with it. At the Office of Censorship, Jack Lockhart noted that "Neither the Army nor the State Department likes [White's article]." To them, White's long-awaited revelation, tentatively called "Now Is the Time to Talk About China," could spark trouble. Trying to gain support, Teddy White observed that the China Affairs Division of the State Department endorsed his ideas. Indeed, John Carter Vincent, the China hand who now headed that division, thought along the same lines as White. Vincent, a forty-three-year-old Foreign Service officer, had spent many years in China. He was now convinced that China was headed for disaster unless Chiang carried out reforms. Vincent, however, spoke for but one faction of his department. More cautious State Department officials worried about White's *Life* article, mainly because his comments could adversely affect "the relations and current negotiations between our two governments."

American military censors had not savaged White's article. Upon appeal they even agreed to restore certain phrases that were mainly "statistical or anecdotal in nature." White, however, continued to worry about the fate of his essay. Impatient with the bureaucracy, he tried to nudge the Board of Review of the War Department's Bureau of Public Relations. General Stilwell, White noted, described American illusions about China as harmful to the United States. Troops who had read about the wonders of Free China spoke bitterly about the reality of serving there. In the War Department, however, concerned officials decided that White's piece was too critical of Chiang. War also objected to White's prediction that Chinese civil strife could result in a postwar confrontation between the Russians and the Americans.

Luce, Billings, and their colleagues heeded the suggestions made by the War Department. Jim Warner, of the Office of Censorship, rejoiced that "considerable rewriting had been done, the general tendency of which was to soften Mr. White's indictment of China and to make the piece less critical of Chiang." The resulting article, called " 'LIFE' Looks at China," represented a compromise. Harry happily observed that "You [White] have undoubtedly written the most important article about China in many years—perhaps ever." Luce hoped that the article "will help to clear the air." He wrote to influential members of his China networks, providing them with advance copies of Teddy White's article. Giving the piece his own spin, Luce promised that the forthcoming article would suppress "none of the 'bad news.' " The White article, Luce claimed, would put the Chinese situation into historical perspective.

Teddy White's famous article did convey some important insights to *Life*'s millions of readers. The United Front, *Life* reported, was weaker than ever. And *Life* admitted that the Communists were a strong force, capable of pinning down a large number of Japanese troops. White's story also revealed that the Ch'en brothers ran a kind of police state, which was on the verge of waging civil war against the Communists. Such statements shocked many Americans, who had heard little about Yenan and its Eighth Route Army or about Chiang's abuses.

Theodore White noted that the number of trucks on China's roads had diminished from 15,000 early in 1942 to perhaps 5,000. White had wanted to discuss the pitiful rice rations allotted to Chinese soldiers, but *Life* was more generous to Chiang's generals. In fact, huge numbers of recruits suffered from tuberculosis, while millions of soldiers had disappeared from the ranks, victims of disease, famine, desertion, and death. White had written about smuggling, corruption, and censorship; a bit of this appeared in his article. In a dramatic appeal, Teddy advised that Americans withdraw their support of the "current regime." *Life* toned this down by adding Luce-like statements that praised Chiang. The final version of White's piece blamed some of China's problems on America's failure to help her.

Henry Luce was still willing to be patient with China. In an editorial appearing in this same May 1, 1944, issue of *Life*, Luce/Jessup argued that Teddy White had produced some shocking truths that would disturb Americans whose view of China was "formed during Madame Chiang K'ai-shek's visit." China remained "a great potential force for freedom and democracy in Asia." Chinese reformers, however, were in for another letdown: the Fifth KMT Central Executive Committee refused to implement serious reforms. Back again in Chungking, Teddy White was surprised and angered to hear that Chiang's censors and bureaucrats were not unhappy about the article—they had expected much worse. Meanwhile, the Japanese Army had launched new strikes across the Yellow River, into Honan. An angry peasantry, which had barely survived the 1943 famine, did not resist the invader, and some peasants even collaborated with the enemy.

Late in May 1944 Congressman Walter H. Judd, once a medical missionary to China, heartily endorsed White's article. He warned, however, against American meddling in China's internal affairs. Rather, he said, the U.S. must make good on its three-year-old promises to aid China. Such assistance would vindicate Chiang's courageous rejection of an alliance with Japan or the Communists. Judd added a personal note that placed a heavy responsibility on Henry Luce's shoulders. "Both America and China are fortunate," wrote Walter Judd, "to have at the head of such important opinion forming organs, a person with your background and firsthand knowledge."

Alfred Kohlberg reacted badly to *Life*'s widely discussed article on China. He wrote to the magazine, claiming that Theodore White had exaggerated the number of Chinese soldiers suffering from tuberculosis and other deadly diseases. Kohlberg also boasted that Chinese troops had killed 688,000 Japanese soldiers, though he did not provide a source for this fantastic figure. A researcher at *Life* checked with Teddy White, who had personally visited five fronts in China. White stood by his (emasculated) story. In retaliation, Kohlberg assembled new files on the men he accused of betraying China. Kohlberg's defendants now included American aid officials who had allegedly misused their funds and undermined China's war effort. Chinese government officials were soon working in tandem with Kohlberg and Judd. This embryonic pro-Chiang propaganda lobby devoted much energy to shoring up American public opinion.

In Washington, the Chinese Ambassador, Dr. Wei Tao-ming, still rejected the idea of sending American military observers to the Communists in Yenan. The plan was, he told the State Department, "ill-advised." Wei blamed the Communists for China's troubles, and he accused the USSR of manipulating the Chinese "rebels." Sadly for Ambassador Wei, Roosevelt was privy to information contradicting his line. Lauchlin Currie's latest memorandum to the President depicted a regime drowning in greed, infighting, and oppression. Currie argued that the U.S. government should disregard Chungking's threats and force the Communists and the Guomindang into an alliance against Japan. In a dramatic flourish, he warned Roosevelt that "another [Spanish Civil War] is in the making." Like other liberals, Currie feared that outside powers could become enmeshed in China's strife. Owen Lattimore, a professor and scholar who had served in Chungking, was no less critical than Currie. Chiang, who had reason to worry about the attitude of his former adviser, had tried to buy him off with a gratuity of $5,000, but Lattimore curtly rejected the gift. Disgust with Chiang was rising in Washington at a time when China was more vulnerable than ever.

In the late spring President Roosevelt decided to send another personal representative to China, his controversial Vice-President, Henry A. Wallace. FDR wanted to remove him from the political debate while the Democrats prepared for their national convention. On June 22, 1944, the Vice-President met with President Chiang Kai-shek. Generalissimo Chiang explained away his many military reverses and attacked the American press for daring to print criticism of his country. Chiang, who knew nothing about the U.S. Constitution, thought that someone should silence his noisy American tormenters. The Vice-President departed, convinced that Chiang could not run postwar China.

Two days after Henry Wallace's ill-fated meeting with Chiang, Foreign Service officer Jack Service predicted that the Guomindang would collapse, and recommended that the U.S. use Lend-Lease as a bargaining chip. Unless Chiang agreed to democratize China, he should no longer receive American help. Service also argued that the pro-Chiang propaganda machine was suppressing the truth about Chinese affairs. He blamed Harry Luce and advised that the U.S. government counter his message. Service himself tried to do so by leaking sensitive material to sympathetic reporters, such as Teddy White.

Among Chiang's American admirers, few harbored more fervent views than General Claire Chennault, who claimed that the Fourteenth Air Force had already sunk a million tons of Japanese shipping. Chennault wanted more of the precious supplies that arrived in Kunming for storage in various depots. Unfortunately, trucking these goods to Chennault's east China air bases proved to be an arduous, inefficient exercise. Critics sympathetic to Chennault agreed that General Stilwell had underestimated the importance of building up the primitive Chinese transportation network. This oversight had left the Fourteenth Air Force and its Chinese defenders undersupplied and isolated. His commander, Chennault believed, was cheating him of final victory. Still, General Marshall had long since warned that Japan, if wounded by Chennault, would lash out at his airfields.

In eastern China, the enemy now launched devastating offensives against the American air bases. Seven airfields ultimately fell after U.S. forces had blown up hangers, supplies, and runways. FDR, who had once shared some of Chiang's illusions about Chennault's strategy, belatedly admitted that "Air power alone cannot stop a determined enemy." China, however, was becoming less important to American strategists, even as it grew more vulnerable to Japanese offensives. In the Pacific the Yanks were moving ever farther westward as Marines hit the beaches on island after island. The powerful eyewitness reports filed by *Time*'s Bob Sherrod provided Americans with some of the best accounts of the savage fighting there. If American bombers could one day use airstrips on islands in the Marianas, they could level much of urban Japan and destroy her maritime commerce. On July 8, 1944, the last Japanese defenders of Saipan yielded to their conquerors. American progress in the Central and Southwest Pacific areas meant that U.S. forces might never land on the China coast.

As Claire Chennault's plans crumbled and Chiang's armies fell back, General Stilwell took the offensive in Burma. His crack Chinese divisions were finally advancing toward the town of Myitkyina, with its important aerodrome. Chiang belatedly supported Stilwell's arduous march, and in early summer he reluctantly agreed to provide him with two more divisions. Stilwell's ranks were filled with soldiers who loved this foreigner who spoke their language and shared their hardships. And Stilwell's American troops struggled to keep up with a man born to lead them. According to a story reported by *Time*'s Jim Shepley, a group of black engineers once noticed a "lean, gaunt, leathery" gentleman fording a stream in some Godforsaken spot. "Look at that poor old man," commented one of the engineers. "Some draft boards will do anything."

The rapid Japanese advance in eastern China offered Chiang a new excuse to withdraw Chinese troops from Stilwell's Burma front. Supported by General Marshall and the Joint Chiefs, the exasperated Stilwell decided that he should succeed Chiang as the commander in charge of all troops, including the Communist forces, engaged in the China theater. Roosevelt agreed to Stilwell's request, and on July 6, 1944, he cabled a sharp message to Chiang Kai-shek. Warning that "the future of all Asia is at stake . . . ," Roosevelt demanded that Chiang appoint Stilwell overall commander in China. Chiang agreed to these terms, but he also indicated that he wanted to work out certain modalities.

Meanwhile Japanese forces pushed relentlessly forward in central China. Teddy White, an anguished chronicler of this drama, donned his war correspondent's uniform and rushed out into the field, where he visited various war zones and scribbled voluminous notes. In an impassioned letter to Harry Luce, White concluded that recent events "have shaken this regime to its foundations." White repeatedly reviled cowardly and incompetent Chinese officers who retreated before forces that their troops sometimes outnumbered by a ratio of seven to one. He informed Luce about officers who stole oxcarts from peasants in order to evacuate their families and property from threatened towns. Only criminals and other riffraff, White added, filled the ranks of the government's army. In order to protect their meager property, peasant bands disarmed these voracious Chinese "soldiers." Inflation ravaged the cities, while corruption drained the economy. Meanwhile, Chiang himself seemed to be strangely passive. Once the Americans cracked the Japanese blockade, White noted, the Generalissimo dreamed that the Chinese armies, armed by the Americans, would move north and take over the whole country, including the Red "liberated" regions.

Facing defeat on several fronts, Chiang's highest officials continued to worry most about the hated Yenan Communists. Unlike the Japanese, the Reds offered the Chinese people both patriotism and the promise of better times. A frustrated General Stilwell watched the Japanese armies advance westward while 200,000 of Chiang's soldiers blockaded the Communist border regions in the north. The Generalissimo's political and military weakness only intensified his fear of compromise with his domestic enemies. The Chinese government, Teddy White reported, believed that it could not co-exist with the Marxist challengers to its legitimacy.

While Chiang's armies retreated, the Communists demanded that he lift the blockade encircling the Yenan region, to equip sixteen (later

Ambassador Joseph P. Kennedy, who, despite his strong anti-interventionist views, became Harry Luce's good friend. *John F. Kennedy Library*

Young John F. Kennedy, soon to be the best-selling author of *Why England Slept*. *John F. Kennedy Library*

China-bound in the spring of 1941,
the Luces receive a scroll from American "China hands,"
men and women who wanted to convey their greetings
to Harry, Clare, and the Chinese people.
Princeton University Library

Rickshaw porters carry Clare Boothe Luce toward Chungking
in the spring of 1941.
Princeton University Library

Henry R. Luce with Theodore H. White, Chungking, 1941.
Houghton Library, Harvard University

Raising money to save China. In 1941, Clare Boothe Luce shows Wendell Willkie, an avid admirer, how one eats with chopsticks.
Cleveland Press Collection Cleveland State University Archives

Generalissimo Chiang Kai-shek, Madame Chiang, General Joseph W. Stilwell, an interpreter, and *Life* correspondent Clare Boothe Luce, 1942.
Cleveland Press Collection/ Cleveland State Univerrsity Archives

Correspondent John Hersey
covers the invasion of Sicily
for *Time*, 1943.
Courtesy of John Hersey

Whittaker Chambers, who
in the 1940s greatly
influenced both Henry R. Luce
and *Time* magazine.
National Archives

Representative Clare Boothe Luce with General Dwight D. Eisenhower, 1944.
Dwight D. Eisenhower Library

At a fund-raiser for United China Relief, David O. Selznick's laughter
and Clare Luce's wit failed to amuse the ever serious Harry Luce.
Princeton University Library

Henry R. Luce and Nelson A. Rockefeller
break ground for the new Time & Life Building, 1957. Their relationship dated
from the late 1930s, when Luce and his media ardently backed one of
Rockefeller's favorite projects, the Museum of Modern Art.
The Rockefeller Center Archive

Henry R. Luce at the age of thirty-nine.
Cleveland Press Collection/Cleveland State University Archives

ten) Red divisions, guarantee political and civil rights, release political prisoners, recognize local governments that had sprung up behind the front, and democratize Free China. Accession to the Reds' proposals would mean recognizing the Communists as the dominant force in the Yellow River valley, Manchuria, and perhaps in the central Yangtze valley. Even Teddy White admitted that if Chiang accepted all these demands, he would be committing political suicide.

White believed that if the Generalissimo wanted to solve his Communist problem peacefully, he would need to make a deal with Stalin. In order to do so, Chiang would have to grant "his" Reds civil and political liberties. Freedom to speak, organize, and propagandize would, however, vastly strengthen the Marxists. Nevertheless, as White saw things, Chiang desperately needed to move away from his peculiar brand of Chinese fascism and toward liberalism. Perhaps naively, Teddy White thought that a democratic Guomindang could then take the lead in unifying China, as it had done twice in the past.

Weakened on all fronts, the Chungking government finally permitted the dispatch of American military observers to Yenan. Headed by the capable Colonel David Barrett, the Dixie Mission, so called because it worked in "rebel" territory, carefully observed the methods, training, and armaments of the Communist Eighth Route Army. As Chungking feared, some Americans were enthusiastic about their new "ally." Jack Service, who was in Yenan, declared that "We have come into a different country and are meeting a different people." From the Generalissimo's viewpoint, moreover, Joe Stilwell was likely to distribute U.S. weapons to the Communists and he would doubtless insist that Chiang lift his blockade of Mao's forces.

By late 1944 American policy was slipping away from the control of Chiang Kai-shek's friends.

American illusions about China, which had peaked during Madame Chiang's visit only seventeen months before, had yielded to bitterness and finger-pointing. What both Pearl Buck and Harry Luce had feared was coming to pass. The Allies were losing China, and Chiang was suffering massive defeats on the battlefield. Although Chiang at first responded sullenly to this terrible new reality, he later talked about reorganizing his battered, bloated army. Teddy White, who was again subject to quick changes of opinion, decided that Chiang might be veering toward reform. Luce was only too happy to agree.

At a July dinner hosted by the China-America Council of Commerce and Industry, Luce saluted H. H. Kung for creating organizations "devoted to Chinese-American friendship. . . ." In his own comments, the wily Kung appealed to Harry Luce's hopes for his beloved China. "I can see," said Kung, "new networks of railroads, highways, steamships, and airways stretching across the Asiatic continent and linking our cities with other parts of the world. I can see far-sighted Americans working side by side with the Chinese." Kung said nothing about democracy or reform. Harry, who longed for the day when he could revisit a liberated Shantung province, was nonetheless moved. Even as Kung spoke at the Waldorf-Astoria, however, his prophecy was turning into ashes in China.

Invariably, *Time* reported on unpleasant truths, only to explain them away. After describing China's plight as a "creeping paralysis," *Time* documented the KMT's suppression of its liberal enemies. The magazine then complained that the annual rate of inflation stood at a staggering 360 percent, though *Time* blamed this disaster on the Japanese blockade. *Time* also described the repression, censorship, and concentration camps that disfigured China, but generously ascribed them to "the stress and strain of China's primary task and great achievement: her resistance to Japan." To Teddy White, this kind of thing was preposterous and dangerous. Americans, he believed, were beguiled by stale illusions, while a convulsion was shaking China.

In mid-August 1944, Theodore White again expressed disappointment at his inability to visit the Communist border regions. He was not alone. For many years, readers of the mainstream American press had received little information about Mao Tse-tung and his guerrillas. In the spring, however, a breakthrough had occurred. A few correspondents, including Israel Epstein, a *Time* stringer, had recently visited Yenan. White, like John Hersey, was a friend of Epstein, and trusted "Eppie's" judgment. In Epstein's Yenan, patriotic landlords charged lower rents since they thereby contributed to building a stronger Eighth Route Army. Peasant families farmed larger plots of land, for enlightened landlords had sold acreage to them. Farmers shared their plows, and as a result they produced a food surplus. This fact particularly impressed Teddy White, who had not forgotten the horrors of the Honan famine.

White could only contrast Epstein's Yenan with the degradation, corruption, and oppression prevalent in so-called Free China. Only recently, for example, White had interviewed the anti-Communist crusader Ch'en Li-fu, who had been fighting the Reds since the 1920s. A xenophobic fanatic, Ch'en had once forced girls with Western-style bobbed hair to parade through the streets with their breasts bared. He had allegedly ordered students beheaded for owning Communist books. Though Ch'en denied he was anti-Western, he failed to convince Teddy White. If Ch'en represented China's dark side, then Yenan was China's hope. In the words of White's mentor, John Fairbank, "Yenan glowed in the distance."

Whatever Harry Luce thought of Teddy White's politics, he knew that his man had come by a major story. In August 1944 White cabled his first detailed reports about Yenan to New York, where *Time* published them. For a time Henry Luce hoped that these Reds might be more Chinese than Marxist, though he remained a skeptic.

If Americans believed that Yenan was not Marxist-Leninist, they were in for a profound shock. Mao, of course, was not taking orders from Stalin, but neither was he a "margarine" or "so-called" Communist or an "agrarian reformer." In truth, Mao Tse-tung and his colleagues were battle-hardened men who proudly called themselves Communists. In name and in structure, the Chinese Communist Party remained Marxist-Leninist in inspiration and goals. True, Mao and Chou spoke often about "democracy," but then so did Stalin.

Facing military disaster, Chiang again agreed to accept General Stilwell as commander of all forces in China; then he stalled. On September 7, 1944, President Roosevelt's special representative arrived in Chungking, where he bravely tried to bring Stilwell and Chiang together. A glamorous, outgoing man—*Time* described him as "ramrodbacked and handsome at 61"—General Patrick J. Hurley knew little about China. Vain and garrulous, Hurley overestimated his own abilities. He viewed criticism as disloyalty and resented people who questioned his recipes for success. It soon became clear that Patrick Hurley and Joe Stilwell were on a collision course. Hurley wanted to believe Chiang; Stilwell despised the Generalissimo. On September 12 Chiang again accepted Stilwell as overall commander in the China theater, but he continued to bicker with Hurley. Chiang wanted an ally who supplied him with American-made goods, dollars, and gold—no questions asked. On September 16, however, Roosevelt warned the Generalissimo that "my chiefs of staff and I are convinced that you are faced in the near future with the disaster I have feared."

In a message that reflected General Marshall's blunt, spare style, FDR accused Chiang of endangering Stilwell's successful offensive in north Burma. The seizure of new roads and airfields had drastically improved the transport situation, and supplies flown over the shorter and safer

"Hump" rose from 18,000 tons in June to 25,000 in July and 30,000 in September 1944. This tonnage would be of no use, however, if the Japanese advanced deep into Yunnan.

On September 19, in the presence of General Hurley, Stilwell delivered a stunning message to Chiang. To Stilwell's joy, Roosevelt's words were harsh. Never had Stilwell so delighted in delivering bad news. Like a schoolboy who had avenged himself on a cruel but incompetent headmaster, the General gloated about his deed:

> I've waited long for vengeance—
> At last I've had my chance.
> I've looked the Peanut in the eye
> And kicked him in the pants.

On September 22, Stilwell again complained to General Marshall, protesting that Chiang had forbidden the American-trained "Y Force to take any further offensive action. . . ." The Japanese, Stilwell noted, were closing in on Kweilin, with its important American airfield, while "we are still waiting for Chiang Kai-shek to make up his mind."

In the event of an inter-Allied political crisis, Chiang would need support, both in Washington and in the American media. The news from the U.S.A., however, greatly dismayed Chinese officials and their friends. In New York, a column by the influential Walter Lippmann of the *Herald Tribune* denounced Chiang for wasting good troops in his blockade of Yenan. He feared that the Russians might respond to Chiang's policy by linking up with the Chinese Communists. Then, warned Lippmann, a civil war could ensue, leading to Chiang's fall from power. Lippmann demanded that Chiang cooperate with the other powers, as they strove to build a better postwar world.

In a memorandum, Clare Luce's adviser, Christopher Emmet, sourly asked, At what cost? Was Guomindang China supposed to behave "like Poland," and face a Communist future? Minnesota Congressman Dr. Walter Judd observed that Henry Luce had "been so right, as our Government has been so wrong, on the most important issue of the Twentieth Century—the nature, the objective, and methods, and the strength of the Communist drive for world conquest."

Despite Emmet's rhetoric and Judd's praise, one fact was clear, however often Harry Luce and his magazines wished it away: China was losing the war.

1944

Two More Losses to FDR

In the winter of 1944, Wendell Willkie had been pursuing the Republican nomination with all-out abandon. In the process, Willkie worked himself into exhaustion. He was smoking, eating, and drinking too much, and he confused the fate of the Republic with his own political future. Through the first half of 1944, Willkie charged, hostile Republicans were spreading the rumor that "Wendell is drinking himself to death." Offended by the loud whispers, Willkie told Luce that he never took more than two drinks at "one sitting." Poor Willkie did not indicate how many "sittings" he engaged in each day, but sadly, there were too many of them. In March Willkie decided to make his stand in Wisconsin. He had narrowly lost the state to Roosevelt in 1940, and now hoped to show his strength in the Midwestern heartland.

In choosing Wisconsin, Wendell Willkie made a terrible blunder. Dewey refused to campaign there, so if Willkie defeated a phantom candidates, party regulars would yawn. If, on the other hand, Willkie lost to absentee candidates (Dewey, plus the marginal draft-MacArthur movement), he was finished. Another political "iffy question" added to Willkie's woes. If the Wisconsin primary became a referendum on

Willkie's one world internationalism, the candidate would find himself in grave danger. Isolationist progressives, who had once rallied to the elder Robert LaFollette, were suspicious of Willkie's global vision. Republican conservatives, moreover, felt that the sometime presidential emissary Willkie had been too close to Roosevelt for too long. Willkie thus risked incurring the wrath of two groups; if they combined against him, he was doomed. He tried to overcome their animosity by barnstorming the state. Willkie delivered forty speeches in thirteen days, an effort that further eroded his health.

Writing for *Life*, which had many readers in the cities, small towns, and farming communities of Wisconsin, John Chamberlain portrayed the candidate as a man who had "made friends among the Negroes, the Jews, the liberal intellectuals, the . . . New Dealers, the foreign correspondents, the labor movement and the civil libertarians." These groups were not necessarily popular among Midwestern Republicans. Wisconsin, *Life* piously concluded, would indicate whether Willkie could break down "the prejudices that can defeat him at the convention. . . ." As if to make matters worse, *Life* proceeded to drive a wedge between prohibitionists and an ever-thirstier Wendell Willkie. A photograph showed Willkie above a caption that alluded to his fondness for beer and scotch. Harry Luce, who raised few objections to the Chamberlain piece, had finally distanced himself from the man whose candidacy *Fortune* had created. Luce, who detested personal unpleasantness, did not confront the volatile Willkie; instead, he sent him a handwritten note which observed that the "event," meaning the primary, was "in the hands of God. . . ."

Wendell Willkie did not win a single Wisconsin delegate. A day after the primary, he suspended his campaign, virtually withdrawing from the race. At first Willkie was gracious as he thanked Harry Luce for his past support. The ex-candidate's mood quickly soured, however, when he read *Time*. Luce did not like losers. The Wisconsin primary, Harry Luce decided, had cleared the air and ended a "long and painful situation." *Time* and *Life* were now blasting the Willkie-ites for their alleged rule-or-ruin philosophy. Anyone who knew his style could see that Luce had personally edited the Willkie material in the post-Wisconsin issue of *Time*. Wisconsin's Republicans, the magazine argued, had reaffirmed their faith in "realistic internationalism." The newsmagazine thanked Willkie for his past services, then asked him to stop blocking the road. Willkie, however, took things very personally. "Naturally," he wrote to Luce, "being human and in view of your many expressions of friendship for me, I thought it appropriate to call your attention to what I . . . thought an undeserved blow at a time when the blows were coming rather thick." Bitterly, Willkie hoped that Luce would "have more luck in shaping the Republican Party than I have had."

Luce humored Willkie, since he was desperately trying to prevent his friend from bolting to Roosevelt. To make matters worse, Wendell Willkie detested Tom Dewey more than ever. Luce tried to mollify him, and invited Willkie to join him for Sunday dinner at the home of his sister, Beth Moore. Willkie, however, would have none of Harry Luce's soothing comments about the future foreign policy of the GOP. At one point the ex-candidate rose from the dinner table in a rage, roaring, "Harry, you may be the world's best editor, but you are certainly the world's worst politician"—a remark for which he later apologized. Wilkie's decline was apparent to many observers, but Harry Luce, perhaps feeling a bit guilty, tried to encourage him. To his troubled friend, Luce pleaded that "you have only just finished Act 1—and, for the country's sake, the play must not be a tragedy."

By May Thomas E. Dewey was winning most of the delegates, though Luce still refused to embrace his candidacy. A competent, honest prosecutor and administrator, the governor came across in *Life* as prissy and cold. Late in May *Life* offended Dewey and encouraged his enemies when the magazine suggested that a Midwesterner might be a stronger candidate. The magazine published an editorial urging that delegates resist the Dewey stampede.

At the end of June, the Luces headed for Chicago, where the Congresswoman was scheduled to address the Republican convention. Harry intended to stay in the background and let Clare bask in her glory. Pledging her "support and loyalty" to candidate Dewey, Mrs. Luce intended to star in a little play of her own creation. She arrived in the fetid, smoke-filled convention hall late in the evening of June 27, looking cool and dazzling. The newsfilm cameramen loved her, as did the still photographers, for she performed so well. Clare was not one more pretty face; rather, she radiated brains, sharpness, and a kind of "if you dare" sauciness. With her girlish braids and her winning smile, she certainly looked younger than her forty-one years.

Speaking to the convention in a tone worthy of an elegant actress, Representative Luce combined artful melodrama with a forceful twist of the knife as she told the story of "G.I. Joe" and "G.I. Jim." In Clare Luce's morality tale, one young American died defending his country; another would return to face an uncertain future. Jim did not complain, if those in power (read: Roosevelt) made false promises or committed blunders. He had gone to fight the Nazis and was ready to die for freedom. But while Jim fought, FDR plotted to stay in power, again violating the two-term tradition begun by George Washington. Speaking in a strong, cultivated voice, Clare Luce entranced the delegates. America, she said, needed leaders who valued the truth more than they relished power. G.I. Jim finally falls in battle, but Clare conjured up his spirit. In a maudlin tone, Clare preciously turned herself into G.I. Jim: "I am the risen soldier," says Jim, evoking Christ. Clare then returned to earth and promised that Joe would come home to create a better, greater America.

The crowd loved the performance, especially when Mrs. Luce attacked Franklin Roosevelt. Harry was proud of his wife and subsequently decided to modify his gag rule, which prevented his magazines from covering her antics. Some Time Incers, however, squirmed in their seats as they endured Clare's histrionic, "cheap" address. One unamused British diplomat sniffed that "Mrs. Luce is held even by some of her admirers to have sunk to a level of sentimental gush which most of her hearers found it difficult to endure."

While still in Chicago, Luce wrote to Willkie, praising the convention that was doggedly ignoring its own 1940 candidate. Luce liked Dewey's acceptance speech, and he approved of the GOP platform, which, among many other things, called for "responsible participation by the United States in a postwar cooperative organization among sovereign nations to prevent military aggression." Luce hoped that Dewey would attack the New Deal for placing social reform above free enterprise. Although John Billings decided that his boss had "moved far to the right," in fact Harry Luce remained a fervent advocate of equal rights for blacks.

The Republican platform contained a demand for a Fair Employment Practices Commission as well as calls for legislation fighting lynching and poll taxes. *Life* was trying to prepare the American people for massive racial change, such as the integration of the armed forces, new civil rights laws, and an end to legal segregation. Luce was not so much moving to the right, as he was suffering from his quadrennial bout of extreme partisan politics. Billings even speculated that Luce himself would one day wish to "fulfill his destiny," perhaps by running for high public office.

Luce continued to support his wife's political career. He gave a $3,000 check to Connecticut Republican Finance Committee treasurer Prescott S. Bush of Greenwich, who was in a position to nurture Clare's ambitions. Representative Luce was engaged in a tough, sometimes nasty reelection campaign. By 1944 she had emerged as a highly partisan Republican. Liberals, socialists, New Dealers, and certain labor leaders regularly felt the lash of her barbed comments, and they wanted revenge. Representative Luce, though, showed no signs of moderating her tone. Clare reacted to FDR like a person bested at her own game. He, too, was a prima donna who felt compelled to dominate a roomful of people; and FDR refused to fall for her charm or looks. Worse still, Roosevelt filled a bigger stage than Clare could ever hope to see.

In her 1944 campaign Clare Luce made the shocking charge that FDR had lied the country into war "because he did not have the political courage to lead us into it." Not content with that twist of the knife, Clare added, "The shame of Pearl Harbor was Mr. Roosevelt's shame." Mrs. Luce had also begun to crusade against communism, wildly charging that 50,000 American Communists had infiltrated the Democratic Party. Clare Luce then ridiculed the "Broadway to Browder Axis," which was trying to defeat her. She added that Earl Browder, the Communist leader, was the only man who offered 100 percent support to Roosevelt's foreign policy. Various liberal celebrities came into Fairfield County, where they called for Mrs. Luce's defeat. New Dealers attacked her as the "globaloney girl," while Max Lerner of *PM* thought she might be a fascist. Clare loved to swirl about in the midst of this highly public emotional turmoil, and she relished the campaign.

Clare Luce tried to have it both ways. She coined unkind phrases about FDR, which were calculated to win the support of isolationists. The righteous Congresswoman then fended off charges from outraged internationalists by calling herself the first apostle of a postwar alliance with Great Britain. Clare Luce narrowly won reelection, but only because she laced her vitriol with heavy doses of good political sense. The Congresswoman, for example, had been careful not to antagonize labor's rank and file. Mrs. Luce had in 1943 voted to uphold Roosevelt's veto of a controversial antistrike bill. She also spoke a good deal about the need to adapt wartime industrial plants to civilian postwar needs. Ahead of her time in many ways, she suggested that Congress install automatic tally machines and hire professionally trained staffers.

Despite her aversion to FDR, Clare Luce appreciated the greatness of Eleanor Roosevelt. Mrs. Roosevelt, like Clare, was independent and outspoken. Displaying eloquence and generosity, Clare later wrote that ". . . I think she is a very great lady." She added that "I could only wish I had half her patience, compassion, inflexibility of purpose and, at the moment, physical durability." Clare Luce correctly predicted that Mrs. Roosevelt would be remembered "long after people have forgotten that she was wrong about some of her political-economic ideas."

At Time Inc., Harry Luce's senior colleagues were dismayed by his increasingly authoritarian manner. Besides, Harry was showing signs of incipient deafness, a malady that did not render him more open to unwelcome suggestions or interruptions. And to the distress of some of his colleagues, Harry Luce continued to attack Roosevelt with gusto. After branding the President a liar, Harry gave him little credit for his prewar or wartime leadership. At best, Luce concluded, FDR had done his job with "average courage or average efficiency. . . ." In Billings' understated words, "Luce is not 'sweetly reasonable' on the subject of FDR." These fulminations alarmed some of Harry's associates, who feared a repeat of the 1940 debacle. Jack Jessup warned that if *Life* sounded too partisan, the magazine would undermine its own credibility, especially among millions of GIs. Restraining Luce was not easy, however.

At one point Harry Luce opposed publishing a Roper survey because the poll revealed Roosevelt making gains. He compromised, however, and Time Inc. printed the results of both the Gallup and the Roper polls, even though the latter looked better for Roosevelt. In Washington, Felix Belair, who had to deal with the White House, even provided Press Secretary Steve Early with an advance copy of the Roper poll. And when Dewey tried to hire Jack Jessup as a speechwriter, Luce said no. Harry, however, still wanted to publish an editorial in *Life* that would endorse Dewey. Dan Longwell thought that this piece, tentatively called "The Case Against Roosevelt," would hurt the magazine. Instead, Jessup suggested drafting an editorial in favor of FDR, to be followed by one making the case for Dewey. Early in September, Luce commissioned three editorials, one for Dewey, one for Roosevelt, and one containing *Life*'s endorsement.

Colleagues could sometimes rein in Harry Luce by pointing out that too much partisanship would provoke sharp rebukes from hostile media. Luce disliked negative publicity about his company, and it was blooming all around him. One wag summed up the indictment: "*Time*," he noted, "is impartial. Fifty percent of its space is used to attack Roosevelt, fifty percent to praise the Republicans." Walter Winchell, the powerful, nationally syndicated gossip columnist, claimed that *Life*'s Dan Longwell prevented any pro-FDR staffer from messing with the magazine's "pro-Dewey captions." Though managing editor

Longwell, who admired Roosevelt, knew that the story was false, this kind of attack bothered Luce. A naive man, Luce did not see that his partisanship inevitably provoked equally unfair counterattacks.

In the early autumn, Henry Luce reviewed some interesting developments on the foreign policy scene. Between August 21 and October 7, 1944, delegations representing the Big Four powers convened in the comfortable setting of Dumbarton Oaks, an estate in Georgetown. There, they discussed the structure of the international organization later known as the United Nations. To Luce's satisfaction, the Republicans adopted a positive approach to the ongoing talks. While the diplomats deliberated, John Foster Dulles, representing candidate Dewey, met three times with Cordell Hull. Dulles agreed that "setting up a permanent structure for peace" was not a fit subject for partisan debate. This new bipartisanship effectively removed the issue of the United Nations from the campaign. Dewey followed suit, and Hull could soon thank him for this "heartening manifestation of national unity. . . ."

In a long piece by John Chamberlain, *Life* hailed Dulles as the next Secretary of State. Harry Luce urged Billings to defend the lawyer against "smear journalism." The magazine therefore said little about Dulles' prewar work for clients with interests in Nazi Germany, but rather selected facts that led to a palatable conclusion: Dulles was a Christian and a Republican internationalist. Chamberlain also failed to probe Dulles' involvement in America First, during a time when his law firm drew up the incorporation papers for that movement. For the first time, a broader public became aware of John Foster Dulles, as filtered through Time Inc.'s lens.

At Dumbarton Oaks, the various delegations agreed to establish a Security Council, a General Assembly, and various related agencies. Five powers—the U.S., Britain, Russia, China, and France—would occupy permanent seats on the Security Council. Great-power domination of the Council was a foregone conclusion, and Harry Luce did not see the international organization as a panacea for the world's ills. Instead, he operated from the premise that a strong, virtuous, and *sovereign* America could help the world. Yes, Luce would work within the United Nations framework, but only when it was feasible to do so. The Luce publications praised Dumbarton Oaks as "positive and bipartisan." Privately, however, Luce still voiced mistrust of Hull and Roosevelt, feeling that they intended to revert to some kind of isolationism once the war had ended.

Throughout the campaign Harry Luce felt frustrated. Hemmed in by the Dulles/Hull agreement, he looked for vulnerable chinks in Roosevelt's armor. He therefore paid close attention to a Board of Inquiry, which was investigating the Pearl Harbor debacle. Luce suspected that Roosevelt's alleged malfeasance might be exposed, but he failed to make much of the story. *Life* also had in its files many photographs that revealed a shockingly wan and ill Roosevelt. The country was at war, however, so the magazine usually published pictures that showed Roosevelt looking reasonably well. *Life*, which had happily suppressed unpleasant facts about Dulles, reluctantly did something similar for FDR.

Henry Luce had been spending four months trying to convert Wendell Willkie into a Dewey supporter. "I hope," Luce had written in June, "that you will be urged to take a leading part in the common task and that you will see your way to do so." But on August 20, 1944, Willkie exchanged hostile telegrams with candidate Dewey. While Secretary Hull prepared to meet with Dulles, the New York Governor was trying to set up a similar meeting between Willkie and Dulles. "I wish," Willkie fumed, "I had known of your desire for my views prior to your original statement [about the forthcoming Dulles/Hull meeting]."

Before Labor Day, Harry Luce sent invitations to Dewey's campaign manager, Republican National Committee chairman Herbert Brownell, and to Wendell Willkie. Brownell, a brilliant political operative, badly wanted Willkie's support. Luce hoped that Willkie and Brownell could dine with him at the Waldorf. Both men accepted Luce's invitation, though they did so with profound misgivings. Herbert Brownell knew that this encounter would not be pleasant. And though Willkie now thought that Dewey might win, he still mistrusted him. As a courtesy, the Dewey campaign provided Willkie with an advance copy of the speech that would signal the onset of the fall campaign. An internationalist himself, the resourceful Brownell hoped that Willkie would laud Dewey's foreign policy statement as a reasonable contribution to the national debate.

Wendell Willkie duly arrived at the Waldorf, as promised. He agreed that Dewey's speech was acceptable—then launched into an assault against the candidate's character. An uncomfortable Herbert Brownell now had to listen to a diatribe against the man he was trying to put in the White House. After dinner, the three men sipped whiskey. Fueled by the high-octane liquor, Willkie now lashed out in all directions. Finally, around midnight, he left the suite. Brownell, exhausted, flopped onto a couch. Neither he nor Harry Luce said anything for several minutes. Drained, both men grimly hoped that Willkie had rid his system of accumulated bile. Goaded by Luce, Willkie would presumably rally to the standard-bearer of his own party. Herbert Brownell later heard that Willkie had subsequently called a close confidant, Indianapolis publisher Eugene Pulliam. According to Brownell, Willkie told Pulliam that he would endorse the Republican candidate in a radio broadcast. He never made the endorsement.

Several days before Christmas 1943, Luce had placed an early-morning phone call to Felix Belair, hoping to set up an appointment with General Marshall. When this tactic failed, he solicited the help of the resourceful C. D. Jackson, who had served with General Eisenhower. Like Belair, Jackson could do nothing for Luce. Harry again wrote to Marshall, laying out the whole painful history of his travel ban. Marshall's office turned the matter over to General Surles, who called presidential aide James Barnes. Surles asked if the President had changed his mind. Barnes went to see Roosevelt, who commented that he would "probably" permit Luce to make his trip to the Pacific theater. Barnes informed Luce, implying that the President wanted Harry to request the change in policy. General Surles then called the publisher on Friday, May 12, suggesting that Harry schedule an appointment to see the President. Luce indicated that he would follow Surles' advice, but the saga now took a bizarre turn.

Harry Luce duly called the White House, which told him "that there was no use coming to see the President if it was on this subject [of the trip]." Otherwise, as "Pa" Watson told Luce on June 2, he was welcome. Luce, sensing some "funny business," then contacted Surles, hoping that Marshall would answer his letter of April 28. Then, armed with the Chief of Staff's approval, he could move to lift the ban. An annoyed General Surles believed that Luce was merely building a record of this sordid affair, but he did contact Marshall.

After a delay of more than a month, the Chief of Staff, using words supplied by General Surles, wrote a cool note to Luce, reaffirming existing policy. On this same June 7, 1944, FDR talked about seeing Henry Luce in "a week or ten days." The President wanted to discuss a *March of Time* newsreel on the postwar economy, but Roosevelt did not intend to argue about Luce's trip to the Pacific. Harry was furious, but being ever restless, he decided to revisit Britain before the beginning of the fall campaign. He still did not realize that Roosevelt saw him only when he needed something from Time Inc.

Anxious to go to Britain, Henry Luce now faced some strange difficulty when trying to revalidate his passport. John Billings, after speaking to Allen Grover, darkly suggested that "it is being held up at the

White House!" Billings described this Administration as "Government by personal whim!" a charge that contained a good deal of truth. FDR was, Billings added, a "tough bastard." In making inquiries about Luce's elusive passport, Felix Belair contacted the State Department, which tried to fob him off. State told Belair on August 30 that "another Government agency" was checking Luce's application. Belair, however, had learned the identity of that "agency" from veteran *Time* source Ed Stettinius. The White House was again the culprit, for Roosevelt had personally prevented the issuance of Luce's passport. Alarmed, Felix Belair quickly called Steve Early's press office, reminding his contact that other publishers had indeed gone overseas.

Roosevelt finally relented, and Steve Early decided that Luce could make his visit to Britain. On August 31, 1944, Luce obtained his passport, though the ban on his travel to the Pacific and China remained in force.

Before his departure, Harry Luce met with Willkie at the University Club. While Willkie was wavering in his support for Dewey, he promised not to decide about the endorsement before Harry returned from England. On September 1 Luce left on his overseas voyage, seemingly unaware of Willkie's precarious health. Upon his return to New York, Luce learned that Willkie had suffered an apparent heart attack while rushing through Grand Central Station. He had checked into the Lenox Hill Hospital, where he underwent a thorough checkup. Doctors discovered a bad case of colitis and exhaustion, and insisted that he remain in the hospital for a protracted period of rest, without seeing visitors.

On October 2 the ailing Willkie contacted an anxious Harry Luce. The invalid indicated that he hoped to see Luce in the near future. Luce and Willkie exchanged some notes, but Harry respected the wishes of his friend's doctors. Meanwhile, political circles buzzed with speculation about the phantom Willkie endorsement. With or without Willkie, Luce forced himself to muster some enthusiasm for Thomas Dewey. "Yes," wrote *Life*, "it is time for a change; Dewey deserves the independent vote." President Dewey, *Life* argued, would not be stymied by conservatives in Congress; isolationism was dead, and Dewey would preserve the essential reforms of the New Deal. At no point did *Life* praise Dewey for his ideas, vision, or foreign policy expertise, because he seemed to lack all three.

Wendell Willkie died on October 8, 1944, before anyone knew for sure what he would do. His friend's death saddened Harry, who undertook to raise money for the Wendell Willkie Memorial Fund. The

October 16 issue of *Time* bade farewell to Willkie in a special section entitled "Heroes." In tribute to Willkie, *Time* also reprinted his famous "We the People" essay.

Harry Luce told anyone who would listen that Willkie had intended to cast his ballot for Thomas E. Dewey, but the widely syndicated columnist Drew Pearson claimed the opposite. And in this kind of draw, only Franklin Roosevelt won. Mitch Davenport particularly angered Luce, when he said that Willkie would have voted for Roosevelt. Despite Harry's impassioned pleas, Davenport, the aristocratic editor who had helped to create the Willkie phenomenon, deserted to FDR. Even worse, Davenport helped to form a group called Independent Republicans for Roosevelt and delivered speeches on its behalf.

Though Allen Grover had long been "more of a democrat than a republican," Luce was hurt when he, too, announced his intention of again voting for the President. As Grover had explained to Billings months earlier, ". . . I do not think that the President is a son-of-a-bitch—nor that the republic is in danger because of the New Deal." More bad news arrived. Walter Lippmann endorsed FDR, as did Senator Joseph Ball, Republican of Minnesota. Harry Luce, who had helped to lead the Republican Party away from its prewar isolationism, could only feel bitter about these defections.

As in the case of China, blind hope and faith were Harry Luce's constant guides. As late as October 25, he believed against all contrary evidence that, in Clare's words, ". . . Dewey is definitely going to win this election." Once again, however, Roosevelt easily won. The Luces did enjoy one sweet moment, however. Clare trailed in her congressional race for much of the evening of November 7, and Roosevelt carelessly remarked that her defeat was a good thing for the country. More returns came in, however, and Clare Luce won reelection. Her defeated opponent, Margaret E. Connors, wrote to FDR, regretting that she "did not get rid of one thorn" in Roosevelt's flesh.

Now, as in 1940, the victorious Roosevelt struck back at Luce. Once again a petty incident recorded by *Time* sparked the President's rage. When casting his ballot in Hyde Park, FDR had allegedly cursed a malfunctioning voting machine. *Time* picked up the story and printed it. Certain clergymen, upset by FDR's blasphemous expletive, complained to the White House. Roosevelt replied that "In view of the falsity of the story, I do not think it is necessary to pay any more attention to it."

The Revolt Against
Whittaker Chambers

For several hours on January 27, 1944, senior Time Inc. personnel, assembled in a "Round Table on Russia," and discussed America's postwar relationship with the Soviet Union.

Raymond Buell, Harry Luce's foreign policy adviser, argued that it was better to stop aggression early than to wait until a general war was the only option left. Buell was anticipating, even cheering on the formation of two antagonistic blocs, anti-Soviet and Soviet. This prospect troubled two senior editors, Jack Jessup and John Osborne, who favored some kind of tripartite agreement between Britain, the U.S., and Russia. *Fortune*'s Kurt Bloch also refused to lend credence to rumors imputing imperialist aims to the Soviet government. True, the Russians would covet the Baltic states, but not Istanbul or ports on the Persian Gulf. Charles Stillman was not so sure, for in his view, Stalin's policy represented a new form of Czarist imperialism. By contrast, most of *Time*'s foreign correspondents held that the postwar Soviet Union could, if treated properly, become a more open society.

After dinner Harry Luce joined the Round Table. He felt that a general settlement of European security questions must occur before one could address specific issues. He also decided that the Soviets would have to accept Western-style plebiscites in countries that they occupied. This process, in Luce's view, must prevail even in territories now controlled by enemy states. Cutting to the heart of the matter, Luce then suggested the following approach to the Russian question: if the Soviets annexed or bullied their neighbors, the West would have to isolate Russia, denying her any assistance after the war.

Harry Luce was thrashing about, much as he had done back in 1938, when he wrestled with the German challenge. Having read Buell's academic memoranda, Henry Luce concluded that Russia had always been a militaristic state. Stalin, in his view, had no intention of creating a peace-loving society devoted to the production of consumer goods. Luce was right, of course, but his comments that night discomforted many of his colleagues. Kurt Bloch, for one, worried about growing American fears of Russia. With subtle irony, he noted that before both world wars, people had talked about the Russian menace, only to find themselves fighting for their lives against German aggressors.

During these same months, Harry Luce drew closer to his "back of the book" man, a soft-spoken intellectual named Whittaker Chambers. In appearance, Chambers was an unlikely celebrity, with pudgy cheeks and bad teeth. This rumpled ex-Communist had joined Time Inc. back in 1939, after surviving some very trying times. As a young man, he felt ill at ease, unattractive, and out of step with his contemporaries. Tormented by his homosexual tendencies and troubled family history, Chambers early on condemned contemporary society as unjust and doomed. He then turned to Marxism for salvation. The coming victory of socialism and the creation of a new Socialist humanity inspired Chambers.

Whittaker Chambers wrote for various Communist publications, where his intelligence and knowledge helped the movement. A trusted fixture in Communist Party circles, he later received stolen microfilms of government documents and passed them on to Soviet spies. By the late 1930s, however, he had tired of the duplicity, secrecy, and treachery. By his account, he experienced a religious transformation and by 1938 had turned from Marx to Christ. Chambers became a kind of Manichaean, fighting the Lord's battle against the forces of darkness.

After leaving the party, Chambers feared for his life and for the safety of his family. In public he was ever on guard as he looked about for signs of treachery. Chambers sometimes took convoluted paths to his destinations, ducking in and out of subways so as to evade suspected Red agents. In restaurants, he always tried to sit in a corner, with his back to a wall. His fears, which were the products of a troubled personality and a conspiratorial past, took their psychic toll.

Through friends, Whit Chambers found his way to *Time*, which hired him in April 1939. Many Time Incers, including Luce, knew he had been a Communist, but no one was aware of Whit's involvement in espionage activities. Chambers quickly made a name for himself, mainly because Tom Matthews, John Billings, and other senior editors admired his superlative writing ability. Luce often growled that "Goddam Republicans can't write," but now he had found a conservative whose literary style and passion awed him. So long as the boss supported him, Chambers was safe, even in the face of growing criticism.

Whit Chambers did not make friends easily, but once he opened up, he could be kind, informative, and witty. He showed consideration when consoling unhappy staffers, and his intellect, spiced with an unremitting hatred for communism, won him converts. Frederick Gruin, who at first disliked him, came to revere the man he called "Reverend Great Teacher." At Time Inc., Chambers played the role of the countersubversive intellectual. Living in an age when many intellectuals felt drawn to Marxism, Whittaker Chambers quickly turned the back sections of *Time* into an encyclopedia of Communist criminality. Did they not realize, asked Chambers of American intellectuals, that Lenin himself had been the "first fascist"? They did not, answered Chambers, for intellectuals were still flocking to this false religion called communism. Sometimes these same misguided men and women engaged in treason (Chambers would have known).

To Chambers, these people were worshiping an idol that symbolized "total depravity." In 1940 his Stalin was an unscrupulous killer of 5 million peasants, and his Soviet Union was a fascist and ultraimperialist state, bent on destroying the democracies. For the so-called idealists who fought Franco in Spain, Chambers expressed special loathing. These volunteers were, he spat, "salon Bolsheviki," who, "drawn like flies by the smell of blood, swarmed down on Spain in 1936." At Time Inc., as elsewhere, the Spanish Republican cause had inspired great devotion among leftists and liberals of every stripe. Chambers was making enemies.

By 1942 Whit Chambers, a prodigious worker, was writing most of the "back of the book" himself. He suffered from all kinds of stress, and had to commute between his working farm northwest of Baltimore and New York. In November he suffered a heart attack, which laid him up for several months. He never again enjoyed robust health.

By his own account, Henry Luce rarely read the "back of the book," but Chambers attracted his notice. Luce began to discuss politics and religion with this strange man, who invariably wore a creased black suit with a gray tie. Chambers impressed Harry with his sense of history, which Luce defined as the "science of knowing where we have been." Invariably, the two men wound up discussing Christianity, communism, liberalism, and the American future. Chambers took Luce to be a serious and spiritual man, albeit a naive one. He was ever grateful to Harry for having given him a chance to put his life together.

To Luce, Chambers could provide a counterforce to the many liberals and social democrats and Communists who worked at Time Inc. Communism, Chambers taught, was a nihilistic force attempting to eject God from man's soul, through every foul method devised by sick minds. Harry Luce did not accept every one of Whittaker Chambers' insights, but he made Chambers a member of the Senior Group, rendering him eligible for generous profit-sharing bonuses.

In 1941 Henry Luce had not viewed Soviet Russia as an impediment to his American Century. The current military situation, plus the coming election in the U.S.A., changed his mind. By 1944 Luce came to see that this great secular "religion," communism, might bid fair to contest Christian America in an unforeseen struggle for global supremacy. Luce, however, was still willing to listen to men like John Osborne and Jack Jessup, who hoped that the West would be able to work with the postwar Soviet Union. Yet Chambers would in the end undermine their arguments, for he convinced Harry of a great truth: Communists, manipulated by Stalinists, were at war with decent men in many countries, especially America and China.

As Harry Luce became more suspicious of liberals who reviled Chiang's government, Whit Chambers egged him on. As early as 1941, Chambers had attacked U.S. leftists for portraying Chinese Reds as "liberals." As the press grew more critical of Chiang, Luce could not fail to be impressed by Whit's arguments. Chambers, who did not even trust the FBI, believed that the Communists had already infiltrated the government and society at all levels. Luce himself feared Communist machinations within the Time Inc. unit of the Newspaper Guild, and Chambers had clearly attracted the intense hatred of the local Reds. Darkly, Chambers talked about a coming Roosevelt purge, with people like himself in the dock. Another voice reinforced Chambers' message. Luce now listened carefully to editor Willi Schlamm, an Austrian refugee and ex-Communist turned anti-Communist. Schlamm, who told Luce all about the conspiratorial, ruthless tactics of his former comrades, wanted to create a magazine that would wean liberals away from the

Soviet Union. Luce did not commit himself, but did suggest that
Schlamm pursue his idea.

Harry Luce's growing mistrust of the Soviets shocked *Fortune*'s Kurt
Bloch. *Time*, after all, had been pretty evenhanded in its coverage, and
Life had sometimes glorified Russia's struggle. During their long hours
of discussion at the Waldorf, many of Harry's colleagues shared Bloch's
apprehension. Undeterred, Luce argued that people feared "communism" for the same reason they mistrusted Roosevelt's social programs.
New Dealers, Luce believed, were enthusiastic about social reform
but ambiguous about capitalism. So to Luce it was logical that the
Communists were supporting FDR for a fourth term. Luce also brought
up the subject of Soviet espionage in the U.S.A. Jack Jessup countered
this point by noting that British Intelligence operated here, too, an
interjection that did nothing to mollify his boss.

Allen Grover, an inveterate Roosevelt fan, protested against Luce's
Red-baiting attacks on the New Deal. So did John Osborne. Luce then
suggested that an aggressive foreign policy provided the U.S. with the
best answer to the Soviets and their friends. Once Americans felt secure,
he added, they would not fear Russia. Luce again suggested that if
Russia wanted to join his proposed Atlantic and Pacific regional blocs,
she would do so on Western, i.e., American, terms.

Back in 1941, Harry Luce had not imagined that his American Century would encompass a large and permanent military establishment.
Now, faced with the Soviet challenge, he adjusted his ideas to suit the
perceived postwar threat.

By the spring of 1944, Henry Luce saw a chance to use the Communist issue against the Democrats. Many American Catholics, Willi
Schlamm observed, favored the New Deal but were vehemently anti-
Communist. If the GOP rejected reactionary social policies, the Republicans could appeal to Catholics on the basis of their anticommunism.
This argument impressed Luce, as did Clare's strident and unfashion-
ably premature anticommunism. A Republican political appeal to alienated "ethnic" Catholics would indeed yield high dividends to the GOP,
but not until 1952.

For more than two and a half years, Time Inc. had been receiving
numerous cables from Moscow—moving, graphic accounts of a suffering but brave people. The Russians, Richard Lauterbach assured New
York, merely wanted to see friendly governments to the west. The
Poles, by rejecting the Curzon Line marking the Russo-Polish border,
had shown themselves to be the tools of a "semi-fascist clique in Lon-

don." John Osborne, who read many of these cables while editing
Foreign News, was not unsympathetic to Lauterbach. He was, however, subject to the influence of Harry Luce, Ray Buell, and their grim
Waldorf conferences. So Lauterbach became irritated, as *Time* increasingly expressed sympathy for the anti-Soviet London Poles. The Russians, who closely monitored the Luce press, grew alarmed, then angry.

In Moscow, Dick Lauterbach found that he could no longer get good
photographs from his Soviet contacts or obtain permission to visit the
front. Important military and political personalities were too busy to
see him. When the Soviets thought they could use him, however, they
involved him in their machinations. In early 1944 Lauterbach and other
foreign correspondents visited the infamous Katyn Forest, where Polish
officers had been mysteriously butchered in 1940 or 1941. Lauterbach,
as the Russians had hoped, convinced himself that the Nazis had murdered the Poles, probably in the summer of 1941. He duly cabled New
York with "proof" of German perfidy, concluding that "If the shoe
fits the Nazis then let them wear it."

Two weeks later, *Time* cautiously vented its doubts about the Soviet/
Lauterbach version of the Katyn Forest story. After the piece appeared,
an unnamed *Time* correspondent received a query from Soviet Ambassador Andrei Gromyko: "Who makes the policy on Russia for TIME
Inc. magazines?" Policy, claimed Luce spokesman Eric Hodgins, did
not come down from above. *Time*'s approach to an issue was subject
to modification if dissenting writers or editors could convince superiors
of their wisdom and their accuracy. Actually, Luce—harried, impatient,
and preoccupied—was less accessible than ever. And he was groping
for a new foreign policy.

Harry Luce, having put up with Laird Goldsborough's cynical indifference to fascism for far too long, now decided to launch a preemptive
strike at communism. When John Osborne departed for Rome on assignment, Whittaker Chambers took his place. For fifteen years, in
Chambers' melodramatic phrase, he had been waiting for the opportunity. He could now carry his crusade to Foreign News where, he
believed, Wertenbaker, Osborne, and other perceived fellow travelers
were dishing out watered down bolshevism to their many readers. Since
Chambers was a compelling writer, Tom Matthews raised no objection
to his promotion.

Happily established in his new office, Chambers literally remade
Foreign News, sometimes out of whole cloth. When men in the field
protested, Chambers darkly ascribed treacherous motives to them. Nor

would he compromise. Many correspondents believed that social reform and Socialist governments offered Europe its best hope for the
future. Nonsense, replied Chambers; these movements were chaotic
preludes to Communist takeovers. Sometimes Chambers went too far,
and *Time* would apologize to an irate reader.

Chambers' enemies soon included Charles Wertenbaker, Walter
Graebner, Richard Lauterbach, and to a lesser extent, John Osborne.
Time Inc. had just opened a permanent Moscow bureau, where correspondent John Hersey feared that *Time*'s growing anti-Sovietism could
block his access to vital sources. Hersey viewed Chambers as a skilled
writer whose effusions were the products of a charlatan's warped mind.
Yet even if Chambers were paranoid, the fact remains that leftists and
Communists hated him. Some researchers refused to check for him.
When Chambers needed news clippings about the Communists or Russia, they mysteriously disappeared from the morgue. Other staffers
stole his notes or committed similar acts of mischief. But Chambers
attracted devoted followers, too.

Whittaker Chambers annoyed correspondents and co-workers by
pushing their deadline back to Friday night. Then, copy in hand, he
turned his office into a kind of cell. For the next two days, behind a
locked door, he wrote and rewrote. Assisted by Marjory Smith or
another loyal researcher, Chambers worked day and night, pausing to
gulp down endless cups of black coffee. In a marathon relieved only
by the occasional nap, Chambers would finish his copy. On Monday
morning, colleagues coming to the office might run into Chambers,
who was shaving or washing himself after forty-eight hours in his
office. His words, Tom Matthews observed, sparkled, and John Billings
concluded that "Whit puts on the best show in words of any writer
we've ever had."

Chambers soon tripled the size of Foreign News and converted it to
the cause of unambiguous anticommunism. The stress, however, further worsened his precarious health. A heavy smoker, he also remained
overweight and paid no attention to proper nutrition. The all-night
writing sessions took their toll, but Chambers refused to lessen his load.
He intended to leave his mark on the postwar world.

Much of *Time*'s attention now shifted from the battlefields of Western
Europe to countries liberated by the Red Army. In August and September 1944, the Polish Home Army launched a revolt against the Nazis.
To the east of Warsaw, the Red Army stood by as the Germans brutally
suppressed the uprising. In the Balkans, the Communists worked their
will without much regard for the wishes of Western representatives.
All these examples of Communist perfidy were grist for Chambers'

mill. In other situations, however, the lines were less clearly drawn, so Chambers arbitrarily adjusted them. From France, Charles Wertenbaker reported that local governments, even Communist-led ones, functioned well. Chambers and *Time* proceeded to describe the same towns as places where chaos reigned and Red rioters ran amok. Cables from occupied Greece called the Communist-led National Liberation Front a popular force that offered a democratic program to the Greek people. The National Liberation Front was, replied Chambers, a tool of "diehard leftists."

Walter Lippmann was also worrying about an expansionist, totalitarian Soviet Union. He warned that the world could not exist "half democratic and half totalitarian." At *Life*, Jack Jessup and Dan Longwell were not ready for this approach, and Luce told Lippmann that his brief work was "too anti-Russian." Privately, diplomat George Kennan spoke even more bluntly than did pundit Lippmann, noting that the Soviets were running things as they pleased in countries "liberated" by the Red Army. After returning to the Moscow embassy late in 1944, Kennan became convinced that the Soviets, like the Russian czars before them, wanted to create a large sphere of influence "in certain areas of Europe. . . ." Unless confronted by Western firmness, the Soviets, Kennan predicted, would march to the Atlantic. The concerns expressed by realists like Lippmann and Kennan showed Luce that Chambers might not be as far removed from reality as his critics alleged. Soon, *Life* published a controversial article that made Lippmann seem moderate by comparison.

Henry Luce greatly admired William C. Bullitt, the erstwhile Ambassador to France. Bullitt was bright, self-assured, and long a premature anti-Communist. Luce himself was intimately involved in the production of Bullitt's article, which *Life* called "The World from Rome." Bill Bullitt claimed that clever Romans, including Pope Pius XII, had graced him with their sophisticated insights into the coming world disorder. He sketched out an apocalyptic scenario in which Soviet barbarians, working through puppets in each country, made a bid for global hegemony. Bullitt's melodramatic article displayed his flair for both foresight and exaggeration. In his script, the Communists took over every Eastern European country, from Finland and Poland in the north to Czechoslovakia in the west and Bulgaria in the south. Bullitt hoped that the West would respond by establishing a European association. Such a move might prevent war; otherwise the conflagration would come in fifteen years. Harry Luce referred to the article as prophetic and courageous, and in fact, Bullitt's shocking article was one of the opening salvos in what in 1947 came to be called the Cold War.

John Hersey cabled New York, enclosing *Pravda*'s response to Bullitt's article. In good Stalinist prose, the Communist Party newspaper attacked Bullitt as a spy, pro-Nazi, liar, and cheat. Though they were more temperate in tone, most of *Time*'s foreign correspondents were also angered by the Bullitt piece. John Osborne cabled home, charging that it was a "travesty" and a "disgrace. Letters to the editor were overwhelmingly negative in their response to Bullitt. Most attacked the former diplomat for endangering the antifascist alliance. For three years, Americans had heard about the heroic Soviet ally, and most Americans believed that the U.S. could work with its partner after the war. Now, Bullitt told them to prepare for a possible war with Russia.

John Billings also thought highly of the Bullitt essay. The editorial director, who had once opposed using *Life* as a political force, was now proud of the magazine's potency. The *New York Daily News* and the Hearst press loved Bullitt, too, but Mac Ingersoll's ultraliberal *PM* launched heavy counterattacks. The academic Max Lerner, an influential columnist for *PM*, attacked Bullitt as a warmonger, compared him to Joseph Goebbels, and labeled him "psychotic." Bullitt was, Lerner decided, a man with a "trivial mind and tortured personality." Moving on to Henry Luce, Lerner made some shrewd observations. Luce, he noted, had not been a labor-baiter, and had been fair-minded in his treatment of both de Gaulle and Tito. And *Fortune*, Lerner admitted, had "followed a policy of mild business liberalism." Something, however, was changing, for in Max Lerner's opinion, Luce was clamping down on free debate at Time Inc. Lerner feared Luce's growing power and questioned his commitment to American pluralism.

Max Lerner was not merely speaking for himself. The apparent change in Harry Luce frightened the influential members of the National Council of American-Soviet Friendship, among them conductor Leopold Stokowski, Mayor Fiorello H. La Guardia, and Interior Secretary Harold Ickes. On October 14 the council sent an open letter to Henry Luce, in which it reviled *Life* for making anti-Soviet propaganda. Fearing Luce's "powerful and influential" press, the signatories, including Albert Einstein, appealed to him in vain in the name of Allied solidarity.

No one resented the Luce/Bullitt axis more than John Hersey. Since he had left Yale almost a decade before, Hersey had labored loyally for Luce. He had discovered Teddy White in China, ably helped to edit Foreign News, and served bravely and well as a war correspondent in the South Pacific theater and in Italy. His books about the fighting on Bataan and Guadalcanal won Hersey a large readership. From Italy,

Hersey had cabled home stories about the GIs as they liberated towns and fought their way northward against entrenched German defenders. There, he conceived the idea for a novel to be called *A Bell for Adano*. Published by Knopf in 1944, this moving story recounted an episode in the life of an Italian village. Liberated from the Fascists, the people turned to the Americans for help finding a replacement for their expropriated church bell. A happy, funny, and moving tale, *A Bell for Adano* became a best-seller, earned a Pulitzer Prize, and changed John Hersey's life. He wanted to write, not for *Time*, but for his own public. Luce, however, had other ideas, for he still saw John Hersey as the future managing editor of *Time*.

John Hersey's sale of his work to outside publishers bothered Luce. Harry was acting like a jealous father, proud of Hersey's success but afraid of losing him. Clare did not help matters any, either. She assembled the books written by Time Inc. employees, and had them bound in richly embossed leather covers. On the binding of each volume were "inscribed" the words "Written on *Time*'s time." Presented to the authors, one can only note that Clare had once again packaged nasty words in beautiful trappings.

From Harry Luce's viewpoint, Moscow was to be a way station on John Hersey's road to a top-floor office at Time Inc. Hersey, however, disliked company politics and despised Whittaker Chambers. Though not a doctrinaire leftist, much less a Communist, John Hersey was sympathetic to the Russian people. He also believed that Americans could not "impose a democracy which is not quite a democracy upon the rest of the world." In carefully crafted cables, Hersey dispatched his rich material to New York, where Whittaker Chambers angrily rejected most of it.

John Hersey bore a double burden: he had to submit to Soviet censors, then undergo surgery at the hands of Foreign News. By this autumn of 1944, he watched with horror as *Time* either ignored or butchered his cables. Hersey, however, was no less principled than Chambers, and he remained committed to his viewpoint. Months later, Hersey still insisted that the Russians believed in their government; their writers wrote without anyone standing over them, gun in hand. Having seen miserable poverty in China and mass bloodletting in the Pacific and Italy, Hersey wanted to believe that Soviet society might offer an alternative to human failure. He was idealistic and in some ways naive, but to Chambers he was a dupe of Soviet propaganda. The short fat editor was on a collision course with the tall young correspondent. By hiring brilliant, strong-minded writers, whether of the left like Hersey or the right like Chambers, Luce was inviting a battle. Yet in this case the outcome was predictable. Henry Luce felt that Whittaker Chambers understood one big truth; the correspondents were haggling about this or that detail.

Luce wanted to bring John Hersey home, where he could serve as a senior editor. The prodigal son refused to return to New York on Luce's terms, and Hersey bluntly informed Luce of his political disagreements with *Time*. Unfortunately for Luce's peace of mind, the grumbling about Chambers was growing louder, and Harry Luce might have to confront all the charges of bias. Around Time Inc., Chambers was quoted as having supposedly said "Truth doesn't matter" when dismissing allegations of factual inaccuracy in his work.

In November, Chambers provoked another battle royal. *Time* correspondent Dick Lauterbach, who had returned to New York from Russia, was preparing to publish a book about his Soviet experience. He wanted to tell his story without interference from Whit Chambers, whom he denounced as a liar. Lauterbach, however, did agree to show the manuscript to the editorial people on the thirty-first floor. In his view the Kremlin wanted peace, cooperation with America, and all manner of good things for humanity. Lauterbach demanded that the U.S. display more faith in Russian goodwill. Unabashedly sympathetic to the Soviets, "The World from Moscow" in due course landed on the desk of Allen Grover. Lauterbach was two years out of date, for by 1945 Luce and *Time* wanted no part of his vision. *Time*'s Soviet Union was still heroic; it was just no longer virtuous.

Allen Grover pointedly observed that Dick Lauterbach's line contradicted Time Inc.'s current policy and suggested that the author change a particularly offensive chapter. Lauterbach refused, whereupon Grover warned him of serious consequences. Luce liked some of Lauterbach's reporting, but he was becoming impatient with Time Incers who published books or articles or gave speeches that contradicted policies propounded by *Time*. A few months later, Harry Luce told Allen Grover that if Lauterbach held such a low view of *Time*, then those concerned should discuss his future.

The great battle over Whittaker Chambers and the Soviets raged on the Balkan front, too. Earlier than most American publications, *Time* and *Life* understood the importance of Yugoslavia's Marshal Josip Broz Tito and his Communist partisan movement. *Time* now stationed two correspondents, John Phillips and Troyan Pribichevich, in Belgrade. Pribichevich cabled New York, indicating that General Draža Mihailovich's anti-Communist Serb Chetniks had sometimes collaborated with the Nazis. From London, Walter Graebner cabled New York, reporting that Tito intended to act independently of both Britain and

Russia. By the autumn of 1944, however, *Time* was growing suspicious of Tito. Foreign News now implied that Moscow was trying to shove aside the Chetniks so that Tito's Communists could take over all of Yugoslavia. Chambers then convened a meeting during which he accused Pribichevich of being a Communist. Luce refused to fire "Prib," but *Time* continued to offer readers Chambers' version of Yugoslav developments.

Whit Chambers foresaw the collapse of the wartime alliance. In his view, the West needed to gird itself for a generation-long struggle. If it did not do so, he claimed, the Reds would one day celebrate "other, global anniversaries." Chambers blamed the Americans for failing to intervene while Stalin worked his will in Eastern Europe. Luce was now unwilling to make more concessions to the Soviets. And when the new Secretary of State, old *Time*-friend Edward R. Stettinius, spoke of "non-interference" in foreign countries, Luce denounced this as "despicable stuff." He wrote Stettinius off as a bureaucrat, in over his head, and feared that American inaction was weakening Europe's democrats. As a result, Luce predicted, the Soviets would take over.

From London, Walter Graebner tried to warn Harry Luce against undue hysteria. "I think you'd find," he told his boss, "that most of your foreign correspondents agree with me." Back home, Kurt Bloch, no leftist, alerted editor T. S. Matthews to inaccuracies disfiguring *Time*'s Foreign News. *Time*, for example, completely distorted an article that had appeared in *The Economist*. The newsmagazine made it seem as if the British publication favored a hard-line policy toward the Soviets, when this was not the case. Such veteran editors as Manfred Gottfried and Tom Matthews expressed concern that *Time* might turn into a propaganda sheet. Though Matthews admired Chambers as a writer, he was not willing to sacrifice *Time*'s reputation on the altar of antibolshevism.

Reluctantly, Harry Luce agreed to authorize a dispassionate review of all the complaints filed against Chambers. John Billings, ably assisted by researcher Connie Burwell, would retrieve relevant cables received since August 1. Burwell would then compare *Time*'s Foreign News to the original dispatches and make a note of what Chambers had used or discarded. She would also list cases in which *Time* changed the spirit of a report while citing isolated facts culled from it. Apprised of the Billings survey, the anti-Chambers correspondents weighed in with a barrage of letters. They attacked Chambers' gruesome descriptions of Russia, which invariably contained stock phrases like "swoop of the paw" and "honey for the bear." Chambers' enemies even claimed that Goebbels' Nazi newspaper, *Das Reich*, had parroted *Time*'s Foreign News. Dick

Lauterbach accused Foreign News of distorting his account of Russia's coming involvement in the war against Japan. Walter Graebner warned that *Time* was turning Americans against Russia while Britain worked to cooperate with her. Allen Grover coldly replied that Luce wanted things this way, and that was that.

An exasperated John Hersey, meanwhile, went on strike, announcing that he would no longer write for Whittaker Chambers' Foreign News. News bureau chief David Hulburd warned Hersey that unless he changed his mind, he would have to forward his defiant cable to Luce and Matthews. The threat was clear, and Hersey backed off. He informed Hulburd that out of loyalty to him and to Matthews, he would indeed file copy for Foreign News. At the same time, Hersey made his case to Billings, accusing Foreign News of gross unfairness. Though he continued to file his cables, Hersey now avoided political commentary. Mostly, he described Moscow's cultural life, such as the premiere of Dmitri Shostakovich's new symphony.

After reviewing Connie Burwell's notes, John Billings concluded that Chambers had often failed to use material supplied by the correspondents. As Burwell observed, John Hersey's "political guidance in many instances has not been followed." Sometimes, Billings argued, the adversaries were quibbling about the use of a word or a phrase, but more fundamental beliefs were at stake. *Time*'s reporters, Billings observed, thought that the Soviets were peace-loving; Chambers believed otherwise. Pointing to Soviet behavior in liberated Poland, the editorial director decided that Chambers was right. He had made up his mind before receiving Burwell's report.

The correspondents' timing hurt them, for Henry Luce feared the Communist shadow now looming over Eastern Europe and Germany. The hated Roosevelt had won yet another term in office, and Luce was in no mood for another leftist assault, however virtuous its paladins might be. Privately, Harry Luce conveyed his admiration to the triumphant Whittaker Chambers, who was writing "by far the best reading in the issue."

Harry Luce formally replied to Billings in early January 1945. While he praised both Chambers and the correspondents, he sided with Foreign News. Luce did admit that FN was too quick to brand every local disturbance as Red-inspired, but Harry was unyielding on the major issue. In the past, Luce concluded, people had paid too little attention to Russia. And thanks to the widespread hunger for peace, the Soviets were able to manipulate public opinion. Russia, Luce had decided, was overrunning Eastern Europe while radical forces worldwide were launching a "leftist attack on the Chinese government."

Chiang, Mao,
and *Time* at a Crossroad

By the late summer of 1944, American officials were exploring new approaches to the China problem. The "Dixie Mission," or Army Observer Group, consisting of Army and diplomatic personnel, was fully operative at the end of September. Foreign Service officer John Paton Davies, Jr., returned from Communist Yenan convinced that "The future of China is theirs rather than Chiang Kai-shek's." He also believed that the overthrow of Chiang might result in a democratic China, which could wage a more effective war. On September 28 the Office of Strategic Services estimated that the Chinese Communists fielded an army of almost a half million men, while their militias contained another 2 million fighters.

While Teddy White awaited a chance to visit the Communists in Yenan, developments at *Time* affected his future. Whittaker Chambers, the new head of Foreign News, wanted no part of the "agrarian liberal" illusion. To Chambers, a Communist was a Communist. A possible alternative to White began to emerge in the person of Frederick Gruin, a diligent writer who was prepared to follow guidelines laid down by Chambers and Harry Luce. Meanwhile, Annalee Jacoby, the talented

and politically active widow of Melville Jacoby of *Time*, joined White
in Chungking at the end of September. She shared his politics and soon
became Teddy's lover. They worked out a rough division of labor by
which Teddy would cover the war fronts, including the border regions
around Yenan. Jacoby would tend to the murky world of Chungking's
politics, where White had come to so much grief. Their relationship
made life bearable for White and Jacoby, but editorial policies adopted
in New York soon caused them much anguish. At one point Jacoby
secured a rare interview with Chiang himself. To her dismay, *Time*—
or rather Chambers—fabricated the questions and answers attributed
to Jacoby and Chiang.

In Chungking, Chiang's minions were engaged in a campaign of
harassment and intimidation. Thomas Chao, who worked for the
Chungking propaganda apparatus, circulated a scurrilous manuscript
about the foreign correspondents. Chao's awkward essay smeared men
like Harrison Forman, who had helped White cover the Honan famine,
and denigrated the reporters who hoped to visit Yenan. Calling Teddy
White an embezzler, Chao's vicious "Fifteen Years as a Reporter" provided fodder for Japanese radio propaganda. While White dismissed
the reactionary Chao as a good-for-nothing, *Time* enraged Teddy by
printing articles that hailed signs of liberalization in China. White and
Jacoby grew more disgusted with their employer, for they knew that
the military situation was disastrous. On September 28 Teddy White
told Time Inc. that China stood in danger of being bisected by the
Japanese offensives.

Three days earlier, Chiang Kai-shek had informed the White House
of his refusal to accept General Stilwell as commander of all Allied
forces in the China theater. Though willing to receive a different American officer as overall commander, Chiang "requested [Stilwell's] relief
from duty in this area." General Marshall, meanwhile, was studying a
stinging cable from Stilwell. Chiang, he concluded, had no intention
of waging war against Japan. The "Gimo" was, added Stilwell, engaged
in a racket, trying to bilk the U.S.A. for money and arms. Chiang did
not, Stilwell added, want to work with the Communists, nor did he
wish to democratize China.

On October 5 Roosevelt suggested to Chiang that Stilwell remain in
command of Chinese forces in Burma and Yunnan, and the President
refused to name another American officer as commander of Allied
forces in China. On October 11 the Generalissimo, in a bitter litany of
charges, accused Stilwell of incompetence and insubordination. This
indictment was unfair and one-sided, though Stilwell's provocative
stance had made him persona non grata. At one point the General,

speaking of Chiang, angrily told Teddy White that "this ignorant son of a bitch has never wanted to fight Japan."

Patrick Hurley nevertheless warned Roosevelt that "if you sustain Stilwell in this controversy, you will lose Chiang Kai-shek and possibly you will lose China with him." Hurley recommended that a less controversial officer replace Stilwell. Roosevelt, in poor health and involved in a reelection campaign, wearily agreed. On October 18, 1944, the President informed Chiang that he was "issuing instructions to recall General Stilwell from the theater immediately." Writing to his wife, Win, Stilwell was bitter. "The politicians are in full command," he noted, "so this kind of monkey business is to be expected." To Teddy White, Stilwell's removal was a personal blow to a man he had come to love and a catastrophe for both China and the United States. As White saw things, an unreconstructed, failed Chinese government had pushed aside one of the last obstacles to its further military deterioration. Like Luce, White failed to see Stilwell as a relic of a policy that was bound to fail: an American could not take over China's war effort, which Stilwell had almost done, and remake it in his own country's image.

Finally, *Time* bore witness to the military debacle in China. In "Disaster Unalloyed," the newsmagazine portrayed a China on the verge of collapse. The U.S. forces had just demolished a $70 million air base at Kweilin, southeast of Chungking, where Japanese troops were poised to strike. Yet, to Teddy White's growing dismay, Luce stubbornly insisted that Chiang was a hero of the Chinese resistance. Harry, White believed, was adopting absurd, self-defeating policies.

On October 21, 1944, Joseph Stilwell flew out of Chungking for the last time. Ironically, within two weeks, Stilwell-trained Chinese forces had crossed the Irrawaddy River and were on the verge of opening a major land route to China. Chiang, however, had won his battle against Stilwell, and Teddy White feared that newly confident Guomindang flunkies would prevent him from visiting Yenan. He wasted no time, and on the very next day he boarded an American courier plane and flew to remote north China. At noon on October 28, while White busied himself in the border regions, the White House announced Stilwell's removal from the China command. General Albert C. Wedemeyer, a talented staff officer, would henceforth be Chiang's deputy, in charge of U.S. forces in the China theater. Though he was bitter about Stilwell's fate, Teddy White decided that the U.S. had replaced "one of her best-beloved soldiers [Stilwell] with a fresh crackerjack team."

The Stilwell removal had attracted worldwide attention, and Chiang's many enemies, from Tokyo to New York, were having a field day. It was now easy for Chungking's critics to portray Chiang as a moody, unreliable loser who had broken his one link to military reality. Brooks Atkinson, of the *New York Times*, had generously smuggled Teddy White's colorful, uncensored account out of China and delivered it to *Time*. Chinese officials were watching American public opinion with great alarm, and the last thing they needed—or expected—was an attack by *Time*.

On the other side of the world, an exultant Teddy White found Yenan a "remote, inaccessible, awe inspiring. . . ." spectacle. White noticed that people there seemed more energetic and younger than their counterparts elsewhere. He enjoyed easy access to his hosts, and he talked, drank, ate, and sang with them. White portrayed these men as products of the Chinese revolution of the 1920s. They had suffered together during a brutal civil war, but since the "epic grandeur" of their Long March, Mao Tse-tung's hardened revolutionaries had become highly energized "pragmatists." Teddy saw the comradeship that inspired Chu Teh, Chou En-lai, and Mao and other veterans of the Long March. White described Mao himself as a kind of teacher who spoke in a homely, conversational style, laced with occasional histrionics. White also sensed that he had encamped in the middle of a "field headquarters," whose troops would one day break camp and march on to new conquests.

Before the Long March to Yenan, White concluded, Chinese nationalism had touched the cities and a few adjacent areas, while the peasants continued to live their traditional lives. Then the Communists came to the border regions, where they reorganized rural society along more just and democratic lines. The Communist Eight Route Army, White decided, enjoyed overwhelming support in the countryside. Marrying social justice to anti-Japanese nationalism, Teddy White's Reds had forged a dynamic social force. They had thereby proven that modern Chinese could be actors in history, not merely victims of it. After seeing so much corruption in Chungking, White happily saluted the Communists' "ostentatious display of fiscal honesty," which "comes as a shocking and welcome surprise. . . ." These men were, said White, humane visionaries. He was convinced that the Communists, after their victory, would accept the will of the people.

Teddy White believed in the "social control of production," but he was no Communist. He supported civil liberties and hated dictatorship. On the other hand, he was too quick to forgive or brush aside tendencies whose implications he did not understand. Teddy admitted that he did not know the extent of Yenan's dependence on Soviet Russia, but he was willing to give Mao the benefit of the doubt. Though repelled by the endless panegyrics to this powerful figure, White overlooked the implications of the Maoist cult. Instead of analyzing the ominous purges that disfigured Yenan, White tended to see the Communists as nationalists, reformers, and revolutionaries, above all, as Chinese. He contrasted them with the dismal leaders of modern China, and in this light, they shone. Teddy White, who had spent five years fighting Chungking's censors, feared Chiang's authoritarianism, not Yenan's "so-called" communism.

White was opposed to dogmatism and suspicious of windy theories drawn from foreign sources. To his relief, he found that these Reds did not slavishly follow foreign models. Mao Tse-tung, for example, insisted that his cadres understand Chinese society. The Communists were no Robin Hoods, White conceded, but they had, he decided, "unlocked the key to Chinese history. . . .": He described his Communist hosts as men who had created an "integrated military and political movement" unique in modern China. White saw the Communist Party as a vast communications network. Defying the lethargy and confusion of old China, Yenan's thirty to forty thousand Communist cadres had drawn town and country together. Mao's men and women could quickly contact guerrillas in the hills or underground fighters engaged in sabotage work against foreign armies. Making use of captured weapons, the Communists moved quickly in their relentless battle against Japanese troops. Peasant militias, armed with everything from pitchforks to Japanese tommy guns, harassed the invader. After jotting down lurid stories of Japanese atrocities, White told how farmers retaliated with crude mines, which they placed outside the gates of Japanese garrisons.

Though White and his friends in the Foreign Service reported what they saw and heard in Yenan, they too often overlooked the totalitarian nature of Communist rule. Most Communists, including the charming Chou, spoke to foreigners about democracy and civil liberties, expressing goodwill toward the United States. Even Colonel Barrett, of the Dixie Mission, did not fully appreciate Mao's commitment to Communist ideology. Yet, if one listened closely, a foreigner could hear the truth. John Fairbank met an outspoken Chinese Communist, who proudly declared that "I am a totalitarian." Even the beguiling Chou En-lai admitted that "we consider the Soviet Union the greatest democracy in the world." Teddy White himself recorded, but let pass uncontested, Mao's comment that in his future China, anyone could express his or her opinion—except for "enemies of the people." Mao did not further define this ominous phrase.

Teddy White cabled New York on November 10, 1944, after he had returned to Chungking from Yenan. His vivid report was a journalistic coup, but if Teddy hoped to influence *Time*'s coverage of the Stilwell dismissal, he was in for one more shock. In New York, Fred Gruin, edited by Whit Chambers and reviewed by Harry Luce, wrote copy. At his disposal were various cables, which reflected a certain ambivalence about the removal of General Stilwell. Cabling from Washington, correspondent Jim Shepley portrayed Stilwell as a blunt infantryman "plunked down smack in the middle of a bubbling mess of Asiatic intrigue. . . ." Forced to choose between Stilwell and Chiang, Harry Luce, like Roosevelt, chose the Generalissimo.

Time's cover on Stilwell, dated November 13, 1944, bemoaned the declining state of relations between China and the United States. *Time* decided that this deterioration would hurt China, but "might be catastrophic" for the U.S.A. Harry Luce was listening to Congressman Walter Judd, not to correspondents like Teddy White or Annalee Jacoby. Citing Judd, *Time* blamed Washington for placing demands on Chiang that no head of state could accept. *Time*'s Stilwell was a strong, gruff soldier, ill-suited to diplomatic pursuits.

The newsmagazine parroted the Generalissimo's proud, pathetic line, "The Americans want me to be a slave . . . [and] they treat me as if I were a thief!" In *Time*'s view, Chungking was "ruling high-handedly in order to safeguard the last vestiges of democratic principles in China." In effect, Chiang had suppressed democracy in order to save it. *Life* therefore blamed the following people for China's troubles: (1) American meddlers, (2) Americans who failed to provide China with adequate aid, (3) Americans who threatened to use Lend-Lease assistance as a form of pressure on Chiang, and (4) American journalists, some of whom were Communists or pro-Communists. To Luce, and to *Life*, China was an American problem; it was clearly ours to lose.

Soon after returning from Yenan, Teddy White read about *Time*'s Stilwell cover in an intercepted Domei (Japanese news agency) dispatch. Enemy propagandists, citing *Time*, happily described the Stilwell clash as an American attempt to overthrow Chiang. Bitterly, Teddy attacked *Time*'s Stilwell cover as "the worst bit of journalism I have ever seen in America." White badly needed to clarify his relationship with Harry Luce. In a lengthy letter to Luce, he admitted that signs of Communist intolerance frightened him. White tried to be fair. He even acknowledged that the KMT had a more powerful army than the Communists (this was questionable). White described Chiang as the symbol of Sino-American friendship and credited him with resisting Japan. Calling for a "tremendous regeneration of the spirit of politics," White looked for inspiration to China's engineers, doctors, and professional people. Sadly, Chiang did not seem willing to turn to this vast pool of talent and goodwill. Teddy concluded his conciliatory comments by graciously thanking Luce for enabling him to become the "best informed correspondent in China. . . ."

Then Teddy White took the offensive, and attacked Chiang's "inhuman fascist machine." Dismissing hopes for reform as illusory, White brutally told Luce that the future of China probably lay in the hands of Mao's Communists. An offended Harry Luce denied that he was a Guomindang supporter, but *Time* immediately struck back at those who shared Theodore White's views. The newsmagazine singled out radical journalists Edgar Snow and Agnes Smedley for special condemnation. Snow, whose revelations about Yenan had once intrigued *Life*, now found himself ridiculed as a man who converted Communist oppression into "agrarian reforms." When *Life* was assembling a portfolio of photographs for White's long-awaited article on Yenan, Agnes Smedley refused to share her pictures with the magazine. She denounced Luce's American Century as imperialist and denied that the Yenan Reds were in the least totalitarian.

Before long, Agnes Smedley rejoiced that "The regime which *Time, Life*, and *Fortune* have chosen to champion is crumbling." She had actually discussed China with Harry Luce, back in 1942. At that time, she described him as a fascinating man, but one who was infinitely gullible on the subject of China. In powerful articles published by *The Nation, PM*, and other left-of-center publications, Agnes Smedley now accused the Luce publications of lying about the situation in China. Like other concerned observers with left-wing views, she feared the growing influence of the Luce press.

At the other end of the spectrum, textile importer Alfred Kohlberg, last seen arguing before Luce's "Special Committee," was again embroiled in controversy. Like Harry Luce, he was anxious to expose left-wing disinformation about Chiang's China. Kohlberg viewed Brooks Atkinson, of the *New York Times*, with particular suspicion, but he also indicted the more liberal *New York Post* for alleged distortions. Kohlberg thereby helped to unleash a venomous debate. Though his charges against the UCR had alienated Harry Luce, Kohlberg now found an ally in Representative Clare Boothe Luce. In a speech that delighted Chiang Kai-shek, she denounced certain unnamed Americans for denying adequate aid to China. These people, Clare argued, were plotting to turn China over to the Communists. The public battle over China was turning uglier.

Teddy White owed his career to Harry Luce, but he was coming of age as a man and a journalist. Given to hero-worship, he was torn between his respect for Professor Fairbank and his affection for Harry Luce. White had finally come to see Luce as a doctrinaire apologist for Chiang Kai-shek, whom the correspondent described as "corrupt, wicked and worthless." A mutual sense of betrayal set in, as White and Luce began to talk past each other. Theodore White did not pay enough attention to Luce's skeptical analysis of the Chinese Communists. Harry, however, refused to believe that the corruption infecting the Guomindang could be ascribed to men like Chiang, Soong, and Kung. Why, Teddy White wondered, did Harry refuse to see things that were apparent to John Fairbank? In the White/Fairbank view, Luce's support for Chiang was making the Chinese leader more rigid; he stumbled ever onward, toward civil war and his own destruction. *Time*, however, remained stubbornly optimistic. His passion for China had brought Teddy White to Harry Luce's attention, but a generational conflict now exacerbated their political differences. Teddy White was not yet thirty years old; at forty-six, Luce was passing into ripe middle age. Luce liked to test younger men to see if they placed loyalty to his company ahead of their own ambitions. If correspondents sought fulfillment by following his rules, then they thrived.

Personally, White was in a bad way. Never too strong physically, he smoked too much and sometimes drank excessively. He badly needed a change of scene, perhaps a drastic one. Several years later, Teddy White's crude architectural metaphor recalled the disappointment and rage engulfing him in 1944 and 1945. "With bricks," White wrote, "you can build a temple to god, or you can make a brick shithouse. And in [Luce's] China stories he used most of the facts his correspondents sent to build a brick shithouse." Despite his affection for Harry Luce, White began to look for a way out of Luce's elegantly designed ceramic defecatorium.

Henry Luce had wrongly decided that Teddy White had taken the side of the Communists, that he wanted to overthrow Chiang. Still, he did not want to lose this superb reporter, for White's dispatches had gained new respect and a wider readership for *Time* and *Life*. White threatened to resign, however, so Harry worked out yet another compromise. He agreed that White's recent experience in Yenan merited a major piece in *Life*. After his article about Yenan appeared in *Life*, White would write about military affairs and human interest stories, Luce decreed. He could leave Chinese politics to others.

For the moment Luce wanted to mollify White, for he recognized a sensational story when he saw one. Besides, a single article in *Life* could scarcely negate the impact of *Time*'s constant barrage of anti-Communist rhetoric. Time Inc. therefore heavily promoted its December 18, 1944, issue of *Life*, which contained Teddy White's "Inside Red China." This piece offered readers a revealing glimpse of life within Mao's empire of 40 million souls. Although White's editors toned down some of his excited prose and omitted many of the details sprinkled through his cables, *Life* faithfully expressed White's belief that the Communists wanted to cooperate with the United States. In the coming weeks, though, White sourly concluded that *Life*'s article had been a sop tossed his way by a disdainful Henry Luce. Luce, however, now gave White a big raise—$2,500—and Teddy agreed to stay with *Time* until the end of the war. The truce prevailed, though *Time* continued to undercut almost everything Teddy believed about China. Ever on the prowl for good news from Chungking, *Time* foresaw "a sweeping reform of China's war production . . . ," and hoped that China would now receive more aid.

A lot of people shared the perplexity of Philip Jaffe, editor of the leftist journal *Amerasia*, especially when they read Teddy White's article in *Life*. "Certainly," Jaffe observed, "the things Time-Life has published in the past two months cannot all be true."

General Albert Wedemeyer, Stilwell's successor, quickly learned that Chiang and his government could be difficult allies. Wedemeyer observed that many generals and officials wallowed in "graft and inefficiency," which cost Chinese soldiers their lives. The General also warned that "it would be wrong for China supinely to sit back and expect us to do the fighting alone." Although Wedemeyer and his staff were working hard to reform the Chinese Army, they stumbled over roadblocks at every turn. In his most trenchant comment, Wedemeyer told General Marshall that "Self-sacrifice and patriotism are unknown quantities among the [Chinese] educated and privileged classes." The Chungking government did not see these reports. In fact, Chiang's court rejoiced in the presence of Albert Wedemeyer, who appeared to be infinitely less difficult than the prickly Stilwell.

When the Japanese advances stalled, as they did in December and

January, *Time* credited China's resistance. This misled many people, who now thought that Chiang was growing stronger, when in fact Japan was weakening. Facing an American onslaught elsewhere, Tokyo could not finish off Chiang's battered armies. *Time*, encouraged by this sign of "progress," tried to improve the image of the Chinese government. In a lavish cover story, fifty-year-old T. V. Soong emerged as "the symbol of Chinese cooperation with the West." As always, *Time*'s Chiang was attempting to solve problems that others had caused.

To *Time*, General Hurley's ascendancy in Chungking augured well for Chinese unity. Hurley, who was then Roosevelt's special representative, had flown to Yenan on November 7. Upon landing, he emitted a Choctaw war whoop, reminiscent of his Oklahoma boyhood. Ever the can-do American, Patrick Hurley persisted for two days and two nights until the Communists seemed ready to make a deal. Mao (who privately called the ebullient Hurley "the clown"; others called him "the big wind") agreed to work for unity in the war against Japan. He insisted on a coalition government, however, which would include his Communists. In addition, a reformed United National Military Council would include "representatives of all anti-Japanese armies." Mao also demanded that supplies obtained from foreign powers "be equitably distributed" to all anti-Japanese armed forces.

Hurley returned to Chungking, where Chiang quickly rejected Yenan's program. T. V. Soong, whom a disappointed Hurley blamed for Chiang's recalcitrance, scornfully dismissed the Yenan agreement. "The Communists," Soong added, "have sold you a bill of goods." More ominously, Soong warned Hurley that "Never will the National Government grant the Communist request." Instead, the government offered to incorporate the Communist forces into a reformed National Army, as equals. The National Military Council would remain supreme, though "some high ranking officers from among the Communist forces" would become members. The government would recognize the legality of the Communist Party, and guarantee civil liberties except in cases involving "the specific needs of security in the effective prosecution of the war against Japan." General Hurley, who was formally named Ambassador on November 17, 1944, seemed taken aback, but he ultimately blamed Yenan, not Chungking, for the impasse.

At home, Harry Luce was busily constructing a network dedicated to Chiang's defense. A few days after *Time*'s Stilwell cover appeared, an enthusiastic Luce hoped that Congressman Walter Judd would "write us a real big time piece on Chiang Kai-shek and embattled China." Judd shared important data on China with Luce; the two men reinforced each other's suspicion of Yenan and of U.S. foreign policy. As more liberals and leftists attacked Chiang for his alleged corruption and incompetence, Judd and Luce formed an alliance that endured for many years. Judd and Luce did not stand alone, however. John Foster Dulles, Thomas Dewey's foreign policy adviser, was also speaking out on China. Grimly alluding to the growth of Chinese communism, Dulles denounced those who would force Chiang into an unsound compromise with the Reds. Dulles asked for Luce's opinion of the speech, which borrowed heavily from the Luce/Judd litany. Harry, of course, could only rejoice that a Republican statesman, other than Clare Luce or Walter Judd, was committing himself to the troubled Chinese cause.

In Chungking, Ambassador Patrick Hurley was working to unify China so that a strengthened China could prepare for her postwar job as one of Roosevelt's "Four Policemen" of the world. The possible entry of the USSR into the Pacific war added a new sense of urgency. Patrick Hurley still wanted to believe in Stalin and Molotov, who had earlier assured him of their goodwill toward Chiang. Hurley therefore paid heed to pleasant gossip in Chungking, where insiders talked of Stalin's willingness to meet with Chiang Kai-shek. Presumably, the "so-called Communists" in Yenan, shunted aside by the Soviets, would soon be willing to make a deal with Chiang. Otherwise, Hurley feared, Chiang's regime, weakened by war and internal strife, could present the Soviets with a tempting target. Russian intervention then might involve the Soviets in a nasty confrontation with Chiang's American protectors.

Hurley wished to be helpful, but under no circumstances would he put pressure on Chiang Kai-shek. Indeed, he wanted to isolate Yenan, and that meant cracking down on liberal diplomats like Jack Service and John Paton Davies. If the Communists no longer expected American help, Hurley believed, they would be willing to deal with Chiang. John Fairbank, Teddy White's revered mentor, could not have disagreed more. Dr. Fairbank argued that the United States was backing men "who were so busily digging their own graves and trying to pull us in with them." Like his friends Service, Davies, and Fairbank, Teddy White believed that the inflexible Chiang, backed by the U.S., would drive Mao into the arms of the Soviets. White provided Jack Service and John Paton Davies with tidbits gathered in the course of his work, which they exchanged for information gleaned from diplomatic cables and embassy chitchat.

The China debate was growing nastier, both in the United States and in Chungking. In a letter to General Marshall, Wedemeyer described the "problem of handling the press" as "acute and dangerous." In the

words of David Hulburd, who received Teddy White's cables at Time
Inc., "for a long time . . . the U.S. press and U.S. correspondents were
bountiful in their praise of China, and idealized the Gissimo and those
around him to the exclusion of any objectivity." Only the leftist press,
Hulburd admitted, had subjected the Chiang regime to closer examination. Chiang's American friends feared that the American public might
now become disillusioned and, ultimately, indifferent.

Frustrated by his inability to hammer out a Yenan-Chungking compromise, Ambassador Hurley grew more suspicious of the Observer
Group ("Dixie Mission"). In January 1945 he told President Roosevelt
that General Wedemeyer's political officers had been hatching evil plots
in the General's absence. The Ambassador also charged that the guilty
Foreign Service officers favored sending American paratroopers to lead
U.S.-armed Communist guerrillas. According to Hurley, Yenan had
learned of the plan, so Mao saw no need for further negotiations with
the Chungking government. Hurley recommended that the President
solicit Soviet support for Chiang. A chastened Yenan would presumably sign an agreement acceptable to Chungking.

Patrick J. Hurley's hopes rested on illusions. Mao Tse-tung and
Chiang Kai-shek were both ruthless men. They might cut a deal if they
wielded the same amount of power, but Chiang was clearly in decline,
while Yenan was rapidly expanding. Fear of an ever weaker Japan could
no longer preserve their tenuous unity. Presiding over a growing power
base, Mao believed that his movement held the key to China's future.
He might turn command of his armies over to an American if the
Guomindang granted him enormous concessions, but Mao would never
hand his armies over to Chiang himself. Refusing to give up, Ambassador Hurley ignored the fact that the two sides had twice been allies,
only to see their partnership fail. Yenan and Chungking, Hurley concluded, both wanted democracy. In fact, neither Yenan nor Chungking
understood that Western term, but both knew how to make Hurley
momentarily happy.

In January Hurley helped to effect a change in the Army Observer
Group. Colonel Barrett, who got on well with his Chinese hosts in
Yenan, yielded to Colonel Morris De Pass, who had close ties to the
Guomindang. De Pass, following Hurley's instructions, delivered a
harsh message to the Communists. Yenan, he warned, would receive
no support from the U.S.A. until the Communists reached an
agreement with Chiang. Good news came from the south, too. The
tonnage flown to China over the Hump showed a marked increase,
from 14,472 tons in January 1944 to 46,482 tons a year later. Presumably, a stronger Chinese government, bolstered by Hurley's unswerv-

ing support, could change Yenan's attitude. The Ambassador suddenly felt encouraged: Communist negotiator Chou En-lai implied that the Communists might participate in the multiparty consultative conference proposed by the Chinese government.

Back in the United States, Harry Luce again tried to get his travel ban lifted so he could visit the Far East. In January 1945 his friend James Forrestal, now Secretary of the Navy, intervened with President Roosevelt on Luce's behalf, but to no avail. It looked as if Harry would not see China while Franklin D. Roosevelt remained President, and FDR's term would not end until noon on January 20, 1949.

1945

Toward
Confrontation with
Soviet Russia

By 1945 editor in chief Henry R. Luce was advocating a harder line toward Russia. At the same time, he was worried about alienating some of his leading correspondents. He especially wanted to salvage John Hersey. Early in the year, Harry made some superficial concessions to the dissident correspondents, whose outstanding work had greatly contributed to *Time*'s success. Editorial director John Shaw Billings assured a skeptical Charles Wertenbaker that Whittaker Chambers had agreed to show more subtlety when writing about "the specific communist politics in various countries." Allen Grover still lamented the rise of this second Goldsborough, but Chambers retained Harry's confidence and admiration.

Luce decided that a new International section, under the moderate John Osborne, would handle stories dealing with communism and other multinational issues. Whittaker Chambers, however, continued to edit Foreign News and greatly influenced other departments of *Time*. Whit was not mollified, however, for he felt that he was being undercut by evil forces that had gained Luce's ear. The Osborne compromise bought some time, but the big problem remained unresolved. Clearly,

John Hersey would not trim his political views to fit the Luce/Billings line. In fact, he seemed to show his contempt for it by sending cables calculated to annoy Chambers and Luce.

In the middle of January 1945, John Hersey described wartime Russia as confident and powerful. Her people, Hersey informed New York, believed that their system had passed a cruel test. Hersey lauded unselfish Russians, who were fervently "dedicated to the state and nation." He even sympathized with Soviets who argued that their press was "freer and truer than the United States press. . . ." In America, he noted, the press was beholden to "owners, stockholders and advertisers" (perhaps Hersey was thinking of Harry Luce when he wrote those provocative words). The Russian economy, Hersey added, would revive after this terrible war. Throughout the Hersey cable, doubts surfaced about the current state of American capitalism. The correspondent clearly felt hostile to the status quo at both Time Inc. and in the United States. Whether he was right or wrong about the Soviet system—and in this cable, Hersey was mostly wrong—this bold young man would never align himself with the Luce/Chambers axis. Graebner, Wertenbaker, and Hersey all placed their faith in varieties of democratic socialism. They felt that peace with Russia was possible in a better postwar world. *Time* had no use for this point of view. Luce's growing insistence on minimal conformity reflected his frustration with an incorrigible world. Overburdened with work and more remote from most of his writers and editors, Luce sought comfort in the ideological certainties offered by Whittaker Chambers and Willi Schlamm.

Clare Luce was now receiving instruction in Church doctrine from Father Fulton J. Sheen, who taught at the Catholic University. Harry was not displeased, though he had no intention of converting. He had, Luce once noted, long since found his own way. A dramatic figure with deep-set, penetrating eyes, Sheen greatly impressed those who knew him. He believed that the world was engaged in a spiritual war. A priest given to speaking blunt words, Sheen regularly denounced "pinks" and "fellow travelers," who "are trying to impose upon America the very scum which Russia rejected." In his powerful book *Philosophies at War*, Sheen debunked the widespread euphoria about the heroic Soviet ally. The priest's rhetoric colored Representative Luce's speeches, and advocates of friendship with Russia feared Clare Luce's impact on her husband's thinking. Soviet communism, virtually ignored by Luce in 1941, had taken center stage.

Early in 1945, a group of Congressmen formed a new House of Representatives Committee on Un-American Activities. Many liberals, and some Communists along with their "fellow travelers," were attempting to derail the new committee. A few years earlier, *Life* would doubtless have opposed its establishment, for the Luce magazines had regularly lambasted the very similar Dies Committee. In this winter of 1945, however, Henry Luce noticed that many opponents of the committee were the same people who bad-mouthed the government of China and supported the appeasement of Soviet Russia. Denouncing "New York liberals," Luce wanted to "expose" Communists and fellow travelers who cloaked themselves in the Bill of Rights. Karl Mundt of South Dakota, a ranking Republican on the committee, spotted his opening, and worked to win the support of the Luce publications. In fact, Henry Luce was well disposed toward the committee, and soon did yeoman work on its behalf. The liberal Republican Ray Baldwin, Governor of the Luces' home state of Connecticut, had doubts about the committee, but Harry, an important constituent, won him over to Mundt's side. Luce had moved to the right out of fear of Russia.

Had Harry Luce and *Life* joined the Congressman's enemies, it is quite possible that the House witch-hunters might have gone out of business. Instead, Congress set up the controversial committee, which would enjoy a long, controversial, and demagogic life.

In January 1945 Harry Luce responded with enthusiasm to a speech delivered by Senator Arthur H. Vandenberg, a Michigan Republican. A senior figure and former isolationist, "Van" skillfully blended his new internationalism with a realistic appreciation of the Russian problem. Vandenberg was unwilling to accept a Soviet *Diktat* in Eastern Europe. Luce's new hero proposed that the West challenge the Soviet Union in the following way. Since Russia talked endlessly about her need for security, the Allies should together disarm and police Germany. Vandenberg knew that this offer appealed to Americans, too. Having achieved security, Vandenberg continued, the Soviets would be expected to cease acting unilaterally in Eastern Europe. In Vandenberg's view, final territorial settlements must result from a joint Allied "postwar review."

At Time Inc., Harry Luce attended a meeting of his advisory committee on foreign policy. With his approval, the committee commissioned memoranda on Russia, one of which would come from Whittaker Chambers. A few days later, Ray Buell called for Western countermeasures aimed at blocking the further expansion of Russian despotism. Even in places like Cuba, Buell noted, Communist parties were promoting the goals of Soviet foreign policy. The more suspicious side of Harry Luce spoke through a Stalin cover story, crafted by Chambers for *Time*. Referring to the Soviet dictator as a man who had killed millions, *Time* bemoaned Western inaction in the face of this tyrant's program. Long before people spoke of an "Iron Curtain," *Time* delineated an 800-mile front that was bisecting Europe. In memorable words, *Time* concluded that a "specter was haunting Europe—the specter of World War III." Could Vandenberg's proposed policy prevent war?

Early in February 1945, a haggard and sick Franklin Roosevelt arrived in the Crimea, where he met with Churchill and Stalin. To a suspicious Harry Luce, this Yalta conference presented the wartime coalition with one last chance. For a few weeks Luce could not make up his mind. Had the conference failed or succeeded? In the middle of the month, Luce rudely exploded when Tom Matthews expressed too much enthusiasm about the outcome of the conference. Matthews, a wealthy and aristocratic man who had precious little time for Harry's bad manners, thereupon called Luce an incompetent and threatened to resign. Luce quickly regretted his outburst; he promised John Billings that he would apologize to Matthews.

A day later, hard-liner Ray Buell provided Harry Luce with a surprisingly optimistic analysis of the Yalta meetings. Luce respected Buell's judgment, and for a moment he ignored Chambers. *Life* subsequently hailed Yalta as a "success," even though Russia insisted on building a security buffer around her western borders. In Washington, *Time* correspondent Robert T. Elson had a long, off-the-record talk with powerful presidential assistant James F. Byrnes, who had attended the Yalta meetings. Byrnes was optimistic, for he looked forward to a peace conference based on what he understood of the Yalta accords. In principle, the West had accepted the Russian insistence on reparations, though the modalities remained to be worked out.

Other insiders saw things quite differently. Yalta had shocked diplomat George Kennan, an expert on Soviet Russia. He felt that the planned allied occupation of Germany, combined with Soviet demands for reparations, could lead to the Russian absorption of the entire country. After the Yalta reprieve, Time Inc. tilted away from its unwonted optimism. At *Fortune*, John Davenport, who was more conservative than his brother Russell, now advocated support for the British Empire. Luce, a staunch opponent of European imperialism, appears not to have objected. In fact, Harry seemed willing to contemplate, though not yet endorse, a future alliance between *any and all* anti-Soviet states. Again, he moved to the right out of fear of Russia.

Late in February, John Hersey, freshly returned from Russia, engaged in important talks with Harry Luce. Hersey expressed his frustration with *Time*, which he accused of harming U.S. relations with Russia.

We must, Hersey argued, "allay [Russia's] suspicions and get along with it in 'Give-and-take.' " John Hersey was particularly enthusiastic about former Vice-President Henry A. Wallace, advocate of the Century of the Common Man and a proponent of better relations with Russia. Luce scoffed at the idea of putting Wallace on the cover of *Time*, fearing that if he did so, Wallace's supporters would decide to run him for President, presumably in 1948. Relations between Hersey and Luce remained tense; more than ever, Hersey longed to leave Time Inc., perhaps when the war ended.

John Hersey and other dissident correspondents reacted with shock to a bizarre, oddly persuasive piece that appeared in *Time* on March 5, 1945. In a fable entitled "Ghosts on the Roof," *Time* offered readers a Whittaker Chambers nightmare. Luce had not approved or disapproved of its publication; he left the decision up to Tom Matthews.

At the Livadia Palace near Yalta, where the Big Three are convening, the wraiths of Czar Nicholas II and his courtiers perch on the roof. Like vultures, they loom over the diplomatic proceedings. Nicholas proudly compares Stalin to Peter the Great, then praises the dictator for extending the reach of Russian power to Eastern Europe and the Balkans. In Chambers' fable, the Czar thinks ahead to settling scores with Chiang, subverting the West, and taking over Germany. Then, with Britain and America in a state of economic collapse, the Communists would prevail there, too.

"Ghosts" was written in a heavy-handed, sarcastic style, reserving its most bitter jibes for those fools who did not realize that, among Communists, "peace may be only a tactic of struggle." Chambers declared that "Two faiths are at issue," as good struggled against a criminal conspiracy. The publication of "Ghosts" enraged John Hersey. In Moscow, he discovered that Soviet officials canceled long-planned interviews, effectively depriving him of his sources. Dan Longwell, seeing Hersey slip away from Time Inc., blamed Luce and his hard-line policies.

A lunch with the Secretary of State did nothing to allay Harry Luce's concerns about American passivity. According to Edward R. Stettinius, Roosevelt had accepted the Soviet demand for a sphere of influence in Eastern Europe. The Poles could have any government they wished, so long as it was friendly to the Soviet Union. "The President," Stettinius added, "has put all his chips on the World Organization." In fact, Stettinius had persuaded Roosevelt that the Russians would insist on the Security Council veto. Stettinius, however, was optimistic, for he believed that Russia had "definitely decided to be a 'citizen of the world.' " Harry Luce, after lunching with Stettinius, thought that his friend should resign rather than put up with what the Secretary himself called FDR's "double-talk."

Like most Americans, Harry Luce assumed that President Roosevelt would preside over the end of the war in Asia. *Time*, however, knew that there was something terribly wrong with FDR. Frank McNaughton had cabled New York on March 2, reporting that Roosevelt showed "a marked loss of weight." FDR's wrists, McNaughton added, "seemed to have lost their beefy, rugged marks of strength." The President's skin drooped in folds, while his body lacked buoyancy. FDR's voice sounded "weak," McNaughton added. Luce, however, made no reference to Roosevelt's health or to its policy implications. His magazines, as they had during the campaign, took care not to alarm the public—or encourage the enemy. *Life* did note that Roosevelt looked "gray and thin," but quickly added that the President was also "chatty and sure of himself."

A few weeks after "Ghosts" appeared, President Roosevelt joined Whittaker Chambers' Czarist wraiths. He died in Warm Springs, Georgia, on April 12, 1945. Upon learning the news from Tom Matthews, John Billings called Harry Luce, who at first refused to believe him. The next morning Luce spent several hours discussing the political implications of Roosevelt's death. *Time* paid an eloquent tribute to the man who had "brought his nation triumphantly through a great war and started it on the road to peace." *Life* captured some wonderful scenes of Americans convulsed with grief at the news of FDR's passing. Luce, however, refused to mourn, then or later. As he once put it, it was his duty to go on hating Roosevelt, who ". . . kept me, wholly without moral justification, physically isolated from the global war. . . ." Within four weeks, Italians had executed Mussolini, Hitler had committed suicide, and Germany had collapsed.

Despite *Life*'s tribute, Luce had finally concluded that FDR's final legacy, Yalta, was a disaster. Indeed, *Life* now placed little faith in Roosevelt's last hope, the United Nations. Luce worried about the "big-power veto," and feared for the fate of small nations. More bluntly than Senator Vandenberg, Luce attacked the Dumbarton Oaks agreements for failing to secure human rights, freedom, and justice. Referring at the end of April to the coming United Nations conference in San Francisco, *Life* hoped that the delegates would remedy the defects of Dumbarton Oaks. Clearly, Luce had drawn a line. On one side stood American power and the cause of justice and freedom; over the other loomed the darkening shadow of Soviet imperialism.

John Billings believed that "for our purposes [President Harry S. Truman] may prove better than Roosevelt." Late in the spring, Luce learned more about the new President, and what he read offered some encouragement. In June, after a weekend spent with Truman, *Time* correspondent Edward Lockett cabled a detailed report to Bob Elson, who forwarded it to Luce. Truman, Luce learned, did not merely succeed FDR; he seemed to be his opposite. Before embarking on a respite from his labors, Harry Truman would tell reporters, "leave that Mr. President shit in the office." In Eddie Lockett's account, Truman emerged as a salty, profane little cuss, who described de Gaulle of France as a "dumb bastard" and a "stuckup asshole." The President enjoyed two rounds of drinks after dinner, then sipped bourbon and played cards until past midnight. Meanwhile, he shared his views with Lockett and a few other favored reporters.

Truman had little use for the Poles, but his comments about the Russians sounded like a repudiation of FDR's Yalta policy. Stalin would be a strong opponent, but he, Truman, could talk tough to him and bring the Soviet leader to heel. The U.S., said Harry Truman, was the number one power, and "we're going to stay that way." Though clearly suspicious of the Soviets, Truman hoped to sign a German peace treaty, then reduce the size of the U.S. defense establishment. The latter point bothered Luce, but at least this President shared some of his suspicions of Soviet behavior—in Europe. As for China and the Far East, Luce had no idea what Truman intended to do there.

Representative Clare Luce now seized the initiative. In a series of historic radio addresses, delivered between May 31 and July 17, 1945, she fired powerful salvos in her anti-Communist crusade. Clare spoke in precise, cold words, and her message was simple: the Communists were murderers and the Russian people were slaves. Mrs. Luce predicted that the Soviets would try to conquer Germany. Clare also claimed that progressives like Archibald MacLeish were selective in denouncing aggression. They had waxed indignant in the case of Nazi Germany, but remained silent in the face of Soviet transgressions. Testing tactics that later defaced American politics, Mrs. Luce occasionally took the words of American liberals out of context and compared them to the writings of Communists. Clare Luce had crisply outlined a program for confrontation, not just with the Soviets, but with all liberals who sought to come to terms with the USSR. *Time* continued to give prominent coverage to Clare Luce ("Congresswoman *v.* Russia"), and hailed her warnings against Soviet domination of Europe. *Pravda* called Mrs. Luce a Fascist, as did some American leftists. The Hearst newspapers, which Harry Luce had always despised, praised Mrs. Luce, while Alfred Kohlberg described her as the "American Winston Churchill."

By late May 1945, Harry Luce was thinking hard about the postwar implications of the struggle for the Pacific. *Time* now warned against the danger of a Red *cordon sanitaire*, stretching from the Turkish Straits, through Iran, India, and Tibet, all the way across Sinkiang, Outer Mongolia, and Manchuria. Meanwhile, Ray Buell drafted a memorandum that summed up much of Luce's thinking. He intended to send it to his old friend, White House press secretary Charles G. Ross.

The Russians, Buell argued, had violated the Yalta agreement on Poland; they were now trying to take over Germany. Unless a new policy curbed Soviet ambitions, there would be war within "ten or fifteen years." The Buell memorandum urged that the West (1) merge its German zones into one unit: this came about early in 1947; (2) make plans for the massive rehabilitation of France and Italy: this occurred after 1947; (3) end Lend–Lease to Russia unless Stalin changed his policy: this was done between May and August 1945 (4) keep 1 million men in Europe, not the 400,000 announced by the War Department: this did not happen; (5) land U.S. forces in Korea: this occurred; (6) let the Japanese people decide the future of their Emperor, after the end of the war with Japan: this became implicit Allied policy a few months later; (7) demilitarize Japan, but do not encourage Soviet participation in Far Eastern hostilities or occupation agreements: the first took place, but the Russians did enter the war; (8) strengthen Chiang, but not the Chinese Communists: this represented American policy, though it was never implemented to Luce's satisfaction; and (9) guarantee Japanese access to markets in Southeast Asia for Japan's textiles and manufactured goods: this became one of the bases of Japan's emergence as a great economic power. Luce and Buell, looking beyond the hatreds of the day, advocated bringing Germany and Japan into a renewed world trading system based on capitalism and democracy.

John Billings was nervous about the Buell memorandum. To outsiders, Harry's suggestion might smack of disloyalty or worse. After all, while Americans stormed ashore on bloodstained beaches in the Pacific, moving ever closer to Japan's home islands, Time Inc. seemed to be thinking about a compromise with the hated enemy. Luce, after hearing Billings, apparently decided to treat Buell's memorandum as an internal document. The memorandum, however, remained available for his editorial guidance. Luce's plan for confrontation, so radical in 1945, became national policy by 1948. His publications played a substantial role in preparing the public for this fateful shift.

With Franklin Roosevelt dead, Luce could finally visit the Pacific theater of war. General Douglas MacArthur issued Luce an invitation, as did Secretary of the Navy Forrestal. Harry also received special clearance to visit the Philippines and Okinawa. He expected to leave San Francisco for Pearl Harbor on May 22, 1945, and log 30,000 miles in about thirty days. Accompanied by *Time* senior editor Roy Alexander and a public relations officer named Lieutenant James Britt, Luce spent three days at Pearl before flying to Kwajalein and Guam. Harry inspected the paved roads built on Guam, the new harbors, the gleaming warships, and the mighty bombers. *Life*, he believed, had not exaggerated when it boasted to American readers of all this hard-won glory. In Guam, Harry enjoyed another surprise as he waited to board the carrier *Yorktown*.

Luce knew that his son, Ensign Henry ("Hank") Luce III, was serving on a destroyer escort somewhere in the Pacific. After making an inquiry, Harry discovered that the *McGinty* was anchored in the harbor. Father and son were able to chat for a few short minutes before both returned to duty. Back on the *Yorktown*, Luce received an invitation to address the assembled crew. In eloquent remarks, Harry thanked the men for their dedication, high spirits, patriotism, and assistance. Many of his listeners doubtless read *Life* or a pony (local) edition of *Time*.

In letters to John Shaw Billings, Harry Luce marveled at the rapid extension of American power. Billings noted in his diary that Luce was "bursting with ideas about Pacific coverage. . . ." The frontier, Luce argued, now extended from Manila to Okinawa, "and it will never be moved back from there." Some of Luce's gaudier language may have reflected the influence of General MacArthur, with whom he spoke for four hours in Manila. "This," he wrote of American hegemony in Asia, "is the political geography for the next round of the human drama."

On June 24, 1945, Harry Luce arrived back in New York. He convened his senior editors and provided them with new leads. In a series of articles published between June and September, *Life* concluded that the United States had worked wonders in the Philippines, and as a consequence, Filipinos loved Americans. Luce saw the Philippines as the western anchor in a new strategy for the Pacific. *Life* advocated the construction of a vast naval base on Leyte Gulf, which would have access to the sea in two directions, east and west. Thanks to his friend-ship with Navy Secretary Forrestal, Luce could expect a friendly hearing in Washington.

Henry Luce came away convinced that the U.S. could quickly win the war in the Pacific. By the deft use of psychological warfare, he argued, Japan could be induced to surrender. Otherwise, he warned, the war would drag on for another year, and 20 million Japanese (*sic*) would die. Anxious to end the conflict without Russian help, Luce badly wanted to explore the possibility of an early Japanese surrender, so on July 6, 1945, Harry Luce traveled to Washington, where he met with President Truman. The President, however, thought that the publisher was merely making a courtesy call. He brusquely ended the discussion before Luce could argue his case for a quick conclusion of the war against Japan.

The war continued, and Henry Luce continued to grapple with prob-lems related to postwar reconstruction. The new United Nations char-ter, he admitted, was a pleasant surprise. Calling the document a "great improvement" over Dumbarton Oaks, Luce praised its commitment to justice under law, and to human rights. *Time* called the charter a document "written for a world of power, tempered by a little reason." Luce, however, feared the Soviet Union more than he revered the United Nations, and he wondered whether the Russians would use their veto to exclude the West from any say in Eastern Europe. By the middle of the summer, *Time* was worrying about the precipitous withdrawal of American troops from Europe. When only a small num-ber of U.S. forces remained to police Germany and Austria, *Time* warned, armed minorities might launch revolutions throughout the continent. And Britain, financially strapped and pressed for manpower, would be left alone to secure the entire Mediterranean region.

While Henry Luce fretted about Japan and Russia, the Hersey situa-tion festered. Teddy White heard that John Hersey had confronted an angry Harry Luce, telling him that *Pravda*'s international coverage was more accurate than the stories appearing in *Time*. Hersey, moreover, wanted to travel where and when he wished, and write what he felt. On July 11 Dan Longwell announced that John Hersey had resigned. Hersey, who refused to follow Luce's line on Russia, agreed to write some articles for *Life*, but from Harry's viewpoint this was a poor tradeoff. A potential managing editor of *Time* had become a free-lancer for *Life*, in an arrangement that left both parties unhappy. When an esteemed protégé placed his freedom before the interests of Time Inc., Luce felt betrayed, and he refused to address the real grievances that had led to Hersey's resignation. Absent the Russian uproar, John Hersey would have departed at some point, but perhaps not so soon, and not under these bitter circumstances.

On this same July 11, Harry Luce was back in Washington, where he trudged from office to office, meeting with a total of thirty-three Senators. He argued that the Japanese troops were no longer the equals of the ferocious defenders of Tarawa, Saipan, and Iwo Jima. His attempt to end the war with Japan led nowhere, but Luce refused to give up. He noted that certain government officials believed that Japan might surrender if she could retain her Emperor. Luce brought his urgent message to the attention of Navy Secretary Forrestal, who shared his fears about Russia.

Even before President Truman met Stalin at Potsdam in July 1945, Henry R. Luce had decided that the USSR was America's "No. 1" problem. As a powerful state and the center of world Marxism, the Soviet Union, Luce continued, enjoyed great advantages. She could fabricate propaganda in the United States, where both labor and the media were often friendly to the USSR. Americans, by contrast, could not penetrate the Soviet Union. In addition, the Soviets were determined to play an aggressive role in the world; America seemed undecided about its future course. Luce did, however, ascribe two great advantages to the United States: this nation was the most productive country in the world, and foreign nations knew that we did not want to dominate them. Jack Jessup toned down some of Luce's rhetoric, so *Life*'s latest editorial on "America and Russia" issued warnings while still waving the olive branch in Stalin's direction.

Harry Luce's growing fear of Russia sometimes proved costly to Time Inc. The end of the war meant that Eric Hodgins was on the prowl for new talent. He had heard good things about one Harrison Salisbury, a young United Press correspondent in Moscow. Salisbury rejected Time Inc.'s offer, however, explaining that "I don't think I'd be happy here." Hodgins explained the reason for Salisbury's reticence: "At issue: Russian policy." Harry Luce's hard line did not go uncontested inside his company, either. Tom Matthews soon reported that "The whole Junior Staff is anti-Republican. They are suspicious of management, of Luce, and of Luce policy. That's the way the younger generation is."

Some voices expressed dismay at his approach to world affairs. Charlie Wertenbaker reported from Potsdam that, despite blunders and misunderstandings, the Russian and Americans got along fine together. Though describing Russia as "powerful, mysterious and on the March," C. D. Jackson also believed that American honesty, bolstered by firmness, could effect a better relationship. Jackson, however, like John Osborne, was attuned to Luce's moods. When Harry moved toward confrontation with Russia, C.D. and Osborne followed in his footsteps.

During this summer of 1945, Whittaker Chambers continued to commute to New York from his Maryland farm, driving himself to the breaking point. One Monday morning in August, a "grey and shaky" Whit Chambers arrived in his office. He had apparently suffered a heart attack on the train. Luce had been worrying about the health of his overworked senior editors, and Chambers' illness confirmed his fears. Chambers returned to his farm, where he wrote polemical book reviews and cover stories for *Time*. For the moment, John Osborne edited Foreign News, but Chambers' line remained intact.

Time grimly observed that the world was dividing into two hostile blocs. Wendell Willkie's "One World" and FDR's Four Policemen echoed like faint, distant, and irrelevant reminders of yesteryear's hopes. In sadness, Archibald MacLeish wrote to Nelson Rockefeller, complaining that "Mr. Luce's boys have been prepared to find a bomb-bearing Russian under every bed on the planet, and they're making a vigorous search."

Chiang's
Illusory Triumph

At Yalta, Stalin had indicated that Russia would enter the Pacific war two or three months after the collapse of Nazi Germany. China, however, would pay a price for Soviet belligerency. The Yalta "Agreement Regarding Japan" internationalized the Chinese port of Dairen, and permitted the use of Port Arthur by the Soviet Navy. The agreement also decreed that a joint Chinese-Soviet company would operate certain key Manchurian rail links. The Soviets would sign a pact of friendship and alliance with the Chinese government. FDR had not felt obliged to inform the Chungking government of its future concessions to the Russians.

The Big Three knew that these gifts would require Chiang's eventual assent, which FDR agreed to secure "on advice from Marshal Stalin." The President also told Stalin that Ambassador Hurley and General Wedemeyer were making progress, though the Guomindang were even more recalcitrant than the so-called Communists. Like his envoy Patrick Hurley, Roosevelt assumed that Stalin could control his Chinese. This was a remarkable assumption, since FDR and Hurley had proven incapable of dominating *their* Chinese in the ruling Guomindang.

Ambassador Hurley returned to Washington in February. In his absence several Foreign Service officers, including George Atcheson, chargé d'affaires in Chungking, drafted a joint telegram to the State Department. These officers favored cooperating with (and supplying) the Communists, even if Chiang objected to such a policy. Otherwise, they claimed, China would lurch toward a civil war in which the Communist forces would involve the Soviets. When Hurley found out about the Atcheson telegram, he was furious. Demanding the reassignment of the perpetrators, Hurley insisted that Washington endorse his policy. The President ultimately supported Hurley, who continued to back Chiang Kai-shek while trying to mediate an agreement between Chungking and Yenan.

The departure of the American liberals affected Chiang's perception of U.S. policy, for their disappearance from Chungking and Yenan signaled the end of American pressure for real reform. *Time*, however, was again voicing optimism about Chiang's future. The newsmagazine decided that Chiang was prepared to convene a National Assembly, on November 12, 1945. This body, *Time* added, would draft a constitution for China, *subject to later approval by the Guomindang*. The Communists would gain legal status, *if* they placed their armies and administration under the authority of the central government.

Like *Time*, Ambassador Hurley insisted on using hope as his guide when sorting out stubborn or recalcitrant facts. True, there was good news on the war front. In February, "Stilwell's Dream"—the reopened, expanded Burma Road—became a reality, and the blockade of China ended. While Chiang was allegedly stronger, Hurley believed that the "strength of the armed forces of the Chinese Communists has been exaggerated." In fact, China was not stronger; rather, more American aid poured into that country. Hurley still believed that Chiang should reform his government only *after* the Allies had won the war. On March 9 Chou En-lai rebuffed Chungking as he angrily denounced Chiang's long-promised People's Congress as "deceitful, China-splitting and one-party controlled."

At this critical juncture, Harry Luce received a devastating letter about both *Time* and China. Written in Calcutta by a Time Incer named Mary Johnston Tweedy, the note implied that *Time* was harming China more than helping her. Tweedy believed that the magazine bore a special responsibility since *Time* devoted so much coverage to the war there. She also concluded that *Time* "will have an important effect on U.S. public opinion [regarding] China."

As Mary Tweedy told the story, people no longer believed *Time* when it reported on China. Instead, well-informed readers cited U.S.

military advisers who freely spoke of a Chinese government "composed of thieves and cutthroats." Chiang's army, according to the same men, would be worthless in the event of American landings on the coast of China. These officers reported that Chiang was hoarding arms and men for a war against the Chinese Communists. China, they joked, should not be one of the "Big Four," but one of the "big 64" (nations). Mary Tweedy, who was no radical, believed that "the dewy-eyed opinion of the Communists is quite unrealistic." Still, she quoted a source who moaned that "It's too bad that Luce still thinks of China as though it was a mission." One critic, she added, scornfully called Harry the "[William Randolph] Hearst of the intelligentsia." Nothing could have offended Luce more, but during this same month, Harry Luce received a second troubling memorandum.

Finis Farr, who had served as editor of *Time*'s press department, had been attached to General Stilwell's staff and knew the Chungking foreign press corps. "Extremely intelligent, sensible, and responsible," Farr was highly critical of *Time*'s Stilwell cover for implying that the General did not "have enough sense to respect a really great man & sovereign ruler: i.e., Chancre Jack." (The latter was a contemptuous name for Chiang, commonly used by Americans stationed in the China-Burma-India theater.) Farr attacked *Time* for building up an "obsolescent Chinese politician," Chiang, "who is not China." Most wounding of all was Farr's comment that "there are many [readers in Asia] who simply do not believe some of the things they see in *Time*. . . ." In searching for a villain, Farr discovered Whittaker Chambers, whom he unkindly described as a "disfrocked Communist." Teddy White, meanwhile, was also telling friends that *Time*'s prestige had hit an "all-time low" among U.S. civilian and military personnel based in China. White griped about "inaccuracies, errors, and misuses of the copy Annalee and I send in," especially since the appearance of the Stilwell cover story. Henry Luce respond in his own way to the criticisms voiced by Mary Tweedy, Finis Farr, and Teddy White.

On March 12, 1945, Luce circulated Tweedy's letter to his Management Executive Committee. In a stunning sentence, Henry R. Luce admitted that his approach to the China problem might be wrong. Ultimately, however, he was unable to abandon his Christian partnership with the Chiangs and the Soongs, especially when Communists and other critics damned him for maintaining it. Harry Luce quickly snapped back and reaffirmed *Time*'s support for the Guomindang. As Theodore White later put it, "the home office never changed its position to accord with the gradual change in that of its field correspondents."

More than ever, Luce heeded the views of Willi Schlamm, Whittaker Chambers, Walter Judd, Lin Yutang, and John Foster Dulles. Teddy White felt abandoned, and looked for a way out of his isolation.

Stilwell was gone, Yenan was again closed to White, and his friends in the Foreign Service had departed or were preparing to leave China. Teddy White felt that it was easier "ducking Jap bullets than working in Chungking." Though he liked Luce and admired General Wedemeyer, he was clearly persona non grata to Ambassador Hurley, a *Time* favorite. When Wedemeyer flew to Yenan, the foreign correspondents asked that Teddy White be allowed to represent them. Chiang himself vetoed the idea, and Hurley supported his decision. Worse still, Hurley accused White of writing scripts for Communist propaganda broadcasts. When Teddy protested to Hurley, the Ambassador called him a "subversive little son-of-a-bitch." Not unreasonably, White concluded that "people of our [Jewish] faith are odious to him."

White wanted to get out of China; perhaps he could cover Russia for a few months. Luce told him to stay in Chungking. Half on leave and half irrelevant after six exciting, frustrating, and exhilarating years in war-torn China, Teddy White clearly needed a rest. He suffered from various ailments, but as a "bureau chief," White had to handle diverse and petty chores. These tasks required him to supervise messenger boys, account for travel expenses, hire stringers, and worry about salaries and volatile exchange rates. Everything was going badly for White, as one fallen idol after another revealed feet of clay or exited the China stage. Chiang had started out as a hero and had evolved into a symbol of corruption. Luce, White's patron and protector, had proven to be stubborn, and wrong. Only Annalee Jacoby, who had come to despise Luce and Chambers, helped Teddy muddle through the next few months.

White and Jacoby, now friends rather than lovers, mused about writing a book revealing the real situation in China. It might not be a bestseller, Teddy noted, but he and Annalee felt compelled to offer their report to the American people. The proposed book would contain all the observations that *Time* had refused to print. By leveling with the reading public, White would set the record straight—and avenge himself on both Chiang and Foreign News. Writing to John King Fairbank, Teddy declared that he would not work in China "so long as the present government remains in power." He added that "I'm blacklisted. . . ."

Pleading for Fairbank's respect, White cried out, "I'm not a Communist, not a Luce-man, not a pen-prostitute." He then resolved that "I will never write about China for [Time Inc.] again, nor will they use my name to cover their policy." Henry Luce quickly dismissed most of White's complaints about Chiang's regime. He felt betrayed and later decided that "I should have fired [White] immediately. . . ." Luce became convinced, in his words, that White "had gone over to the side of the Communists in China."

Teddy White now dreamed about visiting a great country of which he had seen little—the United States of America. During his imagined tour of the U.S., he hoped to write some free-lance pieces about everything except politics. Though angry at Luce and contemptuous of *Time*, one side of Teddy White hesitated to cut the umbilical cord. So White roamed around the Pacific, covering battlefronts. Harry Luce agreed that Teddy had earned the right to see the final American assault against Japan.

On April 2, 1945, Ambassador Hurley, who had been visiting Washington, reiterated his support for the Chungking government. The U.S., he pledged, would not recognize or arm other forces. Hurley returned to China by way of Moscow, where he met with Stalin on April 15. The Ambassador told the Soviet leader about American plans to train and equip thirty-six Chinese divisions, which would be part of a united army commanded by Chiang Kai-shek. To Hurley's satisfaction, Stalin appeared to approve. Despite the pall cast by Roosevelt's death three days before, Hurley came away from the meeting filled with optimism. Ambassador W. Averell Harriman, however, believed that Hurley put too much faith in Stalin's promises. And George Kennan, chargé d'affaires in Harriman's absence, thought that Stalin's sweet words could raise unrealistic expectations in Washington. *Time*, however, insisted that China was growing stronger, and praised Chiang for democratizing his country. The magazine noted that China's delegation to the forthcoming United Nations conference in San Francisco included liberals, intellectuals—and Communists. If Chiang was reforming his government, then now was the time to solve China's Communist problem.

Mao Tse-tung's recent words were not reassuring. In his April 23 address to the Seventh National Congress of the Chinese Communist Party, Mao attacked the "old China" and cheered the onward march of his country toward communism. The Communist leader's words about building a new China omitted all mention of the Guomindang. Instead, he boasted of his 1,210,000 Communist Party members, who now, he claimed, ruled over 95,500,000 people. "The center of gravity in China," Mao concluded, "does not lie anywhere else; it lies right here [in Yenan]." The next day Mao attacked the Guomindang for its "reactionary policy of active repression." He denigrated the contribution of the Chungking government to the war effort, and described the Communists as "the most faithful spokesman of the Chinese people."

In late April a Teddy White mailer to Time Inc. confirmed some of Mao's claims. The Reds, White informed New York, were on the move, from points near Shanghai in the south to the north China coast. He reported that the big story in China was the expansion of Communist authority, ". . . a power that comes from direct popular support." Yenan, White reported, was unhappy about General Wedemeyer, who was creating a "superb Chinese army." This planned thirty-nine-division "Alpha force" included the five divisions molded by General Stilwell. Yet the bulk of this new force was far from battle-ready.

An unsigned and impeccably anti-Communist source, probably dating from the early summer of 1945, confirmed much of Teddy White's reporting. This anonymous essay was directed to the Luces, who appear not to have taken it seriously. The report freely acknowledged that "The Chinese Communist Movement" had provided "individuals, especially the laborers and peasants, with greater economic opportunities than the Kuomintang Nationalists provide. . . ." Clare's informant added that "the Communists enjoy wider popular support in the areas held by their own armies than do the Nationalists in their areas of control."

Teddy White still hoped that American forces might land on the China coast, where they would require the help of 600,000 Communist guerrillas. In fact, General Douglas MacArthur would bypass China altogether, as American forces converged on the Japanese home islands from the Central Pacific and the Philippines. If Chiang hoped that a large American force would save him from defeat in the coming civil war, he was fooling himself. And that internal clash was sure to come, for, as White revealed, the negotiations with Yenan were taking place in an "air of unreality." *Time* dismissed this grim view of things, but its upstart rival, *Newsweek*, did not. According to a piece written by China hand Harold Isaacs, Chiang's "semi-medieval tyranny" lived in a fantasy world.

Chiang Kai-shek was deeply suspicious of *any* rival power base, be it Communist, democratic, or foreign. This Henry Luce could not grasp, for he wanted to believe all the fine words about democracy and progress rolling off Chiang's corroded propaganda presses. White, to his boss's regret, was too pessimistic about Chiang and his reforms and too optimistic about Yenan. "Too bad," Luce concluded in a note to Billings, "that [White's reporting] comes packaged in Communist [trappings?]."

Harry Luce did not realize that a rapid termination of hostilities against a crippled Japan would leave Chiang with a poorly trained and equipped army. Nor did he grasp the implications of Chinese Communist expansion beyond the border regions around Yenan. Confront Chiang's weak forces with a sudden end to the war and renewed Communist expansion, and one had a recipe for disaster.

In a widely noted article published by the *Reader's Digest*, Congressman Walter Judd warned about the need to prevent the Soviet Union from absorbing East Asia. If, Judd argued, the Red Army dominated China the way it did Eastern Europe, "then Russia and her satellites will be irresistible." Harry Luce thereupon decided that *Time* should devote four full pages to a Walter Judd speech in which the Congressman predicted the outbreak of a new Asian war.

Lauding Chiang's contribution to the Allied war effort, Judd attacked the propaganda war being waged against the Chungking government. Cutting through the rhetoric ("so-called Communists") used by both the left and General Hurley, Judd noted that the Chinese Communists were not agrarian reformers. Rather, Mao's people followed the Moscow line. Judd was right to call the Yenan revolutionaries Communists, but he was wrong when he equated their Leninist rhetoric with obedience to Moscow. In his conclusion, Judd flogged a dead policy. Instead of putting pressure on Chiang, he advised that Washington push the Communists toward a peaceful settlement. This might be hard to do, for, as *Time* admitted, Red guerrillas were even penetrating Kwangsi in southern China. And the Communists were crossing the Yellow River, moving into the Shantung Peninsula and then down the coast.

If and when American forces ever landed in China, *Time* asked in despair, how would they deal with these aggressive Communists? The United States, the magazine concluded, would have to make a "momentous political decision." In early June, Ray Buell brought more ill tidings. Despite Chungking's "growing liberalism," he concluded, "the political news from China seems to be worse." In a dispatch, Teddy White documented the rampant corruption, cynicism, and boondoggling infecting the recent congress of the Guomindang. The Communists, White added, were expanding in the Shanghai area. *Time* did not deface its columns with White's brickbats.

On June 9, 1945, Ambassador Hurley sent an important telegram to

Washington. Sources cited in his report indicated that the Japanese were in full retreat, and in their wake, the Guomindang and the Communists were rushing to fill the vacuum. As a result, clashes "between the two parties are reported to have occurred in nearly every province in Central and Eastern China." According to analysts working in the U.S. embassy, Chiang, in secret meetings held during the Sixth Guomindang Congress, had advocated the extermination of the Communists. He wanted to rid China of the Reds before the unpredictable Americans landed on the China coast. Ironically, the Communists had become equally intractable. If they had to fight Chiang, they, too, wished to do so before the arrival of pro-Guomindang American troops.

His subordinates' comments about Chiang's plan enraged Patrick Hurley. In his view, the troublemakers in his embassy were either Communists or people who were "apparently" trying to "bring about the collapse of the National Government of China." If American "ideological crusaders" (meaning pro-Communists) would only behave themselves, China could avoid civil war. In response, Hurley rid himself of dissenting embassy personnel. Now, Teddy White wrote, "cowards, ignoramuses and stooges" took the place of men like Davies and Service. Yet *Time* remained stubbornly optimistic about China.

Dr. Owen D. Lattimore, a leading academic expert with vast experience in China, dissented. He warned President Truman against continuing the government's open-ended support for Chiang Kai-shek. Lattimore, who had once advised the Generalissimo, feared that Chungking's rigidity would result in civil war. Russia, Lattimore added, might then intervene on the side of the Communists. In a bland reply, Truman, who was preoccupied with the final stages of the Pacific war, tried to reassure Lattimore. Everything, the President said, was working out fine.

Lattimore made an appointment to see Truman on July 3, and in a dramatic memorandum, he argued that the imminent division of China into two spheres might one day result in war between the United States and the Soviet Union. Chiang, Lattimore argued, could prevent this by giving the Communists several places in a coalition cabinet. Lattimore, however, told Truman that Chiang, relying on long-term American support, wanted to crush the "bolshevik menace." His Guomindang advisers, Lattimore continued, told Chiang that conservative Republicans would soon triumph in the United States, "and that Henry Luce, Walter Judd, etc., have guessed the trend correctly."

Despite the efforts of Luce and his allies in the media, however, Chiang's image abroad was growing darker. Alarmed, the Generalissimo wrote a rare personal letter to Harry Luce, complaining that the American press stressed Chungking's defects while ignoring "our efforts to correct those shortcomings. . . ." Chiang then thanked Luce for his "fair presentation" of the facts about China. He clearly felt that *Time* provided the accurate exception to the grim rule about the American media. Ambassador Hurley now developed a plan to counteract this negative criticism of the Chungking regime. He intended to invite Henry Luce to China. Luce, having seen the "truth about China," would, Hurley hoped, return to the States more committed than ever to Chiang's cause. He would then be in a position to say "I was there," and his words would gain badly needed credibility for the Chiang regime. The new Secretary of State, James F. Byrnes, however, rejected Hurley's proposed invitation to Luce. Byrnes explained that the Hurley proposal smacked of favoritism, but he also suspected that Luce, a partisan Republican, would try to hurt the Truman administration.

Chiang Kai-shek's vaunted Fourth People's Political Council was supposed to culminate in a constitutional process worthy of a modern country. Opening on July 7, 1945, the council met with ridicule at the hands of Mao Tse-tung, whose Communists boycotted it. The National Assembly, scheduled to convene on November 12, would, Mao added, "probably end up like this [council]." Mao, who now described Patrick Hurley as an "imperialist," blamed the collapse of negotiations upon the "Hurley-Chiang racket." Certainly, Chiang had no intention of sharing power with these Communists. He wanted to gain control of their army, then grant them some vague form of "legal status." Mao would have none of this, especially since his illegal state was rapidly expanding. He also made new demands for democracy in China, knowing full well that Chungking would never accede to them. Ridiculing Chiang as "our monarch," Mao taunted him for being unwilling "to introduce democratic reforms." Mao also attacked American policy as articulated by General Hurley. His line was, warned Mao, "leading China to a crisis of civil war." Suddenly, *Time* grew pessimistic and claimed that "Open civil war in China seems inevitable."

Teddy White was now earning about $10,000 a year, and for a young man of modest background, this was a fortune. Yet he saw himself as a victim of Time Inc., akin to the talented Foreign Service officers purged by the ignorant Hurley. White was now ashamed of working for Harry Luce. As he put it, "I feel like a prostitute. . . ." Annalee Jacoby concluded that "I think it's hopeless." Harry Luce had in the meantime dispatched a more cooperative colleague to China.

Charles J. V. Murphy, a tough, self-assured editor at *Fortune*, arrived in Chungking, where Jacoby found him to be a "prejudiced pompous ass." Treating her like an "office girl," Murphy expected her to file large amounts of his copy. An exhausted, frustrated Jacoby told White that Murphy constantly contradicted her, though he knew little about China. At other times, the newcomer repeated facts known to Jacoby for many weeks, treating them as great revelations from secret sources. Calling Teddy White a "Red," Charles Murphy expressed his high regard for General Hurley. He had lunch with the Ambassador, who would no longer see Jacoby or White.

Jacoby realized that Luce must have descended into a state of extreme Russophobia if had sent Murphy to China. ". . . I hate his [Murphy's] guts," she muttered. Told that *Time* planned to do a cover story on Chiang, Annalee Jacoby responded that she heard that it "stinks." After learning that White was supposed to confer with Luce in New York, Jacoby urged that Teddy not jump to the snap of Harry's whip. Luce, she argued, obviously wanted to remove him from the China bureau, else why would he ask that White return to New York? Annalee recommended that Teddy counter by again inviting Luce to Chungking.

Like other reporters covering the Pacific theater, Teddy White expected to witness a bloody assault on the Japanese home islands. The atomic attack on Hiroshima on August 6, 1945, took White and his colleagues by surprise. Harry Luce, however, who was hoping to end the Pacific war without Soviet intervention, spied an opportunity. On August 8 Luce, accompanied by former Ambassador Joseph Kennedy, called on New York's Francis Cardinal Spellman, hoping that Spellman would prevail on President Truman to offer Japan a brief respite. Luce would let the Japanese keep their Emperor, because in a few years Hirohito would "bear no resemblance to the Emperor-image" with which Americans had become so "recently and unhappily familiar." Henry Luce, however, was swimming against the American current, which was vehemently "anti-Jap." Certainly, his proposal showed courage and was prophetic, but it would have raised the hackles of Americans who had served in the Pacific.

Luce's plan for Japan, for example, resulted in a clash with *Time's* crack correspondent Bob Sherrod, who had landed with the Marines on many a Pacific island. There was no point, Harry Luce argued, in prolonging the war by insisting on the removal of Hirohito. Sherrod disagreed, for he had seen evidence of atrocities committed in the god-emperor's name. The Emperor Hirohito, Sherrod insisted, "is the core of the Japanese cancer." In fact, even after American newsreels had shown scenes of horror in liberated Nazi concentration camps, 82 percent of those Americans polled by Gallup described the Japanese as "more cruel" than the Germans.

Luce's plan to freeze Moscow out of the Far East now failed, for on August 9 the Americans destroyed Nagasaki with a second atomic bomb. On the same day, the Soviet Union informed Japan that a state a war now existed between the two nations. The course of events spared Harry Luce serious embarrassment, for his readers would not have reacted well to an editor who favored giving Tokyo some more time to think. Five days after Nagasaki, Japan capitulated. America's China crisis, however, was just beginning. This may explain Luce's irritation in a moment of triumph.

During a lunch at the Waldorf, eighteen Time Inc. editors celebrated the imminent victory. When the call arose for a toast, the usually reticent John Shaw Billings jumped up and raised his glass to "the man who so ably led us to victory—Henry R. Luce." Offended and embarrassed, Luce growled, "Thank you. Now let's get back to work."

Back in Chungking, Teddy White warned against undue euphoria. "Unless China is organized . . . ," he wrote, "Asia is still in a ferment and there is no peace." In his prescient dispatch, White listed the problems confronting China. To whom would the Japanese armies surrender? Would the Red Army, which was invading Manchuria, return this vast land to Chiang? How could China master her skyrocketing rate of inflation? How would millions of refugees return to their homes in distant river valleys and coastal towns? What help would the United States offer to China? White could not even pretend to know the answers.

The Chinese government had anticipated a long campaign against Japan, probably ending in 1946. By then, Chiang's government expected to field thirty-six American-trained divisions, which would quickly move north. The sudden surrender of Japan caught Chiang by surprise and left him unprepared to reassert his power. Accordingly, the War Department issued new instructions to General Wedemeyer. By an order dated August 10, the American command was to assist Chiang when he reasserted control over regions previously occupied by Japanese forces.

Two days later, in a report to Harry Luce, Teddy White wrote that China's fragile unity was in full dissolution. Mao's General Chu Teh had already declared that the Communists would disarm Japanese garrisons in regions that the Reds controlled. Chiang chastised Chu Teh in terms usually reserved for an errant schoolboy: "You have issued the wrong order, very wrong indeed, and will have to reject it resolutely." The Communists were unimpressed. Apparently they intended to seize all of north China, denying the crucial Yellow River valley and other regions to Chiang's forces. *Time*, meanwhile, worried about the rapid, blitzkrieg-like entry of the Red Army into Inner Mongolia, Korea, and Manchuria. Victory in Asia had left problems in its wake.

1945

Henry Luce's
Ambiguous Victory

Time and *Fortune* and *Life* had made the name Henry R. Luce synony-
mous with success and innovation. World War II turned him into the
great phenomenon of the publishing industry. Time Inc., claimed Eric
Hodgins, now published two magazines that were really the "national
newspapers." The company was, he added, America's "largest publisher of news on a national scale." Once a rewrite sheet, Time Inc.
now claimed (with much exaggeration) that a *Time* story begins "where
the newspapers leave off." By Time Inc.'s estimates, more than 30
million people were reading or looking at one or more of Luce's magazines.

In June 1941 *Life* was already printing 3.2 million copies each week.
The magazine enjoyed an impressive, perhaps unique "renewal of sub-
scription" rate of over 80 percent. By the time of Pearl Harbor, *Life*
sold more than 3.5 million copies, thereby passing the old *Saturday
Evening Post* in circulation. By July 1942 the war had brought *Life* an
influx of new readers, pushing its circulation to 3.9 million. The magazine was achieving other "firsts," as well. In September 1942 *Life* dis-

patched copy to its Chicago printers by airplane, thus cutting twelve hours off the picture magazine's tight production schedule. *Time*'s circulation passed a million each week, and by 1945 it had climbed to 1,270,500 per issue. Eight thousand theaters screened *The March of Time*, as did 3,000 more in foreign countries. The radio version of "The March of Time" claimed 8 million listeners.

By 1945 *Life* had long since passed its competitors in the amount of advertising devoted to food, clothes, liquor, drugs, and toiletries, and was closing in fast in jewelry and tourism. And *Life* was the first popular magazine to foresee a postwar investment boom in something called television. The magazine promised improvements in video reception, and bigger screens. Practicing what it preached, Time Inc.'s treasurer, Charles Stillman, purchased 25,000 shares of the General Precision Equipment Company, which made television components. Stillman predicted that these shares would double in value after the end of the war, and he was a shrewd man. Harry Luce gave Stillman plenty of leeway, but he failed to appreciate television's potential impact on the nation. Devoted to the printed word, Luce mistakenly claimed that "we should consider ourselves in competition with Hollywood and the radio. . . ."

Luce's company employed 1,177 people in its New York editorial offices. The Chicago operations of the company (production and circulation) paid another 890 staffers. At the time of Pearl Harbor, Time Inc. showed current assets of $22,561,000, against current liabilities of only $8,569,000. Gross income had climbed to a record $45,047,879.34, which rose to $74,157,211 by 1945. Profits were also huge. Each share of common stock earned $3.95, and dividends paid a princely $2.50 per share. Like Luce, Stillman rejected the dire prophecies of those who expected a postwar crash. Though the early postwar period would be a tough one for the nation and for Time Inc., Luce's optimism was vindicated. By 1946, for example, he himself owned 250,000 shares of Time Inc. common stock, valued at about $30 million. Luce expanded his Savings and Profit Sharing Plan, which matched or exceeded employee contributions. In 1945 Time Inc. became the first company to provide its employees with medical coverage under a plan devised by the United Medical Service, Inc.

Luce continued to pay up to 50 percent of the salaries owed employees who were serving in uniform. These people, after all, would one day return home, having lived through experiences that would profit them, the company, and America. Roy Larsen proposed taking some of the brightest ex-officers and making them advertising representatives for

Life. There, these young men of ability would prove themselves by selling ad space to big retailers. Later, they would emerge as top salesmen and managers. Larsen's scheme worked out well.

The war began to change some of Time Inc.'s personnel policies, too, though old ways of thinking endured. Hobbled by the manpower shortage, the company began to think of recruiting female journalists. Ed Thompson checked out the journalism classes at Ohio State University and found five good possibilities. Some of these young women defied the old Time Inc. norms. Mary Agnes Vavrek, of Cleveland, for example, was "Second or third generation Slav but supposed to be very bright and persistent. . . ." When Thompson spoke to students about recruiting "college-girl office girls" at low salaries, he received a cold shoulder. American expectations were rising thanks to incipient prosperity. This recruitment problem bothered Luce, because "I do not feel that women and womanhood are represented in *Life*." He wondered why women did not push "more vigorously to the top." Perhaps they were afraid of bumping into a glass ceiling, which Luce, like many contemporary employers, had built but could not see. Ultimately, things began to change, but not until many years of pressure had eroded traditional prejudices.

Harry Luce thought that bigger was usually better, and in this he was a man of his time. Despite Luce's aversion to FDR, his company's expansion followed in the wake of the President's victories. Under Franklin Roosevelt, America had become the world's permanent great power. A bit of symbolism illustrates the ties that bound the company to the country. Soon after the war, one Boyce Price, a former major in the U.S. Army, became John Billings' assistant. Price was responsible for analyzing the policy content of *Time* and *Life*. During the war, this young man had been in charge of the Map Room in the White House, where he briefed Harry Luce's nemesis, Franklin D. Roosevelt, on the daily military situation. So the man who told FDR what American armed forces were doing all over the world made the transition from Roosevelt to Luce.

Luce was proud of Time Inc.'s work in covering this "first truly global war," a war in which *Life*'s staff had traveled a million miles in one year (1944). In a rare sentimental moment, Luce saluted Walter Graebner, "who *lived* the Blitz; Bob Sherrod . . . who *lived* the Marine Corps . . . Teddy White who . . . became, as *Time*'s correspondent, the unrivaled walkie-talkie encyclopedia on embattled China. Thanks to their work, Luce's magazines were in demand throughout the world.

During the war, the State Department flew copies of *Life* in diplomatic pouches to ambassadors stationed in many foreign cities. Emperor Haile Selassie of Ethiopia and King Ibn Saud of Saudi Arabia received gold-embossed albums containing *Life*.

Special ("pony") editions of *Time* reached servicemen and women stationed in countries from Britain to China. In Australia, for example, the magazine was printed weekly about ten days after the U.S. edition had appeared. Robert Sherrod, who supervised the early stages of the Australian operation, observed that the company expected to lose $10,000 during the first year of this edition. The Army, however, was anxious to distribute the magazine, and Luce wanted to reach overseas Americans. Teddy White, after visiting Australia, urged the expansion of this project.

Before his disillusionment with *Time*, White reported that soldiers "manhandle" *Time* until each copy is worn out. "There is nothing," White wrote in 1942, "that Time Incorporated could do for the morale of the U.S. forces in the Far East that would be of greater value than sending out copies of *Time* and *Life*." By the end of 1944, the twenty-one pony editions enjoyed a total circulation of 750,000 copies. And by the end of the war, *Life* had an overseas military circulation of 625,000 copies. At the request of the Army, Time Inc. was giving away magazine subscriptions to wounded men recuperating in hospitals all over America. *Time* claimed that in a survey, 63 percent of the men in the U.S. armed forces named *Life* their favorite magazine. *Collier's* ran a poor second, with 28 percent of the vote.

This expansion only whetted Harry Luce's appetite, and Time & Life International now became his pet project. Luce expected that Americans abroad would live up to his standards. Through the editions published by TLI, Americans would stay in touch with their homeland and learn what they needed to know about the United States and the world. Soon after the war, C. D. Jackson reached an agreement with the government by which the U.S. earmarked dollars for the purchase of *Time* and *Life* by people in Holland, Norway, and other countries strapped for hard currency. Wherever Americans traveled, there Henry Luce intended to plant Time Inc.'s flag. Though it often lost money, Harry insisted on supporting TLI, and in a decade, the circulation of *Time's* (civilian) international edition had grown from 145,200 copies to 390,000.

Teddy White's happiness over the defeat of Japan could not distract him from the impending crisis in China. While jubilant crowds in Times Square celebrated America's victory in the Pacific, a worried Teddy

White concluded that the "destiny of China may be decided for better or worse for a generation." Though White again declared that it was crazy for Time Inc. to offer unconditional support to Chiang Kai-shek, *Time* again celebrated China's onward rush toward "democracy and unity."

General Order No. 1, approved by President Truman and issued by the Emperor Hirohito on August 15, addressed the nettlesome issue of the Japanese surrender. By command of the Allies, Japanese forces in Manchuria and Korea (north of the 38th parallel) were to be disarmed and interned by the Soviet Union. The Allies authorized Chungking to accept the surrender of Japanese units throughout the rest of the China Theater of Operations. Naively, Washington hoped that the local Communists would assist Chiang's government in carrying out this arduous task. The United States also agreed to provide Lend-Lease assistance to China for another six months. In addition, American Marines, Navy personnel, and transport units were landing in China, where they would help to maintain order. U.S. forces would also transport Chinese troops to formerly occupied regions. The War Department, however, warned its commanders not to become embroiled in China's internal clashes. The Americans thus refused to help Chiang occupy towns situated to the rear of Communist units active in northern and central China.

Ambassador Hurley again moved to mediate the dispute between Chungking and Yenan. Chiang invited the Communist leader Mao Tse-tung to visit him, and the two enemies, who had not met since the Guomindang's bloody purge of the "Red bandits" in 1927, soon agreed to resume talks. A few weeks later, Chiang talked grandly about restoring the United Front of 1924. The negotiations resulted in a communiqué, in which both sides pledged to work for constitutional development and military reunification. While Mao, however, discussed peace and unity, Communist guerrillas were on the move in China's fields, villages, and towns. In some places they cut rail links, thereby preventing Chungking from restoring its authority over vital regions of the country. And the Communists often seized warehouses filled with ammunition stored by Japanese or Chinese "puppet" forces.

Communist guerrillas remained wary of the port-based American forces, whom the rebels accused of helping the Guomindang. The Communists retaliated by refusing to let U.S. personnel land at Chefoo, in Henry Luce's native province of Shantung. Tension begat more tension. The Chinese government wanted to station forces in the fine port at Dairen, but the Soviets would not let Chungking do so. Communist guerrillas then moved into Mukden in Manchuria, with the tacit approval of the Red Army. The Russians agreed to the evacuation of

Manchuria on January 3, 1946, but their promise left open the question as to who would control its rich deposits of coal, lead, copper, and zinc. Everything seemed uncertain.

At this point a flurry of cables between Chungking and New York crossed the airwaves. Teddy White pleaded that he be recalled to New York so he could make his last appeal to Luce. He hoped to make a convincing case for a peaceful, democratic solution to the Chinese dilemma. Luce's anger grew, however, when he read Teddy White's cables, which he curtly dismissed as the work of "an ardent sympathizer with the Chinese Communists." For years, Harry Luce had been a lonely prophet, arguing that China would prevail when so many others anticipated her collapse. He intended to savor this moment, and White would not be allowed to spoil it. Luce reminded White that Chiang had fought against Japan for eight years, longer than anyone else.

Harry suggested that *Time* ask White "to try for one brief moment to imagine himself as a non-partisan or even pro-Chiang man." "We realize," Luce added with sarcasm, that "this might be an unreasonable request in view of your avowed partisanship." Teddy White received another warning. If he could not do a "professional objective job," Luce might have to cancel *Time*'s planned cover on Chiang. White responded with alacrity. Affronted by Luce's slaps at his professionalism, Teddy defended himself. "I resent," he wrote, "being called [an] 'avowed partisan.' " White protested that he opposed both communism and fascism. What he wanted for China was a compromise that promoted democracy and peace. Otherwise, he warned, that country was headed for civil war.

Luce had already decided that he wanted a new team in postwar China. Among his prospective rookies was William Gray, who received an outline of *Time*'s China policy for purposes of orientation. Luce, without any hint of humor, noted that Time Inc. was nonpartisan—but supported Chiang. *Time*, he added, favored the liberal elements in China, *so long as they were loyal to the government*. Luce did not want his people to have anything to do with propaganda advocating the overthrow of the Chungking regime.

Teddy White was finally ordered home to New York to talk about his future. He would be delighted, he responded, to return for a good discussion with Harry. In fact, Teddy still hoped that Luce would visit China, where he might be able to deflect him from taking a road leading to disaster. In Chungking, White would doubtless try to pry Harry Luce out of the hands of Hollington Tong, H. H. Kung, the Chiangs, and other doomed wraiths haunting U.S. policy in China. Teddy could then introduce Harry to his friend Chou En-lai, or perhaps take him to conferences with Sun Fo or other dissidents. White, whose indecision confused, then angered the home office, cabled New York, stalling for time. He expressed perplexity over what was really an unambiguous command, but as usual both White and Luce drew back from the implications of their disagreement.

In Luce's view, the Communists had contributed something to the war against Japan, but not as much as they claimed. According to Harry Luce, the Generalissimo wanted to form a coalition containing several parties, while the Communists adhered to a one-party system. Luce had long since concluded that Yenan believed in Soviet-style "democracy," and followed the Russian line. *Time* admitted, however, that Yenan did field an army of 470,000 men, and governed regions containing 70 million people (the accurate figure was far higher). Even if Chiang agreed to Mao's proposals, how, Luce asked, could he trust these ambitious Reds? They had not kept their word before, so why would they do so now?

On August 27, 1945, Foreign News decided that the Communists were part of a "conspiracy to seize the Chinese government." Luce, who had upbraided White for his pessimism, was finally worrying about Yenan. On this same day Teddy White received a reminder from Time Inc. Right after he returned to Chungking from his trip to Japan, he was to fly home to the States. In an evasive reply, White promised to come home as soon as he could secure a seat on a military transport plane. Writing to David Hulburd, Teddy declared that he looked forward to a talk with Harry. Then, after telling John Fairbank that he would never again work for Luce in China, White reversed himself. If he and Harry could "settle the basic principles" of China coverage, White would continue to report for Time Inc. First, however, Teddy headed for Tokyo Bay, where General MacArthur turned the Japanese capitulation into a spectacular drama.

White covered the moving ceremony of surrender, which took place on September 2 aboard the battleship *Missouri*. Among those present was a gaunt General Joseph Stilwell. For a brief moment, the mercurial White was euphoric over the prospects for a better world. After returning to Chungking, he described himself as a man who was "viewing the promised land of China, which is entirely free for the first time in a decade."

Teddy was still not anxious to confront Harry on his own turf. Coyly, White asked if he was to meet Luce in China or India? New York, of course, had repeatedly informed White that he was to return to Rockefeller Center. In a note to Luce, John Billings observed that White wanted to "dally around in post-war China." He suggested that

Time Inc. get tough with Teddy if he did not respond to its summons. On the margin of Billings' note, Luce scrawled a single word: "Okay." On September 4 an irritated Allen Grover ("Luce's Vice-President in Charge of Luce") told White to gather his belongings, then fly to New York.

On September 3 *Time* published its long-planned cover story on Chiang Kai-shek. After a few weeks of doubt, *Time* disparaged the Communists as ragtag guerrillas who had not yet seized a single big city. *Time*, which was regularly attacking Stalin for his behavior in Eastern Europe, hoped that the Soviets would help, or at least not harm, Chiang Kai-shek. Russia and China, pledging friendship and cooperation, had indeed committed themselves to a policy of noninterference in each other's internal affairs. In August China had conceded control of Outer Mongolia to the Russians while granting Moscow naval concessions in Dairen and Port Arthur. The two powers would jointly own the Manchurian railroad systems, while the USSR pledged to withdraw from Manchuria within three months. Stalin recognized the Chungking regime as the government of all China and promised that any aid he provided to China would go through Chiang Kai-shek. *Life* soon boasted that "the present prospects of China are a vindication of American policy in Asia. . . ."

Ambassador Hurley, replete with two cases of scotch, had gone to Yenan and brought the Communist leader Mao Tse-tung back to Chungking. In early September *Time* believed that Mao might come to terms with Chiang. In fact, a weak Chinese government faced an internal revolt, widespread disaffection, and a powerful, ideologically hostile neighbor. The Generalissimo himself privately admitted that he required *sixty* modern divisions for pacification purposes alone. Secretary of State Byrnes, however, indicated that the U.S. might complete its wartime program by equipping thirty-nine Chinese divisions. But what good would these troops really do Chiang? They would take the field long after they were needed. Besides, these Chinese soldiers were training to fight an enemy like Japan; they would be useless in the counterinsurgency campaign that might become a sad fact of life in 1946.

General Wedemeyer, meanwhile, recommended that the War Department shut down the China Theater of Operations by December 15. He feared that the further presence of Marines would offend the Soviets, who would then extend their stay in Manchuria. Wedemeyer was also afraid of being sucked into a Chinese civil war. At the State Department, Under Secretary of State Dean Acheson wanted to assist the Chinese government without becoming involved in a war. Nor did he wish to support an authoritarian, undemocratic administration. At home, many liberals, leftists, Communists, fellow travelers, and people of goodwill demanded that the U.S. get its military men out of China.

Owen Lattimore counseled caution and tried to undercut Ambassador Hurley. During the second half of 1945, Lattimore made a detailed study of public opinion, the media, and the China issue. Americans, Lattimore noted, were growing more suspicious of Soviet aims, but they "refuse to be anti–Chinese Communist." U.S. opinion, Lattimore wrote, was "hostile to the attempt to suppress the Chinese Communists by civil war." Why? Because, he explained, Americans think that Chiang's government "is full of crooks and militarists." Most of the press did not agree with Luce, and many other newspapers ignored China for long periods of time.

Harry Luce needed to convince Americans that their country should participate fully in what *Time* called China's renaissance. Luce did have allies in this endeavor. Charter members in new network were Alfred Kohlberg, Patrick J. Hurley, Walter Judd, and Chiang's agents, registered and unregistered, in the United States. Harry Luce now became the prime voice of this fledgling "China Lobby." Luce himself began to denounce the Chinese Communists with growing passion. Perhaps they were, as Kohlberg and Judd alleged, part of a broader conspiracy.

Though not entirely persuaded of the un-Chinese nature of Mao's party, Luce was coming to see the Yenan Communists as tools, witting or not, of Soviet imperialism. Chiang remained Luce's favorite fighter for liberation from the foreign yoke. *Time* cogently noted that "The driving force of Asiatic nationalism and anti-colonialism is one of the strongest political factors in the world today." Luce, however, failed to understand that many Chinese saw Mao, not Chiang, as their liberator. And sadly, he could never admit that some Chinese viewed the Americans as imperialists or exploiters. Those who believed such a lie, Luce argued, must be people who did not "think like Chinese." Seduced by misplaced hopes and confused by incomprehensible forces, both *Time* and Luce continued to play down the strength of the Communists.

Time believed that tormented China might be on the eve of her long-awaited era of peace. The magazine's persistent bouts of euphoria annoyed Ray Buell, who had finally rejected Luce's optimism. Concluding that "the economic and political future of China is dubious," Buell tried to alert his colleagues to the danger at hand. Harry Luce, however, did not want to hear warnings; he was ever scanning the horizon in search of that shining Christian city on a distant China hill. If it were not for those annoying Communists and their Soviet protectors, he believed, China would already be taking her rightful place in his American-ordered world.

These were the waning days of a surface "United Front," in which Mao was supposedly Chiang's ally. Mao, who had flown to Chungking, now talked about a settlement with the Guomindang. Readers of *Life* saw a smiling Chiang, toasting Mao Tse-tung. The Soviets were supposedly cold-shouldering the Communists in Manchuria. Chinese troops, flown to the north by American air transport, were taking over provinces previously occupied by Japan, on behalf of the Chungking government. ". . . last week," wrote *Time*, "the ancient land of China was bright with hope." *Life* wrote of happy crowds in Shanghai, who had returned to the liberated city. *Life* mentioned some of Shanghai's poverty and human misery, but ignored the Communists, who exploited these social inequities.

Teddy White, who was so disgusted with *Time*'s pie-in-the-China-sky reporting, did have some rare good news for Annalee Jacoby. He had received word of Whittaker Chambers' absence from the office. After learning of Chambers' heart attack, White gloated that Whit "may be off the desk for a month." Despite this respite, the other news from Time Inc. was all bad. Finally, on September 18, 1945, Teddy White began his long trip home.

In New York he found a preoccupied Harry Luce, who was anxious to leave for China. The young reporter did not get much of a chance to rehash his old arguments with Luce. Instead, White agreed to take six months off, during which time he and Annalee would complete their book. Teddy remained a nominal if inactive employee of Time Inc. He expected to see Harry Luce again, but both men sensed that these waltzes were futile, for the music had long since faded away.

Teddy White had a story to tell; Harry Luce had a sermon to preach. One vocation necessarily undercut the other.

The Chinese government badly needed Henry Luce's support in the ongoing battle for American public opinion. Accordingly, Harry received an invitation from President and Madame Chiang Kai-shek, for the Chinese Ambassador believed that Luce's visit "will be of mutual benefit to China and the United States. . . ." On September 29, 1945, a very happy Henry Robinson Luce left the United States on the first leg of his long journey to the land of his birth. Harry landed at the shabby airport near Chungking on Saturday, October 6, where high Chinese and American officials greeted him.

The next day, Harry attended church in "Tibbets Theatre," a place replete with symbols. Tibbets Theatre was now U.S. Army headquarters in Chungking. Named after a GI who had died of meningitis, the theater had once served as a Methodist missionary compound. Where American soldiers now played softball on an adjacent field, a bomb had fallen during Luce's 1941 visit. No place could bear stronger witness to Harry's trinity: Christianity-America-China. There was one down note, however. Luce, a great aficionado of sermons, found this one to be mediocre. Later in the day, things improved, for Harry enjoyed tea with Dr. Kung. Luce and his Chinese host rejoiced in their common victory over Japan.

Luce then called upon the Chiangs, who had invited him to dinner. A special treat awaited Harry, who loved to discuss abstruse philosophical and religious subjects. Luce was able to enter into a dialogue with Chiang, who discoursed on the Chinese concept of freedom. An enchanted Luce listened to the Gissimo explain that freedom meant acting according to one's nature, like a fish in water. (Luce was unaware of the fact that Mao was also fond of the fish-in-the-water simile.) Men, said Chiang, "should behave without improper restraint but also without artificiality." Luce did not think through this interesting proposition. In fact, the Generalissimo implied that *someone* would have to make sure that people acted "without artificiality." This throwback to the Guomindang concept of "tutelage" seemed dated, given the expectations of so many Chinese.

Luce departed in a happy frame of mind, convinced that the Chiangs knew that their government had, in Madame's words, "a terrible responsibility not to disappoint the hopes of the people." Unfortunately, the other China surfaced to spoil a few hours of Luce's day. Harry had a painful interview with Annalee Jacoby, during which they discussed the tattered relations between Teddy White and his boss. Luce, referring to the White/Jacoby team, concluded that "we should not have allowed this situation to continue so long."

On Monday, October 8, Harry Luce attended an important dinner hosted by General Chang Shih-chung. The American was the only foreigner in the hall, which contained 300 guests. The center of attention was the Communist leader Mao Tse-tung, who was present because Ambassador Patrick Hurley still hoped to broker a settlement between the Guomindang and the Marxists. Harry Luce observed Mao closely. In his dairy, Harry described Mao as a man with a heavy, peasantlike face. He compared Mao's plebeian appearance to that of Chiang's officers, who presumably displayed more noble features. Mao was clad in a "sloppy blue-denim garment," which "contrasted sharply with his host's snappy beribboned uniform." When Mao spoke, he began slowly and even hesitated; by the time he was ready to conclude, the Communist leader was engaged in a "full-voiced shout." Remarkably, he pledged himself to a peaceful solution of the problems at hand and declared that China should find "unity under Chiang Kai-shek." Henry Luce did speak briefly with Mao. The Communist leader seemed to know who Luce was, and expressed surprise at his presence. Mao gazed at Luce "with an intense but not unfriendly curiosity," but his remarks, Harry noted, consisted of "polite grunts."

Chiang's other friends were more forthcoming. Marshal Feng Yu-hsiang, a Christian general whom Luce had met back in 1932, told the publisher that almost all Chinese were grateful to America. They "knew" that Japan had bombed Pearl Harbor because the United States was defending the integrity of China. Dr. Fu Sze-nien, acting president of the National University of Beijing, said that *Time* and *Life* had brought about a change for the better in the Chinese government.

Luce held happy reunions with United China Relief personnel, including Dwight Edwards, but not everyone he met was sanguine about the future. With a sense of urgency, a man Luce identified as Chiang Kai-ngnau declared that he was about to fly to Manchuria, where he was empowered to tackle difficult problems. A former banker with influence in the government, Chiang asked that Luce approach Chiang Kai-shek and urge him to liberalize his government. The Communists, added Chiang Kai-ngnau, had ideas that were spreading "throughout the nation."

Henry Luce's incorrigible curiosity had in the past served him well. However, he did not confront Chiang Kai-shek. Nor did he ever demand the right to visit the border regions, where he could have observed the Communist "state" firsthand. In the case of China, Harry did not want to undermine the certainties that inspired and guided his thought. America must save China, and Chiang was the only instrument at hand. So Luce thought about how he could help, not criticize, the Chungking government, and once again an opportunity evaporated.

His aide, Wes Bailey, wrote of Henry Luce that "I don't think any foreign visitor . . . has been so welcome in China since Marco Polo. . . ." Chiang's government went out of its way to make sure that cheering children, medal-bedecked generals, smiling politicians, and applauding newspaper editors greeted Luce like a benevolent head of state.

The *Beijing Chronicle* explained why Chungking had gone to so much trouble. Luce, the newspaper observed, published "articles on China which greatly influenced American public opinion in favor of China." His reception in China moved and inspired Henry Luce.

In a telegram home, Luce decided that China needed "three or four ships to carry coal from Manchuria to Shanghai to get the wheels of industry started there. . . ." Then he spoke about dispatching a hundred American businessmen and ten missionaries to China, where they could restore her economy and society. Charles Stillman, Time Inc.'s gifted treasurer, had been proposing since 1941 that Time Inc. and other corporations dispatch zealous young businessmen and technicians to China, where they would instruct managers of the struggling industrial cooperatives. Both Luce and Stillman saw this proposal as part of "the hoped-for extension of the United States into the world after the war." The United States, they seemed to say, could redeem China. A few more missionaries, generals, dollars, and sympathetic articles, and the Americans would save their valiant ally. Harry hoped to get things moving, for Americans had a "great stake in peace and progress here."

"Problems [in China] are terrific," Luce decided, but they are by no means insoluble." Clare Luce shared her husband's bright mood. "How well Harry and his father built," wrote Clare, "in this matter of our friendship and understanding with the Orient!" If Luce failed, the defeat would break his heart.

Representative Walter Judd, along with his colleague Clare Luce, had been waging a bitter fight against men and women who wanted to remove U.S. forces from China. Judd soon began to spy a connection between these left-wingers and Communist subversives in the Army, government, and media. On its surface, the *Amerasia* scandal seemed to vindicate Judd's hunch. Early in 1945, government officials noticed that an article published by the journal *Amerasia* seemed almost identical to material contained in a report written by an OSS official. Subsequently, the FBI decided that Philip Jaffe, editor of *Amerasia*, had obtained the document from persons employed by the Office of Naval Intelligence and the Department of State. The FBI broadened its investigation and concluded that John S. Service and others were involved in the illicit transfer of government documents. Though two of the defendants pleaded guilty and paid fines, the other targets were exonerated.

Jack Service's arrest shocked Teddy White, who was still *Time*'s Chungking bureau chief. As White knew, most of the material appearing in *Amerasia* was available elsewhere, and had no real national security interest. In White's view, the government was trying to purge men for speaking the truth about America's failed China policy. White, who had regularly exchanged information with Service and Davies, might himself become a target. By contrast, the *Amerasia* case confirmed the fears of treachery harbored by Alfred Kohlberg and Walter Judd.

In China, Ambassador Hurley concluded that this alleged conspiracy showed that a fifth column had infiltrated the government and was working to destroy his China policy. Like these men, Harry Luce became convinced that a worldwide, Communist-inspired propaganda campaign was subverting China's image. Luce concluded that if it were not for the Communists and the Soviet Union, "we would have a surcease from the politics of crisis." Actually, Mao's forces were making alarming progress, but they usually did so without the benefit of large-scale Soviet aid.

While in China in October 1945, a suspicious Harry Luce met with another leading Communist, Chou En-lai, but the encounter went badly. Harry, who did not value charm highly, was among the few Westerners unmoved by Chou's pleasing manners. As in so many matters that challenged Luce's shibboleths about China, Harry's famed curiosity was again absent. Perhaps he felt that Chou had nothing to teach him about freedom or anything else. Chou politely complained of Time Inc.'s attitude toward his party. Far from apologizing, Luce replied "that was too bad because we had a world-wide battle on our hands with world-wide left-wing propaganda—and it was just as nasty as skunk." Luce and Chou parted, having settled nothing.

After his stay in the temporary capital, Henry Luce, accompanied by Charles J. V. Murphy, Wesley Bailey, and others, flew to Chengtu, northwest of Chungking. Luce was hoping to visit West China College, in Chengtu. An American lieutenant who accompanied his party delighted Luce by telling him that the pony edition of *Time* "had been a life-saver." The young officer's praise contradicted the sour warnings about *Time*'s diminished credibility received from Farr, Tweedy, White, and their ilk. Luce felt encouraged, for he wanted to publish his magazines in a free, postwar China. Despite the immense difficulties confronting this project, Luce hoped to establish a branch of Time-Life International in Shanghai. Wesley Bailey pointed out that it would be easier to publish in MacArthur's Tokyo, but Luce wanted no part of that idea.

After listening to the junior officer's words of praise, Harry Luce got into a Jeep, which promptly broke down. A truck filled with GIs passed by, stopped, then took Bailey and Luce aboard. The ride was bumpy, but the conversation bothered Luce much more than the discomfort. As they roared through the hilly Szechuan countryside, the cynical GIs ridiculed China, *his* China. Passing a battalion of armed Chinese soldiers, one wag yelled, "The war's over; so now you're going to fight!" The same character claimed that the Chinese had hidden many aircraft while they "were yelling for more airplanes to be brought over the hump." After surviving this ordeal, Luce arrived in Chengtu. There, he heard that the Chinese ran two whorehouses, one fair and one good. He made no inspections. Instead, Harry toured the college campus, where he took tea with some of the students. The next day, Luce arrived in Sian, where he visited a Buddhist pagoda and a nearby village. As the guest of the governor, Harry enjoyed certain rare amenities, such as a hot bath.

On October 13, 1945, Harry Luce began his journey back to haunts that meant so much to him and his family. He arrived in Tsinan at night. The next day he visited Cheloo University, where Harry heard sad news. The Japanese Army had desecrated Cheloo's chapel by using the building as a grain storage depot. Still, it felt good to be back in Shantung for the first time since 1932. Luce then traveled to Beijing, where 1,000 Marines were helping to maintain order. The *Chronicle* greeted Luce with a lengthy lead editorial in which the newspaper hailed him as a friend who loved China. In Beijing, the mayor hosted a wonderful dinner for Harry Luce. Like the others, Luce played *gam-bei*, a contest that involved drinking glass after glass of highly potent alcohol. According to the Central News Agency, Luce "emptied his cup so many times that an extra cup might have put him under the mahogany." By the next morning, Luce had fully recovered, and he enjoyed a busy day. He visited several local editors and granted an interview to the press corps. Luce then dined at the French embassy before revisiting his father's old campus at Yenching University.

Two days later, Harry Luce, sailing aboard a U.S. Navy ship, docked in Tientsin, temporary home to 25,000 Marines. Luce visited Marine headquarters, where his reputed influence almost cost Harry his life. A disturbed Marine, convinced that Luce's magazines were responsible for keeping him in north China, loaded his M-1. He then aimed the rifle at the back of Harry's neck. Another Marine, William R. Hasbrook, persuaded his buddy to lay down the gun. Years later he wrote to Luce, describing the incident. An astounded Harry Luce responded that "It's a curious feeling to learn years later that your number was almost up." Luce thanked Hasbrook for "your interference in changing the signals."

On October 19 local authorities welcomed Harry Luce to Tsingtao, where he stayed at the Edgewater Hotel. Harry conferred with Charles Murphy, dined in the governor's mansion, and visited with President James McConaughy of United China Relief. Here, where he had passed many summer weeks as a child, Luce swam in the Pacific. He recalled the Tsingtao of his youth, and again admired its "magnificent port." Returning from his reveries, Luce gloried in the presence of 3,000 to 5,000 Marines and sailors, and celebrated the patriotism and optimism reflected in the faces and cheers of thousands of Chinese schoolboys and girls.

Luce spent little or no time conversing with workers, peasants, or dissidents. Instead, he dined with Major General Robert B. McClure, head of the Chinese Combat Command, with mayor this or governor that, and discussed matters with Chiang's generals. Dining on the USS *Alaska* under a full moon, Harry Luce could bask in the happy triumph of American power. When he toured Chinese cities, he saw the signs of Japanese defeat: abandoned homes, warehouses, and arsenals. Though a million Japanese soldiers still needed to be disarmed, interned, and repatriated, Luce felt that they would soon be a bad memory. He dismissed the Japanese as cruel invaders who had merely interrupted Chiang's march toward a modernity nurtured by the Christian West.

During these precious days of remembrance and hope, an enchanted Harry Luce again wired Billings, noting with excitement that "We have a great opportunity here to offset much mediocre reporting and to develop journalistically new territory." Since he had helped to write the Stilwell cover, Fred Gruin, now an ardent disciple of Whittaker Chambers, had become *Time*'s resident China specialist. Luce believed that Gruin was ready to cover that troubled land, while Wes Bailey could handle a number of business-related publishing chores in Shanghai. There was no room for Teddy White in this pretty picture, for Charlie Murphy would play the key role on Time Inc.'s new team. Since Murphy knew little about China, he scrupulously followed Harry Luce's guidelines. Harry's pointers won Murphy the confidence of the Chungking government, whose viewpoint he adopted and disseminated. At times, Murphy sounded more pro-Chiang than did Harry Luce himself. Murphy's long essays would subsequently appear in many issues of *Life* and *Fortune*.

To Harry Luce, the Chiang government remained the legitimate heir to the 1911 revolution, which had put China on the path toward modernity and progress. The coming weeks, *Time* wrote, would be decisive ones, for government forces were poised to move north, as far as Manchuria. Luce, who had failed to confer with Communist commanders or visit disputed rural regions, disastrously underestimated the rebels' strength. Instead of informing himself of the truth, Luce blindly parroted his sources in the Chinese government. The Communists, Harry wrote, might be trying to break out into Outer Mongolia. In fact, that distant, arid country would not be the scene of decisive confrontations; Outer Mongolia was fixed in the Soviet orbit.

Despite his obstinate optimism, Luce heard unsettling rumors about the entry of Communists into Hopei and Shantung. The rebels had also seized Japanese weapons and ammunition stored in Soviet-occupied towns, while Red Army soldiers looked the other way. No matter; *Time* expressed faith in the outcome of China's recent troubles. Henry Luce insisted that Chungking, backed by the United States, would surmount all challenges, including the Communists' sabotage of the northern railroad lines. By late November 1945, Luce boasted, "Crack government armies, mostly U.S.-equipped and U.S.-trained, will have arrived in North China." As he put it, "The reoccupation of China by the Chinese with American aid is something . . . unique in history." Luce concluded that "There's at least one more *Time* cover in this."

Time's "Report on China" loosely based on copy filed by Bill Gray, was one product of Luce's enthusiasm. Gray was an independent-minded reporter, but *Time*'s editors produced the desire result. ". . . the U.S.," wrote *Time*, "has gone too deeply into the China affair to duck all responsibility for what may ensue." By this logic, which appealed to Luce, the United States *should* intervene; once it had done so, the U.S. *must* remain, to finish the job. Like John McCloy, Luce thought that Chiang would have plenty of time for reforms "after he has got peace." America must not abandon its old friend just when the presence of American troops, the gift of American arms, and a solid infusion of American dollars could yield a great victory.

In October 1945, while Henry R. Luce was enjoying his pilgrimage to China, *Life*'s Jack Jessup made an important discovery. His source, Harvard President James B. Conant, had been head of the wartime National Defense Research Committee, which advised the government on the atomic bomb. Experts, reported Jessup, believed that Russia would test an atomic bomb at some point between 1950 and 1960 (the correct date was 1949). Nuclear proliferation could not be prevented, and the bomb would be used, despite fear of reprisal by the other side. Mutual inspection, according to Conant, offered the only way out of this looming catastrophe. More bad news was on the way, too. Secretary of State James F. Byrnes failed to conclude a peace treaty on

Germany, while the Soviets were demanding 3 million tons of German steel as reparations.

In the autumn of 1945 Harry Luce read a disturbing memorandum written by correspondent Samuel Welles. Welles did not name his source, but it appears to have been diplomat George Kennan or someone familiar with Kennan's views. Welles' interviewee concluded that Stalin would not give up his expansionist goals in return for economic aid. Welles' contact also advocated a standoffish attitude on the part of the West; any other demeanor would be misinterpreted as appeasement. Those who shared this hard-line view worried that Secretary of State James F. Byrnes remained too enthusiastic about making a deal with the Russians.

Harry Luce felt that Americans were unprepared for an aggressive foreign policy. After the Depression and a world war, people were most concerned about jobs, prices, shortages, and their readjustment to normal lives. In a sense, Harry was back in 1939, only this time Russia had replaced Germany as the Great Threat. Once again Luce decided that he would have to sound the alarm. Some friends and acquaintances watched with dismay as Henry Luce became the pioneer Cold Warrior in the American mainstream media. Figures so diverse as Henry Wallace, Archibald MacLeish, and diplomat Joseph Grew rushed to dismiss Luce's claim that Soviet ambitions threatened basic Western interests.

Henry R. Luce was advocating a new foreign policy, one based upon anticommunism, massive assistance to suffering peoples, and the use of exports as a stimulus to the American economy. There was to be no return to the disarmament and withdrawal that had marked the post–World War I era. As part of his plan, Luce now envisaged a long-term military buildup supported by appropriate institutions of national security. Opposing the loud calls to bring the boys home, Harry demanded that the Truman administration keep the Marines in northern China. The United States, Luce argued, must intrude further into the affairs of Asia and move to block Russian domination of Europe.

In an important *Life* editorial on "National Security," the magazine predicted that the next war might be won by guided, pilotless super-bombers, carrying atomic weapons. *Life* did not identify the Soviet Union as their target, but readers could fill in the blank. With the Office of Strategic Services going out of business, *Life* also favored the creation of a new central intelligence office. *Life*, which in 1941 had looked forward to a post-Fascist world of peace and abundance, had become an early prophet of the permanent national security state.

What would happen, however, if Henry Luce, who was so concerned about the parasitical growth of federal power, found himself supporting a cause that mandated a vast increase in the size of government? And could the American global mission come into conflict with the conscience of patriotic Americans who were loyal to their country? Irony and introspection were not Luce's strong points; he did not get around to posing these questions, much less answering them.

Five years after his proclamation of a benevolent, unipolar world order called the American Century, his perception of events convinced Henry Luce that he must confront new, profound challenges in Europe and Asia.

1994

The American Century
in Retrospect

Speaking of his new, postwar China, Henry Luce playfully asked, "What *is* this riddle-less riddle?" To him there was no longer a question, only an answer: American power, combined with the Chinese spirit, guaranteed the future happiness of both nations. U.S. troops, like the Reverend H. W. Luce and his wife, Elizabeth in 1897, had come to China in order to redeem a people. All Chinese of goodwill loved Americans.

Henry Luce began his long trip home on October 29, 1945. His itinerary showed an estimated arrival date of November 1, when he would land in San Francisco. Among many memorable images, one remained with Harry forever. Writing that "Incredible military power is represented by the Stars and Stripes," Luce long recalled his days in Tsingtao as an "autumn so rare and bright [that it] makes the heart joyful." Years later, Harry Luce, speaking with emotion to executives at Time Inc., remembered those days in Shantung back in 1945: "I tell you very solemnly," said Luce, "if American affairs had been entrusted to Major General [Lemuel] Shepherd and to me, China would not now be Communist." Either the American Century saved China or it remain unfulfilled. But in fact, Chiang, not Roosevelt or Truman, was "losing" China.

Harry Luce and Teddy White were taking different paths, and in 1946 the young correspondent left Time Inc. As events soon proved, Luce and White were both right and both wrong about China. Luce correctly suspected Yenan of harboring totalitarian ambitions that would assume xenophobic, anti-American forms. He was wrong, however, to over-look so much of the oppression and corruption destroying Chiang's regime from within. Driven by faith, Luce put aside his obligations as a reporter.

Teddy White, who was rightly sickened by Chungking's corruption, hailed Yenan in terms that were too bright by half. If Chiang Kai-shek was bad, White seemed to think, then Mao Tse-tung must be better. He devoted little time to pondering the totalitarian ideology and disci-pline that had energized the Communist state within a state. Still, Teddy White was realistic in doubting whether well-intentioned Americans could remake a society whose convulsions defied their understanding.

Ironically, until he left China, Teddy White still fell prey to a liberal version of Henry Luce's misplaced optimism. He assumed that a leftist, democratic coalition, which included the Communists, would create a better world for most Chinese. In fact, China was caught in a time warp in which a failed authoritarian regime did battle against an embryonic totalitarian movement. Perhaps the story could not have yielded a happy ending, no matter who won the incipient civil war, and no matter what the United States did. Maybe Mark Twain was right back at the turn of the century, when he argued that "We have no more business in China than in any other nation that is not ours." Harry Luce hoped that the curtain was rising on Chiang's long-awaited era of liberal reform, but China's entry into the American Century was taking place only in Luce's mind.

Two might-have-beens make the unfolding tragedy even more tanta-lizing. When the Reverend Luce wrote his remarkable outline of the Yenan movement in 1940, the Communists were not yet the major players they later became. Had Dr. Luce lived beyond 1941, he might have conveyed some of his realistic views about these Marxists to his influential son.

Franklin Roosevelt contributed to Harry Luce's inability to recognize the disaster confronting Chiang. By barring Luce from the China the-ater, FDR made it impossible for Theodore White to show Harry what was happening to the Chungking regime. Luce, one recalls, had last seen China in the spring of 1941, when heroic resistance and surface political unity defined the war effort against Japan.

Harry Luce, who had at first been indifferent to the Nazis, saw Hitler's Central Europe and returned to the United States convinced that war was inevitable—and desirable. Perhaps Luce would not have changed his mind about China. Yet one wishes that he had seen wartime China in 1943, with Teddy White as his guide through Honan and Chungking. Had Luce come home with a realistic appraisal of developments in China, he might not have launched his debilitating postwar search for scapegoats. Then the American public would have been better served. Through no fault of his own, that was one trip that Harry Luce never made.

As more rot set in, and Chiang's China grew weaker, Luce, who was sitting in New York, ignored or played down most unpleasant facts and searched for the whipping boys responsible for Chungking's failure. Imbued with faith in his version of China and blissfully ignorant of the situation in the rural areas of the country, Luce deluded himself and ill-served his readers. By 1947 Luce's magazines were taking the road that led to the bitter, partisan wrangles that disfigured the national debate between 1949 and the mid-1950s. If Chiang fell, then Communists, or conspirators, or a lack of American help were to blame. Pursuing this line, an embittered Henry Luce found ready allies in his quest for American villains.

Luce's obsessive wrongheadedness about Chiang had its roots in factors that were far more important than FDR's travel *Verbot*. The fact is that Henry Robinson Luce knew a lot about China, but did not understand the forces molding its history in the 1940s. He did not grasp the drives that inspired millions of its people and made them hunger for change. Luce did not know the urban Chinese masses or understand the aspirations for land and dignity motivating hundreds of millions of Chinese peasants. He assumed that Chiang Kai-shek did, so Harry let the Guomindang speak for the mute masses. Luce knew a lot about Chinese religion and philosophy, about Confucius and the Shanghai stock exchange, about the geography of Shantung, about the Kungs and the Chiangs and the Soongs—but he did not know the new China, a country that was in a state of upheaval. Luce's China—the China of the Reverend Luce and of T. V. Soong—was doomed.

Recall that Harry Luce grew up in a Christian American compound, walled off from the Chinese masses that surrounded it. Chinese were people to be converted, they were servants, they were co-religionists— but they were different. Luce attended a British school, then left for America, not to return to the land of his birth until 1932. He did not

revisit China until 1941, and could not return again until after World
War II. Luce had by then long since forgotten most of his boyhood
Chinese. From the 1930s, he associated almost exclusively with Chinese
elites, usually Christian, and often bankers, statesmen, publishers, diplomats, and propagandists.

The fact is that love for his imagined China eroded Luce's greatest
journalistic strength, which was his phenomenal curiosity. Henry
Luce's China was a product of his narrow circle of friends, projected
onto the pages of his magazines. Harry reminds one of Goethe's tragic
character Faust, who in one enchanted but deluded moment pleads:

> Oh, let them prevail,
> The wondrous images,
> That my eye has projected before me.

Luce's curiosity, married to his strong-willed moral certainty, had
resulted in marvelous innovations that changed the world of publishing
and popular culture. In the case of China, Luce failed to read warning
signs that Teddy White and many others tried to make him see. Why?
Because Henry Luce was morally certain that American-influenced,
Christian elites were fated to bring China into the modern world.

The man who would ask a dinner guest twenty questions about his
or her profession or work day showed no desire to see Yenan or investigate the debilitation undermining the Guomindang. When forced to
inhale the stench of Chinese corruption, Luce had a ready response: the
Japanese, or the Communists, or a lack of American aid had created a
pathological situation that was not the fault of the Chinese elites. Certainty overruled curiosity. To say that those leaders failed was to admit
that America-in-China had failed, and this Luce could never do.

With marvelous certainty, Henry R. Luce had predicted the defeat of
the Nazis when Hitler bestrode Europe and the United States possessed
a puny army. Now he refused to see the coming debacle in Asia, when
all signs pointed to Chiang's fall. The Paul Revere of 1941 later became
an embittered man searching for scapegoats to blame over the "loss"
of his China.

Between the 1930s and the present, friends and enemies alike have
spoken with awe of Harry Luce's achievements and influence. After
Luce's death, Time Inc.'s vice-president Eric Hodgins referred to his
late boss as "the towering editorial genius of the twentieth century." A
rival publisher, John Cowles, described Luce as exercising an "enor-

mous amount of influence." Robert Hutchins, president of the University of Chicago and perhaps the most controversial and important university educator of his day, claimed that Luce's magazines did more to mold the American character than "the whole education system put together." Carl Sandburg, a poet and folklorist revered by generations of Americans, named Henry Luce the "greatest journalist of all time." Even Luce's old nemesis, William Randolph Hearst, believed that "There can no longer be any doubt that *Time* is the world's outstanding journalistic venture to date." Contrarian views were easy to find, and by and large they achieved greater notoriety.

Franklin D. Roosevelt ascribed far too much power to Time Inc.'s magazines. He sometimes acted as if Henry Luce could unseat his Administration, but Luce failed to do so. A broad array of liberal writers condemned Henry Luce's magazines for contributing to the smugness, drift, and belligerence they ascribed to the postwar United States. A generation later, the distinguished writer W. A. Swanberg, reflecting the passions engendered by the Vietnam War, came close to blaming Luce for creating the China Lobby, the "Who lost China?" witch-hunts, and of course, the Vietnam intervention. One suspects that Henry Luce's influence, though considerable, was not so all-encompassing as Roosevelt, Hutchins, or Swanberg made it out to be.

What then was the nature of Luce's power over American public opinion? Wars, politics, international affairs, and social changes forced the nation to confront various choices. At their best, *Time* and *Life* and *Fortune* helped the people and their leaders face the great issues of the day. In 1940 and 1941, for instance, Harry Luce played a striking and persistently effective role in preparing the American people for entry into the Second World War. Sometimes, as in the case of the 1940 "destroyer deal," Luce acted effectively on two levels. While winning public support for a daring measure, he also helped to convince FDR that the proposed agreement with Churchill was good politics.

Among many examples of his success one recalls the story told by General George C. Marshall. The Army's Chief of Staff, not a man given to exaggeration, told Dan Longwell that *Life* had been crucial in winning congressional approval for a vital appropriation. This bill provided for $110 million to be earmarked for new weapons that were essential in 1940 to the Army's emergency modernization program. Had Luce endorsed such a program in 1937, however, he would have acted in vain, for the time was not ripe.

During the war *Life* captured the imagination of millions of people at home and at the war fronts. *Life*'s war embodied sacrifice and heroism, but the glossy magazine also promised a future laden with automobiles, jobs, television sets, and much good food and drink. By linking victory to a promised golden age of the American consumer, *Life* boosted both civilian and military morale.

Henry Luce was the greatest prophet of consumerism in American history, and his hour finally struck in the 1940s and the 1950s. Luce, however, was selling more than refrigerators. His magazines' relentless attacks on lynching, the poll tax, and segregation in the armed forces and society began to bear fruit. Luce, a prime mover in the campaign for a permanent Fair Employment Practices Commission, would live to see the enactment of civil rights legislation he had long espoused. A look at some of Henry Luce's other failures and successes, however, is equally illustrative.

Harry Luce hoped to defeat Roosevelt and tried mightily to do so in 1940 and 1944. In these signal cases, Harry Luce failed. Why? Because the public and most of the politicians were not ready to see things as Luce saw them. Hence they were not willing to follow his political recommendations. Then, when China fell, Luce's drumbeat caught the ear of more politicians and a growing number of opinion makers. Suddenly Luce was able to influence policy, during an increasingly anti-Communist era. Though he was filled with contempt for the "demagogue" Senator Joseph R. McCarthy, Luce's strident rhetoric about China prepared the way for the Red-hunter from Wisconsin. Luce's China Lobby helped to decimate the State Department, as frightened politicians and cabinet officers purged foreign policy of badly needed China experts.

When Harry Luce tried to interest General Dwight D. Eisenhower in the presidency between 1945 and 1948, nothing happened. Luce's arguments flattered but failed to impress Eisenhower. But when Luce backed "Ike" after 1950, he helped to convince the General that he should run. Why the difference? In 1948 Americans were proud of their winning war effort and sensed that good times were in the offing. In 1952 a bloody, indecisive war in Korea and an unpopular Administration made a President Eisenhower a realistic possibility. Suddenly, after he and his magazines helped to secure Ike's nomination and election, Henry R. Luce was hailed or reviled as a kingmaker. He succeeded in 1952, however, only because people were ready for his message, not because his media had the power to force it upon the nation.

By 1948 Henry Luce sensed that history, which had moved so rapidly, had already bypassed his expansive vision of 1941. Just when hegemonic global power seemed to lie within Luce's—and America's—

reach, a new threat emerged to block his enjoyment of it. As Luce had anticipated, the United States had defeated the Axis, fed much of the world, and had advanced the cause of capitalism, and sometimes of democracy. The tragic element in all of this was the rise of communism in Eastern Europe and China, and with it, the Cold War. Luce had been among its earliest prophets back in 1944 and 1945, but that long conflict eroded the ecumenical generosity that had inspired and informed his "American Century."

Many Americans enjoyed prosperity after 1950, but they also found themselves embroiled, directly and through proxies, in an endless array of "small wars," which engendered fear, bloodshed, inflation, and, sometimes, defeat. The growing middle class had an unpleasant companion—the specter of nuclear annihilation. Apocalyptic trepidation was supposed to end with the defeat of the Axis. Instead, a new kind of anxiety became more universal and lasted for more than two generations. Harry Luce never worked out this problem, a fact that may explain his occasional annoyance when anyone brought up the "the American Century" concept after 1947. Slowly at first, then at an alarming pace, the Cold War undermined the self-confidence and peaceful development essential to Harry Luce's original idea of American globalism.

Though his United States won the Cold War twenty-four years after his death in 1967, it paid a terrible price for victory in lives, social cohesion, and fiscal stability. Perhaps Luce sensed this, because he could not wait to end the Cold War. He was impatient, and sometimes Harry even toyed with—and rejected—the dangerous idea of preventive war.

By the time of his death early in 1967, Henry R. Luce felt that the mood of the country had turned sour. Fortunately for him, he did not live to see his American Century enter an age marked by a divisive and ultimately lost war in Vietnam, even more violent racial turmoil, and political scandal at the highest levels.

Men and women, Henry Robinson Luce taught, must try to build the Kingdom of God on earth. They are, he believed, sinners and are doomed to fall short of their glorious goal, but they must keep striving. Luce's kingdom on this earth was to be called the American Century, and it achieved much, though not so much as its author hoped. His was a great vision, and the fate of Henry Luce's shining city on a hill tells an inspiring but troubling story.

Certainly, Harry Luce was blinded by his illusion of a Chiang-led, Christian China allied with the American big brother. His stubborn commitment to the Guomindang worked to the detriment of two nations. But if Luce was sometimes wrong about Chiang and the American place in Asia, then it is important to remember that this man was right about Hitler and many other major challenges.

Achievements quickly come to mind. Harry Luce published three highly innovative magazines that affected the reading habits and culture of many Americans for several decades. *Fortune* helped to create a modern capitalist entrepreneurial ethic that proved effective in the postwar world. Luce insisted that black Americans must have full civil rights, when most of the country preferred to look away. There, too, he was ahead of his time, to his enduring credit. Luce demanded that the Nazis be stopped, and America intervene against them, when only 20 percent of the U.S. population favored war with Germany. At times against their will, the Luce media prepared Americans for war. Luce's magazines later waged war on the home front, and they did so to great effect. By virtually creating the Willkie candidacy and by his actions between 1944 and 1952, Luce helped to convert the Republican Party into an internationalist entity. Harry Luce correctly foresaw the emergence of an expansionist Soviet Empire. He did so at a time when most of the press preferred to dream of peace and salute the heroic Soviet ally.

Through a troubled time, in bad times and good, Luce's American Century insisted that American farmers feed the hungry of the world, while other Americans taught skills to peoples who needed them. Here, too, he proved to be a prophet with honor. An examination of popular support for postwar American food aid, of the Marshall plan, and of the Peace Corps shows that Harry Luce had not labored in vain.

Henry Robinson Luce's idealistic patriotism and faith in human progress resulted in these great achievements, but they also led him into defeats and disappointments. The experience of this unusual, sometimes great man teaches us a valuable lesson about the place of our nation in a sometimes intractable world. It appears as if history will never culminate in global hegemony exercised by one nation, no matter how righteous, powerful, and rich it may be. Even after the American victory in World War II, and the Western triumph in the Cold War, renewed prophecies of the "end of history" and of a peaceful "new world order" appear to have been misplaced.

NOTES

ABBREVIATIONS

AFSC	Archives of the American Friends Service Committee, Philadelphia, PA
CBL	Clare Boothe Luce
CS	Connecticut State Library, Hartford, CT
DCL	Manuscripts Department of the Baker Library at Dartmouth College, Hanover, NH
DDEL	Dwight D. Eisenhower Library, Abilene, KN
DJSB	The diary of John Shaw Billings, in the papers of John Shaw Billings, at the South Caroliniana Library, Columbia, SC
DRBCUL	Department of Rare Books, Cornell University Library, Ithaca, NY
FDRL	Franklin D. Roosevelt Library, Hyde Park, NY
FHLSC	Friends Historical Library at Swarthmore College, Swarthmore, PA
FRUS	Department of State, *Foreign Relations of the United States*
GARLSU	Special Collections Department of the George Arents Research Library at Syracuse University, Syracuse, NY
GCMF	Library of the George C. Marshall Foundation, Lexington, VA
HHL	Herbert Hoover Library, West Branch, IA
HIWRP	Archives of the Hoover Institution on War, Revolution, and Peace at Stanford University, Stanford, CA
HLHU	Houghton Library at Harvard University, Cambridge, MA
HRL	Henry R. Luce
HSTL	Harry S. Truman Library, Independence, MO
JFKL	John F. Kennedy Library, Boston, MA
MCWSHS	McCormick Collections, Wisconsin State Historical Society, Madison, WI
MDLLIU	Manuscripts Department of the Lilly Library at Indiana University, Bloomington, IN
MDLOC	Manuscript Division of the Library of Congress, Washington, DC
MDUVL	Manuscripts Department of the University of Virginia Library, Charlottesville, VA
MHS	Division of Archives and Manuscripts of the Minnesota Historical Society, St. Paul, MN
MLBU	Department of Special Collections of the Mugar Library at Boston University, Boston, MA

MMAL	MacArthur Memorial Archives and Library, Norfolk, VA
MOB	Museum of Broadcasting, New York, NY
NARA	National Archives and Records Administration, Washington, DC (RG stands for Record Group)
NYPL	Manuscripts Division of the New York Public Library, New York, NY
RAC	Rockefeller Archive Center, North Tarrytown, NY
RBMLCU	Rare Books and Manuscript Library, at Columbia University, New York, NY
RRUR	Department of Rare Books, Manuscripts and Archives of the Rush Rhees Library at the University of Rochester, Rochester, NY
RWWLEU	Special Collections Department of the Robert W. Woodruff Library at Emory University, Atlanta, GA
SCDKLUO	Special Collections Department of the Knight Library, University of Oregon, Eugene, OR
SCL	Manuscripts Division of the South Caroliniana Library at the University of South Carolina, Columbia, SC
SGMMLPU	Seeley G. Mudd Manuscript Library, Princeton University, Princeton, NJ
SMLYU	Division of Manuscripts and Archives of the Sterling Memorial Library at Yale University, New Haven, CT
SWCL	The Peace Collection in the Swarthmore College Library, Swarthmore, PA
WSHS	Archives Division of the State Historical Society of Wisconsin, Madison, WI
YDSLAM	Archives and Manuscripts Department of the Divinity School Library, Yale University, New Haven, CT
YIVO	Archives of the YIVO Institute for Jewish Research, New York, NY

PREFACE

xi **War in the Philippines:** "Mark Twain on American Imperialism," *Atlantic Monthly*, April 1992, pp. 49ff.

xii **"That is not ours":** Mark Twain, interview with the *New York World*, October 14, 1900, ibid., p. 59.

xiii **What a man:** DJSB, March 8, 1950 (SCL).

CHAPTER ONE

1 **Fry one of the eggs:** CBL, "The White House," in the papers of CBL, container 1 (MDLOC).

2 **Their impressions of the evening:** HRL, "War Diary," in the papers of HRL, box 86; and CBL, "The White House," in the papers of CBL, container 1 (MDLOC).

3 **Damaged or sunk:** William L. Langer and S. Everett Gleason, *The Challenge to Isolation: The World Crisis of 1937–1940 and American Foreign Policy* (Gloucester, Mass.: Peter Smith, 1970), vol. II, p. 744.

3 **Inessential:** Robert Dallek, *Franklin D. Roosevelt and American Foreign Policy 1932–1945* (New York: Oxford University Press, 1979), p. 243.

3 **White's meeting with Roosevelt:** Walter Johnson, *The Battle Against Isolation* (Chicago: The University of Chicago Press, 1944), pp. 91–100.

3 Destroyer for bases deal: William Allen White to Francis Pickens Miller, July 25, 1940, in the papers of Francis Pickens Miller, box 25, folder May–August 1940 (MDUVL).

3 Win public support: Eichelberger to William Allen White, July 5, 1940, in the papers of Clark M. Eichelberger, box 50; White, telegram to HRL, July 5, 1940, ibid., box 48; and memorandum from Mr. Weeks to Eichelberger et al., July 9, 1940, ibid.

4 White to Sherwood: William Allen White to Robert E. Sherwood, July 26, 1940, in Walter Johnson, ed., *Selected Letters of William Allen White 1899–1943* (New York: Henry Holt, 1947), pp. 409–410.

4 Demanded the dispatch of destroyers: Press release of the Committee to Defend America (CDA), in the papers of Clark M. Eichelberger, box 49 (NYPL).

5 The Century's offices: Johnson, *The Battle Against Isolation*, p. 116.

5 Common hatred: Francis P. Miller to Mark Lincoln Chadwin, August 21, 1964, in the papers of Francis P. Miller, box 47, folder 1945–1965 (MDUVL).

5 A free system of production: The "Tentative Draft," July 12, 1940, in the papers of Francis P. Miller, box 26, folder 1934–1967 (MDUVL).

6 Assist England in every way: Memorandum of the meeting at the Columbia Club, July 11, 1940, in the papers of Fight for Freedom, box 69 (SGMMLPU).

6 Invaded from the Atlantic: Memorandum of Meeting, July 25, 1940, ibid., box 25, folder May–August 1940.

6 Miller on the Battle of the Atlantic: Minutes of the Advisory Policy Committee of the CDA, September 9, 1940, in the papers of Clark M. Eichelberger, box 49 (NYPL).

6 Moral responsibilities: Francis P. Miller, *Man from the Valley: Memoirs of a 20th-Century Virginian* (Chapel Hill: University of North Carolina Press, 1971), p. 95.

7 Hitlerian interference: HRL, memorandum of July 18, 1940, the Time-Life-Fortune papers, in the John Shaw Billings collection (SCL).

7 On Roosevelt and the Luce publications: *The Complete Presidential Press Conferences of Franklin D. Roosevelt* (New York: Da Capo Press, 1972), vol. IV, p. 170. On the influence of magazines on the campaign, see Paul F. Lazarsfeld et al., *The People's Choice: How the Voter Makes Up His Mind in a Presidential Campaign* (New York: Columbia University Press, 1948), pp. 134–136.

8 On Time Inc.'s coverage of the Democratic convention: *Life*, July 29, 1940; DJSB, July 18, 1940 (SCL).

9 St. Lucia: Langer and Gleason, vol. II, p. 750.

9 The May 29 decision: Joseph P. Lash, *Roosevelt and Churchill 1939–1941: The Partnership That Saved the West* (New York: W. W. Norton, 1976), p. 203.

9 The Foreign Office: Sir Llewellyn Woodward, *British Foreign Policy in the Second World War* (London: Her Majesty's Stationery Office, 1970), vol. I, pp. 361–363.

9 Knox and defense: Lash, p. 205.

10 Benjamin Cohen: Langer and Gleason, vol. II, p. 745.

10 Refused to embrace: Franklin D. Roosevelt to Frank Knox, July 22, 1940, in Elliott Roosevelt, ed., *F.D.R.: His Personal Letters 1928–1945* (New York: Duell, Sloan and Pearce, 1950), vol. II, pp. 1048–1049.

10 **Luce argues for the quid pro quo:** Mark Lincoln Chadwin, *The Hawks of World War II* (Chapel Hill: University of North Carolina Press, 1968), pp. 84–85, passim.

10 **Wednesday afternoon conversation:** "Questions for Thursday Evening," ibid.

10 **Luce on the concessions:** Ibid., p. 85. Chadwin claims that Luce made his dramatic proposal on July 25, but this could not have been the case. Relevant documentation, leads me to conclude that Luce made his proposal *before* July 25.

11 **Defending the British Isles:** George Watts Hill, "Memorandum of Meeting held July 25th at the Century Club, New York," written on July 26, 1940, in the papers of Francis P. Miller, box 25, folder May–August 1940 (MDUVL).

11 **The United States needs naval bases:** Francis P. Miller, Notes on Conversation during meeting, July 25, 1940, ibid.

12 **Now had a plan:** Langer and Gleason, vol. II, p. 747.

12 **The Gallup poll:** Robert E. Cleary, "Executive Agreements in the Conduct of United States Foreign Policy: A Case Study: The Destroyer-Base Deal" (New Brunswick, NJ: Ph.D. dissertation, Rutgers University, 1962), p. 148.

12 **Lothian alerts the Foreign Office:** Woodward, vol. I, p. 362.

14 **On** *The March of Time* **and** *The Ramparts We Watch*: Raymond Fielding, *The March of Time 1935–1951* (New York: Oxford University Press, 1978), chapters 8 and 11.

15 **The meeting between Luce and Roosevelt:** Interview with CBL, in the W. A. Swanberg collection, box 18 (RBMLCU).

16 **CBL cites Roosevelt:** Michael R. Beschloss, *Kennedy and Roosevelt: The Uneasy Alliance* (New York: W. W. Norton., 1980), p. 211.

16 **Luce's annoyance with Roosevelt:** The interview with William Benton, in the W. A. Swanberg collection, box 18, folder on interviews (RBMLCU).

17 **Press the President:** Martin Gilbert, *Winston S. Churchill, Volume VI, Finest Hour 1939–1941* (London: Heinemann, 1983), p. 688.

17 **Would not be believed:** Langer and Gleason, vol. II, p. 748.

17 **America is doomed:** Lord Lothian to Shepardson, July 28, 1940, with a memorandum, in the papers of Whitney Shepardson (FDRL).

17 **The importance of Caribbean bases:** *Time*, July 29, 1940; and Gilbert, vol. VI, pp. 687–688.

18 **Tonnage lost:** Philip Goodhart, *Fifty Ships that Saved the World: The Foundation of the Anglo-American Alliance* (Garden City, NY: Doubleday, 1965), p. 165.

18 **Churchill appeals to Roosevelt:** Churchill's cable of July 31, 1940, cited in Winston S. Churchill, *Their Finest Hour* (Cambridge, MA: Houghton Mifflin, 1949), pp. 401–402.

19 **The Century men meet FDR:** Langer and Gleason, vol. II, p. 749. See also Charles G. Ross, "Inside Story of 'Propaganda Engine,' " *St. Louis Post-Dispatch*, September 22, 1940.

19 **The Knox-Lothian conversation:** Harold L. Ickes, *The Secret Diary of Harold L. Ickes, III, The Lowering Clouds 1939–1941* (New York: Simon & Schuster, 1954), p. 283. For another, very similar version of the conversation, see John Morton Blum, *From the Morgenthau Diaries: Years of Urgency 1938–1941* (Boston: Houghton Mifflin, 1965), p. 177.

19 **Lothian did not yet know this:** Lash, p. 207.

19 **Sale to the United States:** Woodward, vol. I, pp. 364–365.

20 **An impediment overcome:** B. Mitchell Simpson, III, *Admiral Harold R. Stark: Architect of Victory, 1939–1945* (Columbia: University of South Carolina Press, 1989), p. 53.

20 **Roosevelt's account of the Cabinet meeting:** *F.D.R.: His Personal Letters 1928–1945*, vol. II, pp. 1050–1051.

20 **Atlantic Coast:** *The Secret Diary of Harold L. Ickes*, III, p. 292, August 2, 1941.

20 **Agreeable to us:** Churchill to Lothian, August 3, 1940, in Churchill, *Their Finest Hour*, pp. 402–403.

20 **Authorize the use:** The President's note, dated August 13, 1940, in *F.D.R.: His Personal Letters 1928–1945*, vol. II, p. 1052.

20 **Ninety-nine-year leases:** Churchill, *Finest Hour*, p. 407.

20–21 **Face-saving compromise:** Ibid., pp. 410–414.

21 **Jackson's opinion:** *The Public Papers and Addresses of Franklin D. Roosevelt*, 1940 Volume, *War—and Aid to the Democracies* (New York: Macmillan, 1941), p. 405.

21 **Roosevelt on the agreement:** Ibid., p. 391.

21 **Widely felt:** Churchill (August 15), cited by Goodhart, p. 165.

22 **Declaring war:** Churchill, *Finest Hour*, p. 404.

22 **Lothian on the agreement:** James R. M. Butler, *Lord Lothian, Philip Kerr, 1882–1940* (London: Macmillan, 1960), p. 298.

22 **The threat of American intervention:** Churchill, *Finest Hour*, pp. 521–522.

22 **At a crucial moment in the war:** Churchill to Roosevelt, April 24, 1941, in Churchill, *The Grand Alliance* (Boston: Houghton Mifflin, 1950), p. 143.

23 **In a favorable sense:** Churchill to Roosevelt, in Churchill, *Grand Alliance*, p. 146.

CHAPTER TWO

24 **On the youth and education of Henry W. Luce:** "Candidate Papers of Henry Winters Luce" before the Presbyterian Board, 1896, in the papers of B. A. Garside, box 2 (HIWRP); and "In the Interest of the Kingdom" (presumably written by Garside in 1942), in the United China Relief Collection, box 65 (SGMMLPU). Garside was Henry W. Luce's friend, co-worker, and biographer. His writing about Luce tends to be worshipful, but he often provides important and accurate information. See his *One Increasing Purpose: The Life of Henry Winters Luce* (London: Fleming H. Revell, 1948), pp. 23–28. John Hersey's comments about the Reverend Luce are more negative. See Hersey's essay on HRL in *Life Sketches* (New York: Alfred A. Knopf, 1989).

25 **On Luce's call:** Garside, pp. 21–22.

25 **On Luce's vocation:** HRL to Members of the China Colleges Committees, February 15, 1940; and the Associated Boards for Christian Colleges in China, *An Impressive Service: The Story of the Christian Colleges of China* (February 1940), in the Anita McCormick Blaine papers, box 388, folder on HRL (MCWSHS).

25 **On Mateer:** HRL, "The Christianity of the Missionary," speech delivered in San Francisco, September 11, 1946, sponsored by the World Mission of the Christian Church.

25 **On Elizabeth Root:** Garside, pp. 58–60.

26 **Hersey's evocation of the missionaries:** John Hersey, *The Call* (New York: Alfred A. Knopf, 1985), p. 120.

27 **The Luces' activities in China:** The memorandum from Dr. Luce to Dr. Barstow, February 4, 1933, in the papers of Henry W. Luce, microfilm frame 17509, Hartford Seminary Foundation, Case Memorial Library, Hartford, CT.

27 **Luce and his servants:** Interview with Mrs. Maurice T. Moore, in the W. A. Swanberg collection, box 18 (RBMLCU).

27 **On the challenge of China:** Jerry Israel, " 'For God, for China and for Yale'—The Open Door in Action," *American Historical Review*, vol. 75/3 (February 1970), p. 805.

27 **Western ideals in China:** Hersey, *The Call*, p. 200.

27–28 **The United States and the Open Door:** Paul A. Varg, *The Making of a Myth: The United States and China 1897–1912* (East Lansing: Michigan State University Press), pp. 22–28.

28 **The Luces and the Boxer Rebellion:** W. A. Swanberg, *Luce and His Empire* (New York: Charles Scribner's Sons, 1972), pp. 22–24; and Garside, pp. 94–98.

28 **American policy toward China:** Nathaniel Pfeffer, "The United States and China: Politics of Sentimentality," in Peter Spackman and Lee Ambrose, *The Columbia University Forum Anthology* (New York: Atheneum, 1968), pp. 38ff.

28–29 **The Luce children and their household:** The interview with Sheldon Luce, in the W. A. Swanberg collection, box 18 (RBMLCU). Kenneth Stewart's very useful articles on Luce's background appeared in *PM* (New York) on August 27 and September 3 and 10, 1944.

29 **Young HRL:** HRL, letters to his family 1903–1922, copies in the papers of W. A. Swanberg (RBMLCU).

29 **Anecdotes about Harry Luce's childhood:** Interview with CBL, in the W. A. Swanberg collection, box 18 (RBMLCU).

30 **Beth Moore and HRL as children:** John Kobler, "The First Tycoon and the Power of the Press," *Saturday Evening Post*, November 6, 1965; and the W. A. Swanberg collection, box 18, interviews (B. A. Garside, September 3, 1968) (RBMLCU).

30 **The McCormicks:** "First Families of Chicago," *Herald-Examiner*, November 27, 1932; interviews with Henry W. Luce and Elizabeth L. Moore, February 22, 1934, and February 25, 27, 1937, box 33, in the Nettie F. McCormick Papers (MCWSHS); and the Anita McC. Blaine Papers, box 389, Henry W. Luce folder (MCWSHS). See also Garside, pp. 113–124.

30–31 **The Reverend Luce's fund-raising:** Robert T. Elson, *Time Inc.: The Intimate History of a Publishing Enterprise 1923–1941* (New York: Atheneum, 1968), p. 23, note 4.

31 **The Reverend Luce's paternal advice:** H. W. Luce to Harry Luce, October 11, 1914, in the papers of B. A. Garside, box 2 (HIWRP).

31 **The Reverend Luce's opinion of Mrs. Nettie McCormick:** H. W. Luce to McCormick, March 14, 1907, in the papers of Harold F. McCormick, box 17, Correspondence 1907 (MCWSHS).

32 **Luce and Rockefeller:** Luce lunched with Rockefeller on January 30, 1907. See the Nettie F. McCormick Papers, box 24, folder on Mr. and Mrs. Henry W. Luce 1906–1922 (MCWSHS). This folder contains two especially im-

portant letters, from Nettie McCormick to Henry W. Luce, December 14, 1906, and to Elizabeth R. Luce, January 31, 1907. See also Swanberg, pp. 25–26, and Garside, p. 150.

32 Bringing Christianity to Asia: See HRL, comments welcoming Bishop Chen Wen-yuan, Madison Avenue Presbyterian Church, March 6, 1944, in the papers of HRL, Correspondence, box 75 (MDLOC).

32 Harry Luce in school: HRL, citations from letters to his family, 1903–1922, in the papers of W. A. Swanberg (RBMLCU); and Elson, pp. 24–25.

32–33 Harry Luce's Americanism: The papers of W. A. Swanberg, box 18, interviews (B. A. Garside, September 3, 1968) (RBMLCU); and HRL, "An American Story," 1950, in John K. Jessup, ed., *The Ideas of Henry Luce* (New York: Atheneum, 1969), pp. 376–379.

33 Harry Luce's exuberant patriotism: Elson, p. 27.

CHAPTER THREE

35 Harry Luce at Hotchkiss: The letters of Henry R. Luce 1903–1922, p. 6, in the folder "Interests and Family," box 17, in the papers of W. A. Swanberg (RBMLCU).

35 The scholarship boy and his Chinese background: Garside, *One Increasing Purpose*, p. 27; and Elson, *Time Inc.*, pp. 29–31.

36 Harry Luce and his America: Swanberg, *Luce and His Empire*, pp. 31–34.

37 Harry Luce and sports: HRL, address at the sales convention of *Sports Illustrated*, Carefree, AZ, May 11, 1965, in the private papers of Sidney James. See also H. W. Luce to Harry Luce, September 29, 1914, in the papers of B. A. Garside, box 2 (HIWRP).

37 The Luces in contact: H. W. Luce to Harry Luce, September 29 and October 29, 1914, in the papers of B. A. Garside, box 2 (HIWRP).

37 Further contrasts between Luce and Hadden: Elson, p. 16.

38 American hegemony after the war: Excerpts from HRL's letters, in the W. A. Swanberg collection, box 17, folder on interests and family (RBMLCU).

38 Hadden and Luce at Hotchkiss: Elson, p. 31. See also the interview with Douglas Hadden, May 24, 1950, in the papers of Dorothy Sterling (SCDKLUO). Briton Hadden was his first cousin.

38 Luce's calling to journalism: Swanberg, p. 34.

38 Luce's job in journalism: Letters of HRL, #448, Interests and Family, box 17, in the papers of W. A. Swanberg (RBMCCU).

38 Luce at the *News*: *Yale Daily News*, March 7, 1917.

39 Debate about going to war: "Do the People Want War?," ibid., March 6, 1917.

39 Luce, work, and ROTC: Interview with Mrs. Maurice T. Moore, in the W. A. Swanberg collection, box 18 (RBMLCU).

39–40 Luce in camp: Interview with John M. Hincks, ibid.

40 Smoking: Luce was addicted to nicotine all of his adult life. For a theory about the causes of addiction among American smokers, see Kathleen Cushman, "Addicted to 'Getting Normal,' " *Atlantic*, October 1991, pp. 131–132.

40 Luce in the autumn of 1918: Mrs. Nettie F. McCormick to Elizabeth R. Luce, October 1, 1918, in the Nettie F. McCormick papers, box 24, folder on Mr. and Mrs. Henry W. Luce 1906–1922 (MCWSHS). See also Swanberg,

p. 42, for Luce's comment about the Bolshevik menace. On Luce at Yale, see Morehead Patterson, ed., *History of the Class of Nineteen Hundred Twenty* (New Haven, CT: Tuttle, Morehouse and Taylor, n.d.), pp. 269–271.

40 **HRL, "On the Integrity of Mind":** *Yale Literary Magazine*, vol. 85/5 (February 1920).

41 **"When We Say America":** Patterson, pp. 447–450.

41 **Luce most brilliant:** John Shaw Billings, Scrapbook 57, p. 259, in the papers of John Shaw Billings (SCL). Luce, commenting in 1948, regretted that "When I went to Yale, the last thing they tried to tell me was the truth—the philosophic truth." See also Patterson, pp. 269–271.

41 **Hadden heading south:** Elson, p. 50.

42 **Harding:** HRL, in the papers of Henry Robinson Luce, box 86, unpublished memoir of Republican conventions (MDLOC).

42 **Luce and Mrs. McCormick:** Interview with Henry R. Luce in the Nettie F. McCormick papers, box 33 (MCWSHS).

42 **Luce on America's future:** The letters of Henry R. Luce 1903–1922, p. 15, in the papers of W. A. Swanberg (RBMLCU). See also Swanberg, p. 45.

42 **Luce at Oxford:** Elson, p. 51.

43 **Faith and reason:** Henry Luce III, "The Faith of Henry R. Luce," *Dedication Addresses, The Center of Theological Inquiry*, Reports from the Center, Number 2 (Princeton, 1985), p. 3.

CHAPTER FOUR

44 **Luce in Chicago:** HRL, interview, box 33, in the Nettie F. McCormick papers (MCWSHS).

44–45 **Hecht on Luce:** Elson, *Time Inc.*, p. 53.

45 **Luce's early career in journalism:** The W. A. Swanberg collection, box 19 (RBMLCU)

45 **Luce and the origins of his newsmagazine:** Elson, p. 56.

45 **Preparing to publish a newsmagazine:** Ibid., p. 4; and Swanberg, *Luce and His Empire*, p. 50.

45 **The Luce/Hadden prospectus:** "TIME The Weekly News Magazine (A Prospectus)," in the W. A. Swanberg collection, box 19, uncatalogued material 1921–1952 (RBMLCU). *Time* early on ended the practice of acknowledging specific newspaper sources except in a few rare cases.

46 **The attitudes expressed by the early *Time*:** *Time* (dummy issue), December 30, 1922.

46 **The attitudes of Luce and Hadden toward journalism:** Sterling, "The Luce Empire," p. 17, in the papers of Dorothy Sterling (SCDKLUO).

47 **Luce's bias:** John K. Jessup, *The Ideas of Henry Luce*, p. 7.

47 **Luce's attempt to raise money:** The official Time Inc. biography of HRL, October 1956, p. 4, in the private papers of Sidney James. For a list of the preferred shareholders and their holdings, see the papers of A. J. Liebling, Munves notes, TM VII (DRBCUL).

47 **Hadden's role in soliciting investors:** The W. A. Swanberg collection, box 18, interviews (John M. Hincks, pp. 2–6) (RBMLCU); also relevant are HRL to Anita McC. Blaine, September 6, 25 and October 6, 23, 1922, in the Anita McC. Blaine papers, box 388 (MCWSHS).

48 **Manfred Gottfried:** Elson, pp. 60–62.

48 Harry Luce's work habits: Davenport, "History of TIME, INC." (undated memorandum to Mr. Hodgins), in the papers of Russell W. Davenport, box 36 (MDLOC).

48 Luce's attempt to solicit the names of distinguished individuals: HRL's letter to Baruch, n.d., in the papers of Bernard M. Baruch, box 176 (SGMMLPU).

48 The solicitation of potential subscribers: Roy E. Larsen's circular letter of December 26, 1922, and his letter to Mrs. Emmons Blaine, January 31, 1923, in the papers of Anita McC. Blaine, 1E, box 691, folder *Time* (MCWSHS). See also Elson, pp. 9, 64.

49 *Time* on Victor Emmanuel III: *Time*, July 30, 1923, p. 10.

49 *Time* on Prohibition: *Time*, March 11, 1929, p. 16, noted in the A. J. Liebling papers, Munves notes, TM IV (DRBCUL). On the Luces' disagreements over alcohol, see Elson, p. 114.

49 Larsen and the promotion of *Time*: Elson, p. 69.

50 Mr. Mohney: Charles C. Mohney to Time Inc., October 22, 1923, and Lisabeth Davis to "Dear Sir," October 22, 1923, in the Daniel Longwell collection, box 70 (RBMLCU).

50 Roosevelt and *Time*: FDR to HRL, August 13, 1923, and Luce to Roosevelt, August 23, 1923, in the Papers of Franklin D. Roosevelt Concerning Non-Political Affairs, Group 14/Box 7 (FDRL). Copy in the Sterling papers (SCDKLUO).

50–51 Harry Luce and Lila Hotz: Interview with Lila Tyng, in the W. A. Swanberg collection, box 18 (RBMLCU).

51 The death of Mrs. McCormick: HRL to Anita McC. Blaine, October 8, 1923, in the papers of Anita McC. Blaine, box 704/folder on HRL (MCWSHS); and Henry Winters Luce to Blaine, November 27, 1923, ibid., box 389, folder on Henry Winters Luce.

51 Lila R. Hotz: Lila R. Hotz, premarital letters to Luce (excerpts), in the W. A. Swanberg collection, box 17, Henry R. Luce and Lila R. Hotz folder (RBMLCU).

51 Luce and his marriage: Interview with Mrs. Maurice T. Moore, in the W. A. Swanberg collection, box 18 (RBMLCU).

51–52 Marriage and "honeymoon": 1956 Time Inc. biography of Luce, p. 5; Munves notes, in the papers of A. J. Liebling, TM VI (Hobson, p. 2) (DRBCUL). Some of Hotz's letters to Henry R. Luce may be consulted in the W. A. Swanberg collection, box 17, folder on HRL and Lila Hotz (RBMLCU).

51 *Time* and its readability: James P. Wood, *Magazines in the United States* (New York: The Ronald Press, 1956), p. 206.

51 The expansion of *Time*'s staff in the 1920s: Elson, pp. 67–69.

52 Luce on religion: The interview with Dr. Francis Brown, in the W. A. Swanberg collection, box 18 (RBMLCU).

52 Hadden's style: Munves notes, TM VI, in the papers of A. J. Liebling (DRBCUL).

52 *Time*'s invention of playful new words: Elson, pp. 83–90; and James Baughman, *Henry R. Luce and the Rise of the American News Media* (Boston: Twayne, 1987), p. 44.

52 "Peter Mathews": Robert Sherrod's letter to the editor, *The Smithsonian*, May 1991.

52 *Time*'s circulation figures: Elson, pp. 77–96.

52 Growing circulation: Ibid., p. 94.

53 Preparing copy: Ibid., p. 109; and Munves notes, TM VI (interview with J. S. Martin), and TM VII, in the papers of A. J. Liebling (DRBCUL).

54 *Time*'s method: Baughman, pp. 43, 59; and the W. A. Swanberg collection, box 17, W.A.S. folder (RBMLCU).

54 *Time*'s upscale audience: Baughman, pp. 34–51.

54 *Time* and the early days of radio: The interview with John M. Hincks, in the W. A. Swanberg collection, box 18, interview folder (RBMLCU).

55 Luce and the Hadden shares: The Munves notes, TM VI, in the papers of A. J. Liebling (DRBCUL); interview with John Shaw Billings (November 9, 1968), in the W. A. Swanberg collection, box 18, interview folder (RBMLCU); and Elson, pp. 120–124.

CHAPTER FIVE

56–57 Luce, capitalism, and *Fortune:* HRL to Ferdinand Eberstadt, December 9, 1942, in the Ferdinand Eberstadt papers, box 103 (SMMLPU). On Luce's plans for *Fortune,* see Lloyd Morris, *Postscript to Yesterday* (New York: Harper & Row, 1965), pp. 311–318; oral history interview with Eric Hodgins, Columbia University Oral History Project, p. 51.

57 Luce and spiritual values: Jessup, p. 95.

57 Luce on leadership: Address by HRL, Rochester, 1928, in the W. A. Swanberg collection, box 18, folder on the speeches of HRL 1920–1932 (RBMLCU).

57 "You must educate your conscience": Scrapbook 57, "Analecta," p. 367 (1951), in the papers of John Shaw Billings (SCL).

57 Luce and Burke: Jessup, *The Ideas of Henry Luce,* pp. 100–101.

57 Luce on the public interest: HRL, "An Admonition" and "The Tycoon," ibid., pp. 218–221.

57–58 The founding of *Fortune:* Elson, *Time Inc.,* pp. 128–129.

58 Owen Young: Ibid., p. 143.

58 Advertisers and *Fortune:* Ibid., pp. 134–140.

58 *Fortune*'s prospects: Davenport, *History of TIME, INC.,* in the papers of Russell W. Davenport, box 36 (MDLOC). John K. Jessup, who knew Luce well, tells us that he "operated on the assumption that freedom is the real source of efficiency. . . ." Managing editor Parker Lloyd-Smith might not have been efficient, but his product was spectacular. See Jessup, p. 23.

58 *Fortune* during the Depression: Archibald MacLeish, "The First Nine Years," in Daniel Bell et al., *Writing for Fortune* (New York: Time Inc., 1980).

58 Ingersoll and Luce: Munves notes, TM VI (J. S. Martin, 3), in the papers of A. J. Liebling (DRBCUL). Hodgins: Oral History, p. 82. On the New Deal, see Jessup, p. 235.

58 Luce and the search for journalistic talent: Elson, p. 137.

59 Russell Davenport on his experience at *Fortune:* Davenport to Mumford, February 5, 1940, in the papers of Lewis Mumford, Special Collections, Van Pelt Library, University of Pennsylvania.

59 On Davenport: Obituary in the *New York Times,* April 20, 1954.

59 Luce and industrial photography: Elson, p. 136.

59 Bourke-White's interview with Luce: HRL and Bourke-White, exchange

of telegrams, May 1929, in the papers of Margaret Bourke-White, box 24, folder on Luce (GARLSU).

60 **Bourke-White and *Fortune:*** Vicki Goldberg, *Margaret Bourke-White* (New York: Harper & Row, 1986), p. 102.

60 **Bourke-White on her early days at *Fortune:*** Margaret Bourke-White, *Portrait of Myself* (New York: Simon & Schuster, 1963), pp. 63–76.

60 **Luce's willingness to tolerate political dissenters:** See Hodgins, Oral History, p. 57. MacLeish called Luce a "truly generous publisher": See his scrawled comment on HRL, November 6, 1933, in the papers of Archibald MacLeish, box 8 (MDLOC).

60 **Luce's work rules:** HRL, memorandum to the staff of *Fortune*, April 13, 1933, in the W. A. Swanberg collection, box 18 (RBMLCU).

60 **Hodgins as an editor:** Elson, pp. 214–216; Baughman, *Henry R. Luce*, pp. 71–73; and Hodgins' comments cited by John K. Jessup, "The Best Writing Job in the Country," in *Writing for Fortune*, p. 16.

61 **Research at *Fortune:*** Elson, pp. 146–47.

61 **The socioeconomic status of *Fortune*'s readers:** Baughman, pp. 67–74.

61 **Rumors about *Fortune:*** Elson, p. 150.

62 **"Ought to lose an account . . .":** Ibid., p. 209.

62 **On Time Inc.'s financial condition:** Munves notes, II, in the papers of A. J. Liebling (DRBCUL).

62 **On Billings and *Time:*** HRL to John Shaw Billings, November 1, 1933, the Time-Life-Fortune papers, I, folder 5, in the John Shaw Billings collection (SCL). See also the interview with Manfred Gottfried, June 19, 1968, and with Noel F. Busch, January 22, 1969, in the W. A. Swanberg collection, box 18 (RBMLCU).

62 **Billings' early career at Time Inc.:** John S. Billings, "Recollections of Time and Life and Luce," two tapes recorded in January 1966, T73/a/b (SCL). See also Elson, pp. 156–158.

63 **The expansion of Time Inc.:** Elson, pp. 389–392. Mary Fraser, who headed the research department, warned Luce against becoming an isolated boss, working amid people whom he did not know.

63 **Time Inc. and radio:** ibid., pp. 154, 175, 183; and Baughman, pp. 74–76.

64 **American good works in China:** Jonathan D. Spence, "China on the Verge," *New York Review of Books*, July 18, 1991, p. 40.

64 **Luce's trip to China:** Notes made by Mr. Luce on his trip to China, July 1932, in the W. A. Swanberg collection, box 20, folder on HRL, 1920–1932, speeches (RMBLCU).

65 **China's progress:** Dr. Arthur N. Young, a financial adviser to the Chiang government, praised it for being efficient and progressive. See Patricia Niels, *China Images in the Life and Times of Henry Luce* (Savage, MD: Rowman, 1990), p. 79.

65 **Luce's return to Chefoo:** Diary of Leslie R. Severinghaus, cited in the W. A. Swanberg collection, box 18; for Luce's account of his 1932 trip, see his rough notes for a speech delivered on November 17, 1932, Ibid., box 20, folder on HRL 1920–1932, speeches (RBMLCU).

66 **On LaGuardia:** John Chamberlain, *A Life with the Printed Word* (Chicago: Regnery Gateway, 1982), p. 72.

66 ***Time*'s changing style:** Baughman, pp. 42, 56.

66 *Time*'s establishment of bureaus outside New York: Munves notes, TM VI, in the papers of A. J. Liebling (DRBCUL).

66 Billings' years with *Time:* John S. Billings, "Recollections." See also the Time-Life-Fortune papers, I, folder 4, in the John Shaw Billings collection (SCL).

66 Time Inc.'s incentives: Munves notes, TM II (DRBCUL). The figures on Time Inc. also come from the Munves/Liebling notes.

CHAPTER SIX

67 Clare Luce's youth: Wilfrid Sheed, *Clare Boothe Luce* (New York: E. P. Dutton, 1982), p. 38; and Ralph G. Martin, *Henry and Clare: An Intimate Portrait of the Luces* (New York: G. P. Putnam's Sons, 1991), chapter 3.

68 Without central heating: Swanberg, *Luce and His Empire*, p. 136.

68 "No good deed": Sheed, p. 22.

68–69 Luce's encounters with Clare Boothe: Interview with Allen Grover, May 23, 1968, in the W. A. Swanberg collection, box 18 (RBMLCU).

69 Harry's infatuation with Clare: Interview with CBL, ibid.

69 Luce's personal anguish: Swanberg, pp. 114–116. See also John S. Billings, "Recollections." T73/a/b (SCL).

69 Luce's separation: The W. A. Swanberg collection, box 18, folder on interviews (Allen Grover) (RBMLCU).

70 The Luces' anguish: Correspondence between HRL and Lila H. Luce, ibid., box 17 (RBMLCU).

70 Clare Boothe's personal situation in the early 1930s: Sheed, p. 56. On Luce's income in 1936 see Munves notes on *Time*, in the papers of A. J. Liebling (DRBCUL).

70 The origins of *Life:* John R. Whiting and George R. Clark, "The Picture Magazines," *Harper's Magazine*, vol. 187, no. 1117, June 1943. On the purchase, see Baughman, *Henry. R. Luce*, p. 90. On Clare's earlier plans for a magazine, see Goldberg, *Margaret Bourke-White*, p. 174.

70 Daniel Longwell: Munves notes, TM VII, in the papers of A. J. Liebling (DRBCUL).

71 Longwell and Missouri: Upon his retirement to Neosho in 1954, Longwell became a kind of local celebrity. See "Back to the Old Farm with a New Philosophy of Living," the *Kansas City Star*, December 4, 1955, and March 16, 1958.

71 Longwell's career in publishing: The notes written and dictated by Daniel Longwell, typed in March 1970, presumably by his wife, Mary Fraser, in the Daniel Longwell collection, box 71, folder "Biography" (RBMLCU).

71 Longwell's career: See the obituary in the *New York Times*, November 22, 1968. See also the memo re: "History of Life Magazine," in the Daniel Longwell collection, box 68 (RBMLCU).

71 Longwell, Luce, and Clare Boothe: Mary Fraser Longwell to W. A. Swanberg, March 10, 1969, in the W. A. Swanberg collection (RBMLCU).

72 Luce's concept of *Life:* HRL, memorandum to all members of the editorial staff of *Life*, May 16, 1938, in the Margaret Bourke-White collection, box 27, folder on HRL (GARLSU). Wilson Hicks, who became Billings' picture editor at *Life*, should be consulted. See his *Words and Pictures: An Introduction to Photojournalism* (New York: Harper, 1952), especially pp. 3–59.

72 *Life* **in the making:** Loudon Wainwright, *The Great American Picture Magazine: An Insider History of Life* (New York: Alfred A. Knopf, 1986), p. 29. On Luce as promoter, see William F. Buckley, Jr., "The Life and Time of Henry Luce," *Esquire*, December 1983, p. 254.

72 **Korff:** Wainwright, p. 27; and Jackson Edwards, "One Every Minute: The Picture Magazines," *Scribner's Magazine*, May 1938.

73 **The Luces' divorce:** Munves notes, TM VII, in the papers of A. J. Liebling (DRBCUL).

73 **Luce's dress habits and Clare's influence on them:** The William Benton interview, in the W. A. Swanberg collection, box 18 (RBMLCU).

73 **Mepkin:** Interview with Marcia Davenport, in the W. A. Swanberg collection, box 18 (RBMLCU).

73 **Luce and Greenwich:** Dorothy Sterling, "The Luce Empire," chapter 5 (SCDKLUO); and Swanberg, pp. 133–134.

73 **Prospectus:** Time Inc., "A Prospectus for a New Magazine," in the papers of the National Broadcasting Company, box 50, folder Time Inc. (WSHS).

74 **Staffing** *Life:* Wainwright, chapter 3, specifically page 50. On Billings' view of Martin's womanizing, see his scrapbook, item number 57, in the papers of John Shaw Billings (SCL).

74 **Billings' problems:** John S. Billings, "Recollections." T73/a/b (SCL).

74 *Life* **and its organization:** *Editorial Organization and System for LIFE,* October 19, 1936, in the W. A. Swanberg collection, box 18, folder with uncatalogued correspondence, 1932–1939 (RBMLCU).

74 **Bourke-White's arrangement with Luce:** Letter of agreement between Time Inc. and Bourke-White, September 3, 1936, in the Margaret Bourke-White collection, box 50, folder on Time Inc. 1935–1937 (GARLSU).

74 **Bourke-White in Montana:** Bourke-White, *Portrait of Myself,* pp. 141–149. On Luce's choice for the cover photo, see Daniel Longwell to T. George Harris, May 10, 1956, in the Margaret Bourke-White collection, box 27, folder on Longwell (GARLSU); and Goldberg, p. 178.

74 **Bourke-White's politics:** William L. Howard, "Dear Kit, Dear Skinny: The Letters of Erskine Caldwell and Margaret Bourke-White," *Syracuse University Library Associates Courier,* XXIII, 2 (Fall 1988), pp. 25–26.

75 *Life's* **attitude toward photographers:** George Eggleston to Longwell, June 3, 1937, i, in the Daniel Longwell collection, box 26, folder on miscellaneous correspondence (RBMLCU).

75 **Bourke-White and Luce:** John S. Billings, "Recollections." Bourke-White believed that since much of her work for *Life* never appeared in the magazine, it was "wasted." For Bourke-White's temporary break with Luce, see her letter to Mr. Weiss, February 27, 1940 ("not sent"), in the Margaret Bourke-White collection, box 26, folder headed "Life Resignation" (GARLSU).

75 **Publishing** *Life:* Edwards, p. 20. On the printers, see Goldberg, p. 174.

75 **The early issues of** *Life:* Baughman, p. 95.

75 *Life's* **commitment to contemporary American art:** The Cranbrook-Life exhibition of contemporary American painting took place in Bloomfield Hills, MI, May 17 to June 2, 1940. Also relevant is MacLeish to HRL, October 16, 1939, in papers of Archibald MacLeish, container 14 (MDLOC).

75 **Billings on Longwell:** DJSB, September 8, 1949 (SCL).

75 **Hicks and** *Life's* **pictures:** Elson, *Time Inc.,* p. 305; and Wilson Hicks,

Speech to Managing Editors, Louisville, 1940, the Time-Life-Fortune papers, in the John Shaw Billings collection (SCL).

75–76 John Shaw Billings: Wainwright, p. 105. On Billings' likes and dislikes, see David Cort, *The Sin of Henry R. Luce: An Anatomy of Journalism* (Secaucus, N.J.: Lyle Stuart, 1974), p. 115.

76 Working with Luce et al. at *Life*: *The Reminiscences of Andrew Heiskell*, in the Oral History Research Office, Columbia University (1990), pp. 59, 190.

76 Busch: Ibid., pp. 56, 178. Heiskell, p. 54, is the source of the quote about Busch as a "British" dilettante. See also Wainwright, p. 112, and the comments of Laura Z. Hobson, cited in Munves notes, Hobson 3, TM VI, in the papers of A. J. Liebling (DRBCUL).

76 Christ in *Life*: *Life*, December 28, 1936.

77 The Post Office objected: John S. Billings, "Recollections."

77 Abortion: *Life*, January 11, 1937.

76–77 Censors: DJSB, March 5, 1942. Billings reports that Boston banned an issue of *Life*.

78 Larsen: John S. Billings, "Recollections." See also Elson, pp. 338–342.

78 Time Inc. and *Life*'s financial woes: Edwards, p. 21.

CHAPTER SEVEN

79 Luce and the Roosevelts: HRL, "Indispensable Man," speech delivered at the University of Chicago, April 19, 1933, in Jessup, *The Ideas of Henry Luce*, pp. 338–339.

79 Roosevelt walking: *Time*, March 13, 1933. On Luce's concept of the hero, see Scrapbook 57, p. 361, in the papers of John Shaw Billings (SCL).

80 Luce's impression of Roosevelt: Elson, *Time Inc.*, pp. 207–208; and Swanberg, *Luce and His Empire*, pp. 106–107.

80 Writing to Billings: HRL to John S. Billings, November 1, 1933, the Time-Life-Fortune papers, I, folder 5, in the John Shaw Billings collection (SCL). On moral intelligence and molding history, see Scrapbook 57, p. 308, ibid. Long after Luce had ceased to admire Roosevelt, he remembered FDR's "easy charm." See HRL, report on his trip to Brazil (1947), in Jessup, p. 359.

80 Luce, Grover, and Early: The correspondence in OF 3618, *Fortune* magazine folder (FDRL).

80 Private initiative and public law: Elson, p. 191. Luce retained urban historian Lewis Mumford as a consultant to *Fortune*. Mumford, who was interested in the relationship between housing and urban culture, subsequently provided both *Fortune* and *Architectural Forum* with valuable material.

81 Luce, the White House, and problems with *The March of Time*: HRL to Louis M. Howe, and Stephen Early to Charles J. Gilchrist, January 15, 1934, OF 2442, March of Time. See also Luce to Early, January 21, 1935, and Early to Luce, January 22, 1935, in the papers of Stephen Early, box 10, Luce folder. Also relevant is Louis de Rochemont to Marvin H. McIntyre, May 15, 1935, OF 2442. On *March of Time*'s treatment of FDR, see Roosevelt to Rochemont, November 4, 1936, PPF 3338, *Time* magazine, March of Time (FDRL).

81 Roosevelt and the *Fortune* polls: The White House advance copy of the *Fortune* press release on the 1936 election: OF 3618 (FDRPL); and Elson, pp. 223–224. On Roosevelt's gratitude, see Roosevelt to Elmo Roper, August 2, 1938, PPF 5437 (FDRPL). On Roosevelt's interest in the press, including magazines, see Richard W. Steele, "The Pulse of the People: Franklin D. Roosevelt and the Gauging of American Public Opinion," *Journal of Contemporary History*, IX, no. 4 (October 1974), pp. 197–198. For Roper's comments on Luce, see the interview with Roper, November 25, 1969, in the W. A. Swanberg collection, box 18 (RBMLCU).

81 **Time on Roosevelt:** Elson, p. 257. On Early, see Delbert Clar, " 'Steve' Takes Care of It,' " *New York Times Magazine*, July 27, 1941. On Luce's objection to Eleanor Roosevelt, see HRL, unpublished manuscript, Speeches and Writings File, box 86, in the papers of Henry Robinson Luce (MDLOC).

81 **Farley and the Luce publications:** The Oral History Interview with George Tames, Washington, D.C., June 11, 1980, p. 9 (HSTL). On Farley, see H. Horan to John S. Billings, August 25, 1937, and Horan to Roy Larsen, August 28, 1937, in the Time-Life-Fortune papers, I, folder 12, in the John Shaw Billings collection (SCL). See also Betty H. Winfield, *FDR and the News Media* (Urbana: University of Illinois Press, 1990), pp. 114–115.

82 **Mrs. Sara Roosevelt and *Life*:** Wainwright, *The Great American Magazine*, p. 45.

82 **Roosevelt's attacks on business:** "Business-in-Government," *Fortune*, February 1938, p. 58. On hatred for the business world, see Cort, *The Sin of HRL*, p. 18.

82 **Ickes and Luce:** The Diaries of Harold Ickes, reel 2, pp. 1649–1652, July 27, 1936 (MDLOC).

82 **Luce and the New Deal:** HRL to MacLeish, June 26, 1942, in the papers of Archibald MacLeish, box 14 (MDLOC). See also the address of HRL before the Ohio Bankers Association, Cleveland, November 10, 1937, in Jessup, p. 229.

82 **Luce on freedom of the press:** HRL, speech delivered at Williamstown, Mass., before the Institute of Human Relations, September 2, 1937, in the Post-Presidential papers of Herbert Hoover/Individual/HRL (HHPL).

82–83 **Luce's philosophy of the press:** Thomas Griffith, *How True* (Boston: Little, Brown, 1974), p. 98. On Luce's rejection of impartiality, see Jessup, pp. 56–57; and HRL to Dewey, October 4, 1938, in the papers of Thomas E. Dewey, Series I, box 53, folder 1 (RRLUR). On serving the nation, see the diary of John Shaw Billings, November 14, 1952 (SCL). See also HRL, remarks at a dinner of *Time*, New York, November 14, 1952, in Jessup, p. 71.

83 **Luce and Ortega:** José Ortega y Gasset, *The Revolt of the Masses* (New York: W. W. Norton: 1932). See also Sterling, "The Luce Empire," chapter 5 (SCDKLVO), and Baughman, *Henry R. Luce*, pp. 111–114.

83 **Luce on Mussolini:** Jessup, p. 232. On "Roosevelt the First," *Fortune*, May 1938, p. 182.

83 ***Life* on Dies:** *Life*, ". . . Dies smear . . . danger of wide Red hunt," November 6, 1939. On Shirley Temple, see *Life*, September 5, 1938.

83 **Anticommunism and attacks on Roosevelt:** Robert E. Herzstein, *Roosevelt and Hitler: Prelude to War* (New York: Paragon House, 1989), pp. 84–85.

83 **The expansion of Time Inc.:** Elson, p. 334. Luce's office: John S. Billings, "Recollections of Time and Life and Luce," T73/a/b (SCL).

84 ***Fortune* on "Business-in-Government":** *Fortune*, September 1938, p. 64.

84 **Luce in the late 1930s:** "Man of the Week," *New York Post*, April 16, 1938.

85 **Luce, Macdonald, and U.S. Steel:** Elson, pp. 254–255.

85 Luce, labor, and management: "America in 1938 Needs Fewer Men with Guns & More Men of Good Will," *Life*, October 24, 1938.

85 John L. Lewis: *Fortune*, April 1939. On Billings' reaction to Ingersoll, see Baughman, p. 110.

85 Migrant workers: " 'I Wonder Where We Can Go Now,' " *Fortune*, April 1939.

85–86 *Life*'s labor coverage: *Life*, May 3 and July 12, 1937, on the CIO. On the Albany yards, see *Life*, October 4, 1937.

86 On the Guild: "Time Inc. and the Newspaper Guild," August 12, 1949, in the papers of Dorothy Sterling (SCDKLUO). See also the interview with Bernard Barnes, November 3, 1969, in the W. A. Swanberg collection, box 18 (RBMLCU). On Luce's pay scale, see Chamberlain, *A Life with the Printed Word*, p. 65.

86 On the status of Luce's employees: John S. Billings, "Recollections."

86–87 On Luce and *High Time*: Copies of *High Time* may be consulted in various collections, including Ms. vol. bd. 66, in the John Shaw Billings collection (SCL). Three issues appeared between the end of January and May of 1939. Years later, former *Time* managing editor Thomas S. Matthews criticized Luce for using the contradictory phrase "Free speech in confidence." He also claimed that Luce exhibited authoritarian tendencies. See Matthews' review of Elson's *Time Inc., Atlantic*, vol. 222/6, December 1968, p. 128.

87 The New Deal and *Fortune*'s polls: The *Fortune* Survey: XXII, July 1939.

87 Public attitudes toward government and business, according to the polling data: "What Should Congress Do Now?" *Fortune*, April 1938, p. 102. See also *Fortune* press release of October 27, 1938, OF 2602 (FDRPL).

87 Roosevelt in the polls: *Life*, "Do You Approve in General of F.D.R.?" June 27, 1938.

87 The New Deal and relief: "The March of Time" (radio), November 18, 1938, R87:1008 (MOB). On the term "welfare state," see Sterling, "The Luce Empire," chapter 8 (SCDKLUO). On "handouts," see the interview with Elmo Roper, November 25, 1969, in the W. A. Swanberg collection, box 18 (RBMLCU). For examples of *Time*'s approach, see the issue of October 3, 1938, which treats alleged nepotism.

88 On the Democratic dinner: "Happy Drinkers in Mr. Roosevelt's Recession," *Life*, January 24, 1938.

88 Comparing FDR to Hitler: *Life*, "Speaking of Dictators," November 18, 1938.

88 Luce rejoicing over the downfall of the New Deal: *Fortune*, February 1938, p. 59. On Baruch, see *Life*, March 14, 1938 ("Baruch Admonishes New Deal. . . .").

88 Luce bangs his fist: Interview with Laura Z. Hobson, August 26, 1939, in the W. A. Swanberg collection, box 18 (RBMLCU).

88 Luce's concept of happiness: Luce's scrawled note to Longwell, asking him to obtain books checked off on the attached list, June 7, 1935, in the Daniel Longwell collection, box 29, folder on Henry R. Luce (RBMLCU). See also Henry R. Luce to Barton, April 26, 1942, in the papers of Bruce Barton, box 1, folder on the Advertising Federation of America (WSHS).

88 Luce and the Klan: *Time*, December 30, 1922, p. 5. On the Scott lynching, see Elson, p. 89.

89 *Time* and Marcus Garvey: *Time*, June 11, 1923, and December 12, 1927.

89 Paul Robeson: *Life*, January 11, 1937.

89 *Life*'s tour of the South: Daniel Longwell, telegram to Robert Sherrod, August 26, 1936; and Longwell, memorandum to Sherrod, August 18, 1936, i, in the Daniel Longwell collection, box 29, Sherrod folder (RBMLCU).

90 The minority problem in the U.S.: *Life*, October 3, 1938.

90 "The American Way": *Life*, February 15, 1937.

90 Restoring the South to the nation: *The March of Time*, V, 10, April 1939. On Luce's hostility to regionalism: Hodgins, Oral History, p. 107.

90 Blacks dancing: *Life*, December 14, 28, 1937.

91 On the Memphis fair: *Life*, November 10, 1941.

CHAPTER EIGHT

92 Prejudices of their time: *Time*, April 21, 1924.

92 Luce and the Jews: HRL, memorandum to publishers and managing editors, December 26, 1938, in the papers of the John Shaw Billings (SCL).

93 Jassy: "The Riot Cause," *Time*, December 30, 1922 (dummy).

93 The retraction of a libel against Jews: *Time*, March 7, 1938.

93 Jews and Communists: *Time*, July 30, 1923.

93 The future of the German Jews: *Time*, September 29, 1930. Time Inc. was not always so blind. A radio program, "The Voice of Time," evoked the virulence of Hitler's anti-Semitism. Expulsion, listeners heard, would be the Jews' fate in Hitler's Third Reich.

94 Blum as Jew: Eric Hodgins, Oral History, p. 103. On Léon Blum, see *Time*, June 15 and July 13, 1936.

94 *Time* on the Jews: Sterling, "The Luce Empire," chapter 2, in the papers of Dorothy Sterling (SCDKLUO).

94–95 Anti-Semitism in the U.S.: Herzstein, *Roosevelt and Hitler: Prelude to War*, pp. 160–163.

94 The plight of the Jews: *Time*, February 6, March 13, April 10, June 5, 1933.

94 German-Jewish refugees: *The March of Time*, I, 7, October 18, 1935.

94 The age and class cohort running Time Inc.: (hear) John S. Billings, "Recollections of Time and Life and Luce," T73/a/b (SCL).

95 Billings and the Jews: DJSB, March 19 and December 6, 1940, February 3, 6, 1941 (SCL).

95 *Time* and the Jews: Elson, *Time Inc.*, pp. 167–168.

95 MacLeish's proposal: MacLeish, memorandum to Luce, November 12, 1935, in the papers of Archibald MacLeish, container 8 (MDLOC).

95 MacLeish's arguments: MacLeish, memorandum to Luce, with copies to Ingersoll, Hodgins, and Grover, November 14, 1935, in the papers of Archibald MacLeish, ibid.

95 Luce's comments on the MacLeish proposal: Harold D. Lasswell papers, General Files, Commission on Freedom of the Press, Series I, box 27 (SMLYU).

95 Jewish leaders: I. M. Rubinow to Waldman, November 14, 1935, files of the American Jewish Committee/347/box 11/EXO-29; and Archibald MacLeish to H. Schneiderman, December 24, 1935, and Schneiderman to MacLeish, December 27, 1935, and January 2, 1936 (YIVO).

95 The book version of the *Fortune* articles: *Jews in America* (New York: Random House, 1936).

96–97 **Fortune, arms, and neutrality:** Elson, pp. 216–218. See also Eric Hodgins' account in his interview with Swanberg, the W. A. Swanberg collection, box 18 (RBMLCU).

97 **War dead:** *Life*, August 30, 1937.

97 **American attitudes toward the possibility of war:** Hedley Donovan, *Right Places, Right Times* (New York: Holt, 1989), p. 42. On the Roper polls, see Elson, pp. 223–224.

97 **On the U.S. Army:** *The March of Time*, I, 5, August 16, 1935, "Army."

97 **Pearl Harbor:** *Life*, April 26, 1937.

98 **Time on the Spanish war:** *Time*, July 13 and August 31, 1936.

98 **Men of property:** Laird S. Goldsborough to Archibald MacLeish, January 23, 1937, in the W. A. Swanberg collection, box 18 (RBMLCU).

98 **The dispute over Spain:** Elson, p. 249.

98 **The Ingersoll-Goldsborough debate:** Ralph McA. Ingersoll to Laird S. Goldsborough, August 25, 28, 1936 (copies to Billings), and Billings to Ingersoll, August 28, 1936, the Time-Life-Fortune papers, I, folder 9, in the John Shaw Billings collection (SCL).

98–99 **The Luce-MacLeish discussions about Spain:** HRL to Archibald Mac-Leish, December 21, 1936, in the W. A. Swanberg collection, box 18 (RBMLCU). See also MacLeish to HRL, January 25, 1937, in the papers of Archibald MacLeish, container 8 (MDLOC).

98–99 **Life on the Spanish war:** *Life*, July 12, 1937 (on Cordoba); July 17, 1937 (on the origins of the revolt), and January 24, 1938 (on the fall of Teruel).

99 **The "Quarantine" speech:** *Time*, October 18, 1937.

99 **Luce in Montclair:** HRL, address delivered on December 4, 1937. Speeches and Writings File, box 74 (MDLOC); another version is stored in the papers of John Shaw Billings, Scrapbook 48 (SCL).

99 **Ideals worth dying for:** Jessup, *Ideas of Henry Luce*, pp. 101–103.

99 **The U.S. thirty years hence:** HRL, address delivered on December 4, 1937. Speeches and Writings File, box 74 (MDLOC); another version is stored in the papers of John Shaw Billings, Scrapbook 48 (SCL).

100 **Rollins College:** Address by HRL at Rollins College, February 21, 1938.

100 **Luce editorial director:** Elson, p. 333.

100 **"Christmas in Naziland":** *Life*, December 22, 1937.

100 **Inside Nazi Germany:** *The March of Time*, IV, 6, *Inside Nazi Germany*; Elson, p. 384; and Baughman, *Henry R. Luce*, p. 114. For a more detailed evaluation of the film, see Raymond Fielding, *The March of Time* (New York: Oxford University Press, 1978), pp. 187–201.

101 **Goldsborough in decline:** Patricia Divver's analysis of *Time*, 1938, pp. 1–2 [1953], the Time-Life-Fortune papers, in the John Shaw Billings collection (SCL).

101 **Austrian crisis:** *Time*, February 7, 21, 28, 1938.

101 **Trapped Jews:** *Life*, April 18, 1938.

101 **Anti-Jewish graffiti:** Ibid.

101 **Ingersoll and Norris on foreign policy:** Patricia Divver, analysis of *Time*, 1938, p. 4 [1953], the Time-Life-Fortune papers, in the John Shaw Billings collection (SCL).

101 **Documentary on Japan in China:** *The March of Time*, I, 9, December 13, 1935.

101–102 **On executions:** *Life*, December 28, 1936.

101–102 *Time* **on Chiang:** *Time*, November 11, 1935, and August 3, 1936.

102 *Life* **on Soong:** "China's Soong," *Life*, March 24, 1941.

102 T. V. Soong and China: *Life*, March 8, 1937.

102 Christianity in China: Francis Cho-min wei, "Rooting the Christian Church in Chinese Soil" (New York: Union Theological Seminary, 1945).

102 China's future: *Time*, October 4, 1937. See also *The March of Time*, IV, 1, September 10, 1937.

103 Snow's photographs: "First Pictures of China's Roving Communists," *Life*, January 25, 1937.

103 Snow on the Long March: *Time*, January 10, 1938.

103 Small child crying: *Life*, May 16, 1938. INS made the film for Hearst, but Movietone News purchased the reel.

104 The Japanese soldier: *Life*, August 30, 1937.

104 Flooding the fields: *Life*, June 20, 1938; *Time*, November 7, 1938. On refugees, see *Life*, January 10, 1938.

104 Gloating about the damage: *Life*, October 17, 1938.

104 On Japan as a rival: MacLeish to Henry R. Luce, February 15, 1936, in the papers of Archibald MacLeish, container 8 (MDLOC).

104 Eliot on war with Japan: George Fielding Eliot, "The Impossible War with Japan," *American Mercury*, September 1938; and Eliot, "U.S. Watches Japanese Policy in the Pacific," *Life*, December 4, 1939. On Pearl Harbor, see *The March of Time*, III, 12, July 9, 1937.

CHAPTER NINE

106 Luce's trip to Europe: Luce's extensive notes on his trip to Europe, dated 22 June 1938, the Time-Life-Fortune papers, in the John Shaw Billings collection (SCL).

107 Luce's impressions of the Czechs: *Life*, May 30, 1938. On news coverage, see John S. Billings, memorandum to all writers, May 12, 1938, the Time-Life-Fortune papers, I, folder 13, in the John Shaw Billings collection (SCL).

108 Luce and the Czech crisis: Elson, *Time Inc.*, pp. 353–354. See also "Czechoslovakia," in *Fortune*, August 1938.

108 Ingersoll: The October 28, 1938, memorandum on the subject of Goldsborough, probably by Ingersoll, with responses from Luce, in the W. A. Swanberg collection, box 18 (RBMLCU).

108 Luce on Munich: DJSB, September 29, 1938 (SCL). See also *Life*, October 3, 10, 1938.

108 *Time* **on Chamberlain's apparent triumph:** *Time*, October 3, 17, 1938.

108–109 *Reichskristallnacht* **in** *Life*: *Life*, November 28, 1938.

109 *Time* **on the mistreatment of Jews:** *Time*, December 5, 1938 (Sachsenhausen); and *Time*, November 28, 1938.

109 "The March of Time" on the pogroms: "March of Time" (radio), November 18, 25, 1938, R87:1008 (MOB).

109 FDR's recall of the U.S. Ambassador: Unidentified letter from a State Department source to Cudahy, November 17, 1938, in the papers of John Cudahy, correspondence 1933–1940, 1943 (WSHS).

109 On the refugee issue: *The March of Time*, V, 5, "The Refugee—Today and Tomorrow."

109 **The Policy Committee:** Elson, p. 360.

109 **Luce and the Policy Committee:** Ibid., pp. 363–381.

109 **Luce on the Hitler threat:** Chamberlain, *A Life with the Printed Word*, p. 67. On Luce as the conscience of the company, see Swanberg, *Luce and His Empire*, pp. 163–164.

109 **The announcement about Goldsborough:** HRL, memorandum to all *Time* writers and editors, December 8, 1938, in the W. A. Swanberg collection, box 18 (RBMLCU).

109–110 **Goldsborough's leave:** Luce announced his decision on November 18. On Goldsborough, see John S. Billings, "Recollections of Time and Life and Luce," recorded in January 1966, T73/a/b (SCL). On November 21 *Time* came close to calling Munich a total failure. See Wainwright, *Great American Magazine*, p. 103.

109–110 **The sabbatical for Goldsborough:** HRL, memorandum to the staff, December 19, 1938. The Christmas issue was dated December 26, 1938. For reader reaction, see Sterling, "The Luce Empire," chapter 2 (SCDKLUO).

110 **Goldsborough's decline:** The diary of John Shaw Billings, in the papers of John S. Billings, entries for January 15 and March 11, 1942 (SCL); and Patricia Divver, "The Ideology of TIME Magazine, II, A Research Report on TIME during the period 1936–1944" (March 1953), in the papers of John S. Billings, Ms. vol. bd., 66 (SCL); DJSB, August 22 and November 13, 1940 (SCL); and the *New York Times*, February 15 and March 2, 1950.

110 **The Hitler cover:** Baughman, *Henry R. Luce*, p. 111.

110 *Time* **deriding Chamberlain:** *Time*, January 2, 1939.

110 *Life* **on Churchill:** *Life*, January 9, 1939.

111 *Time* **on the naval buildup:** *Time*, February 20, 1939.

111 *Life* **on Wilson's legacy:** "He Would Save Democracy for the World," *Life*, January 16, 1939.

111 *Life* **on American attitudes toward intervention:** *Life*, January 2, 1939.

111 **Poland:** *Time*, February 27, 1939.

111 **Roosevelt's plans for revision:** *Time*, April 17, 24, 1939. On public attitudes toward cash and carry, see *Fortune*, May 1939, pp. 104–108.

112 **Attacks on isolationists:** Frederic Sondern, Jr., "Lindbergh Walks Alone," *Life*, April 3, 1939.

112 **Tom Matthews at** *Time:* Matthews, *Name and Address: An Autobiography* (New York: Simon & Schuster, 1960), pp. 216–222.

112 **Matthews' view of Luce and** *Time:* Thomas S. Matthews, "Some Recollections of T. S. Matthews," Oral History Research Office of Columbia University, 1958 and 1959, p. 66.

112 **Luce and his editors debate:** Swanberg, pp. 164–165.

113 **The Gibbs profile of Luce:** *The New Yorker*, November 28, 1936, Profiles. See also James Thurber, *The Years with Ross* (New York: Grosset & Dunlap, 1959), pp. 214ff.

113 **The** *Los Angeles Times:* Elson, pp. 460–461. This appraisal appeared in 1941.

114 **Dwight Macdonald, " 'Time' and Henry Luce":** *Nation*, May 1, 1937.

114 **Luce on** *Time's* **influence:** Swanberg, p. 142.

114 *Life's* **readership:** Wainwright, p. 114.

114 **A new class of millionaires:** Elson, pp. 401–402.

114 *Life's* **marketing and sales:** Howard Black to Mr. Witmer of NBC, August 11, 1937, box 54, National Broadcasting Company Records (WSHS).

114 **Billings on Hitler:** DJSB, June 29, 1939 (SCL).

114 **Howe on Luce:** Quincy Howe, *The News and How to Understand It: In Spite of the Newspapers, In Spite of the Magazines, in Spite of the Radio* (New York: Simon & Schuster, 1940), pp. 148–155.

115 **Brown on *Life:*** *American Mercury*, December 1938, pp. 404ff.

115 **Barzun on *Time:*** Baughman, p. 172.

CHAPTER TEN

116 **Luce's address:** HRL, speech before the Fashion Group, April 20, 1939, in the W. A. Swanberg collection, box 20, HRL, 1933–1939, speeches and writings (RBMLCU).

117 **Wage war against the U.S.A.:** Polls summarized in *The Gallup Poll* (New York: Random House, 1972–), I, pp. 141–157.

117 **Moral sentiments:** Elson, *Time Inc.*, p. 406.

117 **Bartlett:** *Time*, April 10, 1939.

117 **A long war:** *Time*, May 15, 22, 29; June 5, 12, 1939.

117 **Lindbergh:** *Time*, June 19, 1939.

118 ***Life*'s financial tribulations:** Elson, p. 334.

118 **Eleanor Roosevelt on Clare Luce's work:** Eleanor Roosevelt, reviewing *Kiss the Boys Goodbye*, December 22, 1938, in the papers of the John Shaw Billings (SCL). See also Eleanor Roosevelt to Clare Luce, January 19, 1939, in the papers of CBL, container 840 (MDLOC).

118 **Margin for Error:** Sheed, *Clare Boothe Luce*, pp. 72–73. On Clare's alleged hints of anti-Semitism, see Charles Graves to CBL, n.d. (probably 1939), in the papers of CBL, container 840 (MDLOC).

118 **Strengthen Roosevelt:** Rhodes to Missy LeHand, April 20, 1939, PSF 3338; and the June H. Rhodes file, PPF (FDRL).

118–119 **Roosevelt's fear of anti-Semitism:** Hans von Hentig to FDR, October 8, 1939; James Rowe, Jr. to the President, October 30, 1939; FDR to James Rowe, October 31, 1939; and Rowe to Lowell Mellett, November 8, 1939 (FDRL).

119 **The *St. Louis:*** *Time*, May 22, 1939.

119 **Immigration policy:** Ibid.

119 **John Gunther:** "Chaim Weizmann," *Life*, June 12, 1939.

119 **Luce and the Jews:** Interview with Laura Z. Hobson, in the W. A. Swanberg collection, box 18 (RBMLCU).

119 **Davenport:** Russell W. Davenport, "Anti-Semitism in the U.S.?" Address delivered at Hunter College, August 4, 1938.

119 ***Fortune*'s research on anti-Semitism:** Russell W. Davenport, memorandum to HRL et al., May 10, 1939; and Ralph D. Paine, Jr., memorandum to Luce et al., May 12, 1939, in the papers of Russell W. Davenport, container 33 (MDLOC)

120 **Advertising:** Davenport to HRL, June 20, 1939, in the papers of Russell W. Davenport, container 36 (MDLOC).

120 **Too damn smart:** Helen Walker and Judith Pequignot, memorandum to Mitch (Davenport), July 13, 1939, in the papers of Russell W. Davenport, container 33; and Davenport to Luce, August 4, 1939, ibid., container 36 (MDLOC).

120 **Heiskell:** The March 6, 1939, issue of *Life* ("Americanism Masqueraders")

denounced a rally held by the German-American Bund. The attack on *Life* can be consulted in the papers of the John Shaw Billings, Ms. vol. 48 (SCL).

121 **Business circles and war:** Roland N. Stromberg, "American Business and the Approach of War 1935–1941," *The Journal of Economic History*, 13, no. 1 (Winter 1953), pp. 58ff. Luce told Billings that Roosevelt was "dull" and "uninspired." See the DJSB, May 19, 1939 (SCL).

121 **Longwell and the fleet:** DJSB, May 16, 1939 (SCL).

121 **Longwell and *Life*:** Ibid., May 25, August 22, and September 21, 1939 (SCL).

121 **The Round Table:** "THE TIME INC ROUND TABLE," in the papers of Russell W. Davenport, container 40 (MDLOC).

122 **Lippmann's evolution:** Francine Curro Cary, *The Influence of War on Walter Lippmann, 1914–1944* (Madison: The State Historical Society of Wisconsin, 1967), p. 35.

123 ***Time* on *Lippman*: Time**, September 27, 1937.

123 **Lippmann and his *Life* article:** Ralph Paine, Jr., to Lippmann, June 6, 1939; and Rachel Albertson to Lippmann, January 5, 1940, in the Walter Lippmann papers, selected correspondence 1931–1974, group no. 326, series no. III, box 85, folder 1338 (SMLYU). The contract called for a fee of $750, but Luce paid Lippmann $1,000.

124 **Luce in trouble with the Paris press:** Etienne de Nalèche to the editor of TIME, n.d.; HRL to the president of the Paris Press Syndicate, n.d.; and copy of cable to Luce from Rochemont, n.d., in the papers of Sherry Mangan, bMs Am 1816 (1054) (HLHU). See also Munves notes, TM V, "Complaints," in the papers of A. J. Liebling (DRBCUL). In addition: René de Chambrun to Rochemont, July 10, 1939; cable from Mangan to Krug, July 14, 1939 (copy), and July 15, 1939 (copy); cable from Rochemont to Heiskell, July 19, 1939; Georges Bidault, "La trahison," *L'Aube*, July 19, 1939; and Henry Walter to Rochemont, July 25, 1939, in the papers of Sherry Mangan, bMs Am 1816 (1054) (HLHU).

CHAPTER ELEVEN

126 **Luce's account of his trip to Europe, August 17, 1939:** The W. A. Swanberg collection, box 20, HRL, 1933–1939, speeches and writings (RBMLCU).

127 ***Time* on Poland:** *Time*, August 28 and September 4, 1939.

127 **Jack Benny and Winston Churchill:** Elson, *Time Inc.*, pp. 408–409.

127 **Luce and Larsen:** Luce picked good managers, such as C. D. Jackson, Andrew Heiskell, and Roy Larsen. He discussed major business problems with them and continued to involve himself in important financial and managerial decisions. See *The Reminiscences of Andrew Heiskell*, pp. 74, 226, 267–269. Luce remained chairman of the board until 1942, when his able brother-in-law, attorney Maurice T. Moore, assumed that position.

127 **Billings on Luce and his pro-British slant:** DJSB, September 15, 26, 1939. On a correspondent in London, see ibid., January 17, 1940 (SCL).

127 **American attitudes toward neutrality and the war:** The Gallup Organization .0172.002 (October 1939), Roper for Fortune Magazine .0010.014 (October 1939), and Robert E. Sherwood, *Roosevelt and Hopkins: An Intimate History* (New York: Harper and Brothers, 1948), p. 128.

127 Polls on the repeal of the arms embargo: *The Gallup Poll*, I, pp. 178–185.

127 Luce on the war: HRL, speech before the Senior Group, September 21, 1939, in the W. A. Swanberg collection, HRL, 1933–1939, speeches and writings (RBMLCU).

128 On the U.S. Army's strength: War Department, Bureau of Public Relations, "Biennial Report of the Chief of Staff of the United States Army, July 1, 1939, to June 30, 1941 to the Secretary of War," July 3, 1941, in the papers of Grenville Clark ML 7 (90), Marshall, Gen. George C (DCL).

128 Marshal and Time Inc.: The papers of George C. Marshall, box 87, folder 9 (GCMF), which contains correspondence exchanged by Marshall and Time Inc.

128 Roy Alexander: Elson, p. 468.

129 Time Inc. and G-2: G-2 based its information on the latest reports received from military attachés. See Buell to Allen Grover, May 15, 1940, in the papers of Raymond Leslie Buell, box 15 (MDLOC).

129 The Round Table and economic policy: "How Can the U.S. Achieve Full Employment?" *Fortune*, October 1939.

129 *Time* on the war: *Time*, October 2 (on the Maginot Line), October 9 (on British workers), October 23 (on aviation), and October 30, 1939 (on the Western Front).

129 *Fortune* on a German victory: "America's Stake in the Present War and the Future World Order," *Fortune*, January 1940.

129–130 American attitudes at the end of 1939: *The Gallup Poll*, I, poll of December 31, 1939.

130 If Britain fell: *Time*, November 20, 1939.

130 Luce and the Christian Foreign Service: Luce to Archibald MacLeish, December 23, 1939, PPF 6403 (FDRL); PPF 3338 (FDRL); Roosevelt to MacLeish, January 5, 1940, and Emory Ross to MacLeish, January 12, 1940, in the papers of CBL, container 840 (MDLOC).

130 Luce and his appointment with FDR: Stephen Early, memorandum to Gen. Watson, January 25, 1940, PPF 3338, saying that Luce had urgently asked for an appointment. Harold Horan of Time Inc. was Luce's emissary. See also PPF 2442, which indicates that Luce would telephone Watson when he arrived in Washington (FDRL). See the President's Appointments, January 26, 1940, in Accession No. 9786, box 17, daily schedule (MDUVL).

130–131 Luce and Frankfurter: DJSB, January 24, 1940, where Billings refers to Luce's worshipful attitude toward Frankfurter's intellect.

131 Aircraft: *Fortune*, March 1940 (on aviation and steel), especially "The Aircraft Boom."

132 Luce the interventionist: DJSB, March 12, 1940 (SCL), and Elson, p. 416.

132 French censorship: Mangan to David Hulburd, March 21, 1940, in the papers of Sherry Mangan, 27 (HLHU).

132 Luce's trip to Europe: DJSB, April 9–13, 1940 (SCL). On Clare, see Swanberg, *Luce and His Empire*, pp. 173ff.

132 The Luce message to Larsen: HRL, cable to Roy Larsen, May 9, 1940, the Time-Life-Fortune papers, folder Luce trips, in the John Shaw Billings collection (SCL). See also Elson, pp. 418–419, and Swanberg, pp. 172–173. On rumors about Norway, see *Time*, April 22, 1940; on the setback for the Allies, see *Time*, May 13, 1940.

133 **The Luce message of May 2:** HRL, cable to Time Inc., May 2, 1940, in the W. A. Swanberg collection, box 18 (RBMLCU).

133 **Republican attitudes toward the war:** *The Gallup Poll*, vol. I, pp. 222–223, referring to questions asked between April 25 and May 10, 1940, that is, before the German attack on the Low Countries and France.

133 **Luce in Brussels:** Isabella Van Meter, memorandum, May 10, 1940, the Time-Life-Fortune papers, folder Luce trips, in the John Shaw Billings collection (SCL). See also Elson, p. 420.

133 **The Luces during the Blitz:** *The Reminiscences of Andrew Heiskell*, pp. 227ff. and 815.

133 **Luce on the German breakthrough:** Cables from HRL on May 11, 12, 1940, the Time-Life-Fortune papers, folder Luce trips, in the John Shaw Billings collection (SCL).

134 **Billings dazed:** DJSB, May 10–16, 1940 (SCL).

134 **Luce leaves France:** Elson, p. 421.

134 **William Allen White:** William M. Tuttle, Jr., "William Allen White and Verne Marshall: Two Midwestern Editors Debate Aid to the Allies Versus Isolationism," *Kansas Historical Quarterly*, XXXII, 2 (Summer 1966), pp. 201ff.

135 **A dangerous proposal:** DJSB, May 20, 22, 1940 (SLC).

CHAPTER TWELVE

136 **Luce's radio address:** Text of speech by HRL, May 22, 1940, in the W. A. Swanberg collection, box 21, HRL, speeches 1940–1941 (RBMLCU); and *Life*, May 27, 1940, "Threat of German victory . . ." On Millis, see *Time*, same date.

137 **Ready to make sacrifices:** HRL to B. A. Garside, May 25, 1940, in the Archives of the United Board for Christian Higher Education in China (RG 11), box 14, folder 344 (YDSLAM).

137 **Sabotaged coverage:** Mangan to Andrew Heiskell, May 23, 1940, in the papers of Sherry Mangan, box 27 (HLHU).

138 **Heiskell's background:** *The Reminiscences of Andrew Heiskell*, pp. 5ff.

138 **Rescue of the old:** Address by Churchill to the House of Commons, June 4, 1940, in Winston S. Churchill, *Blood, Sweat, and Tears* (New York: G. P. Putnam's Sons, 1941), p. 297.

138 **June 1 appointment:** White House log of telephone calls, May 31, 1940, in Accession No. 9786, box 2, May 1940, memos to General Watson (MDUVL); and Mr. Early's press conference on June 1, 1940, Scrapbook 9, in the papers of Stephen T. Early (FDRL).

138 **Luce patronized:** Interview with William Benton, in the W. A. Swanberg collection, box 18 (RBMLCU).

138–139 **June 1 speech:** HRL, address over WABC and full Columbia network, June 1, 1940, OF 2442 (FDRL).

139 **Hoover:** Luce sent Hoover a copy of the speech, see PPI, box 411, folder 3200 (1) [HHPL].

139 **"America and the World":** *Life*, June 3, 1940.

139 **Fled south:** Mangan to Ralph Paine, May 29, 1940, and to Maria Weber, May 30, 1940, in the papers of Sherry Mangan, box 27 (HLHU). See also

Mangan to Richard de Rochemont, June 11, 1940, ibid. Re. Billings: DJSB, June 7, 10, 1940 (SCL).

139 Too bad, too bad: DJSB, in the papers of John S. Billings, June 13, 14, 17, 1940 (SCL).

140 Lisbon: Mangan to Richard de Rochemont, June 11, 1940, in the papers of Sherry Mangan, box 27 (HLHU); *Reminiscences of Andrew Heiskell*, pp. 79–86; *f.y.i.*, December 29, 1967 (published by Time Inc.); and Elson, *Time Inc.*, p. 424.

140 Dewey led the pack: Richard Norton Smith, *Thomas E. Dewey and His Times* (New York: Simon & Schuster, 1982), p. 301.

140 Willkie the businessman candidate: *Life*, December 13, 1937.

141 Davenport and Willkie: Swanberg, *Luce and His Empire*, p. 170; Marcia Davenport, *Too Strong for Fantasy* (New York: Charles Scribner's Sons, 1967), p. 261; "Profiles: Unconquerable," *The New Yorker*, April 22, 1991; see also Sterling, "The Luce Empire," chapter 3. On Willkie, see *Time*, July 31, 1939.

141 *Fortune* on Republican prospects in 1940: "The Republican Party: Up from the Grave," *Fortune*, July 1939.

141–142 Dewey and *Time*: *Time*, May 25, 1936.

142 Had to know him: "Tom Dewey," *Life*, October 31, 1938, and *Time*, February 26, 1940. On Dewey and the other Republicans in 1940, see Nicol C. Rae, *The Decline and Fall of the Liberal Republicans from 1952 to the Present* (New York: Oxford University Press, 1989), pp. 29–37. See also DJSB, April 3, 1940 (SCL). Billings and most of his colleagues disliked Dewey.

142 Photogenic Willkie: *Life*, April 22, 1940.

142 Davenport resigning: Sterling, "The Luce Empire," chapter 5 (SCDKLUO).

143 Taft and Dewey on foreign policy: Smith, p. 304.

143 Luce and the Willkie nomination: HRL, unpublished manuscript, Speeches and Writings File, box 86, in the papers of Henry Robinson Luce (MDLOC).

143 The grass roots: Baughman, *Henry R. Luce*, p. 124.

144 Luce debates foreign policy: DJSB, June 20, 1940 (SCL). On the draft, see the Gallup polls published on June 24 and July 10, 1940, in *The Gallup Poll*, I, pp. 229–232.

144 Heated discussions at Time Inc.: DJSB, July 11, 12, 1940 (SCL). For Luce's comment about Roosevelt, see the interview with Noel F. Busch, in the W. A. Swanberg collection, box 18, (RBMLCU). On the luncheon at Louis XIV, see DJSB, December 4, 1940 (SCL).

144 Billings resented Luce: DJSB, June 11, 13, 1940 (SCL).

144 Opinion on entry into World War I: Hadley Cantril, "America Faces the War," PF 857 (FDRL).

145 Luce at the 1940 convention: HRL, unpublished manuscript, Speeches and Writings File, box 86, in the papers of HRL (MDLOC). See also Sterling, "The Luce Empire," chapter 5 (SCDKLUO).

145 *Time* on Willkie: *Time*, June 24, July 8, August 5, September 16, 1940.

145 China's needs: Raymond L. Buell, correspondence with Tusan-sheng chien, container 11, in the papers of Raymond Leslie Buell, unprocessed (MDLOC).

145 *Life*'s hostility to Japan: "Japan Races U.S. for Power in Big Ships," *Life*, April 29, 1940; and Newsfronts, *Life*, August 7, 1939. See *March of Time*, "Crisis in the Pacific," VI, 5, December 1939.

145 *Life* **on Chinese stamina:** *Life*, November 14, 1938.

146 **Fear of Japanese moves:** *Time*, March 4 and July 1, 1940. On Konoe, see *Time*, July 8, 1940.

CHAPTER THIRTEEN

147 **Luce and the White House rumor mill in June 1940:** The Diaries of Harold Ickes, reel 3, p. 4540, June 29, 1940 (MDLOC). On the press liaison, see Richard W. Steele, *Propaganda in an Open Society: The Roosevelt Administration and the Media, 1933–1941* (Westport, Conn.: Greenwood Press, 1985), pp. 104–105.

149 **The destroyers:** For Churchill's original request, see Churchill to Roosevelt, May 15, 1940, in Francis L. Loewenheim et al., *Roosevelt and Churchill: Their Secret Wartime Correspondence* (New York: E. P. Dutton, 1975), pp. 94–95.

149 **Polls on aid to Britain and entry into the war:** "The *Fortune* Survey: XXXII—The War," *Fortune*, July 1940 (supplement). On Gallup, see *The Gallup Poll*, vol. I, p. 233, (July 19).

149 **Roosevelt concluded that further aid:** For an examination of Roosevelt's oratorical salesmanship, see Ernest Brandenburg, "Franklin D. Roosevelt's International Speeches, 1939–1941," *Speech Monographs* 16 (1949).

149 *Life* **on aid to Britain:** *Life*, July 1, 1940, Newsfronts of the World. On polling data, see *Fortune*, July 1940 (supplement). See also DSJB, July 5 and 9, 1940 (SCL).

149 **Meeting at the Columbia Club, July 11, 1940:** The papers of Fight for Freedom, box 69 (SGMMLPU).

150 *Time* **on the U.S. declaring war:** *Time*, July 22, 1940.

150 **British children:** Ibid.

150 **Visit to Cordell Hull:** Elson, *Time Inc.*, p. 435.

150–151 **Marshall unavailable:** Marshall to Henry R. Luce, July 13, 1940, in the papers of George C. Marshall, box 74, folder 43 (GCMF).

151 **Luce's dislike for Roosevelt's approach:** DJSB, July 19, 1940 (SCL).

151 **Extending American protection:** HRL, Memorandum to Senior Group, July 18, 1940, in the Time-Life-Fortune papers of John Shaw Billings (Luce, 7108) (SCL); and John S. Billings, memorandum to Mr. Luce, July 19, 1940, ibid. See also DJSB, July 23, 1940 (SCL).

152 **On the possible fall of Britain:** *Time*, July 22, 1940. *Time*'s article paraphrased the words of Luce, Miller, and their colleagues in the Century Group.

152 **Walter Lippmann:** *Life*, July 22, 1940, pp. 65ff. See also the Walter Lippmann Papers, Selected Correspondence 1931–1974, Group 326, Series III, box 85, folder 1338 (SMLYU).

152 **Luce's promise of coverage:** Francis P. Miller to HRL, July 23, 1940, and Luce to Miller, July 25, 1940, in the papers of Fight for Freedom, box 69 (SGMMLPU). On the quid pro quo, see Whitney H. Shepardson to HRL, February 3, 1959, in the W. A. Swanberg collection, box 19 (RBMLCU).

152 **Major Eliot:** "The Defense of America," *Life*, July 8, 15, 1940.

152 *Life* **on Joseph Kennedy:** *Life*, October 11, November 22, December 20, 1937.

152–153 **Luce and Kennedy:** HRL, Oral History, p. 7 (JFKL). See also Baughman, *Henry R. Luce*, p. 101; Swanberg, *Luce and His Empire*, p. 154; and Beschloss,

Kennedy and Roosevelt, p. 109. On *Life*'s citation of Kennedy, see the issue of March 14, 1938. See also *Time*, June 10, 1940.

153 Kennedy's disaffection: Beschloss, p. 16.

153 Joseph Kennedy on Roosevelt's alleged warmongering: The Ambassador tended to believe these charges. See his "autobiographical manuscript," wherein he deals with the *White Book*, in the papers of James M. Landis, box 51 (MDLOC). Many other isolationists shared the same belief, which, though exaggerated, contained some truth. See Marshall, creator of the No Foreign War Committee, to D. M. Linnard, January 21, 1941, in the Verne Marshall papers, No Foreign War Committee (HHPL).

153 Kennedy staying in England: Michael R. Beschloss, *Kennedy and Roosevelt: The Uneasy Alliance* (New York: Harper & Row, 1987), pp. 213–221.

154 Jack Kennedy: *Time*, September 18, 1939.

154 On the Kennedy thesis: David E. Koskoff, *Joseph P. Kennedy: A Life and Times* (Englewood Cliffs, NJ: Prentice-Hall, 1974), pp. 403–404; and Nigel Hamilton, *JFK: Reckless Youth* (New York: Random House, 1992), Part 6.

154–155 The senior thesis: John F. Kennedy, "Appeasement at Munich (the Inevitable Result of the Slowness of Conversion of the British Democracy to a Rearmament Policy)," honors thesis at Harvard, March 15, 1940, in the Personal Papers of John F. Kennedy, Harvard Records 1935–1940 (JFKL). In future years, *Why England Slept* caused Jack Kennedy some embarrassment, and he regretted publishing it. Still, it scarcely merited the harsh condemnation visited upon it by Professor Harold Laski, Kennedy's former tutor. Laski, writing to Joseph P. Kennedy, called the book "immature" and superficial, and added that it had "no real structure." (Koskoff, p. 404, cites Laski's comment.)

155 Joseph Kennedy on publishing a book: James MacGregor Burns, *John Kennedy: A Political Profile* (New York: Harcourt, Brace, 1959), pp. 42–44. See also David Nunnerly, *President Kennedy and Britain* (New York: St. Martin's Press, 1972), pp. 15–24.

155 Promotion: Broadcast interview with John F. Kennedy, R76:0418 (MOB).

CHAPTER FOURTEEN

156 The Ramparts We Watch: Louis de Rochemont to Longwell, December 13, 1938, i, in the Daniel Longwell collection, box 28, folder D (RBMLCU). In November 1939, 68 percent of those polled believed that U.S. intervention in the First World War had been a mistake.

156 The imminent release of *The Ramparts We Watch*: DJSB, June 12, 1940 (SCL); and Longwell to Roy Larsen, July 10, 1940, in the Daniel Longwell collection, box 28, folder on Larsen (RBMLCU). On Larsen's interest in the film, see DJSB, June 29, July 6, 20, 1940 (SCL).

156–157 Roosevelt and *The Ramparts We Watch*: The official invitation to the Roosevelts to attend the world premiere of *The Ramparts We Watch*, at Keith's Theater, July 23, 1940, may be consulted in OF 2442 (FDRL). On Roosevelt and the film industry, see Steele, *Propaganda in an Open Society*, pp. 156–157.

157 *Fortune*'s poll: Elson, *Time Inc.*, p. 435. See also *Life*, August 5, 1940, on conscription and the destroyer situation.

157 Ickes and the Luce appointment: The Diaries of Harold Ickes, reel 4, pp. 4640–4641, July 27, 1940 (LOC).

157 The Luces visit Roosevelt: HRL, "War Diary," July 27–July 30, 1940,

HRL, unpublished manuscript, Speeches and Writings File, box 86, in the papers of HRL; and CBL, "The White House," in the papers of CBL, box 1 (MDLOC).

158 **Luce's role in the press campaign:** HRL to Lippmann, July 29, 1940, in the Walter Lippman Papers, Selected Correspondence 1931–1974, Group 326, Series III, box 87, folder 1376 (SMLYU).

158 **On the battle over conscription:** J. Garry Clifford and Samuel R. Spencer, Jr., *The First Peacetime Draft* (Lawrence: The University Press of Kansas, 1986), particularly chapters 10 and 11.

158 *Life* **and the campaign for selective service:** *Life*, August 5 (conscription) and September 9 (volunteers), 1940.

158 **Longwell on the American attitude toward intervention:** Longwell to HRL, August 5, 1940, i, in the Daniel Longwell collection, box 29, folder on Henry Luce, 1940–1947 (RBMLCU). On the polling data cited here, see the folder on Gallup Polls, 1940, in the papers of Grenville Clark (DCL).

159 **Larsen on Time Inc.'s financial future:** Roy Larsen to the Staff of Time Inc., July 26, 1940, in the Daniel Longwell collection (Larsen) (RBMLCU).

159 **The New York Post:** Archer Winston in *New York Post*, September 20, 1940.

159 **Beard on** *The Ramparts We Watch:* Charles A. Beard, "Time and Archibald MacLeish" (microfilm file on *Ramparts*, source not legible), in the Museum of Modern Art's Film Division, New York.

159 **Ferguson attacks** *The Ramparts We Watch:* Otis Ferguson, "At Your Own Risk," *New Republic*, August 5, 1940, p. 189.

159 **World-Telegram:** William Boehnel in *New York World-Telegram*, September 20, 1940.

159 **Interventionist coverage of the censorship dispute:** See *New York Post*, August 22, 29, 1940; *Variety*, September 4, 1940; and *New York Times*, September 19, 20, and October 2, 1940.

159 **Censorship and** *The Ramparts We Watch:* This account of public reaction to *Ramparts* closely follows my *Roosevelt and Hitler: Prelude to War*, pp. 341–344.

160 **John Kennedy:** Landis to Joseph P. Kennedy, July 17, 1940; and Kennedy to Landis, August 6, 1940, in the papers of James M. Landis, box 24 (MDLOC).

160 **Luce's reading of the Kennedy book:** HRL, memorandum to Gottfried and Matthews, September 19, 1940, the Time-Life-Fortune papers, in the John Shaw Billings collection (SCL). After reading Kennedy's book, the isolationist Frank Waldrop concluded that "England slept because England was a democracy." In his foreword, Harry Luce wrote as if he and Waldrop had read two different books.

160 **The New York Times and the Kennedy book:** S. T. Williamson, "Why Britain Slept While Hitler Prepared for War," *New York Times Book Review*, August 11, 1940, p. 3. See also the review in *Time*, August 12, 1940.

160 **Luce and Willkie:** Swanberg, *Luce and His Empire*, pp. 177–178.

161 **Mollify the isolationists:** Willkie to Tobey, September 9, 1940, and Tobey to Willkie, October 1, 1940, in the papers of Charles Tobey, box 7 (DCL).

161 **The Administration and defense:** "U.S. Defense: The Armed Forces," *Fortune*, September 1940. See *Life*, September 9, 16, 1940.

161 **Luce speaking privately:** HRL to George Backer, September 6, 1940, in the papers of Dorothy Sterling (SCDKLUO). For Luce's comment, see Elson, p. 435.

161 *Time* **praising Willkie:** *Time*, September 16, 1940. See also DJSB, November 5, 1940 (SCL).

CHAPTER FIFTEEN

162 Luce on Willkie's nomination: Elson, *Time Inc.*, p. 428. See also Davenport, *Too Strong for Fantasy*, p. 282.

162 Willkie campaigning: Davenport, pp. 269–283.

163 Luce and the Willkie coverage: Thomas S. Matthews, Oral History Project interview, p. 79.

163 *Time's* **coverage of Willkie:** Divver, "Analysis of *Time*'s Contents (1940)" (1953), the Time-Life-Fortune papers, in the John Shaw Billings collection (SCL); HRL to Gottfried, Norris, and Matthews, September 18, 1940, ibid.; and Thomas Matthews, *Name and Address*, pp. 253–254.

163 Defense and politics: Robert A. Divine, *Foreign Policy and U.S. Presidential Elections 1940–1948* (New York: New Viewpoints, 1974), p. 29.

164 *Life* **on Willkie:** Heiskell to Longwell, Hicks, and Kay, September 23, 1940, i, in the Daniel Longwell collection, box 28, Heiskell folder (RBMLCU). See also DJSB, September 19, 1940 (SCL), and Elson, p. 442.

164 Willkie losing his voice: *Life*, September 30 (with Willkie on the cover).

164 Wallace on *Time's* **coverage:** HRL, telegram to Wallace, September 25, 1940, in the microfilm edition of the papers of Henry A. Wallace (FDRL).

164 Luce on Willkie's virtues: Elson, p. 438.

164 Roosevelt was lying: HRL, unpublished manuscript, p. 10, Speeches and Writings File, box 86, in the papers of Henry Robinson Luce (MDLOC).

164 *Time* **on the Battle of Britain:** *Time*, October 7 (on the air battle), October 14 (on Londoners in the Tube), and October 28 (on an Anglo-American alliance). In early November *Time* exaggerated the damage inflicted on German industry by the RAF.

165 Luce and Lippmann on the endorsement: HRL to Lippmann, September 24, 1940, in the Walter Lippmann Papers, Selected Correspondence 1931–1974, Group 326, Series III, box 87, folder 1376 (SMLYU). See also Smith, *Thomas E. Dewey*, p. 330.

165 *Time* **on Roosevelt in the lead:** *Time*, October 7, 1940.

165 The Clare Luce/Thompson debate: CBL's challenge to debate Thompson, October 22, 1940, in the papers of Dorothy Thompson, Series I, container 14 (GARLSU); and CBL's speech, October 15, 1940, in the Willkie MSS. (MDLLIU). See also Thompson's diary, October 10, 1940, Series VIII, box 1, folder 1938–1949, in the papers of Dorothy Thompson (GARLSU). On the debate, see also Marion K. Sanders, *Dorothy Thompson: A Legend in Her Time* (Boston: Houghton Mifflin, 1973), p. 269.

165 FDR on Thompson: Roosevelt, May 6, 1941, telegram on the occasion of a dinner honoring Dorothy Thompson, PPF 6650 (FDRL).

166 Smaller breasts: Scrapbook 57, in the papers of the John Shaw Billings (SCL).

166 *Europe in the Spring:* *Time*, October 7, 1940, containing a review of *Europe in the Spring.*

166 Anne Lindbergh: Anne Morrow Lindbergh, *War Within and Without: Diaries and Letters* (New York: Harcourt Brace Jovanovich, 1980), p. 148.

166 Reactions to *The Wave of the Future:* Robert Wood (head of America First)

to Mrs. Lindbergh, October 11, 1940, and Charles A. Lindbergh, Jr., to
Wood, October 13, 1940, in the papers of Robert Wood, correspondence file,
box 9, Lindbergh 1940 (HHPL). Dulles wrote to Mrs. Lindbergh on October
8, 1940: See the papers of John Foster Dulles, selected correspondence and
related material, box 19 (SGMMLPU). On opposition to *Wave of the Future*,
see Laura Z. Hobson to HRL, December 12, 1940, Ms. Collection Hobson
(RBMLCU). Richard B. Scandrett also wrote a powerful rebuttal: see his
letter to Mrs. Charles A. Lindbergh, January 22, 1941, PPF 1080 (FDRL).

166 Harry's mother endorses FDR: Elizabeth R. Luce to Thompson, n.d.;
Thompson to Mrs. Luce, October 26, 1940, in the papers of Dorothy Thompson, Series I, container 19 (GARLSU).

166 Thompson's view of Luce: The papers of Dorothy Thompson, diary entry
for October 10, 1940, in Series VIII, box 1, 1938–1949.

166 The Luces' donations to Willkie's campaign: A. Hehmeyer, memorandum for Mr. Luce, October 31, 1940, in the papers of CBL, container 454
(MDLOC).

167 *Time* on Kennedy's return: *Time*, November 4, 1940.

167 The Luces' concept of a deal: Divine, p. 77. Beschloss and Hamilton offer
their own interpretations of the Kennedy/FDR deal, and I draw upon their
accounts in my narrative.

167 Luce and his disappointment over the Kennedy endorsement: DJSB,
November 26, 1940, inter alia (SCL).

167 Frankfurter on Roosevelt: Frankfurter to FDR, November 3, 1940, in
Franklin D. Roosevelt, *Roosevelt and Frankfurter: Their Correspondence
1928–1945* (Boston: Little, Brown, 1968), pp. 548–549.

167 *Time* on the last stage of the campaign: *Time*, October 21 (Willkie cover
story) and November 4, 1940, "The train rolled on."

167 *Fortune*'s polling: Time Inc. to John F. Royal, November 19, 1940, in the
papers of the National Broadcasting Company, box 80, file on Time Inc.
(WSHS).

167 Luce on the results of the election: Elson, p. 444; HRL to Time Incers,
November 6, 1940, and to John Billings, November 8, 1940, the Time-Life-
Fortune papers, in the John Shaw Billings collection (SCL). See also DJSB,
November 7, 1940 (SCL).

167 *Life*'s appeal for national unity: Raymond Clapper's article "What About
Unity?" *Life*, November 18, 1940.

168 Early on the *Fortune* poll: Early, telegram to HRL, September 5, 1940, in
the papers of Stephen Early, box 10 (FDRL).

168 FDR reprimands Luce: Elson, p. 443.

168 On the Luce/Roosevelt exchange: *Time*, November 11, 1940. See the draft
of a letter from FDR to HRL, November 20, 1940, PPF 3338; Roosevelt,
memorandum for Stephen T. Early, December 3, 1940; William D. Hassett,
memorandum for Lowell Mellett, December 5, 1940; Hassett, memorandum
for Mellett, December 7, 1940; Mellett to HRL, December 7, 1940; HRL to
Mellett, December 11, 1940; Anne Foster to Hassett, December 13, 1940;
Stephen T. Early, memorandum for the President, December 23, 1940; HRL
to Lowell Mellett, December 24, 1940; Mellett, memorandum for the President, December 28, 1940; and Roosevelt, memorandum for Mellett, December 31, 1940 (FDRL).

170 **On the Hoover plan:** Chadwin, *The Hawks of World War II*, p. 135.

170 *Time* **and the plans to feed Europe:** *Time*, August 19, 26, 1940.

170 **The Quaker position on feeding Europe:** Richard Wood, "Facts about Famine," September 20, 1940, in the papers of the Friends Peace Committee (PYM), Series 6, box 41 (SWCL).

170 **Luce, the Hoover plan, and** *Life* : HRL to Hoover, September 21, and Hoover to Luce, September 22, 1940; Hoover to Luce, October 27, 1940, and Luce to Hoover, October 30, 1940, in the papers of Herbert Hoover, PPI, box 411, folder 3200 (1) (HHPL).

170 **Clare defends the food plan:** Armstrong to Clare B. Luce, November 27, 1940, in the papers of Hamilton Fish Armstrong, box 139 (SGMMLPU).

170 *Life* **on the food plan:** DJSB, December 12, 1940 (SCL); and *Life*, December 23, 1940, "Hunger."

170 **Luce leaves the Century Group:** Elson, p. 436; and Chadwin, p. 113.

170 **Time Inc. and Lend-Lease:** *Time*, January 6, 1941. See "Roosevelt," in *Life*, January 20, 1941.

171 *Time* **puts pressure on Roosevelt:** *Time*, February 10, 1941.

171 **Lovell on the race issue:** Malcolm R. Lovell to Clarence Pickett, December 26, 1939, American Friends Service Committee, Administration, Individuals, Malcolm Lovell (Quaker Service Council), 1940 (AFSC).

172 **The abortive phone call:** DJSB, December 24, 1940 (SCL).

173 *Time* **banned:** The United Press dispatch of May 13, 1939, in the papers of the Jewish Community Relations Council of Minnesota, box 64 (MHS).

173 **Billings' account of the evening with Luce and Lovell:** See DJSB, January 2, 1941 (SCL). See also the FBI Memorandum Re. Malcolm R. Lovell, July 31, 1942 (FDRL).

174 *Time* **opposing the peace offensive:** *Time*, January 6, 1941, lead story in National Affairs.

174 **Roosevelt trying to get rid of Lovell:** FDR, memorandum to E.R., January 21, 1941, in PSF, box 177, folder Anna Eleanor Roosevelt (FDRL). On Lovell and Cudahy, see DJSB, January 14, 28, 1941 (SCL).

174 *Life* **and Lend-Lease:** *Life* even attacked Luce's friend Joseph P. Kennedy for his opposition to parts of the Lend-Lease legislation. The magazine later compensated for this affront by letting Kennedy have a full page where he could make his case. See " 'Stay Out of War,' " *Life*, January 27, 1941; and Longwell, memorandum to HRL, January 14, 1941, in the Daniel Longwell collection, folder of correspondence with HRL, 1941 (RBMLCU).

174 **Luce too busy:** DJSB, September 3, 5, 14, 1940. On the Senior Group, see ibid., December 20, 1940 (SCL).

174 **Luce on U.S. belligerency:** Swanberg, *Luce and His Empire*, p. 177. Later, Luce criticized Willkie for promising peace.

175 **Democracy and free enterprise:** HRL, address at the Coca-Cola dinner, New York, November 8, 1940, in the W. A. Swanberg collection, box 21, folder on HRL, speeches, 1940–1941; and Swanberg's interview with Allen Grover, May 1, 1969, ibid. (RBMLCU).

175 **Luce's globalism:** Noel Busch to Lippmann, February 13, 1941, in the Walter Lippmann Papers, Selected Correspondence 1931–1974, Group 326, Series III, box 85, folder 1338 (SMLYU).

175 *Fortune* **and Luce on the global prospect:** "The U.S. and the World,"

Fortune, September 1940, p. 42. See also DJSB, December 23, 1940 (SCL). Billings' version of Luce's draft may be consulted in the Time-Life-Fortune papers, in the John Shaw Billings collection (SCL). On idolatry, see HRL, remarks at a dinner of *Time* editors, New York, November 14, 1952, in Jessup, *Ideas of Henry Luce*, p. 70.

CHAPTER SIXTEEN

177 Pasadena speech: HRL, speech to the Association of American Colleges, January 9, 1941, in the W. A. Swanberg collection, box 21, folder on speeches 1940–1941 (RBMLCU). On the genesis of Luce's "American Century" article, see Alexander Hehmeyer to Bernhard Knollenberg, March 24, 1941, in the papers of Yale in World War II, Series I, Number 5, container 78 (SMLYU).

178 Luce on the American frontier: DJSB, June 29 and July 12, 1951 (SCL).

178 Feeding the world: Buell to Henry R. Luce, January 23, 1941, in the papers of Raymond Leslie Buell, box 15 (unprocessed) (MDLOC).

178 The Tulsa speech: Address by HRL at the annual dinner of the Mid-Continent Oil & Gas Association (Kansas-Oklahoma Division), January 11, 1941, in the W. A. Swanberg collection, box 21, folder on speeches, 1940–1941 (RBMLCU).

178 The Pittsburgh speech: HRL, address delivered at the National Automobile Association banquet in Pittsburgh, January 22, 1941, in the papers of Russell W. Davenport, container 76 (MDLOC).

179 James' comments and suggestions: James to HRL, February 5, 1941, in the private papers of Sidney L. James.

179 Billings on Luce and his magazines: DJSB, January 31, February 1, 12, 1941 (SCL). See also Swanberg's interview with Roy Alexander, in the W. A. Swanberg collection, box 18 (RBMLCU); and Davenport, memorandum to Henry Luce, January 28, 1941, in the papers of Russell W. Davenport, container 76 (MDLOC). For Longwell's view, see his letter to HRL, January 17, 1941, in the Daniel Longwell collection (RBMLCU).

179 "The American Century": Time-Life-Fortune papers, I, folder 21, in the John Shaw Billings collection (SCL).

180 Linen on Luce: James A. Linen, Jr., to Henry R. Luce, March 27, 1941; and to Elizabeth Luce, July 31, 1942, in the papers of B. A. Garside, container 2 (HIWRP).

180 Lippmann on "The American Century": Lippmann to Dr. Henry W. Luce, September 26, 1941, in the Walter Lippmann Papers, Selected Correspondence 1931–1974, Group 326, Series III, box 87, folder 1375 (SMLYU); and Allen R. Alderson to Franklin D. Roosevelt, February 20, 1941, OF 2442 (FDRL).

180 Hornbeck: Hornbeck, note on "The American Century," February 17, 1941; and Hornbeck, memorandum to Sumner Welles, February 18, 1941, in the papers of Stanley K. Hornbeck, box 281 (HIWRP).

181 Reaction to "The American Century": Letters on "The American Century" in the papers of HRL, box 113 (MDLOC).

182 Opposition to "The American Century": Baughman, *Henry R. Luce*, p. 135. See also Freda Kirchwey, "Luce Thinking," *Nation*, March 1, 1941.

182 Barton vs. Luce: Barton to Henry Luce, March 4, 1941, in the papers of Bruce Barton, box 40, folder Henry R. and CBL (WSHS).

182 Norman Thomas: Swanberg, *Luce and His Empire*, pp. 182–183.

182 Luce and Wallace: HRL, address to the Academy of Political Science, New York City, November 12, 1941, the W. A. Swanberg collection, box 21 (RBMLCU). On Wallace's reaction to "The American Century," see Wallace to HRL, May 16, 1942, in the Henry A. Wallace papers at the University of Iowa, reel 23 (FDRL).

182 Villard vs. Luce: Oswald G. Villard, "Are We to Rule the World?," *Nation*, March 26, 1941. See also his "President of the World?," April 9, 1941, also in *Nation*.

182 Thompson and Luce: *New York Herald Tribune*, March 14, 1941; and Dorothy Thompson to HRL, March 14, 1941, in the papers of CBL, container 840 (MDLOC). See also Baughman, p. 120.

183 Nazi reaction to "The American Century": James B. Stewart to the Secretary of State, January 24, 1942, in RG 226, M-1499/43 (NARA). Richard Sallet's article was entitled "American Century?" It appeared in the *Völkischer Beobachter* on January 15, 1942.

183 Fortune: *Time*, June 9, 1941, on "The American Century"; and August 18, 1941, promoting *Fortune*. See *Time*, August 25, 1941, for this remarkable prediction.

183 Reader reaction to *Life*'s "volcano": *Life*, March 10, 1941.

184 *Time* on polled Americans: *Time*, July 28, 1941.

184 Longwell: Longwell to HRL, February 21, 1941, in the Daniel Longwell collection (RBMLCU).

184 Dorothy Thompson on Luce: Thompson, " 'The American Century,' " *New York Herald Tribune*, February 21, 1941; Thompson to unidentified person, March 4, 1941, in the papers of Dorothy Thompson, Series II, box 1 (GARLSU).

184 The Hunger debate: A transcript of Thompson's broadcast of March 16, 1941, is preserved in the papers of Dorothy Thompson, Series VII, box 15, folder 1941 (GARLSU). See also "Belgium Is Hungry," *Life*, June 2, 1941.

184 Roosevelt, the food plan: *Complete Presidential Press Conferences of Franklin D. Roosevelt*, XVII, 136, February 18, 1941. Quaker activist Clarence Pickett continued to work on refugee problems with Mrs. Roosevelt. See Aydelotte to Edgar P. Dean, February 13, 1941, in the papers of Frank Aydelotte, Series III, box 30 (FHLSC).

184–185 Thompson's food plan: Thompson to Luce, March 12, 1941, in the papers of Dorothy Thompson, Series II, box 1 (GARLSU).

185 FDR vetoes the food plan: Clarence E. Pickett's Journal, January–December 1940, entries for April 20, 23, 1941 (AFSC). See Roosevelt's account in his note of April 18, 1941, in PPF 2143 (FDRL).

CHAPTER SEVENTEEN

186 Luce on the Pacific: HRL, memorandum to the managing editors of *Time*, June 14, 1940, i, in the Daniel Longwell collection, Luce folder 1940–1947 (RBMLCU). See also Robert A. Divine, *Foreign Policy and U.S. Presidential Elections 1940–1948*, pp. 22–23.

186 **Luce on U.S. policy toward Japan:** HRL, speech to the Cleveland Advertising Club, April 5, 1941, in United China Relief, Inc., and United Service to China, papers, box 41 (SGMMLPU).

186 **Luce on the Chinese:** HRL, speech at the Advertising Club banquet, April 5, 1941, in the W. A. Swanberg collection, box 21 (RBMLCU).

187 *Life* **on Hitler and Russia:** *Life*, July 15, 22, 1940.

187 **The matching gift plan:** Edward Carter to HRL, October 24, 1939, in the papers of the Institute of Pacific Relations, box 29 (RBMLCU).

188 **Important recruits:** Vincent Sheean to David Sarnoff, March 5, 1941, in the papers of the National Broadcasting Company, box 86, folder on UCR (WSHS); and B. A. Garside, memorandum to HRL, April 8, 1941, in United China Relief, Inc., and United Service to China, papers, box 2, folder on agencies (memoranda, 1940–1941) (SGMMLPU).

188 **Most of the China relief agencies:** "Five Years of United China Relief," September 20, 1945, in United China Relief, Inc., and United Service to China, Papers, box 2 (SGMMLPU). On Luce's view of united charity appeals, see Scrapbook 57, in the papers of John Shaw Billings (SCL).

188 **Missionaries in China:** *Time*, January 17, 1938.

188 **Luce and INDUSCO:** HRL to Hornbeck, November 13, 1939, in the papers of Stanley K. Hornbeck, box 281 (HIWRP); Stimson to Luce, November 20, 1939, in the Henry L. Stimson Papers, reel 99, frame 765 (SMLYU); HRL, draft letter of January 26, 1940, in the Archives of the United Board for Christian Higher Education in China, box 13, folder 298 (YDSLAM). See also Nym Wales, "Old China Hands," *New Republic*, April 1, 1967.

189 **Luce and his relief funds:** HRL to Willkie, January 6, 16, 20, 1941; and Luce to the Coordinating Committee, January 15, 1941, in the Willkie MSS. (MDLLIU). See also HRL to Hu, February 14, 1941, in the papers of Stanley K. Hornbeck, box 281 (HIWRP). Hu Shih gave Hornbeck the letter on February 17. On Willkie and China, see Wendell Willkie to HRL, February 28, 1941, in the Willkie MSS. (MDLLIU).

189 **White as a youth:** Interview with John K. Fairbank, in the papers of David Halberstam, relevant to *The Powers That Be* (MLBU).

190 **Fairbank:** Interview with Theodore White, ibid.

190 **White on Fairbank:** Theodore H. White, *In Search of History: A Personal Adventure* (New York: Warner Books, 1981), p. 75.

190 **Fairbank on White:** John King Fairbank, *Chinabound: A Fifty-Year Memoir* (New York: Harper & Row, 1982), p. 156.

190 **Fairbank's introductions:** Theodore H. White to John K. Fairbank, December 17, 1936; Randall Gould to Fairbank, July 29, 1937; and Fairbank to White, May 7, 1939, in the Time-Life Correspondence 1940–1946 of Theodore H. White (HLHU).

191 **White and the IPR:** Theodore H. White to Edward C. Carter, September 8, 1938, in the papers of the Institute of Pacific Relations, B, catalogued correspondence, White, Theodore (RBMLCU).

191 **Like so much garbage:** White, p. 89.

191 **White on the Chinese government:** Ibid., p. 103.

191 **White leaving Tong:** White to Hollington Tong, December 18, 1939, in the Time-Life Correspondence 1940–1946 of Theodore H. White (HLHU).

191 **Hersey going to China:** Edward C. Carter to Henry R. Luce, April 10,

1939, in the papers of the Institute of Pacific Relations, box 29 (RBMLCU). See also Elson, *Time Inc.*, p. 470.

191 **White's impressions of Hersey:** White, p. 116.

192 **Resigning from his job with Tong:** Theodore White to John Hersey, December 24, 1939, in the Time-Life Correspondence 1940–1946 of Theodore H. White (HLHU).

192 **Problems covering China, including censorship:** John Hersey to Theodore H. White, June 8, 1939; White to David Hulburd, June 9, 1939; Hulburd to White, July 10, 1939; White to Hersey, July 21, 1939; White to Hersey, November 24, 1939; and Thomas Krug to White, January 29, 1940, ibid.

193 **White's fears about repercussions in China:** White to David Hulburd, August 29 and November 7, 1939; Thomas Krug to White, November 17, 1939; White to John Hersey, November 24 and December 4, 1939; and Hersey to White, February 7, 1940, ibid.

193 **White's love for his work:** White to Hersey, October 2, 1940, ibid.

193 **The Soong sisters and the demonstration:** White to Hulburd, April 6, 1940, ibid.

193 **Himmler-like activities:** White's dispatch of June 1, 1940, in the papers of CBL, container 509 (MDLOC).

194 **Stupid or cruel:** White, p. 146.

194 **China turning to Russia or Japan:** White to Hulburd, April 5, 1940, in the Time-Life Correspondence 1940–1946 of Theodore H. White (HLHU).

194 **China and British appeasement:** White to Hulburd, July 24, 1940, ibid. On White in Hanoi, see his letter to Thompson, September 7, 1940, ibid.

194 **Soong vs. Kung:** White to John and Wilma Fairbank, October 2, 1940, in the Time-Life Correspondence 1940–1946 of Theodore H. White (HLHU).

194 **White on Chiang:** White's dispatch of June 1, 1940, in the papers of CBL, container 509 (MDLOC).

194 **White on Madame Chiang:** White dispatch of June 1, 1940, on politics in China, ibid.

195 **Peace feelers:** Dispatches of Theodore White, July 24, 1940, through January 26, 1941, in the Time-Life Correspondence 1940–1946 of Theodore H. White (HLHU).

195 **New offensives:** Theodore H. White to David Hulburd, December 6, 1940, ibid.

195 **Impressions of Shansi:** White, pp. 132ff.

196 **White on Stalin and Chiang:** White to San Francisco office of the IPR, n.d.; and to David Hulburd, April 5, 15, 1940, in the Time-Life Correspondence 1940–1946 of Theodore H. White (HLHU).

196 **Hopes for land reform:** White to John and Wilma Fairbank, October 2, 1940, ibid.

196 **Depths of misery:** White's dispatch of June 1, 1940, in the papers of CBL, container 509 (MDLOC).

CHAPTER EIGHTEEN

198 **The Reverend Luce and his seminars:** Files pertaining to the Reverend Luce in the Hartford Seminar Foundation, microfilm frames 17529–17618, and *A Brief Outline of the History of Chinese Communism*, in the Archives of the

United Board for Christian Higher Education in China, box 15, folder 353 (YDSLAM).

200 Chou and Tung: Theodore H. White, *In Search of History*, p. 162.

200 Chiang, Japan, and the Communists: White to David Hulburd, August 20, 1940, January 26, and March 2, 1941, in the Time-Life Correspondence 1940–1946 of Theodore H. White (HLHU).

200 On civil war and the situation in the spring: White's dispatch of March 15, 1941, in the papers of CBL, container 509 (MDLOC).

200 *Time* on the incident involving the New Fourth Army: *Time*, February 3, 1941.

200 *Time*'s account of the fighting: *Time*, February 10, 1941.

201 The Communists: Mao Tse-tung, "The Chinese Revolution and the Chinese Community Party" (1939), in Dan N. Jacobs and Hans H. Baerwald, *Chinese Communism: Selected Documents* (New York: Harper & Row, 1963), pp. 40–41.

201 Luce's work for China, and his goals: HRL to B. A. Garside, December 27, 1938; Garside to Luce, January 12, 1939; Luce's donation to the Emergency Committee, dated March 23, 1939; Garside to Allen Grover, April 4, 1939; Garside (?) to Grover, June 30, 1939; and Grover to Garside, December 28, 1939, Archives of the United Board for Christian Higher Education in China, box 14, folders 340–343 (YDSLAM). On the morality of the American mission to China, see "A Program for Service: The China Colleges and the Crisis," memorandum to United China Relief from ABBCCC, ca. 1941, ibid., box 254, folder 615. On Luce's 1940 gifts, see B. A. Garside (?) to Alexander Heymeyer, January 29, 1941, ibid., box 15, folder 345.

201 Snow: *Time*, March 10, 1941.

201 White's concerns about Chiang: White, dispatch of April 11, 1941, in the papers of CBL, container 509 (MDLOC).

202 Currie in China: *Time*, March 24, 1941.

203 Currie to Roosevelt: Lauchlin Currie, report to FDR, March 15, 1941, in PSF Diplomatic files, box 27 (FDRL). See also Michael Schaller, *The U.S. Crusade in China 1938–1945* (New York: Columbia University Press, 1979), pp. 48–53.

203 Currie on Luce: Patricia Neils, *China Images in the Life and Times of Henry Luce*, p. 86.

203 China's struggle: Eliot Janeway, "Roosevelt vs. Hitler," *Life*, May 5, 1941.

203 Luce and *Time* on a wider war: *Time*, April 21, 28, 1941.

203 Gallup: *The Gallup Poll*, I, February 1941, p. 266.

203 Statistics on China's needs: Currie to Chiang Kai-shek, May 2, 1941 (enclosing a message from Roosevelt), in the papers of Lauchlin Currie, box 1. On confusion regarding Chinese needs, see Currie to Harry Hopkins, October 27, 1941, ibid. (HIWRP).

203 Founding of UCR: "Outline of United China Relief, Inc., for Board Members of Participating Agencies," April 2, 1941, in the papers of CBL, container 509 (MDLOC).

203 Dewey: Relevant materials can be consulted in the papers of Thomas E. Dewey, Series 4, box 189, folder 2 (RRUR).

204 Publicity for UCR: William B. Miller, memorandum to Niles Trammell, March 7, 1941; and Trammell to Vincent Sheean, March 10, 1941, in the papers of the National Broadcasting Company, box 86, folder UCR (WSHS).

204 Halted Japan: HRL, address at the Books and Authors luncheon, New York, April 8, 1941.

204 Luce preparing for his China trip: Memorandum to HRL, December 4, 1940, signature illegible, in the papers of CBL, container 454 (MDLOC).

205 Luce's journey: "Itinerary—Trip to China," April 24, 1941, in the papers of CBL, container 509 (MDLOC). See also interview with Roy Alexander, in the W. A. Swanberg collection (RBMLCU); and White, p. 170.

205 Luce and Johnson: Johnson to Henry R. Luce, March 22, 1940; Luce to Johnson, April 12, 1940; and Johnson to Luce, April 13, 1940, in the papers of Nelson T. Johnson, container 38 (MDLOC). On Johnson's view of the Japanese threat, see Schaller, p. 18.

206 Luce on China's needs: HRL, "China to the Mountains" (photographs by CBL), *Life*, June 30, 1941. See also John S. Service, Oral History Interview No. 386 (HSTL).

206 Chinese suffocated in their shelters: *Life*, July 28, 1941. See also HRL, draft speech, apparently intended for delivery before the New York City Presbytery, November 10, 1941, in the W. A. Swanberg collection, box 21 (RBMLCU).

206 Need for a tougher U.S. policy: DJSB, February 13, 1941, where Billings seems to be parroting Luce's views on Japan (SCL). On the embargo, HRL, address to the Foreign Policy Association, New York, November 29, 1941, in the W. A. Swanberg collection, box 21 (RBMLCU).

CHAPTER NINETEEN

207 On White and Luce: Interview with John Hersey, in the papers of David Halberstam, relevant to *The Powers That Be* (MLBU).

207 White's experience with Luce in 1941: Interview with Theodore H. White, ibid.; and Theodore White to "Bob," June 22, 1941, in the Time-Life Correspondence 1940–1946 of Theodore H. White (HLHU). See also interview with White, October 2, 1969, in the W. A. Swanberg collection (RBMLCU).

208 Back of the book: Interview with White, in the papers of David Halberstam, relevant to *The Powers That Be* (MLBU).

208 Luce's meeting with Chiang: Elson, *Time Inc.*, p. 470. See also the hand-written notes of Clare Luce, in the papers of CBL, container 1 (MDLOC).

209 Luce on the Chinese soldier: DJSB, May 20, 1941 (SCL); Elson, p. 471. See also HRL, address to the Commonwealth Club, June 5, 1941, in the W. A. Swanberg collection, box 41 (RBMLCU).

209 Warnings of xenophobia: Johnson to Henry R. Luce, April 21, 1941, in the papers of Nelson T. Johnson, container 39 (MDLOC). See also Neils, *China Images in the Life and Times of Henry Luce*, p. 73.

209 Chiang's speeches: *Time*, review of *China Fights On—War Messages of Chiang Kai-shek*, July 14, 1941.

209 *The March of Time*: "China Fights Back," *March of Time*, VII, 11, June 1941.

210 Luce and White discuss their professional relationship: Interview with Theodore White, in the papers of David Halberstam, relevant to *The Powers That Be* (MLBU).

210 *Time* on MacArthur: *Time*, August 4, 1941.

211 White and Luce argue: DJSB, June 11, 1941 (SCL).

211 **Chinese love for America:** Address by HRL at the China Relief dinner, New York, March 26, 1941, in the W. A. Swanberg collection, box 21, HRL, speeches, 1940–1941 (RBMLCU).

211 **Luce's opposition to Chiang's critics:** HRL, address at the Commonwealth Club, San Francisco, June 5; and his broadcast on WABC and full network, June 11, 1941, in the W. A. Swanberg collection, box 21, folder with speeches 1940–1941 (RBMLCU).

211 **Luce on the Chinese Communists:** HRL, address in New York City, June 18, 1941, in Jessup, *Ideas of Henry Luce*, pp. 194–198.

211 **Luce on the Burma Road workers:** HRL, address at UCR dinner in Chicago, June 24, 1941, in the Willkie MSS. (MDLLIU).

212 **Bloch:** Bloch, memorandum to Raymond W. Goldsmith, July 12, 1941, in the papers of Kurt Bloch, box 3, folder 6 (SCDKLUO).

212 **Wang and Luce:** Dr. Wang Shih-chieh to Henry R. Luce, June 18, 1941, in the papers of CBL, container 454 (MDLOC).

213 **Madame Chiang quoted:** Luce's June 18 speech for UCR, in the W. A. Swanberg collection, box 21 (SGMMLPU). See also HRL, address in Buffalo, July 1, 1941, in the Willkie MSS. (MDLLIU).

213 **UCR fund-raising at Time Inc.:** Ruth Berrien et al., memorandum to all members of the staff, October 5, 9, 1941, in the papers of John Hersey; and B. A. Garside to HRL, report of November 6, 1941, in United China Relief, Inc., and United Service to China, Papers, box 48 (SGMMLPU). See also Otis P. Swift to Hoffman, with enclosures, April 1, 1941, in the papers of Paul G. Hoffman, box 49, folder on UCR (HSTL); and HRL, memorandum to Larsen et al., June 16, 1941, in the papers of Russell W. Davenport, container 76 (MDLOC).

213 *Life* **on Madame Chiang:** *Life*, June 30, 1941.

213 **International Harvester:** List of donations of $1,000 or more, in the papers of Anita McCormick Blaine, McCormick Collections, 1E 704 (MCWSHS).

213 **Luce, Buck, and Mrs. Blaine:** Pearl S. Buck to Mrs. Emmons Blaine, March 31, 1941; Robert J. Thorne to Mrs. Blaine, July 2, 1941; and HRL to Mrs. Blaine, October 4, 1941, ibid., box 388.

214 **Madame Chiang on America's challenge:** Madame Chiang to Clare Luce, August 15 and October 23, 1941, in the papers of CBL, container 840 (MDLOC).

214 **Luce less critical of Roosevelt:** HRL, memorandum to publishing and managing editors, June 19, 1941, in the W. A. Swanberg collection, box 18 (RBMLCU).

214 **Luce and Stimson:** The diary of Henry Stimson, entry for June 13, 1941 (MDLOC).

214 **Luce on China:** HRL, address to the Foreign Policy Association, New York, November 29, 1941, in the W. A. Swanberg collection, box 21 (RBMLCU). See also interview with Theodore White, in the papers of David Halberstam, relevant to *The Powers That Be* (MLBU); and Clare Boothe, "Wings Over China," *Life*, September 8, 1941, and *Time*, June 9, 1941.

214 **China *must* be helped:** *Life*, June 23, 1941.

214–215 **UCR rally:** HRL, memorandum to Wendell L. Willkie, October 3, 1941, in the Willkie MSS. (MDLLIU). See also Luce to Willkie, November 19, 1941, ibid.

215 **Celebrities cheer China:** *Life*, September 1, 1941.

215 **UCR's fund-raising:** HRL to Wendell Willkie, November 19, 1941, with enclosure, in the Willkie MSS. (MDLLIU). See also Progress Report, May 5, 1941, as well as documents concerning activities later in the year, in United China Relief, Inc., and United Service to China, Papers (SGMMLPU).

215 **Cue on Luce:** *Cue*, July 26, 1941, cited in the Time Inc.–related papers of Dorothy Sterling (SCDKLUO), along with comments made by Wesley Bailey on Luce and UCR.

CHAPTER TWENTY

217 **Luce and the CFD's finances:** Jackson to Ernest Angell, November 22, 1941, in the papers of C. D. Jackson, 1931–1967, container 33, Council for Democracy (DDEL).

218 **Jackson's penchant for storytelling:** DJSB, March 29, 1941 (SCL).

218 **Jackson the crusader:** Edward G. McGrath, "The Political Ideals of Life Magazine" (Ph.D. Dissertation, Syracuse University, 1961), p. 92. On Jackson's going on leave, see DJSB, August 10, 1940 (SCL). See also Jackson's obituary, *New York Times*, September 20, 1964; Elson, *Time Inc.*, p. 187; and Jackson to "Isabella," November 28, 1944, in the papers of C. D. Jackson, 1931–1967, container 13 (DDEL).

218 **Jackson plans to work for the CFD:** C. D. Jackson to HRL, March 14, 1941, in the papers of C. D. Jackson, 1931–1967, container 35, the Council for Democracy (DDEL).

219 **Combatting subversive propaganda:** Presidential memorandum for Harry Hopkins, March 7, 1941, OF 1661 (FDRL).

219 **MacLeish on the CFD:** Ernest Angell to the Board of Directors, October 15, 1941, in the papers of Hamilton Fish Armstrong, box 114 (SGMMLPU). MacLeish expected to consult with the board on October 20, 1941.

219 **Mellett on private groups:** Lowell Mellett, "Government Propaganda," *Atlantic Monthly*, September 1941, p. 312.

219 **Cudahy's contract with *Life*:** John S. Billings to John Cudahy, January 3, 1941; and Cudahy to Billings, February 4, 1941, the Time-Life-Fortune papers, in the John Shaw Billings collection (SCL).

220 **The White House watching Cudahy:** Berle, Jr., memorandum for FDR, February 20, 1941, in the papers of A. A. Berle, Jr., State Department Subject File, 1938–1945/Roosevelt, F.D., 1941, box 67; FDR memorandum for the Under Secretary of State, February 21, 1941, OF 2442; and for Stephen T. Early, February 22, 1941, PPF 3338 (FDRL).

220 **He's a newspaperman:** *The Complete Presidential Press Conferences of Franklin D. Roosevelt*, XVII, p. 167, March 4, 1941. See also the interview with Noel Busch, in the W. A. Swanberg collection (RBMLCU).

220 **Roosevelt on Cudahy:** Alexander Weddell to Sumner Welles, March 2, 1941; Welles, memorandum to FDR, March 2, 1941, containing Weddell's letter; and FDR, memorandum to Welles, March 19, 1941, PSF Departmental/ State Department/Sumner Welles January–May 1941/Cudahy (FDRL).

220 **Luce on Cudahy's mission:** Undated (probably March or April), unsigned memorandum, probably by Luce to Billings, in the Daniel Longwell collection (RBMLCU).

221 **The embassy on Cudahy:** Sumner Welles, telegram to FDR, April 11, 1941, in PSF Departmental/State Department/Sumner Welles, January–May 1941 (FDRL).

221 **The May 4 meeting:** National Archives Microcopy, T-120/330/2444170-322; conversation of May 4, 1941, in the Department of State, *Documents of German Foreign Policy* (Washington, D.C., Government Printing Office, various dates), D, XII, pp. 704ff.

221 **Goebbels:** Clippings concerning "U.S. Invasion Study Admitted by Nazis," in the papers of John Cudahy (WSHS).

221 **John Cudahy on Belgium:** "Leopold, Coward or Hero?" Ibid. Cudahy's draft article: Dave H. Morris to Miss LeHand, May 20, 1941; LeHand to Morris, May 31, 1941; and "Proposed Article for *Life* Magazine and North American Newspaper Alliance," by John Cudahy, OF 548 (FDRL).

222 **Saving children:** Hoover to Noel Busch, May 9, 1941, in the papers of Herbert Hoover, PPI, box 309, 2480-B (HHL).

222 **Cudahy's conversation with Hitler:** *Documents of German Foreign Policy*, D, XII, 854ff.; and related material in the Brammer Collection, Zsg 101/22 October 11, 1941 (Bundesarchiv, Koblenz).

222 **Billings on Early:** DJSB, May 27, 1941 (SCL).

222 **Roosevelt on Cudahy's activities:** Sumner Welles, memorandum of conversation with Lord Halifax, June 22, 1941; Welles, memorandum to FDR, June 24, 1941; and FDR, memorandum to Welles, June 25, 1941. For related materials, see PSF Departmental/State Department/Sumner Welles 1941 (FDRL).

222 **Matthews on Cudahy:** DJSB, June 7, 1941 (SCL). See also Buell to HRL, memorandum of June 12, 1941, in the papers of Raymond Leslie Buell (unprocessed) (MDLOC); and Matthews' comment in the papers of the John Shaw Billings, Ms. vol. bd. 50 (SCL).

222 **Cudahy's interview with Hitler:** John Cudahy, "A Man on a Mountain," *Life*, June 23, 1941. On Roosevelt's request, see his memorandum to General Watson, June 26, 1941, in the Time Magazine File, PPF 3338 (FDRL). Later in the year Cudahy published his account of the interview in *The Armies March: A Personal Report* (New York: Charles Scribner's Sons, 1941).

222 **Cudahy passed on information:** John Cudahy to Cordell Hull, June 14, 1941, in PSF Departmental/State Department/Sumner Welles January–May 1941 (FDRL).

223 **Kay on the isolationists:** Hubert Kay, "Boss Isolationist: Burton K. Wheeler," *Life*, May 19, 1941.

223 **Taylor on Lindbergh:** DJSB, May 15, 1941 (SCL). See Roger Butterfield, "Lindbergh," *Life*, August 11, 1941.

223 **Robert Wood:** Elson, p. 479.

223 **Coughlinites:** *Time*, October 13, 1941.

223 **A dead bunny:** HRL to Laura Z. Hobson, September 20, 1941, in Ms. collection Hobson (RBMLCU).

223 **Chiang on Hitler invading Russia:** Chiang's comments, passed on to Roosevelt on or about May 12, 1941, in the papers of Lauchlin Currie, box 1 (HIWRP). See also *Time*, June 23, 1941.

224 **Bourke-White in Moscow:** Elson, pp. 475–476. See Margaret Bourke-White, *Portrait of Myself*, pp. 174–187.

224 **Hicks on Life:** Elson, p. 473. Hicks spoke in June 1941.

224 Luce on Roosevelt's caution: HRL to Hoover, July 16, 1941, in the papers of Herbert Hoover, PPI, box 411, folder 3200 (1) (HHL).

224 The Allies might win: Press report dated August 29, 1941, ibid.

224 Polls taken after the invasion of Russia: *The Gallup Poll*, vol. I, July 14 and September 1, 1941, pp. 289, 296.

224 More sanguine: Press report dated August 8, 1941, Office of the Secretary (including CNO and JAG), General Correspondence, 1940–1942, box 76 (RG 80, NARA).

224 A myth shattered: The press report dated September 5, 1941, Office of the Secretary (including CNO and JAG), General Correspondence, 1940–1942, box 76 (RG 80, NARA).

225 Hersey: *Time*, September 29, 1941.

225 Aid to Russia: *Time*, September 22, 1941.

225 *Life* on atheism: *Life*, November 10, 1941.

225 CFD accused of warmongering: *Uncensored*, August 23, 1941, in the papers of C. D. Jackson, 1931–1967, container 35, Time Inc., Council for Democracy, Inc. (DDEL).

226 Nye on *The March of Time*: He was referring to "Peace—by Adolf Hitler." See *Hearings Before a Subcommittee of the Committee on Interstate Commerce United States Senate*, 77th Congress, first session, on S. Res. 152, p. 37.

226 *Life* on the Nye committee: *Life*, September 22, 1941.

226 Longwell on *Life*: Longwell, memorandum to Ralph Paine, February 21, 1941, in the Daniel Longwell collection (RBMLCU).

226 Grover's new task: Allen Grover, memorandum to publishers and managing editors, March 21, 1941, in the Daniel Longwell collection (RBMLCU).

227 Marshall on public opinion: Marshall to Green Peyton, January 14, 1941, in the papers of George C. Marshall, box 87, folder 9 (GCMF).

227 A modern landing operation: *Life*, August 4, 1941.

227 Bored young soldiers: *Life*, December 23, 1940.

227 Venereal disease: *Life*, October 13, 1941.

227 Fleischmann's: *Life*, October 27, 1941.

228 Rubber imports: *Life*, November 24, 1941.

228 Controversy over *Fortune*: Interview with William Benton, in the W. A. Swanberg collection (RBMLCU). See also the relevant Luce quote, cited by Hedley Donovan, *Right Places, Right Times* (New York: Henry Holt, 1989), p. 102.

228 The Forum: *Fortune* Forum of Executive Opinion, 1st proof, July 26, 1940.

228 The Forum and its clients: Eric Hodgins to Stettinius, May 28, 1940; and Stettinius to Hodgins, May 31, 1940, in the papers of Edward R. Stettinius, box 636, folder on *Fortune* (MDUVL). See also Roland N. Stromberg, "American Business and the Approach of War," *Journal of Economic History*, XIII (1953), pp. 74–77. The Hodgins citation is from his oral history, p. 85.

228 Wertenbaker giving full support: See the folder on *Fortune*, in the papers of Edward R. Stettinius, box 636 (MDUVL).

228 Stettinius and Wertenbaker: Ibid., box 622, folder on 1938.

229 Wertenbaker and Marshall: C.E.T., memorandum to Marshall, March 23, 1942, in the papers of George C. Marshall, box 92, folder 9 (GCMF).

229 Stimson and Luce: Stimson to HRL, September 10, 1941, in the Henry L. Stimson papers, reel 104 (SMLYU).

229 FDR on *Life*'s alleged errors: FDR, July 12, 1941, confidential note for filing, War, box 78, reproduced in Munves notes, TM X, in the papers of A. J. Liebling (DRBCUL).

229 River Rouge plant: *Life*, August 19, 1940.

229 Labor: *The March of Time*, VII, 5, December 1940; and DJSB, August 15, 1941 (SCL).

229 General Motors: *Time*, January 27, 1941.

229 Janeway on Negroes: Eliot Janeway, "Roosevelt vs. Hitler," *Life*, May 5, 1941.

230 Raymond: *Life*, August 11, 1941.

230 On the state of the Army: Press release of the War Department, Bureau of Public Relations, August 7, 1941, in the papers of Grenville Clark ML 7 (90) (DCL).

230 Lobbying for extension: Marquis Childs, interview with the Columbia University Oral History Project, p. 127.

230 Photographs of Marshall: C. M. Adams, memorandum to Marshall, October 18, 1940, in the papers of George C. Marshall, box 87, folder 9 (GCMF).

230 G-2: DJSB, August 13, 1941 (SCL).

231 Arrange this: Lt. Col. Ward H. Maris, memorandum to Marshall, January 2, 1941, in the papers of George C. Marshall, box 92, folder 9 (GCMF).

231 Marshall on Time Inc.'s magazines: George C. Marshall to A. E. Eggleston, July 8, 1941, ibid., box 74, folder 31 (GCMF). Marshall was willing to have *Life* cite his words, but his public relations people advised otherwise. See W. T. Sexton, memorandum of July 15, 1941, ibid.

231 The Navy and Longwell: H. R. Stark to Longwell, November 18, 1940, in the Daniel Longwell collection, box 69 (RBMLCU). For an example of *Life*'s influence, see *New York Herald Tribune*, October 27, 1940, which cited *Life*.

232 Forrestal and Life: Forrestal to Daniel Longwell, November 7, 1940, in the papers of James V. Forrestal, box 53 (SGMMLPU). For an example of *Time*'s treatment of Forrestal, see the issue of August 10, 1942.

232 Forrestal and Luce: Forrestal to Henry R. Luce, October 31, 1941, in the papers of James V. Forrestal, box 54; and Forrestal, Navy Day speech at the Union League Club in Philadelphia, October 27, 1941, ibid., box 5 (SGMMLPU).

232 Forrestal on the postwar order: James V. Forrestal to HRL, October 31, 1941, ibid., box 54; and Navy Day speech, October 27, 1941, ibid., box 5.

CHAPTER TWENTY-ONE

234 Time Inc. views Latin America: MacLeish to Russell W. Davenport, December 2, 1939, in papers of Archibald MacLeish, container 6, Davenport folder (MDLOC).

234 Life on Brazil: Wainwright, *The Great American Magazine*, p. 77.

234 Fortune's influence: Archibald MacLeish, memorandum to Henry Luce et al., in the papers of Russell W. Davenport, container 36 (MDLOC).

234 Fortune on Mexico: "Mexico in Revolution," *Fortune*, October 1938.

234 Roosevelt and Latin America: G. Hass, *Von München bis Pearl Harbor* (Berlin, 1965), p. 41; and N. P. Macdonald, *Hitler Over Latin America* (London, 1940), pp. 23, 71.

234 The Nazi threat: Macdonald, pp. 32–57; and William E. Dodd, *Ambassador Dodd's Diary* (New York: Harcourt Brace, 1941), pp. 362–363.

234 The origins of the Rockefeller office: Draft history of the Office of Coordinator, in the Rockefeller Family Archives, Civic Series, Government Hemisphere, box 50, folder 3, chapter 1 (RAC).

235 *Time* on Rockefeller: *Time*, May 22, 1939; and Elson, *Time Inc.*, p. 382.

235 Luce at MOMA: Relevant material in the Rockefeller Family Archives, Civic Series, box 8 (RAC).

236 Rockefeller angry at *Fortune*: Davenport to Nelson A. Rockefeller, September 13, 1939; Rockefeller to Davenport, September 20, 1939; and correspondence re. the *Fortune* article, in the papers of Russell W. Davenport, container 36 (MDLOC).

236 *The March of Time*: Nelson A. Rockefeller, memorandum to Steve Early, April 1, 1941, enclosing his Program of the Communications Division, in the records of the Office of Government Reports, Executive Division, box 889 (RG 44, NARA).

236 Expropriations: Memorandum from the research department, May 1, 1941, in the papers of Russell W. Davenport, container 36 (MDLOC).

237 Time Inc.'s boast: Elson, p. 453.

237 Trippe's boast: Juan T. Trippe to FDR, April 30, 1941, OF 2442 (FDRL); and P. I. Prentice to FDR, August 6, 1941, ibid.

237 *Life* on Trippe: Noel Busch, "Juan Trippe," *Life*, October 20, 1941.

237 The M.I.D. observers: Records of the Military Intelligence Division, box 50, file 10919-48 31A (RG 165, NARA).

238 *Life* supported Rockefeller: *Life*, June 2, 1941.

238 Luce and the Rockefeller committee: Sidney Hyman, *The Lives of William Benton* (Chicago: The University of Chicago Press, 1969), pp. 218–237.

238 Bowers: Interview with Claude Bowers, the Columbia University Oral History Project, p. 128.

238 Luce's magazines warn: *Life*, June 9, 1941, contains a good example, "Roosevelt on Americas." Roosevelt's carefully crafted comments on the threat to the Americas may be consulted in *The Complete Presidential Press Conferences of Franklin D. Roosevelt*, vol. 13: pp. 111–112, 462–463; vol. 15: pp. 278–361, 413–414, 502, 571; vol. 16: p. 97; and vol. 18: pp. 260–264. For writers supporting Roosevelt's tactics, see among many examples Howell M. Henry, "The Nazi Threat to the Western Hemisphere," *South Atlantic Quarterly*, XXXIX, 4 (October 1940); Lawrence and Sylvia Martin, "Nazi Intrigues in Central America," *American Mercury*, LIII (July 1941); and John Gunther, *Inside Latin America* (New York: Harper & Brothers, 1941).

238 Hart Preston: "Nazis in Chile," *Life*, June 30, 1941. Sherry Mangan, who had been cynical about the U.S. passion for Latin America, changed his mind. "Such a comfort to have Preston here," wrote Mangan, "and thus have projects turn into pictures instead of disappointments." See Mangan to Wilson Hicks, January 23, 1941, in the papers of Sherry Mangan, box 27 (HLHU).

238 Bowers on *Life*: Claude Bowers to FDR, July 19, 1941, OF 303 (FDRL). For a summary of the Bowers/Roosevelt correspondence on Aguirre and *Life*, see ibid., OF 2442.

239 Hopkins: Harry Hopkins, memorandum to FDR, November 24, 1941, PSF Diplomatic, box 26 (FDRL).

239 **Roosevelt attacks** *Time:* OF 2442, containing the *Time*/Chile file, summary
   of items variously dated October 31, November 3, 11, 15, 1941 (FDRL); and
   press release of November 25, 1941, containing Roosevelt's statement about
   Time's transgression. The offensive article appeared in *Time*, November 17,
   1941.

239 **Luce answers Roosevelt:** Luce's public reply, printed by the *Washington Post*
   on November 26, 1941, and carried on the Associated Press wire. See also
   Walter Graebner (a director of Time and Life Ltd., in London) to John G.
   Winant, December 1, 1941, in the papers of John G. Winant, box 224, folder
   on *Time* and *Life* (FDRL).

CHAPTER TWENTY-TWO

240 **Theodore Roosevelt on the Navy:** Theodore Roosevelt to Roosevelt,
   May 10, 1913, in the papers of Franklin D. Roosevelt, Assistant Secretary
   of the Navy, Personal Correspondence, Roosevelt, Theodore and Mrs.
   (FDRL).

240 **Luce at Pearl Harbor:** HRL to Longwell, n.d., but probably June 1941, in
   the Daniel Longwell collection (RBMLCU).

240 **Sherrod on Hawaii:** Sherrod/Japan, June 12, 1941, in Wendell, memorandum to Sherrod, December 11, 1941, on "U.S. Japanese Background," in
   the papers of Robert L. Sherrod, Series I, box 9, Time Inc., 1941–1943
   (GARLSU).

241 **Luce on FDR's Far Eastern policy:** HRL to John Osborne, September 18,
   1948, the Time-Life-Fortune papers, II, folder 117, in the John Shaw Billings
   collection (SCL).

241 **The battle of the Pacific under way:** See *Time*, June 30, 1941, and Wendell,
   memorandum to Sherrod, December 11, 1941, on "U.S. Japanese Background," in the papers of Robert Sherrod, I, 9, Time Inc. (GARLSU).

241 **On the U.S. position:** William L. Langer and S. Everett Gleason, *The
   Undeclared War 1940–1941* (New York: Harper & Row, 1953), p. 469.

241 **Japan could not conquer:** *Time*, March 31 and May 5, 1941, in Wendell,
   memorandum to Sherrod, December 11, 1941, on "U.S. Japanese Background, in the papers of Robert Sherrod, I, 9, Time Inc. (GARLSU).

241 **The Axis powers combined:** *Time*, April 28, 1941, and Lyons memo,
   April 19; Wendell, memorandum to Sherrod, December 11, 1941, on "U.S.
   Japanese Background," ibid. See also unsigned memo, April 23, 1941, and
   Time, May 5, 1941, ibid.

241 **Smoking rubble:** *Life*, July 21, 1941.

241 **On Japan's defiant attitude:** Nobutaka Ike, ed., *Japan's Decision for War:
   Records of the 1941 Policy Conferences* (Stanford: Stanford University Press,
   1967), pp. 77–89.

241 **Favored an embargo:** Press report dated July 24, 1941, Office of the Secretary (including CNO and JAG), General Correspondence, 1940–1942, box
   76 (RG 80, NARA).

242 **MacArthur returns:** Waldo Heinrichs, *Threshold of War: Franklin D. Roosevelt and American Entry into World War II* (New York: Oxford University
   Press, 1988), p. 131; and Paul Schroeder, *The Axis Alliance and Japanese-
   American Relations: 1941* (Ithaca: Cornell University Press, 1958), pp.
   173–176.

242 **Confrontation was replacing appeasement:** Secretary Hull's Report, dated August 17, 1941, in the Department of Defense, *The "Magic" Background of Pearl Harbor* (Washington, D.C.: Government Printing Office), III, pp. 13–14; Heinrichs, p. 162; Gordon W. Prange, *At Dawn We Slept: The Untold Story of Pearl Harbor* (New York: McGraw-Hill, 1981), pp. 169–191; Langer and Gleason, *The Undeclared War*, pp. 694–695; and Dean Acheson, *Present at the Creation: My Years in the State Department* (New York: Norton, 1969), pp. 26–27. See also Cordell Hull to Joseph Grew, August 25, 1941, in FRUS, 1941, vol. IV, p. 394; and the State Department's Report, August 28, 1941, in DOD, "*Magic*," vol. III, p. 28. See also Miwa, "Japanese Images," in Iriye, *Mutual Images*, p. 119; Ambassador Grew's report, September 4, 1941, in DOD, "*Magic*," vol. III, pp. 41–42; and Ambassador Nomura's report, September 4, 1941, ibid., p. 45.

242 **Editorials supported Roosevelt:** Press reports dated August 15 and 29, 1941, Office of the Secretary (including CNO and JAG), General Correspondence, 1940–1942, box 76 (RG 80, NARA). Eden cited by Christopher Thorne, *Allies of a Kind: The United States, Britain and the War Against Japan 1941–1945* (London: Hamish Hamilton, 1978), p. 69.

242 **The U.S. at war:** *Life*, November 10, 1941, and *Time*, October 20, 1941.

243 **Longwell on war:** Longwell, memorandum to HRL, November 3, 1941, in the Daniel Longwell collection (RBMLCU).

243 **Lovell's letter:** Malcolm R. Lovell to William J. Donovan, November 11 and 13, 1941, in the Microfilm Copy of Files Selected for Filming by General William J. Donovan, Director of the Office of Strategic Services, 1941–1945 (RG 226, NARA).

243 *Life* **on MacArthur:** Clare Boothe, "Destiny Crosses the Dateline," *Life*, November 3, 1941; and "MacArthur of the Far East," December 8, 1941.

243 **Good stuff:** DJSB, October 18, 1941 (SCL).

244 **Luce hit by the doorknob:** The interview with John Hersey, in the papers of David Halberstam, relevant to *The Powers That Be* (MLBU).

244 **Clare Luce's article:** Longwell's notes on the authorized history of Time Inc., pp. 3–4, in the Daniel Longwell collection (RBMLCU).

244 **Sherrod on the Marshall press conference:** Sherrod to David Hulburd, November 15, 1941, in the papers of Robert L. Sherrod, Series I, box 14, folders 1940, 1941 (GARLSU).

244 **MacArthur in the Philippines:** Heinrichs, p. 204.

244 **On the Philippines in American strategy:** Waldo Heinrichs, "Franklin D. Roosevelt and the Risks of War, 1939–1941," in Warren I. Cohen and Akira Iriye, eds., *American, Chinese, and Japanese Perspectives on Wartime Asia 1931–1949* (Wilmington, DE: SR Books, 1990), pp. 168–169.

244 **Marshall's strategy:** Forrest C. Pogue, *George C. Marshall, Ordeal and Hope* (New York: The Viking Press, 1966), pp. 202–203.

245 **Marshall's mistaken optimism:** Other insiders, such as Cordell Hull, soon heard that the Army needed another five weeks and the Navy an extra three and a half months. See A. A. Berle, *Navigating the Rapids, 1918–1971: From the Papers of Adolf A. Berle* (New York: Harcourt Brace, 1973), p. 379, entry for December 1, 1941.

245 **Sherrod's account:** Sherrod, memorandum for David Hulburd, November 15, 1941, in the papers of Robert L. Sherrod, Series I, box 14, folder 1940–1941 (GARLSU). See also *Life*, November 24, 1941.

245 FDR and the coming of war: John G. Winant to Cordell Hull, November 26, 1941, in FRUS, 1941, IV, p. 665. See also Langer and Gleason, *The Undeclared War*, pp. 884–891.

245 New information from Stimson: Henry L. Stimson, memorandum for the President, November 26, 1941, in the papers of George C. Marshall, box 80, folder 30 (GCMF).

245 The Ten-Point program: Langer and Gleason, *The Undeclared War*, pp. 894–900.

245 Kimmel and an air attack: John H. Bradley et al., *The Second World War: Asia and the Pacific* (West Point: 1984), pp. 47–48.

246 Lack of range and sabotage threats: Ariel Levite, *Intelligence and Strategic Surprises* (New York: Columbia University Press, 1987), pp. 77–79; Frank P. Mintz, *Revisionism and the Origins of Pearl Harbor* (Lanham, Md.: University Press of America, 1985), pp. 98–101; and Gordon W. Prange et al., *Pearl Harbor: The Verdict of History* (New York: McGraw-Hill, 1986), Appendix 5, p. 656.

246 The Navy Department: Memorandum of conversation by Sumner Welles, November 27, 1941, in FRUS, 1941, IV, pp. 666–667; and for the war warning, see OPNAV TO CINCAF, CINCPAC, November 27, 1941 (27337 CR 0921), Department of Defense, in "*Magic*," IV, Appendix, A-117. See also Henry L. Stimson, *On Active Service in Peace and War* (New York: Harper, 1948), pp. 389–390.

246 Marshall's message: OPNAV TO COM PNNCF, COM PSNCF; Info to CINCPAC, COM PNCF, November 29, 1941 (290110 CR 066), in DOD, "*Magic*," IV, Appendix, A-119; and OPNAV TO COM PNNCF, COM PSNCF; Info to CINCPAC, COM PNCF, November 29, 1941, 290110 CR 066, ibid.," IV, Appendix, A-119.

246 Japanese knew this: Prange, pp. 423–429.

246 Missing carriers: David Kahn, "The United States Views Germany and Japan in 1941," in Ernest R. May, ed., *Knowing One's Enemies: Intelligence Assessment Before the Two World Wars* (Princeton: Princeton University Press, 1984), pp. 483–490.

246 On the approach of war: Heinrichs, *Threshold*, p. 217; and Hull to Winant, December 2, 1941, FRUS, 1941, IV, p. 711. Stanley Hornbeck, the State Department's adviser on public relations and a longtime expert on the Far East, argued on November 27 that the odds were five to one against war before December 15. See Memorandum of November 27, 1941, FRUS, p. 673. While Hornbeck mused about peace, Hull was warning Grew that he might soon have to pack his bags. See Hull to Grew, November 28, 1941, ibid., p. 682; and Hull, Memorandum of Conversation, November 29, 1941, ibid., p. 687.

246 Gallup: *The Gallup Poll*, I, December 10, 1941, p. 311, based on interviews conducted about ten days earlier.

246 *Time* on the Japanese people: *Time*, December 8, 1941. See DJSB, December 6, 1941 (SCL).

246 *Life* on the coming of war: Elson, *Time Inc.*, pp. 482–483. See also Longwell to HRL, November 21, 1941, in the Daniel Longwell collection (RBMLCU).

247 Dumbo: Hodgins, Oral History Project interview, p. 109.

247 Destroy their codes: Kahn, "U.S. Views," in May, p. 498. On the imminence of war, see also Myers (Canton) to Hull, December 1, 1941, FRUS, 1941, IV, p. 704.

247 Churchill: Kahn, "U.S. Views," in May, p. 500.

247 The Japanese note: Heinrichs, *Threshold*, p. 218; and Pogue, p. 225.

248 Yamamoto: Cited by Bradley, p. 61.

248 Audacious Japanese: *Time*, December 15, 1941. See also *Life*, same date.

248 At the office: DJSB, December 7, 1941 (SCL). See Teddy White's undated (probably 1948 or 1949) memorandum to Liebling, Munves notes, TM X, in the papers of A. J. Liebling (DRBCUL).

CHAPTER TWENTY-THREE

249 Death of the Reverend Luce: Elson, p. 484; Baruch, telegram to HRL, December 8, 1941, in the papers of Bernard M. Baruch, box 192 (SGMMLPU); and DJSB, December 8, 1941 (SCL). White to Joseph Liebling, n.d., but probably 1949, in the Time-Life Correspondence 1940–1946 of Theodore H. White (HLHU). For Elizabeth Luce's comment, see her letter to Mr. Decker, December 29, 1941, in the Archives of the United Board for Christian Higher Education in China (RG 11), box 14, folder 337 (YDSLAM). See also Elson, *Time Inc.*, pp. 483–484.

249 Germany first: *The Gallup Poll*, vol. I, December 23, 1941, p. 312.

250 McNaughton: McNaughton, dispatch to James McConaughy, November 28, 1942, in the papers of Frank McNaughton, box 3 (HSTL).

250 Luce bitter toward FDR: DJSB, December 11–13, 1941 (SCL).

250 Luce corresponds with FDR: OF 2442, OF 3338, OF 7093, and PPF 6677 (FDRL), for the correspondence, which dates from December 16 to 22, 1941.

250 Germans bombing New York City: *Life*, December 29, 1941.

251 *Life* advised: *Life*, January 26, 1941. On Japan's racial crusade, see *Life*, October 19, 1942.

251 Germans and Japanese converge: *Life*, March 2, 1942.

251 Like a losing game: DJSB, March 9, 19, 1942 (SCL).

251 Shell the West Coast: *Life*, March 9, 1942.

251 Rubber shortage: *Life*, June 8, 1942.

251 Internment of Japanese-Americans: *Life*, April 6, 1942.

251 Victory over the enemy: Conversation with Mr. McCloy, April 15, 1942, in the Transcripts of Director's Conversations of 1941–1945, Bureau of Public Relations, entry 265, box 1, (RG 107, NARA).

252 Hollywood war: *Life*, May 18, 1942.

252 Labor problems: *Time*, July 6 and August 24, 1942.

252 Price control problems: *Life*, May 11, July 13, September 14, 1942. See also DJSB, July 15, 1942 (SCL).

252 Scrap metal: *Life*, September 14, 1942.

252 On the rubber program: *Time*, July 27, 1942; HRL to Baruch, August 10, 1942; and Baruch to Luce, August 12, 1942, in the papers of Bernard M. Baruch, box 192 (SGMMLPU).

252 All vacations canceled: DJSB, April 24, 1942 (SCL).

252 Real historians: *Life*, September 16, 1942.

252 Corregidor and Ginger Rogers: DJSB, February 16, 17, 20, 1942 (SCL).

253 Luce and *Life:* DJSB, September 8, 1942 (SCL).

253 No drinking: Felix Belair, memorandum to the staff, May 13, 1941, in the papers of Robert L. Sherrod, Series I, box 9, folder on Time Inc., 1931–1943 (GARLSU).

253 **Belair's complaints:** The interview with Roy Alexander, in the W. A. Swanberg collection, box 18 (RBMLCU).

254 **Galbraith as source:** McNaughton, dispatch to James McConaughy, November 13, 1942, in the papers of Frank McNaughton, box 3 (HSTL).

255 **Cargo Ship:** *Life*, December 7, 1942.

255 **Time Inc. and the armed forces:** DJSB, December 10, 1941 (SCL).

255 **The origins of the BPR:** The War Department, Adjutant General's Office, memorandum on the subject of the Creation of the War Department Photonews Board, January 13, 1942, 263/228 (RG 319, NARA).

255 **The BPR:** Sherman Miles, memorandum for the Assistant Chief of Staff, G-1, June 12, 1940; and for the Chief, Public Relations Branch, G-2, June 14, 1940, in the records of the P.I.D., box 2 (RG 165, NARA). See also War Department, Press Section, memorandum to the press, July 24, 1940, in the records of the Office of the Secretary of War, 74A/11 (RG 107, NARA); and "Bureau of Public Relations," in General Services Administration, National Archives and Records Service, *Federal Records of World War II*, I (*Civilian Agencies*) (Washington, D.C.: National Archives, 1950), pp. 80–85. On the responsibilities of the BPR, see War Department Circular No. 59 and the BPR's policy book for Army public relations officers, in the Records of the Army Staff, 1939–, Chief of Information, Public Information Division, entry 263, box 227 (RG 319, NARA).

255 **Contingency plan:** Summary of press conference instructions issued by Brig. Gen. Alexander Surles on December 7, 1941, 7:30 P.M., prepared for Secretary Knox by the Office of Public Relations, in the records of the Office of the Secretary of the Navy (including CNO and JAG), General Correspondence, 1940–1942, box 77 (RG 80, NARA).

255 **Accreditation:** R. Ernest Dupuy, memorandum for the Director, BPR, October 23, 1941, in the records of the P.I.D., box 3 (RG 165, NARA).

255 **Time Inc. and accreditation:** Sherrod, memorandum for David Hulburd, December 17, 1941, in the papers of Robert L. Sherrod (GARLSU). See also agreement with the BPR, the Time-Life-Fortune papers, in the John Shaw Billings collection (SCL).

255 **Life's unique photographers:** Robert T. Elson, *The World of Time Inc.* (New York: Atheneum, 1973), p. 44.

256 **Early alarmed:** Stephen Early to K. T. Keller, October 19, 1942, OF 2442 (FDRL).

256 **Longwell and the armed forces:** DJSB, July 22 and October 7, 1942 (SCL).

256 **Longwell and *Life*'s artists:** Longwell, memorandum to Irene Saint re. *Life* and Art, April 24, 1968, in the Daniel Longwell collection (RBMLCU). See also DJSB, July 9, 1943 (SCL).

256 **Tom Lea:** *Life*, June 11, 1945.

256 **Luce and Surles:** The Transcripts of Director's Conversations of 1941–1945, Bureau of Public Relations, entry 265, box 1 (August 17) (RG107 NARA).

256 **Thompson jokes:** Elson, *World of Time Inc.*, p. 188.

257 **Confidential material lying about:** George Tames, "Washington Photographer for the New York Times 1945–1985," Oral History Interviews, 1988,

Senate Historical Office, Washington, D.C. See also John S. Billings, memorandum to Time Inc. editors, January 24, 1945, Time-Life-Fortune papers, in the John Shaw Billings collection (SCL).

257 The Army and Price: Marshall to Byron Price, September 17, 1945, in the papers of George C. Marshall, box 39, folder 2 (GCMF). See also Henry T. Ulasek, compiler, *Records of the Office of Censorship* (Washington, D.C.: National Archives, 1953).

257 Price on Roosevelt: Price, memorandum of August 3, 1942, Notebooks, in the papers of Byron Price, box 4, folder 5 (WSHS).

258 Hodgins: N. R. Howard to Byron Price and JHS, April 7, 1942, in the records of the Office of Censorship, 3, 1009 (RG 216, NARA).

258 Price on Luce's men: Price's Notebooks, reference 152, August 26, 1942, in the papers of Byron Price, box 3, folder 5 (WSHS). On the movements of the President, see Eric Hodgins to Jack Lockhart, July 29, 1944; and Lockhart to Hodgins, December 8, 1944, in the records of the Office of Censorship, Index to Administrative Subject File, III, box 1107 (RG 216, NARA).

258 Price on Luce: The unpublished memoirs of Price, section IX, in the papers of Byron Price, box 4, folder 11 (WSHS).

258 Hodgins and the atomic bomb: Atomic bomb, early 1944 inquiries, notebooks, ibid., folder 4.

258 Premature disclosure: List of violations compiled by Time Inc., July 31, 1944; and Eric Hodgins, memorandum to Mr. Luce et al., August 1, 1944, the Time-Life-Fortune papers, in the John Shaw Billings collection (SCL).

258 Longwell and the Navy: Forrestal to Henry R. Luce, May 11, 1944, in the papers of James V. Forrestal, box 61 (SGMMLPU).

258 Future of the world: HRL to James V. Forrestal, September 21, 1944, ibid.

258 *Life* getting first crack: DJSB, May 26 and July 25, 1942 (SCL).

259 *Life* scoops the field: DJSB, January 26, 28, 1944 (SCL).

259 Secret work: DJSB, October 7, 1942 (SCL).

259 Recognition: *The Reminiscences of Andrew Heiskell*, p. 103; and the *U.S. Army-Navy Journal of Recognition* (on microfilm, in the manuscripts division of the WSHS). See also DJSB, March 13, 1942 (SCL); and Elson, *World of Time Inc.*, p. 40.

259 OSS and Time Inc.: L. C. Houck, memorandum to R. DeVecchi, November 25, 1943; DeVecchi to Houck, January 22, 1944, in the records of the OSS, 092, box 61, folder 10; and 092, box 318, folder 9 (RG 226, NARA).

259 Requesting a list of personnel: Robert DeVecchi to Ralph D. Paine, May 5, 1944, ibid.

259 Dulles: J. Mildred Schwarz to Allen Dulles, April 14, 1942, ibid.

259 Jackson: DJSB, October 6, 1942 (SCL).

260 Luce on Eisenhower: Ibid., November 7, 1942 (SCL).

260 Lovett: Ibid., July 1, 1943 (SCL).

260 G-2 and Surles: Conversations of February 19 and September 27, 1944, in the Transcripts of Director's Conversations of 1941–1945, BPR, entry 265, box (RG 107, NARA).

260 Honest fundamental understanding: HRL to Marshall, January 19, 1942, in the papers of George C. Marshall, box 15, folder 7 (GCMF); and "America's New Army," in *The March of Time*, VIII, 9 (April 1942).

260 *Life* on Marshall: *Life*, October 3, 1943, and January 3, 1944.

260 **Karsh and Marshall:** The office memorandum to Gen. Marshall, April 11, 1944, in the papers of George C. Marshall, box 92, folder 22 (GCMF).

261 **Shepley and Marshall:** Correspondence related to McAvoy and Shepley, in the Records of the Army Staff, Public Information Division, Decimal Files of General Correspondence, 000.7/318, box 39 (RG 165, NARA); the correspondence between Surles, Marshall, and Eisenhower, November 15, 1944, 000.7/655, ibid.; and the relevant conversation, dated December 15, 1944, in the Transcripts of Director's Conversations of 1941–1945, Bureau of Public Relations, entry 265, box 3 (RG 107, NARA).

261 **Luce too busy:** C. D. Jackson to HRL, April 13, 1945, in the W. A. Swanberg collection, box 18 (RBMLCU). The complaining party was *Time* correspondent Bill Walton. See also DJSB, September 2, 1942 (SCL); and Elson, *World of Time Inc.*, pp. 203–208.

261 **The list of the war dead:** *Life*, July 5, 1943.

262 **"Jap skull":** *Life*, May 22 and June 12, 1944, Letters.

262 **Lynd:** *Life*, February 15, March 1, September 20, 1943.

262 **Capa and Bourke-White:** Elson, *World of Time Inc.* pp. 46–54. See also Mr. Lockhart, memorandum to Mr. Howard, February 8, 1943, in the records of the Office of Censorship, Index to Administrative Subject File, III, box 1034 (RG 216, NARA).

262 **New era:** *Time*, November 23, 1942.

262 **We're all anti-Semitic:** DJSB, December 11, 1946 (SCL).

263 **Jewy-looking Jews:** Ibid., March 21, 1942, and the entries for March 15, 1942, and April 14, 1944. For Billings' views on job discrimination, see ibid., June 23, 1944, and July 22, 1946.

263 **Jew woman:** Ibid., August 10, 1943, and January 1, 1944 (SCL).

263 **Subversive persons and movements:** "Voices of Defeat," *Life*, April 13, 1942.

263 **Posen and Lodz:** *Time*, November 27, 1939.

263 **Stories about atrocities committed against Russians:** *Life*, February 23, 1942.

263 **Stories on Himmler:** *Time*, October 11, 1943, and February 12, 1945.

263 **Rabbi Wise on extermination:** Deborah E. Lipstadt, *Beyond Belief: The American Press and the Coming of the Holocaust, 1933–1945* (New York: Free Press, 1986), p. 180.

263 **Two million Jews:** Gallup Organization .0287.012 (interview dates January 9–14, 1943).

264 **American Jewish Congress:** *Time*, March 8, 1943.

264 **Bloch's knowledge:** "Werner" to Bloch, April 23, 1943, in the papers of Kurt Bloch (SCDKLUO).

264 **Lauterbach:** *Time*, August 21, 1944.

265 **Public view of the Holocaust:** I am grateful to the Yankelovich organization for supplying me in 1989 with charts based upon Gallup Polls conducted in January 1943 and November 1944.

CHAPTER TWENTY-FOUR

266 **Cruelty and folly:** Luce's comment in C. Stuart Heminway, *Twenty Years with Nineteen Twenty*, p. 312.

266 **Luce on a liberal epoch:** HRL, address to the Advertising and Sales Club

of Toronto, April 28, 1942, in the W. A. Swanberg collection, box 21 (RBMLCU); HRL, commencement address at Grinnell College, May 31, 1942, in the W. A. Swanberg collection, box 21 (RBMLCU); and HRL, speech before the Open Meeting of the United War Fund Campaign for 1943, Boston, January 4, 1943, in the papers of HRL, speeches (MDLOC).

266 **Unlimited duration:** HRL, address at the Ohio State University commencement, Columbus, June 11, 1943, in the W. A. Swanberg collection, box 2 (RBMLCU).

267 **Luce on idealism and the American idea:** HRL to Barton, April 2, 1943, in the papers of Bruce Barton, box 40, folder on HRL (WSHS); and HRL, address at the *Yale Daily News* dinner, New Haven, February 16, 1942, in the W. A. Swanberg collection, box 21 (RBMLCU).

267 **Luce on the interdependent world:** HRL, address at the Dayton Art Institute, June 12, 1943, in the W. A. Swanberg collection, box 21 (RBMLCU), and DJSB, April 21, 1944 (SCL).

267 **Luce on the postwar economy:** HRL to Roy Alexander, February 22, 1945, the Time-Life-Fortune papers, I, folder 49, in the John Shaw Billings collection (SCL).

267 *Life* **on the future:** "Jobs for Veterans" and "*Life* in the Kitchen," *Life*, August 9, 1943.

267 **Luce on postwar industry:** The comments of HRL at a *Fortune* dinner, May 17, 1944, the Time-Life-Fortune papers, I, folder 34, in the John Shaw Billings collection (SCL).

267 **Luce and Keynes:** Elson, *World of Time Inc.*, p. 21.

268 *Life* **on Saudi Arabian oil:** *Life*, February 28, 1944.

268 **Hoffman and Luce:** Cover story in *Time*, September 6, 1943.

268 **Jessup on the economy:** *Life*, September 13, 1943.

268 **Planning the postwar world in 1941:** HRL to Raymond L. Buell et al., July 10, 1941, in the papers of Russell W. Davenport, container 76 (MDLOC).

268 **Advising Luce:** The Q Department folder in the Daniel Longwell collection, box 27 (RBMLCU).

268 **Luce and the uses of the postwar materials:** HRL, memorandum to the senior editors of *Time*, October 22, 1943, the Time-Life-Fortune papers, I, folder 30, in the John Shaw Billings collection (SCL).

268 **Luce, Jessup, and the Postwar Department:** HRL to the Staff, August 3, 1942, in the papers of Raymond Leslie Buell (unprocessed), carton 15 (MDLOC).

268 **Luce and the Policy Formulation Committee:** HRL, memoranda of May 12 and June 10, 1943, the Time-Life-Fortune papers, I, folder 27, in the John Shaw Billings collection (SCL).

268 **The 1944 committee:** Sterling, "The Luce Empire," chapter 6, in the papers of Dorothy Sterling (SCDKLUO). Writing to Buell after the war, Luce commented that "Our respect and admiration for the job you have done remains undiminished." Raymond Leslie Buell died in 1946 from a brain tumor.

269 **Sensitive materials:** Charles Stillman, memorandum of January 7, 1942 (misdated 1941), in the papers of Raymond Leslie Buell (unprocessed), carton 15 (MDLOC).

269 **Clare on postwar planning:** Clare Luce to Streit, September 23, 1942, in the papers of Clarence K. Streit, box 66 (MDLOC).

269 **Wallace and Roosevelt:** Henry A. Wallace to FDR, June 11, 1942, in the papers of Franklin D. Roosevelt, OF 4351 (1) (FDRL).

269 **Willkie and Luce:** Wendell Willkie to HRL, draft of October 7, 1943, in the Willkie MSS. (MDLLIU).

269 **Luce and postwar:** Minutes of the Postwar Committee, February 19, 1943, in the papers of Dorothy Sterling (SCDKLUO).

269 **Grover and the Luce memorandum:** Allen Grover to Buell, November 5, 1943; and HRL, memorandum to the Policy Committee, November 3, 1943, in the papers of Raymond Leslie Buell (unprocessed), carton 15 (MDLOC).

270 **Luce's God:** *Life*, April 10, 1944.

270 **Zero hour:** *Life*, January 10, 1944.

270 **Luce and Britain:** HRL to Ed (Thompson?), July 22, 1943, in the Time-Life-Fortune papers, I, folder 29, in the John Shaw Billings collection (SCL).

271 *Time* **on Australia:** *Time*, March 30, 1942.

271 **On Nehru:** "Nehru of India," *Life*, December 11, 1939.

271 **Freedom for India:** HRL, "England Revisited," April 1, 1942, in the Willkie MSS. (MDLLIU).

271 **Nehru arrested:** *Time*, August 17, 1942.

271 **Not unmindful:** Correspondence between Graebner and the Air Ministry, May 28, 1941, in the papers of Walter Graebner, box 1, folder 3 (WSHS).

271 **Lies about Britain:** Brendan Bracken to Walter Graebner, November 26, 1941, ibid., box 1, folder 2.

271 **Britain weaker:** "Conversation with Henry R. Luce," Military Intelligence Division W.D.G.S., March 18, 1942, in the records of the Office of Strategic Services, 16, box 69, no. 14494 (RG 226, NARA).

272 **Luce on England:** HRL, "England Revisited," April 1, 1942, in the Willkie MSS. (MDLLIU).

272 **Go easy on Britain:** DJSB, February 14, 1942 (SCL). See also H. G. Nicholas, ed., *Washington Despatches, 1941–1945: Weekly Political Reports from the British Embassy* (Chicago: The University of Chicago Press, 1981), p. 46 (June 20, 1942).

272 **Future of the empire:** DJSB, August 12, 1942 (SCL).

272 **Davenport editorial:** *Life*, October 12, 1942.

272 **Free trade:** HRL, memorandum to managing editors, August 17, 1943, the Time-Life-Fortune papers, I, folder 29, in the John Shaw Billings collection (SCL).

272 **Martin on Luce:** File cards of Raymond L. Buell, Luce, Henry R., November 12, 1942, in the papers of Raymond Leslie Buell (unprocessed) (MDLOC). See also *The Reminiscences of Andrew Heiskell*, p. 100.

273 **Isolationists attack Luce:** *New York Times*, October 24, 1942.

273 **Refuting the critics:** DJSB, October 18, 1942 (SCL).

273 **Luce contrite:** HRL, statement of October 15, 1942, the Time-Life-Fortune papers, I, folder 25, in the John Shaw Billings collection (SCL).

273 **Bartlett's response:** *Life*, October 26, 1942.

273 **Uproar over the open letter:** Elson, *World of Time Inc.*, pp. 23–33.

273 **Luce on the Indian right to freedom:** File cards of Raymond L. Buell, Luce, Henry R., January 25, 1945, in the papers of Raymond Leslie Buell (unprocessed) (MDLOC).

273 *Time* **on Churchill:** *Time*, August 17, 1942.

273 **Polls:** Special Service Division, Research Branch, Army Service Forces, War Department, *What the Soldier Thinks*, ii, August 1943, pp. 79–83.

274 **Luce's plan for Britain:** HRL, memorandum to the Senior List, December 8, 1945, in the papers of C. D. Jackson, 1931–1967, container 57 (DDEL).

274 **Luce's early anticommunism:** Swanberg, *Luce and His Empire*, pp. 90–91. On the Russians as sloppy and boorish, see Elson, *Time Inc.*, p. 172, and HRL, "Notes on U.S.S.R" (August 1932), in the W. A. Swanberg collection, box 20, folder on HRL 1920–1932, speeches (RBMLCU).

274 **Genghis Khan:** *Time*, December 1, 1941.

275 **Luce complaining about Russia:** DJSB, September 23, 1942 (SCL).

275 **Willkie on Russia:** *Time*, October 26, 1942.

275 **Germans losing the war:** *Time*, December 14, 1942.

275 **Americans and Russians:** *Time*, January 4, 1943.

275 **Luce in Washington:** HRL, Memoranda summarizing conversations held in Washington, D.C., on February 1–3, 1943, in Jessup, *Ideas of Henry Luce*, p. 349. Contrast Luce's skepticism about the Soviets with FDR's optimism: Adlai E. Stevenson, memorandum of April 30, 1942; Frank Knox to FDR, May 1, 1942; and FDR to Knox, May 4, 1942, PSF Navy, Knox folder (FDRL).

277 **Venomous lies:** Robert Lippin to Graebner, April 5, 1943, box 1, folder 3, in the papers of Walter Graebner (WSHS).

277 **Gallup on Russia:** *Time*, July 25, 1943.

277 **No** *cordon sanitaire:* *Time*, March 15 and April 12, 1943.

277 **Katyn:** *Time*, April 26, 1943, and May 17, 1943.

278 **Luce on Russia and freedom:** HRL, memorandum to managing editors, August 17, 1943, the Time-Life-Fortune papers, I, folder 29, in the John Shaw Billings collection (SCL).

278 *Time* **worries about Russian ambitions in Germany:** *Time*, August 30, 1943.

278 **Moscow Declaration:** "Moscow Agreement," *Life*, November 15, 1943.

278 *Time* **praises FDR:** *Time*, November 29, 1943.

279 **Buell on Russia:** Raymond L. Buell, Summary, January 21, 1944, in the papers of Dorothy Sterling (SCDKLUO).

279 **Buell's critics:** P. Prentice, memorandum to Mr. Jessup, January 18, 1944, the Time-Life-Fortune papers, in the John Shaw Billings collection (SCL).

279 **Raymond Buell and relations with Russia:** Agenda for the meeting of January 26, 1944, in the papers of Dorothy Sterling (SCDKLUO).

280 **Luce and MacArthur:** HRL to Douglas MacArthur, June 8, 1944; and Noel Busch to Luce, May 24, 1944, in the papers of CBL, container 455 (MDLOC).

CHAPTER TWENTY-FIVE

281 **White on Chiang:** White to David Hulburd, August 3, 1942, in the Time-Life Correspondence 1940–1946 of Theodore H. White (HLHU).

281 **White and Soong:** White to T. V. Soong, January 10, 18, 1942, ibid.

282 **Stilwell's defeat:** Barbara Tuchman, *Stilwell and the American Experience in China 1911–1945* (New York: Bantam, 1972), p. 305.

282 **Gauss:** Ibid., p. 336.

282 **Marshall's concerns:** Marshall to AMMISCA, April 12, 1942, and the exchange of letters between Chiang and FDR, in the Franklin D. Roosevelt Papers, Map Room File, box 10, folder 1 (FDRL).

283 **Clare Luce on Stilwell:** "Life's Reports," *Life,* April 27, 1942. See the Stilwell diary, February 21, 1942, in the papers of Joseph W. Stilwell, box 21 (HIWRP).

283 **Stilwell and his troops:** Tuchman, pp. 4–5, 164–165, 218–219.

283 **Stilwell on Chiang:** Herbert Feis, *The China Tangle: The American Effort in China from Pearl Harbor to the Marshall Mission* (New York: Atheneum, 1967), p. 37.

283 **Chiang on Stilwell:** Tuchman, p. 341.

283 **Chiang's plans:** Schaller, *The U.S. Crusade in China,* p. 89.

283 **The U.S. in China–Burma–India:** Maurice Matloff, *Strategic Planning for Coalition Warfare* (Washington, D.C.: Department of the Army, 1959), p. 15.

283 **Clare Luce and Berle:** A. A. Berle, Jr., memorandum of conversation with Mrs. Luce, May 5, 1942; and Stanley K. Hornbeck, memorandum of May 7, 1942, in the papers of Stanley K. Hornbeck, box 281 (HIWRP).

284 **Chennault:** White, *In Search of History,* pp. 185–187.

284 **Stilwell happy about Chennault:** Stilwell, entry for March 4, 1942, in the papers of Joseph W. Stilwell, box 21 (HIRWP).

284 **Trying to manure:** White, p. 190.

285 **Prostitutes:** Ibid., p. 187.

285 **Chennault vs. Stilwell:** Tuchman, p. 429.

285 **Chungking propagandists and Luce:** The Minister of Foreign Affairs, Republic of China, to HRL, May 19, 1942, in the papers of CBL, container 841 (MDLOC).

285 **A new sun:** HRL, address delivered in Rochester, April 22, 1942, in the W. A. Swanberg collection, box 21 (RBMLCU); see also Jessup, *Ideas of Henry Luce,* pp. 198–201.

285 **Rowe:** Buell, memorandum to the Post-War Research Committee, June 8, 1942, in the papers of Raymond Leslie Buell (unprocessed) (MDLOC).

286 *Time* **praised Kung:** *Time,* November 9, 1942.

286 **Buell on China:** Raymond L. Buell, memorandum on Pacific relations in the postwar world, revision dated July 7, 1942, Office of Censorship, Administrative Division—Service Section, I, box 416, File 012D Censorship Review, *Fortune* (RG 216, NARA).

286 **Legend vs. reality:** White to Charles Wertenbaker, June 19, 1942, in the Time-Life Correspondence 1940–1946 of Theodore H. White (HLHU).

286 **Currie on China:** Currie, memorandum of November 10, 1942, in the Lauchlin Currie papers, and memorandum to FDR, November 13, 1942, box 5 (HIWRP).

286 **Currie on Stilwell:** Lauchlin Currie to George C. Marshall, September 14, 1942, ibid., box 1; and Feis, pp. 43–44.

286 **White on the lack of reforms:** Theodore H. White, Chungking Cable no. 43, November 29, 1942, in the papers of Dorothy Sterling (SCDKLUO).

287 **Luce worried about China:** DJSB, February 13, 1943 (SCL).

287 **We fail totally:** HRL, address at St. Thomas Church, New York, December 13, 1942, United China Relief, Inc.; and United Service to China, Papers, box

48 (SGMMLPU). On this event, see Mrs. John K. Sloan to HRL, December 8, 1942, ibid.

287 Luce speaking in the dark: David Hulburd to Roy Larsen, April 9, 1942, the Time-Life-Fortune papers, I, folder 22, in the John Shaw Billings collection (SCL).

287 Clare Luce's blurb: CBL, cable to Stilwell, June 26, 1942, and related correspondence in Records of the Army Staff, Public Information Division 1924–1946, Decimal Files of General Correspondence, box 3/000.7–46 (RG 165, NARA).

288 Hollywood and UCR: United China Relief, Inc., and United Service to China, papers, box 49 (SGMMLPU).

288 Luce and Selznick: HRL to O.P. (Swift), n.d., ibid., box 48.

288 UCR fund-raising: B. A. Garside to James L. Crider, September 19, 1945, enclosing "Five Years of United China Relief," in United China Relief, Inc., and United Service to China, papers, ibid.

288 Madame Chiang coming to the U.S.: *Life*, February 25, 1943.

288 Luce's reception committee: HRL, telegram to William W. Lockwood, February 10, 1943, in the papers of the Institute of Pacific Relations, B, catalogued correspondence (A-L) (RBMLCU); HRL, telegram to Wendell L. Willkie, February 8, 1943, in the Willkie MSS. (MDLLIU). See also HRL, telegram to Kohlberg, February 15, 1943, in the papers of Alfred Kohlberg, box 114, folder on Clare Boothe and Henry Robinson Luce to 1947 (HIWRP).

289 Madame Chiang in Washington: *Life*, March 1, 1943. See also DJSB, February 24, 1943 (SCL).

289 Madame Chiang and the dinner: Interview with Wesley Bailey, in the W. A. Swanberg collection, box 18 (RBMLCU).

290 Bailey: Luce was grateful to his discreet, efficient young assistant. As usual, he had trouble thanking a person directly. Instead, he presented Bailey with a gift of seventy shares of common stock in Time Inc. Many years later, Bailey informed W. A. Swanberg that this equity had helped to send his daughter to Syracuse University.

290 First Lady of China: The volume can be consulted in the papers of Paul G. Hoffman, box 49, United China Relief file (HSTL).

290 Incompetence and corruption: The anonymous memorandum on China, dated March 9, 1943, may be consulted in the papers of CBL, container 509 (MDLOC).

291 On the Honan famine: White, pp. 193ff.

291 Authorities had done little: Theodore H. White, cable no. 114, in the records of the Office of Censorship, III, 1107 (RG 216, NARA). On the danger to himself, see White, p. 199.

291 Loyang office: White to David Hulburd, April 15, 1943, in the Time-Life Correspondence 1940–1946 of Theodore H. White (HLHU).

291 Exorbitant prices: Embassy in Chungking to the Secretary of State, April 15, 1943, in the records of the Office of Strategic Services, file 37758/390 (RG 226, NARA).

291 Saved a few thousand lives: Fragment of a manuscript on the civil war, written late in 1944, Time-Life Correspondence 1940–1946, in the papers of Theodore H. White (HLHU).

292 Currie forwarded copies: Currie, memorandum to Eleanor Roosevelt, May 8, 1943, and to FDR, May 10, 1943, in the Lauchlin Currie papers, box 5 (HIWRP). See also Lauchlin Currie to Harry Hopkins, June 10, 1943, ibid.

292 Ch'en brothers: White to T. and P. Durdin, June 1, 1943, in the Time-Life Correspondence 1940–1946 of Theodore H. White (HLHU).

293 Fire White: White to Charles Wertenbaker, July 4, 1951; and White to A. J. Liebling, n.d., but probably 1949, ibid.

293 Fairbank on the Ch'en brothers: Fairbank, *Chinabound*, pp. 245–263.

293 Rising star: White, *In Search of History*, p. 240.

293 Would turn to the Soviet Union: John Paton Davies, "The China Hands in Practice: The Personal Experience," in Paul G. Lauren, ed., *The China Hands' Legacy: Ethics and Diplomacy* (Boulder, CO: The Westview Press, 1987), p. 41.

293 Foreign Service officers: Neils, *China Images*, p. 113; Warren I. Cohen, *America's Response to China* (New York: Wiley, 1980), p. 172; and Schaller, p. 116.

293 Undisputed leader: Tuchman, p. 461.

293 Sevareid: Eric Sevareid, *Not So Wild a Dream* (New York: Alfred A. Knopf, 1947), pp. 313–319.

293 The need for an outside source: Neils, pp. 104–106.

293 Pearl Buck: *Life*, May 10, 1943.

293 Buck on democracy, with Luce's view of her proposed article: Cited by Neils, pp. 104–105.

294 Headed for ruin: Tuchman, p. 452.

294 Foreign loans: E. J. Kahn, *The China Hands: America's Foreign Service Officers and What Befell Them* (New York: The Viking Press, 1975), p. 99.

294 Lodge: Lodge made his statement on September 30, 1943.

294 Long-range happiness: HRL, memorandum to managing editors, August 17, 1943, the Time-Life-Fortune papers, I, folder 29, in the John Shaw Billings collection (SCL).

294 Mighty upsurge: *Time*, July 12, 19, and September 20, 1943. On Luce and White, see Elson, *World of Time Inc.*, pp. 120–122.

294 The peasant is China: White to David Hulburd, July [?] 1943, in the Time-Life Correspondence 1940–1946, June 1943–November 1944, in the papers of Theodore H. White (HLHU).

294 White on the plight of China: White, p. 210.

294 White and Sun Fo: White to *Fortune*, November 12, 1943, the Time-Life Correspondence 1940–1946, in the papers of Theodore H. White (HLHU).

295 Bloch argued: Kurt Bloch, memorandum to HRL, October 11, 1943, in the papers of CBL, container 454 (MDLOC).

295 To improve the situation: HRL to T. V. Soong, November 26, 1943, in the papers of T. V. Soong, box 6, folder on HRL (HIWRP).

295 Luce and Japan: *Life*, July 16, 1943; and HRL, memorandum to Davenport et al., September 1, 1943, in the papers of Russell W. Davenport, container 76 (MDLOC).

295 Chiang and the Soviets: *Time*, October 25, 1943. See also Feis, pp. 86–95.

295 After joint consultation: Ibid., p. 99.

295 Allied pressure: Ibid., p. 88.

296 Hurley's report to Roosevelt: Patrick J. Hurley to FDR, November 20,

1943, in the Franklin D. Roosevelt Papers, Map Room File, box 165, folder A16-3/China (FDRL).

296 Roosevelt's irritation with Chiang: Schaller, p. 151.

296 Men to carry on: Cited by Kahn, *China Hands*, p. 101.

296 Roosevelt disgusted with Chiang: Schaller, p. 154.

296 Troops who fought badly: Tuchman, p. 514.

296–297 Kohlberg investigates medical relief: Correspondence in the Alfred Kohlberg file, records of the American Bureau for Medical Aid to China, container 38 (RBMLCU).

297 Kohlberg and EMSTS: Alfred Kohlberg, telegram to George Bachman, August 15, 1943, ibid. See also Kohlberg to Madame Chiang, August 25, 1943, ibid.

297 Report on the living and health conditions in the two group armies at the Ichang front, January 8, 1944: Material contained in Kohlberg file (2) (RBMLCU).

298 Kohlberg and Edwards: Edward C. Carter to Lennig Sweet, April 28, 1943; and Donald D. Van Slyke, proposal presented to the UCR-ABMAC conference of December 7, 1943, ibid.

298 Lin backing Kohlberg: Lin Yutang, telegram to Alfred Kohlberg, January 23, 1944, ibid.

298 Kohlberg to directors: Kohlberg to the directors of UCR, February 5, 1944, in the papers of Alfred Kohlberg, box 189, folder on United China Relief (HIWRP).

298 Kohlberg to Special Committee: Alfred Kohlberg to Paul G. Hoffman, HRL, and James G. Blaine, April 5, 1944, in the records of the American Bureau for Medical Aid to China, container 38, file on Alfred Kohlberg (RBMLCU).

298 Edwards: HRL to Willkie, August 25, 1942, in the papers of Wendell L. Willkie (MDLLIU).

298 Report of the Special Committee, February 15, 1944: James McConaughy, telegram to Alfred Kohlberg, February 25, 1944; and Kohlberg to McConaughy, April 21, 1944, in the United China Relief–United Service to China, papers, box 46, folders on Alfred Kohlberg (SGMMLPU).

299 Sun Fo: Sun Fo's speech is reproduced in *The Amerasia Papers: A Clue to the Catastrophe of China*, published in 1970 by the Subcommittee to Investigate the Administration of the Internal Security Act and Other Internal Security Laws (Washington, D.C.: Government Printing Office), I, 416.

299 Chiang and *China's Destiny*: Robert P. Martin, memorandum to David Hulburd, January 4, 1944, in the papers of CBL, box 509 (MDLOC).

299 Gauss: Ambassador Gauss to the Secretary of State, April 18, 1944, in the General Records of the Army Staff, Public Information Division 1924–1946, Decimal Files of General Correspondence, box 39/000.7/79–80 (RG 165, NARA).

299 Chiang accuses: Chiang Kai-shek to FDR, March 17, 1944, and Roosevelt to Chiang, March 20, 1944, in the George C. Marshall papers, box 60, folder 43.

299 Fraudulent and lying: Department of State, memorandum of conversation between Secretary Hull and Ambassador Wei, June 24, 1944, in the papers of Edward R. Stettinius, box 724, folder on China, October 1943 (MDUVL).

See also Director of OSS Donovan to Grace Tully, enclosing a report on
Chiang Kai-shek, dated April 4, 1944, in PSF Safe File, box 4; and Report by
the Research & Analysis branch of the OSS, June 16, 1944, in PSF (OSS),
box 168, folder April–July 1, 1944 (FDRL).

299 Fascist countrymen: White to Butsy, February 15, 1944, in the papers of
Theodore H. White (HLHU).

299–300 White's opinions: White's dispatches and the comments of his Chinese censors, in *The Amerasia Papers: A Clue to the Catastrophe of China*, I, 358–381.

300 Censors: "Reasons for Censoring Theodore H. White's Article on Chinese
Communist Party," in the papers of Theodore H. White, the Time-Life
Dispatches, series 1A (HLHU).

300 So-called Communists: Tuchman, p. 590.

300 Disabuse Americans: Department of State, memorandum of conversation,
February 14, 1944, in the papers of Edward R. Stettinius, box 724, folder on
October 1943—China (MDUVL).

300 Bloch's pessimism: Kurt Bloch, memorandum to White, March 31, 1944,
in the papers of Theodore H. White, Time-Life Correspondence 1940–1946
(HLHU).

300 Confirmed the pessimistic prognosis: Bob Sheehan, cable of January 22,
1944, in dispatches to *Time* (HLHU).

300 I value so highly: HRL, cable to H. H. Kung, March 3, 1944, in the papers
of Lauchlin Currie, box 5 (HIWRP).

CHAPTER TWENTY-SIX

302 Dewey and Willkie: Smith, *Thomas E. Dewey and his Times*, p. 346.

302 The onslaught: *Life*, April 30, 1942.

302 In need of a foreign policy: *Life*, October 19, 1942.

302 Willkie's internationalism: Robert A. Divine, *Second Chance: The Triumph
of Internationalism in America during World War II* (New York: Atheneum,
1967), pp. 105–106.

302 Widening Willkie's circle of contacts: HRL to Wendell L. Willkie, November 9, 1942, and related correspondence with Emory Ross, in the Willkie
MSS. (MDIU).

302 Barton and Dewey: *New York Herald Tribune*, January 23, 1942; and Barton
to Herbert Brownell, August 20, 1942, in the papers of Bruce Barton, box
17, folder on Thomas E. Dewey (WSHS).

302 After much hesitation: CBL to J. Kenneth Bradley, July 31, 1942, in the
Willkie MSS. (MDLLIU).

303 Supported by her husband: The interview with CBL, in the W. A. Swanberg collection, box 18 (RBMLCU).

303 Billings on Clare: DJSB, February 12, 1943 (SCL).

303 Clare's campaigns: Sheed, *Clare Boothe Luce*, p. 92. See also DJSB, August
14 and September 3, 1942 (SCL).

303 Time Inc. and Clare Luce's campaign: Sterling, "The Luce Empire,"
chapter 11, in the papers of Dorothy Sterling (SCDKLUO).

303 Campaign coverage: *Time*, September 21, 1942.

303 Madame Chiang and Clare Luce: Madame Chiang to CBL, October 6,
1942, in the papers of CBL, container 841 (MDLOC).

304 A close-up on Clare: John Billings to David Hulburd, September 25, 1942, the Time-Life-Fortune papers, I, folder 25, in the John Shaw Billings collection (SCL).

304 Pride in her victory: HRL to Baruch, November 14, 1942, in the papers of Bernard M. Baruch, box 192 (SGMMLPU).

304 McNaughton on the elections: McNaughton, report to James McConaughy, November 5, 1942, in the papers of Frank McNaughton, box 3 (HSTL).

304 *Time* on Willkie: *Time*, January 4, 1943.

304 Sport of kings: Elson, *World of Time Inc.*, p. 71.

304 Willkie and Chamberlain: Wendell Willkie to HRL, May 28, 29, 1943.

304 Dewey and Luce: HRL to Dewey, February 7, 1943, in the papers of Thomas E. Dewey, Series 4, box 107, folder 17 (RRLUR).

304–305 Dewey, Willkie, and Warren: Barton, memorandum to William Benton, September 14, 1943, in the papers of Bruce Barton, box 72, folder on Wendell Willkie; and John F. Neylon to Barton, August 24, 1943, ibid., box 57, folder on the Republican Party (WSHS)

305 A glamor boy: *Time*, July 5, 1943.

305 Willkie in the Midwest: *Time*, July 25, 1943.

305 Willkie's *One World*: *Time*, August 16, 1943.

305 Economic waste: HRL to Wendell Willkie, August 2, 1943, in the Willkie MSS. (MDLLIU).

305 Luce on the Democrats: Notes on "The Present Situation of the Republican Party," in the papers of Russell W. Davenport, container 76 (MDLOC).

305 Foreign policy sleep: *Life*, March 22, 1943.

305 Barton on the nomination: Barton to Thomas E. Dewey, July 2, 1943, in the papers of Bruce Barton, box 17, folder on Thomas E. Dewey (WSHS).

305 Luce on the regular Republicans: HRL to Wendell Willkie, June 3, 1943, in the Willkie MSS. (MDIU).

305 Luce's plans for 1944: HRL, memorandum of August 23, 1943, and Manfred Gottfried, memorandum to HRL, August 29, 1943, the Time-Life-Fortune papers, I, folder 29, in the John Shaw Billings collection (SCL).

306 Luce's impressions of Dulles: Richard Challener, interview with HRL, July 28, 1965, in the John Foster Dulles Oral History Project (SGMMLPU).

306 Dulles and the Council: Divine, pp. 36–37.

306 Dulles on sovereignty and liberty: Dulles, "The Christian Forces and a Stable Peace," published by the National Board of the Young Men's Christian Associations of the United States, January 25, 1942, in the papers of John Foster Dulles, selected correspondence and related material, box 20 (SGMMLPU). See also his remarks delivered at the meeting of the National Peace Conference in New York City, March 17, 1941, ibid.

306 The Six Pillars of Peace: *Discussion of Political Propositions* by John Foster Dulles et al., Commission to Study the Bases of a Just and Durable Peace (New York: 1943), in the papers of Thomas E. Dewey, series X, box 15, folder 2 (RRLUR). On the Six Pillars, see also Divine, p. 160.

307 Dulles and FDR: Material on the meeting with Roosevelt, March 26, 1943, in the papers of John Foster Dulles, selected correspondence and related material, box 22 (SGMMLPU). Soviet system and peace: Divine, pp. 36–37.

307 Dulles in *Life*: John Foster Dulles, "A Righteous Faith," *Life*, December 28, 1942.

307 **Senator Ball:** McNaughton, cable to James McConaughy, March 13, 1943, in the papers of Frank McNaughton, box 3 (HSTL).

307 *Time* **on Ball and Fulbright:** *Time*, June 21, 1943.

307 **On the Ball Resolution:** Divine, pp. 92–102.

307 **Vandenberg's past votes:** *"Vandenberg and Isolationism,"* with a memorandum from Burwell to Billings, commented on by Luce, January 17, 1944, the Time-Life-Fortune papers, I, folder 32, in the John Shaw Billings collection (SCL).

307 **Karl Mundt:** *Time*, February 1, 1943.

307 **The debate about the world organization:** Dispatches to James McConaughy, March 26, 1943, to September 25, 1943, in the papers of Frank McNaughton, boxes 3 and 4 (HSTL).

307 **Would offend no one:** *Time*, September 13, 1943.

307 **McNaughton on Spangler:** McNaughton, dispatch of February 1, 1944, in the papers of Frank McNaughton, box 4 (HSTL).

307 **Spangler angry at** *Time:* Harrison E. Spangler to HRL, September 21, 1943, the Time-Life-Fortune papers, I, folder 30, in the John Shaw Billings collections (SCL).

308 **Hostility to Willkie:** Grover W. Dalton to Wendell L. Willkie, September 1, 1943, in the papers of Bruce Barton, box 72, folder on Willkie, Wendell (WSHS)

308 **Liabilities:** Smith, p. 384.

308 **By way of Wall Street:** Ibid., p. 387.

308 **Dewey and the British alliance:** *Time*, September 13, 1943.

308 **Vying with Willkie:** *New York Times*, September 6, 1943.

308 **His compromising heart:** *Time*, September 20, 1943.

308 **Spangler old and slow:** Stanley High to DeWitt Wallace, September 10, 1943, in the papers of Bruce Barton, box 57, folder on the Republican Party, 1943 (WSHS)

308 **Among sovereign nations:** *New York Herald Tribune*, September 8, 1943; and Divine, pp. 120–135.

309 **The grand perspective:** HRL to Wendell Willkie, May 9, 1944, in the Willkie MSS. (MDLLIU).

309 **The Big Four:** Department of State, press release of the Joint Four-Nation Declaration, November 1, 1943, in the papers of John Foster Dulles, selected correspondence and related material, box 23 (SGMMLPU).

309 **Hull on the international organization:** Divine, pp. 155–176.

309 **Planning the world organization:** Ibid., pp. 182–198.

309 **Dulles and the four-nation declaration:** Dulles, "Analysis of the Moscow Declarations . . . ," in the papers of John Foster Dulles, selected correspondence and related material, box 22 (SGMMLPU).

309 **Dulles and world government:** John Foster Dulles to HRL, September 29, 1943, ibid.

CHAPTER TWENTY-SEVEN

310 **Luce on Roosevelt:** HRL, memorandum to John S. Billings et al., April 30, 1942, the Time-Life-Fortune papers, I, folder 23, in the John Shaw Billings collection (SCL); and Elson, *World of Time Inc.*, p. 59.

310 **Eleanor Roosevelt's sons:** *Life*, December 29, 1941.

310 *Life* **and Theodore Roosevelt:** *Life,* September 27, 1943.

310 **FDR and** *Time's* **wisecracks:** S. R. Fuller to Harry Hopkins, February 27, 1941; and FDR to Fuller, March 4, 1941, OF 2616 (FDRL).

311 **Roosevelt and the Brazil incident:** Correspondence contained in the papers of Stephen T. Early, box 31, folder on *Life* (FDRL); and DJSB, January 7, 1942 (SCL).

311 **On the airfield imbroglio:** FDR to Early, January 20, 1942, in the papers of Stephen T. Early, box 31 (FDRL).

311 **Roosevelt on the Rio episode:** FDR, memoranda to Early, January 7, 17, 1942, Munves notes, TM X, in the papers of A. J. Liebling (DRBCUL).

312 **Billings on Roosevelt:** DJSB, January 6, 1942 (SCL).

312 **Longwell on Roosevelt:** Ibid., January 8.

312 **Marshall and Luce:** Ibid., January 21.

312 **Roosevelt is the government:** Ibid., February 14.

312 **The Egyptian incident:** Sumner Welles to FDR, March 7, 1942; and Roosevelt, memorandum to Stephen T. Early, March 12, 1942, Munves notes, in the papers of A. J. Liebling (DRBCUL).

312 **Build a complete case:** Elson, *World of Time Inc.,* p. 10.

313 **The Luces and Turkey:** Correspondence in the Office of the Secretary of War, Safe File, 741, box 2 (RG 107, NARA).

313 **Mrs. Luce's sharp tongue:** Letter from "another voter," to the *New York Sun,* June 28, 1943.

313–314 **Gervasi and Clare Luce:** The W. A. Swanberg collection, box 18 (RBMLCU).

314 **British reaction:** *Washington Despatches,* p. 153, February 21, 1943; see also CBL to unidentified correspondent, November 19, 1943, in the papers of CBL, container 454 (MDLOC).

314 **Luce,** *Time,* **and** *Fortune* **on the globaloney debate:** Correspondence between HRL and Henry A. Wallace, in the Henry A. Wallace papers at the University of Iowa, reel 24 (FDRL).

314 **Harry Luce on globaloney:** Sterling, "The Luce Empire," chapter 10, in the papers of Dorothy Sterling (SCDKLUO).

314 **Clare Luce to the President:** CBL to the President, for release on March 7, 1943, in the papers of Dorothy Thompson, series I, container 19, folder on Luce, Clare Boothe (GARLSU).

314 **Harry Hawes:** File on Clare Luce, in the Stephen T. Early papers, box 31 (FDRL); for Dietz's poem, see PPF 8342, ibid.

315 **Clare Luce on de Gaulle:** *Time,* July 19, 1943. For her important speech on foreign policy, see the June 24, 1943, *Congressional Record,* Proceedings and Debates of the 78th Congress, First Session.

315 **Luce's account of his application:** HRL to George C. Marshall, April 27, 1944, in the papers of C. D. Jackson, 1931–1967, container 57, folder on HRL, 1943–1948 (DDEL).

315 **Luce looking forward to his trip:** DJSB, March 23, 1943 (SCL).

317 **Hersey and Roosevelt:** Correspondence relating to John Hersey in the papers of Franklin D. Roosevelt, PSF Navy/Diplomatic, Frank Knox Folder (2), box 62 (FDRL).

318 **Luce, Arnold, and Surles:** Transcripts of Director's Conversations of 1941–1945, Bureau of Public Relations, March 26, 1943, entry 265, box 1 (RG 107, NARA).

318 Luce appeals to Marshall: HRL to Marshall, March 27, 1943; and Marshall to Luce, March 31, 1943, in the papers of George C. Marshall, box 74, folder 43 (GCMF).

319 Luce visits Stimson: The diaries of Henry L. Stimson, entry for March 29, 1943 (MDLOC).

319 McCloy and Grover: John McCloy, memorandum to Stephen T. Early, in the papers of Franklin D. Roosevelt, Map Room File, box 162, folder 3 (FDRL).

319 Early and McCloy: Summary of Early's memorandum of August 26, 1943, in PPF 3338 (FDRL).

319 Stimson and Luce: Diaries of Henry L. Stimson, entry for September 27, 1943 (MDLOC).

319 Empty-handed: DJSB, May 14, 1948 (SCL).

320 Luce's appointment on November 8: Correspondence in PSF Confidential, box 6 (FDRL).

320 Kennan and Portugal: OF 442, box 1, folder on Portugal (FDRL).

320 The presidential dossier: OF 2442, where the Kennan material follows the correspondence concerning Luce's visit to the White House (FDRL). See also Luce's defiant memorandum to managing editors, November 1, 1943, the Time-Life-Fortune papers, I, folder 31, in the John Shaw Billings collection (SCL).

320 Luce and the November 8 appointment: The papers of Edwin M. Watson, box 21, folder on November 1943, daily schedule (MDUVL); and Mr. Early's Press and Radio Conference of November 8, 1943, scrapbook 16, in the papers of Stephen T. Early (FDRL).

320 Roosevelt's meeting with Luce: HRL to George C. Marshall, April 27, 1944, in the papers of C. D. Jackson, 1931–1967, container 57, folder on HRL, 1943–1948 (DDEL).

320 Censorship: OF 1773, box 1 (FDRL).

320 Belair and Surles: Transcripts of Director's Conversations of 1941–1945, Bureau of Public Relations, November 12, 1943, entry 265 (RG 107, NARA).

321 Bureaucratic procedures on travel: FDR, memorandum of November 20, 1943, and related memoranda, in the papers of Franklin D. Roosevelt, Map Room File, box 162, folder 3 (FDRL).

321 Luce on "Führer" Roosevelt: HRL, memorandum to Charles Wertenbaker, February 2, 1944, the Time-Life-Fortune papers, I, folder 32, in the John Shaw Billings collection (SCL).

321 Mrs. Luce and Italy: Transcripts of Director's Conversations of 1941–1945, Bureau of Public Relations, conversation of February 20, 1944, entry 265, box 4 (RG 107, NARA).

321 *Life* on Willkie: "Willkie's Speech," *Life*, October 25, 1943.

321 The Bricker cover: Elson, *World of Time Inc.*, p. 72.

321 Luce on idealism: HRL to Daniel Longwell, December 19, 1943, in the papers of Russell W. Davenport, container 76 (MDLOC).

321 Clare on politicians: Clare Luce, memorandum to HRL, December 20, 1943, in the papers of CBL, container 454 (MDLOC).

321 *Time* on Dewey and Warren: *Time*, January 31, 1944, and related materials in the papers of Thomas E. Dewey, Series 4, box 185, folder 15 (RRLUR).

322 Ann Brokaw killed: The W. A. Swanberg collection, box 18 (RBMLCU).

322 Luce on *Time* in the 1944 campaign: HRL, memorandum of February 10, 1944, the Time-Life-Fortune papers, I, folder 32, in the John Shaw Billings collection (SCL).

322 Luce on Willkie: Elson, *World of Time Inc.*, p. 80.

322 Life on Dewey: *Life*, February 28, 1944, and March 20, 1944.

322 Letter on the Dewey photograph: Letter of Merrill Bieley, *Life*, April 10, 1944.

322 Willkie in the polls: *Time*, March 6, 1944.

322 Luce on Willkie: Elson, *World of Time Inc.*, p. 93; HRL to Wendell Willkie, March 18, 1944, in the Willkie MSS. (MDIU).

322 Clare Luce and MacArthur: Clare Luce to Sherrod, July 25, 1977, in the private papers of Robert L. Sherrod.

323 An Asia-firster: *The Reminiscences of Andrew Heiskell*, p. 809.

323 Luce on MacArthur: HRL, memorandum to Roy Larsen et al., January 31, 1944, the Time-Life-Fortune papers, I, folder 32; and Luce, memorandum to John S. Billings, April 25, 1944, ibid., in the John Shaw Billings collection (SCL).

323 MacArthur and the Luces: Correspondence file on the Luces in the papers of Douglas MacArthur, SWPA: Official Correspondence (RG 3, MMAL).

323 Clare Luce on MacArthur: Clare Luce to Oswald G. Villard, October 7, 1943 (HLHU).

323 MacArthur in the Luce publications: *Time*, October 30, 1944.

323 MacArthur and a conspiracy: DJSB, March 29, 1945 (SCL).

323 MacArthur vs. *Time*: Ibid., March 27, 1945. (SCL).

323 Man of the Year: *Time*, January 1, 1945.

CHAPTER TWENTY-EIGHT

324 White awaiting Luce: White to David Hulburd, November 12, 1943, in the Time-Life Correspondence 1940–1946 of Theodore H. White (HLHU).

325 White on corruption: DJSB, March 21, 22, 1944 (SCL).

325 Luce on China: HRL, memorandum to Teddy White, April 3, 1944, in the papers of Theodore H. White (HLHU); and HRL, memorandum to John Shaw Billings, March 24, 1944, and to Theodore H. White, April 3, 1944, the Time-Life-Fortune Papers, I, folder 33, in the papers of John Shaw Billings (SCL).

325 Chiang and reforms: HRL, memorandum to John S. Billings et al., March 24, 1944, in the W. A. Swanberg collection, box 18 (RBMLCU).

325 A better regime: White to HRL, n.d., but probably late March or early April 1944, in the papers of Theodore H. White, Time-Life Correspondence 1940–1946 (HLHU); see also Theodore H. White to HRL, March 23, 1944, ibid.; and Israel Epstein for Teddy White, May 13, 1944, in the papers of Philip Jaffe, box 16, folder 4 (RWWLEU).

326 Statistical in nature: White to Charles Wertenbaker, n.d., in the papers of Theodore H. White papers, Time-Life correspondence 1940–1946 (HLHU).

326 The reality of serving there: Theodore H. White to the Board of Review of the BPR, War Department, April 5, 1944, ibid.

326 The Office of Censorship: Jack Lockhart to Time Inc. re. Teddy White, April 15, 1944, in the Office of Censorship, box 1107 (RG 216, NARA). For correspondence related to the White article and its censors, see the General

Records of the Army Staff, Public Information Division 1924–1946, Decimal Files of General Correspondence, box 35 (RG 165, NARA); and Office of Censorship, Administrative Division—Service Section, box 458 (RG 216, NARA).

326 **Clear the air:** HRL to B. A. Garside, April 26, 1944, in United China Relief—United Service to China, papers (SGMMLPU).

327 **Perspective:** HRL, April 26, 1944, in the papers of Wendell L. Willkie (MDLLIU).

326–327 *Life* **on Chiang:** "News From China," *Life*, May 1, 1944.

327 **Resist the invader:** White, *In Search of History*, p. 221.

327 **Judd:** Judd to HRL, May 22, 1944, and Luce to Judd, May 25, 1944, in the papers of Walter H. Judd, box 31, folder on HRL (HIWRP).

327 **Kohlberg:** Kohlberg to the editor of *Life*, April 28, 1944, and Beulah Holland to Kohlberg, June 16, 1944, in the papers of Alfred Kohlberg, box 111, folder Life Magazine (HIWRP).

328 **Wei on Yenan:** Department of State, memorandum of conversation, May 8, 1944, in the papers of Edward R. Stettinius, box 724, folder October 1943–China (MDUVL).

328 **Looming civil war:** Currie, memorandum for the President, June 15, 1944, in the Lauchlin Currie papers, box 5 (HIA).

328 **Lattimore rejected the gift:** Kahn, *The China Hands*, p. 102.

328 **Wallace and his advisers:** Schaller, *U.S. Crusade in China*, p. 160.

328 **Wallace on Chiang:** Correspondence between HRL and Wallace, August 1949, in the Henry A. Wallace papers at the University of Iowa, reel 46 (FDRL). On Wallace and Stilwell, see Tuchman, *Stilwell and the American Experience in China*, p. 596.

329–330 **Chennault and Stilwell:** "United States Military and Lend-Lease Relations with China from 1941 through September 1944," in the papers of Whiting Willauer, box 4 (SGMMLPU).

330 **Some draft boards will do anything:** Jim Shepley, cable to Eleanor Welch, November 1, 1944, in the papers of Philip Jaffe, box 16, folder 4 (RWWLEU).

330 **The future of all Asia:** Schaller, p. 165.

330 **Marshall and Chiang re. the China command:** Jim Shepley, cable to Eleanor Welch, November 1, 1944, in the papers of Philip Jaffe, box 16, folder 4 (RWWLEU).

330 **Facing defeat on several fronts:** White, p. 223.

330 **The Chinese Communists as a threat:** Theodore H. White to HRL, July 21, 1944, the Time-Life-Fortune Papers, I, folder 38, in the papers of John Shaw Billings (SCL).

331 **White on Chiang:** Fragment of a letter dating from the late summer or autumn of 1944, in the papers of Theodore H. White, correspondence 1940–1946 (HLHU).

331 **Meeting a different people:** Schaller, pp. 183–191.

331–332 **Kung:** "A Notable Event in American-Chinese Relations: Dinner to his Excellency Dr. H. H. Kung," given by the China-America Council of Commerce and Industry, Inc., July 27, 1944.

332 **Harry moved:** HRL, speech welcoming Bishop Chen Wen-yuan, Madison Avenue Presbyterian Church, March 6, 1944, in the papers of HRL, correspondence, box 75 (MDLOC).

332 **Her resistance to Japan:** *Time*, July 10, 1944.

332 **Epstein:** White, wireless of August 11, 1944, Time-Life Dispatches 1944, series IA, in the papers of Theodore H. White (HLHU).

332 **Epstein on Yenan:** Chungking cable from Israel Epstein to Teddy White, August 19, 1944, in the papers of Philip Jaffe, box 16, folder 4 (RWWLEU).

333 **Failed to convince Teddy White:** White to Annalee Jacoby, August 5, 1944, in the papers of Theodore H. White, correspondence 1940–1946 (HLHU).

333 **Yenan glowed:** Fairbank, *Chinabound*, p. 266.

333 *Time* **on Yenan:** *Time*, August 28, 1944.

333 **American illusions:** John S. Service, *The Amerasia Papers: Some Problems in the History of US-China Relations* (Berkeley: Center for Chinese Studies, 1971), p. 85.

333 **Ramrodbacked:** *Time*, December 4, 1944.

333 **Hurley, Stilwell, and Chiang:** Feis, *The China Tangle*, pp. 181–187. See also Matloff, *Strategic Planning for Coalition Warfare 1943–1944*, pp. 476–477.

333 **Stilwell on Chiang:** Joseph W. Stilwell, *The Stilwell Papers* (New York: William Sloan Associates, 1948), p. 327.

334 **Figures on tonnage:** Tuchman, p. 618.

334 **Kicked him in the pants:** White, p. 226.

334 **At what cost?:** Emmet to CBL, September 12, 1944, in the papers of Christopher Emmet, box 86, folder on Clare Luce (HIWRP).

334 **Judd to Luce on the Communists:** Judd to HRL, August 4, 1944, in the papers of Walter H. Judd, box 31, folder on HRL (HIWRP).

CHAPTER TWENTY-NINE

335 **Luce on the rumors:** HRL to Willkie, June 10, 1944, ibid.

335 **Willkie's sittings:** Wendell Willkie to HRL, June 9, 1944, in the Willkie MSS. (MDLLIU).

336 **Chamberlain on Willkie:** John Chamberlain, "Wendell Willkie," *Life*, April 3, 1944.

336 **Willkie after the primary:** *Life*, April 17, 1944.

336 **Painful situation:** HRL, telegram to Jackson, April 12, 1944, in the papers of C. D. Jackson, 1931–1967 (DDEL).

336 *Time* **on Willkie's defeat:** *Time*, April 17, 1944.

337 *Time* **on the primary:** Divine, *Second Chance*, pp. 188–189.

337 **Willkie at the dinner table:** Luce's unpublished manuscript on the 1944 campaign, p. 12, in the papers of HRL (MDLOC).

337 **Willkie's apology to Luce:** Willkie to HRL, May 9, 1944, in the Willkie MSS. (MDLLIU).

337 **Luce's reply to Willkie:** HRL to Willkie, May 10, 1944, ibid.

337 **A Midwestern candidate:** *Life*, May 22, 1944.

337 **Clare Luce and the cameras:** Film no. 6 Bailey/1944 Republican Convention, in the papers of Thomas E. Dewey (RRLUR); and the newsfilm clips in "Thomas E. Dewey, a Career of Public Service," Dewey campaigns, film 38, reel 1, ibid.

337–338 **G.I. Jim:** Tape of Mrs. Luce's speech to the Republican National Convention, Chicago, June 27, 1944, SRT 50-54 (61-62) (FDRL).

338 **Harry proud:** DJSB, June 27, 1944 (SCL).

338 **British embassy:** *Washington Despatches*, p. 380, July 2, 1944.

338 Far to the right: DJSB, July 19, 1944 (SCL).

338 The platform: Raymond Buell, memorandum to Daniel Longwell, June 29, 1944, in the papers of Dorothy Sterling (SCDKLUO).

338 Luce's ambitions: DJSB, January 31, 1945 (SCL).

338 Luce and Bush: HRL to Prescott S. Bush, August 14, 1944, in the papers of CBL, container 455 (MDLOC).

339 Lied us into war: *Time*, November 20, 1944.

339 Clare Luce, Browder, and FDR: Draft of a speech, probably delivered in early October 1944, in the papers of CBL, container 520 (MDLOC).

339 Clare Luce, Communism, and Roosevelt: CBL, address to the 4th District Convention, Greenwich, Conn., August 9, 1944, in the papers of Ferdinand Eberstadt, box 103 (SGMMLPU).

339 Clare Luce on Mrs. Roosevelt: Clare Luce to Baruch, March 2, 1945, in the papers of Bernard M. Baruch, correspondence, box 70 (SGMMLPU).

340 Luce and his mannerisms: DJSB, July 20, 22, and September 9, 1944 (SCL).

340 Luce on Roosevelt: HRL, memorandum of September 26, 1944, in Jessup, *Ideas of Henry Luce*, pp. 351–353.

340 Sweetly reasonable: DJSB, September 20, 1944 (SCL).

340 Luce's associates on political dangers: Elson, *World of Time Inc.*, pp. 75–77.

340 Belair and the poll: Felix Belair to Stephen Early, August 16, 1944, in OF 3618 (2), folder on *Fortune*, 1940–1944 (FDRL).

340 Dewey and Jessup: DJSB, August 25, 1944 (SCL).

340 Jessup on editorial tactics: John K. Jessup to HRL, August 30, 1944, the Time-Life-Fortune papers, I, folder 40, in the John Shaw Billings collection (SCL).

340 Luce and the editorial endorsement: DJSB, August 25, 29, 1944 (SCL).

340 *Time* is impartial: Sterling, "The Luce Empire," chapter 11, in the papers of Dorothy Sterling (SCDKLUO).

340 Longwell and Winchell: Daniel Longwell, memorandum to John S. Billings, October 26, 1944, in the Time-Life-Fortune papers, I, folder 42, in the John Shaw Billings collection (SCL).

341 *Time* on Dumbarton Oaks: *Time*, August 28 and September 4, 1944.

341 Dulles on Dumbarton Oaks: Statement dictated over the telephone, August 15, 1944, and related materials, in the papers of Thomas E. Dewey, Series X, box 15, folder 3 (RRLUR).

341 Dulles on partisan debate: John Foster Dulles to Barton, September 27, 1944, in the papers of Bruce Barton, box 18, folder on John Foster Dulles (WSHS).

341 Hull thanking Dewey: Cordell Hull to Dewey, September 4, 1944, in the papers of Thomas E. Dewey, Series IV, box 52, folder 5 (RRLUR).

341 Dulles and Life: John S. Billings to Roy Larsen, September 12, 1944, the Time-Life-Fortune papers, I, folder 41, in the John Shaw Billings collection (SCL).

341 Smear journalism: HRL, memorandum to John S. Billings, November 17, 1944, the Time-Life-Fortune papers, I, folder 43, in the John Shaw Billings collection (SCL).

341 Dulles and America First: Dulles to Edwin S. Webster, February 7, 1941, in the papers of John Foster Dulles, selected correspondence and related material, box 20 (SGMMLPU); and Dulles to Joseph R. Dillinger, December 4, 1945, ibid., box 26.

341 Dumbarton Oaks: The Department of State, Publication 2223, Conference Series 60.

341 *Time* on Dumbarton Oaks: *Time*, October 23, 1944.

341 Luce's mistrust: HRL, memorandum to Manfred Gottfried, July 28, 1944, in the Time-Life-Fortune papers, I, folder 37, in the John Shaw Billings collection (SCL).

342 Luce on the Pearl Harbor inquiry: HRL to Tom Matthews, August 25, 1944, ibid., folder 40.

342 Roosevelt ill: David Hulburd to White, October 23, 1944, the Time-Life Correspondence 1940–1946, in the papers of Theodore H. White (HLHU).

342 Roosevelt's appearance: *Life*, May 29, 1944, where FDR looks healthy.

342 The common task: HRL to Wendell Willkie, n.d., but probably June 27, 1944, in the Willkie MSS. (MDLLIU). See also Barton, memorandum of a conversation with H. V. Kaltenborn, July 27, 1944, in the papers of Bruce Barton, box 57, folder on the Republican Party (WSHS).

342–343 Dulles, Dewey, and Willkie: Dulles to Ruth Simms, June 15, 1943, in the papers of John Foster Dulles, selected correspondence and related material, box 22 (SGMMLPU). On the Dulles/Willkie meeting: Willkie to Dewey, and Dewey to Willkie, August 20, 1944, in the papers of Thomas E. Dewey, Series X, box 47, folder 4 (RRLUR). Also relevant is Dulles, memorandum of August 21, 1944, in the papers of John Foster Dulles, selected correspondence and related material, box 23 (SGMMLPU).

343 Belair and Marshall: Transcripts of Director's Conversations of 1941–1945, Bureau of Public Relations, December 22, 1943, entry 265, box 3 (RG 107, NARA).

343 Marshall, Luce, and Roosevelt: Correspondence and memoranda contained in the papers of George C. Marshall, box 74, folder 44 (GCMF).

343 "Funny business": Henry Luce to Jackson, June 2, 1944, in the papers of C. D. Jackson, 1931–1967, container 57 (DDEL).

343 FDR and *The March of Time:* OF 3338 (FDRL).

343–344 Luce's passport: DJSB, August 30, 1944 (SCL). See also file memo by Early, August 31, 1944, in the papers of Stephen T. Early, August 31, 1944, box 10 (FDRL).

344 For Dewey's side of the story: Smith, *Thomas E. Dewey*, p. 415. On Luce and the Willkie endorsement: HRL's notes with political reminiscences, in the papers of HRL (MDLOC). Particularly important is Herbert Brownell (with John P. Burke), *Advising Ike: The Memoirs of Attorney General Herbert Brownell* (Lawrence, KS, 1993), p. 57.

344 *Life* endorses Dewey: *Life* editorials, October 2, 9, 1944; Roger Butterfield's article, October 9, and *Life*'s appeal to independents, October 16, 1944.

345 Willkie would have voted for Roosevelt: DJSB, February 16, 1953 (SCL).

345 Davenport's defection: E. Kendall Gillett to Barton, September 28, 1944; and Barton to Gillett, October 2, 1944, in the papers of Bruce Barton, box 72, folder on Wendell Willkie (WSHS).

345 Grover and FDR: DJSB, November 7, 1944 (SCL).

345 Grover on Roosevelt: Allen Grover to Billings, June 8, 1944, the Time-Life-Fortune papers, I, folder 35, in the John Shaw Billings collection (SCL).

345 Luce and Ball: HRL to Joseph Ball, October 21, 1944, in the papers of John Foster Dulles, selected correspondence and related material, box 24 (SGMMLPU).

345 **Clare Luce on Dewey:** CBL to Lawrence, October 23, 1944, in the papers of David Lawrence, box 74 (SGMMLPU).

345 **One thorn:** Connors to FDR, November 15, 1944, in the file on Margaret E. Connors, PPF (FDRL).

345 **Voting machine incident:** President's note of December 6, 1944, cited in PPF 3338 (FDRL).

CHAPTER THIRTY

346 **Debate about Russian policy:** *Life*, January 31, 1944.

347 **Chambers' appearance and style:** Interview with Marjory Newlon, Munves notes, TM VI, in the papers of A. J. Liebling (DRBCUL).

348 **Can't write:** Donovan, *Right Places, Right Times*, p. 102.

348 **The Chambers era at Time Inc.:** Patricia Divver, "The Ideology of TIME Magazine, II: A Research Report on TIME during the period 1936–1944" (March 1953), in the papers of John Shaw Billings Ms. vol. bd., 66 (SCL).

348 **Gruin and Chambers:** Ibid.

348 ***Time's* anticommunism:** *Time*, September 18, 1939; January 1, 22, July 22, and October 28, 1940.

348 **"Total depravity":** *Time*, January 21, 1941.

348 **Smell of blood:** *Time*, September 30, 1940.

348 **Chambers' health:** Elson, *World of Time Inc.*, pp. 104–106.

349 **Where we have been:** Scrapbook 57, p. 230, in the papers of John Shaw Billings (SCL).

349 **Roosevelt purge:** Whittaker Chambers to Herbert Solow, n.d., in the papers of Herbert Solow, box 1 (HIWRP).

349 **Schlamm's magazine:** DJSB, February 23, 1945 (SCL).

350 **Against the Democrats:** Barton, memorandum to Herbert Brownell, August 24, 1944, in the Bruce Barton papers, box 9, folder on Herbert Brownell (WSHS).

351 **Lauterbach's contacts:** Richard Lauterbach to John S. Billings, March 21, 1944, the Time-Life-Fortune papers, I, folder 33, in the John Shaw Billings collection (SCL).

351 **German perfidy:** Richard Lauterbach, cable of January 26, 1944, in Dispatches to Time Magazine (HLHU).

351 ***Time* on Katyn:** *Time*, February 7, 1944. See also Richard Lauterbach, "Graves in the Forest," reprinted in Gordon Carroll, ed., *History in the Writing: By the Foreign Correspondents of* Time, Life *and* Fortune (New York: Duell, Sloan & Pearce, 1945).

351 **Hodgins on policy-making:** Eric Hodgins, memorandum to Gottfried et al., March 9, 1944, in the W. A. Swanberg collection, box 18 (RBMLCU).

351 **Chambers and his crusade at Foreign News:** Interview with Max Ways, ibid.

351–352 **Chambers and his colleagues:** Swanberg, *Luce and His Empire*, pp. 215–232, 256.

352 **Chambers' writing:** Sterling, "The Luce Empire," chapter 10 (SCDKLUO). See also the interviews with John Barkham and Francis Brown, in the W. A. Swanberg collection, box 18 (RBMLCU).

353 **Greece:** *Life*, September 4, 1944.

353 **Chambers on Greece:** Sterling, "The Luce Empire," chapter 10.

353 Lippmann: Walter Lippmann to John Foster Dulles, April 29 and July 10, 1944, in the papers of John Foster Dulles, selected correspondence and related material, box 24 (SGMMLPU). See also Divine, *Second Chance*, pp. 124–126, 178–182.

353 Lippmann's view of Russia: *Time*, September 25, 1944. Luce rejects Lippmann's article: Ronald Steel, *Walter Lippmann and the American Century* (Boston: Little, Brown, 1980), p. 410.

353 Kennan: David Mayers, *George Kennan and the Dilemmas of U.S. Foreign Policy* (New York: Oxford University Press, 1989), pp. 86–96.

353 Bullitt: DJSB, March 8, 17, 1944 (SCL).

353 Bullitt's article: William C. Bullitt, "The World from Rome," *Life*, September 4, 1944.

354 Pravda: John Hersey, Cable no. 7, September 5, 1944, from Moscow to *Time*, in the papers of Dorothy Sterling (SCDKLUO).

354 Osborne: John Osborne, cable to David Hulburd, October 1, 1944, the Time-Life-Fortune papers, I, folder 41, in the John Shaw Billings collection (SCL). See also Elson, *World of Time Inc.*, p. 99.

354 The Bullitt controversy: Daniel Longwell to John S. Billings, September 6, 1944; and Billings to Roy Larsen, September 12, 1944, in the Time-Life-Fortune papers, I, folder 41, in the John Shaw Billings collection (SCL).

354 Lerner: Max Lerner, "Where Is *Life* Going?" (September 11, 1944) and "O *Time*, O *Life*" (September 17, 1944), in *Public Journal: Marginal Notes on Wartime America* (New York: The Viking Press, 1945), pp. 295–302.

354 The petition: "An Open Letter to Henry R. Luce of *Life* Magazine," October 14, 1944, the Time-Life-Fortune papers, I, folder 42, in the John Shaw Billings collection (SCL).

354 Luce and Hersey: HRL to John S. Billings, May 5, 1944, ibid., folder 34.

355 Hersey on democracy: "Tests for 1941," drafted by John Hersey for the *Hotchkiss Alumni News*, II, no. 2, January 1941.

355 Hersey on Russian writers: John Hersey to John S. Billings, February 1945, the Time-Life-Fortune papers, I, folder 50, in the John Shaw Billings collection (SCL).

356 Disagreements with Luce: John Hersey to HRL, November 14, 1944, and Luce to Hersey, ibid., I, folder 42.

356 Truth doesn't matter: Sterling, "The Luce Empire," chapter 10, and interview with John Scott, May 24, 1950, in the papers of Dorothy Sterling (SCDKLUO).

356 Lauterbach on Russia: Richard E. Lauterbach, *These Are the Russians* (New York: Harper & Brothers Publishers, 1945), pp. 328–359.

356 Lauterbach vs. Grover: Interview with Richard Lauterbach, December 16, 1949, in the papers of Dorothy Sterling (SCDKLUO). See also DJSB, November 14, 17, 20 and December 7, 1944 (SCL).

356 Luce on Lauterbach: HRL to Allen Grover, July 30, 1945, in the Daniel Longwell collection, box 29 (RBMLCU).

356 Chambers and the Chetniks: Sterling, "The Luce Empire," chapter 10, and related notes (SCDKLUO).

357 Russian expansion: *Time*, November 6, 13, 20 and December 4, 25, 1944.

357 Luce and Stettinius: HRL to John K. Jessup, December 7, 1944, and to David Hulburd, December 8, 1944, the Time-Life-Fortune papers, I, folder 44, in the John Shaw Billings collection (SCL).

357 **Graebner warns Luce:** Walter Graebner to HRL, December 2, 1944, ibid.

357 **Bloch:** Kurt Bloch to T. S. Matthews, December 5, 1944, ibid.

357 **Burwell/Billings:** "December 1944 revolt of foreign correspondents against Chambers, Foreign News Editor," n.d., in the W. A. Swanberg collection, box 18 (RBMLCU).

358 **Grover and Graebner:** Elson, *World of Time Inc.*, p. 107.

358 **Hersey's "strike":** John Hersey to David Hulburd, December 13, 1944, and Hulburd to Hersey, same date; Hersey to John Billings, December 16, and to Hulburd, same date; the Time-Life-Fortune papers, I, folder 45, in the John Shaw Billings collection (SCL).

358 **Billings' conclusion:** John Billings to Henry R. Luce, with the survey by Miss Burwell, ibid., I, folder 48. See also the Burwell materials in the W. A. Swanberg collection, box 18, folder on uncatalogued material, 1945–1947 (RBMLCU).

358 **Billings' draft:** John Billings, draft memorandum of December 21, 1944, the Time-Life-Fortune papers, I, folder 46, in the John Shaw Billings collection (SCL).

358 **Luce praising Chambers:** HRL to Whittaker Chambers, January 17, 1945, ibid.

358 **Red-inspired disturbances:** HRL, memorandum to John Billings, January 6, 1945, ibid., folder 48.

CHAPTER THIRTY-ONE

359 **Dixie Mission:** David D. Barrett, *Dixie Mission: The United States Army Observer Group in Yenan, 1944* (Berkeley: Center for Chinese Studies, 1970).

359 **Davies on the future:** White to Charles Wertenbaker, n.d., in the papers of Theodore H. White (HLHU).

359 **Wage a more effective war:** Harry Hopkins, memorandum to FDR, enclosing the Davies memorandums of August 30 and September 8, 1944, in the Map Room File, box 165, folder 2 (FDRL).

359 **The OSS on Free China:** William Donovan to the President, September 28, 1944, PSF Subject File (OSS) (FDRL).

359 **Chambers on liberal illusions:** Steven W. Mosher, *China Misperceived: American Illusions and Chinese Reality* (New York: Basic Books, 1990), p. 61.

359 **Gruin and Chambers:** Annalee Jacoby to White, August 2, 20, 1944, in the papers of Theodore H. White, Time-Life correspondence 1940–1946 (HLHU).

360 **Jacoby joined White:** See Theodore H. White to David Hulburd, September 28, 1944, ibid.

360 **Jacoby interview:** Walter Sullivan, ". . . The Crucial 1940's," in *Nieman Reports*, XXXVII, 1 (Spring 1983), p. 31.

360 **Chao's book:** The manuscript copy may be consulted in the papers of Philip Jaffe, box 16, folder 6 (RWWLEU).

360 **White and Chao:** Theodore H. White, cables of October 2, 6, 1944, in the Time-Life Correspondence 1940–1946 of Theodore H. White (HLHU).

360 **Danger of being bisected:** White to David Hulburd, September 28, 1944, ibid. See also *Time*, October 2, 16, 1944.

360 **Democratic China:** Joseph Stilwell to the Chief of Staff, September 26, 1944, cited in Munves notes, TM VIII, in the papers of A. J. Liebling (DRBCUL).

361 Ignorant son of a bitch: White, *In Search of History*, p. 234.

361 Lose China: Feis, *The China Tangle*, pp. 198–199.

361 This kind of monkey business: Joseph W. Stilwell, *The Stilwell Papers* (New York: W. Sloan Associates, 1948), p. 345.

361 White on Stilwell: White, p. 233.

361 "Disaster Unalloyed": *Time*, October 9, 1944.

361 Kweilin falling: *Time*, October 16, 1944.

361 Wedemeyer: Records of the Army Staff, Public Information Division, 1924–1946, Decimal Files of General Correspondence, entry 000.7/380, box 39 (RG 319, NARA).

361 Crackerjack team: Theodore H. White, cable of December 29, 1944, in the Dispatches to Time Magazine (HLHU).

362 Evaded the censors: White, p. 236.

362 White in Yenan: Chungking cable no. 23 (notation for November 8), sent November 21, 1944, in the papers of Theodore H. White, Series 1A, Time-Life Dispatches 2, 1944—CP (HLHU).

362 White on Mao: White, chapter 5.

362 White on the honesty of the Communists: White, fragment of a manuscript on the civil war, Time-Life Correspondence 1940–1946, in the papers of Theodore H. White (HLHU).

363 Fairbank encounter: *Chinabound*, p. 271.

363 Greatest democracy: Barrett, p. 65.

364 Enemies of the people: White, p. 259.

364 Returned from Yenan: Theodore H. White, cable of November 10, 1944, in the Dispatches to Time Magazine (HLHU).

364 Plunked down: Cable from Jim Shepley to Eleanor Welch, November 1, 1944, in the papers of Philip Jaffe, box 16, folder 4 (RWWLEU).

364 Americans to blame: *Life* editorial of November 13, 1944.

364–365 White on the Stilwell cover: White, p. 271; and White to Joseph Liebling, n.d., Time-Life Correspondence 1940–1946, in the papers of Theodore H. White (HLHU).

365 Regeneration of the spirit: White, cable to Harry Luce, November 21 or 22, 1944, ibid.

365 Is crumbling: Janice R. MacKinnon, *Agnes Smedley* (Berkeley: University of California Press, 1988), p. 287.

365 Concerned radicals: The comments of M. Lindsay, in the papers of Theodore H. White, Time-Life Dispatches 1944, Series 1A (HLHU). See also Feis, p. 206, note 12.

365 Clare Luce on China: Theodore H. White, cable of October 14, 1944, Dispatches to Time Magazine (HLHU).

366 Corrupt, wicked, and worthless: Theodore H. White to Sterling, December 31 (no year, but probably ca. 1949), in the papers of Dorothy Sterling (SCDKLUO).

366 *Time* optimistic: *Time*, November 27, 1944.

366–367 Trouble with White: *St. Louis Post-Dispatch*, October 28, 1949, and the summary notes in the papers of Dorothy Sterling (SCDKLUO).

367 Until the end of the war: White to Mom and Gladys, January 17, 1945, in the Time-Life Correspondence 1940–1946 of Theodore H. White (HLHU).

367 Cannot all be true: Jaffe to D. W. Bishop, December 22, 1944, in the papers of Philip Jaffe, box 43, folder 5 (RWWLEU).

367 **Wedemeyer on the China situation:** General George C. Marshall, memo-randum for the President, December 3, 1944, in the papers of Franklin D. Roosevelt, Map Room File, container 165, China A-16-3 (FDRL).

367 **Do the fighting alone:** Theodore H. White, cable of December 29, 1944, in Dispatches to Time Magazine (HLHU).

367 **Among the privileged classes:** George C. Marshall, memorandum for the President, December 20, 1944, containing Gen. Wedemeyer's letter dated December 10, 1944, in the Franklin D. Roosevelt Papers, Map Room File, box 165, folder China A16-3 (FDRL). See also Wedemeyer to Soong, Decem-ber 31, 1944, in the papers of T. V. Soong, box 9, folder on Albert C. Wedemeyer (HIWRP).

368 **Chiang:** *Time*, December 18, 1944.

368 **Called Hurley the clown:** Kahn, *China Hands*, p. 124.

368 **Negotiations:** Feis, pp. 214–216.

368 **Judd on embattled China:** HRL to John S. Billings, November 17, 1944, the Time-Life-Fortune papers, I, folder 43, in the John Shaw Billings collec-tion (SCL).

368–369 **Judd, Luce, and Yenan:** Judd to HRL, December 23, 1944, and Luce to Judd, January 4, 1945, in the papers of Walter H. Judd, box 31, folder on HRL (HIWRP).

369 **Dulles on China:** Dulles to HRL, January 29, 1945, in the papers of John Foster Dulles, selected correspondence and related material, box 27 (SGMMLPU).

369 **Hurley and an agreement:** William D. Leahy to Marshall, November 9, 1944, in the papers of George C. Marshall, box 71, folder 31 (GCMF). See also Schaller, *U.S. Crusade in China*, pp. 190–195.

369 **Digging their own graves:** Fairbank, p. 316.

369 **Opposed to Hurley's view:** Elson, p. 142.

369 **White and the Foreign Service officers:** Stephen R. MacKinnon and Oris Friesen, *China Reporting: An Oral History of American Journalism in the 1930s and 1940s* (Berkeley: University of California Press, 1987), pp. 69–70.

369 **The China debate:** *Foreign Despatches 1941–1945*, pp. 447–448, November 5, 1944.

369–370 **Wedemeyer and the press:** George C. Marshall, memorandum for the President, December 20, 1944, in the Franklin D. Roosevelt Papers, Map Room File, box 165, folder on China A16-3 (FDRL).

370 **To the exclusion of objectivity:** David Hulburd to White, October 23, 1944, in the Time-Life Correspondence 1940–1946 of Theodore H. White (HLHU).

370 **Hurley's view:** Schaller, pp. 205–206.

370 **Further negotiations:** William Leahy, memorandum for Marshall, January 15, 1945, in the papers of George C. Marshall, box 71, folder 31 (GCMF).

370 **Solicit Soviet support:** Schaller, p. 206.

370 **Chungking's decline:** Tuchman, *Stilwell and the American Experience in China*, p. 650.

370 **Until they had reached an agreement:** Schaller, pp. 206–207.

370 **Tons a year later:** Feis, p. 205, note 10.

371 **Consultative conference:** Ibid., p. 223.

371 **Forrestal and Luce:** James V. Forrestal, memorandum to the President,

January 2, 1945, in the papers of Franklin D. Roosevelt, Map Room File, box 163, folder 3 (FDRL).

CHAPTER THIRTY-TWO

372 **Billings and Wertenbaker:** John S. Billings to Charles Wertenbaker, January 15, 1945, the Time-Life-Fortune papers, I, folder 48, in the John Shaw Billings collection (SCL).

372 **Chambers undercut:** John S. Billings to HRL, June 20, 1945, ibid. See also Elson, *World of Time Inc.*, p. 110.

373 **A cruel test:** John Hersey, cable to *Life*, January 17, 1945, in the papers of Dorothy Sterling (SCDKLUO).

373 **Antifascist left:** Interview with Charles and Lael Wertenbaker, September 20, 1950, ibid.

373 **Sheen on communism:** Fulton J. Sheen, *Philosophies at War* (New York: Charles Scribner's Sons, 1944), p. 87.

374 **Mundt and his committee:** Rep. Karl Mundt to HRL, January 20, 1945; HRL to Mundt, January 24, 1945; Luce to Baldwin, January 24, 1945; Baldwin to Luce, January 31, 1945, in the papers of Gov. Raymond Baldwin, General Files 1939–1948, in RG 69:10/17 (CSL); and "Un-American Activities," *Life*, March 26, 1945.

374 **Vandenberg's speech and reaction to it:** McNaughton, cable to Don Bermingham, January 12, 1945, in the papers of Frank McNaughton, box 6 (HSTL). See also Smith, *Thomas E. Dewey and His Times*, p. 441.

374 **Appealed to Americans, too:** *Life*, November 20, 1944.

374 **Vandenberg's view:** "Vandenberg's Speech," *Life*, January 22, 1945.

374 **Luce's reaction to Vandenberg's plan:** HRL to managing editors, January 26, 1945, the Time-Life-Fortune papers, I, folder 48, in the John Shaw Billings collection (SCL).

374 **Memoranda on Russia:** Buell to Whittaker Chambers et al., February 7, 1945; and Buell, memorandum to HRL et al., February 9, 1945, in the papers of Raymond Leslie Buell (unprocessed) (MDLOC).

374 **Buell on Cuba:** Raymond L. Buell, memorandum to HRL, February 5, 1945, ibid.

375 **Eight-hundred-mile front:** *Time*, February 5, 1945.

375 **Would apologize:** DJSB, February 14, 1945 (SCL).

375 **Optimistic analysis:** Ibid., February 19, 1945.

375 **A security buffer:** *Life*, February 26, 1945.

375 **Byrnes:** Robert T. Elson to David Hulburd, March 1, 1945, the Time-Life-Fortune papers, I, folder 50, in the John Shaw Billings collection (SCL). On Byrnes at Yalta: Robert L. Messer, " 'Et Tu Brute!' James Byrnes, Harry Truman and the Origins of the Cold War," in Kendrick A. Clements, ed., *James F. Byrnes and the Origins of the Cold War* (Durham, NC: The Carolina Academic Press, 1982), pp. 29–35.

375 **Kennan:** Mayers, *George Kennan and the Dilemmas of U.S. Foreign Policy*, p. 101.

375 **Davenport:** Buell to Whittaker Chambers et al., with copies to Luce and Billings, March 5, 1945; and John Davenport to Buell, n.d., in the papers of Raymond Leslie Buell (unprocessed) (MDLOC).

376 Luce on the chances of getting along with Russia: DJSB, February 26, 1945 (SCL).

376 Tense relations: Ibid., entry for March 8, 1945 (SCL).

376 "Ghosts": *Time*, March 5, 1945.

376 Longwell and Hersey: DJSB, May 4, 1945 (SCL).

376 Luce and Stettinius: Ibid., March 19, 1945.

377 McNaughton on Roosevelt: McNaughton, cable to Don Bermingham, March 2, 1945, in the papers of Frank McNaughton (HSTL).

377 *Life* on Roosevelt: *Life*, March 12, 1945.

377 From the global war: HRL to Thomas L. Matthews, January 16, 1947, the Time-Life-Fortune papers, II, folder 92, in the John Shaw Billings collection (SCL).

377 *Life* on the defects of the United Nations: *Life*, April 30, 1945.

378 Billings on Roosevelt's death: DJSB, April 12, 1945 (SCL).

378 Lockett on Truman: Edward Lockett, dispatch to Robert T. Elson, June 11, 1945, the Time-Life-Fortune papers, I, folder 58, in the John Shaw Billings collection (SCL).

378 Clare Luce on Russia: "Leaning Over Backward in Europe," remarks of the Hon. CBL (Washington, D.C.: Government Printing Office, 1945). See also *New York Journal-American*, February 20 and June 18, 1945, *New York Herald Tribune*, May 28, 1945.

378 Clare Luce: *Time*, July 30.

378 Soviet communism in Europe: *Time*, July 2, 9, 16, 23.

379 Kohlberg: Kohlberg to CBL, May 22, June 4, July 10, 1945, in the Alfred Kohlberg collection, box 114, folder on Clare Boothe and Henry Robinson Luce to 1947 (HIWRP).

379 Manchuria: *Time*, May 28, 1945. Raymond Buell was already warning Luce against the coming Soviet domination of Manchuria, north China, and Korea.

379 Buell's thoughts on foreign policy: Buell to HRL et al., May 23, 1945, containing a memorandum to Charles G. Ross, dated May 21, 1945, in the papers of Raymond Leslie Buell (unprocessed) (MDLOC).

379 Billings' concerns about Luce and Japan: DJSB, May 25, 1945 (SCL).

380 Britt and Luce's trip: John Billings to HRL, May 18, 1945, and Brantz Mayor to HRL, ca. May 20, 1945, the Time-Life-Fortune papers, I, folder 56, in the John Shaw Billings collection (SCL).

380 *Yorktown*: Luce's remarks, in the W. A. Swanberg collection, box 21 (RBMLCU).

380 Pacific coverage: DJSB, June 11, 1945 (SCL).

380 The Philippines: *Life*, June 4, 1945.

381 Luce on the Pacific theater: W. A. Swanberg collection, box 18 (RBMLCU); and DJSB, June 11, 21, 24, 27; July 3, 11, 12, 1945 (SCL).

381 Luce and the President: Elson, p. 133. See also DJSB, July 6, 1945 (SCL).

381 *Time* on the Charter: Divine, *Second Chance*, p. 297. For Luce's view of the U.N., see HRL, address to the Michigan State Bar Association, Grand Rapids, October 30, 1952, in the W. A. Swanberg collection, box 21 (RBMLCU).

381 *Time*'s concerns about Britain and Europe: *Time*, July 16, 30, 1945.

381 *Pravda* more accurate than *Time*: White to Annalee Jacoby, probably early September 1945, correspondence, in the papers of Theodore H. White (HLHU).

381 Longwell on Hersey's resignation: Daniel Longwell to *Life* writers, July 11, 1945, the Time-Life-Fortune papers, I, folder 65, in the John Shaw Billings collection (SCL).

382 Luce in Washington: DJSB, July 11, 12, 1945 (SCL).

382 No longer the equals: HRL to Sherrod, July 13, 1945, in the papers of Robert L. Sherrod (GARLSU).

382 America and Russia: *Life*, July 30, 1945; and HRL, memorandum to senior editors, July 16, 1945, the Time-Life-Fortune papers, I, folder 60, in the John Shaw Billings collection (SCL).

382 Hodgins on Salisbury: Eric Hodgins, report on employment, September 21, 1945, the Time-Life-Fortune papers, I, folder 65, in the John Shaw Billings collection (SCL).

382 Matthews on the junior staff: Evaluation of the staff, late 1945 or early 1946, ibid., folder 70.

382 Jackson: HRL, memorandum to Roy Alexander et al., August 1, 1945, in the papers of C. D. Jackson, 1931–1967, container 84, speeches to 1945 (DDEL).

383 Chambers' illness and its aftermath: John S. Billings to HRL, August 21, 1945, the Time-Life-Fortune papers, I, folder 64, in the John Shaw Billings collection (SCL).

383 *Time* on blocs: *Time*, September 17 (on the peace negotiations), October 15 (on the world of blocs), November 26, 1945 (on the triumph of collectivism).

383 MacLeish citation: MacLeish to Nelson A. Rockefeller, August 10, 1945, in the papers of Archibald MacLeish, container 19 (MDLOC). See also MacLeish to Samuel Rosenman, August 8, 1945, ibid.

CHAPTER THIRTY-THREE

384 On advice from Marshal Stalin: Feis, *China Tangle*, pp. 249–250.

384 Were even more recalcitrant: Ibid., p. 244.

385 Involve the Soviets: Ibid., pp. 268–269. See also Warren I. Cohen, *America's Response to China* (New York: Wiley, 1980), p. 177.

385 Sustain Chiang: Tuchman, *Stilwell and the American Experience in China*, p. 655.

385 Under the authority of the central government: *Time*, March 12, 1945.

385 Has been exaggerated: Ambassador Hurley to the Secretary of State, July 10, 1945, cited by John S. Service, *The Amerasia Papers* (Berkeley: Center for Chinese Studies, 1971), p. 88.

385 One-party controlled: Feis, p. 276.

386 Chancre Jack: Frank Norris, memorandum to Luce, Larsen, and Matthews, March 26, 1945, in the W. A. Swanberg collection, box 17, folder W.A.S. (RBMLCU).

386 The things they see in *Time*: Frank Norris, memorandum to HRL et al., ibid., box 18, uncatalogued correspondence 1945–1947 (RBMLCU).

386 Among U.S. civilian and military personnel: White to David Hulburd, February 9, 1945, Time-Life Correspondence 1940–1946, in the papers of Theodore H. White (HLHU); and White to Hulburd, April 18, 1945, ibid.

386 Damned him for it: HRL, memorandum to Management Executive Committee, March 12, 1945, the Time-Life-Fortune papers, I, folder 51, in the John Shaw Billings collection (SCL).

386 Changed its position: Theodore H. White to Sterling, December 31, no year but probably ca. 1949, in the papers of Dorothy Sterling (SCDKLUO).

387 A *Time* favorite: White to Gladys and Mama, April 30, 1945, Correspondence, in the papers of Theodore H. White (HLHU).

387 White could not go to Yenan: Munves notes, TM I, *Time* notes, in the papers of A. J. Liebling (DRBCUL).

387 Odious to him: White to Mom and Gladys, July 17, 1945, Correspondence, in the papers of Theodore H. White (HLHU).

387 White in Chungking: White, *In Search of History*, pp. 280–281.

387 To cover their policy: White to John K. Fairbank, February 18, 1945, Time-Life Correspondence 1940–1946, in the papers of Theodore H. White (HLHU).

388 Luce felt betrayed: Interview with Noel Busch, in the W. A. Swanberg collection, box 18 (RBMLCU).

388 Should have fired White: HRL, interviewed by the *St. Louis Post-Dispatch*, October 28, 1949, in the papers of Dorothy Sterling (SCDKLUO).

388 Other forces: Cohen, p. 178.

388 Unrealistic expectations: Feis, pp. 286–287.

388 Liberals and intellectuals: *Time*, April 9, 1945.

388 Mao and the party congress: Mao Tse-tung, *Selected Works* (New York: International Publishers, 1956, 4 volumes), IV, pp. 241–243; and Feis, pp. 288–292.

389 Mao on the Guomindang: "On Coalition Government," ibid., pp. 304ff.

389 Alpha force: Theodore H. White, telegram to Eleanor Welch, n.d. but late 1945, in the Time-Life Correspondence 1940–1946 of Theodore H. White (HLHU).

389 Their areas of control: "The Chinese Communist Movement," in the papers of CBL, container 509 (MDLOC).

389 Air of unreality: HRL, memorandum to John S. Billings, April 23, 1945, in the W. A. Swanberg collection, box 18 (RBMLCU).

389 Isaacs: Kenneth E. Shewmaker, *Americans and Chinese Communists* (Ithaca: Cornell University Press, 1971), p. 174.

390 Will be irresistible: Walter H. Judd to Buell, May 25, 1945, in the papers of Raymond Leslie Buell (unprocessed), carton 3 (MDLOC).

390 Toward a peaceful settlement: *Time*, June 18, 1945. See also Raymond Buell to Walter H. Judd, June 6, 1945, in the papers of Raymond Leslie Buell (unprocessed), carton 3 (MDLOC).

390 Communists were expanding: White, dispatch of May 28, 1948, the Time-Life dispatches, June 1943–November 1944, in the papers of Theodore H. White (HLHU).

390–391 Hurley's comments: Telegram from Ambassador Hurley, June 9, 1945, in the papers of Harry S. Truman, PSF (HSTL).

391 Lattimore and Truman: Owen Lattimore to Truman, June 10 and July 14, 1945, in the papers of Harry S. Truman, White House Central Files, Confidential File, State Department, Correspondence, 1952, box 3 (HSTL).

392 A fair presentation: Chiang Kai-shek to HRL, June 20, 1945, in the papers of CBL, container 841 (MDLOC).

392 Byrnes rejected the idea: Shewmaker, p. 176.

392 Mao denigrated the council: Mao Tse-tung, *Selected Works*, IV, p. 324.

392 A crisis of civil war: Ibid., pp. 328–329.

392 Seems inevitable: *Time*, July 16, 1945.

392 Feel like a prostitute: White to Mom and Gladys, July 17, 1945, Correspondence, in the papers of Theodore H. White (HLHU).

393 The piece stinks: Annalee Jacoby to Theodore H. White, August 1, 1945, ibid.

393 Japanese cancer: Robert Sherrod to HRL, August 10, 1945, and HRL to Sherrod, August 11, 1945, the Time-Life-Fortune papers, I, folder 62, in the John Shaw Billings collection (SCL). Luce and the Emperor: Elson, *World of Time Inc.*, pp. 134–137.

394 A toast to Luce: DJSB, August 10, 1945 (SCL).

394 Chiang's unprepared divisions: Feis, p. 356.

395 Reject it resolutely: *Time*, August 27, 1945.

395 Denied to Chiang's forces: Theodore H. White, cable to Time Inc., August 12, 1945, the Time-Life-Fortune papers, I, folder 63, in the John Shaw Billings collection (SCL).

395 *Time* worried: *Time*, August 20, 1945.

CHAPTER THIRTY-FOUR

396 Newspapers leave off: Robert T. Elson, *World of Time Inc.*, p. 477.

396 On Time Inc. in 1942: "Facts about *Life*," June 1941, Time-Life-Fortune papers, in the papers of John Shaw Billings (SCL). See also DJSB, January 2, February 25, July 2, 1942.

397 The production facilities: Ibid., September 26, 1942.

397 Advertising: Elson, *World of Time Inc.*, p. 448.

397 Television: *Life*, September 22, 1941. Billings was unconvinced. This great movie and camera buff argued with Roy Larsen, who believed in the future of television. Appropriately, Billings departed from *Life* just as television was becoming a national obsession. See DJSB, August 9, 1943 (SCL).

397 Stillman: Elson, *World of Time Inc.*, p. 35.

397 Hollywood: DJSB, July 7, 1944 (SCL).

397 Employment at Time Inc.: "MEMORANDUM FOR U.S. EMPLOYMENT SERVICE: The News Publishing Activities of TIME Incorporated," the Time-Life-Fortune papers, I, folder 25, in the John Shaw Billings collection (SCL).

397 Luce's wealth: DJSB, October 18, 1946 (SCL).

397 Profit-sharing: Roy Larsen to the Staff of Time Inc., February 24, 1941, with enclosure, in the papers of Robert L. Sherrod, Series I, box 9 (GARLSU).

397 Young ex-officers: *The Reminiscences of Andrew Heiskell*, p. 117.

398 Thompson: Edward K. Thompson, report of February 27, 1942, the Time-Life-Fortune papers, I, folder 22, in the John Shaw Billings collection (SCL).

398 To the top: HRL to Daniel Longwell, August 12, 1944, ibid., folder 39.

398 Boyce Price: DJSB, January 24, February 5, 7, 1946 (SCL).

398 First truly global war: HRL to John S. Billings, December 29, 1945, in the papers of Dorothy Sterling (SCDKLUO).

398 *Life*'s staff: John Billings to Roy Larsen, September 12, 1944, the Time-Life-Fortune papers, I, folder 41, in the John Shaw Billings collection (SCL).

399 Sending out *Time* and *Life*: White to David Hulburd, June 14 and October

11, 1942, in the Time-Life Correspondence 1940–1946 of Theodore H. White (HLHU).

399 Time Inc. overseas: Sterling, "The Luce Empire," chapter 7, uses these figures (SCDKLUO).

399 Collier's: Time, September 21, 1942.

399 TLI: "So We Went Abroad . . ." (May 1956), in the papers of James Parton, box 121 (HLHU).

399 Strapped for hard currency: "ES, May, 1948," in the papers of Dorothy Sterling (SCDKLUO).

400 For a generation: Theodore H. White, cable to David Hulburd, August 14, 1945, the Time-Life-Fortune papers, I, folder 63, in the John Shaw Billings collection (SCL).

400 The Communists in Shantung: Feis, *China Tangle*, pp. 365–366.

401 Flurry of cables: John Shaw Billings, cable to Gottfried and others, August 14, 1945, the Time-Life-Fortune papers, I, folder 63, in the John Shaw Billings collection (SCL).

401 White's cables, with Luce's response: Theodore H. White, cable to Time Inc., August 11, 1945, ibid., folder 62, and HRL to Dana Tasker, August 13, 1945, ibid., folder 63.

401 Avowed partisanship: HRL to Theodore H. White, ibid., August 14, 1945.

401 Responded with alacrity: Theodore H. White to Time Inc., ibid., August 15, 1945.

401 Luce did not want: HRL to William Gray, August 16, 1945, in Jessup, *The Ideas of Henry Luce,* pp. 190–191.

402 Immediate return to the States: Theodore H. White to Time Inc., August 25, 1945 (read by Luce); and Eleanor Welch to White, August 27, the Time-Life-Fortune papers, I, folder 63, in the papers of John Shaw Billings (SCL).

402 Settle the basic principles: White to David Hulburd, August 27, 1945, in the Time-Life Correspondence 1940–1946 of Theodore H. White (HLHU).

403 Scrawled the word okay: John S. Billings, undated note to HRL, the Time-Life-Fortune papers, I, folder 66, in the John Shaw Billings collection (SCL).

403 On the treaty: *Time,* September 3, 1945.

403 Policy in Asia: *Life,* September 10, 1945.

403 Might come to terms: *Time,* same date.

404 Lattimore's advice: Owen Lattimore, memorandum to Ambassador Pauley, November 28, 1945, in the papers of Harry S. Truman, President's Secretary's File (HSTL).

404 Tormented China: *Time,* September 3, 1945.

404 The future is dubious: Buell, memorandum to A. W. Jones, October 4, 1945, in the papers of Raymond Leslie Buell (unprocessed), carton 7 (MDLOC).

405 Bright with hope: *Time,* September 24, 1945.

405 Shanghai: *Life,* same date.

405 Of mutual benefit: The Chinese Ambassador to the Acting Secretary of State, September 26, 1945, in the records of the Department of State, 811.79600/ Reservations/9-2145 (RG 59, NARA).

405 Luce headed for China: *Time,* October 8, 1945.

406 Interview with Jacoby: HRL, cable to John Billings, probably October 7, 1945, in the W. A. Swanberg collection, box 17, folder on W.A.S.

(RBMLCU); see also HRL to John S. Billings, October 8, 1945, the Time-Life-Fortune papers, II, folder 66, in the John Shaw Billings collection (SCL).

407 **Since Marco Polo:** Interview with Wesley Bailey, in the W. A. Swanberg collection, box 18 (RBMLCU).

408 **Published articles:** Ibid.

408 **The wheels of industry:** HRL, telegram to Clare Luce, October 9, 1945, in the papers of CBL, container 455 (MDLOC).

408 **Stillman:** Charles L. Stillman, memorandum to HRL, June 5, 1941, in the papers of John Hersey, copy provided by Mr. Hersey.

408 **How well Harry and his father built:** CBL to Garside, October 11, 1945, in the papers of B. A. Garside, box 2 (HIWRP).

408 **Communist subversives:** Walter H. Judd, interviewed by Paul Hopper, Oral History Interview at Columbia University, p. 77.

408 *Amerasia:* Athan G. Theoharis, *The Boss: J. Edgar Hoover and the Great American Inquisition* (Philadelphia: Temple University Press, 1988), pp. 259–261. See also Oral History Interview with John S. Service, 386 (HSTL).

408 **White on *Amerasia:*** Undated cable, probably June 1945, from Jacoby and White, in the papers of Theodore H. White (HLHU).

409 **Publish his magazines in China:** Interview with Wesley Bailey, in the W. A. Swanberg collection, box 18 (RBMLCU).

410 **Two whorehouses:** Mr. Luce's Chungking Diary, October 1945, in the papers of C. D. Jackson, 1931–1967, container 57, folder on Time Inc., HRL, 1943–1948 (DDEL).

410 **Hailed him as a friend:** Interview with Wesley Bailey, in the W. A. Swanberg collection, box 18 (RBMLCU).

410 **Under the mahogany:** Elson, *World of Time Inc.,* p. 144.

410 **Changing the signals:** Ibid., p. 145.

411 **Magnificent port:** HRL, memorandum to the Senior List, November 12, 1945, in the papers of CBL, container 455 (MDLOC).

411 **New territory:** HRL, cable to John R. Billings, October 25, 1945, in the W. A. Swanberg collection, box 17, folder on W.A.S. (RBMLCU).

412 **Decisive confrontations:** HRL to Eleanor Welch, October 27, 1945, the Time-Life-Fortune papers, II, folder 67, in the John Shaw Billings collection (SCL).

412 **North China:** HRL and Charles J. V. Murphy, cable to Eleanor Welch, October 27, 1945, in the W. A. Swanberg collection, box 17, folder on W.A.S. (RBMLCU).

412 **Something . . . unique:** HRL, cable to John Billings, probably October 7, 1945, ibid.

412 **For what may ensue:** *Time,* November 12, 1945.

412 **After he has got peace:** HRL to John K. Jessup, November 13, 1945, in the papers of C. D. Jackson, 1931–1967, container 57 (DDEL).

412 **Conant:** John K. Jessup to John S. Billings et al., October 17, 1945, the Time-Life-Fortune papers, I, folder 66, in the John Shaw Billings collection (SCL). See also Louis Liebovich, *The Press and the Origins of the Cold War, 1944–1947* (New York: Praeger, 1988), pp. 91–92.

413 **Welles:** Sam Welles, memorandum to John Osborne, November 10, 1945, in the papers of C. D. Jackson, 1931–1967, container 57 (DDEL).

413 **Debate over Russia:** *Time,* June 4, 11, 1945.

413 **Central intelligence:** *Life,* September 17, 1945.

EPILOGUE

415 Loved Americans: HRL, cable to John Billings, October 19, 1945, in the W. A. Swanberg collection, box 17, folder on W.A.S. (RBMLCU).

415 Tsingtao and the American presence in China: HRL, speech to Time Inc. executives, May 4, 1950, ibid., box 21.

415 Makes the heart joyful: HRL, memorandum to the Senior List, November 12, 1945, in the papers of CBL, container 455 (MDLOC).

416 That is not ours: Mark Twain's interview with the *New York World*, October 14, 1900, cited in "Mark Twain on American Imperialism," *Atlantic Monthly*, April 1992, p. 59.

418 Hodgins: Interview with Eric Hodgins, in the W. A. Swanberg collection, box 18 (RBMLCU).

418 Cowles: Baughman, *Henry R. Luce*, p. 81.

419 Hutchins: John Kobler, *Luce: His Time, Life, and Fortune* (Garden City, NY: Doubleday, 1968), p. 2. On the effect of *Time*'s classroom materials, see James A. Linen, "A Letter from the Publisher," *Time*, October 17, 1949, p. 19.

419 Sandburg: Sherrod to Luce, February 22, 1940, in the papers of Robert L. Sherrod, Series I, box 14 (GARLSU).

419 Hearst: Bill Rich to HRL, January 15, 1942, in the papers of CBL, container 841 (MDLOC).

419 Marshall told Longwell: George C. Marshall to Longwell, July 19, 1940, in the Daniel Longwell collection, box 69 (RBMLCU). See also C. D. Jackson, memorandum to Ed Thompson, August 19, 1940, ibid.

INDEX